*teach yourself...*
# PowerBuilder 5

The icon can be a stock icon or an icon contained in a bitmap file (ICO). Figure 5.41 shows an example of drag and drop. This is the second window from the **CONTROLS.APP** example.

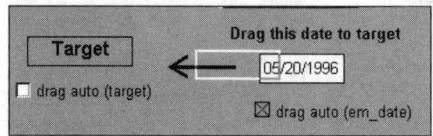

*Figure 5.41  Dragging the date.*

In this example, the user has just clicked on and begun to drag the **em_date EditMask**. The default drag icon is displayed here (the ghost outline rectangle). In Figure 5.42, the drag has been initiated in the listbox and a standard Rectangle icon is being used for the display.

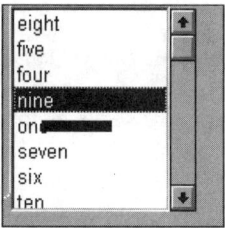

*Figure 5.42  Dragging an item from the listbox.*

If you drag the pointer to a location that cannot serve as the target object, the icon changes to the No-Drop icon. Figure 5.43 shows the No-Drop icon as it is displayed if you drag the pointer to the title bar of the window, which is not a valid target area.

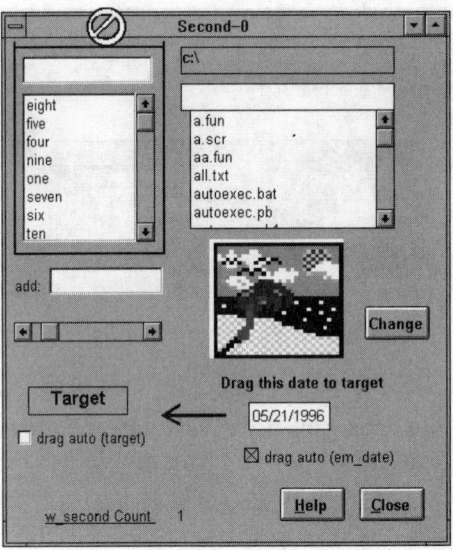

**Figure 5.43**  *The Not Valid icon.*

The PowerBuilder controls that can serve as target objects have the following events:

+ `DragDrop`—Occurs when drag mode is on and the pointer drops an object within the target control.
+ `DragEnter`—Occurs when drag mode is on and the dragged object enters the target control.
+ `DragLeave`—Occurs when drag mode is on and the dragged object leaves the target control.
+ `DragWithin`—Occurs when drag mode is on. This event is triggered periodically while an object is dragged within the target control.

Scripts in these events determine the effect of the drag-and-drop function.

The `DragEnter` event is also triggered for CommandButtons and PictureButtons in another instance. If the button's drag mode is off and the button's `DragAuto` attribute is set, a `DragEnter` event is triggered (rather than a `Clicked` event) when the user clicks the button. Because of this action, it is usually better to change the drag mode programmatically rather than setting the `DragAuto` attribute.

*teach yourself...*

# PowerBuilder 5

### David McClanahan

A Subsidiary of
Henry Holt and Co., Inc.

**MIS:Press**
A Subsidiary of Henry Holt and Company, Inc.
115 West 18th Street
New York, New York 10011
http://www.mispress.com

Copyright © 1997 by MIS:Press

Printed in the United States of America

All rights reserved. No part of this book may be reproduced or transmitted in any form or by any means, electronic or mechanical, including photocopying, recording, or by any information storage and retrieval system, without prior written permission from the Publisher. Contact the Publisher for information on foreign rights.

**Limits of Liability and Disclaimer of Warranty**

The Author and Publisher of this book have used their best efforts in preparing the book and the programs contained in it. These efforts include the development, research, and testing of the theories and programs to determine their effectiveness.

The Author and Publisher make no warranty of any kind, expressed or implied, with regard to these programs or the documentation contained in this book. The Author and Publisher shall not be liable in any event for incidental or consequential damages in connection with, or arising out of, the furnishing, performance, or use of these programs.

All products, names and services are trademarks or registered trademarks of their respective companies.

**teach yourself... and the ty logo are registered.**

First Edition—1997

**Library of Congress Cataloging-in-Publication Data**

```
McClanahan, David.
    Teach yourself...PowerBuilder 5 / by David McClanahan.
       p.   cm.
    ISBN 1-55828-474-5
    1. Application software--Development. 2. PowerBuilder.
  I. Title.
  QA76.76.D47M388    1996
  005.2'76--dc21                                          96-46896
                                                             CIP
```

MIS:Press and M&T Books are available at special discounts for bulk purchases for sales promotions, premiums, and fundraising. Special editions or book excerpts can also be created to specification.

For details contact:     Special Sales Director
                         MIS:Press and M&T Books
                         Subsidiaries of Henry Holt and Company, Inc.
                         115 West 18th Street
                         New York, New York 10011

10 9 8 7 6 5 4 3 2 1

**Associate Publisher:** *Paul Farrell*         **Copy Edit Manager:** *Shari Chappell*
**Executive Editor:** *Cary Sullivan*           **Production Editor:** *Natalie Fortin*
**Editor:** *Michael Sprague*                   **Copy Editor:** *Suzanne Ingrao*

# Introduction ..................................................................................1
Using this Book ........................................................................2
Using the Example Applications ...............................................2
The Database ...........................................................................3
Installing the Examples (See Appendix B) ................................3
Additional Information ............................................................4

# Chapter 1: Introduction to PowerBuilder 5 ...............5
The Development Environment ...............................................6
    The PowerBuilder Painters ..................................................6
    Displaying Text Labels in the Toolbars ................................7
    Displaying PowerTips ..........................................................9
    Displaying MicroHelp ..........................................................9
Customizing the Presentation Style ........................................10
Online Help ............................................................................11

      Find Option .................................................................................12
      Creating Bookmarks ....................................................................14
      Using the Help Button ................................................................14
      The Help Option ........................................................................15
   The Context-Sensitive Popup Menu ..................................................15
   The PowerBuilder Painters................................................................16
      Overview of PowerBuilder Painters .............................................17

## Chapter 2: Programming in PowerBuilder 5 ...........21

   The PowerScript Language ...............................................................22
      PowerScript Text..........................................................................22
      Line Continuation .......................................................................23
      Comments ..................................................................................23
      Dot Notation ..............................................................................24
      Identifiers ...................................................................................26
      Data Types .................................................................................27
      Arrays.........................................................................................28
   Variable Scope Options ....................................................................29
      Global Scope ..............................................................................29
      Local Scope ................................................................................30
      Instance Variables .......................................................................30
   Using Dot Notation with Instance Variables ....................................31
      Variable Access Levels ................................................................32
      The Shared Scope.......................................................................32
      Labeling Scope in Identifiers......................................................33
      Passing Variables in Function Calls ............................................33
   PowerScript Language Statements....................................................34
      The IF Statement .......................................................................34
      Operator Precedence ..................................................................35
      The CHOOSE CASE Statement ................................................36
   LOOPING Constructs.....................................................................37
      The FOR…NEXT Loop .............................................................39

| | |
|---|---|
| The HALT Statement | 40 |
| The RETURN Statement | 40 |
| PowerBuilder Functions | 40 |
|     User-Defined Functions | 40 |
|     The Object Browser | 46 |
| The PowerScript Painter | 47 |
| The Drop-Down List Boxes | 48 |
|     Select Event Listbox | 49 |
|     Paste Global Listbox | 49 |
|     Paste Instance Listbox | 49 |
|     Paste Shared Listbox | 49 |
|     Paste Argument Listbox | 50 |
|     Paste Object/Window Listbox | 50 |
|     Edit Menu Paste Options | 50 |
|     Paste SQL | 51 |
|     Paste Statement | 52 |
| Entering and Editing Text | 53 |
|     Selecting Text | 54 |
|     To Cut, Copy, Clear, or Replace Selected Text | 55 |
|     Pasting Text | 55 |
|     Keyboard Shortcuts for the Cut and Paste Functions | 55 |
| The PowerScript Painter Menu Options | 56 |
|     File Menu | 57 |
|     Edit Menu | 57 |
|     Search Menu | 58 |
|     Declare Menu | 58 |
|     Design Menu | 58 |
| Import and Export | 58 |
|     Exporting Text | 59 |
| Compiling PowerScript Code | 59 |
|     Customizing the Editor | 61 |
| Context-Sensitive Help | 62 |

The Object Browser ................................................................................63
    Selecting Another Object ...............................................................67
    Editing Function Declarations ......................................................68
The PowerScript Debugger ....................................................................69
    Adding a Breakpoint .......................................................................70
    Running the Debugger ....................................................................72
    Displaying and Modifying Variables ............................................73

## Chapter 3: Creating PowerBuilder Applications ...... 75

A PowerBuilder Application ................................................................76
The Application Painter .........................................................................76
    Application Programs and Application Objects .......................77
    PowerBuilder Application Libraries ............................................77
    The Application Executable ..........................................................78
Properties, Events, and Functions ........................................................78
Application Object Properties ..............................................................79
    Dot Notation Addressing ...............................................................79
Application Object Events ....................................................................79
The Application-Level Events ...............................................................80
    The Application Open Event .........................................................80
    The Application Close Event ........................................................80
    The Application Idle Event ...........................................................80
    Application Object Functions .......................................................81
    The Application SystemError Event ............................................81
    The Application Error Object .......................................................81
The Application Initialization File ......................................................83
Building an Application .........................................................................85
    Creating a New Application ..........................................................85
    Developing the Exercise Applications ........................................86
Example: FirstApp .....................................................................................86
    Opening the FirstApp Application ..............................................87
    Running FirstApp .............................................................................88

FirstApp—Step-by-Step ..................................................................91
Run the Application ......................................................................95
Create an Executable ....................................................................96
Run the Executable from Windows................................................98
Library Painter ......................................................................................99
What's Next .........................................................................................100

## Chapter 4: Creating Windows ..................................101

Window Painter ..................................................................................102
The Window Painter Dialog Box ..............................................103
The 3D Look ...............................................................................104
Window Painter Toolbars ..........................................................104
The Style Toolbar .......................................................................105
Setting Color Options ................................................................105
Defining a Window's Style .................................................................107
The Window Type ......................................................................108
The Main Window .....................................................................110
The Child Window .....................................................................111
The Popup Window ...................................................................111
The Response Window ..............................................................111
The MDI Frame Window ...........................................................112
Sheets and Menus ......................................................................113
Recommendation for Sheets and Menus ..................................113
MDI Sheet Window Types ........................................................114
MDI Frame with Microhelp ......................................................114
Other Window Attributes ..................................................................115
Resizing the New Window ........................................................116
Other Window Options .....................................................................119
Saving the Window ............................................................................119
The Window Painter Popup Menu ...................................................120
Window Scripts ..........................................................................120
Window Events ...................................................................................120

Window Functions ..................................................................................... 121
Window Attributes .................................................................................... 122
Window Variables ..................................................................................... 122
Example: FirstWin ..................................................................................... 125
    Running FirstWin ............................................................................... 126
    FirstWin—Step-by-Step .................................................................... 127

## Chapter 5: Window Controls .................................................. 137

Adding Controls to a Window ................................................................. 140
    Working with Controls ...................................................................... 142
    Adding a Control to a Window ......................................................... 142
    Aligning Controls with the Alignment Function ............................. 146
    Adjusting the Spacing of Controls ................................................... 148
    Automatically Sizing Controls .......................................................... 149
The Control Properties Dialog Box .......................................................... 150
    Naming a Control ............................................................................... 151
    Setting Text In a Control ................................................................... 152
    Setting Control Attributes ................................................................. 153
Accelerators for Controls .......................................................................... 153
Change an Attribute ................................................................................. 155
Duplicating a Control ............................................................................... 156
PowerBuilder Units (PBUs) ...................................................................... 157
Colors in PowerBuilder Applications ...................................................... 158
    Color Values ........................................................................................ 158
    The 3D Look ....................................................................................... 160
    Show Invisibles ................................................................................... 160
Description, Properties, Events, and Functions .................................... 160
The Window Controls ............................................................................... 161
    The Window Controls Example ....................................................... 161
    Controls by Category ......................................................................... 162
    Control Popup Menu Options .......................................................... 163
CommandButtons ..................................................................................... 164

| | |
|---|---|
| Adding a CommandButton to a Window | 165 |
| CommandButton Properties Dialog Box | 166 |
| CommandButton Properties | 168 |
| CommandButton Events | 169 |
| CommandButton Functions | 170 |
| PictureButtons | 171 |
| SingleLineEdit Controls | 172 |
| EditMask Control | 172 |
| Defining Spin Controls | 173 |
| MultiLineEdit Control | 173 |
| RichTextEdit Control | 174 |
| ListBox Controls | 174 |
| DropDownListBox Controls | 175 |
| DropDownPictureListBox Controls | 176 |
| Picture Controls | 176 |
| StaticText Controls | 177 |
| ListView Controls | 177 |
| TreeView Controls | 178 |
| RadioButton Controls | 179 |
| GroupBox Controls | 179 |
| CheckBox Controls | 180 |
| HScrollBar | 180 |
| VScrollBar | 181 |
| Line Controls | 181 |
| Oval Controls | 181 |
| Rectangle Controls | 182 |
| RoundRectangle Controls | 182 |
| Tab Controls | 183 |
| Drag and Drop | 184 |
| Drag-and-Drop Functions | 187 |
| CONTROL1 Example Program | 188 |
| CONTROL1—Step-by-Step | 191 |

Create the Application and Library ..................................................... 191
Create the Main Window ..................................................................... 191
Add Code to the Application Open Event ......................................... 193
Create the w_second Window ............................................................ 194
Return to the w_first Window ............................................................ 195
Return to the w_second Window ....................................................... 200
Run the Application ............................................................................ 206

## Chapter 6: Events, Functions, and User Events ...... 207

Event-Driven Programming ................................................................ 208
    Messages ......................................................................................... 208
Events1: A PowerBuilder Application ................................................ 208
Events1 ................................................................................................. 209
    Experiment with Events1 .............................................................. 211
PowerBuilder Events ........................................................................... 212
    User-Defined Functions ................................................................ 213
    Object-Level Functions ................................................................. 216
    Function Return Value Type ........................................................ 216
    Function Argument List ................................................................ 217
    Standard User Objects and User-Defined Functions ................. 217
    Object Function Access Level ..................................................... 218
    A Sample Function ....................................................................... 218
Defining User Events .......................................................................... 219
    Creating a User Event .................................................................. 219
    Creating a Custom Event ............................................................. 221
    Creating a Parameterized Custom Event ................................... 223
    Mapping a Windows Event .......................................................... 226
    The Other Event ........................................................................... 227
    The Message Object ..................................................................... 228
Initiating Functions and Events ......................................................... 229
Events2 Example Program .................................................................. 231
Events2—Step-by-Step ........................................................................ 231

Create the Application and Library ........................................................ 232
Create the Main Window ........................................................................ 232
Add a Function to w_main ...................................................................... 234
Add Code to the Application Open Event ............................................ 235
Add a User Event to the w_main Window ............................................ 235
Add Code to the w_main Open Event .................................................... 236
Add Code to the ue_init Event ................................................................ 237
Add Controls to the Window .................................................................. 238
Add a User Event to lb_1 ........................................................................ 239
Add Code to the ue_add_item Event ...................................................... 240
Add Code to the sle_1 Modified Event .................................................. 240
Add Another User Event to lb_1 ............................................................ 241
Add Code to the lb_1 we_mousemove Event ........................................ 241
Add Code to the sle_1 DragDrop Event ................................................ 242
Summary .......................................................................................................... 243

# Chapter 7: Embedded SQL ........................................................ 245

SQL Statements .............................................................................................. 246
    Embedded SQL Statements .................................................................... 248
Creating SQL Statements .............................................................................. 248
    Paste SQL .................................................................................................. 249
Cursor SQL Statements .................................................................................. 251
    Declare Cursor .......................................................................................... 251
    Fetch Cursor .............................................................................................. 252
    Update Cursor .......................................................................................... 253
    Delete Cursor ............................................................................................ 254
    Noncursor SQL Statements .................................................................... 254
Query Painter .................................................................................................. 257
    Transaction Objects .................................................................................. 258
    The SQLCode ............................................................................................ 260
The Application Initialization File .............................................................. 261
Example: SQLApp ............................................................................................ 264

## Contents

Running SQLApp ..................................................................................264
Using SQLApp ....................................................................................266
SQLApp—Step-by-Step ..........................................................................268
   Create the Application and Library ..................................................268
   Create the Main Window ...............................................................269
   Add Code to the Application Open Event .........................................270
   Add Code to the Window ..............................................................272
   Add Code to the w_embedded_sql Window ....................................272
   Save the Window and Run the Application ......................................280
   Selecting and Updating Blobs .........................................................280
   UPDATEBLOB SQL Statement .......................................................282

## Chapter 8: Menus .................................................................285

Introduction to the Menu Painter .........................................................285
Creating Menus ..................................................................................287
Adding Menu Bar Items .......................................................................289
   Adding Menu Items ......................................................................289
   Menu Item Events ........................................................................290
   Creating Cascading Menus ............................................................290
   Creating Popup Menus .................................................................292
Menu Item Properties ..........................................................................293
   General Attributes ........................................................................293
   Style Attributes ............................................................................293
   Shortcut Keys and Accelerators .....................................................294
   Toolbar Tab .................................................................................295
   Pictures Tab ................................................................................296
MDI Applications ................................................................................297
Adding MDI Microhelp ........................................................................298
   The MDI Toolbar .........................................................................298
Adding Scripts ....................................................................................299
Previewing the Menu ..........................................................................300
Saving the Menu .................................................................................301

Attaching the Menu to a Window ..................................................................301
Menu Item Attributes .....................................................................................301
Menu Item Functions .....................................................................................302
The Menus Example .......................................................................................302
Menus—Step-by-Step ....................................................................................304
    Create the Application and Library..........................................................304
    The Test Menu ..........................................................................................306
    The Dynamic Menu ..................................................................................307
    The Help Menu .........................................................................................307
    Create the Main Window .........................................................................308
    Add Code to the Application Open Event................................................313
    Add a Function to m_main ......................................................................313
    Add Another Function to m_main ...........................................................315
    Copy Windows to zmenus.pbl ..................................................................316
    The w_environment Window....................................................................319

## Chapter 9: Introduction to DataWindows .............323

DataWindow Concepts....................................................................................323
DataWindow Objects and Controls.................................................................325
    DataWindow Objects ................................................................................326
DataWindow Controls.....................................................................................327
Creating a New DataWindow Object .............................................................328
    DataWindow Creation ..............................................................................329
    The Data Source and Presentation Style..................................................330
    Data Sources..............................................................................................331
    Presentation Style .....................................................................................332
DataWindow Data Sources .............................................................................332
    Quick Select ..............................................................................................333
    The Quick Select Dialog Box ...................................................................334
    Joins ...........................................................................................................335
    Sort Order .................................................................................................335
    Select Criteria............................................................................................336

The SQL Select Data Source Option ................................................. 339
The SQL Toolbox ............................................................................. 340
Joins .................................................................................................. 341
Selecting Columns ........................................................................... 342
Computed Columns ........................................................................ 343
WHERE Clause Criteria .................................................................. 344
Viewing the SQL Statement ........................................................... 346
Group By ........................................................................................... 347
Having ............................................................................................... 348
Order By ............................................................................................ 349
Unions ............................................................................................... 350
Saving a Query ................................................................................. 350
The Query Data Source Option .................................................... 351
The External Data Source Option ................................................ 352
The Stored Procedure Data Source Option ............................... 352
Presentation Styles ................................................................................ 353
Freeform ........................................................................................... 355
Tabular .............................................................................................. 355
Group ................................................................................................ 356
dwstyles.pbl ..................................................................................... 357

## Chapter 10: The DataWindow Painter ................... 359

Enhancing DataWindow Objects ....................................................... 360
Customizing the DataWindow Presentation ............................. 360
Bands ........................................................................................................ 363
The Header Band ............................................................................ 363
The Detail Band ............................................................................... 364
The Summary Band ........................................................................ 364
The Footer Band .............................................................................. 365
Group Bands .................................................................................... 365
Changing the Design ...................................................................... 366
Saving the DataWindow Object ......................................................... 367

Modifying the DataWindow.................................................................................367
    Adding DataWindow Objects.................................................................367
    Selecting DataWindow Objects...............................................................368
    Selecting Multiple Controls ....................................................................368
    Selecting Objects with the Menu Option..............................................368
    Positioning and Sizing Objects ...............................................................369
    Using the Design Grid.............................................................................370
    The Snap to Grid Option ........................................................................371
    The Show Ruler Option ..........................................................................371
    Using the Zoom Option..........................................................................372
    Using the Preview Option ......................................................................372
    Aligning Objects with the Alignment Function...................................373
    Adjusting the Spacing of Objects...........................................................375
    Automatically Sizing of Objects .............................................................375
    The Style Toolbar.....................................................................................376
    Colors .......................................................................................................379
    Setting the Tab Order .............................................................................380
DataWindow Properties ...................................................................................381
    Print Specifications..................................................................................382
Adding Computed Fields..................................................................................382
    DBMS Computations versus DataWindow Computations ..................384
    Predefined Calculated Fields ..................................................................386
    Adding Database Columns.....................................................................387
The Rows Menu.................................................................................................388
    Column Specifications ............................................................................388
    Data..........................................................................................................389
    Prompt for Criteria .................................................................................390
    Retrieve....................................................................................................390
    Filtering and Sorting ..............................................................................391
    Suppressing Repeating Values ...............................................................393
    Update Properties...................................................................................396
Creating Groups.................................................................................................398

Column Attributes ................................................................................ 400
   The Column Popup Menu ................................................................ 400
   The Display as Picture Option ......................................................... 402
   Using Autosize Height ..................................................................... 404
   Using Column Validation ................................................................. 406
Column Edit Styles ............................................................................... 407
   The Default Edit Style ...................................................................... 408
   EditMask Style ................................................................................. 410
   RadioButton ..................................................................................... 412
   DropDownListBox Style ................................................................... 413
   DropDownListBox Attributes .......................................................... 414
   DropDownDataWindow Style .......................................................... 415
Presentation Styles .............................................................................. 418
   Freeform ........................................................................................... 419
   Tabular .............................................................................................. 421
   DataWindow Examples .................................................................... 423

## Chapter 11: DataWindow Controls: Adding DataWindows to Your Applications ......................... 425

   Overview: Using DataWindow Controls ............................................ 426
      DataWindows with a DBMS Source ............................................ 426
      DataWindows With an External Source ...................................... 427
   Adding a DataWindow Control to a Window .................................... 428
      DataWindow Control Popup Menu Options ............................... 429
      Select a DataWindow Object ....................................................... 430
      Modify DataWindow Object ........................................................ 433
      Set the DataWindow Attributes .................................................. 434
   Using DataWindow Controls with a Database .................................. 436
      Connecting to the Database ........................................................ 436
      Disconnecting to the Database ................................................... 437
   Transaction Objects ........................................................................... 437
      SetTransObject .............................................................................. 437

## Contents

- SetTrans .................................................................. 438
- Data Manipulation .................................................. 438
- Database Error Handling in DataWindows ............................ 440
- Updating Data in a DataWindow ..................................... 441
- The DataWindows Edit Control ....................................... 442
  - AcceptText ........................................................ 443
  - Updating a Row in a DataWindow .................................. 444
  - The DataWindow Edit Control ..................................... 444
  - ItemChanged Event ............................................... 445
  - ItemError Event ................................................. 446
- DataWindow Items ..................................................... 446
  - Item Reference by Column Number ................................. 446
  - Item Reference by Column Name ................................... 448
  - Ranges of Item References by Column Number ...................... 450
- Status Codes .......................................................... 451
- DataWindow Programming ............................................... 452
  - Retrieve() ...................................................... 453
  - InsertRow() ..................................................... 454
  - DeleteRow() ..................................................... 455
  - Update() ........................................................ 455
- COMMIT ................................................................ 456
- ROLLBACK .............................................................. 456
  - Sharing Data between DataWindows ................................ 456
  - SaveAs .......................................................... 457
  - Print ........................................................... 458
  - Dynamically Assigning DataWindow Objects ........................ 459
  - Filter Functions ................................................ 459
  - Sort Functions .................................................. 461
  - The Find Function ............................................... 462
- DataWindow Events ..................................................... 464
  - Retrieving Data into a DataWindow ............................... 464
  - Updating the Database ........................................... 465

Printing a DataWindow .................................................................. 466
The Object Browser ...................................................................... 466
DataWindow Control Attributes.................................................... 467
DataWindow Control Events ........................................................ 467
DataWindow Control Functions.................................................... 468
DataStores..................................................................................... 470
Reports.......................................................................................... 470
The DataWindow Example Programs............................................ 471
    Example Requirements ............................................................ 472
    DB_INIT.PBL ........................................................................... 474
    Global Functions...................................................................... 478

# Chapter 12: Multiple Document Interface.............483

The MDIAPP Example................................................................... 484
    The OpenSheet Function ......................................................... 487
    MDI Events............................................................................... 488
Creating an MDI Application......................................................... 489
    Creating the MDI Frame .......................................................... 489
    Creating the Window Parms Structure..................................... 490
    Creating the Sheet Window (w_mdi_sheet) ............................. 491
    w_mdi_frame Instance Variable............................................... 494
    w_mdi_frame Window-Level Functions ................................... 495
    Add Code to the Application Open Event................................ 499
    Creating the Menus ................................................................. 499
    Creating the m_mdi_sheet Menu ............................................ 503
Creating an MDI Template............................................................ 506

# Chapter 13: User Objects ........................................511

User Objects .................................................................................. 512
Types of User Objects ................................................................... 512
    Class Category ......................................................................... 513
    Visual Category ........................................................................ 513

Using Visual User Objects ...................................................................... 514
The Standard User Object ...................................................................... 514
The Example uodemo Program ............................................................. 516
An Example Standard Visual User Object ............................................. 517
Create Object-Level Function fu_disable .............................................. 520
Create Object-Level Function fu_enable ............................................... 521
Create Object-Level Function fu_get_state ........................................... 521
Adding a User Object to a Window ....................................................... 522
Edit the w_main_with_uos CloseQuery Event ..................................... 524
Custom Visual User Objects ......................................................................... 524
The U_DW_NAV User Object ................................................................ 526
Assigning the idw_x DataWindow Value ............................................. 528
Using a Registration Function (or Event) .............................................. 528
The U_DW_NAV_VERTICAL User Object ............................................. 530
The U_DW_NAV_WITH_CLOSE User Object ....................................... 531
The U_LB_WITH_SEARCH User Object ................................................ 533
Custom Class User Objects ........................................................................... 538
Standard Class-User Objects ......................................................................... 542

## Chapter 14: Inheritance ............................................................. 545

Object-Oriented Concepts ............................................................................. 546
Data Abstraction and Encapsulation ........................................................... 546
Classes ...................................................................................................... 547
Objects ..................................................................................................... 547
u_person .................................................................................................. 549
Inheritance ..................................................................................................... 551
u_employee ............................................................................................. 551
Why Inherit? ........................................................................................... 553
Polymorphism ................................................................................................ 554
Object-Oriented PowerBuilder ..................................................................... 555
PowerBuilder Classes .............................................................................. 555
Window Inheritance ...................................................................................... 558

The Snap-to-Grid Option and Inheritance ............................................. 559
Updating the Ancestor ............................................................................ 560
Menu Inheritance ............................................................................................ 561
User Object Inheritance .................................................................................. 564
MDI Inheritance .............................................................................................. 567

## Appendix A: The PowerScript Language ................ 569

Data Types ........................................................................................................ 569
Using Special ASCII Characters............................................................... 573
The NULL Value ....................................................................................... 573
The Any Data Type ................................................................................... 574
Declaring Constants ........................................................................................ 574
The Pronoun Reserved Words ....................................................................... 575
This ............................................................................................................. 575
Parent ......................................................................................................... 576
Using Parent in a MenuItem ................................................................... 577
Using Parent in a User Object ................................................................. 577
ParentWindow .......................................................................................... 578
Super .......................................................................................................... 579

## Appendix B: Using the Example Applications ........ 581

The Example Applications .............................................................................. 582
Run the SETUP Program ......................................................................... 582
The PBINI Application ............................................................................. 585
Viewing the ODBC Configuration .......................................................... 590
Using PBINI to Configure the ODBC .................................................... 591
An Alternate Installation Technique .............................................................. 593
Overview .................................................................................................... 593
Temporarily Delete the Example Database Files .................................. 593
Delete the Old ODBC Data Source ......................................................... 594
Delete the Old Database Profile .............................................................. 595
Create the MCCLAN2 Database ............................................................. 595

Exit PowerBuilder .................................................................................. 597
Delete the Newly Created MCCLAN2 Database Files ........................ 597
Run PowerBuilder ................................................................................... 597
Run the PBINI Application .................................................................... 597
AutoStop .................................................................................................. 598
Installing to a Nondefault Directory ..................................................... 599
The Example Applications ..................................................................... 599
A Word about Programming Style ....................................................... 600

# Index ........................................................................................... 603

# Introduction

If you would like to quickly increase your value as a client/server developer and ensure your employability, becoming proficient with PowerBuilder is probably the best move you can make at this time. The intent of this book is to bring developers, who are already proficient in at least one other language up to speed on PowerBuilder as quickly as possible. It uses a "by-example" approach, providing complete applications to demonstrate each topic. This book will take you from beginning through intermediate programming in the shortest amount of time.

This book is a complete introduction to PowerBuilder 5 and is essentially a condensed version of my much larger book, *PowerBuilder 5: A Developer's Guide*. I have reduced the amount of information to cover the absolute essential knowledge that is required to work as a PowerBuilder developer. You will find that this is still a very concentrated text, and I believe this provides the most information of any introductory PowerBuilder book of comparable length. The material in this book is based on—and has been well tested in—seminars I have been teaching for several years. I believe that working code examples are as informative as the best explanation. In this book, I present dozens of sample applications, each focused on a particular area of PowerBuilder development. These examples are included on the disk that comes with this book.

My goal is to get you up to speed as quickly as possible and to provide the information you need to become a proficient PowerBuilder developer. This material extends into advanced topics that are essential such as User Objects and Inheritance.

## USING THIS BOOK

I will present dozens of sample applications, each focused on a particular area of PowerBuilder development. The examples have been carefully designed to cover all the essential areas of PowerBuilder development. When you have completed the exercises based on these examples, you will have acquired hands-on experience with the most important details of PowerBuilder and will have covered many advanced topics.

Complete source code is provided for each of the examples, and I provide walk-throughs for creating many of the examples. This edition includes a disk. You may use the code in your own applications without limitation (except that you may not use this code for another PowerBuilder book or training). The examples are also intended to serve as a resource for future development.

## USING THE EXAMPLE APPLICATIONS

The disk that comes with this book contains finished versions of all the exercises and a number of other objects you will need to create the example applications (databases, icons, text files, and so on). You should first read the material presented before each example application. Then run the example, try all of the options, and think about how you would create a similar application. Once you understand the application, you should attempt to create your own version of the application (as closely as possible). When you need a hint, refer to the text or examine the example's code.

Most of the examples focus on a particular area of PowerBuilder development (relating to the area covered in the corresponding text). When you have completed the exercise of duplicating each of the examples, you will have acquired real, hands-on experience with all the important aspects of PowerBuilder. You will, for example, have created at least one of every type of object in the Window painter. You will also have a large amount of source code and example objects that you can reuse in your PowerBuilder applications. It is highly recommended that you take time to work through each example.

## THE DATABASE

The examples in this book use the Sybase SQL Anywhere 5.0 database engine that is included with both PowerBuilder and PowerBuilder Desktop. To run the examples, you must have installed the database engine. If you did not, you should run the PowerBuilder installation and install just the database engine, before running these examples.

## INSTALLING THE EXAMPLES (SEE APPENDIX B)

The disk that comes with this book includes a setup program that will install the example files and database on your system. Read Appendix B for instructions on installing the examples. The setup program will create a directory for the examples, such as C:\PB5\MCCLAN2, and it will create the ODBC configuration necessary for the database (all further references assume C:\PB5\MCCLAN2 is the installation directory, so adjust these statements according to the actual location you have chosen). It is highly recommended that you accept the default directory (C:\PB5\MCCLAN2). Many of the objects in the applications and the application profile files assume this to be the directory for the example files. If you must install to another directory, you will have to adjust the path references in the example applications.

After installing the example files, you must run the PBINI example program (found in C:\PB5\MCCLAN2) from within PowerBuilder. This application will update the LibList (the library search path) for the example PowerBuilder applications. Appendix B has detailed information on **PBINI**.

All of the database examples use a Sybase SQL Anywhere 5.0 database C:\PB5\MCCLAN2\MCCLAN2.DB (and MCCLAN2.LOG). The install program can set up the ODBC configuration in most cases.

Throughout this book, we assume that the path to the sample application is C:\PB5\MCCLAN2. If that is not the case (perhaps you placed them in directory D:\pbsample), you will have to adjust all references to C:\PB5\MCCLAN2 accordingly. The **SETUP** program will allow you to place the example files in any directory.

## ADDITIONAL INFORMATION

Most of the material in this book is based on the PowerBuilder seminars I have been teaching over the last few years. I teach three one-week seminars on PowerBuilder development (beginning, intermediate, and advanced). I also teach seminars on other client/server and database-related topics. Good luck with PowerBuilder. I hope you find this book and the example applications useful. I can be reached via email at 72517.1124@compuserve.com.

This method may also be licensed for PowerBuilder training classes. A workbook will also be available. Contact me for more information.

**CHAPTER 1**

# Introduction to PowerBuilder 5

This chapter presents an overview of the PowerBuilder environment, including an introduction to the following topics:

- ✦ The PowerBuilder development environment
- ✦ The online help system
- ✦ The context-sensitive popup menu
- ✦ The PowerBuilder painters

## THE DEVELOPMENT ENVIRONMENT

The PowerBuilder installation program adds a new program group named *Powersoft* to your Windows desktop. In the Powersoft program group, double-click the icon labeled **PowerBuilder 5.0** (or **PowerBuilder Desktop**) to launch the PowerBuilder application.

After you start the application, the initial PowerBuilder window is displayed. Figure 1.1 shows the initial display format, a window with a menu and a toolbar called the *PowerBar*. (If the Welcome window opens first, just close it.)

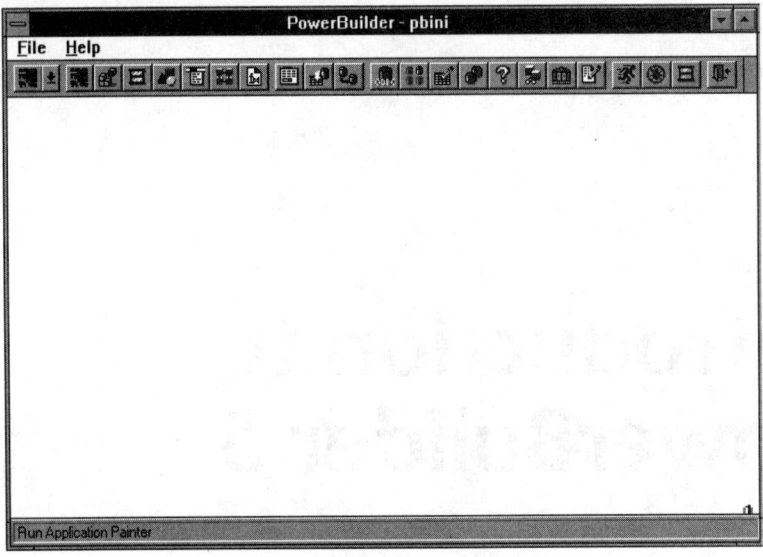

*Figure 1.1* The initial PowerBuilder window.

## The PowerBuilder Painters

A PowerBuilder application consists of many components including windows, controls, functions, and programming code. You develop each component using the various PowerBuilder painters. The PowerBar provides access to the suite of PowerBuilder painters. Each painter provides a development environment for a specific area of development. For example, the Window painter provides the functions you need to develop the graphical user interface. It allows you to create new windows and add controls and other graphical objects

## Introduction to PowerBuilder 5

to these windows. You click on the PowerBar icons to launch the various development environments, each of which works in a certain area of development.

## Displaying Text Labels in the Toolbars

Beginning PowerBuilder developers will not recognize the purpose of all the icons on the PowerBar, but there is a simple solution. You can select an option that displays a text label with each icon on the PowerBar and the other toolbars (which will be introduced shortly). These text labels are useful as you learn your way around the PowerBuilder environment. They make it easier to identify functions on the toolbars until you know what each icon means. To activate this option, click on the PowerBar with the right mouse button to open the popup menu (Figure 1.2).

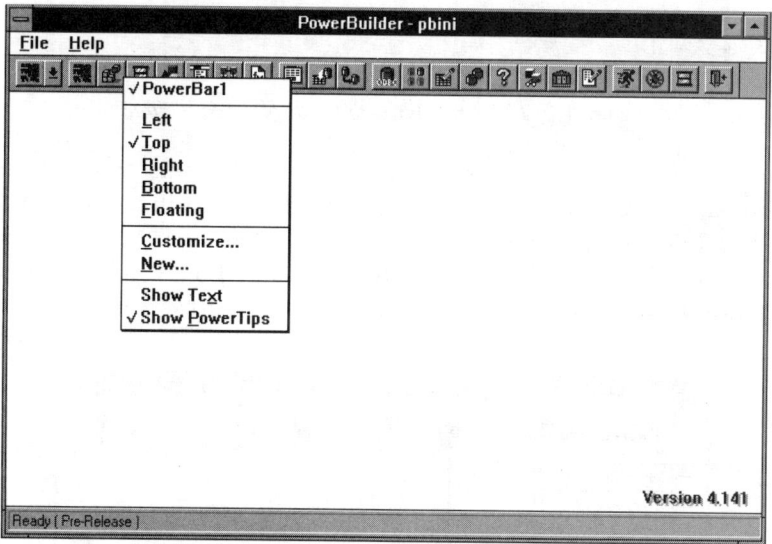

*Figure 1.2* Use the popup menu to control the display of the toolbars.

**NOTE** Take note of this popup menu; it is very useful throughout the development process. You will see many references in this book to the *popup menu* or the *RMB* (right mouse button) popup menu. This popup menu is *context-sensitive*, which means that the contents on the menu change depending on the type of object you have selected.

**8    Chapter 1**

One of the options on this popup menu allows you to toggle the text label for the toolbar icons on and off. Select the Show Text menu option to toggle on the display of the descriptive labels for each icon. A check mark next to the menu option signifies that it is active. Select it again to toggle off the text display option, which removes the check mark. Other options in this popup menu let you select the displayed toolbars, position them (top, bottom, left, right, floating), and create or customize toolbars. Figure 1.3 shows the PowerBar icons with the text display option turned on.

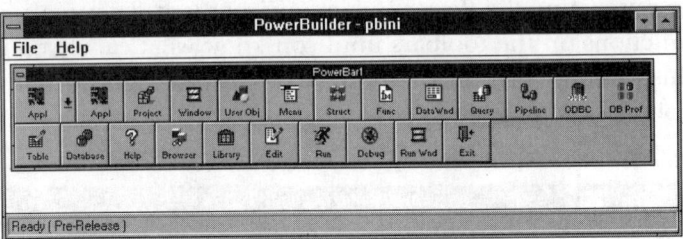

*Figure 1.3  The PowerBar with the display text option.*

You can also set this option with a menu selection in the initial screen. Select the **File|Toolbars** menu option as shown in Figure 1.4. This will open the Toolbars dialog box (Figure 1.5), where you can click the **Show Text** checkbox to toggle on and off the text labels display. In this dialog box, you can also set the **Show PowerTips** option, which I'll describe in the next section.

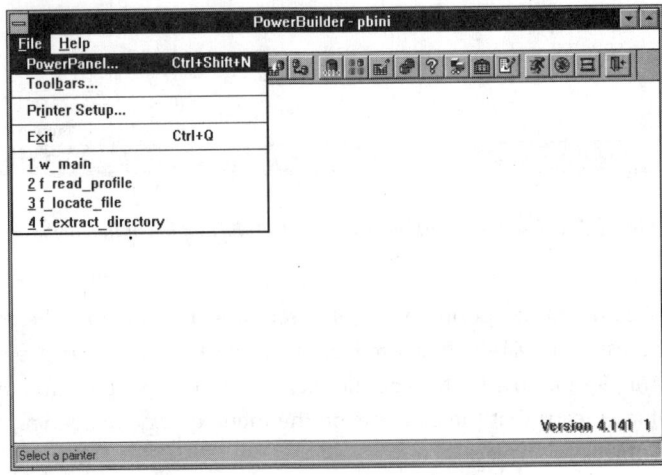

*Figure 1.4  The **File|Toolbars** menu option.*

Introduction to PowerBuilder 5      9

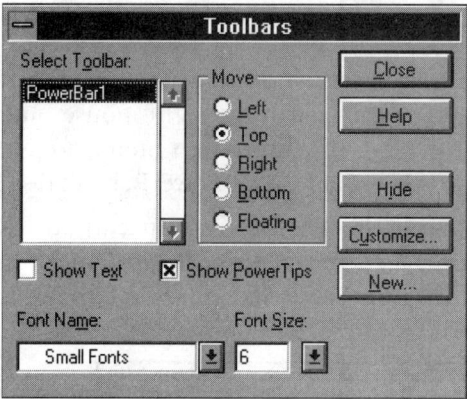

*Figure 1.5*  The Toolbars dialog box with the display text option.

## Displaying PowerTips

An alternative to displaying text on the toolbar icons is to use PowerBuilder PowerTips. This is a standard Windows technique for displaying helpful information about an object. To display a PowerTip for one of the PowerBars (or any toolbar in PowerBuilder), just position the mouse pointer over one of the icons. After about a second, a small yellow popup balloon will open with descriptive text about that icon. In this manner, you can view the same information that the **Show Text** option provides without taking up the additional screen space. If the PowerTip popup menu does not appear, open the Toolbars dialog box (Figure 1.5) and check the **Show PowerTips** option.

## Displaying MicroHelp

For more descriptive help text, click and hold the left mouse button on one of the icons. A message (the MicroHelp text) will appear in the status line of the MDI frame (the bottom line of the PowerBuilder window). If you only want to display the help text and do not want to launch the painter associated with the icon, drag the pointer off the icon while holding the mouse button down. If you slide the pointer off the icon before releasing the mouse button, PowerBuilder will not launch the painter.

## CUSTOMIZING THE PRESENTATION STYLE

You can choose not to display the PowerBar (or any other toolbar). To choose this option, click the PowerBar with the right mouse button. This opens the popup menu (Figure 1.2). On the popup menu, toggle off the PowerBar option by clicking it (**PowerBar1**). The PowerBar will disappear.

Without displaying the PowerBar, you can still access the various PowerBuilder painters by selecting the **PowerPanel** option from the File menu. This opens the PowerPanel dialog box shown in Figure 1.6.

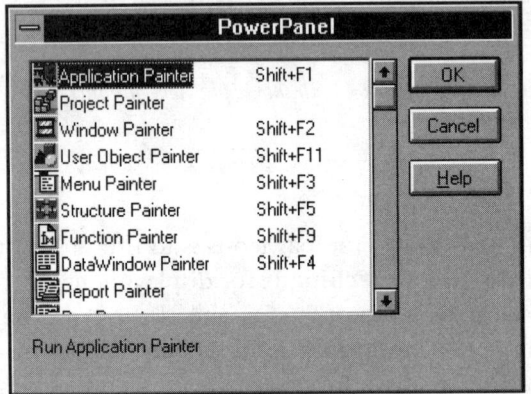 

*Figure 1.6  The PowerPanel dialog box.*

You can also open the PowerPanel drop-down list by clicking the arrow on the PowerBar (Figure 1.6).

The PowerPanel dialog box contains dozens of icons. Clicking any of them will launch one of the painter applications (covered later in this chapter) or perform an action such as arranging the windows.

If you have hidden the PowerBar and wish to make it visible, select the **Toolbars** option from the File menu in the initial screen (Figure 1.4). (This option is available in the Window menu of other painters.) This opens the Toolbars dialog box shown in Figure 1.5.

Select the **PowerBar1** toolbar and click on the **Show** button to display the PowerBar. You can also choose the position of the toolbar and whether or not to show text.

In the Toolbar dialog box, you can also create and customize new toolbars. To customize a toolbar, select the toolbar in the **Select Toolbar** listbox and click the **Customize** button. This will open the Customize dialog box shown in Figure 1.7.

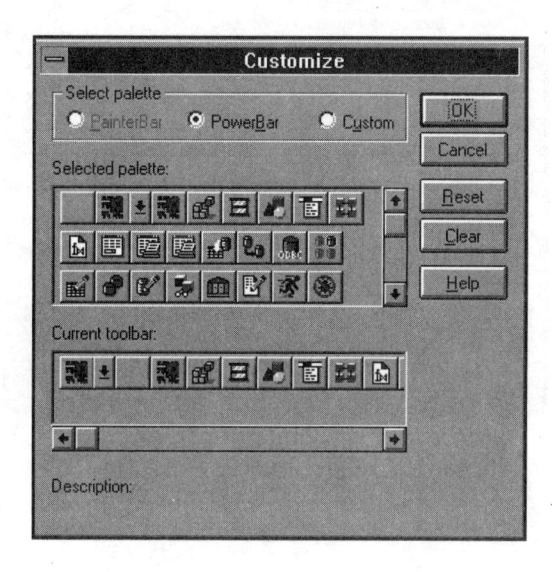

*Figure 1.7  The Customize dialog box.*

In the Customize dialog box, drag the icons from the Selected palette and drop them onto the Current toolbar. When you click on an icon, PowerBuilder will display a description at the bottom of the dialog box. You can remove icons from the current toolbar by dragging them back to the selected palette. You can also reorder the icons by dragging them to the desired location on the toolbar.

## ONLINE HELP

The help system in PowerBuilder is excellent; you can access it in several ways. You can click on the **Help** icon (the question mark) on the PowerPanel or simply press **F1**. Then click on the **Contents** button to open the table of contents shown in Figure 1.8 (this display will vary for different versions of PowerBuilder). In this window you can select a topic, such as **Getting started with PowerBuilder**, to help you find your way through the development environment. You can also search the help index described in the next section.

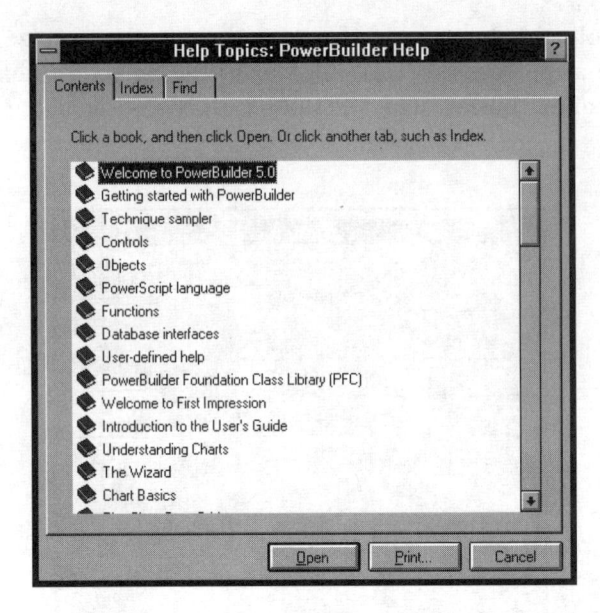

*Figure 1.8* The Help Contents dialog box.

## Find Option

The **Find** option is one of the most useful help system functions. The search function helps you find a specific topic and the related information in the help system. The next paragraphs describe how to use the search function in the help system (these details vary slightly for different versions of PowerBuilder).

### Enter the Search Criteria

From within Help, click on the **Find** tab (**Search** in Windows 3.1) or from within a painter window select the **Help|Search** menu option (**Help|Search for help** is available in all the painters). This opens the dialog window shown in Figure 1.9. Next, enter the search criteria into the input fields (for this example, type **window events**). As you type, the upper listbox presents an index of the choices that best match the text you have entered; see Figure 1.9.

**Introduction to PowerBuilder 5**     13

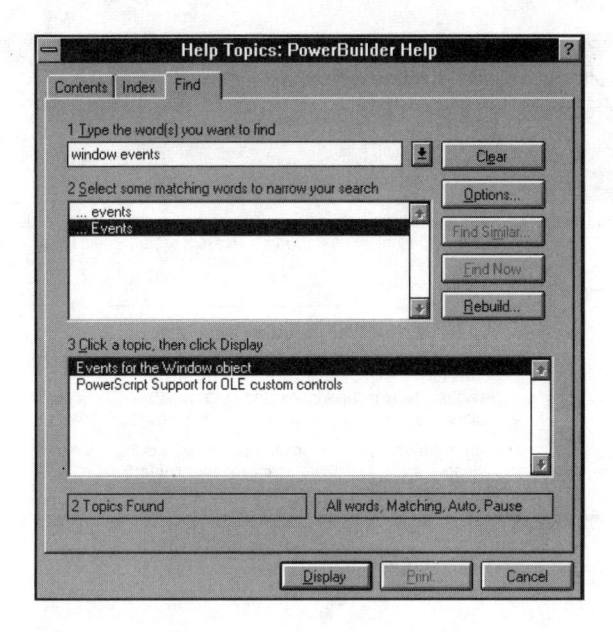

*Figure 1.9  The PowerBuilder help system Search dialog box.*

## Select the Matching Words

After you type each word, click on the best match in the second field (**2 Select some matching words...**) to narrow down the search. In this example, type **window** and click on **Window**; then type **events** and click on **Events**. This will display an entry for "Events for the Window object."

## Select a Topic

Select one of the listed topics (from the bottom listbox) and then click the **Display** (in Windows 3.1) button. This presents the information that is available on the topic (Figure 1.10).

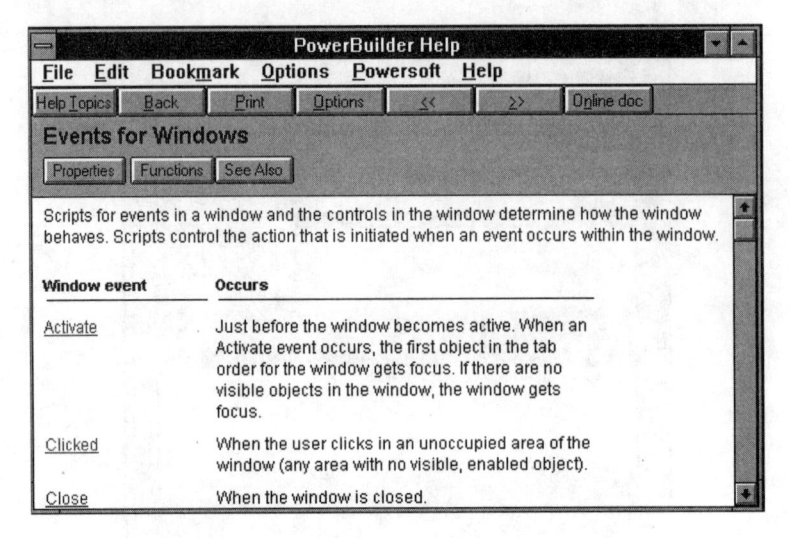

*Figure 1.10 A help topic.*

## Creating Bookmarks

You can place electronic *bookmarks* in the help system so that you can quickly return to a marked entry. After you have found an important entry, create a bookmark by choosing the **Bookmark|Define** menu option and enter a name for the bookmark (or accept the default suggested by PowerBuilder). PowerBuilder adds the name that you assign for a bookmark directly to the Bookmark menu. After that, you can return to any help entry by selecting its name from the menu. To delete the bookmark, choose the **Bookmark|Define** menu option to open the Bookmark Define dialog box, select the bookmark entry, and then click the **Delete** button.

## Using the Help Button

You can also access the help system by clicking on the **Help** button that appears in many dialog windows. Context-sensitive help is available throughout the development process to explain the choices you have at each step. When you are performing an action, such as opening an existing application, you will often see the **Help** button presented as an option. If you click the **Help** button, the help system displays an entry that is specific to the operation you are performing, guiding you though the process and explaining what the options are at each step. Context-sensitive help is also available for the commands and functions in the PowerScript programming language. This will be covered in the section on writing code in the PowerScript language.

## The Help Option

If you click the **Options** button in Figure 1.11, you can set options for the help system. You can also enter more than one word as a search parameter. Here's another tip: If you cannot locate an entry that you expected to find in the index, use the **Find+** option. This will open the Full Text Search window (Figure 1.11), which provides a complete search of the help text.

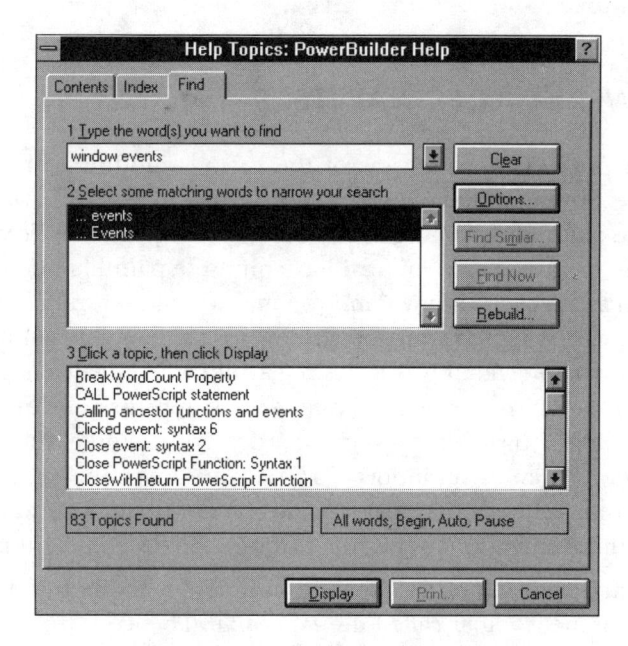

*Figure 1.11* *The help system Find dialog box.*

# THE CONTEXT-SENSITIVE POPUP MENU

You can activate popup menus by placing the pointer on an object and clicking the right mouse button. In this book, this window is referred to as the RMB (right mouse button) menu, or simply the popup menu. You have already seen how the popup menu is used to position the toolbars and toggle the display of text for the toolbar icons. The popup menu is context-sensitive and available throughout the PowerBuilder environment. You often use this menu to set properties of the various PowerBuilder objects. During the design phase, if you click the right mouse button on an object, such as a window or a control, the popup menu will present a different set of options that apply specifically to the type of object you selected. Using the popup menu is often the fastest way to get around in the development process because the pointer is often located near the object with which you are currently working, and the right-mouse click is convenient. As you work your way through the various painters, take time to become familiar with the options that are available in different contexts.

## THE POWERBUILDER PAINTERS

This section presents an overview of the various modules, or *painters*, that make up the PowerBuilder development environment. You will work with each of these painters as you develop your PowerBuilder applications. In the PowerBuilder environment, you can have multiple painters open at the same time (each in a different window) and you may work in several painters simultaneously. You can switch from one window to another by pulling down the Window menu and selecting the desired window. You will encounter some restrictions, however. In a few areas, PowerBuilder appears quite modal, insisting that you complete your work in a specific order. For example, you can only edit the script for one event in a window at a time, and you cannot edit a user object while you have a window open that contains one of these objects. We will point out some of these limitations as we step through the development process.

When you open each of these painter utilities, in addition to the PowerBar you will see another toolbar called the *PainterBar*. The icons that appear on the PainterBar vary for each of the painter utilities. The PainterBar icons are shortcuts to the more important menu options. You can customize the contents of each of the toolbars by adding or deleting icons. You can also control the display of any toolbar, including the PainterBar, by selecting the **Window|Toolbars...** menu option, which opens the Toolbars dialog window (Figure 1.12).

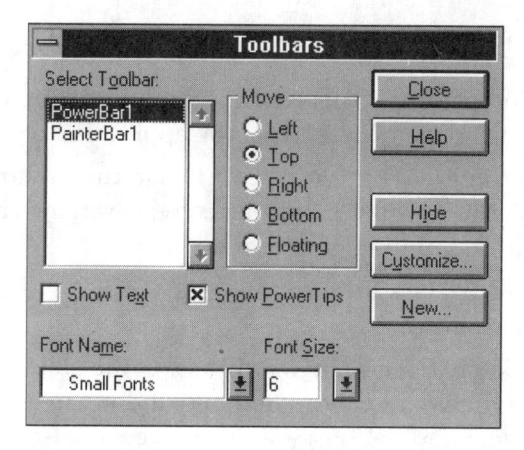

*Figure 1.12  The Toolbars dialog box.*

You can choose to show or hide each toolbar, set their position on the screen, and toggle the text display on and off. (You can also use the RMB popup menu to change the display of the toolbars.) Throughout this book, most of the example screens will show the PainterBar positioned at the left side of the window. Some developers prefer to place it at the bottom of the screen; you can put it wherever you prefer.

## Overview of PowerBuilder Painters

The PowerBuilder painters are the set of development environments you will use to develop PowerBuilder applications. The PowerBuilder initial window (the first screen that opens when you run PowerBuilder) provides a starting point and gives you access to the set of painter utilities (Figure 1.13).

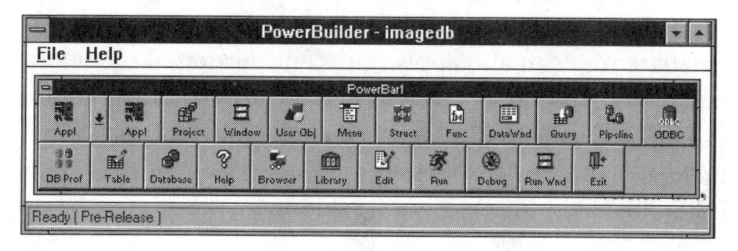

*Figure 1.13  The PowerBar.*

The next section presents a short overview of each painter. Briefly, they are:

- Application painter—This is where you will define the most general application attributes and create the application object itself.
- Window painter—This is where you build the windows that make up your application. You will be able to create windows and add controls to them in an intuitive, graphical manner.
- Menu painter—This is where you create the menus that will be attached to some of your windows.
- DataWindow painter—The *DataWindow* is the object that encapsulates data access for your application. DataWindows are at the heart of most PowerBuilder applications; several chapters will be devoted to them.
- Structure painter—This is where you create composite variables. A *structure* is a set of data elements grouped together as a unit. The set of variables is then referenced by a single name. You can use a structure as a function argument, which will pass the entire structure to the function argument as a unit, reducing the number of arguments necessary in the call. In the structure painter, you create and edit structures.
- Help painter—PowerBuilder has an excellent help system. It also provides context-sensitive help throughout the development process. You should become fluent with this utility.
- Database painter—The Database painter provides a convenient interface to the database. In this painter, you can create tables, indexes, views, extended attributes, validation criteria, and display formats. You can also create, edit, and activate database connection profiles and export and import database definitions.
- Data Manipulation painter—Part of the Database painter where you can execute select, update, insert, and delete operations against the database. You can also apply filters and sorting to the select result set and export and import data to or from a wide range of formats.
- Database Administrator—Lets you enter and execute SQL statements manually. You can save these programs as files for later. The result set is handled as in the Data Manipulation painter.
- Table painter—With this painter you can create and modify database tables and create, alter, and drop primary keys. You can also edit table comments, fonts for table data, headings, and labels.

- Pipeline painter—With this painter you can copy data from one database to another.
- Query painter—With this painter you can graphically create SQL select statements. You can then store these statements in a library where they can be referenced by other objects (such as DataWindows).
- PowerScript painter—This is where you create and edit PowerScript code.
- Function painter—This is where you declare and code your PowerScript procedures. After declaring a function, you will use the PowerScript editor to enter the code. You will call the functions from event scripts or other functions.
- Project painter—This allows you to create and maintain project objects. A project object contains all the information necessary to build application executables.
- Library painter—This is the utility for creating and managing PowerBuilder libraries. *Libraries* are repositories where the components of the applications reside.
- User Object painter—The developer can create a special type of custom object in this painter. After you create custom objects, you can use them as if they were native PowerBuilder controls (such as a command button). This is a more advanced topic, covered later in this book.
- Debugger—The PowerBuilder debugger helps you test your application and provides the features needed to track down and fix programming errors. You can set breakpoints, single-step through the code, examine and change the values of variables, etc.

**CHAPTER 2**

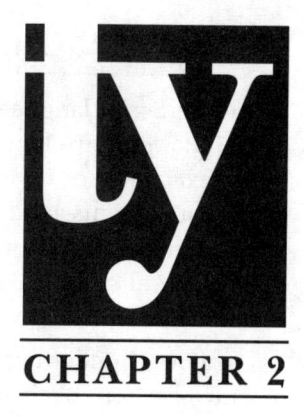

# Programming in PowerBuilder 5

This chapter presents an introduction to programming in PowerBuilder. The first section presents an introduction to PowerBuilder's programming language, PowerScript (often referred to simply as *script*). In this book, we provide all the code for the example applications, so you do not have to know all the information in this chapter to complete those applications. You may, therefore, skip or skim the first section of this chapter. Appendix A provides more details about PowerScript.

This chapter also presents an introduction to the PowerScript editor; read this section carefully because you will use the editor extensively. This is where you enter and edit all of your PowerScript code. The last sections of this chapter cover two very important tools for developing PowerBuilder applications, the *Object Browser* and the *PowerScript Debugger*.

## The PowerScript Language

The PowerScript language has many features that are very similar to BASIC or C. The PowerScript language contains flow-control constructs for the conditional execution of code and to implement looping. For example, the flow control statements are IF, DO, FOR, and CASE. PowerScript has a wide variety of datatypes, with extensions provided to handle database items. You can define a local or global scope for variables. You can also create shared variables that provide one value across different instances of an object.

In PowerBuilder applications, all code execution is triggered by an event or a message sent from another script. This is a fundamental trait of the event-driven paradigm. You can attach PowerScript code to the PowerBuilder application objects (such as windows and command buttons) by writing code for object events or object-level functions. You can also write functions that are used more generally and are available globally. You will write code for the events in which you are interested. In that code you may trigger other events or call other functions (either system or user defined).

### PowerScript Text

You can enter PowerScript text in a free-form fashion. You can add spaces and indent the code to make the code more readable. Generally, each PowerScript statement should be put on its own separate line. You can put multiple script statements on a single line if you separate them with a semicolon. For example:

```
beep(1) ; MessageBox('Note', 'Hello'); beep(2)
```

Script code is case insensitive so that:

```
b_FirstTime =  true
b_firsttime =  True
B_FIRSTTIME =  TRUE
```

are all the same to PowerBuilder. This applies to all identifiers, including function names. `OpenWithParm()` and `openwithparm()` are the same, but you may find the mixed-case version easier to read.

Many developers use the underscore character to delineate words in their identifiers. For example:

```
b_first_time
```

is a Boolean variable; its value tells us if this is the first time through the code. This is the convention followed throughout this book. For the previous example, you could also have used:

```
bFirstTime
```

as the identifier for the Boolean, but you can choose whichever style you prefer. I recommend the first usage, because PowerBuilder will only paste in lowercase. If you use the mixed-case style, you will find that you have to constantly fix up the code pasted into the Script Editor. This chapter includes a set of recommended naming conventions that will make the sharing and maintenance of code easier.

## Line Continuation

You can continue a code statement on the next line by using the continuation character & (ampersand). Place & at the end of the line you wish to continue; it must be the last character on the line. This is easy to remember because & means *AND there is more to follow*. An example of line continuation is

```
MessageBox("Status", "Successfully read " &
                + string(idx) + " lines of text")
```

You cannot break up an identifier by using the continuation character. The following is illegal:

```
i_return = Message&
    Box('note', 'this message')
```

## Comments

PowerScript permits comments to be added in two different forms: in single line and in multiline (block) form. Place a multiline comment between /*

and `*/`. Create a single-line comment using two slashes, `//`. This can appear anywhere on a line and causes the rest of the line to be interpreted as a comment. For example:

```
/*
    here is a multiline
    comment
*/
/* it could also be used for a single line */
// or use this for a single line comment
beep(1) // this adds a comment to the end of a line
```

Block comments can be nested, as in the following example.

```
int i_sum
i_sum = 1 + 2 /* add 1,2,and 4
    /* i_sum will be equal to 7 at the end of this example */
    + 3 */ +4
```

You might expect an error in this example because the final +4 looks like it is dangling on a line by itself. Lines broken up by multiline comments do not need the continuation character.

## Dot Notation

PowerScript allows the direct addressing of objects and their attributes (and functions) by using a *dot notation* syntax. The general form of the dot notation is

```
object_name.attribute_name OR
window_name.object_name.attribute_name
```

For example, you can disable a command button (cb_close) in the Main window (w_main) by setting the button's Enabled attribute to false with the following notation:

```
w_main.cb_close.enabled = FALSE
```

Dot notation is also used for functions. That form is

`object_name.Function_name()`

For example, you can set the focus on the `cb_close` command button as follows:

`cb_close.SetFocus()`

Here are a few additional examples:

1. `st_status.text = "OK"`
    `// set the text attribute`
    `// of static text object`
    `// st_status`

2. `w_main.sle_count.text = "12"`
    `// qualified reference`
    `// made from another window`

3. `w_main.title = "Hello"`
    `// set the window caption`
    `// to "Hello"`

4. `dw_1.Retrieve()`
    `// execute the retrieve`
    `// function for dw_1`

5. `cb_retrieve.Enable()`
    `// enabled a button using`
    `// a user-defined function`

6. `w_main.m_file.m_exit.Disable()`
    `// qualifies window name,`
    `// menu name, MenuItem`

A control name (such as a command button or single-line edit) is known throughout the window and does not need any further qualification within that window. The window name is required if you are making the reference from outside the window. In example 1, the reference does not require a window name to qualify it if it is made within a script in the window or one of its objects. In example 2, the reference is being made from a window other than w_main, and therefore the qualification is required in order to locate the sle_count object.

## Identifiers

*Identifiers* are tags that are used throughout PowerBuilder. They are used to name variables, controls, functions, labels, and other PowerBuilder objects. In PowerScript, identifiers can be up to 40 characters long, must begin with a letter, and cannot contain spaces. In addition to the alphanumeric characters, identifiers may contain the following special characters:

-     –    minus (dash)
-     _    underscore
-     $    dollar sign
-     #    pound sign
-     %    percent sign

It is unusual for a programming language to let the minus sign be a character in identifiers; if you are not careful it can cause unexpected problems. For example:

```
i_len-1
```

is a legal identifier. If you intended this to be an expression where 1 is to be subtracted from the current value of i_len, you are in for a surprise. Consider the following code:

```
i_size = i_len-1
```

When you compile this line of code, you may receive an error stating that i_len-1 is an unknown identifier. This is because PowerBuilder has interpreted i_len-1 to be an identifier and it cannot find a previous declaration for it. Fortunately, you can avoid this type of problem by disallowing the use of the minus sign in identifiers. To do this, uncheck the **Allow Dashes In Identifiers** checkbox in the Properties dialog box (in the Script Editor, choose **Design|Options**). Or, you could set it to **zero** in the **PB.INI** file as follows:

```
PB.INI
[pb]
DashesInIdentifiers = 0
```

This turns off the option, the previous code example is interpreted in the way that you intended, and the script then compiles successfully. You should set this constraint as soon as you install PowerBuilder at your site, so that other developers cannot create identifiers with the dash. Otherwise, their code will fail to compile after you make this change.

## Data Types

PowerScript provides variables, which hold data values for your applications. A variable's *datatype* specifies the type of data stored in the variable. PowerScript offers a wide variety of datatypes to the developer. These data types include Boolean, Integer, Long, Decimal, Real, Character, String, and Real. PowerScript includes a set of date- and time-related datatypes and a binary type called a Blob. See Appendix A for more information on datatypes.

### The Enumerated Datatype

The *enumerated* datatype is a special type used in the PowerScript language. This datatype is used to set characteristics of objects (or controls) and as arguments for functions with a label that is more meaningful than an integer (i.e., `Maximized!`). All the enumerated values are predefined by the PowerBuilder system; you cannot add to this predefined set as in other languages. Enumerated values always end with the exclamation character (!) to signal their special type.

For example, the possible values for the style of arranging windows are `Cascade!`, `Layer!`, `Tile!`, which is far more descriptive than 0, 1, and 2. You could arrange all the currently open windows as follows:

```
w_main_mdi.ArrangeSheets (Cascade!)
```

You can find all the enumerated datatype values using the browser (described later in this chapter). In the browser, select the **Enumerated** tab, click on the type in the objects listbox (such as **arrangetypes**), and then double-click the **Properties** icon. This lists the enumerated values in the correct listbox (see Figure 2.1).

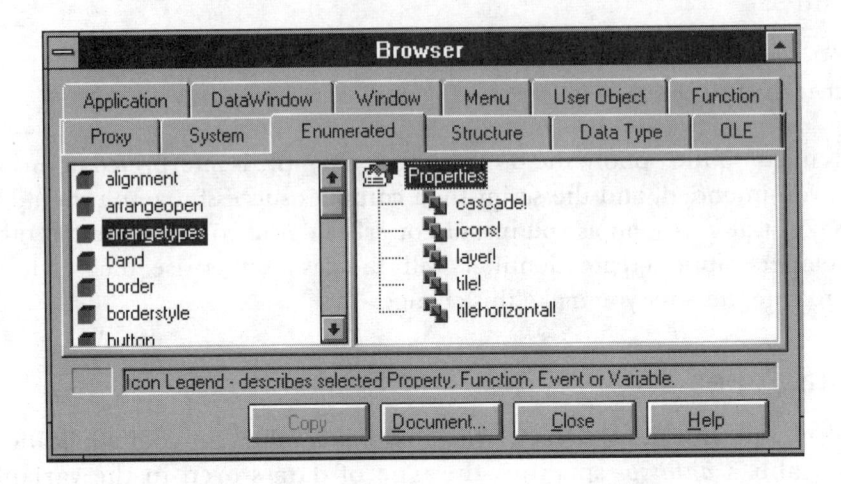

*Figure 2.1 Listing the arrangetypes enumerated values.*

## Arrays

You can create an array of any standard datatype. You can also create arrays of other types, such as windows or user objects. Array notation uses square brackets to enclose the array index. Arrays can also be multidimensional. Array indexes, by default, begin with the value 1 and are bounded by the size of the array. *Unbounded* (variable-length) arrays can be declared by omitting the size from the declaration. This is only permitted with single-dimension arrays:

Examples of array declarations and assignments follow:

```
int i_count[10]
int i_set[3] = {1,2,3}
int i_multi[3,3,3]
i_multi[1,2,3] = 12
i_count[10] = 5
```

## Variable Scope Options

PowerScript variables have several different scoping options that determine the range of visibility. The variable scopes are local, global, instance, and shared.

## Global Scope

The *global* scope is the least restrictive of the scoping options. A global variable will be known (visible and usable) throughout the entire application. You declare a variable as global by selecting **Declare|Global** menu option (from within the Window, User Object, or PowerScript painter). This opens the Declare Global Variables dialog box shown in Figure 2.2. (This can also be reached from the Menu and Function painters.)

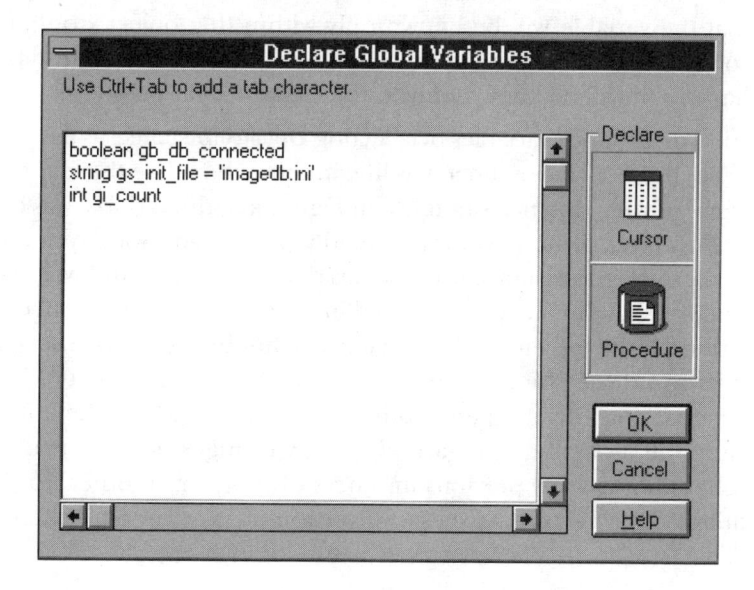

*Figure 2.2 Declaring a global variable.*

Enter the datatype and the name of the variable on a new line in the list box and hit **Enter** to close the dialog box. If you wish to declare multiple variables, use the **Ctrl+Enter** key combination to move to the next line in the listbox instead of closing it. Use the letter *g* to prefix the name of your global variables, such as `int gi_count`.

## Local Scope

The *local* scope is the most common and most restrictive option. When you declare a variable within your script (or function) text, it is defined with a local scope. That variable will only be known in the script (or function) in which it was declared. You should declare most of your variables as local variables, unless you definitely need to extend access to the variable beyond the immediate locality where it was declared.

## Instance Variables

You declare *instance variables* within the context of an object. Instance variables have a scope limited to the object level for that occurrence (instance) of the object. The object level can be application, window, menu, or user-object. This means that the variable will be known only within that object (to that object and the objects that it contains). For example, if you declared an instance variable in a menu, it will be known only to the elements of that menu.

You declare instance variables by selecting **Declare|Instance**, as in Figure 2.3, and entering the declaration on a new line in the listbox. Use the letter *i* to prefix the name of your instance variables. In Figure 2.3, the variable was declared at the window level (from a window named w_main) and was given an initial value of 1. Because the instance variable was declared at the window level, it will also be known to all the objects contained in the w_main window (such as command buttons, listboxes, etc.). This variable will not be visible to other windows or the objects in those other windows (except as noted in the next paragraph). One additional note: if you open another instance of w_main, the initial value of i_count will always be 1, regardless of any changes of value made to the ii_count variable in any previous instances of w_main. In other words, each instantiation of w_main will have its own version of ii_count to manipulate.

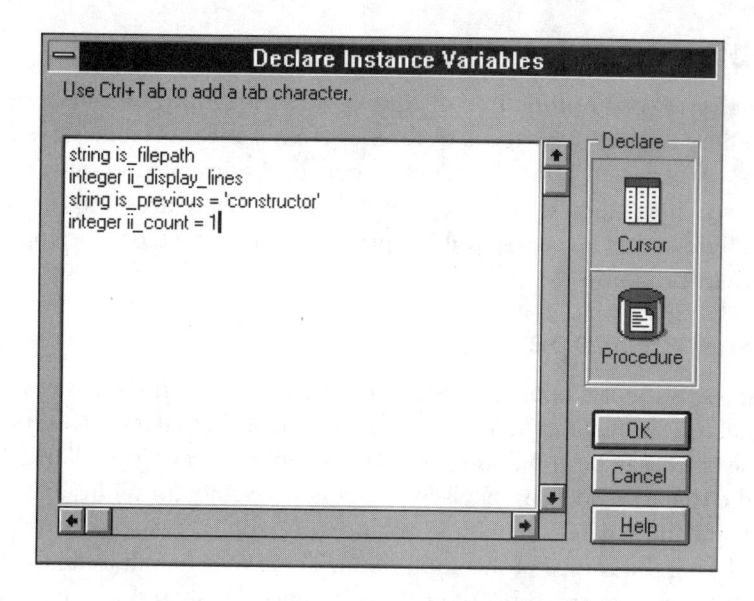

*Figure 2.3* Declaring an instance variable.

## USING DOT NOTATION WITH INSTANCE VARIABLES

You can access an instance variable externally by using dot notation to qualify the object and variable name. For example, in Figure 2.3, the variable ii_count was declared as a window-level instance variable (in w_main). In the window w_other, access this variable as w_main.ii_count. This is generally a practice to be limited as much as possible; it will make maintenance difficult if the ii_count variable is changed. It is even possible to prevent this type of reference by using PowerScript access levels.

## Variable Access Levels

*Access levels* give you another level of control over the scope of instance variables. You can limit or prevent external references to instance variables by setting the variable's access level. The access level is part of the instance variable's declaration and specifies which scripts in the application will have access to the variable. The possible access levels are public, private, and protected. See Appendix A for more information.

## The Shared Scope

*Shared* scope is the last option for a variable scope. A shared scope variable has a scope that is very similar to that of an instance variable in that it is also at the object level (the object can be application, window, menu, or user object). The difference is that the shared scope variable is known and accessible for all instances of that object. Sometimes there are multiple instances of an object (window, menu, or userobject) during the course of the application. There may be values that you would like to maintain and share between these instances. A shared variable retains its value across instances, and therefore the instances of the object share that variable. You could use a shared variable to count the number of times a window is opened.

You declare variables with shared scope by selecting **Declare|Shared**, as shown in Figure 2.4. Use the letter *s* as the prefix for your shared variables. In this example, in the first instance of `w_main`, the initial value of `si_count` is 1. If you open another instance of `w_main`, the initial value of `si_count` is equal to that of the last change of value that had been made to `si_count` in the previous instances of `w_main`.

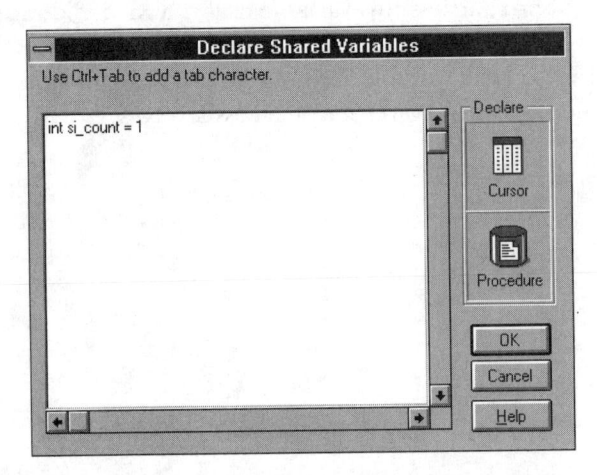

*Figure 2.4 Declaring a shared variable.*

## Labeling Scope in Identifiers

It is recommended that the first letter of your identifiers be a letter that labels the scope of the variable. An underscore is used to set off the scope and datatype from the rest of the variable name:

- g  global
- s  shared
- i  instance
- l  local (This is optional, because it is not actually necessary to recognize local scope.)
- a  argument (This labels a variable as an argument passed to a function when referenced inside the function.)

Here are a few examples:

1. `gs_init_file = "C:\app.ini"   // a global string variable`
2. `ii_count = 1   // an instance integer variable`
3. `si_max_range = 123   // a shared integer variable`
4. `i_count = 1   // a local integer variable`
5. `li_count = 1   // alternative notation for a local integer`
6. `as_name   //a string argument passed to a function`

This naming convention makes it easy to avoid name collisions. If you use the same name for two different variables, it is important that you understand PowerBuilder's order in resolving variables.

## Passing Variables in Function Calls

You can pass variables in function calls either by value or by reference. When passed by value, it is actually a copy of the variable that is made available in the called functions. All changes made to that variable in the called function are limited to the copy, and the changes are not visible back in the calling function.

If the variable has been passed by reference, this works differently. Any change made to the reference variable in the called function will be visible in the calling function because the two functions are actually sharing a reference to a single variable. So all changes are actually made to the original variable in the calling function. This is very similar to how pointers are used in the C language, but the declaration and use are different.

### Declaring a Reference Variable

A *reference variable* is defined when you create the declaration of a function's arguments. When you define a function, you must specify the datatype for each argument, and you must specify whether the argument is passed by reference or by value, as shown in Figure 2.5.

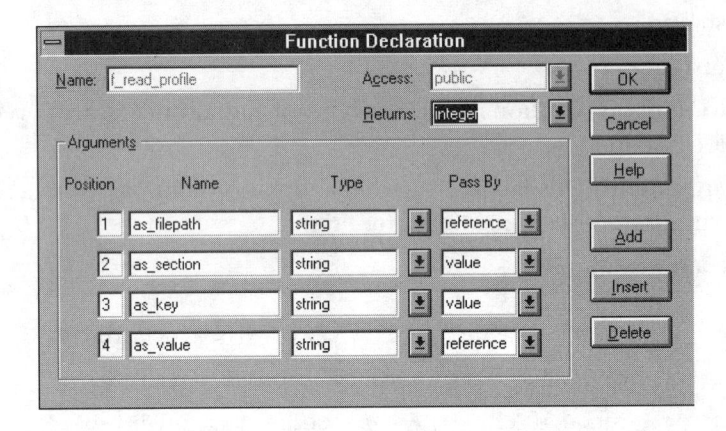

**Figure 2.5** *Declaring a function argument.*

This declaration is all that is required. Neither the calling function nor the called function uses any other notation for the "by reference" variables.

In the case of complex datatypes, such as structures and windows, PowerBuilder will pass the variable as "by reference" even if you declare it as "by value." This is done to conserve memory.

## POWERSCRIPT LANGUAGE STATEMENTS

PowerScript has several statements that provide branching. We will look first at the IF statement and the CHOOSE CASE statements.

## The IF Statement

The IF statement has several different forms, all of which may be familiar to you if you know Basic. The first and simplest form is the single-line version:

```
IF <condition> THEN action
```

This executes the action if the condition is true. Multiple statements can be combined within the action clause with the use of the semicolon (if there is no ELSE clause).

Some examples follow:

```
IF i_count > 99 THEN i_count = 0; beep(1)
IF i_count > 99 THEN i_count = 0 ELSE i_count = i_count + 1
```

The relational operators that can be used for comparison are:

| | |
|---|---|
| = | equal |
| <> | not equal |
| > | greater than |
| >= | greater than or equal |
| < | less than |
| <= | less than or equal |

## Operator Precedence

The order of precedence for the mathematical and relational operators is shown in Table 2.1.

*Table 2.1 Mathematical Operators*

| Symbol | Name |
|---|---|
| ( ) | parentheses |
| +, – | unary |
| ^ | |
| *, / | |
| +, – | |
| the relational operators (including =, <>, and >=) | |
| NOT | |
| AND | |
| OR | |

More complex conditions can be created by using the logical operators AND, OR, and NOT. Parentheses are used, in the same manner as in other languages, to specify the order of the evaluation.

The next form of the IF statement lets multiple statements be grouped together (the ELSE clause is optional):

```
IF <condition> THEN
    <action1>
ELSE
    <action2>
END IF
```

The <action1> and <action2> labels can be replaced by one or more PowerScript statements, for example:

```
IF s_last_name > 'M'   THEN
    i_count = i_count + 1
    beep(1)
ELSE
    i_count = i_count - 1   // or i_count -= 1
    beep(2)
END IF
```

## The CHOOSE CASE Statement

The CHOOSE CASE construct is very flexible and can handle several forms of CASE conditional expressions. It is a better choice and is much clearer and easier to code than using multiple ELSEIF clauses in an IF statement.

```
CHOOSE CASE <expression>
    CASE <item>
        <statementblock>
    CASE ELSE
```

```
        <statementblock>
END CHOOSE
```

The final CASE ELSE clause is optional. The possible forms of the CASE expression are a single value, a list of values, a range of values, a relational operator, or combinations of any of these.

A single value is simply listed after the keyword CASE. To create a list, add additional values with a comma between them, as in CASE 1, 3, 5.

A range of values is expressed using the TO keyword, for example, CASE 1 TO 5. Use the IS keyword with a relational operator, as in CASE IS > 5 or CASE IS <> 'Smith'. You can combine these forms by using commas, as in CASE 1, 11 TO 15, IS >999. Some examples follow:

```
CHOOSE CASE i_count
    CASE 9, 1 to 5
        i_count += 1
    CASE IS > 5
        i_count = 0
    CASE  -1
        i_count = -i_count
    CASE ELSE
        i_count = -1
END CHOOSE
```

## LOOPING CONSTRUCTS

PowerScript has several ways to implement looping. The DO...LOOP construct will be covered first. This has four different forms:

```
DO
    <statementblock>
LOOP UNTIL <condition>
```

```
DO
    <statementblock>
LOOP WHILE <condition>
DO UNTIL <condition>
    <statementblock>
LOOP
DO WHILE <condition>
    <statementblock>
LOOP
```

All forms have DO at the beginning and LOOP at the end of the loop. The placement of the WHILE or UNTIL changes the behavior of the loop. The most significant point to notice is that the first two forms will execute the code inside the loop at least once, because the evaluation is not done until the end of the loop. The statements inside the loop for the last two forms may not be executed at all. The WHILE forms execute the loop as long as the condition is true. The UNTIL forms execute the loop as long as the condition is not true:

```
i_rc = 0
DO WHILE i_rc = 0
    i_rc = dotest()
LOOP
DO UNTIL i_rc = 100
    i_rc = FetchAgain()
LOOP
DO
    i_rc = FetchAgain()
LOOP UNTIL i_rc = 100
DO
    i_rc = FetchAgain()
LOOP WHILE i_rc = 0
```

## The FOR...NEXT Loop

The other looping construct in PowerScript is the FOR...NEXT statement, which is identical to the form that it takes in most versions of the Basic language:

```
FOR <varname>=<start> TO <end> STEP <increment>
    <statementblock>
NEXT
```

A variable is initialized at the start of the loop, and the statements in the statement block are executed. When NEXT is executed, the variable is incremented by the STEP value and the result is then compared against the end value. If the value is still within the start-to-end range, the loop is executed again.

The STEP clause is optional. If the STEP clause is not included, the variable is incremented by 1 if the start value is less than the end value. If the end value is less than the start value, then the loop increments the variable by –1:

```
FOR i_count = 1 TO 10 STEP 2
    dosomething(i_count)
NEXT
```

This first example initializes the i_count variable to 1. Each time through the loop it is incremented by 2 (1,3,5 etc.). The loop executes as long as i_count is less than or equal to 10. The value of i_count is 11 when it exits the loop.

```
FOR i_count = 10 TO 1
    dosomething(i_count)
NEXT
```

In this example, the STEP value has not been specified. It will default to STEP –1, because the start value is greater than the end value. The value of i_count will be 0 when it exits the FOR loop.

## The HALT Statement

The `HALT` statement forces the application to terminate. This is used most often to shut down the application after a serious error has occurred.

`HALT CLOSE` does the same thing, but triggers the application object's `CLOSE` event before terminating.

## The RETURN Statement

The `RETURN` statement causes the script (or event) to end and returns control to the calling procedure (or to the system). In a function, you can specify a return value with this statement, for example:

```
//Function f_calc
i_value = Calc(ai_price)
RETURN i_value
```

# POWERBUILDER FUNCTIONS

PowerBuilder has nearly 500 built-in functions providing a wide range of functionality such as numeric and string processing and data conversion for your applications. You should make a couple of passes through the list of functions in the help system to become familiar with the types of functions available. From your previous programming experience, you will know what kind of functions should be available; often the hardest part of locating a function is finding its name. The browser and help system will ease your search.

## User-Defined Functions

Even though PowerBuilder provides hundreds of built-in functions, you will also need to create functions of your own. You create these user-defined functions in the Function painter. After you have created the user-defined functions, you can call them from your other script code as if they were PowerBuilder built-in functions. User-defined functions are created using the PowerScript language. The process is almost the same as writing code for an event. User-defined functions can have *arguments* (parameters) and a return value and are not associated with an event.

User-defined functions have scope, either global or object level. Global functions have the same visibility as global variables and can be called from anywhere in your application, just like built-in PowerBuilder functions that can be used by any object. Define a function with global scope when it provides a general functionality that may be used by various types of objects in your application.

You can define object-level user-defined functions at the application, window, menu, or user-object level. This type of user-defined function has a scope like PowerBuilder functions that are defined for a specific type of object (like `menuitem1.Check()`). Define a function with an object-level scope when you want to limit the use of that function to a single type of object.

To create or edit a global function, you must use the Function painter. Click the **Func** icon on the PowerBar to create a function. This will open the Select Function dialog box, as shown in Figure 2.6.

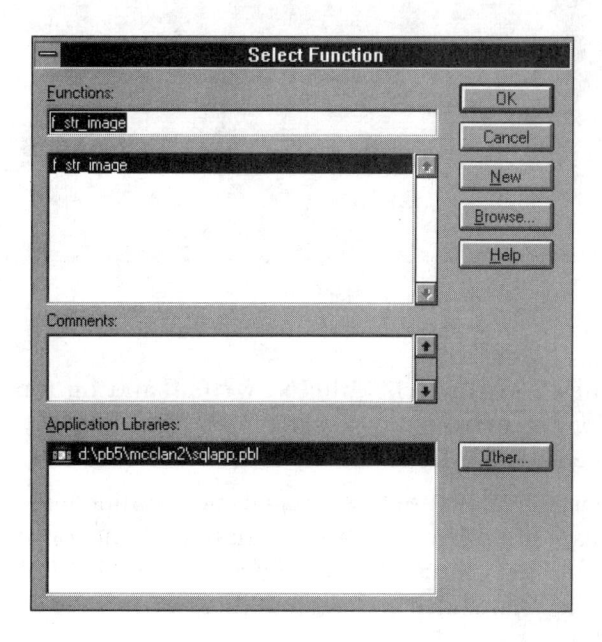

*Figure 2.6 Select Function dialog box.*

In this dialog box, you can edit an existing function by selecting the library and the function name. This opens the Function painter, and you can edit the code. The Function painter is essentially the PowerScript painter with a few variations. When you are in the Function painter, there are only three possible listboxes, the Paste Global listbox, the Paste Window listbox, and the Paste Argument listbox. The Paste Argument listbox contains the names of the function parameters you defined when you declared the function (in the New Function dialog box); this will let you paste the arguments into your code.

Edit the function declaration by selecting **Design|Function Declaration** and click the **Edit** icon **PainterBar**. This opens the Function Declaration dialog box shown in Figure 2.7.

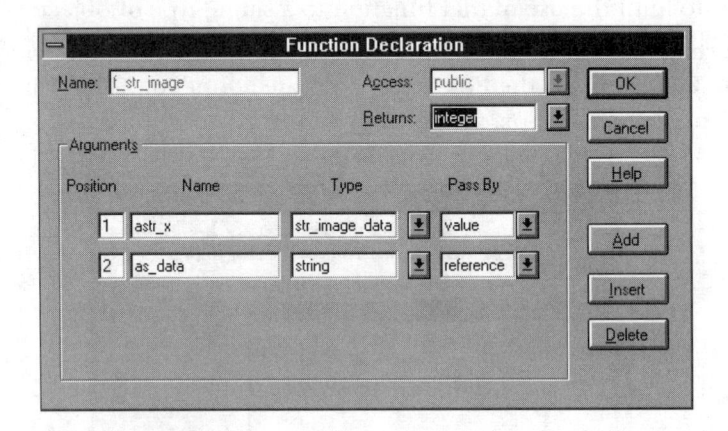

*Figure 2.7  Editing a function declaration.*

To create a new function, click the **New** command button in the Select Function dialog box to open the New Function dialog box, which is essentially the same as the Function Declaration dialog box (Figure 2.7).

In this dialog box, you define a name for the function, select a return type, and add any arguments that are passed in the function call. The recommended convention is to use f_ as the prefix for global functions, such as f_calc_tax. Recommended prefixes for other types of user-defined functions are listed in Table 2.2.

**Table 2.2** *Recommended Function Name Prefixes*

| PREFIX | OBJECT LEVEL | ALTERNATIVE CHOICE |
|--------|--------------|--------------------|
| f_     | Global       |                    |
| fa_    | Application  | af_                |
| fw_    | Window       | wf_                |
| fm_    | Menu         | mf_                |
| fu_    | User-object  | uf_                |

A global function has an access level of public. You can set the access level to public, private, or protected for object level functions.

## *Object-Level Functions*

To create an object-level function, first open the painter for the object for which you intend to define the function. Then choose **Declare|Object Functions**. The actual text for this menu option will vary according to the type of object you are editing. For example, for user objects the menu selection is **Declare|User Object Functions** and for windows it is **Declare|Window Functions**.

This opens the Select Function dialog box, as shown in Figure 2.8. In this dialog box, you can edit an existing function or create a new function.

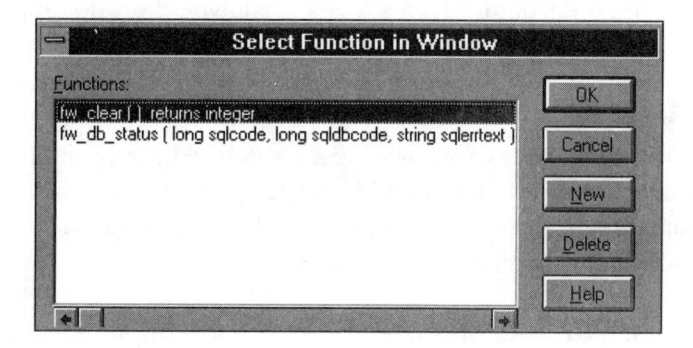

*Figure 2.8 Select Function dialog box.*

Clicking the **New** command button opens the New Function dialog box (similar to Figure 2.7). In the New Function dialog box, you define a name for the function, select a datatype for the return value, and add any arguments that are passed in the function call. For an object-level function, you can also set the access level to public, private, or protected.

The recommended conventions for function name prefixes were given in Table 2.2. I prefer the set under Prefix because all user-defined functions will appear under the letter *f* (for function) in the browser. Other developers use the set of prefixes under Alternative.

### *Function Return Value Type*

Most functions return a value; the default datatype of the return value is an *integer*. A common standard in PowerBuilder is to return a value of 1 to signify success. To choose another datatype for the return value, select from the Returns drop-down listbox. You can also decide not to return a value from the function. This is less usual, but specify this by choosing **None** from the Returns drop-down listbox. You can also ignore the return value if you wish.

### *Function Argument List*

You can define arguments to be used for the function. To define an argument, you name the argument, specify its datatype, and then declare whether the argument is to be passed by value or by reference. Arguments can be user-object datatypes or structures. This type of datatype does not appear in the Type listbox, but if you enter the datatype, it will be allowed. In Figure 2.7, the first argument is a `str_image_data` structure passed by value. The second argument is a string passed by reference so that it may be assigned a value.

As many arguments as you need can be defined for your function. Just click the **Add** command button to add a new argument. Click on **Insert** to add a new argument at the current position in the list. Click on **Delete** to remove the currently selected argument from the list.

### *Standard User-Objects and User-Defined Functions*

Although you cannot define an object-level function at the control level (such as a command button or a listbox), you can define a function for a standard user object. Because the standard user object is based on a standard type of control (such as a command button), you can achieve the desired result. This is essentially the same as adding a method to a class in object-oriented languages.

Even though functions are defined at the object level, you can access these functions from outside the object using dot notation (described earlier). For example, suppose a user-defined function was created for a standard user object based on a command button and this function was used to disable the user object. For this example, assume that the user-object was added to a window and named `cb_close`. The following code can call this function from another object in the window:

```
cb_close.fu_disable ()
```

or from another window by using:

```
w_main.cb_close.fu_disable()
```

## Function Access Level

The access levels for functions are the same as for instance variables. Public access lets the function be referenced externally using dot notation. The private access level restricts access to scripts within the object. The protected access level restricts access to scripts within the object or within objects inherited .from this object.

## A Sample Function

The next example shows the code for a simple window-level function that displays the current database status information in three fields on the window. The function is named `fw_db_status`, has three arguments, and returns 1 if there is no error and 0 if there is a database error.

```
Function:    fw_db_status
Arguments:   al_sql_code      long     by value
             al_sql_dbcode    long     by value
             as_sql_err_text  string   by reference
```

Returns:    Integer

```
st_dbcode.text = string(al_sql_dbcode)
st_sql_code.text = string(al_sql_code)
mle_dbtext.text = as_sql_err_text
IF al_sql_code = 0 THEN
     return 1
ELSE
     return 0
END IF
```

In this book, you may see the previous function declaration presented as follows:

```
//integer fw_db_status(long al_sql_code, long al_sql_dbcode,
ref string as_sql_err_text)
```

After you have created a user-defined function, it is available in the Object Browser for pasting into your code, just like built-in functions. If the function is a global function, select the **Function** tab. If the function is an object-level function, first locate the object in the Windows listbox, and then double-click the **Function** icon. The listing for the function also includes the Argument list.

The global function names also appear on the list of user-defined functions, which is available if you select **Edit|Paste Function** in the PowerScript painter (click the **User-defined** radio button).

## The Object Browser

The PowerBuilder Object Browser is a very powerful tool. It has an icon on the PowerPanel and on the PowerScript Editor PainterBar. You should become familiar with this tool. You will use the Object Browser most often to paste text into your PowerScript code, so it is covered in the next section.

## THE POWERSCRIPT PAINTER

This section introduces the PowerScript painter, the editor you will use to create and edit most of the PowerScript code you write (it is worth your time to become familiar with it). The PowerScript painter is similar in functionality to the Windows' Write editor. Menu options let you cut, copy, and paste text within or between windows; they also provide search and replace functionality from within the file. The PowerScript code you create will automatically be stored within your PowerBuilder application library.

The last section of this chapter introduces the Object Browser, a PowerBuilder utility. With the browser you can quickly locate the name of a specific attribute, function, enumerated value, variable, or object. The Object Browser is convenient for pasting a wide range of values into PowerScript code.

You can open the PowerScript painter from within any PowerBuilder painter in which you need to create or edit code, including the Application, Window, Function, Menu, and User-Object painters.

The first opportunity to use the PowerScript painter (after starting PowerBuilder) is in the Application painter. For this introduction, launch PowerBuilder and open the Application painter by clicking on the **Application** icon on the PowerBar.

NOTE: To explore the editor, you can use the FirstApp application, just be sure that the current application is set to **FirstApp** (check the title bar). If it's not, select the **Open** icon from the PainterBar (or the **File|Open** menu item) and select **FIRSTAPP.PBL** in the File Name listbox and then click **OK**. In the Select Application window, select the **firstapp** application object and click **OK** to open it.

When you are in the Application painter, click on the **Script** icon on the PainterBar to open the PowerScript painter (or choose the **Edit|Script** menu item). This will open the PowerScript painter, as shown in Figure 2.9.

## Chapter 2

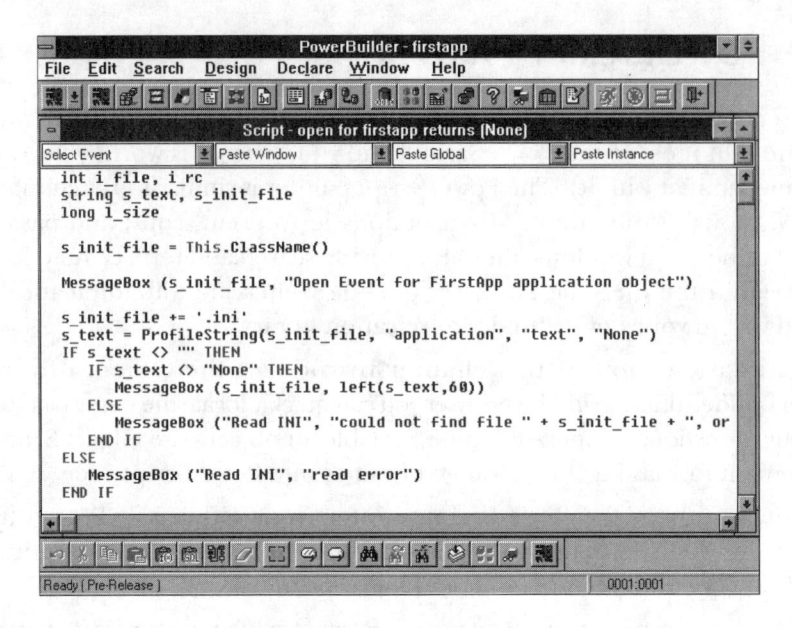

*Figure 2.9  The PowerScript painter.*

The PowerScript painter title bar displays the name of the object (or control) and the name of event for which you are currently coding. It also displays the data type of the return value or None if a value is not returned. Figure 2.9 shows that we are editing the Open event script for the FirstApp application object, and that this event has no return value.

## THE DROP-DOWN LIST BOXES

There are a number of drop-down listboxes in the PowerScript painter. They have labels such as Select Event, Paste Object, Paste Global, and Paste Instance (this is customizable and may be different on your display). Use the Select Event listbox to choose the event for which you are editing code. The other listboxes are used to paste the names of objects, controls, windows, and variables into your script code. Pasting object names in this manner is quick, avoids having to look up a name, and avoids typing errors. You can choose which drop-down lists are displayed in the Properties dialog box for the editor; see the later section on customizing the editor for directions.

**NOTE:** When you are in the Function painter, there are only three possible listboxes: Paste Global, Paste Argument, and Paste Window. The Paste Argument listbox contains the names of the function parameters you defined when you declared the function (in the New Function dialog box).

Use **Ctrl-1**, **Ctrl-2**, **Ctrl-3**, or **Ctrl-4** to drop down any of the drop-down listboxes. Use the **up** and **down arrow** keys to move through the list. Use the **Enter** key to select a highlighted item. The **Escape** key closes the list and cancels the selection.

## Select Event Listbox

The Select Event drop-down listbox contains a list of all the events that apply to the current object (the application object in this example). To change to another event, pull down the listbox list and make your selection. For this example, select the **open event**. The title bar caption should now list the open event (open for firstapp).

When you pull down the Select Event listbox, the list displays an icon next to the names of any events that already contain code (shaded icons are related to ancestor scripts, covered in the chapter on inheritance).

## Paste Global Listbox

The Paste Global listbox allows you to paste into your code the name of any global variables known to the application. Again, the main advantage is that it is quick and avoids your having to look up the name.

## Paste Instance Listbox

The Paste Instance listbox is similar to the Paste Global listbox, except that it lists instance variables instead of globals. This listbox is not available from the Function painter.

## Paste Shared Listbox

The Paste Shared listbox is similar to the Paste Instance listbox, except that it lists shared variables instead of instance variables. This listbox is not available from the Function painter.

## Paste Argument Listbox

The Paste Argument listbox lists the function (or event) arguments so that you can paste them into your code.

## Paste Object/Window Listbox

The Paste Object listbox lets you paste into your code the name of any objects (or controls) related to the object you are currently editing. When editing application-level events, this listbox is labeled Paste Window, and it contains the names of all the windows that have been stored in the related libraries. This listbox is not available from the Function painter.

When you are using the editor in the Window painter, the Paste Object listbox contains the name of the window and all the controls that have been added to the window. This is convenient for pasting in the names of the controls.

When you are using the editor in the User Object painter, the Paste Object listbox lists the name of the object and any related controls (as when creating custom controls).

When you are using the editor in the Menu painter, the Paste Object listbox contains a list of all the menu items that are part of the current menu.

### Paste Window Listbox

The Paste Window listbox is available in the Application object events to allow you to paste window names into your code.

## Edit Menu Paste Options

You will find three other useful paste options in the PowerScript painter Edit menu. They are grouped together as: **Paste Function**, **Paste SQL**, and **Paste Statement**. These functions also have icons on the PainterBar.

### Paste Function

Selecting **Edit|Paste Function** opens the Paste Function dialog box (Figure 2.10). This listbox presents an alphabetized list from which you can select and paste function names into your code. You can display built-in, user-defined, or external functions by selecting the appropriate radio button. The listbox also provides a single-key search, so you can search for the function beginning with a certain letter.

You will find the Paste Function dialog box most useful in the first few weeks of using PowerBuilder as you learn the names of the functions. Later you may find that the Object Browser is more efficient, but it takes more knowledge to use.

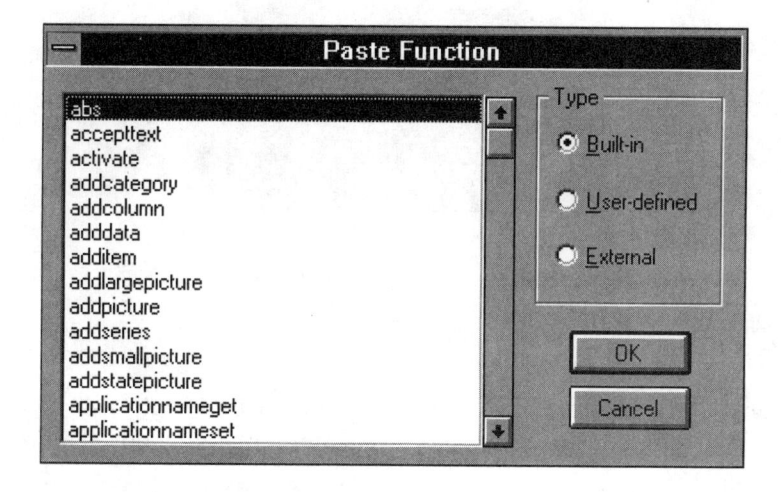

*Figure 2.10* The Paste Function dialog box.

## Paste SQL

To insert a SQL statement into your code, select **Edit|Paste SQL**. This opens the SQL Statement Type dialog window (Figure 2.11). Choose the type of SQL statement you want to create. This opens the SQL painter, which assists in creating the statement. When you have finished, it will paste the SQL statement into your code. This tool is covered later in greater detail.

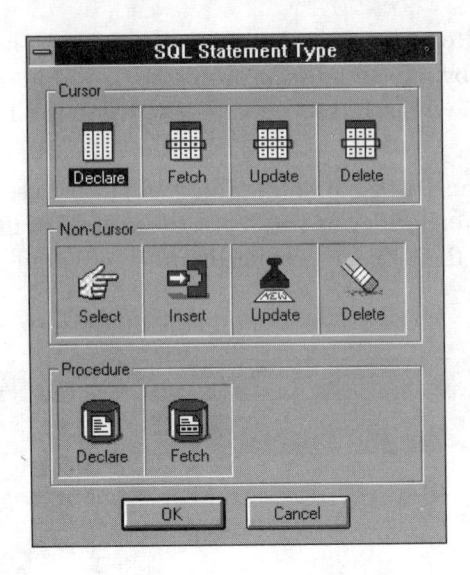

*Figure 2.11* The SQL Statement Type dialog box.

## Paste Statement

To insert one of the logical PowerScript constructs, select **Paste Statement** from the Edit menu. This opens the Paste Statement dialog box (Figure 2.12).

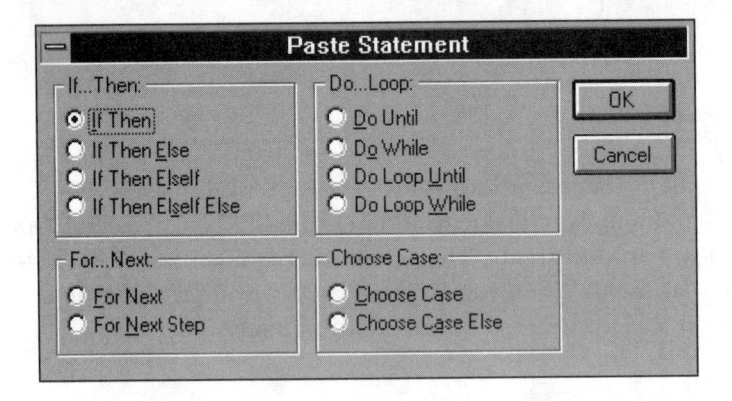

*Figure 2.12* The Paste Statement dialog box.

This window presents the set of PowerScript branching statements (`IF`, `FOR`, `DO`, and `CHOOSE CASE`), with multiple forms of each. If you choose one of these statements and click **OK**, the dialog box pastes a prototype of the statement into your code (Figure 2.13). The editor then selects the first entry (`<condition>` in this example) that you need to complete to use this statement.

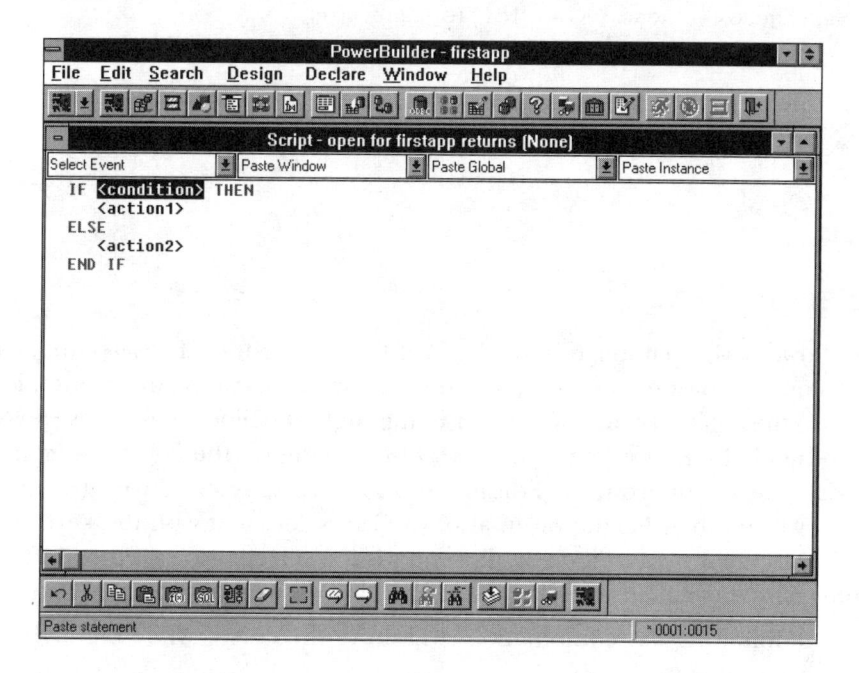

*Figure 2.13 After pasting the IF statement into the script.*

## ENTERING AND EDITING TEXT

Enter a few lines of text into the workspace. For example, the FirstApp uses the following:

```
int i_file, i_rc
string s_text
long l_size
```

```
MessageBox ("FirstApp", "Open for FirstApp")
i_file = FileOpen("firstapp.ini")
IF i_file > 0 THEN
   FileRead(i_file, s_text)
   MessageBox ("Read INI", left(s_text,60))
   i_rc = FileClose(i_file)
ELSE
   MessageBox ("Read INI", "could not find file FIRSTAPP.INI")
END IF
```

## Selecting Text

The PowerScript painter follows the Windows convention for selecting, cutting, copying, pasting, and deleting text. To select text with the mouse, left-click on the text and drag the pointer to highlight the block of text. Use **Select All** to highlight all the text in the script by clicking on the **Select All** icon or choosing **Select All** from the Edit menu. You can also select a word (or string of text) by double-clicking on it; also, you can select text with the keyboard. Place the cursor next to the text that you wish to select and hold the **Shift** key while using the cursor arrows to highlight a word, string, or block of text.

The following key combinations will move the cursor while highlighting (selecting) the text:

- **Left Arrow**—move left one character
- **Right Arrow**—move right one character
- **Up Arrow**—move up one line
- **Down Arrow**—move down one line
- **End** key—go to the end of the current line
- **Home** key—go to the beginning of the current line
- **Ctrl+Home**—go to the beginning of the script (or file)
- **Ctrl+End**—go to the end of the script (or file)

## To Cut, Copy, Clear, or Replace Selected Text

After you have selected text, the selected text can be:

- **Cut**—deleted from the script and placed on the Window's clipboard. Use the **Cut** icon or the **Edit|Cut** menu option.
- **Copied**—copied to the clipboard without removing from the script. Use the **Copy** icon or the **Edit|Copy** menu option.
- **Cleared**—deleted from the script and not placed on the clipboard. Use the **Clear** icon or the **Edit|Clear** menu option.
- **Replaced**—replaced with text copied from the clipboard or typed from the keyboard. To replace the selected text with the contents of the clipboard, use the **Paste** icon or the **Edit|Paste** menu option.

## Pasting Text

You can paste text from the clipboard in one of two ways depending on whether you have a block of text currently selected in the editor:

- **Insert**—if you do not have any text selected, the **Paste** operation inserts the text at the current cursor position on the screen.
- **Replace**—if you have selected a block of text on the screen, the **Paste** operation will replace the selected text with the text currently on the clipboard. The selected text is not copied to the clipboard.

The **Replace** option also works when you type in new text. If you select a block of text and then type a character, the entire block will be replaced by the single character.

## Keyboard Shortcuts for the Cut and Paste Functions

You may already be familiar with the keyboard shortcuts for these functions if you've used other Windows applications. If not, take a minute to memorize them. They are listed in the Edit menu. They are:

- **Ctrl+X**—cut to the clipboard
- **Ctrl+C**—copy to the clipboard

- **Ctrl+V**—paste from the clipboard
- **Delete**—clear, do not copy to the clipboard

Other useful keyboard shortcuts are:

- **Ctrl+Z**—undo (multilevel)
- **Ctrl+A**—select all
- **Ctrl+F**—find text
- **Ctrl+Shift+G**—go to line
- **Ctrl+G**—repeat last find
- **Ctrl+L**—compile script
- **Ctrl+H**—replace
- **Ctrl+W**—close

The most-often-used functions appear on the PainterBar—the first six duplicate functions—have already been discussed. These are **Undo**, **Cut**, **Copy**, **Paste**, **Clear**, and **Select All**. The other functions that appear on the PainterBar are:

- **Comment**—marks the selected text as comment text. This adds a double-slash ("//") to the beginning of each line.
- **Uncomment**—removes the comment characters from the selected text.
- **Paste SQL**—brings up the SQL painter to let you paste a SQL statement into your code.
- **Paste Statement**—brings up the Paste Statement dialog box. You can paste the PowerScript `IF`, `FOR`, `DO`, or `CHOOSE` statements.
- **Browse Object**—brings up the browser. This useful utility is covered later in this chapter.
- **Return**—compiles the current code (if any) and closes the editor.

## THE POWERSCRIPT PAINTER MENU OPTIONS

The PowerScript painter menu bar includes the following pull-down menus:

```
File | Edit | Search | Declare | Design | Window | Help
```

The options on each menu are as listed here.

## File Menu

- **Close**—exits the editor. If changes have occurred, you will be prompted before changes are saved. If you want to save changes, compile the code before exiting.
- **Return**—exits the editor and saves any changes without prompting. If changes were made, compile the code.
- **Import**—inserts a DOS text file in the script.
- **Export**—saves the code as a DOS file.
- **PowerPanel**—displays the PowerPanel.
- **Print**—prints the code.
- **Printer Setup**—lets the user set print options.
- **Exit**—quits PowerBuilder.

## Edit Menu

- **Undo**—multiple-level undo.
- **Cut**—deletes selected text from the script and places it on the Windows clipboard.
- **Copy**—copies selected text to the clipboard without removing it from the script.
- **Paste**—inserts the text on the clipboard.
- **Paste Function**—inserts a PowerBuilder or user-defined function (from a list box selection).
- **Clear**—deletes selected text from the script and does not place it on the clipboard.
- **Select All**—highlights all the text in the script.
- **Comment Selection**—marks selected text as comment text. This adds a double-slash ("//") to the beginning of each line.
- **Uncomment Selection**—removes the comment characters from the selected text.

- **Paste SQL**—brings up the SQL painter, to let you to paste a SQL statement into your code.
- **Paste Statement**—brings up the Paste Statement dialog box. You can paste PowerScript `IF`, `FOR`, `DO`, or `CHOOSE` statements.

## Search Menu

- **Find**—searches for the entered text.
- **Find Next**—repeats the last search.
- **Replace**—finds and replaces.
- **Go to Line**—goes to a specific line number.

## Declare Menu

- **Global Variables**—declares or modifies a global variable.
- **Shared Variables**—declares or modifies a shared variable (see below).
- **Instance Variables**—declares or modifies an instance variable (see below).
- **Application Functions**—declares or modifies an application function.
- **Application Structures**—declares or modifies an application structure.
- **Global External Functions**—declares or modifies an external function.

## Design Menu

- **Compile**—compiles the current script.
- **Select Object**—edits a script for another object.
- **Browse Object**—brings up the browser. This useful utility is covered later.
- **Option**—opens the Properties for the Editor Tab dialog box.

## IMPORT AND EXPORT

You can import ASCII text from a DOS file into your scripts. Insert a file into your script using the **File|Import** menu option. To insert a text file into a script, open the PowerScript editor and select the event you wish to edit. Position the cursor at the point in your code where you want to insert the text. Then select **File|Import**. This opens the File Import dialog box (Figure 2.14).

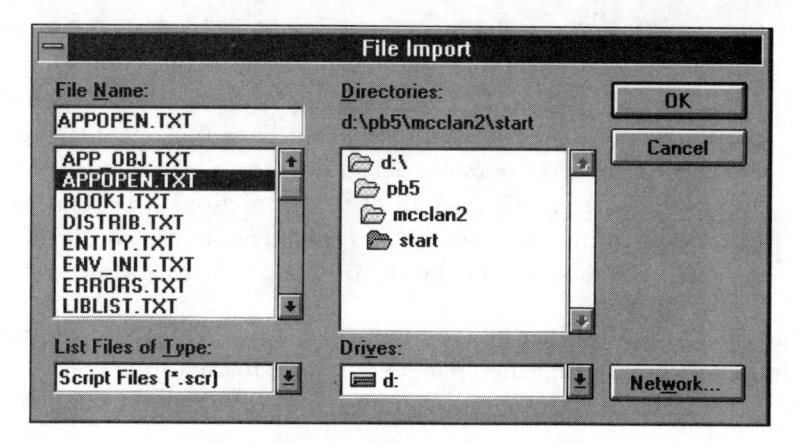

*Figure 2.14  The File Import dialog box.*

You can also choose to replace script code with a file. Select the text in the script (use the **Select All** icon), and then select **File|Import**. This discards the selected current code before reading in the DOS file text.

## Exporting Text

You can also export text from your scripts to a DOS file. To export script text to a DOS file, open the PowerScript editor and select the event you wish to export. You can either export the entire script or a block of text to a file. If you wish to export only part of the script, select the block of text before doing the export; otherwise the entire script will be exported. Next select **File|Export**. This opens the Export File dialog box (essentially the same as Figure 2.14). Enter the file name (after setting the directory) and press **OK**.

## COMPILING POWERSCRIPT CODE

Script code can be compiled using **Design|Compile Script** or by closing a script. In most cases, PowerBuilder will insist that the code be compiled successfully before you leave the editor if you want to save your changes to the code.

If the compile fails, you have three options:

+ Correct the problems reported by the compiler and recompile successfully.

+ Close the editor (using **File|Close**) and do not save the changes. This will discard all changes that have been made in the current session.

✦ Comment out the erroneous line(s) of code. The PowerScript editor provides an easy way to quickly comment out all lines of the text. Use **Edit|Select All** to select all text. Selecting **Edit|Comment Selection** will comment out all the currently selected lines of text. If you choose **Select All** and then **Comment Selection**, this will comment out all the text in the current script. Both of these functions have icons on the PainterBar for quick access. (If you comment out all code, you will still need a valid return statement if the function returns a return value.)

In some cases, PowerBuilder lets you ignore compiler warnings. In this case, you can exit without losing the changes you have made to the code. Do not confuse this option with the choice you must make in the next example.

It is important that you recognize the message in Figure 2.15 and the effect of answering **No**.

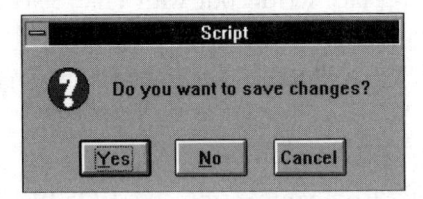

*Figure 2.15* The Exit Script dialog box.

If you have errors in your code and you exit the PowerScript painter and see the message Do you want to save changes?, PowerBuilder will insist that you go back and correct the errors or exit without saving the changes. If you click **No**, all the code changes that you made in the current editing session will be discarded. If you click **Yes** or **Cancel**, you will be returned to the editor.

If the compile error is a minor problem (and not in the Application Open event), PowerBuilder may give you the option of exiting without losing the changes you have made. In this case, you will see the message shown in Figure 2.16.

*Figure 2.16* In this dialog box, you may choose to save the code, even with errors.

If you see this message, choose **Yes** to exit the editor without losing your code changes. You can return later to fix the code.

## Customizing the Editor

You can configure various aspects of the editor by selecting **Design|Option** (while in the editor). This will open the Properties for Editor tab dialog box (Figure 2.17). In this tab dialog box, you can set the font, indentation, coloring, and drop-down lists in the editor.

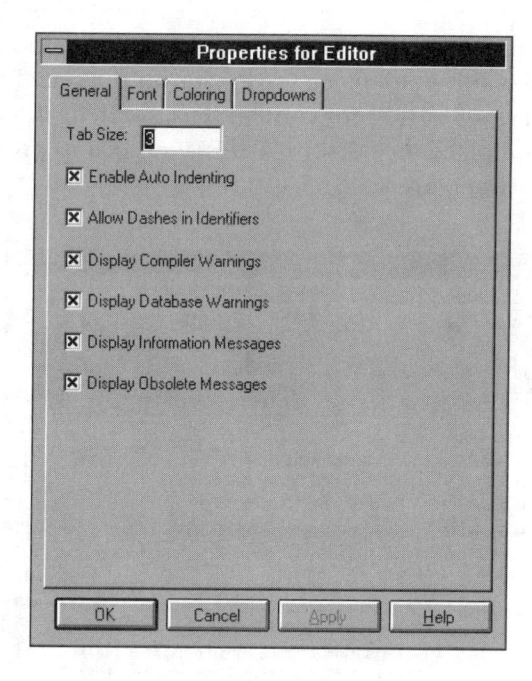

*Figure 2.17* The Editor Properties dialog box.

To set the font, select the **Font** tab and then select the font name, style, size, and other font properties for the selected control or object. You should choose fonts that you know will be on your user's system when you distribute your application. If a font is not on a user's system, a font will be substituted that may be inappropriate.

To set the indention, select the **Indention** tab and enter the number of spaces you wish to indent the code each time you hit the **Tab** key. You can also enable **auto indenting**, which will format the text by indenting as you enter it.

To set the syntax coloring for the editor, select the **Coloring** tab. Then enable **syntax coloring** (if you wish) and assign the colors you want to use for the choices listed in the Set Colors For listbox.

To select the drop-down listboxes, select the **Dropdowns** tab. Then drag and drop the listbox names between the Available Dropdowns listbox and the Selected Dropdowns listbox.

## CONTEXT-SENSITIVE HELP

You can obtain context-sensitive help for any of the built-in PowerBuilder functions. To access this help, place the cursor on the name of a function in your code. Then press **Shift+F1** for context-sensitive help about that function. For example, if you place the cursor on MessageBox and press **Shift+F1,** you will see the display in Figure 2.18.

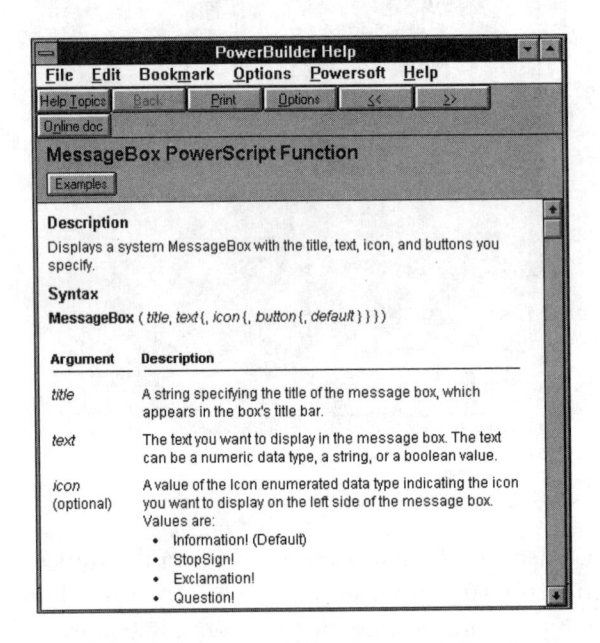

*Figure 2.18 The Help entry for MessageBox.*

This shows the first part of the help system entry for MessageBox (scroll down to read the rest of the text). Each entry typically shows the argument list, explains the use of the function, defines the return value, and provides a short code example. You can copy and paste any of this text into your application by selecting **Edit|Copy**. This will open the Copy dialog box. In this window, you can drag the mouse to select the text you want to copy. Hit the **Copy** button to copy the selected text to the clipboard. From there, you can paste it into your code.

## THE OBJECT BROWSER

The Object Browser is convenient for viewing attributes and pasting a wide range of values into your script. With the browser, you can quickly locate the name of a specific attribute, function, enumerated value, variable, or object. You can select the Object Browser by clicking on the **Browse Object** icon on the PowerScript painter's PainterBar or by selecting **Design|Browse Object**. When you select the Object Browser, the system displays the Object Browser tab dialog box, as shown in Figure 2.19.

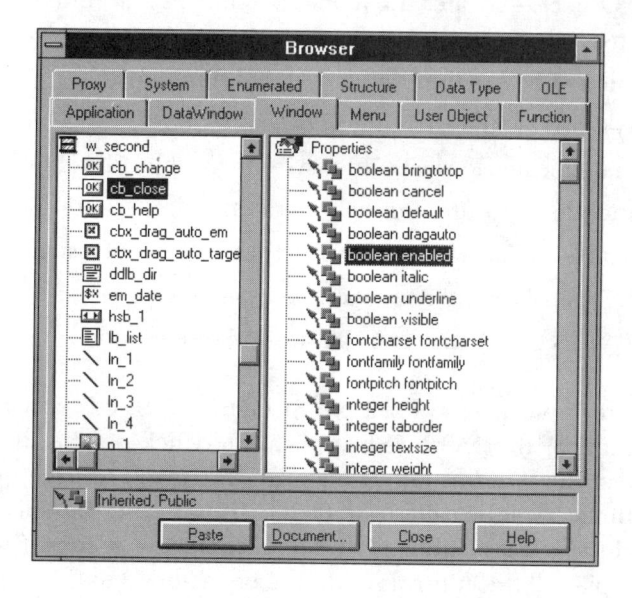

*Figure 2.19  The Browser dialog box.*

This example shows the use of the Object Browser to locate the attribute names for `CommandButton cb_close` in a window named `w_second` (this is from the **EVENTS1.PBL** application). Selecting the **Paste** button would paste `w_second.cb_close.enabled` into the script.

Locating the value you wish to paste takes several steps, and they vary according to the object type you are using.

Select the object type from the set of tabs on the top of the window. The possible types are:

- **Application**—locates external functions and global variables. It is also used for shared or instance variables that were declared at the application, window, or menu level.
- **DataWindow**—information, attributes, and functions relating to DataWindow.
- **Window**—locates a wide range of items—controls, variables, and attributes—contained in a window and the objects within a window.
- **Menu**—locates menu functions or variables.
- **User Objects**—locates the names of controls and functions associated with user objects.
- **Function**—locates user-defined global functions.
- **Proxy**—used with distributed PowerBuilder.
- **System**—locates PowerBuilder system- or object-level functions.
- **Enumerated**—locates PowerBuilder enumerated values.
- **Structure**—locates local variables that are part of a structure.
- **Data Type**—lists the PowerScript data types.
- **OLE**—lists the OLE classes known to PowerBuilder.

If you want to duplicate the example in Figure 2.19, edit any event in the w_first window of the EVENTS1 application. Click on the **Browse Object** icon and select the **Window** tab (see Figure 2.20). You will see two listboxes; the one on the left will be called the Object listbox, and the one on the right will be called the Values listbox. Then double-click w_second (in the Object listbox) to display all the controls that have been added to the w_second window. Click **cb_close** and then double-click on **Properties** in the Values listbox. Scroll down and click on **boolean enabled**. Finally, click on the **Paste** command button to insert this into your script.

As you click on various objects in the Objects listbox, the list of attributes changes in the right-hand listbox (if you expand the **Properties** icon, you can watch the change). Click on the **Functions** icon (in the Values listbox) to see the list of functions that apply to the selected object. If you click in the **Values** listbox (to set the focus) and then type a letter on the keyboard, you can jump to the first entry in the list that begins with that letter. Repeat the keystroke to step to the next function that begins with that letter. This single-key search works in both listboxes.

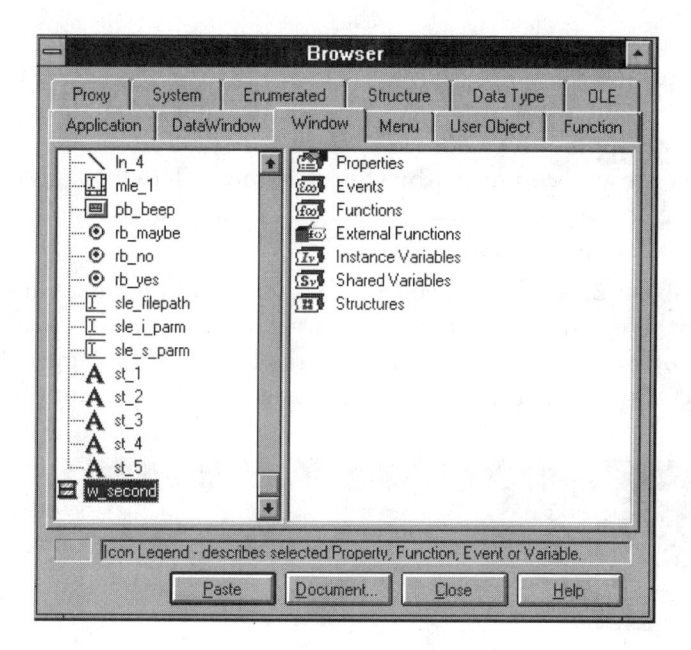

*Figure 2.20  The Browse Object dialog box.*

For example, select a command button from the Objects listbox and a function from the Paste category. Click anywhere in the **Value** listbox and hit the **s** key. The listbox will scroll to the **setfocus** function. If you press the **s** key again, the listbox scrolls to the next entry that begins with the letter *s* (setposition). You can paste any of these values into your code by selecting it and clicking **Paste**.

The browser may seem difficult to use at first, if only because of the huge amount of information that is available through it. It takes some time to learn where all this information is within the browser. The browser can be a more efficient search tool than the help system or the **Paste** function option on the Edit menu because it only displays the functions and attributes associated with the object you have selected, thus reducing the scope of the search. In general, it is easy to use for the following:

- Locating objects, names, attributes, functions, and variables
- Enumerated values
- Standard datatypes
- DataWindow attributes and functions

Use one of the larger applications (such as Imagedb) to explore the browser. While in the PowerScript painter, select the **Browse Object** icon. In the Object Browser, select the **Window** tab; this displays the names of all the windows contained in the application's libraries. Double-click on the name of the main window for the application (in the Objects listbox). This expands the window and lists the controls and objects it contains. Find a DataWindow control and examine its attributes and functions.

The Object Browser is convenient for pasting a wide range of values into your script. With the browser, you can quickly locate the name of a specific attribute, function, enumerated value, variable, or object. Figure 2.21 shows the Object Browser, listing the functions for a command button.

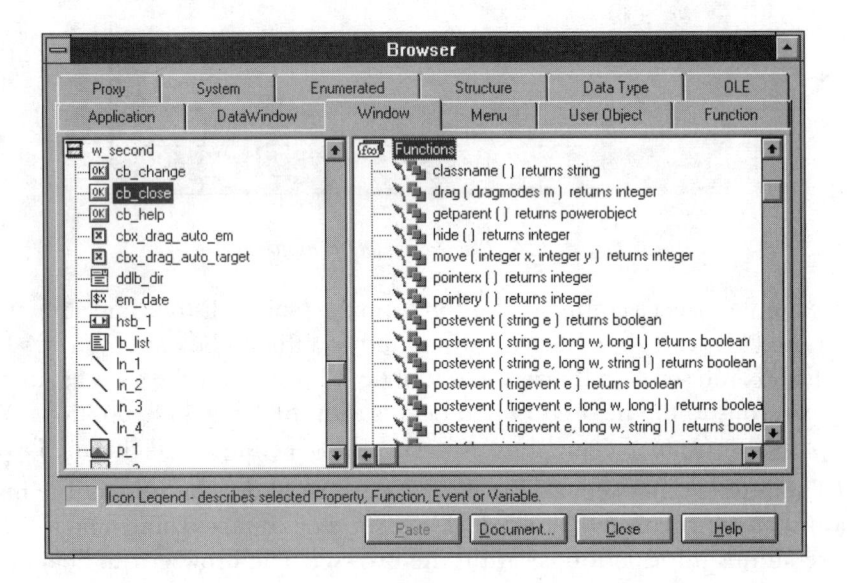

*Figure 2.21 The Object Browser dialog box for functions.*

Click **Paste** to insert the selected item into your script code. Selecting the **OLE** tab option opens a list of the OLE classes known to PowerBuilder (Figure 2.22).

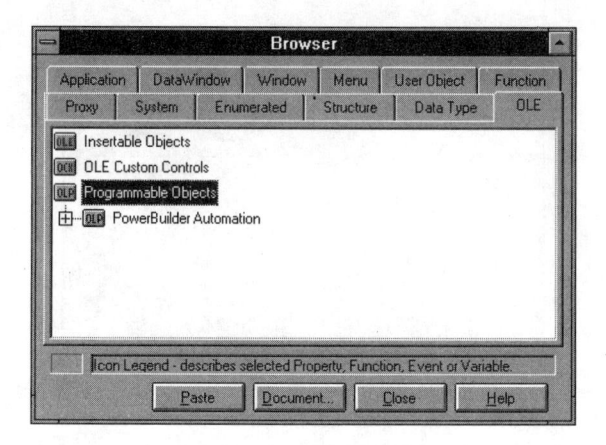

*Figure 2.22  The Browse OLE Classes dialog box.*

## Selecting Another Object

When you are editing an event for a window or for an object in a window (such as a command button or a listbox), you can switch to another object (or the window) by choosing **Select Object** from the Design menu, as shown in Figure 2.23. Selecting this menu item opens the Select Object dialog box, as shown in Figure 2.24.

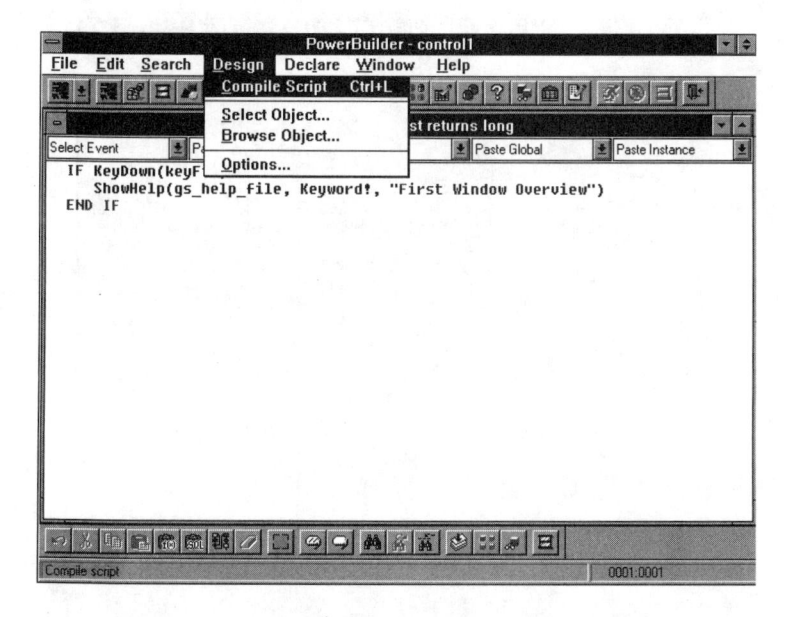

*Figure 2.23  The Design menu with the **Select Object** option.*

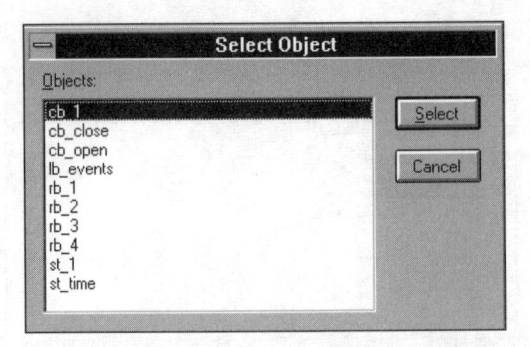

*Figure 2.24  The Select Object dialog box.*

Choose the object in the list and click the **Select** command button. This opens an event in the selected object. From there you may choose a different event if necessary.

## Editing Function Declarations

When you are editing the code for a function (in the Function painter), the third command on the Design menu is changed to **Function Declaration**. Selecting this menu item opens the Function Declaration dialog box, as shown in Figure 2.25.

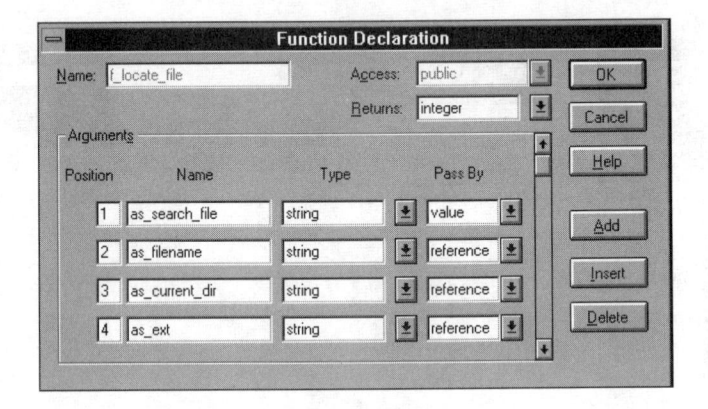

*Figure 2.25  The Function Declaration dialog box.*

The **Function Declaration** command, added to the Design menu when you are editing code for a function, lets you make changes to the declaration of the function. (Make a note of this option; this is one of the questions that arises most often in my PowerBuilder classes.)

That pretty much covers the basics of the PowerScript painter. We're ready to start creating applications. In the next chapter, we'll take a look at another of the PowerBuilder painters—the Application painter—and we'll construct our first PowerBuilder application.

## THE POWERSCRIPT DEBUGGER

The PowerScript debugger provides most of the expected features for debugging, including:

- **Breakpoints**—execution can be stopped at any line of code in your application.
- **Single-step code execution**—steps line by line through the code.
- **Variable access**—examines and changes the value of any variable.
- **Watch points**—defines a list of watch point variables.

The debugger is very good; it provides the basic functions necessary to debug your application. There are a few limitations that you will have to work with in the current version of the debugger. Currently there is no "step-over" function; you can only step into each function. The workaround is to set a breakpoint at the line after the function call. You cannot usefully set breakpoints within the `GetFocus` or `Activate` events, because the debugger would receive the focus and become active. This is a result of the complexity of the event-driven paradigm. You cannot examine variables after the execution of the last line of a script or function. The solution to this is to add an additional line to the code (a return statement will not do).

Start the debugger by clicking on the **Debug** icon on the PowerBar. Before the debugger starts, it displays the Edit Stops dialog box (Figure 2.26).

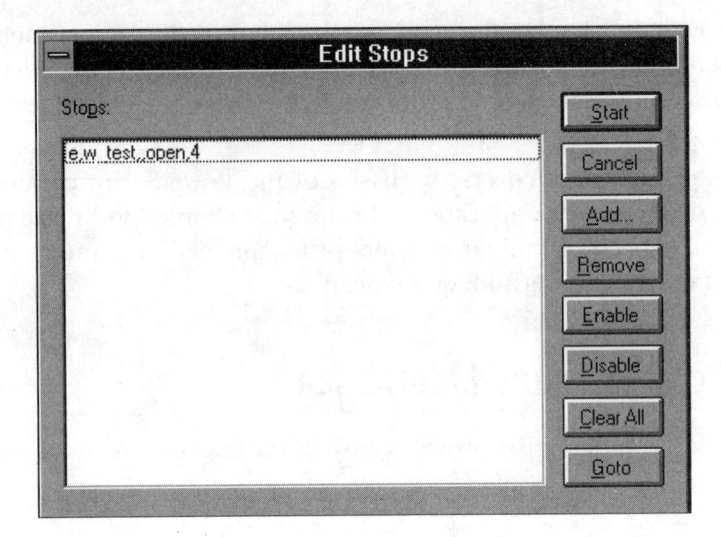

*Figure 2.26 Editing breakpoints.*

In this dialog box, you can add or remove breakpoints and then start the debugger.

## Adding a Breakpoint

To add a breakpoint, click on **Add** to display the Select Script dialog box (Figure 2.27). This helps you find the line of code where you want to set the breakpoint. First, make a choice from the Object Type pull-down listbox. Your choices are **Application**, **Window**, **Menu**, **User Object**, and **Function**. To set a breakpoint in one of the application events, select **Application**. To set a breakpoint in a window or window object event, select **Window**.

Next, select one of the two radio buttons, either **Events** or **Functions**, depending on whether you are looking for an event script or function code. The top listbox presents a list of names. When you select one of these names, the lower listbox lists the related controls or objects (for the events or functions). Make a selection in the lower listbox and the code is displayed in the Debug window. Double-click on any line of code to set the breakpoint; the display adds a stop sign icon to the line. Remove a breakpoint by double-clicking on the line of code.

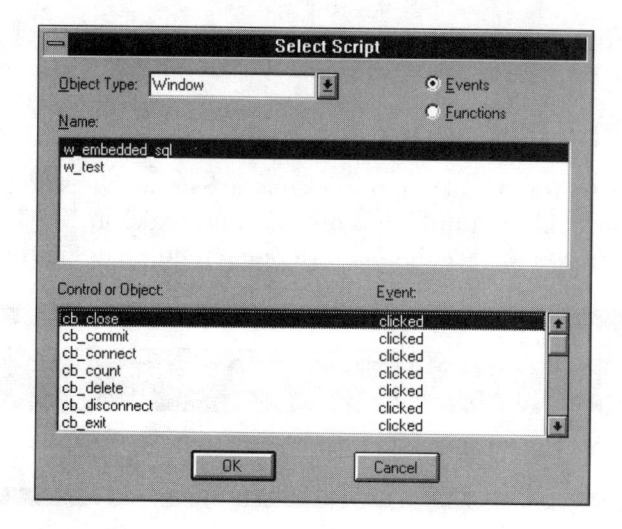

*Figure 2.27 Locating a script.*

You can set additional breakpoints and you can remove, enable, or disable existing breakpoints with the other options in the Edit Stops dialog box. The Stops listbox (in the Select Script dialog box) lists all the currently defined breakpoints and the status of each. The status lists the following:

## Breakpoint Status

- **state**—(e,d) for enabled or disabled
- **object**—name of the object
- **control**—name of the control
- **event**—name of the event
- **lineno**—line number

For example,

```
e,w_main,cb_close,clicked,3
```

lists an enabled breakpoint for the third line of the `Clicked` event for the command button `cb_close` in the window `w_main`.

```
d,w_main,fw_calculate,,2
```

This status is for a disabled breakpoint in the second line of the function `fw_calculate` in the `w_main` window.

## Running the Debugger

After you have set your breakpoints, click on the **Start** icon to start the debugger. The application will run until it hits one of your breakpoints. When you reach any breakpoint, you will see the main Debug screen, as in Figure 2.28.

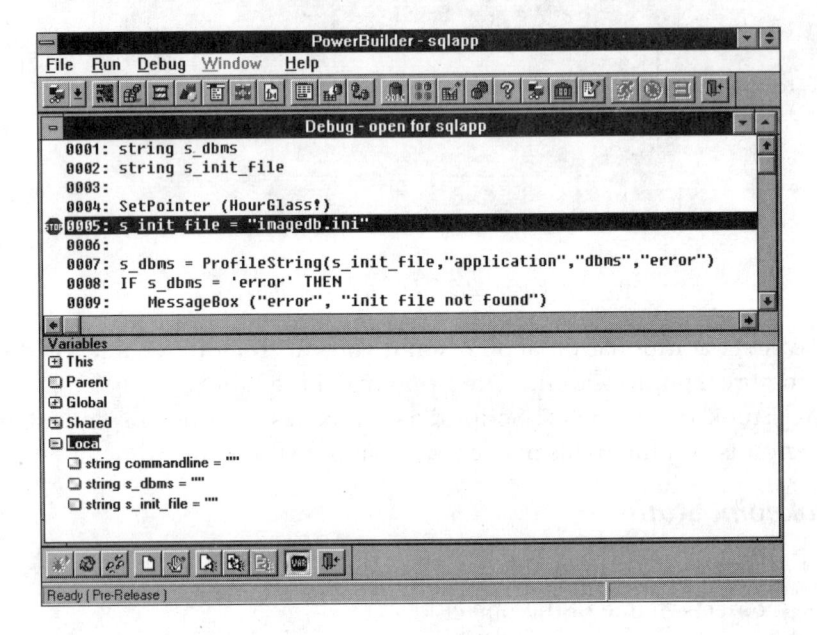

*Figure 2.28  Debugging a script.*

The options on the Debugger PainterBar are:

- **Continue**—Resumes program execution.
- **Step**—Single-steps through the next line of code.
- **Select**—Adds a new breakpoint (or lets you view the code).
- **Edit Stop**—Goes to the Edit Stops dialog box (to add or remove breakpoints).
- **Show Watch**—Toggles the display of the Watch window.
- **Add Watch**—Adds the selected variable to the Watch window.
- **Remove Watch**—Removes the selected variable from the Watch window.
- **Show Variables**—Toggles the display of the Variable window.

## Displaying and Modifying Variables

When execution stops at a breakpoint, you can display any variable in the application in the Variable window. The **Show Variables** icon is a toggle to show or hide the Variable window. To display a local variable, double-click on the **Local variable** icon in the Variable window. The icon expands to show a list of the local variables. If there are many local variables, scroll through this window to locate the ones you are interested in viewing. You can reduce the number of variables you have to view by adding the important variables to the Watch window, as discussed in the next section. To adjust the size of the Watch and/or Variable windows, drag the Watch or Variable title bar with the mouse to adjust the size.

### Locating Window Instance Variables

Window instance variables are contained in the definition of the window instantiated under the global variables list. To find an instance variable, click on the **Global** icon to expand the list. Scroll until you find the window. Click on the window's icon to expand the list of objects inside it and scroll until you find the instance variable.

You can modify the current value for any variable. To do this, locate the variable, and then double-click on its icon. This opens the Modify Variable dialog box, which displays datatype, name, and current value for the variable. Change the value by entering a new value in the New Value listbox. To assign the NULL value to the variable, click on the **Null** checkbox in this dialog box.

### Adding Variables to the Watch Window

To select a set of variables to watch, open the Variable window and click on the type of variable you are interested in watching. You can select from **Global**, **Shared**, **Local**, **This a Parent**. In the Variable window, locate and then click on the variable you want to add to the Watch window. Next, click on the **Add Watch** icon to add the variable to the Watch window.

You can enter a set of variables by clicking on the type (e.g., **Local**); this adds all the variables in the group to the Watch window. To remove a Watch variable, select it in the Watch window and click on the **Remove Watch** icon.

When you hit a breakpoint, the name of the icon will be grayed out in the Watch window, if it is not in the current scope of the breakpoint.

CHAPTER 3

# Creating PowerBuilder Applications

This chapter introduces the creation of PowerBuilder applications. It covers:

- ✦ An introduction to PowerBuilder applications
- ✦ The Application painter
- ✦ PowerBuilder libraries
- ✦ The Project painter
- ✦ Compiling applications
- ✦ The application initialization file
- ✦ Managing application objects with the Library painter
- ✦ A step-by-step example of creating an application

## A PowerBuilder Application

A PowerBuilder application consists of many components, including windows, controls, functions, and PowerScript code. You will develop each of the components by using various PowerBuilder painters. The first painter that you will use in this chapter is the Application painter.

In the Application painter, you can create or modify an application object. Every PowerBuilder application has one—and only one—application object. This object is the starting point; it is the entry point for the entire application.

A typical PowerBuilder application usually contains:

- One application object
- Windows
- Controls
- Menus
- DataWindows
- Functions
- Structures
- Script language programming code
- External resources (icons, initialization file)
- A project

Most of these components reside in PowerBuilder libraries, which are files created by PowerBuilder that have the extension **PBL** (usually called "pibbles" by developers). All of a small application's components may all be stored in a single library, such as **FIRSTAPP.PBL**. Components of larger applications will be stored in multiple libraries. When you create a new PowerBuilder object (such as a window or menu), you save the object into a PowerBuilder library. You can run the application from these libraries in the development environment. Later, when you create an executable, these components will be bound into one or more files. More details about libraries will be discussed in the next section. This chapter presents an introduction to the basics of creating executables.

## The Application Painter

The Application painter is where you define the most general details about each application. In the Application painter, you can create and name the application object, choose an icon to be associated with the application executable, create scripts for application-level events, define the library list, and set the default display characteristics of text (such as the fonts) for the application. The Application painter can also create the application library where the components are stored (you can also create a library with the Library painter). From the Application painter you can also run (execute) or debug the application that you have developed (from within the development environment).

## Application Programs and Application Objects

An application is the program that you develop with PowerBuilder. It includes all of the components that you have created. Each application must include one application object. This application object can reside in any PowerBuilder library that contains the components for the application program. Most often the application object will be placed in a library that has the same name as the application object (**FIRSTAPP.PBL** for the FirstApp object). Creating the application object (and the library) is usually the first step in creating a new application.

The application object holds application-level parameters (such as the default fonts), application-level events, and a list of all the libraries (**.pbl** files) that hold the components for the application program. The application object is sort of a wrapper for the rest of the application components.

## PowerBuilder Application Libraries

You store the application components in one or more PowerBuilder libraries. A library is a special type of repository file created and managed by PowerBuilder. These files always have the file extension of **.PBL**. Small applications can store all of their components in a single library, but most larger applications store their components in multiple libraries. Often, you will share PowerBuilder components, such as windows or functions, across multiple applications. To do this, you will need to place the objects in shared libraries. Normally, these will be on a network file server where they can be reached by all the developers. The components that are not shared and are used only by a single application (or a single developer) may be placed in other local libraries.

For simplicity, most of the example applications in this book use a single separate library. For example, the first application, named FirstApp, is stored in the library **FIRSTAPP.PBL** (you will find it on the CD-ROM that is included with this book).

## The Application Executable

As you develop an application, you can run it from the development environment by clicking the **Run** icon on the PowerBar. When you are ready to distribute the application, you will create an executable version of it. When you create the executable file, PowerBuilder binds the various components into one or more files (for a small application, this is a single file, e.g., **FIRSTAPP.EXE**). Even after creating the executable, additional **DLL** files will be required to run the bound executable. You may distribute these required DLLs with your application executable. You may also want to partition the executables for larger applications into multiple files. You can find more information about creating and distributing applications in the chapter, "Distributing PowerBuilder Applications."

## PROPERTIES, EVENTS, AND FUNCTIONS

Each object (windows, controls, application objects, menu items) in the PowerBuilder system has properties, events, and functions. The help system for objects is organized around these properties, events, and functions—this division will become familiar to PowerBuilder developers.

*Properties* are the attributes that define the characteristics of each object. Properties are data elements that store the characteristics of the object (such as application name). They are variables, like the elements of a structure in other languages. Each object type has a specific set of properties. You can examine and assign values to these properties using the dot notation described earlier or sometimes by calling a function.

*Events* are the triggers that cause the Windows environment to send messages to the various objects in your application. For example, clicking the left mouse button sends a `Clicked` message to the object that is currently under the pointer. If you double-click on the control menu, the system sends a `Close` message to the control menu's window. Each object type has an associated set of events. If you are new to Windows programming, read the chapter on events for a detailed explanation of events and messages.

*Functions* are the procedures provided by PowerBuilder. PowerBuilder functions are similar to those found in developmental libraries that are available for most languages such as C, Pascal, and Basic. These include functions for data conversion, file access, string manipulation, time and date manipulation, and so forth. You call these functions by embedding a call into your script code. Some functions are related to one (or a few) object types, while others are more general and can be used by any object.

## APPLICATION OBJECT PROPERTIES

The application object attributes include:

- `string Appname`—the name of the application object.
- `string MicroHelpDefault`—the text to be displayed in the Microhelp area at the bottom of the application window.

### Dot Notation Addressing

The attributes of PowerBuilder objects can be accessed using the dot notation scheme, `ObjectName.Attribute`. For example, to set the application default MicroHelp, you would use the following line of code:

`myapp.MicroHelpDefault = 'Ready'`

## APPLICATION OBJECT EVENTS

Only six events apply specifically to the application object. The four most important application-level events are:

- `Open(string commandline)`—triggered when the application is started
- `Close`—triggered when the application has been closed
- `Idle`—triggered after a set interval of inactivity (interval set with the `idle( )` function)
- `SystemError`—triggered by a run-time error; in the case of a serious error, you can choose to shut down the application

You may write code for any of these events. At the least you must provide code for the Open event. If you omit this, you will receive an error when you try to run the application. Coding for the other events is optional.

## THE APPLICATION-LEVEL EVENTS

The next section discusses the most important events that occur at the application level. To add PowerScript code to any of these events, first you must open the Application painter. Then click on the **Script** icon on the PainterBar to open the PowerScript editor. Once in the editor, select the event from the Select Event listbox.

### The Application Open Event

The system triggers the Application Open event when you begin to execute your application. The Open event is the first chance you have to execute code and is where you begin to direct the application's execution. Depending on the application, the Open event may perform some initialization, connect the application to a database, or make a call to open the main window (which then takes over). The example applications often only open the main window in the Open event. PowerBuilder requires you to enter at least one line of code in the Application Open event, because there would be no point in creating an application that didn't do anything. The Open event receives one parameter, `CommandLine`, which is a string.

### The Application Close Event

When the user shuts down the application, the system triggers the Application Close event. The Close event gives you a chance to perform any last processing before the application is terminated. In this event, you can clean up, close files, or save parameters that have been delayed.

### The Application Idle Event

The Idle event lets you regain control of the application after the user has been idle for a certain amount of time. You can use the Idle event to perform background processing when the user is not using the workstation. You can also use it to trigger other actions. For example, perhaps you have decided that no one should have a database connection open (without activity) for more than half an hour. You can set the time parameter to 30 minutes in the Application Open event with the following code:

```
Idle(1800)
```

Then you could disconnect the user from the database and close the application, or you could lock the application and display a Password dialog box.

## Application Object Functions

There are only a few application level functions. Here are the most important ones (listed as return datatype and function name):

- `string ClassName()`—returns the name of the application object
- `Boolean PostEvent()`—places the event at the end of the application queue
- `integer TriggerEvent()`—initiates a PowerBuilder event, causing the related script (if any) to be executed

For example, to obtain the name of the application object, you would use the following code:

```
string s_class_name
s_class_name = myapp.ClassName() //"myapp"
```

or to trigger a Idle event

```
myapp.TriggerEvent(Idle!)
```

## The Application SystemError Event

When an error occurs at run time, PowerBuilder triggers the SystemError event. If you do not write a script for this event, the system displays a window with the error number and an error message. If you write a script for this event, that default behavior will be overridden.

## The Application Error Object

The Application Error Object contains information relating to the occurrence of a system error. You can access the Application Error Object only in the application's SystemError event where you examine the Error object attributes to determine the error information, and then decide how to proceed. The Error Object Attributes are (listed as datatype and name):

- `integer Number`—PowerBuilder error number
- `string Text`—error message, a string describing the problem
- `string WindowMenu`—the name of the window (or menu) where the error occurred
- `string Object`—the name of the object where the error occurred, may be the same as WindowMenu
- `string ObjectEvent`—the event in which the error occurred
- `integer Line`—line number of the script where the error occurred

You will often want to display some of the error information on the screen so the user can give you the information you need to determine what caused the error. You usually display the name of the object, the event, and the line of code where the error occurred.

Table 3.1 shows the PowerBuilder error codes that may occur at run time.

*Table 3.1* The PowerBuilder Error Codes

| Error Code | Explanation |
| --- | --- |
| 01 | Divide by zero. |
| 02 | Null object reference. |
| 03 | Array boundary exceeded. |
| 04 | Enumerated value is out of range for function. |
| 05 | Negative value encountered in function. |
| 06 | Invalid DataWindow row/column specified. |
| 07 | Unresolvable external when linking reference. |
| 08 | Reference of array with NULL subscript. |
| 09 | DLL function not found in current application. |
| 10 | Unsupported argument type in DLL function. |
| 12 | DataWindow column type does not match GetItem type. |
| 13 | Unresolved attribute reference. |
| 14 | Error opening DLL library for external function. |
| 15 | Error calling external function. |
| 16 | Maximum string size exceeded. |
| 17 | DataWindow referenced in DataWindow object does not exist. |
| 50 | Application reference could not be resolved. |
| 51 | Failure loading dynamic library. |

## THE APPLICATION INITIALIZATION FILE

Each application should have its own *initialization* file (sometimes called a *profile* file). This file will contain application parameters such as database connection information, default values, and other information that is specific to an application but which you do not wish to hard-code into the application. This lets you change parameters at run time without having to recompile the program.

By convention, the name given to the initialization file, is the same as the application, and the initialization file is given the extension **.INI**. The init file should be placed in the same directory as the application executable (or in the Windows directory). For example, if you create the sample application FirstApp, you will create an init file called **FIRSTAPP.INI**. You will place this in the same directory as the firstapp library and executable, which is **C:\PB5\MCCLAN2**. An initialization file is often called the *ini* file, the *init* file, or sometimes the *dot ini* file (**.INI**).

The format of the profile file is the same as other Windows initialization files and the PowerBuilder **PB.INI** file. The file is organized in sections that are marked with square brackets (around the section label). In each section, a number of entries follow the section label. Each entry has a key (name), equal sign, and a value. An excerpt from **IMAGEDB.INI** follows. The first section is [sqlca], and the first key is dbms with a value of ODBC. This section specifies the default database connection for the Imagedb application. If a key does not apply or you wish to clear its initial value, the value may be omitted. For example, in the **IMAGEDB.INI** sample notice, servername= is not assigned a value:

[sqlca]

dbms=ODBC

database=mcclan2

userid=

dbpass=

logid=

logpass=

servername=

DbParm=ConnectString='DSN=mcclan2;UID=dba;PWD=sql'

[application]

firsttime=no

dbms=sqlca

PowerBuilder supplies functions for reading and writing to these initialization files. There are three functions:

- `ProfileString (filename, section name, key, default)`—reads an entry from the profile file and returns its value as a string.
- `ProfileInt (filename, section name, key, default)`—reads an entry from the profile file and returns its value as an integer.
- `SetProfileString (filename, section name, key, value)`—writes an entry to a profile file as a string.

For example, you could use the following statement to read the value associated with the DBMS key from the SQLCA section into the string variable s_database.

```
s_database = ProfileString("IMAGEDB.INI", "sqlca", "dbms", "none")
```

If you do not include the full path for the initialization file, the system will look in the current directory first. If it does not find the file there, it will search directories in the usual order for Windows applications: first **WINDOWS**, **WINDOWS\SYSTEM**, and then the directory path from the DOS environment. In this case, you will have set the default directory to **C:\PB5\MCCLAN2** when you create or run the example applications, and the file will be found in that directory.

The `ProfileString()` function returns the value associated with a key as a string. `ProfileInt()` returns the value as an integer. If the file, section, or key is not found, the variable will be set to the default value that you assigned as the last (fourth) argument to the function. In the case of an error, an empty string will be returned for `ProfileString`, and a -1 will be returned for `ProfileInt`.

`SetProfileString` will set a value in the profile file. There is no `SetProfileInt` function. Since you are writing to an ASCII text file, you would still use the `SetProfileString` function. This function will create an entry (a key and its value) and a section if they do not exist in the profile file. If the key already exists in the profile file, its value will be updated. `SetProfileString` will not create the profile file if it does not exist. If `SetProfileString` is successful, it returns a 1. If it fails, it will return a -1. These return values are typical of a large number of the PowerBuilder functions:

```
SetProfileString("C:\PB5\MCCLAN2\IMAGEDB.INI","application",
"firsttime","no")
```

This example would set the value of firsttime to no.

> **NOTE** In our examples, we include the database user ID and password for simplicity. This would not be suitable for production applications. You should prompt the user for the password or encrypt it.

## BUILDING AN APPLICATION

In this section, we create a new application. Read through this section to get an overview of the process, and then go on to build the FirstApp example application. FirstApp introduces you to the creation of an application and its executable. The example application simply displays a couple of message boxes on the screen when it runs.

### Creating a New Application

The minimal steps involved in creating a new application are outlined here.

In the Application painter:

1. Define the application object and create the library.
2. Open the script editor and add code to the Open event for the application object.
3. Run the development version of the application to validate it.

In the Project painter:

4. Create an application project.
5. Using the application project, create an executable for the application.

From the Windows desktop:

6. Run the executable version of the application.

Later, when you are creating larger applications, you will add a step (between steps 2 and 3), which will be the largest amount of the development effort. In that step, you will create windows, add controls and/or menus to those windows, and add script code to the events. The following section describes the process in more detail.

## Developing the Exercise Applications

The example programs that came with this book include finished versions of all the exercises. Following the instructions in the introduction of this book, you should have installed the samples (in **C:\PB5\MCCLAN2**).

You should run each example so that you understand exactly what the application does and how it looks. Next, you should attempt to duplicate the example application as precisely as possible. Give your versions of each application library the same name as the sample, but start your applications with the letter z. You are limited to eight character names in the DOS file system so you may have to truncate the name by one character. For example, for FIRSTAPP, create a library named **ZFIRSTAP.PBL**. You can give all the objects (application objects, windows, etc.) exactly the same names as in the exercise text.

You may be able to create each application from the knowledge you have gained by reading the text and by using the help system. If you are not able to complete the exercise in that manner, examine the source code for each application. You can print out a listing of each application for your reference. To do this, select the application in the Application painter to set the current application. Then go to the Library painter and select all the objects in the application (click the **Select All** icon). Select the **Entry|Print** menu option.

In the application documentation, you will find an outline section that contains a brief description of each object in the exercise and all of the script code that is required to complete the application. You can also use this outline section as a source of hints as you work on your application.

## EXAMPLE: FIRSTAPP

FirstApp is a simple application that will demonstrate two of the application events (Open and Close) and the use of an application message box. The message box is an application modal dialog box window that displays a message and then waits for the user to respond by clicking the **OK** button or pressing the **Enter** key. FirstApp will display a message box in the application Open event. It will also attempt to locate and read the **firstapp.ini** file. If it is successful, it will display the text of that file in another message box; otherwise, it will display an error message. Finally, it will display a final message in the application Close event.

## Opening the FirstApp Application

Before you build your version of this application, run the sample application from the PowerBuilder environment. To do this, launch PowerBuilder (if necessary), and go to the Application painter (click on the **Appl** icon on the PowerBar). Click on the **Open** icon on the PainterBar to reach the Select Application Library dialog box shown in Figure 3.1. To open the FirstApp application, you must select the drive, directory, and library where the application object resides.

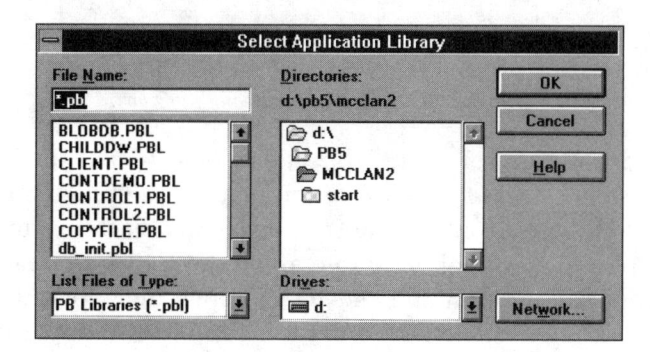

*Figure 3.1* The Select Application Library dialog box.

In this dialog box, use the Drives and the Directories listboxes to navigate to the directory that contains the application library (**D:\PB5\MCCLAN2**, for this example). The File Name listbox displays a list of all the PowerBuilder libraries in the selected directory. You can select a library by highlighting a selection in the File Name listbox, and then click **OK** or just double-click on the library in the listbox. Select the **FIRSTAPP.PBL** library in the listbox and click **OK**. Selecting an application library opens the Select Application dialog box shown in Figure 3.2.

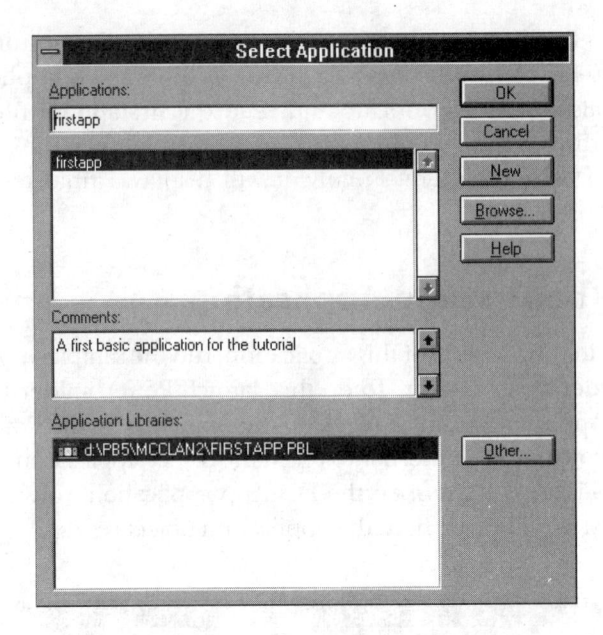

*Figure 3.2  The Select Application dialog box.*

In this dialog box, you select the application object from the library. The dialog box displays a list of the application objects contained in that library. It is possible to have zero, one, or more application objects in a library (most of the examples in this book have one application object in each library). Select the application object and click **OK** to open the application. For this example, the dialog box should display firstapp in the Applications field. Selecting **OK** opens the application and returns to the Application painter. At this point, you can run, debug, or modify the application, as will be covered later in this chapter.

## Running FirstApp

In the Application painter, check that the window caption is Application-firstapp. Click on the **Run** icon to run the application. When the application runs, you will see three different messages on the screen.

1. When the application begins, it triggers the application Open event. You will see a message box announcing the occurrence of the Open event. The message Open for FirstApp should be displayed, as shown in Figure 3.3. Click **OK** to continue.

[Screenshot: firstapp window showing "Open Event for FirstApp application object" with OK button]

*Figure 3.3* The first response window.

2. The code in the application Open event then attempts to read the initialization file (**FIRSTAPP.INI**). If the application successfully locates the file, it displays the init file text, as shown in Figure 3.4.

[Screenshot: firstapp.ini window showing "this is the text in the firstapp.ini file" with OK button]

*Figure 3.4* This window is displayed if the *.INI* file is found.

If the application cannot find the file, then the message is Could not find file FIRSTAPP.INI, as in Figure 3.5. In either case, click **OK** to continue.

[Screenshot: Read INI window showing "could not find file firstapp.ini, or section [application]" with OK button]

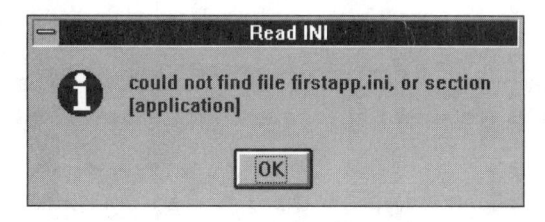

*Figure 3.5* Window displayed if the *.INI* file is not found.

3. When the application has completed the program code in the open event (steps 1 and 2), the application shuts down and finishes. This triggers the application Close event, which displays the message `Close Event for the FirstApp Application`, as shown in Figure 3.6. Click **OK** in this message to allow the application to shut down.

*Figure 3.6* The final response window.

## All the Code You Need

You can complete this application by following the next three steps (the next section steps you through the process):

1. Create a new application library and application object. Name the library **ZFIRSTAP.PBL**.
2. Add the following code to the application Open event:

   ```
   string s_text, s_init_file

   s_init_file = 'firstapp.ini'

   MessageBox ('FirstApp', "Open Event for FirstApp application &
   object")
   s_text = ProfileString(s_init_file, "application", "text", &
   "notfound")
   IF s_text <> "" THEN
      IF s_text <> "notfound" THEN
         MessageBox (s_init_file, left(s_text,80))
      ELSE
         MessageBox ("Read INI", "could not find file " + &
   s_init_file + ", or section [application]")
      END IF
   ELSE
      MessageBox ("Read INI", "read error")
   END IF
   ```

3. Add the following code to the application Close event:

```
MessageBox ("FirstApp", "Close Event for the FirstApp &
Application Object")
```

## FirstApp—Step-by-Step

### Create the Application and Library

Use the following steps to create the FirstApp application and library:

1. Start PowerBuilder (if necessary).
2. If you are not in the Application painter, click on the **Appl** icon on the PowerBar.
3. In the Application painter, select the **File|New** menu option.
4. In the Select New Application Library dialog box:
    a. In the File Name field, fill in the name **ZFIRSTAP.PBL**.
    b. Tab to the directories (or drives) field and set the drive and path to **C:\PB5\MCCLAN2**.
    c. Be sure that the library name is still **ZFIRSTAP.PBL**; if not, correct it.
    d. Click **OK**.
5. In the Save Application dialog box:
    a. In the Applications field, enter **firstapp**.
    b. Tab to the comments field and enter **My firstApp version1**.
    c. Be sure that the application name is **firstapp**; if not, correct it. The bottom listbox allows you to select which library will contain the application object. In this example, we only use a single library, **ZFIRSTAP.PBL**, so there is no choice to make in this case.
    d. Click **OK**.
    e. When prompted if you want to create an Application template, respond **No** (Figure 3.7).

**Chapter 3**

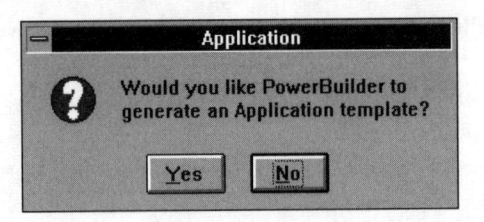

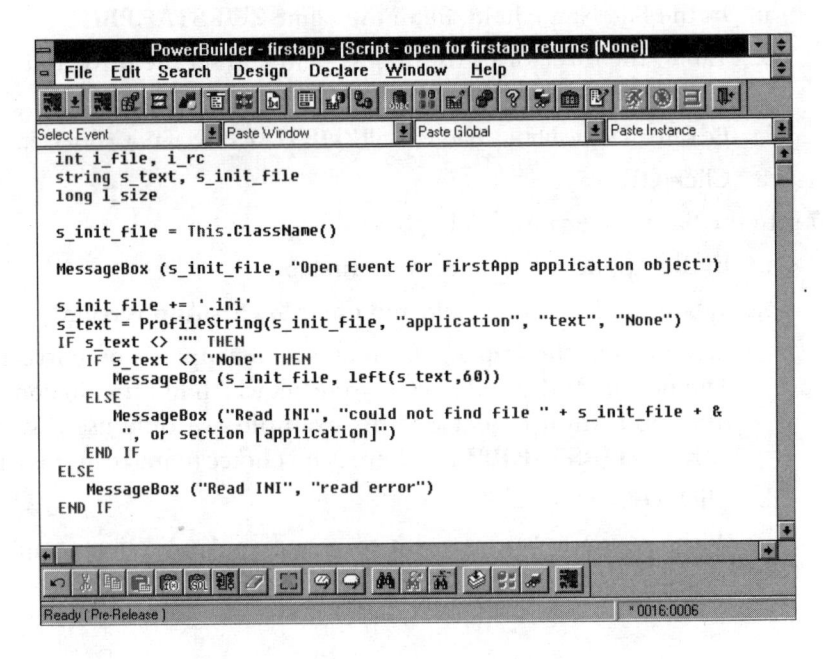

*Figure 3.7  The Open event for the application object.*

You have created the firstapp application object and the zfirstap library.

## Add Code to the Open Event

Code will be added to the Open event in two stages. Follow the next instructions to add a popup window to your first application to announce the Open event. A later step will add code to read the initialization file. To enter code into the Application Open event, open the Application painter (if necessary) and click the **Script** icon on the Application PainterBar. This opens the Script painter, as shown in Figure 3.8.

```
int i_file, i_rc
string s_text, s_init_file
long l_size

s_init_file = This.ClassName()

MessageBox (s_init_file, "Open Event for FirstApp application object")

s_init_file += '.ini'
s_text = ProfileString(s_init_file, "application", "text", "None")
IF s_text <> "" THEN
   IF s_text <> "None" THEN
      MessageBox (s_init_file, left(s_text,60))
   ELSE
      MessageBox ("Read INI", "could not find file " + s_init_file + &
      ", or section [application]")
   END IF
ELSE
   MessageBox ("Read INI", "read error")
END IF
```

*Figure 3.8  The Open event for the application object.*

Figure 3.8 shows the text of the completed example. However, in this step we will only add one line of code. The title bar shows the event (open) and the object (the firstapp application) for which you are entering code. The script editor should display `Script-open for firstapp returns (None)` on the title bar; if not, pull down the SelectEvent drop-down menu and select **Open**.

Edit the code until it matches the following exactly:

`MessageBox ('FirstApp', "Open Event for FirstApp application object")`

When it is correct, click on the **Return** icon or select **File|Close**. This compiles the code. If you mistyped the statement, you will receive an error message.

If for any reason you are unable to complete this step successfully and you wish to exit anyway, you can do one of several things to leave the editor:

1. Double-click on the Control menu (or select **File|Close**) and respond **No** when you are prompted `Do You Want to Save Changes?`
2. Click on **Select All** and then the **Comment** icons on the PainterBar to comment out the line of code so that you can exit.
3. Delete all the code in the Script window, and then exit.

You can then exit. If you return to work on this code later, you can remove the comments by clicking on the **Select All** and then **Uncmnt** icons.

## Add Code to the Close Event

New code will be entered for the Application Close event. Click on the **Script** icon on the Application PainterBar. This opens the Script painter. Pull down the SelectEvent drop-down menu and select **Close**. The script editor should then show `Script-close for firstapp` on the title bar. Next you should type the following line of code (be sure that it matches exactly):

`MessageBox ("FirstApp", "Close Event for the FirstApp Application")`

When it is correct, click on the **Return** icon. If, for any reason, you are unable to do this step successfully, and you wish to exit anyway, click on **Select All** and then **Comment** to comment out all the code. You will then be able to exit.

This line of code was added to show when the Application Close event occurs. It displays the message `Close Event for the FirstApp Application` and waits for you to press the **OK** button.

Now you should run the application from the development environment. Click on the **Run** icon on the PowerBar to execute the application (from within the PowerBuilder development environment). Nothing should go wrong, but if it does, postpone any work on it until you are familiar with the debugger. If everything runs correctly, this will display messages at the Open and Close events. Now you can add the code that will read the initialization file and display the result in another response window.

### Add More Code to the Open Event

Next, add code to read the initialization file. The final result should match the following:

```
string s_text, s_init_file

s_init_file = 'firstapp.ini'

MessageBox ('FirstApp', "Open Event for FirstApp application &
object")
s_text = ProfileString(s_init_file, "application", "text", "not- &
found")
IF s_text <> "" THEN
   IF s_text <> "notfound" THEN
      MessageBox (s_init_file, left(s_text,80))
   ELSE
      MessageBox ("Read INI", "could not find file " + s_init_file + &
         ", or section [application]")
   END IF
ELSE
   MessageBox ("Read INI", "read error")
END IF
```

A few comments on this code are in order. Two string variables are declared. The s_init_file variable is assigned the name of the profile file (**firstapp.ini**). The next line opens a modal response window, with the title FirstApp, an a text. The window contains an **OK** command button (this is the default). When you run the application, the Open event causes this code to be executed. The MessageBox statement displays this window and waits until you click **OK**.

The next line of code attempts to read the file **firstapp.ini**; it will look in the current directory and in directories on your path. If the file was successfully opened, the next section of code reads the text into the string variable s_text and then displays it (the first 80 characters) in another response window. If the application could not find the profile file (probably because the current directory was not set correctly before running the application), the error message is displayed.

## Run the Application

You must exit the editor before you can run the application. PowerBuilder will not let you execute an application while there are any open PowerScript painter windows. After exiting the editor, click on the **Run** icon on the PowerBar to start the application. If you are prompted Save Changes To..., answer **Yes** (this saves the changes you have made to the application). The application begins to execute, and the development environment is minimized showing the Windows desktop (or whatever you were running behind PowerBuilder). When you close the application, the application will quit and the development environment returns to its previous state.

This version of the application is a development version. You can also develop an executable that will run outside the development environment. The executable version of the application requires the PowerBuilder run-time environment to execute. If everything runs, you may go on to create an executable.

If you have any problems, compare your code closely to the code in **firstapp.pbl**. If the application cannot find the **.INI** file, set the current directory to **C:\PB5\MCCLAN2** (or whichever directory you installed the example programs in) before running the program. You can do this in several ways: (1) Reopen the application in the Application painter, (2) set the directory in the Library painter, and (3) open the **FIRSTAPP.INI** file in the text editor (use **Shift+F6**).

## Create an Executable

This step creates an executable version of the application. The executable version is a file (for this example, it is named **ZFIRSTAP.EXE**) that can be executed directly from the Windows desktop without the PowerBuilder development environment. To create an executable, you must create a project for the application. Do this by closing all other PowerBuilder painters and then opening the Project painter by clicking on the **Project** icon on the PowerBar. You must close all other windows before you build a project. In the Select Project dialog box (Figure 3.9), click the **New** button to create a new project (you will later select an existing project in this dialog box to rebuild the executable). You will see the Select Executable dialog box. It should suggest the name **zfirstap.exe** for your executable and select the same directory where the library was created. Click **OK**.

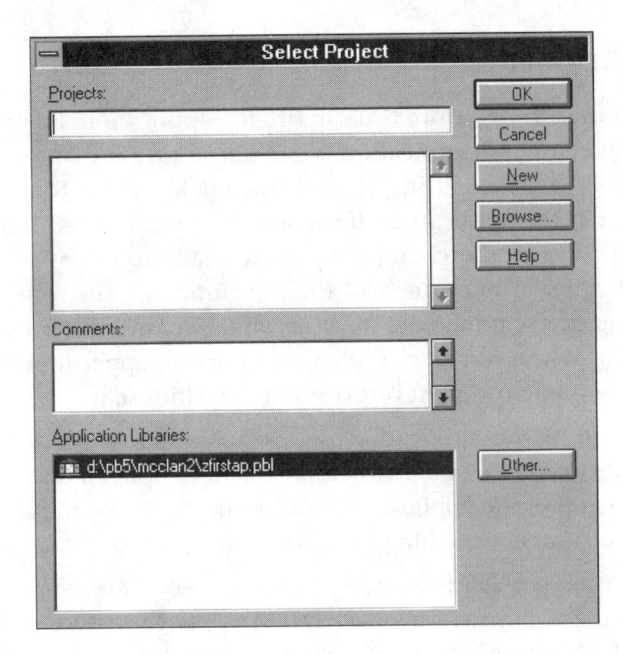

*Figure 3.9  The Select Project dialog box.*

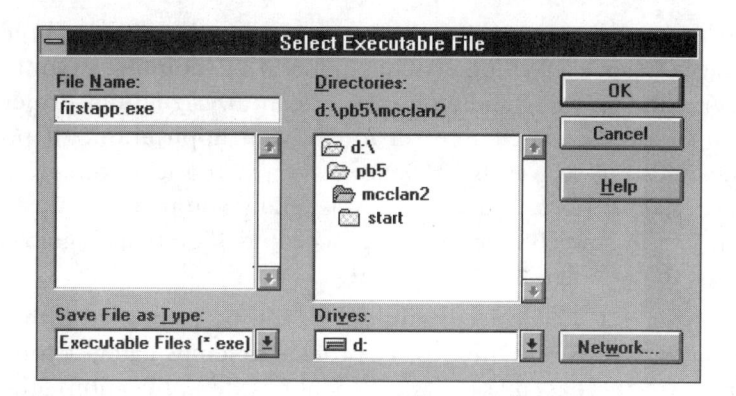

*Figure 3.10  Defining an executable.*

This will open the Project painter, as shown in Figure 3.11.

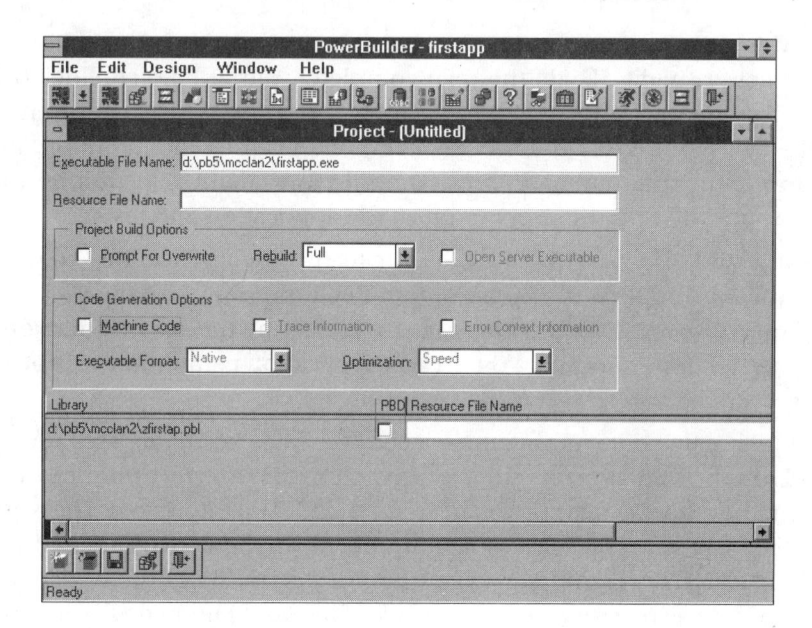

*Figure 3.11  The Project painter.*

Check under the Library listbox to be sure that the correct library (**.PBL** file) is listed. When everything matches Figure 3.11 (pointing to your working directory), click on the **Build** icon or select the **Design|Build Project** menu option to create the executable version of your application. (If prompted to save changes, answer **Yes**. If a MessageBox says `Cannot create run time when another painter is open`, it is telling you that you must close all other windows in PowerBuilder before proceeding. If everything goes correctly, you will see the message `Build Library`.

When you exit the Project painter, you will be prompted with the Save Project dialog box. Name the project **project_firstapp**. Later, if you create a new version of the executable (after updating the application), the system asks if you wish to overwrite the existing **firstapp.exe**; you should answer **Yes**.

## Run the Executable from Windows

Next, you will want to see that the executable was created and can be run outside of PowerBuilder. To do this, exit completely out of PowerBuilder (this is not strictly necessary to run the executable, but the development environment is not required). Do this by selecting the **File|Exit** menu option. In the Windows Program Manager, select the **File|Run** menu selection and then browse until you find the program. Run the application and test it.

You could also use the File Manager to run the application. To do this, select the file and then the menu option **File|Run** or just double-click on the file. You will want to select an icon to represent the application on the Windows desktop. You can do this in the Application painter in the Properties dialog box.

One caveat about running the executable: The executable uses a number of DLLs in the **PB5** directory when it runs. The **PB5** directory must be on your path (in the **autoexec.bat**) or you must set the **PB5** directory to be the working directory for the application when you define the properties for the **ZFIRSTAP.EXE** program item. If you do not follow one of these recommendations, you may receive an error message. This would be a File Error message box with a message something like `Cannot find PBRTF050.DLL`.

## LIBRARY PAINTER

The Library painter manages the PowerBuilder libraries where the application components reside. The Library painter lets you inspect the contents of the libraries, as well as search through them for objects and text. You can move or copy objects from one library to another, delete objects from a library, and perform other types of maintenance. PowerBuilder also lets developers check objects out of the libraries for development. When an object has been checked out, it cannot be modified by another developer. This prevents two or more developers from working on the same object at the same time. When the development has been completed, the developer checks the object back into the library.

To open the Library painter, click on the **Library** icon on the PowerBar. This opens a screen that should look similar to Figure 3.12.

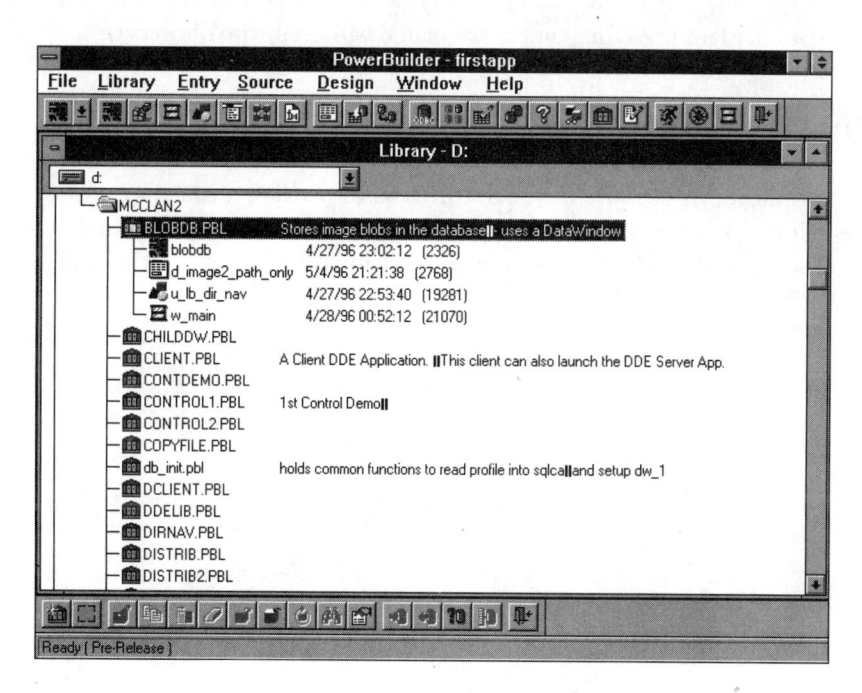

*Figure 3.12  The Library painter.*

You can select the desired disk drive from across the top of the painter window. You navigate through the directory structure by double-clicking on a directory. This will expand the directory display (if the directory contains subdirectories). Once expanded, double-click on a directory to collapse (close) it. Find the library for one of your applications (such as **C:\PB5\MCCLAN2\FIRSTAPP.PBL**). Double-clicking on the **FIRSTAPP.PBL** icon will expand the library, listing its components. This expansion is somewhat similar to the Application painter, but it shows objects by library, not by object. The only component of the **FIRSTAPP.PBL** library is the FirstApp application object (and the Project if you created one). For each object, you should see the modification date, size, and a comment. If you select a larger library, such as **IMAGEDB.PBL**, you will see a greater number of objects (see Figure 3.12). There is a different icon for each type of object (application objects, windows, DataWindows, menus, user objects, functions). To collapse the library, just double-click on it. (If you double-click on one of the application objects, PowerBuilder launches the painter associated with that type of object).

## What's Next

Most applications use one or more windows to provide a interface to the user. The Window Painter is used to create windows and to add controls such as radio buttons to those windows. The next chapter introduces the Window painter.

**CHAPTER 4**

# Creating Windows

Windows present information to and accept input from the user of the application. Most PowerBuilder applications have one or more windows and use them extensively for the user interface. The Window painter provides all the functions the developer needs to create windows and to add controls, such as command buttons and radiobuttons, to those windows. The Window painter is graphical and easy to use.

In this chapter, we cover all the details about building windows. This includes:

- The Window painter utility
- The creation of windows
- Window attributes
- Window events and functions
- FirstWin, an example application

You will spend a great amount of time in the Window painter, and it is important that you become familiar with all of its features. In the next chapter, we cover the addition of controls, such as command buttons, to your windows.

## WINDOW PAINTER

To open the Window painter, click on the Window icon on the PowerBar. This opens the Select Window dialog box (Figure 4.1).

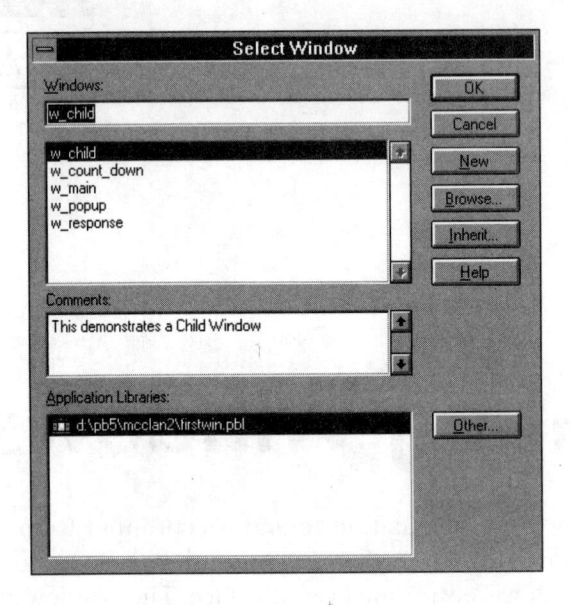

*Figure 4.1  The Select Window dialog box.*

In the Select Window dialog box, you can either open an existing window (to modify it) or create a new one. To create a new window, click the **New** button. (You can create a new window also by using inheritance (by selecting the Inherit button). We cover this option later in the chapter on Inheritance). Clicking the **New** button on the Select Window dialog box creates the new window and opens the Window painter (Figure 4.2).

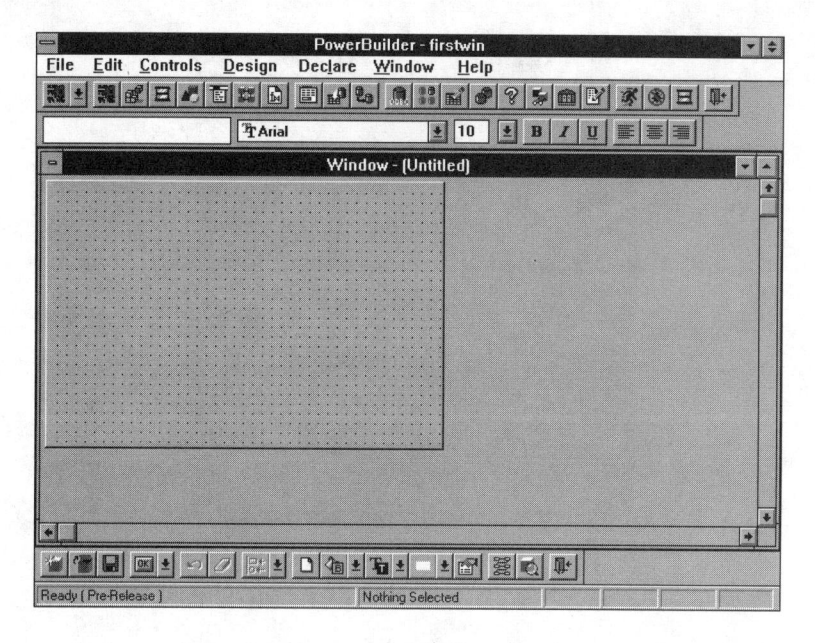

*Figure 4.2  The Window painter.*

## The Window Painter Dialog Box

The Window painter displays the newly created (and as yet unnamed) window. The new window appears as a rectangle in the upper left of the workspace. If you have the grid display turned on, the window will be covered with dots to help you position and align the objects and controls that you add to the window. (To activate the grid, use the **Design|Options** menu option and on the **General** tab click the **Show Grid** and **Snap to Grid** checkboxes; see Figure 4.3). The workspace is the client area of the Window painter where you design the window and add controls and other objects to the window. While working in this window, you are in *design* mode. You can switch to *preview* mode to see the current state of the window with the **Design|Preview** menu option (or use the toggle **Shift+Ctrl+P**).

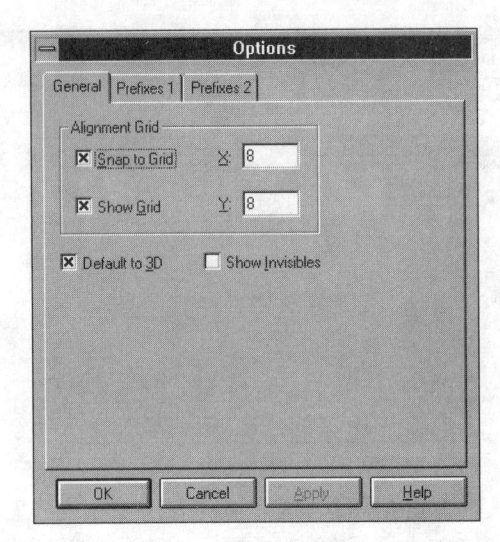

*Figure 4.3  The General Tab Dialog box.*

## The 3D Look

You should select the 3D look as the default for windows. This style gives a three-dimensional characteristic to the controls and sets the default color to **gray**. Gray works very well with the 3D option and will also usually be the choice for your MDI applications. You can set this option in the Window painter by selecting the **Design|Options** menu option and then by setting the Default to **3D** checkbox option on the General tab dialog box (Figure 4.3).

## Window Painter Toolbars

Notice that the Window painter has a number of icons on its PainterBar. One icon, initially displayed with the command button, represents all controls than can be added to a window. If you click the small **down** arrow, it will open a palette that displays icons that represent all the controls or graphical objects you can add to the new window. Just click the type of object and click on the window at the point where you wish to place the object. The icon on the PainterBar will change to the last selected object, so you can easily add several of the same type of objects just by clicking the **icon**. All of these objects are also available under the Controls Menu. Figure 4.4 shows the available controls after clicking the **PainterBar** control arrow icon.

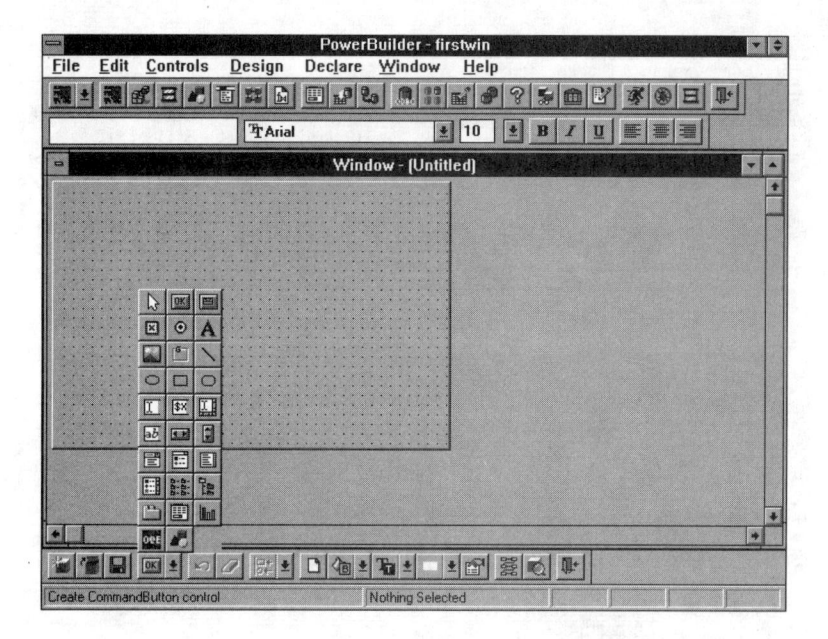

*Figure 4.4  Available controls and object in the Window painter.*

## The Style Toolbar

In the Window painter, you have the option of displaying an additional toolbar, the style (or custom) toolbar. The style toolbar displays and lets you change the attributes of the text on the window, such as the font name, and various options such as underlining, italics, bold, and justification.

## Setting Color Options

Two dropdowns on the PainterBar present a palette of the color choices for the foreground and background colors. Figure 4.5 shows PainterBar with a color dropdown.

To set the color for any object in the window, do the following: select the object(s), click on the **Background Color arrow** or **Foreground Color arrow** and click on a color to set the object's background or foreground color. If you have selected the 3D option, you will not be able to change the color of command buttons, since gray is part of the 3D option.

## Chapter 4

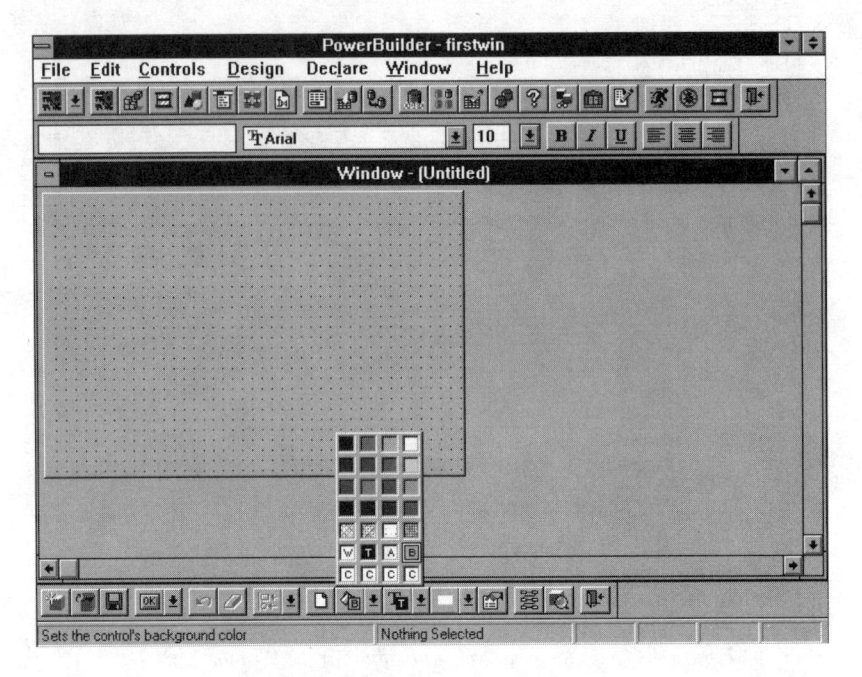

*Figure 4.5* The Style toolbars.

To show (display) the style toolbar, select the **Window|Toolbars** menu option or open the RMB popup over a toolbar. This opens the Toolbars dialog box (Figure 4.6) where you can choose to show, hide, or relocate any of the toolbars, or customize the contents of the PowerBar, PainterBar, and custom toolbars.

You can position any of the toolbars at the top or bottom of the window. You can also choose to display the PowerBar or PainterBar toolbars at the left or right of the window, or as a floating box. The floating toolbar option is especially appropriate for the PainterBar in the Window painter because of the large number of icons contained within it. You can also dock toolbars by dragging a floating toolbar to the position next to another toolbar.

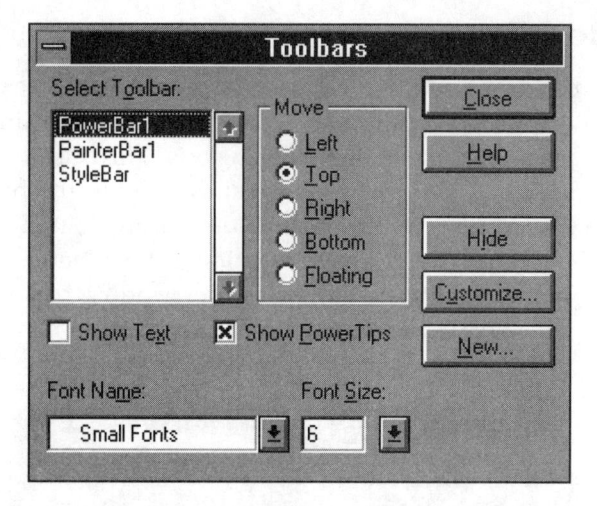

*Figure 4.6  The Toolbars dialog box.*

## DEFINING A WINDOW'S STYLE

A window has a large number of properties that determine its characteristics. These properties define the style of the window and are controlled in various parts of the window's Properties Tab dialog box. Select the **Edit|Properties** menu option from the Window Painter menu or use the RMB popup menu, and then select the **General** tab. This opens the General (window styles) dialog box, as shown in Figure 4.7.

There is also a shortcut to the General (window styles) dialog box, just double-click within the window. If there are other objects in the window (such as buttons) you must be sure to actually click on the window area and avoid the controls.

## The Window Type

The first and most important choice in the General dialog box, is to choose the Window Type. To do this, select one of the types listed in the Window Type dropdown near the bottom of the dialog box. This selection is important because a window's type determines a great deal about the behavior of the window. When you select the type, PowerBuilder will automatically set attributes in this dialog box to match the characteristics of the selected type. The type of window determines its relationship with other windows in your application. Some windows may serve as the parent (or owner) of other parented windows.

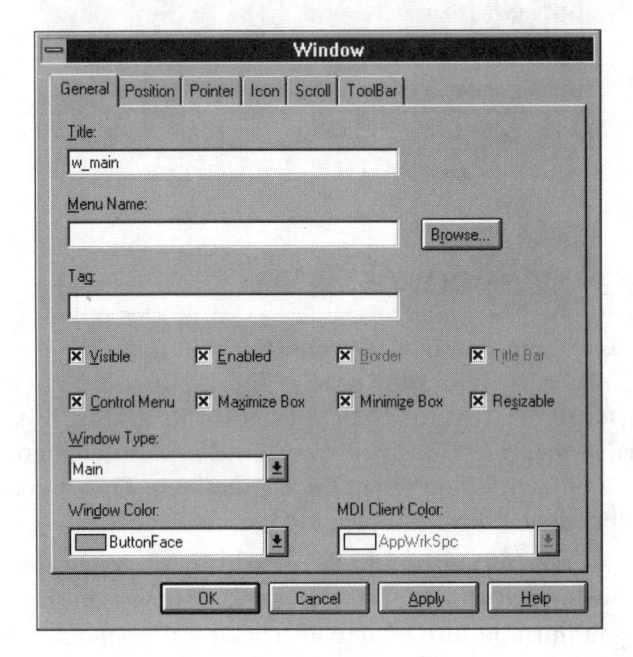

*Figure 4.7* The General (Window Style) dialog box.

The choices for the window types are:

### Main

- A standard, independent overlapping window
- Often used as a base window that holds the application controls and is used to create forms

- May serve as a parent window for child, popup, and response windows
- A main window type can also be an MDI sheet (explained later in this chapter)

## Popup

- A parented window, but can appear outside of parent
- Closed, minimized with parent
- Closed, minimized separately

## Child

- A parented window, which always appears inside its parent
- Can have title
- Does not have menus
- Closed, minimized; maximized within parent
- Closed with parent
- Can never be the active window, so never fires an activate event
- Not often used, now that MDI is standard

## Response

- Is a modal popup window
- Does not have minimize or maximize buttons
- The MessageBox that you have already used is actually a PowerBuilder supplied response box

## MDI

- Multiple Document Interface Frame window
- Contains sheets (child windows, but may be any type except MDI)
- May also opt for MDI with Microhelp

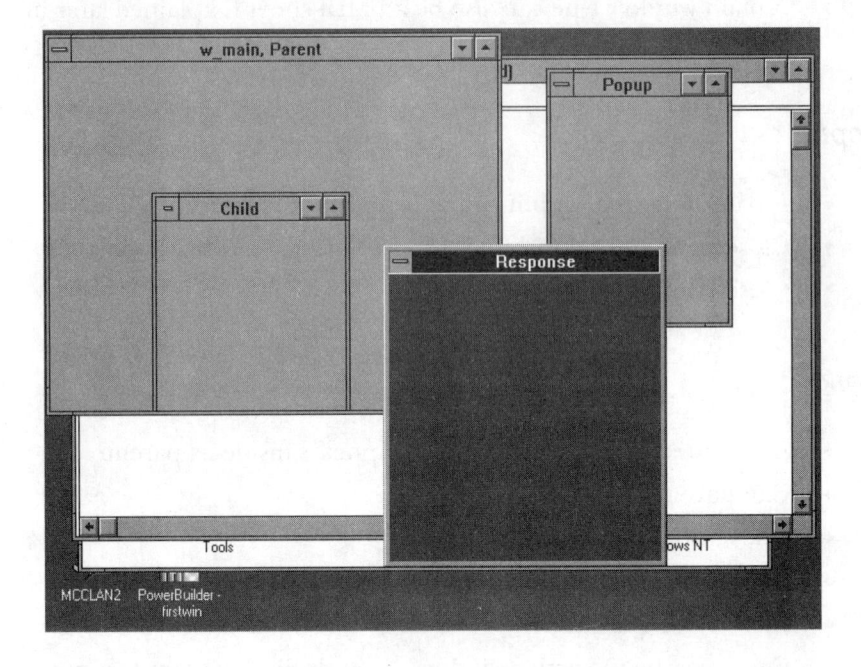

Figure 4.8 shows one of each type of window (except MDI).

*Figure 4.8* The FirstWin application showing a main, child, popup, and response window.

## The Main Window

The main window is usually selected for a window that serves as the primary window in an application. A main window stands as a base window and is not contained in any other window. A main window may be the parent of child, popup, or response windows. In Figure 4.8, the window with the caption "`w_main,Parent`" is a main window.

A main window usually has either a menu or a set of command buttons to present different options to the user. This type of window has a title bar with a caption and has a border. It has an overlapping window style for its presentation. A main window can be resized or minimized. When you set its position, it is set relative to the screen, not to any other window.

## The Child Window

A child window is a dependent window. A child window must be associated with a parent window and can only be presented within the bounds of the parent. A child window can be minimized or maximized within the parent window. If you minimize a child window, its icon will appear in the bottom of the parent window. If the parent is minimized, the child is hidden. When you position a child window, all references are made in relation to the top left corner of the parent window. Child windows cannot have their own menus, but may have a Control Menu. A child window usually has a title bar. In Figure 4.8, you see a child window with the caption "Child." Notice that the bottom of the child window is clipped off by the main (parent) window.

## The Popup Window

A popup window also has a parent window, but it does not have all the limitations of te child window. A popup window's position and display are not limited to the boundary of the parent window. They always appear in front of the parent window and can be minimized separately from the parent (but if the parent is minimized, so is the popup). When minimized, the popup icon appears on Windows' desktop, not inside the parent window. Popups usually have a title bar. Popups are often used to provide additional information or greater detail about an object in the parent window. The window with the caption "Popup" in Figure 4.8 is a popup window. Notice that it appears outside but still on top of the parent main window.

## The Response Window

A *response* window is similar in some ways to a popup window, except that it is application modal. Modal windows require a user response before continuing with the application. When your application opens a response window, the user cannot switch to another window (in the same application) until they close the response window. The response window always presents a message and usually one or more command buttons to the user. They are often used to present error information or to prompt the user to make a decision that is needed before proceeding. A response window cannot have a menu, cannot be resized, and is not scrollable. You can move a response window or close it. Figure 4.8 also contains a response type window.

You often see a response window when you attempt to close a Windows program and have not saved some newly created or modified information. For example, if you are using a text editor where you have created a new text file or have modified an existing file and you attempt to exit the program without having saved those changes, a response window appears. The response window contains a message to warn you that the changed text has not been saved and asks whether you wish to save the changes before closing the program. Figure 4.9 shows a response window from Microsoft Word.

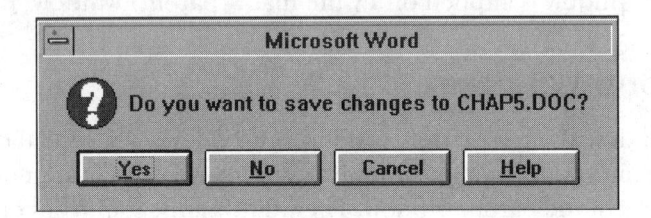

*Figure 4.9* A familiar response window.

The PowerBuilder MessageBox function creates a response window. The response window usually uses the `CloseWithReturn` statement to return to the calling statement with the number of the user's choice.

## The MDI Frame Window

The MDI Frame window may be the most important type of window. Most of the larger Windows applications use the MDI (Multiple Document Interface) application style. Microsoft Word for Windows, Microsoft Excel, and PowerBuilder itself are examples of MDI applications. MDI is a presentation style in which one parent window (called the MDI frame) contains numerous child windows (called *sheets*). In Microsoft Word for Windows, the child windows are the various documents that you are editing, and in Excel, each child represents a spreadsheet.

MDI frames can contain toolbars also and can include Microhelp.

The sheet windows are similar to child windows described earlier. They always appear within the parent frame window, and if you minimize the parent (frame) window, the sheets are also minimized. Sheets can be minimized, maximized, and arranged (tiled, cascaded, or layered) within the frame.

MDI windows are like the main windows discussed earlier, with a number of child windows. The difference is that the MDI style provides greater control in the management of the sheet windows. It automatically provides features, such as scrollbars, as needed.

## Sheets and Menus

The MDI sheet is similar to a child window but does vary a little in style. For example, sheets can have their own menus (but they are displayed on MDI frame). MDI interaction is accomplished primarily through menus. In general and as a point of style, MDI windows do not have command buttons, and you should follow that convention unless you have a good reason to do otherwise.

Sometimes the sheets do not have their own menus. In PowerBuilder applications, a sheet without a menu and/or toolbar inherits them from the previous sheet. If there is no previous sheet, they use the frame's menu and/or toolbar.

## Recommendation for Sheets and Menus

If any sheet in your application has a menu, every sheet should have its own menu. If your sheets do not have menus, they should use the menu (and/or toolbar) on the frame. It is highly recommended that you follow this convention, otherwise it can be very confusing to the user.

The drawback to this technique is a performance penalty. Every time you assign a menu as an attribute on a window, it will load the object into memory. Windows with large menus can take a long time to open; removing menus will make them open quickly.

Another technique is to use the top layer of the menu to represent each sub-application and then enable and disable menu items as sheets are opened or closed. Your application will gain significantly in performance if you have a one-layer menu with a function to handle the enabling and disabling of menu items.

If your menus are vastly different (as in the PowerBuilder application itself), you should have one menu on every sheet as described earlier.

## MDI Sheet Window Types

You might be wondering if there is a MDI sheet window type. The answer is no. When you create a window that is a sheet in a MDI frame, you can select any type except MDI frame, but usually I choose main.

## MDI Frame with Microhelp

The final window-type option is the MDI Frame with Microhelp. As you might expect, this is the same as the MDI Frame type except that it adds Microhelp functionality to your application. Microhelp is a brief text message displayed on the status line at the bottom of the frame window. It is used to give the user assistance on using menus and icons or to present status messages and explanatory information. You can add Microhelp to your MDI applications easily. This is discussed later in the chapter on MDI applications. Figure 4.10 shows an example of an MDI application created with PowerBuilder.

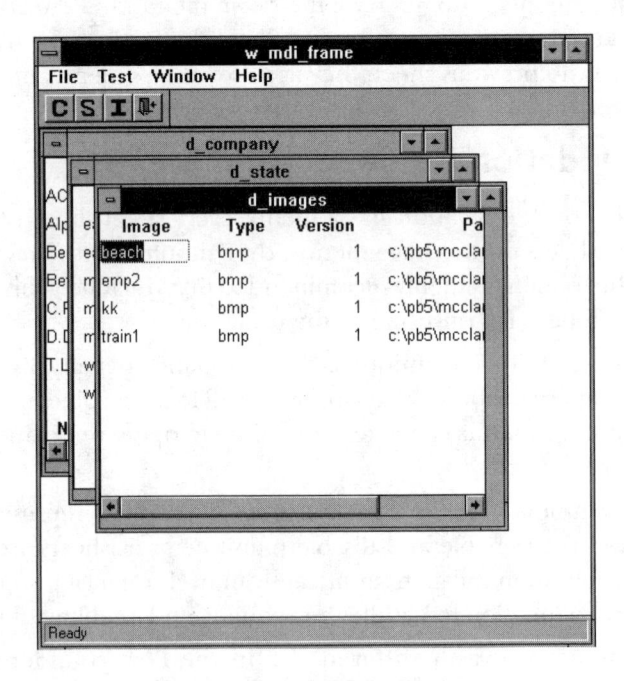

*Figure 4.10* A MDI application.

## OTHER WINDOW ATTRIBUTES

After defining the type of new window, you can proceed to the setting of the other attributes that determine the window's style. The Window Properties dialog box (Figure 4.11) presents the attribute options in a series of checkboxes, edit fields, and several dropdown listboxes. When you select a type for the window, PowerBuilder sets the initial state of the checkboxes and disables some of them. For example, you cannot add a minimize box to a response window, so that checkbox is disabled.

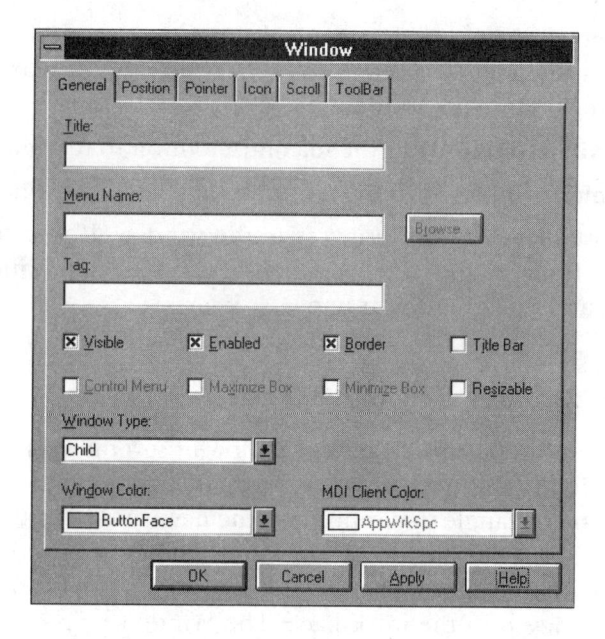

*Figure 4.11* The Window Style dialog box.

The more important options that you have are:

+ **Title**—An edit field, enter the caption that appears in the title bar.
+ **Menu Name**—An edit box for the name of the menu for this window. Clicking the **Browse** button will allow you to select the name of the menu from a list.

- **Window Options**—The next section has eight checkboxes, which have different values depending on the type of window. These attributes are:
  - **Visible**—Makes the window visible (which is usual).
  - **Enabled**—Makes the window active and able to receive user input (which is usual).
  - **Border**—Adds a border to a window. Main windows always have borders.
  - **Title Bar**—Adds a caption bar to a window. Main windows always have title bars.
  - **Control menu**—Adds a control menu to the window, adds functions to allow the user to move, resize (restore, maximize), minimize, or close the window.
  - **Maximize box**—Adds the maximize button to the window.
  - **Minimize box**—Adds the minimize button to the window.
  - **Resizable**—Lets the user resize the window. If selected, it adds a thin frame to the window. The user can resize the window by clicking and dragging this frame.

## Resizing the New Window

You can resize and reposition the new window in several ways. First, you can use the mouse in the painter workspace. To do this, position the pointer at the outer edge of the rectangle that represents the new window until the pointer's shape changes into a double arrow. Then click and drag the edge of the window to expand or contract it. The top and left edges of the window are fixed and cannot be moved in the workspace. The Window painter itself takes up quite a bit of territory on the screen, so you may have to scroll the workspace (using the vertical and horizontal scrollbars) to allow the window to be fully sized and shaped. You can switch from design mode to preview mode to see what the window will actually look like when it is used in an application. To preview the window's appearance, use the **Shift+Control+P** key combination to toggle on the preview mode. The same key combination will return you to design mode. You can also use the **Design|Preview** menu option to switch to Preview mode, and then double-click on the previewed window's control menu to switch back to design mode.

## Window Position Dialog Box

There is another, much easier method for positioning and sizing the new window. In the Window painter, choose the **Edit|Properties** menu option (or activate the RMB popup menu) and select the Position tab dialog box. This action takes you to the Window Position dialog box shown in Figure 4.12. This dialog box is very easy to use, and it gives you a proportional representation of how the window appears on the screen.

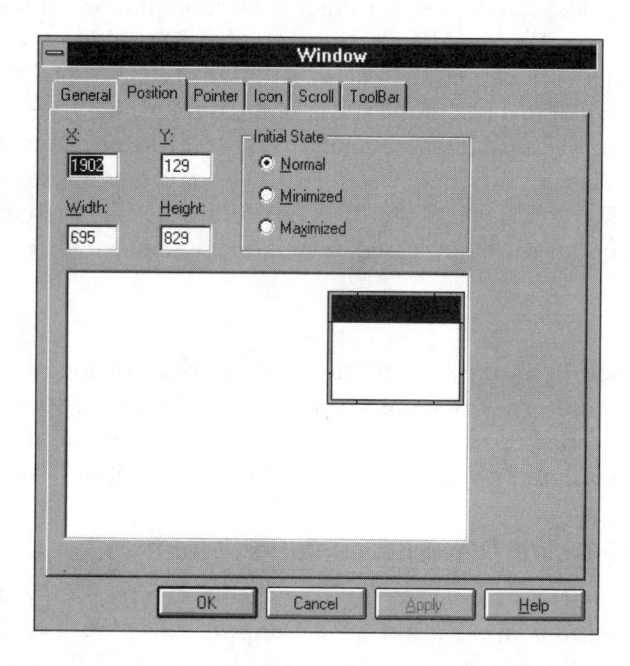

*Figure 4.12  The Window Position dialog box.*

The white rectangular area at the bottom of this dialog box represents the actual display area available on your video screen. In this area, you will also see a rectangle that represents the newly created window. That rectangle shows the window's current position and relative size in the display area. You can use the mouse to position and to resize the window. Click and drag any edge of the window to resize it, or click on the **title bar** of the window and drag to reposition it.

## Automatic Centering

On the Window Position dialog box, you can use two options on the RMB menu (right-mouse click anywhere in the display space on the Position dialog box) to automatically center the window within the display area. Select the first RMB menu option to automatically center the window on the horizontal plane. Select the second RMB menu option to automatically center the window on the vertical plane.

This dialog box also displays the current location and size of the window in PowerBuilder units. You could enter these numbers directly, but that is not very intuitive and there is little reason to do so. The size of a horizontal PowerBuilder unit (PBU) is equal to 1/32 of the width of an average character in the system font. The size of a vertical PBU is equal to 1/64 of the same character. Knowing this you can calculate the size of a standard VGA screen as approximately 2560 horizontal PBUs (80 x 32) by 1536 (24 x 64) vertical PBUs. These numbers are approximate, because they are based on an average size character.

## Initial State

You can also set the initial state of the window in this dialog box. This is the state that the window will assume when it is first opened in your application. The choices for the initial state are normal, maximize, and minimize. Normal is the size that is currently displayed in the Window Position work area.

## Sizing Windows for Different Resolution Monitors

There is an important caveat to consider when sizing the new window. If you are developing your application on a computer that has a different video resolution than the target system, you must be careful. When you run your application on the target systems, what you see may not be what you expected or intended. If you have a high-resolution monitor (for instance, 800 x 600 or 1024 x 768) and create a window that fills the entire screen, you may be surprised to see that when the application is run on a standard VGA system (640 x 480) the window will be too large to fit on the screen. You should also verify that the font type and size are appropriate for the target system. So plan accordingly and run a test early in the development process to be sure that the window(s) will fit. You should also consider choosing the centering options to be sure that the window is positioned correctly. The advantage of using PowerBuilder units based on an average-size character is that the ratio is more accurate on different screen resolution than if you used pixels.

In general, you will find it easier to develop on a lower-resolution screen and deliver to higher-resolution screens, rather than the other way around.

### Scroll Bars

In the Scroll tab dialog box, you can add vertical and/or horizontal scroll bars, and then set the scroll rates for these scroll bars for this window by setting the values in the edit boxes in this dialog box. If you do not enter values (leave them at zero), the default values will be used. The default scroll rate is 1/100 of the window size for each click on one of the scroll bar arrows. The default paging distance is 10 lines of text vertically and 10 columns horizontally. Page scrolling is initiated when you click on one of the **scroll bars** itself.

## OTHER WINDOW OPTIONS

Other tab options allow you to set the remaining window attributes.

- **Pointer**—sets the mouse pointer for this window. PowerBuilder switches to this pointer when the mouse moves it over the window.
- **Icon**—chooses the icon to represent the minimized window.
- **Toolbar**—chooses the position of the toolbar.

## SAVING THE WINDOW

After you have designed the window, you need to save it. To do this, select the **File|Save As** menu option. This opens the Save Window dialog box. Set the PowerBuilder library where you want to store the window and name the window, usually a window is given the prefix `w_`, such as `w_main` or `w_employee`. Add a comment that describes the window.

In general, it is a good idea to save the newly created window as soon as you have defined its major characteristics (such as its type and position).

## THE WINDOW PAINTER POPUP MENU

In the Window painter, you can activate the RMB popup menu by clicking on the right mouse button within the window. The popup menu has the following options:

- **Script**—opens the PowerScript painter to edit an event script
- **Properties**—opens the Properties tab dialog box
- **Paste**—pastes the object(s) in the Clipboard buffer

### Window Scripts

The **Edit|Script** menu option opens the PowerScript painter where you can edit the script for any of the window events. You can also open the editor by selecting the **Script** option on the RMB popup menu.

## WINDOW EVENTS

Windows have over two dozen events, the most important ones are:

- `Activate`—Occurs before the window is made active. The active window receives the keyboard strokes and is displayed with a highlighted title.
- `Clicked`—When you click in a window but not within one of the controls (such as a command button or list box), this event is triggered.
- `Close`—Occurs before the window is deactivated and closed.
- `CloseQuery`—Queries your window, giving the window a chance to handle any last details such as saving any current changes to a file or table. The event occurs before the Close event, and it is possible to refuse to allow the window to close. To do this set the return value to **1**.
- `Key`—When a keyboard stroke occurs and the focus is not within a editing control, the window will receive the event.
- `Open`—This event occurs after the open call has been made to open the window but before the window has been displayed.

- `Resize`—Triggered whenever the window is resized, including the initial sizing when the window is opened.
- `Show`—Triggered before the window is about to be displayed as result of a `Show` function call.
- `Timer`—Occurs at specified intervals as set by the Timer function. The timer event is triggered only if the `Timer()` function was called.

## WINDOW FUNCTIONS

The following are the most important PowerBuilder functions apply specifically to window objects:

- `ArrangeSheets`—a function used for MDI windows. It organizes the sheet windows in a specified style, such as tiled or cascaded.
- `ClassName`—returns the name of the window.
- `Close`—closes a window.
- `CloseWithReturn`—closes the window and returns a value.
- `GetActiveSheet`—returns the window which is the currently active sheet window.
- `Hide`—makes the window invisible.
- `Open`—opens a window.
- `OpenSheet`—opens a MDI sheet.
- `OpenSheetWithParm`—opens a MDI sheet and passes it a value.
- `OpenWithParm`—opens a window and passes it a value.
- `ParentWindow`—returns the window which is the parent window to a given window.
- `PostEvent`—adds an event to an objects message queue (an asynchronous message).
- `Resize`—changes the current size of the window.
- `SetMicroHelp`—assigns the text for the MDI status line and displays it.
- `SetRedraw`—turns on or off the display update for a window.
- `Show`—makes a window visible.
- `TriggerEvent`—sends an event to an objects message queue (this is a synchronous message).
- `TypeOf`—returns the type of the object.

## WINDOW ATTRIBUTES

The following are the most important attributes:

- `Control[ ]`—an array of the objects that are currently contained in a window.
- `ControlMenu`—a Boolean value specifies whether a window has a control menu.
- `Enabled`—a Boolean value that specifies whether a window is currently enabled (able to receive input).
- `Icon`—the name of the icon associated with this window.
- `MenuName`—PowerBuilder's internal name of the menu associated with this window. Do not use this attribute.
- `Pointer`—the name of the pointer icon associated with a window.
- `Title`—the caption for the window.
- `TitleBar`—an internal Boolean value that specifies whether the window has a title bar. This cannot be changed programmatically.
- `Visible`—a Boolean value that specifies whether a window is visible.
- `WindowType`—an enumerated value that returns the current window type.
- `X`—the position of the window, in horizontal PBUs.
- `Y`—the position of the window, in vertical PBUs.

## WINDOW VARIABLES

A window is a PowerBuilder data type (or class). Therefore, you can create variables that are instances of the window data type. These variables have scope, just like other variables. Window objects can have the following scope assignments:

- **Local**—known only in the immediate script containing it.
- **Instance**—owned by an object (such as another window or user object) and visible (accessible) to that object and any other objects within the parent object.
- **Shared**—shared by objects of a certain class.

When you create a new window (w_main, for example), you are actually creating a class (an object type, a new data type) in the Window painter.

Later, when you open the window:

```
open (w_main)
```

you are actually opening an instance of that window. When you created the w_main class, PowerBuilder (behind the scenes) created an instance of the class w_main and gave it the same name (w_main) as the class. This object is what is actually referenced in the open() function.

You could also declare your own instances of w_main as follows:

```
w_main w_main1, w_main2
open(w_main1)
open(w_main2)
open(w_main1) // what does this do?
```

Notice how w_main is used as the data type for the w_main1 and w_main2 variables. The third statement only activates the w_main1 instance (does not fire the open event again). It does not create a third instance of the w_main window type.

You could also create instances of a window by creating an array, as follows:

```
w_child w_child[10]
int idx

FOR idx = 1 to 10
   open(w_child[idx])
   w_child[idx].x = idx * 100
   w_child[idx].y = idx * 100
NEXT
```

This example creates ten instances of a w_child window, cascading the child windows across the parent window.

After creating the instances, you can assign attribute values and call window functions, as follows:

```
open(w_child[1])
open(w_child[2])
w_child[1].x = 10
w_child[1].y = 10
w_child[2].Move(w_child[2].x+100, w_child[2].y+100)
w_child[2].st_status.text = "2"
```

If you need to create a heterogeneous array of windows with mixed types you can use the PowerBuilder window data type:

```
window w_array[2]
string win[2]

win[1] = "w_main"
win[2] = "w_child"
open (w_array[1], win[2])
```

The drawback of this technique is that you cannot reference any objects using the window arrays. So the following statement:

```
w_array[1].cb_close.enabled = false // illegal
```

would create a compiler error. This is because the `w_array` type is a window, which is a generic window that does not contain a command button (`cb_close`). There is a solution. You can "cast" the object to the correct window type before accessing its controls by assigning it to a variable of the correct window type. For example, if you add the following to the previous example, it would work:

```
w_child w_x

w_x = w_array[1]
w_x.cb_close.enabled = False // this works
```

# Example: FirstWin

FirstWin is a simple application that demonstrates each window type (except MDI windows). The main window (w_main) is shown when FirstWin is launched. If you double-click anywhere within the main window, three other windows open, as shown in Figure 4.13.

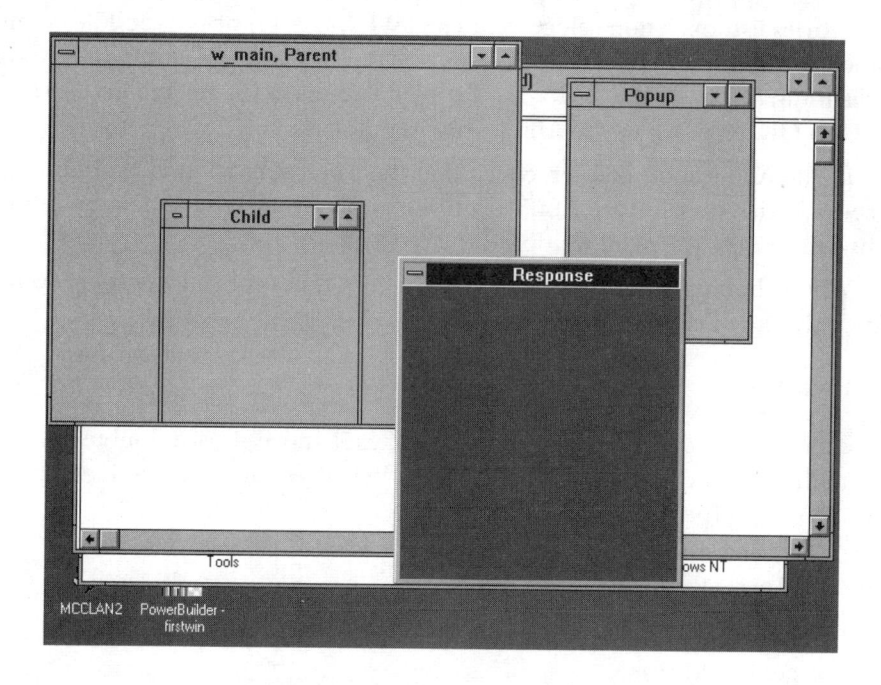

*Figure 4.13  The FirstWin application.*

A child window opens inside the parent (w_main), a popup window opens on top (and perhaps outside) the main window and a modal response window opens in front of all other windows. You must close the response window before you can activate any of the other windows in this application.

Another function demonstrates the Timer event. If you double-click in the child window, a new window, w_count_down, appears. The w_count_down window displays the number 20. Every second the window beeps and decrements the number by one. When it reaches 0 (zero), it closes the application.

## Running FirstWin

Before you build your version of this application, run the sample application from the PowerBuilder environment. To do this, launch PowerBuilder (if necessary), and go to the Application painter (click on the **Appl** icon on the PowerBar). Select the **Open** icon from the Application painter PainterBar. In the Select Application Library dialog box select **C:\PB5\MCCLAN2** in the Directories listbox. Then select the **FIRSTWIN.PBL** library in the File Name listbox and click the **OK** button. This opens the Select Application dialog box and should display "FIRSTWIN" in the Applications field. Select **FirstWin** and click on **OK** to return to the Application painter.

In the Application painter, check that the window caption is "Application-firstwin." Click on the **Run** icon to run the application. When the application runs, you will see the main window displayed on the screen.

When the application launches, it triggers the application Open event. The only line of code in that event is:

```
open(w_main)
```

This code opens the main window and makes it active. If you double-click in the main window, it triggers the double-clicked event. The double-clicked event contains the following code:

```
this.title = 'w_main, Parent'
open(w_popup)
open(w_child, This)
open(w_response)
```

This opens a popup window, a child window, and a response window. The call to open the `w_child` window makes the `w_main` window the parent of the `w_child` using the `This` reserved word. If you left out the keyword `This`, the `w_popup` window would be the parent of the `w_child`, since it would be the activate window at the time `w_child` is opened. So the keyword `This` is used to insure that the `w_main` is the parent of `w_child`.

# FirstWin—Step-by-Step

## Create the Application and Library

1. Start PowerBuilder (if necessary).
2. If you are not in the Application painter, click on the **Appl** icon on the PowerBar.
3. In the Application painter, select the **File|New** menu option.
4. In the Select New Application Library dialog box, set the directory to **C:\PB5\MCCLAN2** and enter the name **ZFIRSTWN.PBL** for the library file name. Click on **OK**.
5. In the Save Application dialog box:
    a. In the Applications field, enter **firstwin**.
    b. Tab to the Comments field and enter My **firstwin version 1**.
    c. Be sure that the Application Library name is still zfirstwn.pbl; if not, select it.
    d. Click on **OK**.
6. PowerBuilder asks if you wish to generate an application template. Click on **No** in this dialog box as we have in all the examples for this book (except one in the MDI chapter).

This returns you to the Application painter. You have created the FirstWin application object and the zfirstwn library.

## Create the Main Window

Click on the **Window** icon on the PowerBar to open the Window painter. In the Select Window dialog box, click on the **New** button to create a new window. In the Window painter, double-click on the new window to open the Window Style dialog box (or select the **Edit|Properties** menu option).

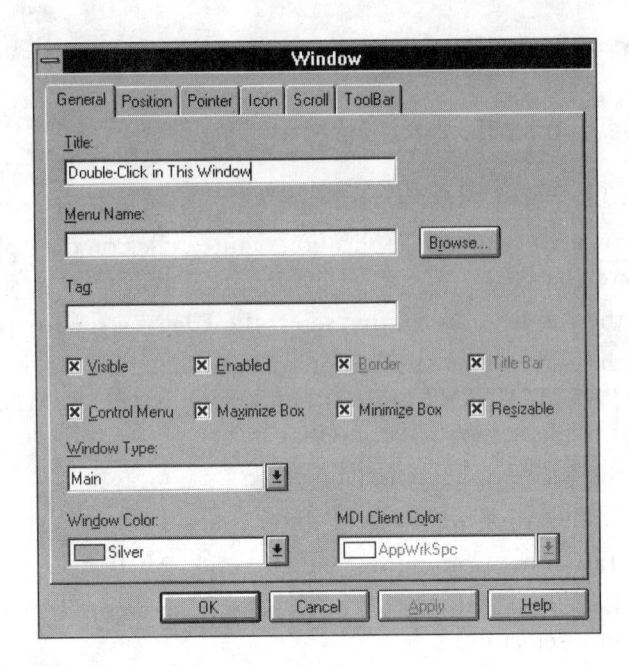

*Figure 4.14  Defining the w_main style.*

In this dialog box, in the Title editbox enter **Double-Click in This Window** as the text. Then select **Main** from the Window Type dropdown listbox. This defines the type for the new window. The other options should match those in Figure 4.14. Set these changes by clicking the **Apply** button.

Next, click the **Position** tab (in the Window Properties dialog box) to open the Window Position dialog box.

In this dialog box, set the position (and size) of the window, as shown in Figure 4.15. The position of a Main window is relative to the display area of your monitor's screen. In this example, the position of the main window is set to the upper left of the screen.

Close the dialog box by clicking on **OK**. In the Window painter, select the **File|Save As** menu option. Check to be sure that the library is set to **ZFIRSTWN.PBL**, and the name w_main and click the **OK** button. Now, close the Window painter.

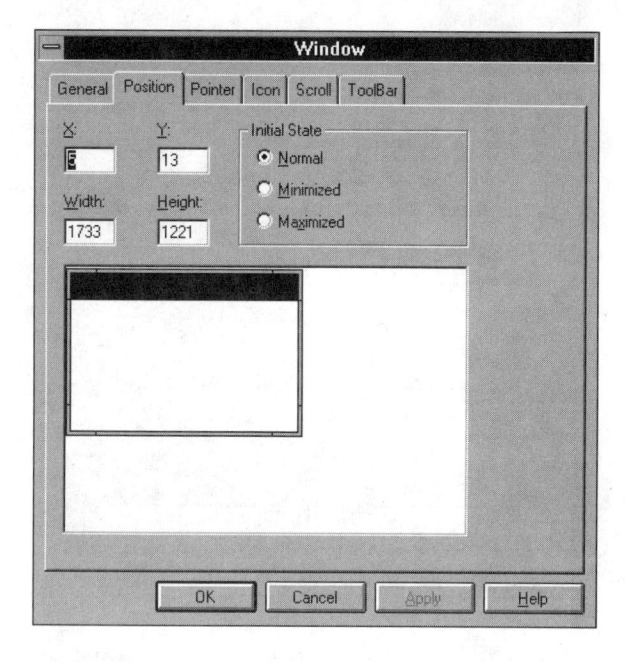

*Figure 4.15  The Window Position dialog box.*

## Create the Child Window

Click on the **Window** icon on the PowerBar to open the Window painter. In the Select Window dialog box, click on the **New** button to create a new window. In the Window painter, double-click on the new window to open the Window Style dialog box.

In this dialog box, enter **Child** as the title bar text. Next, select **Child** in the Window Type dropdown listbox. This defines the type for the new window. The other options should match those in Figure 4.16.

Click the **Position** tab (while still in the Window Properties dialog box) to open the Window Position dialog box.

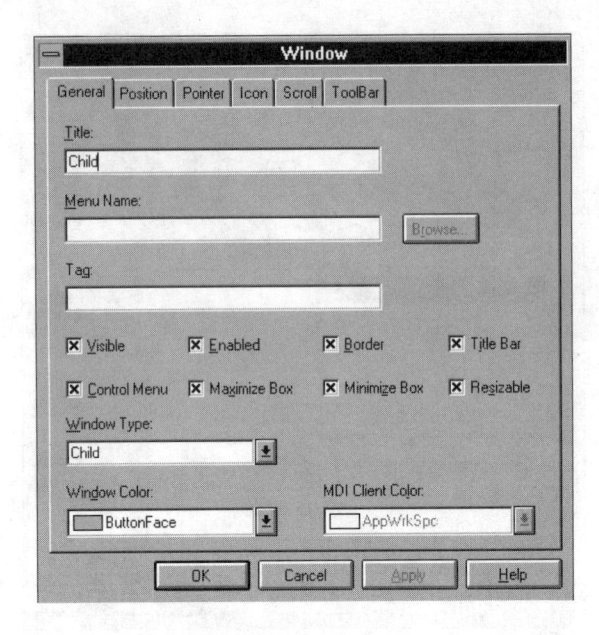

**Figure 4.16** The Window Style dialog box for `w_child`.

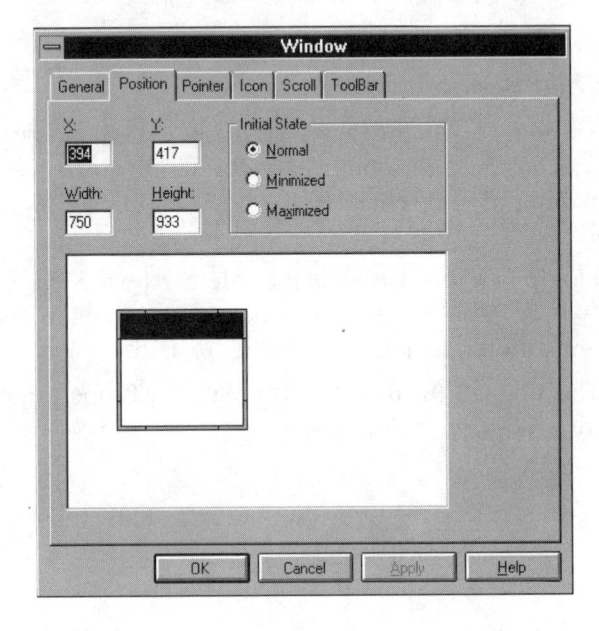

**Figure 4.17** Positioning the `w_child` window.

In this dialog box, set the position (and size) of the window, as shown in Figure 4.17. The position is relative to (and within) the parent window.

Close the dialog box by clicking on **OK**. In the Window painter, select the **File|Save As** menu option. Save the window in the **ZFIRSTWN.PBL** with the name `w_child`. Close the Window painter.

## Create the Popup Window

Click on the **Window** icon on the PowerBar to open the Window painter. In the Select Window dialog box, click the **New** button to create a new window. In the Window painter, double-click on the new window to open the Window Properties dialog box.

In this dialog box, select **Popup** in the Window Type dropdown listbox. This defines the type for the new window. Next, enter **Popup** for the title bar text. The other options should match those in Figure 4.18.

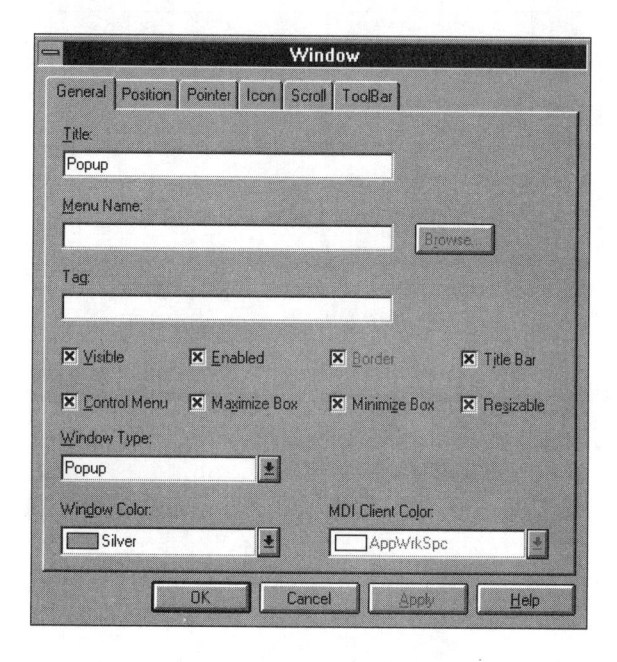

*Figure 4.18* *The Style dialog box for w_popup.*

Click the **Position** tab (on the Window Properties dialog box) to open the Window Position dialog box.

In this dialog box, set the position (and size) of the window, as shown in Figure 4.19. The position is relative to the display area of your monitor. Position the popup on the right side of the screen.

Close the dialog box by clicking on **OK**. In the Window painter, select the **File|Save As** menu option. Save the window in the **ZFIRSTWN.PBL** with the name w_popup. Close the Window painter.

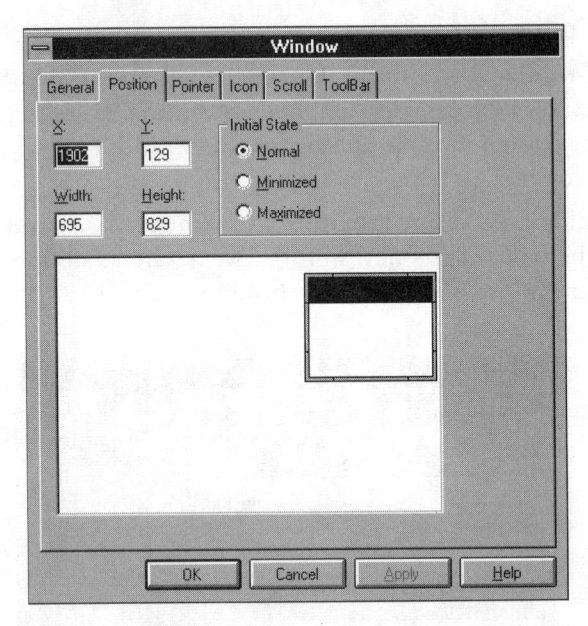

*Figure 4.19 Setting the position of w_popup.*

## Create the Response Window

Click on the **Window** icon on the PowerBar to open the Window painter. In the Select Window dialog box, click the **New** button to create a new window. In the Window painter, double-click on the new window to open the Window Style dialog box.

In this dialog box, select **Response** in the Window Type dropdown listbox. This defines the type for the new window. Next enter **Response** as the title bar text. Select the **red** from the Window Color dropdown listbox (near the top of the list). The other options should match those in Figure 4.20.

Click the **Position** tab (in the Window Properties dialog box) to open the Window Position dialog box.

In this dialog box, set the position (and size) of the window, as shown in Figure 4.21. The position is relative to the display area of your monitor. Position the Response window in the center of the screen.

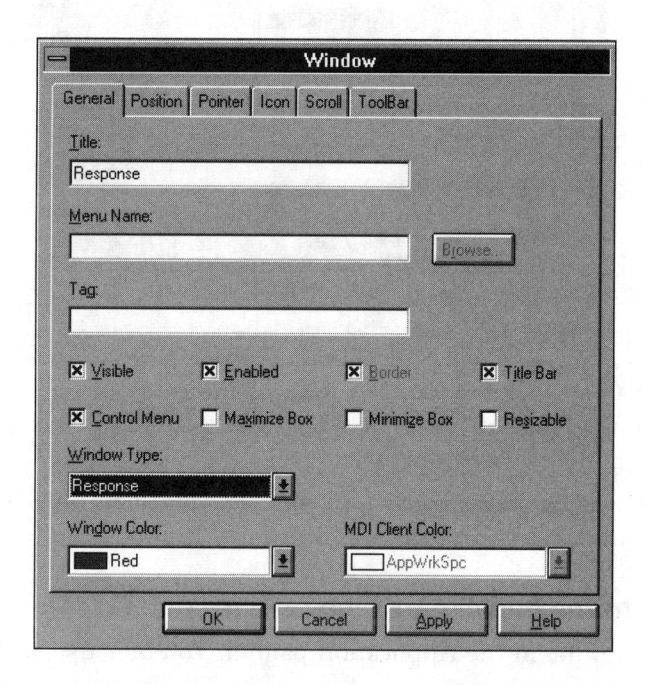

*Figure 4.20 Defining the style for* `w_response`.

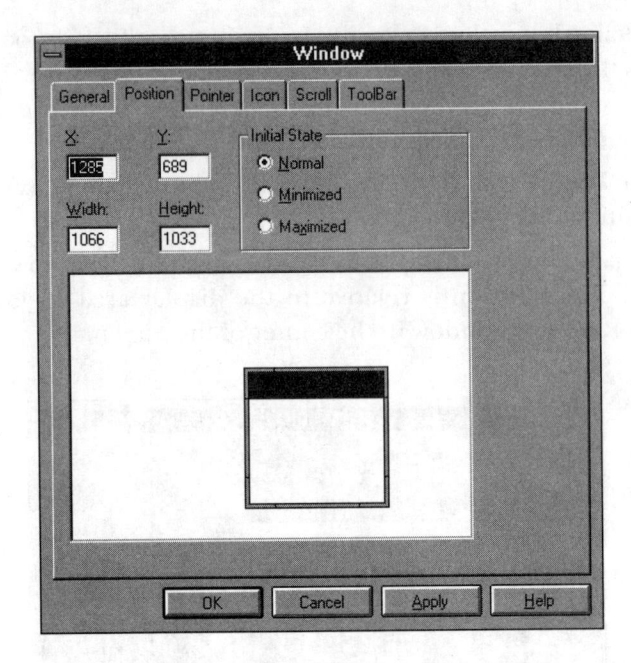

**Figure 4.21** *Positioning the w_response window.*

Close the dialog box by clicking on **OK**. In the Window painter, select the **File|Save As** menu option. Save the window in the **ZFIRSTWN.PBL** with the name w_response. Close the Window painter.

All four windows have been defined. Now you need only add the code necessary to open each window.

### Add Code to the Application Open Event

You should now be in the Application painter. To enter the new code, click the **Script** icon on the Application PainterBar. This opens the Script painter. The Script editor should display Script-open for zfirstwn on the title bar; if not, pull down the **SelectEvent** dropdown menu and select **Open**. Edit the code until it matches the following exactly:

```
open(w_main)
```

When it is correct, click the **Return** icon.

## Add Code to the w_main Window

Next, add code to the `doubleclicked` event in the `w_main` window. Open the Window painter by clicking the **Window** icon on the PowerBar. Select the `w_main` window from the list of windows presented in the Select Window dialog box.

Select the **Script** option from the popup menu to edit the `doubleclicked` event for the window. Be sure to select **doubleclicked** from the Events dropdown data window. Add the following code:

```
this.title = 'w_main, Parent'
open(w_popup)
open(w_child, This)
open(w_response)
```

This opens a popup window, a child window, and a response window when the user double-clicks in this window. Close the editor, and then close the `w_main` window and save the changes.

## Run The Application

Run the application from the development environment. If you are prompted to save the changes, answer yes. If everything runs, create a new executable as you did in the previous chapter. If you have any problems, compare your code closely to the code in the `firstwin.pbl`.

Use this example to clarify the difference between the types of windows.

**CHAPTER 5**

# Window Controls

This chapter explains how to add controls to your windows. The process is similar for many window controls. A number of the procedures for working with controls is common to many different types of controls. The first section of this chapter presents an introduction to working with controls and covers techniques that apply to most of the types of controls that you can add to your windows. The second section provides an example program which uses most of the basic controls. This chapter covers the following topics:

- Adding controls to a window
- Selecting controls
- Positioning and sizing controls
- Undoing control movement and sizing
- Viewing control status
- Using the design grid
- Setting the tab order
- The Control Properties tab dialog box
- Duplicating and copying controls
- PowerBuilder unit of measurement
- Colors for window objects
- The 3D look

The window serves as the background or container for the controls that provide the actual interaction with the user. PowerBuilder offers a wide variety of controls. You will be familiar with most of these control types from using other Windows applications. Figure 5.1 shows a PowerBuilder application with an example of many of the controls that are introduced in this chapter. In these windows are examples of a ListBox, SingleLineEdit, DropDownListBox, StaticText fields, PictureButton, EditMask, RadioButtons, CheckBoxes, command buttons, and a scroll bar.

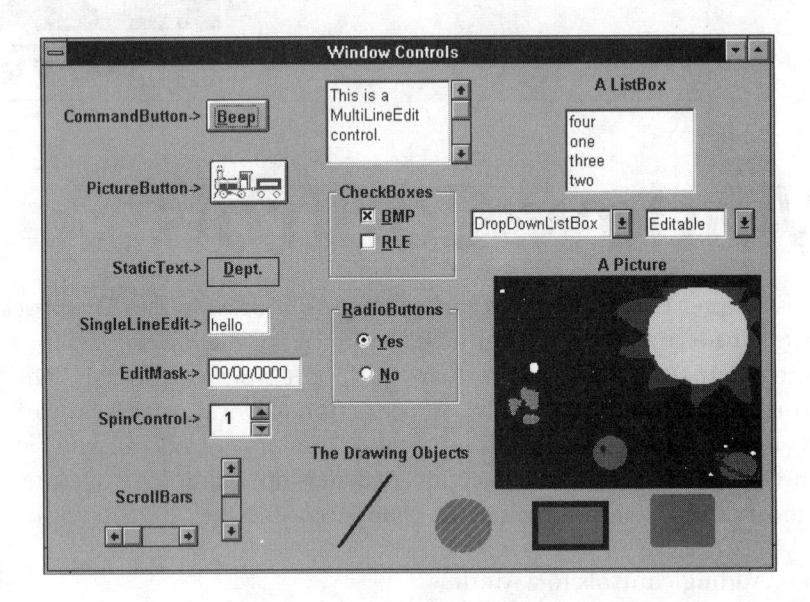

*Figure 5.1 Example window.*

Table 5.1 lists the controls (and other objects) that PowerBuilder provides as options for your windows. The first column contains the type of the control, as you would find it listed in the Controls menu. The second column lists the label for the corresponding icon on the PainterBar. The third column shows the default prefix for naming controls of this type. The final column provides a brief summary of the normal use of each type of control.

*Table 5.1* PowerBuilder Controls and Objects

| Control | PainterBar Label | Prefix | Typical Use |
| --- | --- | --- | --- |
| command button | CmdBtn | cb_ | Used to trigger some action |
| PictureButton | PicBtn | pb_ | Same as a command button |
| CheckBox | ChkBox | cbx_ | Input a choice, toggle an option on or off |
| RadioButton | RadioBtn | rb_ | Input a choice, or select from mutually exclusive set |
| StaticText | StaticTxt | st_ | Label |
| Picture | Picture | p_ | Display |
| GroupBox | GrpBox | gb_ | Gather a set of controls |
| Line | — | ln_ | Cosmetic |
| Oval | — | oval_ | Cosmetic |
| Rectangle | — | r_ | Cosmetic |
| Rounded Rectangle | — | rr_ | Cosmetic |
| SingleLineEdit | SngEdit | sle_ | Display data, input data |
| EditMask | EditMask | em_ | Display data, input data in a specific format |
| MultiLineEdit | MultiEdit | mle_ | Display data, input data Input multiline text data |
| RichTextEdit | RichTextEdit | rte_ | Display data, input data, edit RTF text data |
| HScrollBar | — | hsb_ | Display/input for a range of values, also to display progress |
| VScrollBar | — | vsb_ | Display/input for a range of values |
| DropDownListBox | DrpDnLB | ddlb_ | Display options for selection |
| DropDownPicture | DrpDnPic | ddp_ | Display options for selection with pictures |

*continued*

*Table 5.1 continued*

| Control | PainterBar Label | Prefix | Typical Use |
|---|---|---|---|
| ListBox | ListBox | lb_ | Display options for selection |
| PictureListBox | ListBox | plb_ | Display options for selection with pictures |
| ListView | ListView | lv_ | Display lists for selection |
| TreeView | TreeView | tv_ | Display tree structure for navigation |
| Tab | Tab | tab_ | Display tab dialog box window |
| DataWindow | DataWnd | dw_ | Data interface (usually database), display, and input |
| Graph | Graph | gr_ | Display |
| OleControl | OleControl | ole_ | For implementing OLE controls |
| UserObject | UserObj | uo_ | Varies |
| TabPage | TabPage | tabpage_ | Display tab pages |

You can set these prefixes in the Window painter's Design|Options Tab dialog box (under the tabs Prefixes1 and Prefixes2).

## Adding Controls to a Window

This chapter explains how to add controls to your windows. The process is similar for many of the window controls. The quickest and easiest way to work when building windows is to use the mouse. PowerBuilder is very intuitive and makes excellent use of the mouse and graphical painting of the various objects. Before getting into the details, here is a brief overview of the process.

To add a control to a window, start by selecting the object type from the Control Menu or use the following technique to select an object using the Window painter's PainterBar. On the PainterBar, you will see an icon of a control (or drawing object) with an arrow. Clicking the arrow will open the Control Palette (Figure 5.2). On this palette you can select the control or object that you wish to add to the window. This will close the palette and replace the icon on the PainterBar with the icon you selected (to show you which object will be placed onto the window).

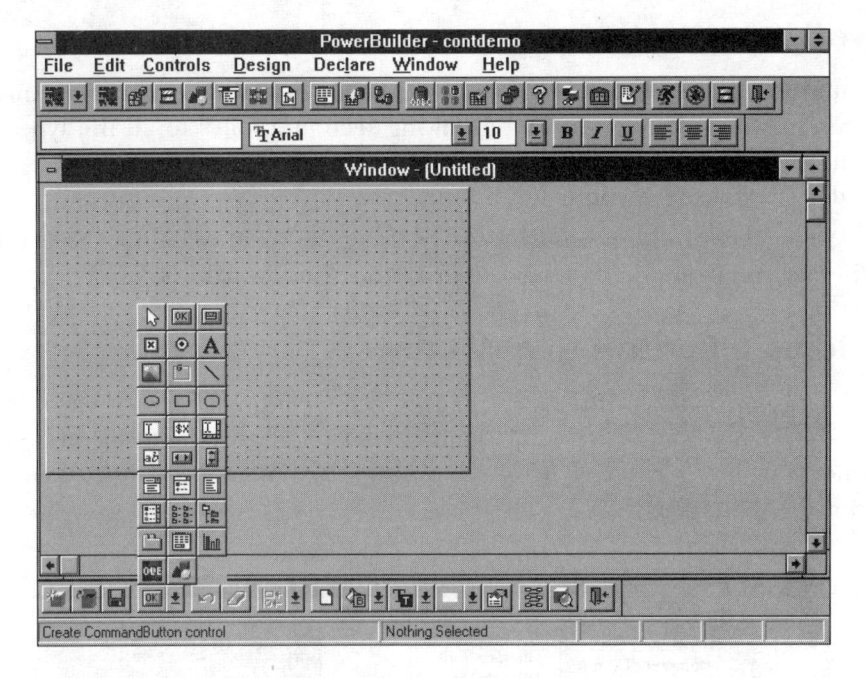

*Figure 5.2  The Control Palette.*

If the PainterBar is displayed on the side of the window, just click the **Control** icon. If the PainterBar is displayed at the top or bottom of the window, the arrow will be a separate icon; in this case, click the **Arrow** icon.

Next, click on the location in the window where you want to place the control (or drawing object) you have selected. If the PainterBar is displayed at the top or the bottom of the window, you can add more controls of the same type by clicking the **Control** icon and then clicking on the window. Controls are easily positioned and sized by dragging the object to position it or by using the sizing handles to resize it.

You then define the attributes of the control. You will assign it a name (or accept a default name). For some types, such as the command button, you can add text as a label or enter data for the control. After you have added two or more controls to a window, you can adjust the relative alignment and size or the controls. You can also define the tab order and accessibility for each.

You will add PowerScript code to some of the control events to define its behavior.

## Working with Controls

A number of the procedures for working with controls is common to many different types of controls. The following section applies to all the types of controls that you can add to your windows. If you want to experiment as you read the text, use the command button.

You add controls to your windows by using the Window painter. Select the **Window** icon from the PowerBar to open the Window painter.

## Adding a Control to a Window

To add a control to a window, click on the corresponding icon on the Controls Palette (Figure 5.2), which you launch by clicking on the **Control** icon on the Window painter's PainterBar. You may also select the control type from the Controls Menu (Figure 5.3).

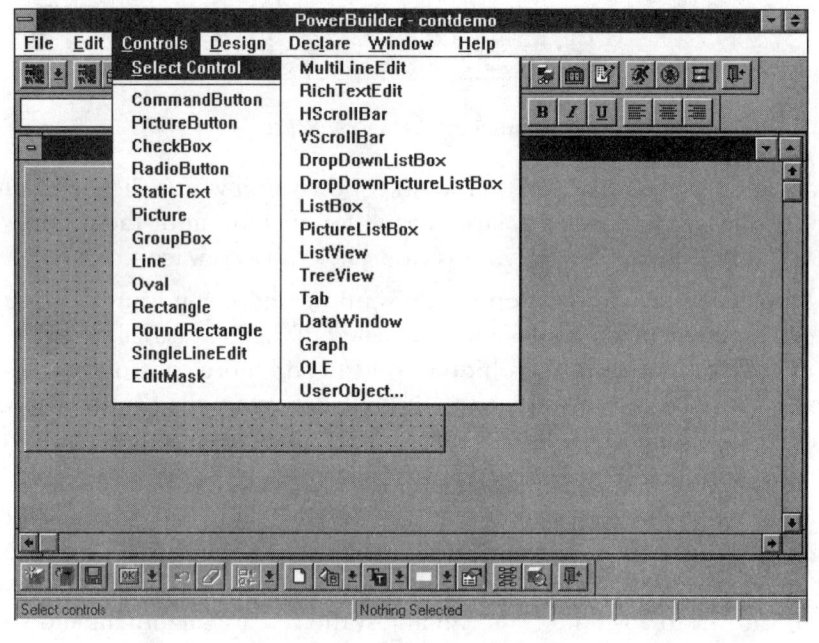

*Figure 5.3* The Controls Menu.

For the command button select the **Controls|CommandButton** menu option. After you have made this choice, click on the point in the window where you want to add the control. The Window painter drops a new control of the selected type (i.e., CommandButton) in the window. The control is given a default name, such as `cb_1`. Figure 5.4 shows the Window painter just after dropping a command button onto the window. Add several more command buttons to the window.

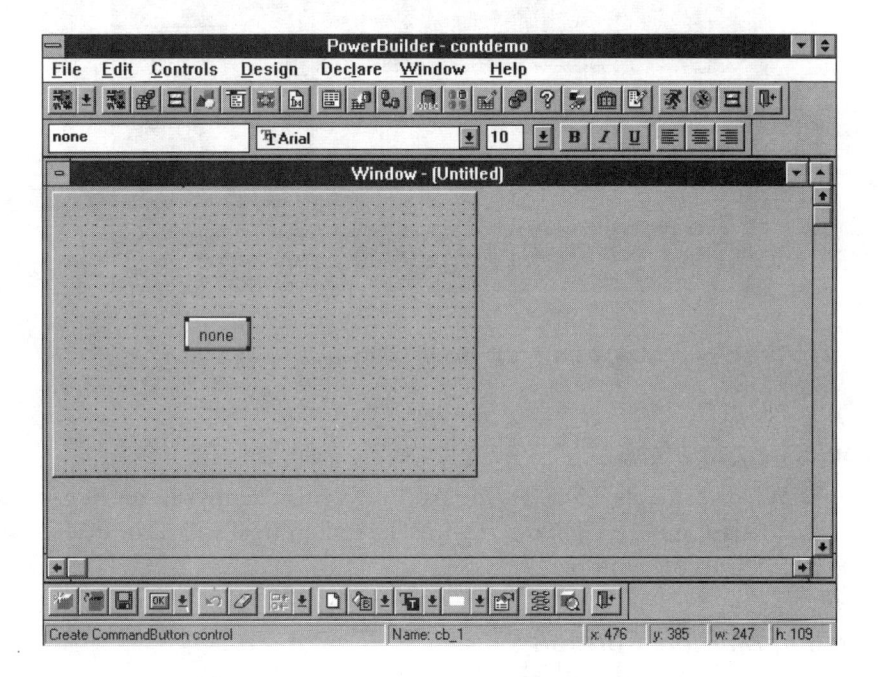

*Figure 5.4  Adding a command button to a window.*

## Selecting Controls

To modify a control, you must first select it. Select a single control by clicking it with the mouse. When you select a control, it is displayed with sizing handles (note the sizing handles on the None button in Figure 5.4). The Tab key can also be used to select a control. Each time that you hit the **Tab** key, the painter selects a different control in the current window. The Tab key will cycle through all the controls, and then start over again.

You can also select one or more controls by selecting **Edit|Control List** to bring up the Control List dialog box (Figure 5.5). This dialog box lists the names of all the objects in a listbox. In that list, highlight the name of each of the objects you wish to select and then click the **Select** button.

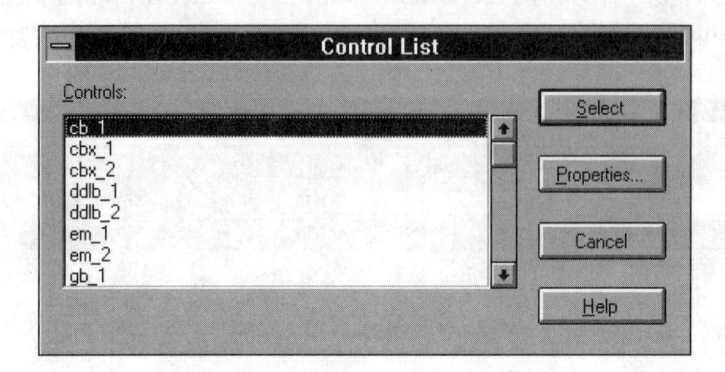

*Figure 5.5* *The Controls List dialog box.*

## Unselecting Controls

To unselect all controls, click on the window's surface anywhere there is no control. A single mouse click on any unselected control will also unselect all other controls in the window.

## Selecting Multiple Controls

There are also several ways to select a set of controls. You can do this by clicking on the first control of the set, and then using **Ctrl+click** to select each of the additional controls. (**Ctrl+click** is a standard technique for selecting multiple items in Windows applications.) A second **Ctrl+click** will unselect a control.

You can also select multiple controls by "lassoing" the controls with the mouse. To do this, click the mouse on the window background and drag the mouse pointer over the items you wish to select. This creates a dotted rectangle and selects all the controls that fall (even partially) within its boundaries.

When you select a set of controls using the lasso method, the placeholder control is the bottom right control in the rectangle, regardless of the order in which the controls were selected.

A shortcut for selecting all the controls in a window is the Edit|Select All menu option (with the shortcut key combination of **Control+A**).

### Positioning and Sizing the Control Button

All controls are positioned in basically the same manner, and they can be moved by using either the mouse or the keyboard. To move a control with the mouse, click within the control and drag it to its new location. To move a control with the keyboard, select the control that you wish to move and use the four arrow keys to position it. The keyboard method for moving controls is useful for making small adjustments to the position of a control that might be more difficult with the mouse. (The snap-to-grid option must be off to make the most precise adjustments with the keyboard).

To resize a control with the mouse, select an object and use the handles that appear around the edges (see Figure 5.4). Drag one of the handles until the control is the desired size. The handles on the corners of the control can resize the object in two dimensions simultaneously, while the other handles can resize in only one dimension (either horizontally or vertically) within the window. To use the keyboard for resizing, select the control you wish to resize and use the four arrow keys while holding down the **Shift** key to resize the control. The movement for resizing with the keyboard is based on the bottom right handle of the control. Therefore, use the right or down arrow to make the control larger and the left or up arrow to make the control smaller.

### Control Status

The status line of the Window painter displays the name, position, and size of the currently selected control (position and size are in pixels). To display the status information for a control, select it. If you select more than one control, the status will display "Group Selected."

### Using the Design Grid

The Window painter can display a grid of dots on the window that help with the alignment and relative sizing of controls. Select this option by choosing **Design|Options** and select the **General** tab on the tab dialog box window (shown in Figure 5.6). In this dialog box, display the grid by clicking the **Show Grid** checkbox. You can also set the distance between the dots (in both the horizontal and vertical planes). The default spacing between dots is 8 pixels, lower values give you finer resolution when placing controls.

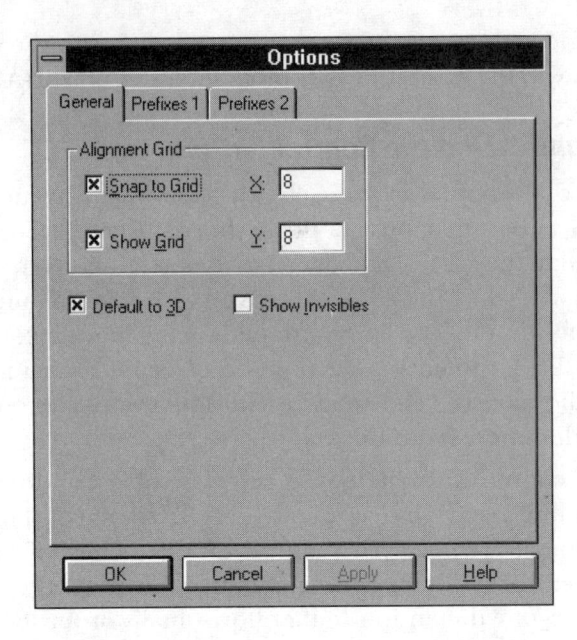

*Figure 5.6* *The Alignment Grid options.*

### *The Snap-to-Grid Option*

Select **Snap to Grid** by clicking the checkbox. By activating this option, the Window painter limits the exact placement of controls. Any controls that you resize or move while this option is active will be placed at the dot that is nearest to the place where you release the control. This makes aligning and sizing controls much easier. If you need to have finer resolution in the placement of the controls, decrease the size of the grid cells by entering smaller values for the x and y grid options. You do not have to make the grid visible to use the Snap to Grid option. This is something to consider if you want to speed up the display speed, because displaying the grid slows down the environment.

## Aligning Controls with the Alignment Function

The Window painter provides a function to automatically align a set of selected controls. To do this, select a set of controls. When you select the controls, you must first select the control that you want to use to govern the alignment of the other controls. After you have selected the controls to be aligned, select **Edit|Align Controls**. This displays the Align Controls cascading menu (Figure 5.7). If the menu option is disabled, it means that you have not selected two or more controls.

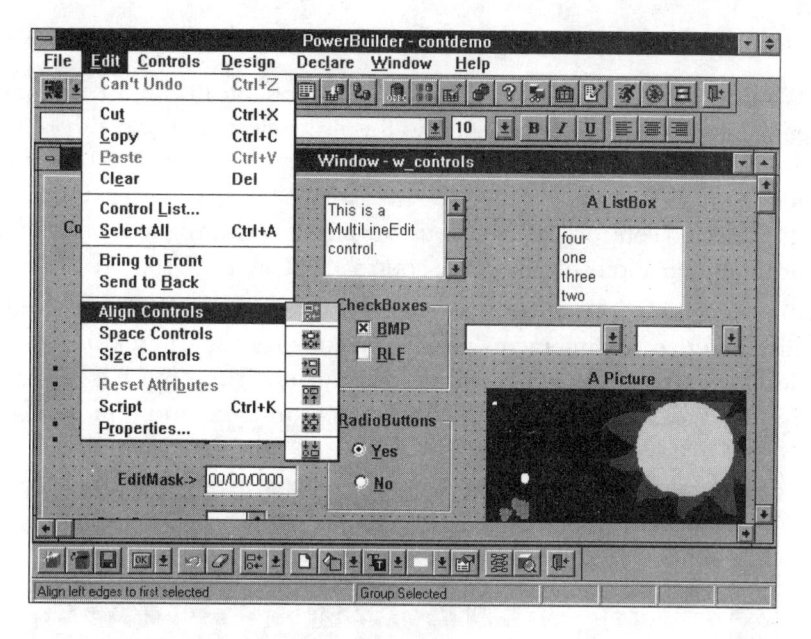

*Figure 5.7  The Align Controls menu.*

You have six choices for aligning controls, three in the vertical plane, and three in the horizontal. Controls can be aligned as follows (listed in the top-down order in which they appear in the cascading menu of Figure 5.7).

Controls can be aligned vertically by:

+ The left edge
+ Centering the controls
+ The right edge

Controls can be aligned horizontally by:

+ The top edge
+ Centering the controls
+ The bottom edge

Remember that the order in which you select the controls determines the result. Be sure that you first select the control that is already in the correct position. After you use this function to align the controls, they still remain selected so that you can reposition the entire group with the keyboard or the mouse. To move the entire set, click and drag any of the selected controls or use the arrow keys. To deselect the group, click somewhere else in the window or hit the **Tab** key.

## Adjusting the Spacing of Controls

The Window painter provides a function to automatically adjust the spacing between a set of selected controls. To do this, first select a set of controls. In this case, it is also important to select the controls in a specific order. The distance between the first two controls that you select will be the spacing that is applied to the other selected controls. So first, set up two adjacent controls to have the correct spacing, and then additively select the controls that are to be spaced similarly.

After you have selected the set of controls, select **Edit|Space Controls**. This displays the cascading menu shown in Figure 5.8. You can set the spacing of the selected controls either horizontally or vertically. This option is most useful for aligning a set of radio buttons, checkboxes, or command buttons.

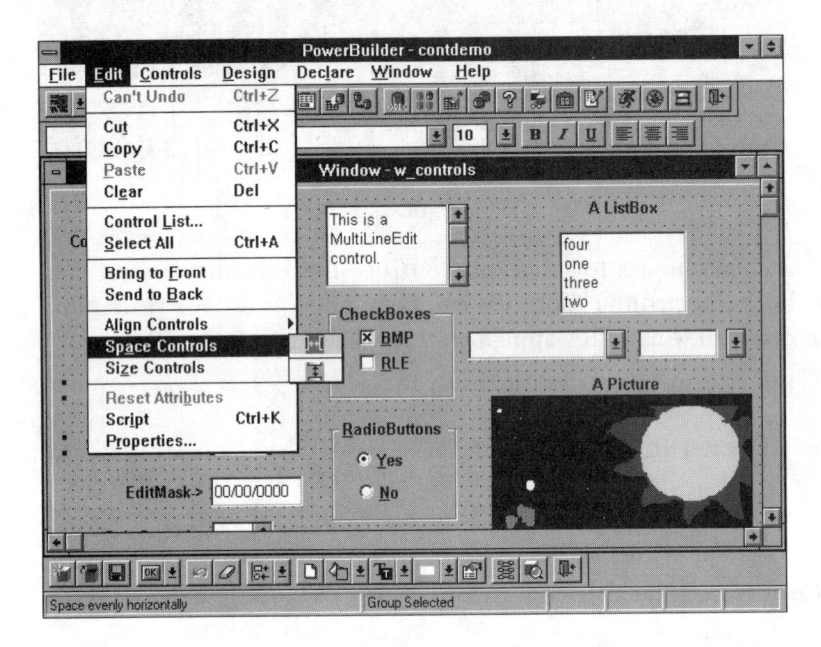

*Figure 5.8  The Space Controls cascading menu.*

## Automatically Sizing Controls

The Window painter provides a function to automatically adjust the size of a set of selected controls to match that of a model control. To do this, first select the control that is the size (in either the horizontal or vertical plane) that you wish to apply to the other control(s). Then additively select the rest of the controls that you want to size.

After you have selected the set of controls, select **Edit|Size Controls**. This displays the cascading menu shown in Figure 5.9.

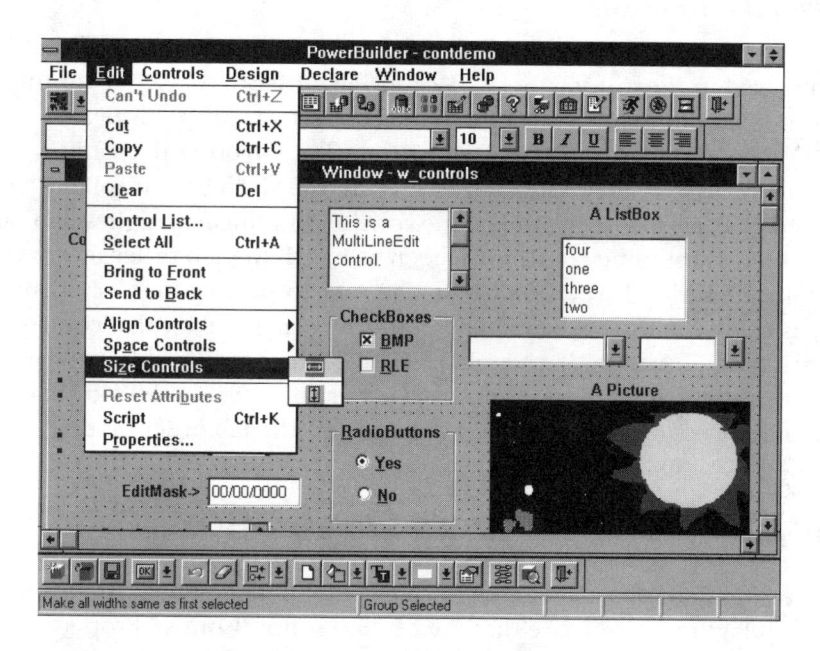

*Figure 5.9* The Size Controls cascading menu.

You can size the control(s) horizontally or vertically. You could, of course, size a control in both dimensions by selecting both functions, one after the other. You will apply the sizing option most often to a set of command buttons.

### Undoing Control Movement or Sizing

One of the more useful features of PowerBuilder 5.0 is its ability to undo the changes caused by aligning, sizing, or spacing controls. When you perform one of these actions, PowerBuilder adds a menu option, Undo Size/Move, to the Edit menu. As long as the items are selected, you can undo the effect of the last operation with **Undo Size/Move**. After selecting it, you also have the option of redoing the action by selecting **Redo Size/Move**.

### Setting the Tab Order

In the Window painter, you can set the tab order for the controls that have been placed in the window. Select **Design|Tab Order** to toggle on (or off) the tab order mode. In tab order mode, each control will be displayed with a number that represents its relative tab order. The tab order determines which control will be selected when the user hits the **Tab** key. The control that will be selected (receive the focus) will be the control with the next highest tab value. After the highest value control has been selected, the tab order moves down through the series. If you don't want the user to be able to select a control, such as fields that cannot be edited, set the tab order to 0 for that control. Not all objects in the window have a tab order (e.g., the drawing objects), it applies only to controls that the user can select. After you have set the tab order, you must select **Design|Tab Order** again to toggle off the tab order mode.

## THE CONTROL PROPERTIES DIALOG BOX

This section describes the Control Properties Tab dialog box. An example is shown in Figure 5.10. Notice that the caption is not "Control Properties," but is labeled the same as the type of the control that is currently selected ("command button" in this example). The exact contents of the Control Properties dialog box varies according to the control type. In the Control Properties dialog box, you can name a control and specify other attributes (which vary with the type of control) such as defining a keyboard accelerator for a control or setting the initial text displayed in the object.

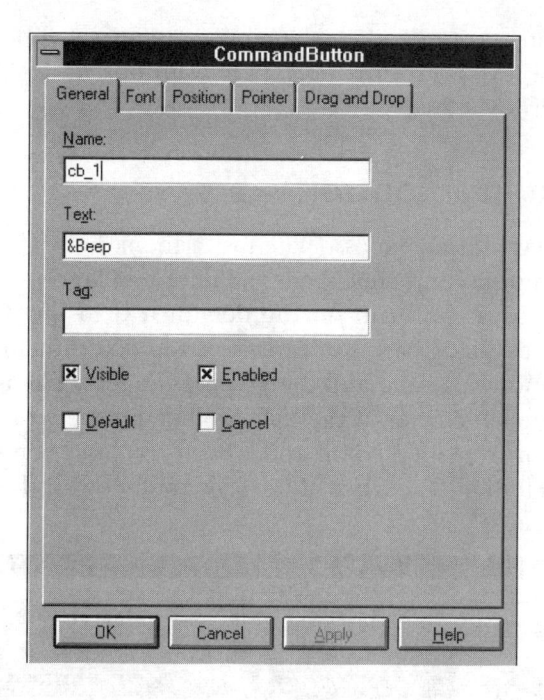

*Figure 5.10  The Command Button Style dialog box.*

## Naming a Control

PowerBuilder assigns a default name to each control when it creates them. You can (and in many cases should) give the control a more descriptive, easier to remember name. To name a control, open the Control Properties tab either by double-clicking directly on the control or by selecting **Properties** from the control's RMB popup menu (right mouse click on the control). The actual caption of the Control Properties dialog box will vary to match the type of control. Figure 5.10 shows an example of the Control Properties dialog box. In this case, it has the caption Command Button, the type of control to be renamed. It is recommended that you use the standard name prefixes for each type of control. You can specify the prefix for any control type if you wish.

The default—and recommended—naming conventions appear in Table 6.1. You can change any prefix in the Design|Options dialog box under the Prefixes 1 and Prefixes 2 tabs.

## Setting Text In a Control

Many controls have static text associated with them. For example, command buttons, radio buttons, and checkboxes all have text labels. If the control has text associated with it, you can set the default text in the Text field of the Control Properties dialog box. You can also enter text directly by selecting an object in the Window painter, and then typing the text. The text is echoed in an edit box in the left corner of the style toolbar. Figure 5.11 shows a window where the text for the Open command button has just been entered. Notice the edit window in the left corner of the style toolbar with the text "Open."

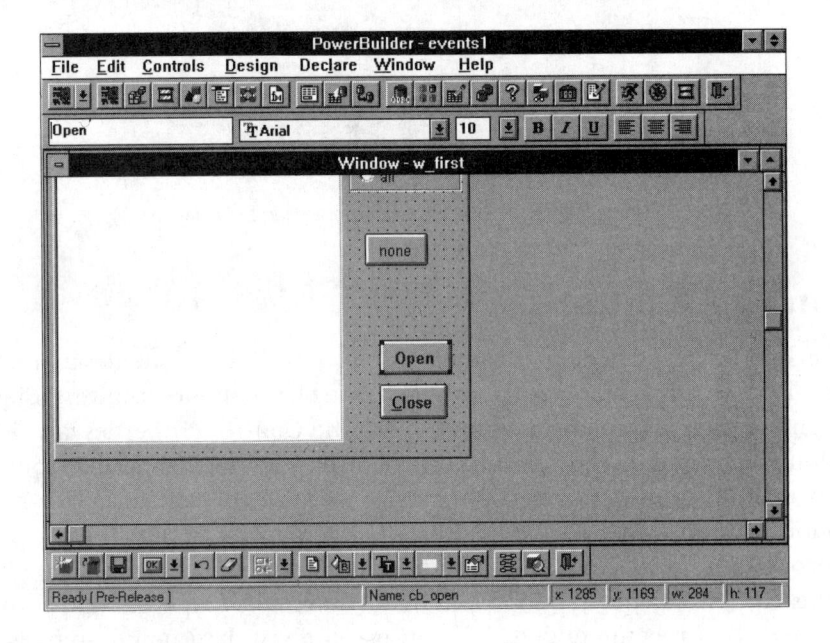

*Figure 5.11 Entered text "Open" for a command button.*

### Setting the Text Style

The style of the text that you enter is determined by the current settings in the StyleBar. This includes the font type, size, and characteristics (bold, italics, underlined, and alignment). You can also set these defaults when you customize PowerBuilder.

## Setting Control Attributes

The other options on the Control Properties dialog box varies greatly among the different types of controls. For most, you will find a set of checkboxes in the General tab section. This set of checkboxes lets you define the initial state of the control. These options vary with the different types of controls; the two most common are:

- **Visible**—Set this checkbox to make the control visible. Obviously, most controls are visible, but occasionally you will need to make a control invisible.

- **Enabled**—If enabled, the control is active and able to receive input. If it is disabled, the control cannot receive input or events. Disabled controls are grayed in color to mark them as inactive. You can enable and disable controls dynamically; you should disable any control if its function does not apply to the current state of the application. For instance, in the SQLApp example, the **Close** command button should be disabled until the **Open** command button has been clicked to open the cursor because you could not close a cursor that has not been opened.

# ACCELERATORS FOR CONTROLS

You can assign an Accelerator key for most of the controls that you create. An *Accelerator key* is a shortcut that lets the user jump directly to that control by pressing a specific key in combination with the Alt key. You cannot assign an accelerator to drawing controls such as lines or rectangles.

You can define an Accelerator key for command buttons, picture buttons, static texts, radio buttons, and checkboxes when you enter the Text field (see Figure 5.12).

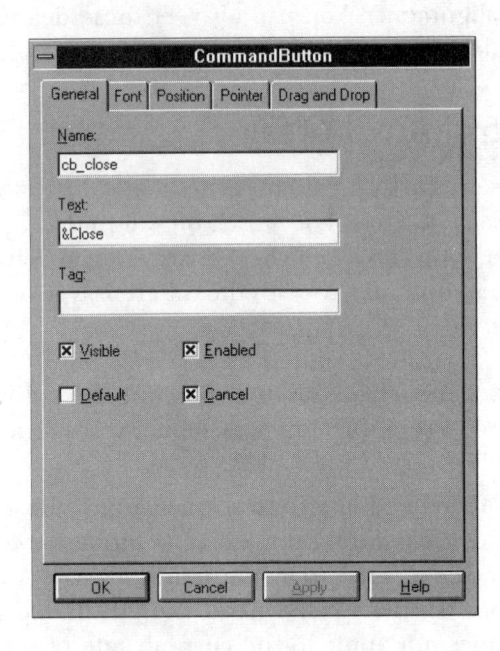

*Figure 5.12 Defining a command button accelerator.*

Insert an ampersand (&) immediately before the character that you want to serve as the Accelerator key. When you run the application, the display will underline the accelerator character to mark it. In Figure 5.12, the letter C is the accelerator. When the user presses **Alt+C**, that command button is selected, receives the focus, and then is sent a Clicked event.

If you use the same Accelerator key for more than one control (in the same window), PowerBuilder ignores that accelerator. If your accelerator doesn't seem to be working, check to be sure that you have not already assigned that key as an accelerator.

You can define an accelerator for a group box in the same manner. However, when you select the accelerator for the group box, the focus is actually given to the checked radio button within the group box (or the first checkbox).

The process of defining accelerators is different for SingleLineEdits, Edit Masks, MultiLineEdits, ListBoxes, and DropDownListBoxes. The Properties tab dialog box for each of these controls has a field for entering the accelerator key, as shown in Figure 5.13. Just enter the letter of the key that you will use as the accelerator for these controls.

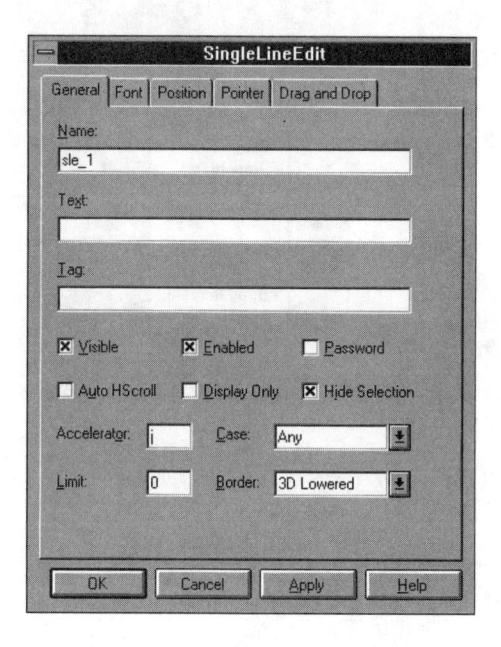

*Figure 5.13* *The SingleLineEdit properties dialog box.*

## CHANGE AN ATTRIBUTE

The RMB popup menu is especially handy during the window design phase because it allows quick access to control functions. Clicking the right mouse button on a control brings up the popup menu. Figure 5.14 shows the popup menu for a command button.

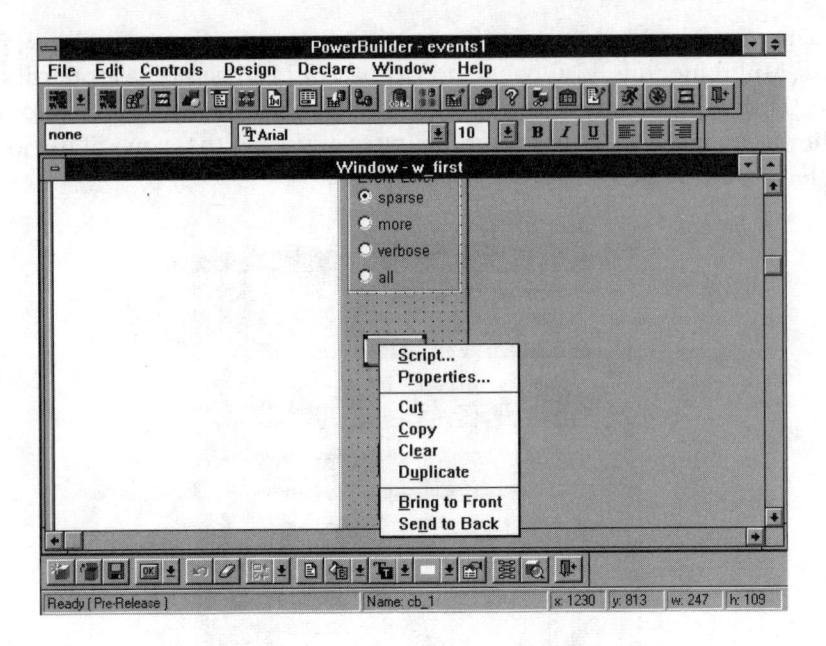

*Figure 5.14  RMB popup for a command button.*

## DUPLICATING A CONTROL

A shortcut for adding several controls of the same type is to duplicate an existing object. This has the advantage of duplicating the size, text, text style, and other properties of the original object. This is the method to use if you wish to create a number of similar controls. There are two ways to duplicate a control. If you want to duplicate a control but do not wish to copy the event PowerScript code (within the control), select the control and do one of the following:

+ Use the **Ctrl+T** key combination
+ Select **Duplicate** from the RMB popup menu

The second method for duplicating controls is to use the Edit|Copy and Edit|Paste menu options. Duplicating a control in this manner also copies the event scripts. When you select Edit|Paste, the control will be placed exactly on top of the original control (because the copy has the same X and Y position values). So you will need to move the duplicate to the correct position.

You can also copy a control from one window to another using the **Edit|Copy** and **Edit|Paste** menu options, but both windows must be open.

## POWERBUILDER UNITS (PBUS)

Many of the measurements used in window, controls, and drawing objects are specified in PowerBuilder units (PBUs). PowerBuilder units are preferable to pixels for setting the size of windows and controls because the number of pixels in a measurement changes with the resolution of the display. PowerBuilder units are calculated on the size of an average character on the screen, which translates better between different resolution displays. The size of a horizontal PowerBuilder unit is equal to 1/32 of the width of an average character in the system font. The size of a vertical PBU is equal to 1/64 of the same character. You can calculate the width of 20 characters as approximately 640 horizontal PBUs (20 x 32). These numbers are only approximate, because they are based on an average-sized character. But it is correct for 20 characters on a standard VGA display (640 x 480), or a higher resolution VGA such as 1024 x 768. The number of pixels would vary greatly between these displays.

You can usually assume that the unit of measure is in PowerBuilder units. There are only a few exceptions. For example, when you set up the Design Grid in the Window (or DataWindow) painter, you define the distance between dots in pixels. When you set the size of the text in your applications, you specify the size as a font point size.

When you create a DataWindow, you can choose the unit of measure. You can select pixels, thousandths of an inch, or thousandths of a centimeter. It is easier to design a report that will be printed if you use the inch or centimeter measurement.

## Colors in PowerBuilder Applications

The Window painter PainterBar presents two palettes (background and foreground colors) for the color choices for the design process. These palettes can be opened by clicking icons on the Window painter PainterBar.

## Color Values

Many PowerBuilder objects have attributes that store colors that are used as foreground or background colors for the object. These attributes have a data type of long. They store the color in a RGB representation, and the long is partitioned into segments for each color component.

The formula for calculating the long is

```
65536 * Blue + 256 * Green + Red
```

PowerBuilder provides a function to ease the calculation of this value. The RGB function accepts three input arguments:

```
long l_value
l_value = RGB(i_red, i_green, i_blue)
```

In this example, you pass in three arguments to specify the color represented by the value `iValue`:

- `i_red`—The value of the red component of the color
- `i_green`—The value of the green component of the color
- `i_blue`—The value of the blue component of the color

Each argument is an integer, with a value ranging from 0 to 255. This value represents the amount of the component (red, green, or blue) that is in the color that you are defining. An example of a basic color set using the RGB function is given in Table 5.2.

*Table 5.2* *Basic Color Set*

| Color | RGB Function |
|---|---|
| Black | - RGB(0, 0, 0) |
| White | - RGB(255, 255, 255) |
| Red | - RGB(255, 0, 0) |
| Red Dark | - RGB(128, 0, 0) |
| Green | - RGB(0, 255, 0) |
| Green Dark | - RGB(0, 128, 0) |
| Blue | - RGB(0, 0, 255) |
| Blue Dark | - RGB(0, 0, 128) |
| Gray | - RGB(192, 192, 192) |
| Dark Gray | - RGB(128, 128, 128) |
| Magenta | - RGB(255, 0, 255) |
| Dark Magenta | - RGB(128, 0, 128) |
| Cyan | - RGB(0, 255, 255) |
| Dark Cyan | - RGB(0, 128, 128) |
| Brown | - RGB(128, 128, 0) |

You can set the colors for most controls except command buttons. Command buttons are defined as gray in color and cannot be changed. You could define the RGB values for a custom color by using the Color dialog box to set the value of a color. In general, this is not required. The choices provided in the ColorBar (and the popup menus) should suffice for most applications.

## The 3D Look

You can (and should) select the 3D look as the default for all your windows. This style gives a three-dimensional characteristic to the controls and creates windows with 3D borders (this will also set the colors of some of the controls in a predefined manner). This is the best appearance for most situations and is standard in many Windows applications. This option also sets the default color to *gray*. Gray works very well with the 3D option and will also usually be the choice for your MDI applications.

You can select this option in the Window painter's Design|Options tab dialog box. Just check the **Default to the 3D option**. Notice the 3D effect of the command button and single-line edit.

## Show Invisibles

Occasionally you will make a control invisible on a window. You can make these controls visible for manipulation by setting the **Show Invisibles** checkbox in the window's Design|Options dialog box.

# DESCRIPTION, PROPERTIES, EVENTS, AND FUNCTIONS

The PowerBuilder help information provides the following information for window controls:

- **Description**—Information about the more important features and attributes of the control will be presented.
- **Properties**—Each type of control has a specific set of attributes (or properties) that defines its exact characteristics. This section lists all of the attributes for the control and provides a brief description of the attribute.
- **Events**—Each control type (except the drawing objects) has a set of events that applies to that type of control. This section lists all the events associated with the control. The events that are most important or unique for each control are marked with bold, underlined text. The last section provides some code examples for some of the events.

- **Functions**—Each control has a set of functions that applies to its type. This section lists all the functions that you will find useful with this type of control and provides a brief description of each function. Many functions can be accessed by more than one type of control.

We present detailed information about the CommandButton in this chapter. Check the help system for the details about the other window controls.

## THE WINDOW CONTROLS

Table 5.3 shows the types of controls that can be added to your windows and those that have events associated with them. This table presents the objects by category. Table 5.4 shows the drawing objects that can be added to your window. These are for decoration only; these objects do not have events.

This chapter covers all the objects listed in these tables, except Graphs, DataWindows, and User Objects. These objects are more complex, and the details about them will be found in later chapters dedicated to those types of objects.

Some of the information that is common between controls is repeated in the section for each control. This will group all the information for each group in its own section, making it easier for you to find the information that you need while working with a particular type of control.

### The Window Controls Example

The control example applications CONTROL1 and CONTROL2 are contained in libraries **CONTROL1.PBL** and **CONTROL2.PBL**. These applications contain an example of every control discussed in this chapter. If you examine these applications and take the time to duplicate each one, you will have created at least one object of each control and will have added code to provide functionality for each of the controls. These examples also cover drag and drop functionality and provide a detailed demonstration of control and window events.

## Controls by Category

*Table 5.3  Controls that Have Events*

| Category | Control Type |
| --- | --- |
| Buttons | CommandButton |
|  | PictureButton |
| Data I/O | SingleLineEdit |
|  | EditMask |
|  | MultiLineEdit |
|  | RichTextEdit |
|  | ListBox |
|  | DropDownPictureListBox |
|  | DropDownPictureListBox |
|  | Picture |
|  | StaticText |
|  | ListView |
|  | TreeView |
|  | Tab |
|  | Graph |
|  | DataWindow |
| Scroll Bars | VScrollBar |
|  | HScrollBar |
| Option Controls | RadioButton |
|  | CheckBox |
|  | GroupBox |
| OLE Controls | OLE |
| User Defined | User Object |

**Window Controls**  163

*Table 5.4* Window Objects without Events

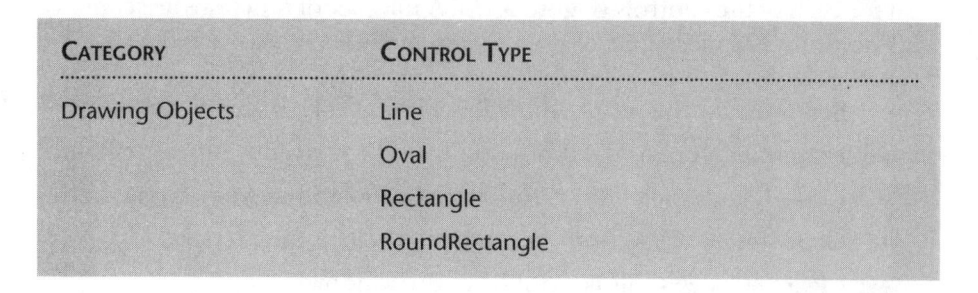

| CATEGORY | CONTROL TYPE |
|---|---|
| Drawing Objects | Line |
| | Oval |
| | Rectangle |
| | RoundRectangle |

## Control Popup Menu Options

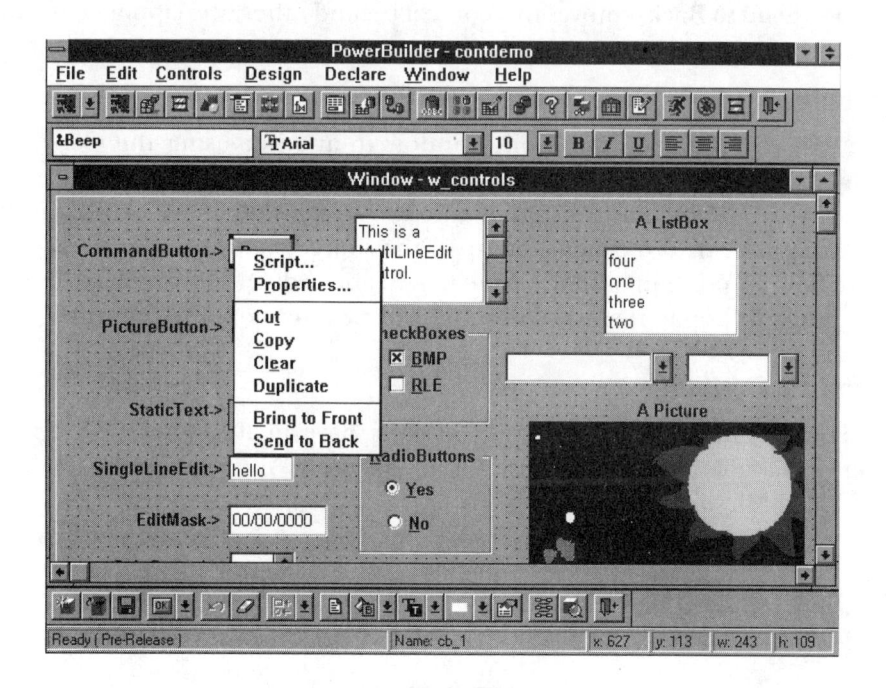

*Figure 5.15* The RMB popup.

The items in the popup menu (right mouse click on the control) vary somewhat for each of the controls (Figure 5.15). A number of functions are common to all controls. For most controls, the popup menu includes the following:

- **Script**—edits the script editor for this control's events.
- **Properties**—opens the Properties dialog box to edit control attributes.
- **Cut**—deletes the control from the window and moves it to the buffer.
- **Copy**—copies this control to the buffer (including scripts).
- **Clear**—removes this control from the window.
- **Duplicate**—makes a copy of this control.
- **Bring to Front**—moves this control to the front of other overlapping controls.
- **Send to Back**—moves this control behind other overlapping controls.

### Copying a Control to Another Window

You can copy controls from one window to another using the **Copy** and **Edit|Paste** menu options. Both windows must remain open until pasted. Note that if you copy and paste a control into the same window, the new duplicate control will be placed exactly on top of the source control (it has exactly the same X and Y positions and the same height and width). The duplicate option (on the RMB popup menu) places the copy next to the source control.

### The Tag Attribute

All PowerBuilder objects, including controls, have an attribute called *tag*. It is a string variable that you can use for any purpose. You may use this field to hold MDI Microhelp text.

# COMMANDBUTTONS

*Figure 5.16* A CommandButton.

*CommandButtons* (or simply, *buttons*) are used to initiate some type of action or respond to a prompt (Figure 5.16). Each CommandButton displays a caption that describes the function it represents. You can click on a **CommandButton** with the mouse or select it (using the **Tab** key) and then press **Enter**. When you click on a **CommandButton**, it appears to be depressed momentarily.

## Adding a CommandButton to a Window

For this example, the steps required to add two buttons to a new window are discussed. The Close button closes the window when the user clicks on it. The second button, cb_open, opens another window when it is clicked. From the Window painter, click on the **PainterBar Control** popup or select **Control|CommandButton**. This tells the Window painter that you are going to add a CommandButton to the window. Next, click in the window where you want to place the button. This drops a CommandButton into the window.

Open the CommandButton Properties dialog box (Figure 5.17) by double-clicking on the new CommandButton. Name the button cb_close and then **Tab** to the Text field and enter a label. If you want to define an accelerator key, place an ampersand before the letter that will be used as the accelerator (&Close). Close the Properties dialog box.

Open the RMB popup menu for the CommandButton, and select the **Script** menu option to write a script for the Clicked event. When the PowerScript painter opens, check to be sure that you are in the Clicked event. If not, pull down the Select Event dropdown listbox and choose the clicked event. In the editor, add the following line of code:

```
Close(Parent)
```

Close the editor by clicking the **Return** icon on the PainterBar. This returns you to the Window painter design window.

Repeat the process to add the second CommandButton. Give this button the name cb_open. Enter the caption text (and accelerator) &Open2. Add the following line of code to its Clicked event:

```
Open(w_second)
```

This will open the w_second window when you click on the **cb_open** button. If you have not yet created the w_second window, you will get a warning

"Ignore compilation warnings." Respond "Yes" to save the script with the unresolved reference.

## CommandButton Properties Dialog Box

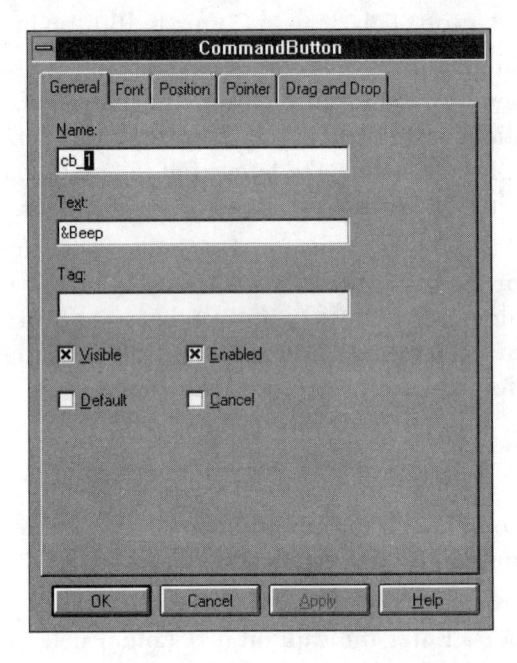

The easiest way to open the CommandButton Properties dialog box is by double-clicking on the **CommandButton** or selecting the **Properties** option from the CommandButton's popup menu. You can also open the dialog box by selecting **Edit|Properties** or **Edit|Control List**. In the Control List listbox, select the control and then click on the **Properties** button. In the CommandButton Properties dialog box (Figure 5.17), enter the name and text caption for the button. You can define one character in the caption to be used as the accelerator by preceding it with an ampersand.

*Figure 5.17* The CommandButton Properties dialog box.

The bottom row of checkboxes is used to set some of the most important attributes. The first two attributes are the standard visible and enable options available for most controls:

- `Visible`—Set this checkbox to make the control visible.
- `Enabled`—When the CommandButton is enabled, it is active, can be selected, and can receive input (such as the Clicked event). If it is disabled, the button cannot receive input or events and will be grayed in color to mark it as inactive.

You can also set the visible and enabled attributes when the program is run. For example:

```
cb_close.enabled = False
cb_open.visible = True
```

The CommandButton dialog box also has checkboxes for two additional properties that apply only to CommandButtons and PictureButtons:

- `Default`—Each window can have one default button. When the user runs your application and presses **Enter**, the button that has been defined as the default for the window will receive a Clicked event (if the focus is not on another button). To mark a button as the default, the button will have a distinct, black outline added to its perimeter. This is a feature of the Windows style. You have seen this often, such as in response windows where an **OK** or **Continue** button can be selected by pressing **Enter**.
- `Cancel`—Each window can also have one Cancel button. When the user runs your application and hits the **Esc** key when the focus is in this window, the button that has been defined as the Cancel button for the window will be clicked just as if the user had clicked on it with the mouse. This button will not be marked in any visible manner (like the Default button), so you should label the button with a caption that suggests its use as a Cancel button.

You should set only one button (either a CommandButton or a PictureButton) as the Default and Cancel buttons on each window. PowerBuilder lets you assign this property to more than one button, so it is up to you as the developer to enforce this constraint.

## CommandButton Properties

The attributes of a CommandButton are:

- `BringToTop`—Sets this Boolean to **true** to place the CommandButton on top of other overlapping controls in this window's front-to-back order.
- `Cancel`—If this Boolean value is set to **true** (and the focus is not on another button), the CommandButton is "clicked" when the user presses **Esc**.
- `Default`—If this Boolean value is set to **true**, this CommandButton is "clicked" when the user hits **Enter** (if the focus is not on another button). The button will also be outlined with a dark rectangle to mark it as the default.
- `DragAuto`—If this Boolean is set to **true**, this CommandButton is automatically set into drag mode when the user clicks on it.
- `DragIcon`—A string containing the name of the icon that is displayed when this button is in drag mode. If you select **None!**, a ghost outline of the control is used.
- `Enabled`—A Boolean value, set to **true** to enable the button, making it active and able to be selected or clicked and to receive events.
- `FaceName`—A string value containing the font name for the CommandButton caption.
- `FontCharSet`—An enumerated value that specifies the font character set for the caption.
- `FontFamily`—An enumerated value that specifies the font family for the button caption.
- `FontPitch`—An enumerated value that specifies the font pitch for the button caption.
- `Height`—An integer value that specifies the vertical size of the button in PBUs.

# Window Controls 169

- `Italic`—A Boolean value set to **true** if the label font is to be italicized.
- `Pointer`—A string containing the pointer icon to be used when the pointer is over this CommandButton.
- `TabOrder`—An integer that specifies the relative tab order for the controls on the window.
- `Tag`—A text string associated with this button that can be used to store the Microhelp text.
- `Text`—The string label (caption) for the CommandButton.
- `TextSize`—An integer that specifies the font size (in points) of the text label (stored as a negative number).
- `Underline`—A Boolean value set to **true** if the text label for this button is to be underlined.
- `Visible`—A Boolean value set to **true** if the button is to be visible (showing).
- `Weight`—An integer that specifies the stroke thickness of the text label font (400 is normal).
- `Width`—An integer value that specifies the horizontal size of the button in PBUs.
- `X`—An integer value that specifies the horizontal position in the window of the button in PBUs.
- `Y`—An integer value that specifies the vertical position in the window of the button in PBUs.

## CommandButton Events

The events associated with a CommandButton are:

- `Clicked`—When you click on a button or select the button and press **Enter**, this event is triggered.
- `Constructor`—Occurs just before the window is made the active window. The window sends a constructor event to all its objects just before the window `Open` event occurs. Do not write code that is dependent on the order in which the constructors are triggered within a window. This is an advanced topic that will be discussed in the chapter on user objects.

- `Destructor`—Occurs when the window is closing. The window sends a destructor event to all its objects just after the window `Close` event occurs.
- `DragDrop`—Occurs when drag mode is on and the pointer drops an object within the CommandButton.
- `DragEnter`—Occurs when drag mode is on and the dragged object enters the CommandButton. If drag mode is off and this button's `DragAuto` attribute is set, a `DragEnter` event is triggered (rather than a `Clicked` event) when the user clicks the button.
- `DragLeave`—Occurs when drag mode is on and the dragged object leaves the CommandButton.
- `DragWithin`—Occurs when drag mode is on, this event is triggered periodically while an object is dragged within the CommandButton.
- `GetFocus`—Occurs just before the CommandButton is selected with the **Tab** key or by clicking.
- `LoseFocus`—Occurs just before the CommandButton loses focus (caused by tabbing away or clicking outside of the button).
- `Other`—All the other Windows events that have not been mapped to PowerBuilder events are routed to this event. You will rarely use this event; user-defined events are a better choice.
- `RButtonDown`—Occurs when the right mouse button is pressed and the pointer is located within the CommandButton.

## CommandButton Functions

The following functions apply to CommandButtons:

- `ClassName`—returns the name of the CommandButton.
- `Drag`—begins or ends drag mode for this button.
- `GetParent`—returns the parent (owning) object as a PowerObject variable.
- `Hide`—makes a CommandButton invisible.

- `Move`—relocates the CommandButton in the window.
- `PointerX`—returns the pointer's horizontal position in the button.
- `PointerY`—returns the pointer's vertical position in the button.
- `PostEvent`—places an event on the CommandButton's event queue and continues (asynchronously).
- `Print`—prints the CommandButton.
- `Resize`—adjusts the size of the CommandButton.
- `SetFocus`—places the focus on the CommandButton, directs keyboard input to the button.
- `SetPosition`—places the CommandButton in the front-to-back display order (relative to other overlapping controls).
- `SetRedraw`—turns on or off the updating of the control if the caption is changed.
- `Show`—makes the CommandButton visible.
- `TriggerEvent`—triggers a CommandButton event immediately (synchronously).
- `TypeOf`—returns the enumerated type of this control (`CommandButton!`).

## PICTUREBUTTONS

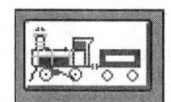

*Figure 5.18* A PictureButton.

*PictureButtons* are essentially the same as CommandButtons, except they display an image (BMP, WMF, or RLE) within the button (Figure 5.18). Choose one image for the enabled state and another for the disabled state of the button. The PictureButton may also contain text that can be aligned horizontally and vertically in the button. The text can also span more than one line in the button.

## SingleLineEdit Controls

A SingleLineEdit control (or edit field) is a rectangular field used for data display and user input (Figure 5.19). The user can type a single line of text into this field. The text may represent a value with any of the PowerBuilder data types. Use this for fields that allow input. If the field is display-only, you might only need a static text field.

*Figure 5.19  A SingleLineEdit.*

## EditMask Control

The mask control is very similar to a SingleLineEdit, but it has a fixed format built into its definition. Examples of common required formats are phone numbers, Social Security numbers, date, and time. Use an EditMask when you wish to format the data that was input and displayed in the control.

*Figure 5.20  An EditMask control.*

The actual mask consists of a number of special characters that determine what can be entered in the field. The exact characters that are used vary according to the type of data being entered.

For a number:

**#**—The number sign is used to represent a digit.
**0**—A zero is used to represent a required digit.

For a string:

**#**—The number sign is used to represent a digit.

**!**—Represents an uppercase character.

**^**—Represents a lowercase character.

**a**—Represents any alphanumeric character.

**x**—Allows any character.

Any other characters in the EditMask are taken literally as punctuation characters used for presentation. For example, the EditMask (###) ###-#### works for phone numbers and ###-##-#### is a Social Security number. !!## allows two uppercase characters followed by two digits, and dd/mm/yyyy is a typical date format.

## Defining Spin Controls

*Spin control* is a control style option for the EditMask. The control is displayed as an edit box with two spinners (the up and down arrows). The arrows are used to increment or decrement the value displayed in the control.

## MULTILINEEDIT CONTROL

MultiLineEdit controls are similar to SingleLineEdits, but as the name implies, they allow multiple lines of text to be entered and presented within the control (Figure 5.21). The MultiLineEdit control has a number of functions that let the control act as a small text editor.

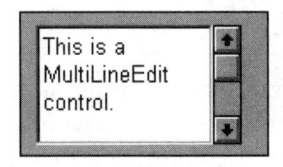

**Figure 5.21** *A MultiLineEdit control.*

## RichTextEdit Control

RichTextEdit controls (Figure 5.22) are similar to MultiLineEdit controls but, as the name implies, they allow text to be entered and presented within the control using the standard Rich Text Format (RTF). This adds functions that lets the control act as a small text editor with formatting.

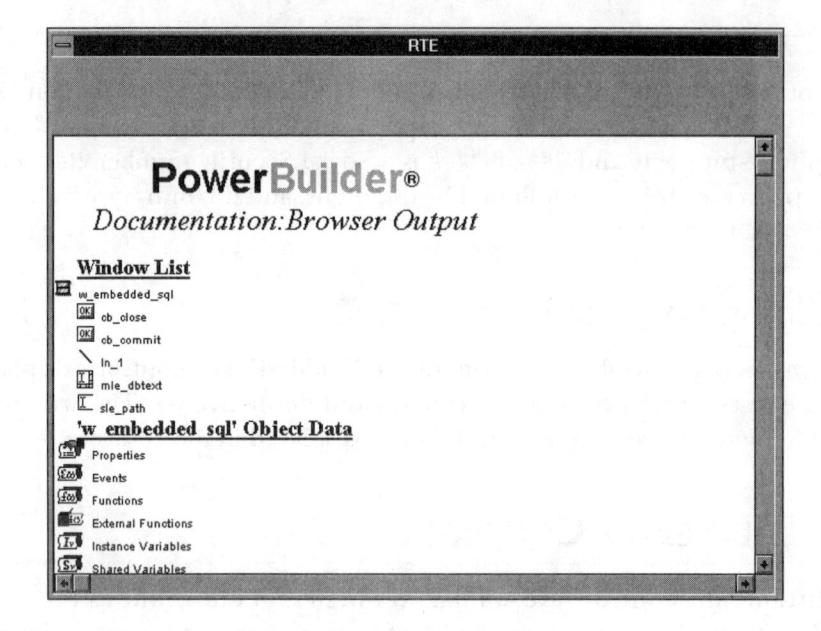

*Figure 5.22  A RichTextEdit control.*

## ListBox Controls

The ListBox control displays a number of items in a list (Figure 5.23). The list can be scrollable. The user can select items in the list by single-clicking an item or by scrolling through the items, and then pressing **Enter**. It is possible to select multiple items. Often, double-clicking on an item is used to trigger an event related to that choice.

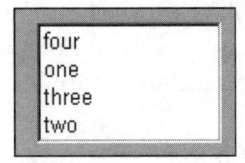

*Figure 5.23  A ListBox control.*

The items on the list can be hard-coded, or you can add items to the list by using the `AddItem` and `InsertItem` functions. The list can be automatically sorted and searched. ListBox controls work well with an associated SingleLineEdit control, where the user enters data into the SingleLineEdit to trigger a search in the listbox.

## DropDownListBox Controls

A DropDownListBox combines a SingleLineEdit control with a ListBox control (Figure 5.24). The ListBox portion of the control can be dropped down (displayed) or closed. The DropDownListBox can be used to display a read-only list for the user to choose from, or it can be set up to allow the input of new values not in the list. To select an item in the list, you can use the scroll bar to locate and then click on the item. You can also use the **Up** and **Down Arrow** keys to scroll through the list. This will select an item as it scrolls.

*Figure 5.24  DropDownListBox controls.*

If the DropDownListBox is set for display only, a search option is provided for items in the list. The ListBox portion will display entries that match the letter typed into the SingleLineEdit part of the control. This matches only on the first letter of the items in the list. If there is more than one item beginning with a character, you can cycle through the items that match in the list by repeating the keystroke. You can also use the **Up** and **Down Arrow** keys to move through the list while in the edit field.

The editable ListBox displays a space between the edit field and the down arrow to mark it as an editable type ListBox. Compare Figure 5.25 to Figure 5.24, which does not have the space and therefore is not editable.

*Figure 5.25  An editable listbox.*

## DropDownPictureListBox Controls

A DropDownPictureListBox allows you to add an icon (picture) for each item in the list (Figure 5.26).

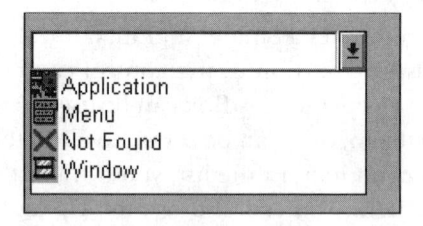

*Figure 5.26  DropDownPictureListBox control.*

## Picture Controls

The Picture control is used to display BMP, WMF, and RLE images in your PowerBuilder applications (Figure 5.27). You can resize the image or invert the image colors. The image is usually on the disk, and it is displayed by assigning the path to the Picture control. You can also read images in from other sources (like a database), and then display the image in the Picture control (by using `Blob` objects). (You could also use OLE to display the image in a OLE server; this is covered in a later chapter.)

*Figure 5.27 A Picture control.*

You may use the Picture control as a passive control used only to display images, or you may let the user click on the image or use drag-and-drop functionality with the control.

## STATICTEXT CONTROLS

StaticText controls are useful for adding labels to windows (Figure 5.28). StaticText controls can also be used to display read-only data (data that is not updatable by the user). In this manner, you can use a StaticText control instead of a SingleLineEdit.

*Figure 5.28 A StaticText control.*

## LISTVIEW CONTROLS

ListView controls are useful for displaying a list of items consisting of text and pictures (Figure 5.29). This control was added with PowerBuilder version 5.

**178** Chapter 5

*Figure 5.29  A ListView control.*

# TREEVIEW CONTROLS

TreeView controls are useful for displaying hierarchical information (Figure 5.30). Each item in a TreeView control consists of text and pictures.

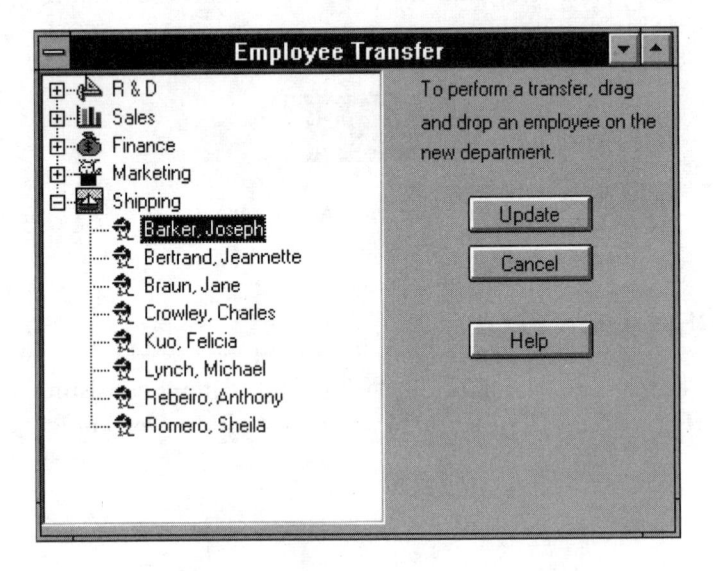

*Figure 5.30  A TreeView control.*

## RadioButton Controls

RadioButton controls are used to select an option (Figure 5.31). RadioButton controls are usually grouped together in a group box, as in this example. Only one of the radio buttons in a group can be selected (checked) at a time. Radio buttons in a group can be managed automatically by PowerBuilder. When you select one of the buttons, it will be checked and the others in the group will be unchecked. You must assign text to label each radio button, placing the text on either the left or the right side of the button.

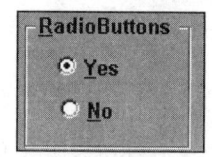

*Figure 5.31 A RadioButton control.*

## GroupBox Controls

GroupBox controls are most often used with radio buttons (Figure 5.32). If you enclose a set of radio buttons within a GroupBox, only one of the radio buttons in the group can be selected (checked) at a time. PowerBuilder automatically provides this management to the GroupBox control. When you select one of the buttons, it is checked and the others in the group are unchecked. You must label each GroupBox, placing the text on either the left or the right of the button.

*Figure 5.32 GroupBox controls.*

You can use group boxes with checkboxes and other controls. In the case of controls other than the RadioButton, this is a cosmetic step, and the functionality described in the preceding paragraph is not provided.

## CHECKBOX CONTROLS

CheckBox controls are used most often to toggle options on and off (Figure 5.33). When you click the checkbox, an *X* is toggled on and then off in the square next to the text. You may group a set of related checkboxes together, but there is no exclusive relationship between the checkboxes as there is when you group radio buttons together.

*Figure 5.33  CheckBox controls.*

You can also create a three-state checkbox that adds a third state to be used to represent a third option (such as "unknown"). The third state is represented in gray in the checkbox square.

You can position the text on the left or right of the square, and the display can be automatically updated when the user clicks (or selects the checkbox with the **Tab** key and presses the **spacebar**).

## HSCROLLBAR

The HScrollBar is a control that is often used to graphically show an amount or percentage (Figure 5.34). For example, you could use the HScrollBar to show the progress as you read in a file or complete some other task. This control is separate from the scroll bars that are used in other controls such as ListBoxes or MultiLineEdits. You could also use the HScrollBar to allow the user to adjust values, such as shades of colors, or to set limits for computation or the number of records to be displayed.

*Figure 5.34  HScrollBar.*

## VScrollBar

The VScrollBar is a control often used to graphically show an amount or percentage (Figure 5.35). For example, you could use a VScrollBar to show the progress as you read in a file or complete some other task. This control is separate from the scroll bars that are used in other controls such as ListBoxes or MultiLineEdits. You could also use the VScrollBar to allow the user to adjust values, such as shades of colors, or to set limits for computation or the number of records to be displayed.

*Figure 5.35 A VScrollBar.*

## Line Controls

Line objects are one of the drawing objects provided to enhance your screens (Figure 5.36). Line objects have attributes and functions, but no events are associated with them.

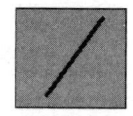

*Figure 5.36 A Line control.*

## Oval Controls

Oval objects are one of the drawing objects provided to enhance your screens (Figure 5.37). Oval objects have attributes and functions, but no events are associated with them.

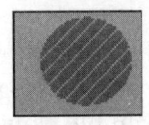

*Figure 5.37  The Oval control.*

## RECTANGLE CONTROLS

Rectangle objects are one of the drawing objects provided to enhance your screens (Figure 5.38). Rectangle objects have attributes and functions, but no events are associated with them.

*Figure 5.38  A Rectangle control.*

## ROUNDRECTANGLE CONTROLS

RoundRectangle objects are one of the drawing objects provided to enhance your screens (Figure 5.39). RoundRectangle objects have attributes and functions, but no events are associated with them.

*Figure 5.39  A RoundRectangle control.*

## TAB CONTROLS

A Tab control is a very powerful and one of the more complex controls (Figure 5.40). Tab controls contain a number of tab pages. Figure 5.40 shows an example with five tab pages. Each tab page is a user object that can contain various controls, text, and pictures. You define tab pages in the Window painter or as user objects (in the User Object painter) before they are inserted into a Tab control.

Each tab has a label, which can be displayed on any side of the Tab control. Tab pages can be selected by bringing the tab page to the front of the display, or tab pages can be opened like a spiral notebook, moving the unselected tabs to the opposite side (horizontally or vertically) of the Tab control.

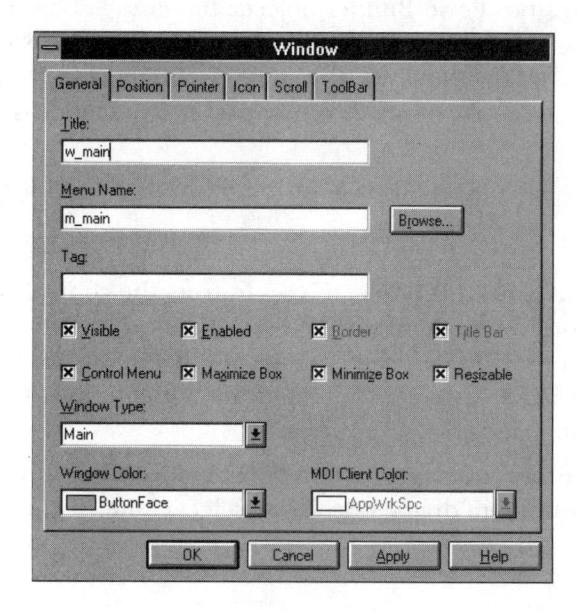

*Figure 5.40  A Tab control.*

You can set the color and font for each tab control.

## DRAG AND DROP

The drag-and-drop function lets the user click on an object and drag an icon representing that object to another location (usually to another object in the application), and then release the mouse button to drop the dragged object at that point. This mouse technique is used to trigger an action in the application in an easy, graphical manner. For example, in a file system, you can copy a file's icon to a directory icon to copy (or move) that file to that directory. Another familiar example would be to drag a file's icon to a trash bin icon to delete it. Drag and drop is a standard Windows interface technique, and it is used in other systems such as Macintosh and The X Window system.

Drag and drop is easily implemented in your PowerBuilder applications. It always involves two PowerBuilder objects: the *dragged* object and the *target* object. The target object is the control to which the object is being dragged. All controls, except for the drawing objects, are draggable. When a control is being dragged, the application's drag mode is on. Drag mode is an application-wide setting.

Each draggable object has two attributes that are used for the drag-and-drop function:

- `DragAuto`—If this Boolean is set to **true**, the control is automatically set into drag mode when the user clicks on it. Otherwise, you must turn on drag mode programmatically. If you set `DragAuto`, the drag mode will also be ended automatically. Otherwise, you must turn it off programmatically.

- `DragIcon`—A string containing the name of the icon displayed when the control is in drag mode. If you select **None!**, a ghost outline of the control is used.

## Drag-and-Drop Functions

Two PowerBuilder functions are used with drag and drop:

- Drag—Begins or ends drag mode for a control.
- DraggedObject—Returns the type of the dragged object.

In our **CONTROL1** example, the drag mode is controlled programmatically for the listbox. The DragAuto attribute for the listbox is set to **false**. A user-defined event traps the drag movement over the list box. The following code was added to the we_mousemove event for the list box:

```
IF Message.wordparm = 1 THEN
    This.Drag(begin!)
fw_update_status ('lb_1.clicked')
END IF
```

In this example, check first to see if the left mouse button is down (wordparm = 1). If that is true, then initiate drag mode for this control.

In the target DragDrop event, the following code is added (excerpt):

```
ListBox      lb_which
CommandButton     cb_which
string       s_text
DragObject obj_which
obj_which = DraggedObject()
CHOOSE CASE    TypeOf(obj_which)
CASE ListBox!
    lb_which = obj_which
    s_text = lb_which.SelectedItem ( )
    This.text = s_text
    lb_which.Drag (Cancel!) // if you used End!
                           // would be recursive!!
END CHOOSE
```

In this code, the `DraggedObject` function is used. This returns the object that was dropped on the target. The `TypeOf` function is used to check if the dragged control is a listbox. If it was, then we get the text for the selected item in that listbox and display it on the target static text.

## CONTROL1 EXAMPLE PROGRAM

The **CONTROL1** example demonstrates a basic set of controls (the new controls added with PowerBuilder 5 will be found in another example, **CONTROL2**). Run the **CONTROL1** program. The `w_first` window will display first, with a number of controls (Figure 5.44). In the top right of the window, you can set an EditMask spin control (`em_count`) to values 0 through 9. The Beep PictureButton will beep the number of times equal to the value of `em_count`. You can disable or enable the `pb_beep` control with the `cbx_enable` checkbox.

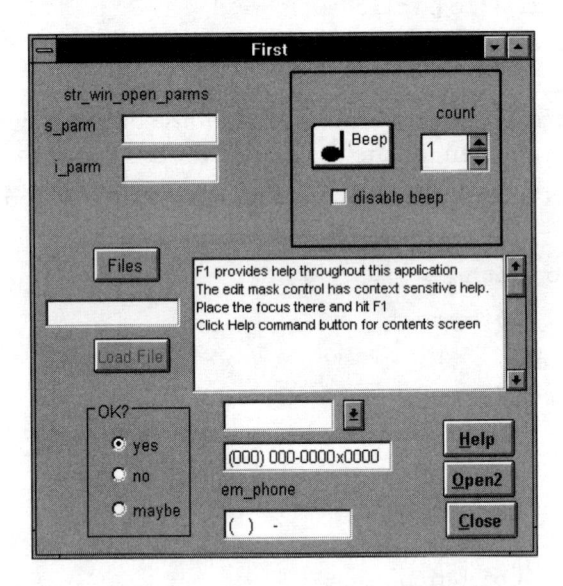

*Figure 5.44 The w_first window.*

The Files button (`cb_file_list`) will open the GetFileOpenName dialog box, where you can navigate through drives and directories to locate any file. If you select a text file (**\*.TXT**) or a profile file (**\*.INI**), the Load File button (`cb_load_file`) is enabled. Clicking **cb_load_file** will load the file (up to 32K characters) and display the file in the `mle_1` multiline edit control.

At the bottom of the `w_first` window, there is a set of radio buttons (with the group label OK?). This demonstrates the automatic action of a radio button group. The dropdown listbox contains the same values as the radio buttons, and selecting an entry in the dropdown listbox will also select the corresponding radio button. This demonstrates detecting the selection in the dropdown listbox and addressing the correct radio button.

The `em_phone` EditMask is designed for the input of seven-digit phone numbers with a three-digit area code. Tab down to this field and enter the number. Notice how this works. The result is a string containing only the ten digits that were entered in this field. Two example EditMask controls demonstrate different data types for the phone number.

At the bottom right of the `w_first` window you will see three buttons. The Help button displays information on this window (more on this in later chapters). The Open2 button (`cb_open`) opens the `w_second` window (Figure 5.45). `cb_open` uses the OpenWithParm function to open the `w_second` window and to pass a parameter to that window. In this case, we pass a structure to `w_second`. The values for the structure are assigned in two single-line edit fields in the top right of the `w_first` window. The third button closes the window and ends the application.

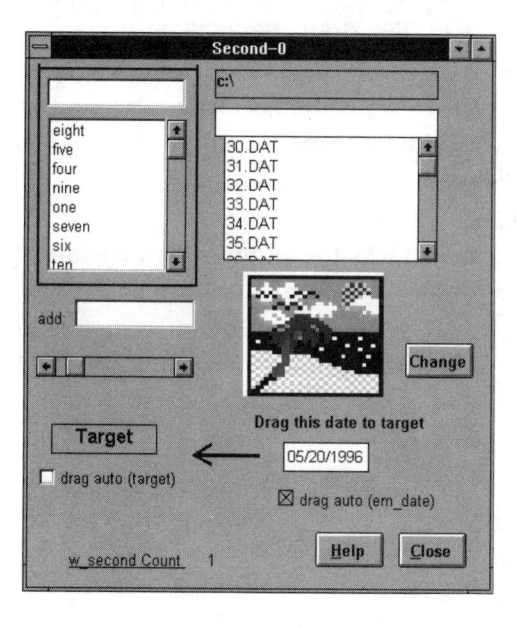

*Figure 5.45* The w_second window.

Click the **Open2** button to open w_second. This window demonstrates other controls and the drag-and-drop functionality. In the top left of w_first, you saw two single-line edit fields where you could enter a string and integer parameter for the w_second window. These values are placed in a structure (str_win_open_parms) that is passed to the w_second window using the OpenWithParm function. This opens w_second and uses the message object to pass parameters to w_second. In this case, we use the message.powerobjectparm variable to carry the str_win_open_parms structure. The powerobjectparm can hold any PowerBuilder object. Examine the w_second Open event to see how the str_win_open_parms structure is retrieved from the powerobjectparm variable.

When w_second opens, its title bar displays the values in the str_open_win_parms structure that is passed with the OpenWithParm function in w_first. If you pass a single character in the s_parm element, w_second will try to use it as the disk drive letter for the directory navigation in the dropdown listbox.

In w_second, enter text in the single-line edit field labeled *add*, and hit the **Enter** key. This will add a new item to the listbox. The top single-line edit provides an incremental search in the listbox. As you type characters, a search will find the first entry in the listbox that matches.

Drag and drop entries from the listbox to the target. The target (a static text field) will display the dropped object. You can also drag from the picture control, the em_date EditMask, and the target itself (if you activate the drag auto (target) checkbox).

The w_second Count field at the bottom of the screen displays a shared w_second variable that tracks the number of times this window has been opened. This value is stored in an instance variable in the w_second window.

The dropdown listbox demonstrates the DirSelect and DirList PowerScript functions. These functions allow you to display and navigate the directories on a disk drive and to select files. The current directory is displayed in the st_path static text field.

# CONTROL1—Step-by-Step

Now you can create your own version of CONTROL1, by following the next set of instructions.

## Create the Application and Library

1. Start PowerBuilder (if necessary).
2. If you are not in the Application painter, click on the **Appl** icon on the PowerBar.
3. In the Application painter, select **File|New**.
4. In the Select New Application Library dialog box, set the directory to **C:\PB5\MCCLAN2** and enter the name **ZCONTRL1.PBL** for the library file name. Click **OK**.
5. In the Save Application dialog box:
    a. In the Applications: field enter **CONTROL1**.
    b. Tab to the comments field and enter **MY CONTROL1 VERSION 1**.
    c. Be sure that the Application Library name is still **ZCONTRL1.PBL**; if not, select it.
    d. Click **OK**.
6. PowerBuilder asks if you wish to generate an application template. Click **No** as in all the examples for this book (except one in the MDI chapter).

This returns you to the Application painter. You have created the CONTROL1 application object and the ZCONTRL1 library.

## Create the Main Window

Click the **Window** icon on the PowerBar to open the Window painter. In the Select Window dialog box, click on the **New** button to create a new window. In

**192** Chapter 5

the Window painter double-click on the new window to open the Window Style dialog box (or select **Edit|Properties**).

In this dialog box, in the Title edit box enter **First**. Then, select **Main** from the Window Type dropdown listbox. This defines the type for the new window. The other options should match those in Figure 5.46. Set these changes by clicking the **Apply** button.

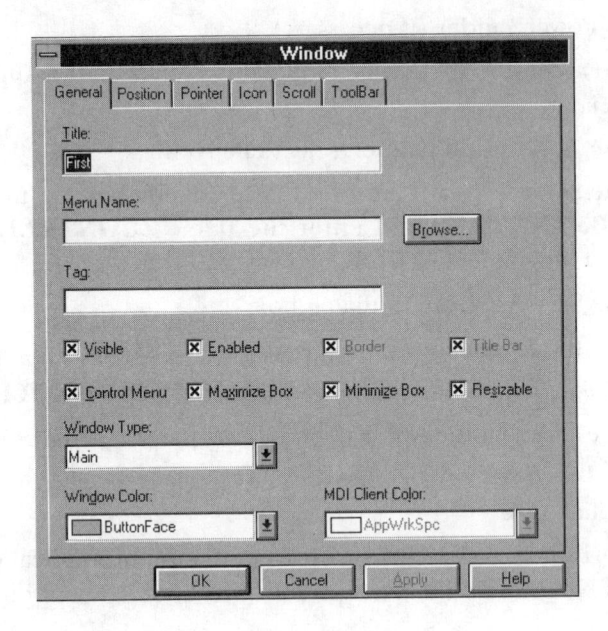

*Figure 5.46 Defining the w_first window.*

Next, click the **Position** tab (in the Window Properties dialog box) to open the Window Position dialog box.

Set the position (and size) of the window, as shown in Figure 5.47. The position of a Main window is relative to the display area of your monitor's screen. In this example, the position of the Main window is at the top left of the screen.

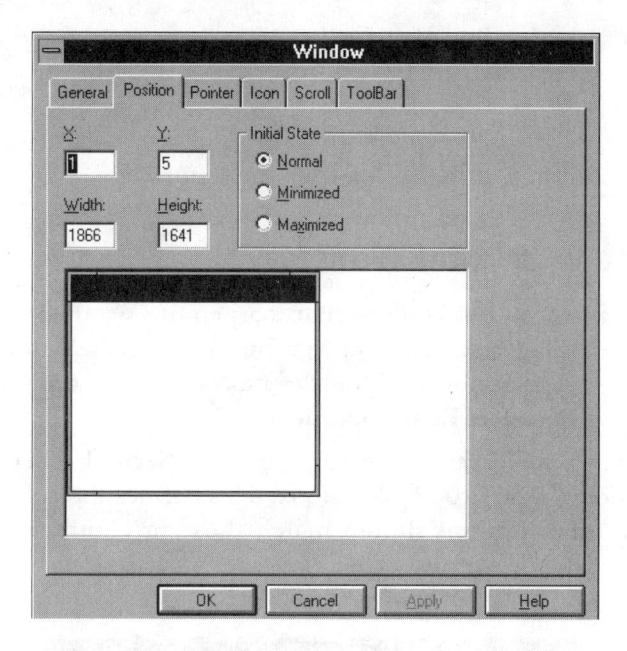

*Figure 5.47* The Window Position dialog box.

Close the dialog box by clicking **OK**. In the Window painter, select **File|Save As**. Check to be sure that the library is set to **ZCONTRL1.PBL**, and then enter the name **w_first** and click the **OK** button.

## Add Code to the Application Open Event

Go to the Application painter (if you did not close it earlier, you can just select it under the Window menu (**Application-CONTROL1**)). To enter the new code, click the **Script** icon on the Application painter PainterBar. This opens the Script Painter. The Script Editor should display *Script-open for CONTROL1* on the title bar; if not, pull down the SelectEvent dropdown menu and select **Open**.

**194** Chapter 5

Enter the following line of code:

```
open(w_first)
```

When you are finished in the editor, click the **Return** icon.

## Create the w_second Window

Click the **Window** icon on the PowerBar to open the Window painter. In the Select Window dialog box, click the **New** button to create a new window. In the Window painter, double-click on the new window to open the Window Style dialog box (or select **Edit|Properties**).

In this dialog box, in the Title edit box enter **Second**. Then select **Main** from the Window Type dropdown listbox. This defines the type for the new window. The other options should match those in Figure 5.48. Set these changes by clicking the **Apply** button.

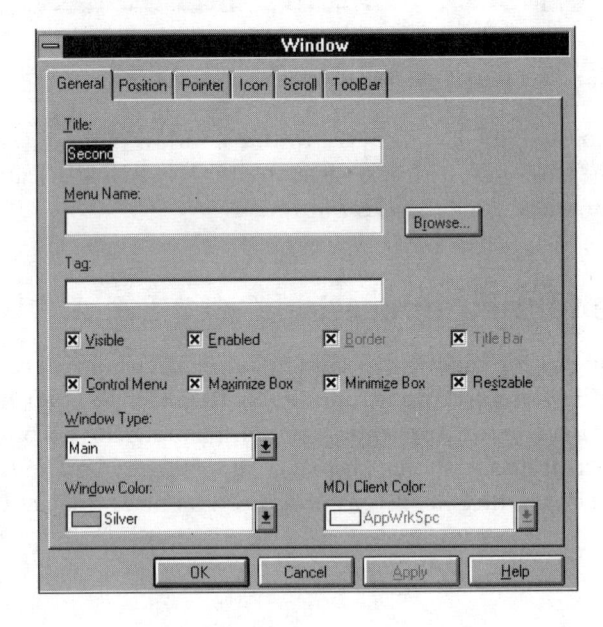

*Figure 5.48 Defining the w_second window.*

Next, click the **Position** tab (in the Window Properties dialog box) to open the Window Position dialog box.

Set the position (and size) of the window as shown in Figure 5.49. The position of a Main window is relative to the display area of your monitor's screen. In this example, the position of the Main window is at the top right of the screen.

Close the dialog box by clicking **OK**. In the Window painter, select **File|Save As**. Check to be sure that the library is set to **ZCONTRL1.PBL**, and then enter the name **w_second** and click the **OK** button. Close the Window painter for w_second. We will return to w_second later.

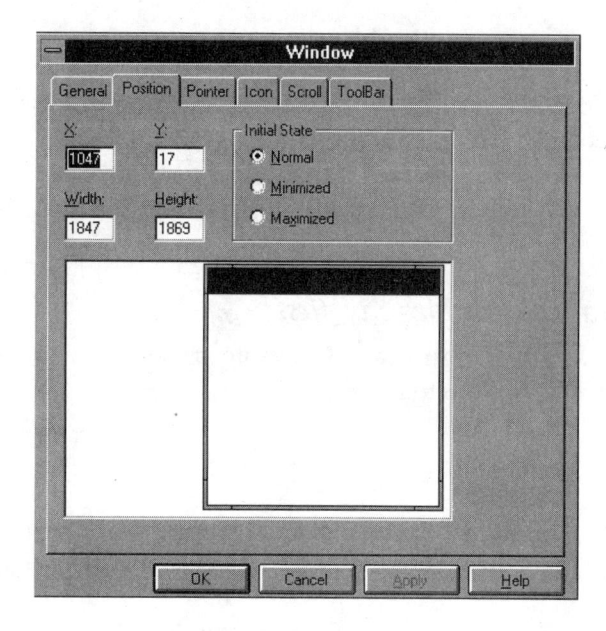

*Figure 5.49* *The Window Position dialog box.*

## Return to the w_first Window

Go to the Window painter for w_first (if you're not already there). Add the controls to w_first. They should be named as follows:

sle_s_parm

sle_i_parm

pb_beep

em_count

cbx_enable

```
cb_file_list
sle_filepath
cb_load_file
mle_1
rb_yes
rb_no
rb_maybe
ddlb_1
em_phone_string
em_phone_number
cb_open
cb_close
```

## Add an Instance Variable to w_first

Now create the following instance variable by selecting **Declare|Instance Variables** and entering the following:

```
int ii_beeps
```

Close the Declare Instance Variables dialog box. This integer will set the number of beeps to be issued by the `Timer` event (after clicking the **pb_beep** button).

## Add Code to the w_first Window Timer Event

Next, you will add code to the `Timer` event in `w_first`. This event will beep the PC's speaker every half second if the instance variable `ii_beeps` is greater than zero. It will then decrement the `ii_beeps` value and turn off the `Timer` event when the `ii_beeps` value is zero.

Open the Script painter (use **Edit|Script** or the RMB popup menu). Select the **Timer** event in the Select Event dropdown listbox. Add the following code:

```
IF ii_beeps > 0 THEN
    ii_beeps = ii_beeps - 1
    beep(1)
```

```
ELSE
    Timer(0)
END IF
```

### Add Code to the w_first Window CloseQuery Event

Next, you will add code to the `CloseQuery` event in `w_first`. This event will close `w_second`, if it is open. Open the Script painter (use **Edit|Script** or the RMB popup menu). Select the **CloseQuery** event in the Select Event dropdown listbox. Add the following code:

```
IF IsValid(w_second) THEN close(w_second)
```

### Add Code to the w_first pb_beep

Next, you will add code to the `Clicked` event in `pb_beep` (in `w_first`). This event will set the `ii_beeps` instance variable to the number of beeps (in `em_count`) and then start the Timer event. Open the Script painter for the `pb_beep` button. Select the **Clicked** event in the Select Event dropdown listbox. Add the following code:

```
int i_rc
ii_beeps = integer(em_count.text)
i_rc = Timer(.5)
```

### Add Code to the w_first cbx_enable

Next, you will add code to the `Clicked` event in `cbx_enable` (in `w_first`). This event will enable or disable the `pb_beep` button:

```
IF This.checked then
    pb_beep.enabled = FALSE
ELSE
    pb_beep.enabled = TRUE
END IF
```

## Add Code to the w_first cb_file_list

Next, you will add code to the `Clicked` event in `cb_file_list` (in w_first). This event will list files in a directory:

```
integer i_rc
string s_pathname, s_filename
cb_load_file.enabled = False
i_rc = GetFileOpenName("Select a file:", s_pathname, &
        s_filename, "INI", "text (*.TXT), *.TXT, ini (*.INI), *.INI")
IF i_rc = 1 THEN
    sle_filepath.text = s_pathname
    IF pos(upper(s_filename), ".TXT") > 0 OR &
       pos(upper(s_filename), "INI") > 0 THEN
            cb_load_file.enabled = True
    END IF
END IF
```

## Add Code to the w_first cb_load_file

Next, you will add code to the `Clicked` event in `cb_load_file` (in w_first). This event will load a file into the `mle_1`:

```
int i_file
long l_len
string s_text
i_file = FileOpen(sle_filepath.text, StreamMode!)
IF i_file > 0 THEN
    l_len = FileRead(i_file, s_text)
    mle_1.text = s_text
    FileClose(i_file)
END IF
This.enabled = False
```

## Add Code to the w_first ddlb_1

Next, you will add code to the `SelectionChanged` event in `ddlb_1` (in w_first). This event will set the corresponding radio button:

```
string s_command
s_command = ddlb_1.text
IF s_command = 'yes' THEN
        rb_yes.checked = TRUE
ELSEIF s_command = 'no' THEN
        rb_no.checked = TRUE
ELSEIF s_command = 'maybe' THEN
        rb_maybe.checked = TRUE
END IF
```

## Add Code to the w_first RadioButtons

Next, you will add code to the `Clicked` event in the set of radio buttons. Add the same line of code to all three RadioButtons. This will select the corresponding item in the dropdown listbox.

```
ddlb_1.selectitem ( This.text, 0 )
```

## Declare str_win_open_parms

Next, you will define a global structure. Click the **Structure** icon on the PowerBar (or PowerPanel). This will open the Structure painter to define a global structure that will be used to carry window `Open` event parameters to w_second. Define the structure as:

```
str_win_open_parms
s_parm string
i_parm integer
```

## Chapter 5

### Add Code to the w_first cb_open

Next, you will add code to the `Clicked` event in the cb_open button:

```
str_win_open_parms str_parms
str_parms.s_parm = trim(sle_s_parm.text)
str_parms.i_parm = integer(sle_i_parm.text)
OpenWithParm(w_second, str_parms)
```

### Add Code to the w_first cb_close

Next, you will add code to the `Clicked` event in the cb_close button:

```
close(Parent)
```

## Return to the w_second Window

Go to the Window painter for w_second. Add the controls to w_second. They should be named as follows:

```
sle_isearch
lb_list
sle_insert
st_path
ddlb_dir
hsb_1
p_1
cb_change
st_target
em_date
cbx_drag_auto_target
cbx_drag_auto_em
st_count
cb_close
```

## Add Code to the w_second Open Event

Go back to w_second. Open the Script painter (in one of w_second's events). The Script Editor should display *Script-open for* w_second on the title bar; if not, pull down the SelectEvent dropdown menu and select **Open**. Enter the following lines of code:

```
str_win_open_parms str_x
str_x = message.powerobjectparm
IF IsValid(str_x) THEN
    This.Title = This.Title + '-' + str_x.s_parm + '-' + &
            string(str_x.i_parm)
        IF Len(str_x.s_parm) = 1 THEN
            IF Upper(str_x.s_parm) >= 'A' &
            AND Upper(str_x.s_parm) <= 'Z' THEN
                st_path.text = str_x.s_parm + ':'
                fw_init_ddlb()
            END IF
        END IF
END IF
si_count = si_count + 1
st_count.text = string(si_count)
hsb_1.position = si_count
```

This code will pull the str_win_open_parms structure off the message object. It will display the value of the structure's two elements on the w_second title bar.

## Add a Function to w_second

Go back to the w_second Window painter. Select **Declare|Window Functions**. Create a new function:

```
public function integer fw_init_ddlb //no arguments
boolean b_rc
```

```
int i_rc
string s_file_spec
s_file_spec = st_path.text + "\*.*"
b_rc = ddlb_1.DirList(s_file_spec,16400, st_path)
IF b_rc THEN
    i_rc = 1
ELSE
    beep(1)
    st_path.text = 'c:'
    b_rc = ddlb_1.DirList(s_file_spec,16400, st_path)
    IF b_rc THEN i_rc = 2
END IF
return i_rc
```

### Add Code to the sle_isearch Other Event

Next, add code to the `sle_isearch`'s `Other` event. In the Script Editor for the `sle_isearch` listbox, select the **Other** event from the SelectEvent drop-down list (at the bottom). Enter the following code for that event:

```
lb_list.SelectItem(this.text, 0)
```

This event will be triggered by the Windows events that are not mapped to PowerBuilder listbox events. One of these events is triggered as each keystroke is entered for the single-line edit. So, we use this event to select the best match in the `lb_list` listbox. A better method would be to define a user event for the `keyup` or `keydown` event. This is discussed in the next chapter.

### Add Code to the sle_insert Modified Event

Next, you will add code to the single-line edit control's `Modified` event. This event is a standard system event that will be triggered when the user types in the single-line edit and then hits **Enter** or **Tab** or clicks the mouse in another editable field. In the Window painter, right-mouse click on the single-line edit to open the RMB popup menu. Select **Script** from the popup menu. This will open the Script Editor for an event in the single-line edit. Select the **Modified** event from the Select Event dropdown list. Add the following code:

```
lb_list.AddItem (This.text)
This.text = ""
```

When you make an entry in the single-line edit field, this code will call the AddItem event in the lb_list listbox. It will pass the string that is currently in the single-line edit (This.text).

Close the editor and run the application. When the w_second window appears, type some items into the single-line editor and watch the results. If the items do not appear in the listbox, check the code in each event carefully.

### Add Code to the cb_changed Clicked Event

Next, you will add code to the cb_change Clicked event. Add the following code:

```
IF p_1.picturename = 'c:\pb5\mcclan2\kk.bmp' THEN
    p_1.picturename = 'c:\pb5\mcclan2\beach.bmp'
    p_1.tag = 'beach'
ELSE
    p_1.picturename = 'c:\pb5\mcclan2\kk.bmp'
    p_1.tag = 'solar'
END IF
```

### Add Code to the p_1 Constructor Event

Add the following code to the p_1 constructor:

```
This.tag = 'beach'
```

## Chapter 5

### Add Code to the lb_list Other Event

Next, add code to the lb_list's `Other` event. In the Script Editor for the `lb_list` listbox, select the **Other** event from the SelectEvent dropdown list (at the bottom). Enter the following code for that event:

```
IF message.number = 513 THEN
     This.Drag(begin!)
END IF
```

This event will be triggered by the Windows events that are not mapped to PowerBuilder listbox events. One of these events is triggered as the mouse moves the pointer across the listbox. We are only interested in this action when the user presses the left-mouse button to signal the beginning of a drag operation. When the left-mouse button is pressed, the message.number will be equal to 513. In that case, we turn on drag mode using the `Drag` function.

### Add Code to the st_target DragDrop Event

Next, you will add code to the target static text control's `DragDrop` event. This event is a standard system event that will be triggered when the user drops an item on the static text field (when the window is in drag mode).

> **NOTE**: Be sure to set the st_target `Enabled` attribute to **true** (check the checkbox in the Properties dialog box). Otherwise, the st_target will not receive the `DragDrop` event.

```
ListBox lb_source
CommandButton    cb_source
EditMask     em_source
Picture      pic_source
string       s_text
DragObject       obj_source
statictext st_source
obj_source = DraggedObject()
CHOOSE CASE      TypeOf(obj_source)
```

```
CASE CommandButton!
    cb_source = obj_source
    s_text = cb_source.text
    This.text = s_text
CASE EditMask!
    em_source = obj_source
    s_text = em_source.text
    This.text = s_text
CASE StaticText!
    st_source = obj_source
    This.text = 'st'
CASE Picture!
    pic_source = obj_source
    s_text = pic_source.tag
    This.text = s_text
CASE ListBox!
    lb_source = obj_source
    s_text = lb_source.SelectedItem ( )
    This.text = s_text
    lb_source.Drag (cancel!)// if you used end! would be recursive!!
END IF
```

This code uses the `TypeOf` function to determine the type of drag-and-drop source variable. That (source) is the only argument passed to this event. The source variable has the data type `dragobject`. All objects that can be the source for the drag-and-drop functionality are descendants of `dragobject` (see the chapter on inheritance for more information). We use the `TypeOf` function to see if the listbox was the source of the drag. If it was, we assign the source to a local variable lb_x (a listbox variable). (This is similar to casting in other languages, such as C.) After this assignment, lb_x is an alias for lb_1. The code ends the drag mode for the window with the `Drag(cancel!)` statement. We do not use `Drag(end!)` because this would trigger another `DragDrop` event and cause a recursive loop. Next, the code uses the `FindItem` function to locate the index for the item. The `DeleteItem` function takes the index to remove the item from the listbox.

### Add Code to the w_second cb_close

Next, you will add code to the `Clicked` event in the **cb_close** button:

```
close(Parent)
```

## Run the Application

Now, run the application. That's all there is to it!

**CHAPTER 6**

# Events, Functions, and User Events

Now that you know the basics about creating applications and building windows, we will discuss the possibilities for adding PowerScript code to your applications. In PowerBuilder applications, you can write PowerScript code both as functions and as scripts for the various events for the objects in your application (including the application object, windows, and window controls). This chapter covers the following topics:

- An overview of event-driven programming
- Understanding PowerBuilder events; the Events1 example application
- Adding PowerScript code to events
- Creating functions
- Creating user events
- An example application, Events2

# Event-Driven Programming

Windows is an *event-driven* environment that is similar to the UNIX-based X Window System and the Apple Macintosh system for the user and developer. In event-driven programs, the application programming is triggered by events that control the execution of its code. Events are conveyed to the application by the Windows system as messages.

## Messages

The operating system receives all events (including hardware and software events), which include keystrokes, mouse movements, and system timer events. The Windows system converts each event into a message and dispatches the message to specific objects (windows, controls, etc.) in the system. Each message has a message type that specifies the type of event that has occurred. The message may also carry other information about the nature of the event.

All the code that you write in a PowerBuilder application will be executed as the result of events. You will write scripts for various events and may then call other code in functions and use other objects in the system. Your PowerScript code can also call the TriggerEvent or PostEvent functions to cause an event to occur, which then sends another message to a specific application object.

The various types of objects in your application will have a set of predefined events that are specific to that object type. For example, windows and many of the window controls have a `Clicked` event. Some of the editable controls have a `modified` event. DataWindows have a `dberror` event. Most object types have `constructor` and `destructor` events.

# Events1: A PowerBuilder Application

This section presents a sample application, Events1. You can find this application on the disk included with this book. This program will make it easy to see and understand events in a PowerBuilder application.

Events1 is a two-window PowerBuilder application that will display a list of the events as they occur in the application. The initial window (w_first) contains a listbox labeled "Events." This listbox will display most of the events that occur in the second window (w_second). When you open the second window, you may have to adjust the position of w_second to the right of the screen, so that you can see the first window's listbox. This listbox will also list a few events that occur in the w_first window (but only after the w_second window has been opened). This is necessary to show the interaction of events as the user switches between the two windows.

Run the Events1 application from the PowerBuilder environment. To do this, launch PowerBuilder (if necessary) and go to the Application painter (click on the **Appl** icon on the PowerBar). Select the **Open** icon from the Application painter PainterBar. In the Select Application Library dialog box, select **C:\PB5\MCCLAN2** in the Directories listbox. Then select the **EVENTS1.PBL** library in the File Name listbox and click the **OK** command button. This should display EVENTS1 in the Applications field of the Select Application dialog box. Select **OK** to return to the Application painter.

In the Application painter, check that the window caption is *Application-events1*. Click on the **Run** icon on the PowerBar (or on the PowerPanel) to run the application. When the application runs, you will see the w_first window on the screen.

## EVENTS1

1. When the application begins, it triggers the Application Open event. The only line of code in the Application Open event is Open(w_first).

2. When the w_first window opens, it should be positioned on the left side of the screen. The listbox will not contain any lines of text until you click the **Open2** command button. Click that button, and a sampling of events will display, as shown in Figure 6.1. Be sure that the w_second window is positioned far enough to the right of the listbox so that you can see the events. Now you can work with the windows and see the resulting events.

**210** Chapter 6

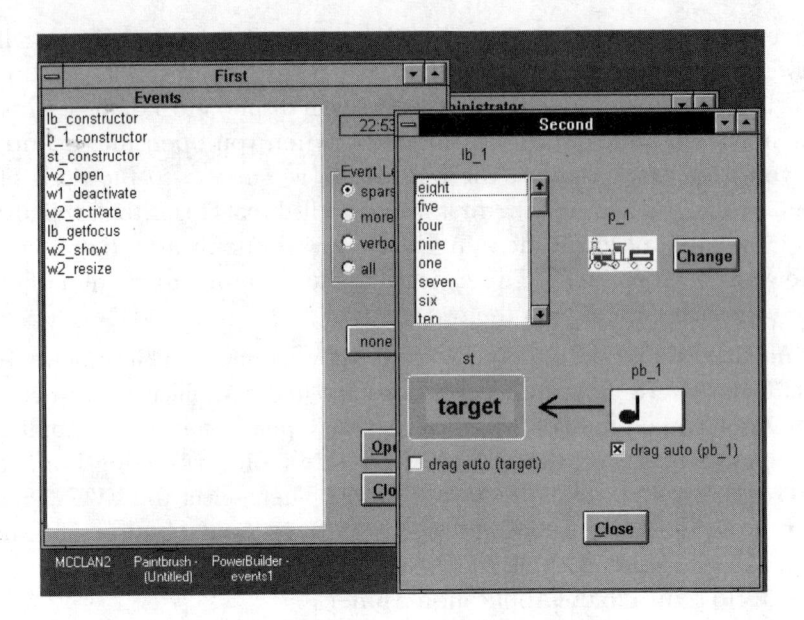

*Figure 6.1 The events1 application.*

When you open the `w_second` window, you will see a series of event messages (they may vary slightly from this description) in the listbox. The first characters of the message tells you to which window and/or object the event belongs. This can be any of the following:

`st`—`w_second`'s static text field, the target for the drag-and-drop example

`lb`—`w_second`'s listbox (lb_1), you can drag a number from this listbox to the target

`p_1`—`w_second`'s picture control

`cb_change`—`w_second`'s Change command button, changes the `p_1` picture

`pb_1`—`w_second`'s picture button, used for the drag-and-drop example

`w2.cb_close`—`w_second`'s close button

`w_1`—This is an event that belongs the `w_first` window

`w_2`—This is an event that belongs to the `w_second` window

The final characters of the message tell you which event was triggered. The original events are interesting and include the following (again note, the exact details may vary slightly from your display):

lb.constructor—When the w_second window opens, all the objects on the window receive the constructor event just before the actual Open event occurs for the window (not all the constructors are listed)

st.constructor—The static text (target) constructor event

p_1.constructor—The picture control constructor event

w2.open—The w_second window open event; note that this occurs only after all the constructors

w1.deactivate—Window, w_first, is sent a deactivate message

w2.activate—w_second window is sent an activate message

lb.getfocus—one of the objects on the window receives the focus (determined by the tag order in the Window painter)

w2.show—w_second is displayed (visible)

w2.resize—w_second is sized (as a result of the open)

## Experiment with Events1

Experiment with the drag-and-drop function. In w_second use the listbox, lb_1, or the **Picture** button, pb_1, to begin the drag. Click on one of these objects and drag to the target. You can set the drag auto attribute on pb_1 or st (target) to see the effect on the events that are generated. Notice that there is no Clicked event for an object when you turn on drag auto.

You can control the number and type of events displayed in the Events listbox. The w_first window has a set of radio buttons that will increase the range of events displayed as the application executes.

If you click back on the surface of the w_first window (leave the w_second window open), w_first will become the active window. This will cause the following events:

w2.deactivate—The w_second window is sent a deactivate message.

w1.activate—The w_second window is sent an activate message.

`w2.xxx.losefocus`—Some object in the w_second window is sent the `losefocus` message.

`w1.clicked`—Only if you clicked on the window (and not on the **None** button).

Try this again. Clear the listbox by clicking the **Open2** button. This time, click back on the **None** button in the w_first window (leave the w_second window open). w_first will become the active window. This will cause the following events:

`w2.deactivate`—The w_second window is sent a `deactivate` message.

`w1.activate`—The w_second window is sent an `activate` message.

`w2.xxx.losefocus`—Some object in the w_second window is sent the `losefocus` message.

`none.getfocus`—If you clicked on the **None** button, it will receive the focus.

`none.clicked`—If you clicked on the **None** button, it will receive this event.

Continue to run the Events1 example until you have a good understanding of these events.

## PowerBuilder Events

Now that you have a good understanding of events, we can briefly mention a few of the more important events where you may insert code. The first event of importance is the Application object's `Open` event. Generally, this event contains initialization code and makes a call to the `Open` function to open the application's first window.

The `Clicked` event is important for many types of window controls. Command buttons will always have code to effect the appropriate action, and many other types of controls also use the `Clicked` event extensively.

The `Clicked` event for menu items will usually have code to effect the action represented by the menu label. We will cover this in detail in the chapter on menus.

The `Window open` event is also of primary importance. When a window opens, you may wish to perform some initialization, perhaps connect to the database. In general, I recommend that you do not place too much code in the `Window open` event, because PowerBuilder will not display the window until all the code in the Open event has executed. If there is a great deal of processing, there can be a noticeable delay, which may confuse the user. So, except for a few simple statements, I generally put the code into one or more functions and then call those functions from a user-defined event that I set up to execute after the window has become visible. I will trigger this event in the window's Open event (using the `PostEvent` function). I will show an example of this later in this chapter in the section on user-defined events. You could also post a function call for the same result.

You can find a list of other events and an explanation of each throughout this book in the section where I discuss each of the PowerBuilder objects.

To write a script for any event, you must first go to the painter for the object (Application, Menu, Window, or User Object) that contains the event. Then open the editor (the **Edit|Script** menu option for some objects or open the RMB popup menu for the object and select the **Script** option).

When the PowerScript painter opens, check the title bar to see that you are in the correct object and event. You can select other events from the Select Event dropdown menu (you can select other objects in the Window painter with the **Design|Select Object** menu item).

## User-Defined Functions

You could place all of your code in Event scripts; however, for better structured programs, you should partition your code into functions (procedures). This section describes the process of creating user-defined functions. After you have created the user-defined functions, you can call them from your other script code just as if they were one of the PowerBuilder built-in functions. User-defined functions are created using the PowerScript language. The process is similar to writing code for an event.

User-defined functions have scope, either at the *global* or *object* level. Global functions have the same visibility as global variables and can be called from anywhere in your application (just like the built-in PowerBuilder functions that can be used by any object). You should define a function with global scope only when it provides a general functionality that may be used by various types of objects in your application.

You can define object-level user-defined functions at the application, window, menu, or user-object level. This type of user-defined function has a scope like the PowerBuilder functions that are defined for a specific type of object (like `listbox.additem()`). Define a function with an object-level scope when you want to limit the use of that function to a single type of object. For example, you could define a function for a window such as `w_customer.fw_get_customer_id()`.

To create or edit a global function, you must use the Function painter. Click on the **Function** icon on the PowerBar to create a new function or edit an existing global function. This will open the Select Function dialog box window, as shown in Figure 6.2.

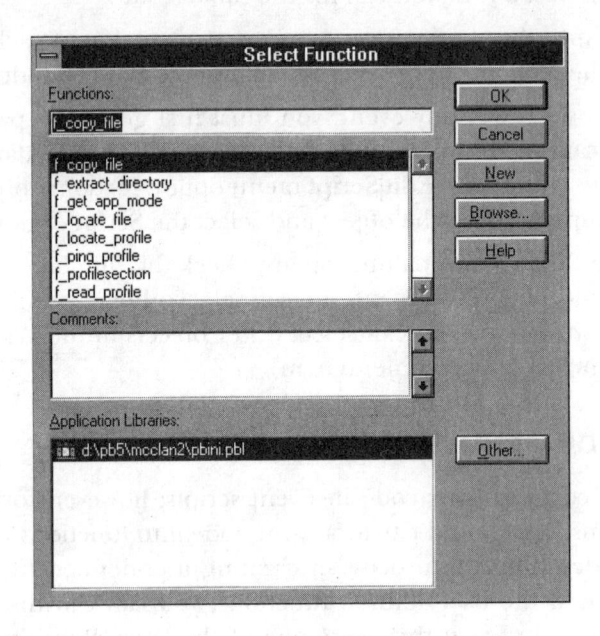

*Figure 6.2 Select Function dialog box window.*

In this dialog box, you can edit an existing function by selecting the library and the function name. This opens the Function painter where you can edit the code. The Function painter is essentially the PowerScript painter with a few variations. When you are in the Function painter there are only two or three listboxes: the Paste Global listbox, the Paste Argument listbox, and perhaps the Paste Window listbox. The Paste Argument listbox contains the names of the function parameters that you defined when you declared the function (in the New Function dialog box); this will let you paste the arguments into your code.

Edit the function declaration by selecting the **Design|Function Declaration** menu option. This opens the Function Declaration dialog box shown in Figure 6.3.

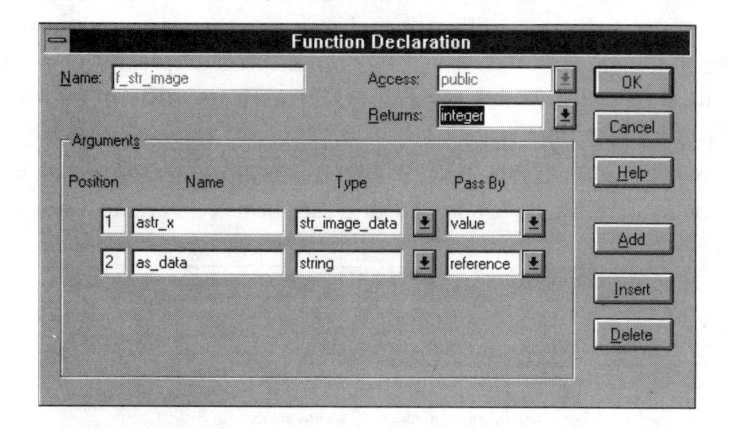

*Figure 6.3 Editing a function declaration.*

To create a new function, click on the **New** command button in the Select Function dialog box window. This will open the New Function dialog window to (essentially) the same display as the Function Declaration dialog window.

In this dialog window, you define a name for the function, select a return data type, and add any arguments that are passed in the function call. The recommended convention is to use f_ as the name prefix for global functions, such as f_calc_tax. A set of recommended prefixes for other types of user-defined functions is listed in Table 6.1. A global function has an access level of public.

*Table 6.1 Recommended Function Name Prefixes*

| PREFIX | OBJECT LEVEL | ALTERNATIVE CHOICE |
|---|---|---|
| f_ | global | |
| fa_ | application | af_ |
| fw_ | window | wf_ |
| fm_ | menu | mf_ |
| fu_ | user object | uf_ |

## Object-Level Functions

To create an object-level function, you must first open the painter for the object where you intend to define the function. Then choose the **Declare|Object Functions** menu selection. (The actual text for this menu option will vary according to the type of object you are editing. For example, for user objects the menu selection is **Declare|User Object Functions** and for windows it is **Declare|Window Functions**).

This opens the Select Function dialog box, as shown in Figure 6.4. In this dialog box, you can choose to edit an existing function or to create a new function.

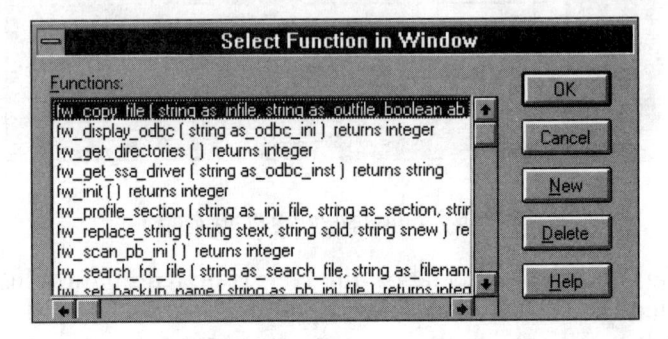

*Figure 6.4  Select Function dialog window.*

Clicking on the **New** command button opens the New Function dialog box (similar to Figure 6.3). In the New Function dialog box, you define a name for the function, select a data type for the return value, and add any arguments that are passed in the function call. For object-level functions, you can also set the access level to **public**, **private**, or **protected**.

The recommended conventions for function-name prefixes are given in Table 6.1. I prefer the first set (under Prefix) because all user-defined functions will appear under the letter $f$ (for function) in the browser. Other developers use the second set of prefixes (under Alternative Choice).

## Function Return Value Type

Usually, you will want your functions to return a value; the default data type of the return value is an integer. A common standard in PowerBuilder is to return a value of 1 to signify success. To choose another data type for the return value, select from the Returns dropdown listbox. You can also decide not to return a value from the function. This is less likely, but you can specify this by choosing **None** from the Returns dropdown listbox. You can also ignore the return value if you wish.

## Function Argument List

You can define arguments to be used for the function. To define an argument, name the argument, specify its data type, and then declare whether the argument is to be passed by value or by reference. Arguments can be any type known to PowerBuilder, including user objects and structures. The user objects and structures that you have defined will not appear in the Type listbox, but you can still enter the data type by typing it into the Type field. In Figure 2.12, the first argument was a `str_image_data` structure passed by value. The second argument is a string passed by reference so that it may be assigned a value.

> **NOTE** All complex objects (such as windows, user objects, and structures) are always passed by reference by PowerBuilder, even if you specify "by value." PowerBuilder does this to conserve memory.

You can define as many arguments as you need for your functions. Just click the **Add** command button to add a new argument to the end of the list. Click on **Insert** to add a new argument at the current cursor position in the list. Click on **Delete** to remove the currently selected argument from the list.

## Standard User Objects and User-Defined Functions

Although you cannot define an object-level function at the standard control level (such as a command button or listbox), you can define a function for a standard user object. Because the standard user object is based on a standard type of control (such as a command button), you can achieve the desired result. This is essentially the same as adding a method to a class in object-oriented languages.

> **NOTE** If you really want to create a function for a standard control, consider using a user-defined event instead. See the section on defining user events later in this chapter for more information.

Even though functions are defined at the object level, you can sometimes access these functions from outside the object using dot notation (described earlier). For example, suppose a user-defined function was created for a standard user object based on a command button and this function was used to disable the user object. For this example, assume that the user object was added to a window and named `cb_close`. The following code can call this function from another object in the window:

```
cb_close.fu_disable ()
```

or from another window by using:

```
w_main.cb_close.fu_disable()
```

You can prevent this type of reference if you wish by using another access level.

## Object Function Access Level

The access levels for functions are the same as for instance variables. *Public* access lets the function be referenced externally using dot notation. The *Private* access level restricts access to scripts within the object. The *Protected* access level restricts access to scripts within the object or within objects that are inherited from this object.

## A Sample Function

The next example shows the code for a simple window-level function that displays the current database status information in three fields on the window. The function is named `fw_db_status`, has three arguments, and returns an integer (1 if there is no error, and 0 if there is a database error).

```
Function:    fw_db_status
Arguments:   al_sql_code       long     by value
             al_sql_dbcode     long     by value
             as_sql_err_text   string   by value
Returns:     Integer
```

```
st_dbcode.text = string(al_sql_dbcode)
st_sqlcode.text = string(al_sqlcode)
mle_dbtext.text = as_sql_err_text
IF al_sqlcode >= 0 THEN return 1 ELSE return 0
```

After you have created a user-defined function, it is available in the Object Browser for pasting into your code, just like built-in functions. If the function is global, select the **Function** tab. If the function is an object-level function, first locate the object in the Objects left listbox (perhaps under the **Window** or **User Object** tab), and then click on the **Functions** icon in the right listbox. The listing for the function also includes the Argument list.

The global function names also appear on the list of user-defined functions, which is available with the **Edit|Paste Function** menu option in the PowerScript painter (click the user-defined radio button).

## DEFINING USER EVENTS

You have seen a number of event types in the example applications. Application objects have six events (including `Open`, `Close`, `Idle`, and `SystemError`), windows have 29 events (`Open`, `Activate`, `CloseQuery`, etc.), and command buttons have 11 events (`Clicked`, `GetFocus`, etc.). Many of these events are mapped by PowerBuilder from the Windows system. PowerBuilder has also added many of its own events. There are many events in the Windows system that are not initially available in your PowerBuilder objects. The `Other` event, found in most objects, is a PowerBuilder event that receives a number of different types of Windows events that have not been explicitly mapped.

You can create your own events (called *user* events) of two types with several categories. User events may also have arguments (parameters) and may have a return value. User events are a basic, essential technique for PowerBuilder development. In this section, we will create both types of user events to demonstrate their use and power.

### Creating a User Event

You create a user event by selecting the **Declare|User Event** menu option that is available from within a number of the painters, such as the Window painter and the PowerScript editor. You define each user event for a specific object, so you must first go to that object (window, control, or user object) and then select the **Declare|User Event** menu option. If you create a user event in the Window painter (say for w_invoice) after clicking on the window (to be sure that no controls are selected), the event will be attached to that window object. If you select a control on the window first and then select **Declare|User Event**, the event will be added to the selected object's events. If you create a user event in the PowerScript editor for a command button event, the user event will be attached to that command button. This defines the scope of the user event.

When you select the **Declare|User Event** menu option, the Events dialog box opens (as shown in Figure 6.5). This dialog window displays the events that are already defined for the current object along with the associated event ID. The Paste Event ID listbox contains all the possible event IDs. This includes all the Windows events for this object, plus 75 custom event IDs for your use.

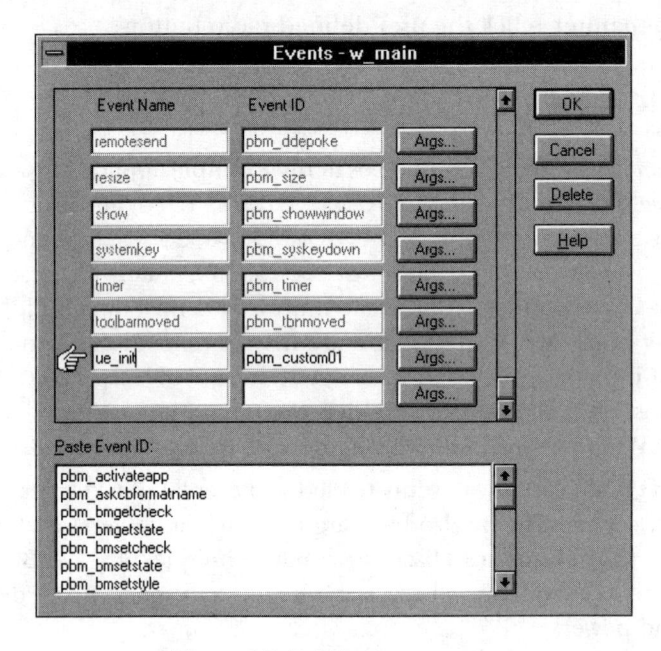

*Figure 6.5* Defining a user event.

## The Predefined System Events

Each object type (class) has a set of predefined system events. You cannot change these events; the name, event ID, arguments, and return value are all fixed. The events listed at the top of Figure 6.5 are predefined system events.

There are several types of user-defined events: user-defined custom events, user-defined parameterized events, and user-defined system events.

### User-Defined Custom Events

The first type of user event is a called a *custom* event. These are events that do not exist in the Windows or PowerBuilder systems. Use the prefix, ue_, for the name of a new custom event. You will assign a value ranging from pbm_custom01 through pbm_custom75 for the event ID. After you have defined this event, you must programmatically trigger the event for it to occur. You trigger this type of custom event in your script code using the TriggerEvent or PostEvent PowerScript functions discussed later.

### User-Defined Parameterized Events

The next type of user event is a type of custom event. Again, these are events that do not exist in the Windows or PowerBuilder systems. Use the prefix, ue_, for the name of this type of event. You will not assign a value for the event ID, and you can define arguments and a return value for the event. After you have defined this event, you must programmatically trigger the event for it to occur. You trigger this type of custom event in your script code using the TriggerEvent or PostEvent PowerScript functions discussed later.

### User-Defined System Events

The final type of event that you can create maps one of the existing Windows system events that is not currently handled (made available to you) by PowerBuilder to a new user event. The Windows system will trigger this type of event and then execute the code that you write for that event. You could also trigger this type of custom event in script code using the TriggerEvent or PostEvent PowerScript functions, but it is not often necessary. Use the prefix we_ for new events that map existing Windows events.

## Creating a Custom Event

The steps to create a custom event are:

- Select the object for which the event is to be defined. For windows and user objects, go to the Object painter. For window controls, open the Script editor in any of the control's events or select the object in the Window painter.

- Select **User Event** on the Declare menu. This will open the Events dialog box.
- Assign a name to the event.
- Assign a custom event ID to the event.
- Close the Events dialog box and write the script for the event.

Figure 6.5 shows the creation of a user event, ue_init. This example event is being created as an event for a window, w_main. Notice that the predefined PowerBuilder events for this window are listed in this dialog window. The event IDs for the predefined events are grayed out, so you cannot change them. All the User Event event IDs are darkened, so you can select and change or delete these events.

To create the custom event, you must first specify a name for the new event. Use the ue_ prefix for the name of a custom event. For this example, we named the event ue_init.

You must then assign an event ID to your new event. For the custom type of event, you must select one of the values reserved for custom user events. You will find these IDs in the Paste Event ID listbox. They range from pbm_custom01 to pbm_custom75. You should start with pbm_custom01 for the first user event you create and use successive custom IDs for the next events that you create. PowerBuilder uses these custom IDs to identify user-defined events internally. You can select any custom ID that has not already been assigned in the object.

After you name the event and assign the event ID, click on **OK**; this closes the dialog window. When you return to the Script editor, pull down the Select Event dropdown listbox and scroll to the very last entries. You will find that the ue_init event has been added to the events for the window. Next you would enter the code for the event. For this event, you would select **ue_init** from the Select Event dropdown listbox and then add then following code (remember that Windows will not trigger the custom event; you must do this in your script code. You can trigger this event by using the TriggerEvent function):

```
TriggerEvent('ue_init')
```

or the `PostEvent` function as:

```
PostEvent('ue_init')
```

From outside this window, you would have to qualify the window as:

```
w_main.TriggerEvent('ue_init')
```

## Creating a Parameterized Custom Event

The steps to create a parameterized custom event are:

- Select the object for which the event is to be defined. For windows and user objects, go to the Object painter. For window controls, open the Script editor in any of the control's events or select the object in the Window painter.
- Select the **User Event** option on the Declare menu. This will open the Events dialog box.
- Assign a name to the event.
- Do not assign an event ID; leave the event ID blank.
- Define the arguments (if any) and the return data type for the event.
- Close the Events dialog box and write the script for the event.

This example event is being created as an event for a listbox, `lb_1`. Notice that the predefined PowerBuilder events for this control are listed in this dialog box. The event IDs for the predefined events are grayed out so you cannot change them. All the User Event event IDs are darkened, so you can select and change or delete these events (Figure 6.6).

**224  Chapter 6**

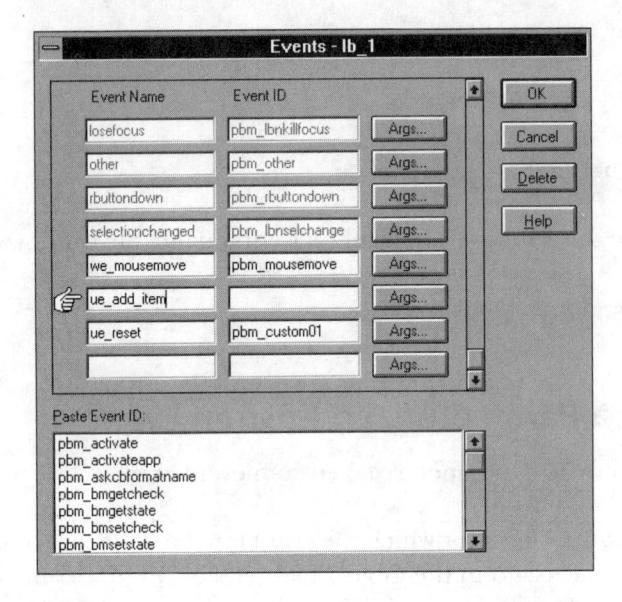

*Figure 6.6 Defining a parameterized custom user event.*

To create the parameterized custom event, you must first specify a name for the new event. Use the `ue_` prefix for the name of a custom event. For this example (in Figure 6.6), we named the event `ue_add_item`.

You do not assign an event ID to a parameterized event; leave the Event ID field blank. Click the **Args** command button to define arguments and the return data type for the event. This opens the Event Declaration window (Figure 6.7).

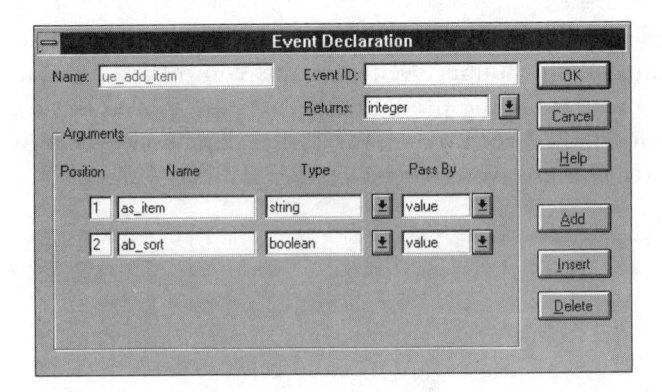

*Figure 6.7 Defining parameters.*

This is similar to the function declaration dialog window. You can define as many arguments as you need for the event. Just click the **Add** command button to add a new argument to the end of the list. Click on **Insert** to add a new argument at the current cursor position in the list. Click on **Delete** to remove the currently selected argument from the list. Check the **Returns** data type and click **OK** when you have finished.

This returns you to the Events dialog box; after you check the **Event Name**, click on **OK** to close the dialog window. When you return to the Script editor, pull down the Select Event dropdown listbox and scroll to the very last entries. You will find that the `ue_add_item` event has been added to the events for the listbox. Next, enter the code for the event. For this event, you would select **ue_add_item** from the Select Event dropdown listbox and then add the following code:

```
int i_rc
This.sorted = ab_sort
i_rc = This.AddItem(as_item)
return i_rc
```

The Paste Argument dropdown listbox will list the parameters for the event and allow you to paste them into your code in the editor. The editor's title bar will display the return data type for the event (*integer* in this example). Remember that Windows will not trigger custom events; you must do this in your script code. You can trigger this event by using the `Event` syntax as follows:

```
i_rc = lb_1.Event ue_add_item (This.text, True)
```

or the `PostEvent` function as:

```
lb_1.Post Event ue_add_item (This.text, True)
```

or:

```
lb_1.Event Post ue_add_item (This.text, True)
```

Notice that when you post the event, there is no return code (because the event does not occur inline).

## Mapping a Windows Event

The second type of user event is used to access existing events in the Windows system that have not been made available in a PowerBuilder event. These events will be triggered by Windows and not programmatically as the custom user events discussed in the previous section.

The steps to map a Windows event are:

- Select the object for which the event is to be defined. For windows and user objects, go to the Object painter. For window controls, open the Script editor in any of the control's events or select the object in the Window painter.
- Open the Events dialog box. You will find the **User Event** option on the Declare menu.
- Assign a name to the event.
- Enter the Event ID. You can locate the event ID for the desired event in the Paste Event ID listbox.
- Close the Events dialog box and write the script for the event.

Figure 6.8 shows an example of this type of event, where we map an existing Windows event. In this case, we are mapping the `pbm_mousemove` event as `we_mousemove` (for this example, it is for `listbox lb_1`). This event will be triggered by the Windows system when the mouse pointer is moved over the object (listbox) that has this event.

First you must name the event. We use the `we_` prefix for the name of this type of event. For this example (in Figure 6.8) we named the event `we_mousemove`. You must then locate the Windows event ID for the existing event. You will find these IDs in the Paste Event ID listbox. You can find more information on these events in the Windows Software Development Kit. If you do not find an event that you are expecting to see in this list, you may be able to trap it in the object's Other event (discussed in the next section).

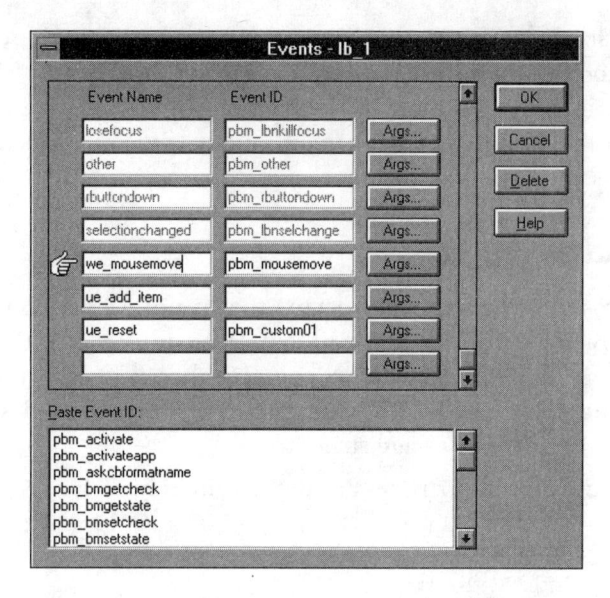

*Figure 6.8 Mapping the Windows* wm_mousemove *event.*

After you name the event and assign the event ID, click on the **OK** command button. This closes the dialog window. When you return to the Script editor, pull down the Select Event dropdown listbox and scroll to the very last entries. You will find that the we_mousemove event has been added to the events for the object. Next, you would enter the code for the event.

This event will be triggered by the Windows system. You do not usually trigger this event by using the TriggerEvent function, but you could trigger it for testing as follows:

```
lb_1.TriggerEvent('we_mousemove')
```

## The Other Event

PowerBuilder doesn't trap every Microsoft Windows event that is available. The events for each object that are not mapped to PowerBuilder events (listed in the Paste Event ID listbox in the previous examples) are routed to the

`Other` event for that object. If you want to access one of these events, you could place code in that event to identify the event that you are interested in trapping. The information that you need to identify the event is located in the PowerBuilder message object. This technique has been replaced by the user-defined events and is not recommended in most cases.

## The Message Object

When a Microsoft Windows event occurs that is not a PowerBuilder-defined event, PowerBuilder populates the global Message object with information about the event. The Message object contains the event information for MS Windows events. The first four attributes correspond to the first four attributes of the MS Windows message structure.

The Message object attributes are defined in Table 6.2.

*Table 6.2* *Message Object Attributes*

| ATTRIBUTE | DATA TYPE | USE |
| --- | --- | --- |
| `Handle` | Unsigned Integer | The event handle. |
| `Number` | Unsigned Integer | Windows event ID. |
| `WordParm` | Unsigned Integer | Event word parameter (from Windows). |
| `LongParm` | Long | Event long parameter (from Windows). |
| `Processed` | Boolean | Set this to **True** in the Other event if you processed the event, otherwise it is sent on the `DefWindowProc`. |
| `ReturnValue` | Long | If you process the event, this is the return value you send to the Windows system. |
| `StringParm` | String | A string. |
| `DoubleParm` | Double | A numeric. |
| `PowerObjectParm` | PowerObject | Any PowerBuilder object. |

**WARNING:** The major drawback to using the `Other` event is that performance can be impacted significantly. This is because a number of events will trigger the `Other` event, and the `IF` statement must be executed for each event. This can result in significant overhead for trapping the event in which you are interested. So only use this technique when absolutely necessary.

## INITIATING FUNCTIONS AND EVENTS

There are several techniques for calling function and events. First, we'll look at a few examples of the simple format. To call a function, you can use the following:

```
i_rc = fw_hello('this is a test')
i_rc = w_main.fw_hello('another test')
```

To call an event:

```
i_rc = lb_1.TriggerEvent('ue_reset')
i_rc = w_main.lb_1.TriggerEvent('ue_reset')
```

or

```
lb_1.PostEvent('ue_reset')
w_main.lb_1.PostEvent('ue_reset')
```

You can use the message object to send and receive values to events. In the next example, a structure is placed in the message object immediately before triggering the `'ue_init'` event. The `message.stringparm` returns a string from the event.

```
message.PowerObjectParm = str_data // where str_data is a structure
i_rc = lb_1.TriggerEvent('ue_init')
s_return_string = message.stringparm
```

## Chapter 6

Inside the `lb_1 ue_init` event, we could see the following code:

```
str_init_data str_init
str_init = message.PowerObjectParm
// at this point the event can use the structure
message.stringparm = str_init.s_name
return
```

However, the new parameterized user events are the preferred technique.

The syntax for the other format for calling object functions and events is:

```
Object-Name.[type]   [Call-Type] [When] Function-Name (arg1, arg2, ...)
```

where:

- `Object-Name` is the label for the object that owns the function or event.
- `type` is what is being called; this can be:
- `FUNCTION` (the default)
- `EVENT`
- `Call-Type` tells PowerBuilder when to bind the call to the function (or event); the options are:
    - `STATIC` (the default) binds the call when the code is compiled
    - `DYNAMIC` only binds at run time
- `When` determines the timing of the call:
    - `TRIGGER` (the default) executes the call immediately
    - `POST` puts the call on the objects event queue and then continues code execution in the current script
- `Function-Name` is the name of the event or function you are calling

The `type`, `Call-Type`, and `When` keywords can occur in any order (after the dot). It is also possible to cascade calls using dot notation as long as each call returns the correct data type for the next function. A few examples follow:

```
i_rc = lb_1.Event ue_add_item(This.text, True)
lb_1.Post Event ue_add_item('delayed', False)
lb_1.Post fw_hello('sending a posted function call')
lb_1.Dynamic Event ue_some_event('hope you find it', 'at run-time')
```

## EVENTS2 EXAMPLE PROGRAM

The Events2 example demonstrates each type of user-defined event and the use of the `PostEvent` and `TriggerEvent` functions. Run the Events2 program. The `w_main` `Open` event will trigger the initial message box, which will display before the `w_main` window is visible. The `w_main` `Open` event also posts an event to display the same message box, but this time (because it is posted to occur after the `Open` event), the `w_main` window will display first with the message box over it. The window function `fw_hello` also displays its message box before the `w_main` is visible.

When the window opens, enter text in the single-line edit field and hit the **Enter** key. This will add a new item to the listbox using a user-defined event and its position in the listbox will display on the single-line edit. If you drag an item from the listbox and drop it on the single-line edit, the listbox will remove the item from the list.

## EVENTS2—STEP-BY-STEP

Now you can create your own version of Events2. Just follow the next set of instructions.

## Create the Application and Library

1. Start PowerBuilder (if necessary).
2. If you are not in the Application painter, click on the **Appl** icon on the PowerBar.
3. In the Application painter, select the **File|New** menu option.
4. In the Select New Application Library dialog box, set the directory to **C:\PB5\MCCLAN2** and enter the name **ZEVENTS2.PBL** for the library file name. Click on **OK**.
5. In the Save Application dialog box:
   a. In the Applications field, enter **Events2**.
   b. Tab to the Comments field, and enter **My Events2 version 1**.
   c. Be sure that the Application Library name is still **zevents2.pbl**, if not, select it.
   d. Click on **OK**.
6. PowerBuilder asks if you wish to generate an application template. Click on **No** in this dialog box, as in all the examples for this book (except one in the MDI chapter).

This returns you to the Application painter. You have created the Events2 application object and the zevents2 library.

## Create the Main Window

Click the **Window** icon on the PowerBar to open the Window painter. In the Select Window dialog box, click on the **New** button to create a new window. In the Window painter, double-click on the new window to open the Window Style dialog box (or select the **Edit|Properties** menu option).

In this dialog box, in the Title edit box enter **Events2** as the text. Then select **Main** from the Window Type dropdown listbox. This defines the type for the new window. The other options should match those in Figure 6.9. Set these changes by clicking the **Apply** button.

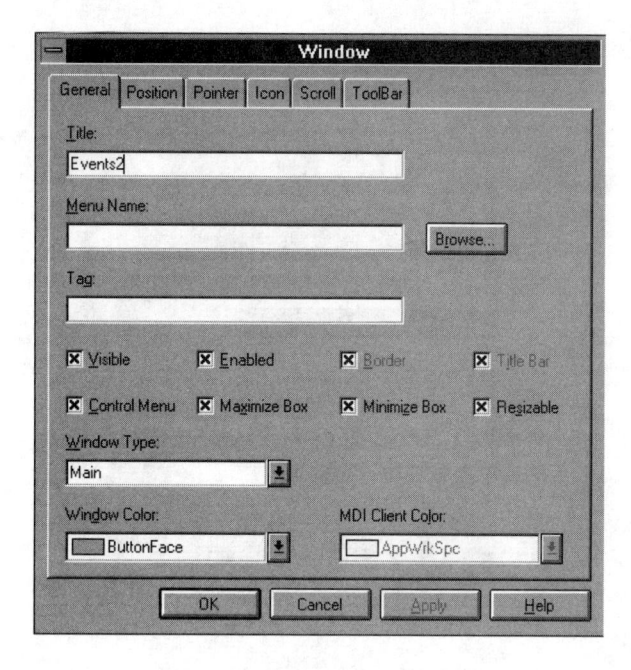

**Figure 6.9** *Defining the* w_main *style.*

Next, click the **Position** tab (in the Window Properties dialog box) to open the Window Position dialog box.

In this dialog box, set the position (and size) of the window, as shown in Figure 6.10. The position of a main window is relative to the display area of your monitor's screen. In this example, the position of the main window is set near the center of the screen. You can exactly center the screen by clicking the right mouse button on the window and selecting **Center Horizontally** and then **Center Vertically**.

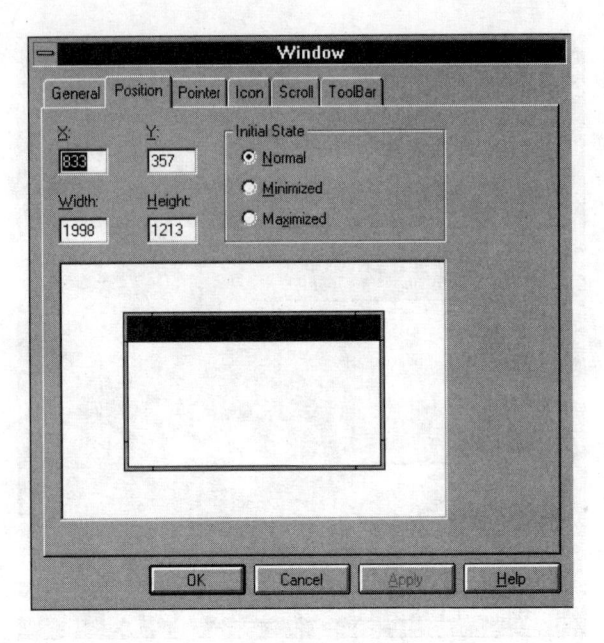

*Figure 6.10 The Window Position dialog box.*

Close the dialog box by clicking on **OK**. In the Window painter, select the **File|Save As** menu option. Check to be sure that the library is set to **ZEVENTS2.PBL** and then enter the name **w_main** and click the **OK** button.

## Add a Function to w_main

Go to the Window painter (if you're not already there). Now create the following function by selecting the **Declare|Window Functions** menu option and then clicking **New** in the Select Function dialog box. The function is named `fw_hello`, has one argument, and returns an integer (1):

| | |
|---|---|
| Function: | `fw_hello` |
| Access: | `public` |
| Returns: | `Integer` |
| Arguments: | `as_text string by value` |

```
MessageBox('fw_hello window-level function', as_text)
return 1
```

Close the window function editor. After you have created this function, it is available in the Object Browser for pasting into your code. To do so, first position the cursor at the point in your script where you wish to paste the code. Next, open the Object Browser, click on the **Window** tab, and click on **w_main** (in the left listbox). Double-click on **Functions** in the right listbox, click on **fw_hello**, and then click the **Paste** button. This will paste the function declaration into your code. You could do this in the `w_main` open script, described next.

## Add Code to the Application Open Event

Go to the Application painter [if you did not close it earlier, you can select it under the Window menu (**Application-events2**)]. To enter the new code, click the **Script** icon on the Application painter PainterBar. This opens the Script painter. The Script editor should display *Script-open for zevents2* on the title bar; if not, pull down the SelectEvent dropdown menu and select **Open**.

Enter the following single line of code:

```
open(w_main)
```

You have just coded one of the standard system events for the Application object. The Application `Open` event is triggered as soon as the application is started. The Application `Open` event has one argument, a command line, and a string. This contains the command line that was sent to the application when it was started. When you are finished in the editor, click the **Return** icon.

## Add a User Event to the w_main Window

Next, you will add a user event to the `w_main` window, so you must return to the Window painter. If the Window painter is still open, just select it from the Window menu (`Window-w_main`). Otherwise, click on the **Window** icon on the PowerBar to open the Window painter. In the Select window, select the **w_main** window and click **OK**.

Open the Script painter (use the **Edit|Script** menu option or the RMB popup menu). To add a new user event, select the **Declare|User Events** menu option. Figure 6.11 shows the declaration for the new event. In the Events dialog box, enter **ue_init** for the Event Name and then click in the Event ID column. Enter **pbm_custom01** for the Event ID. You can type this in or paste it from the Paste Event ID listbox at the bottom of the dialog box. This type of user event has predefined arguments and return value data type. Click on the **Args** button to display this information if you wish to view it. Close the Events dialog box. This new event can only be triggered programmatically. You can use the `TriggerEvent` or `PostEvent` functions to initiate it. In this example, we will use both functions to show the difference in the timing of each and the effect on the display of `w_main`.

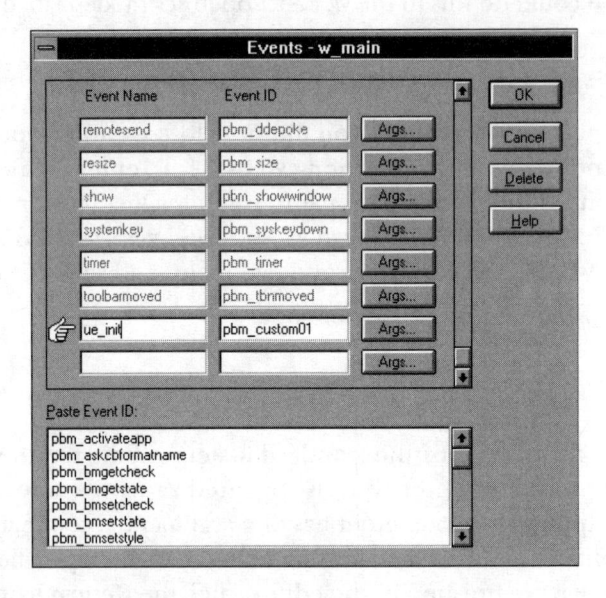

*Figure 6.11 The declaration for the new event.*

## Add Code to the w_main Open Event

You should have returned to the Script painter (in one of `w_main`'s events). The Script editor should display *Script-open for w_main* on the title bar; if not, pull down the SelectEvent dropdown menu and select **open**. Enter the following lines of code:

```
TriggerEvent('ue_init')
This.fw_hello("Triggered in w_main's Open event")
//Post Function fw_hello("Posted in w_main's Open event")
PostEvent('ue_init')
```

The first line of code will immediately send a message to the new `ue_init` event (as soon as the `Open` event begins for the `w_main` window). The second line of code will immediately call the `fw_hello` function. The last line of code will place the message on the `w_main` window's `ue_init` event queue. This event will occur only after the close of the current `Open` event. It is important to understand that the window actually will not be displayed (i.e., be visible) until all the code in the window `Open` event has been executed. (The commented line will also work; it will post a call to the `fw_function`, but in the beta version I am working with as I write this book, it will not work with the last line of code. You can uncomment it and comment out the last line to see the effect.)

## Add Code to the ue_init Event

In the PowerScript editor (assuming that we are still in the `w_main` window `Open` event), select the **ue_init** event from the bottom of the SelectEvent dropdown menu. Notice that the caption reads `Script - ue_init for w_main returns long`. This means that you are currently editing the `ue_init` in the `w_main` window and that the event returns a long value. If you open the Paste Argument dropdown list, you can see the two predefined arguments: the `unsignedlong wParam` and the `long lParam`. (If you do not see the Paste Argument dropdown menu, use the **Design|Options** menu option to open the Properties for Editor dialog box. Then choose the **Dropdowns** tab and drag the **Paste Argument** item from the Available Dropdowns listbox over to the Selected Dropdowns listbox. This will add it to the Script editor.) Add the following code:

```
MessageBox('ue_init event', 'This represents some processing that &
continues until you hit OK')
```

Close the editor. Now run the application. You will see that the message box (which represents any processing that would take place in the `Open` event) is displayed before the `w_main` window becomes visible. It is very important to understand that the `w_main` window will not display until all the code in the `w_main` `Open` event has completed execution. Next, the `fw_hello` function message box will appear. Close the message box, and the `w_main` window appears (the `Open` event has completed after posting the next event). The `ue_init` event fires again, this time as a result of the `PostEvent` call, and the `ue_init` message box appears again (but this time it is over the `w_main` window). So note this point; if you want to display the window as quickly as possible (which is generally the best procedure), don't place initialization code in the `Open` event.

Close the application (double-click on the w_main's control menu to close the window).

## Add Controls to the Window

Next, add the single-line edit and listbox controls to the window. If necessary, open the Window painter, click on the **Window** icon on the PowerBar, and then in the Select Window, select **w_main**.

In the Window painter, add the controls, as shown in Figure 6.12. The default names are `sle_1` and `lb_1`.

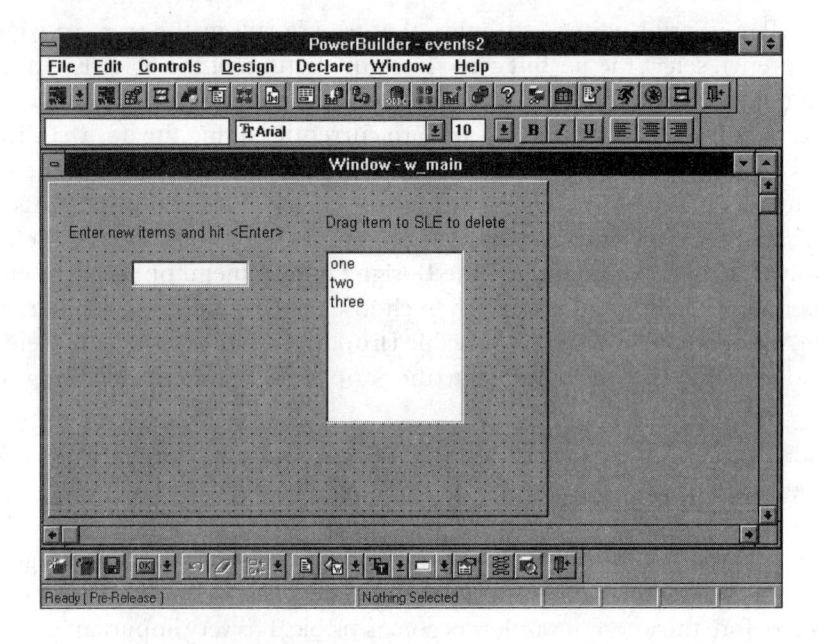

*Figure 6.12 Adding controls to the window.*

The w_main has a single-line edit control and a listbox. The single-line edit control will be used to add items to the listbox. It will also be used as the target for the drag-and-drop functionality in this window. The user can drag any item from the listbox and drop it on the single-line edit to delete the item

**Events, Functions, and User Events** 239

from the list. This requires adding code to two existing events and creating another user-defined event.

## Add a User Event to lb_1

Next, you will add a user event to the `lb_1` (listbox) in the `w_main` window, so you must work in the Window painter. Open the Window painter if necessary. In the window, right-click on the listbox to open the RMB popup menu. Select **script** from the popup menu. This will open the Script editor in an event for the listbox. To add a new user event, select the **Declare|User Events** menu option. Figure 6.13 shows the declaration for the new event, `ue_add_item`. Type **ue_add_item** for the Event Name and do not enter an Event ID. Leaving the Event ID blank signals the creation of a parameterized user event. Now you can define the event arguments and the return value data type. Click on the **Args** button, define the `Returns` data type as an integer, and create two arguments, as shown in Figure 6.7. The first argument, `as_item`, is a string that will be added to the listbox. The second argument, `ab_sort`, is a Boolean value that tells the listbox to sort the items alphabetically if this value is True. Close this dialog box, and close the Events dialog box.

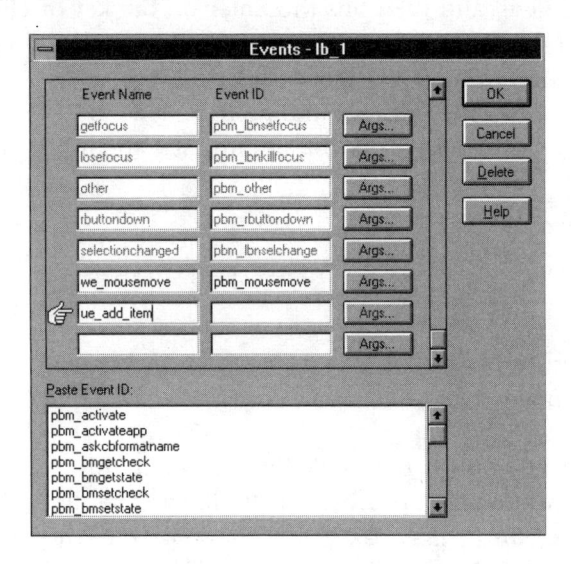

*Figure 6.13  The* `ue_add_item` *event.*

## Add Code to the ue_add_item Event

Next, add code to the `lb_1`'s `ue_add_item` event. In the Script editor for the `lb_1` listbox, select the **ue_add_item** event from the bottom of the SelectEvent dropdown menu. Enter the following code for that event:

```
int i_rc
This.sorted = ab_sort
i_rc = This.AddItem(as_item)
return i_rc
```

This function has added functionality to the listbox. This code will turn on (or off) the sorting and then add the item to the listbox. Now, close the editor.

## Add Code to the sle_1 Modified Event

Next, you will add code to the single-line edit control's Modified event. This event is a standard system event, and it will be triggered when the user types in the single-line edit and then hits the **Enter** or **Tab** key or clicks the mouse in another field. In the Window painter, right-click on the single-line edit to open the RMB popup menu. Select **script** from the popup menu. This will open the Script editor for an event in the single-line edit. Select the **Modified** event from the Select Event dropdown menu. Add the following code:

```
int i_rc, i_len
i_rc = lb_1.Event ue_add_item ( This.text, True)
This.text = string(i_rc)
i_len = len(This.text)
sle_1.selecttext ( 1, i_len)
```

When you make an entry in the single-line edit field, this code will trigger the `ue_add_item` event in the `lb_1` list box. It will pass the string that is currently in the single-line edit (`This.text`). It will also pass a True value for the second argument to sort the items in the listbox. The return value is converted to a string (from an integer) and displayed in the `sle_1` field.

Close the editor, run the application, and when the `w_main` window appears, type some items into the single-line editor and watch the results. If the items do not appear in the listbox, carefully check the code in each event.

## Add Another User Event to lb_1

Next, you will add another user event to the `lb_1` (listbox) in the `w_main` window. This event implements drag-and-drop functionality for the listbox. Open the Window painter if necessary. In the window, right-click on the listbox to open the RMB popup menu. Select **script** from the popup menu. This will open the Script editor in an event for the listbox. To add a new user event, select the **Declare|User Events** menu option. Now declare the new event, we_mousemove. Type **we_mousemove** for the Event Name, and then enter the Event ID, **pbm_mousemove** (you can select this from the Paste Event ID listbox). This creates a new user event, in which you are mapping a Windows event (`mousemouse`). Click the **Args** button to view the arguments and the returns data type. These are predefined by the system and cannot be changed. Close this dialog box, and close the Event dialog box. The name prefix is we_ (instead of ue_) to show that this is mapping a Windows event (we_) (see Figure 6.8).

## Add Code to the lb_1 we_mousemove Event

Next, add code to the `lb_1`'s `we_mousemove` event. In the Script editor for the `lb_1` listbox, select the **we_mousemove** event from the SelectEvent dropdown list (at the bottom). Enter the following code for that event:

```
IF flags = 1 THEN
    This.Drag(begin!)
END IF
```

This event will be triggered repeatedly, as the mouse moves the pointer across the listbox. We are only interested in this action when the user presses the left mouse button to signal the beginning of a drag operation. The flags variable is assigned a value by the Windows system. When the left mouse button is pressed, the flags will be equal to 1. In that case, we turn on the drag mode for w_main using the `Drag` function.

## Add Code to the sle_1 DragDrop Event

Next, you will add code to the single-line edit control's `DragDrop` event. This event is a standard system event, and it will be triggered when the user drops an item on the single-line edit (when the window is in drag mode):

```
string s_text
int i_item
listbox lb_x
IF TypeOf(source) = ListBox! THEN
    lb_x = source
    s_text = lb_x.SelectedItem()
    lb_x.Drag(cancel!)
    i_item = lb_x.finditem ( s_text, 0 )
    IF i_item > 0 THEN
        lb_x.deleteitem ( i_item )
    END IF
END IF
```

This code uses the `TypeOf` function to determine the type of drag-and-drop source variable. That (source) is the only argument passed to this event. The source variable has the data type `dragobject`. All objects that can be the source for the drag-and-drop functionality are descendants of `dragobject` (see the chapter on inheritance for more information). We use the `TypeOf` function to see if the listbox was the source of the drag. If it was, we assign the source to a local variable `lb_x` (a listbox variable). (This is somewhat equivalent to "casting" in other languages, such as C.) After this assignment, `lb_x` is an alias for `lb_1`. The code ends the drag mode for the window with the `Drag(cancel!)` statement. We do not use `Drag(end!)` because it would trigger another `DragDrop` event and cause a recursive loop. Next, the code uses the `finditem` function to locate the index for the item. The `deleteitem` function takes the index to remove the item from the listbox.

That's everything. Now, run the application.

## SUMMARY

In this chapter, you used each type of event. You coded for predefined system events. You created a user-defined system event, which maps existing Window events. You also created a custom user-defined event that used the `pbm_customXX` Event ID and the predefined arguments. You also created a parameterized custom event that was not mapped to any Event ID for which you defined the arguments and return data type. You also wrote an object-level function (`wf_hello`). You triggered and posted calls to events and functions.

**CHAPTER 7**

# Embedded SQL

PowerScript allows the direct embedding of SQL statements for database access. This chapter covers the use of embedded SQL in your PowerScript code, explains the use of transaction objects, which are required for the database interface, and explains how to set up profile files. This chapter presents a complete example of a database application, SQLApp, which shows how to add database access to your applications.

To follow the examples in this chapter, you must have installed the Sybase SQL Anywhere database manager. You must also complete the installation steps for the example application, as described in Appendix B.

## SQL STATEMENTS

You can embed SQL statements directly into your PowerScript code. There are several differences between the format of SQL statements and PowerScript statements.

A SQL statement always requires a semicolon (;) as a delimiter (at the end of each statement). If you need to continue a SQL statement across multiple lines, do not use the PowerScript continuation symbol (the ampersand, &). The omission of the semicolon is enough to signal the continuation of the SQL statement:

```
SELECT count(*) INTO :i_count FROM images;
```

or

```
SELECT count(*) INTO :i_count
 FROM images;
```

Note that any reference you make (within embedded SQL statements) to a PowerBuilder host variable (either a script variable or an object attribute) requires that you mark the identifier by adding a colon (:) to the beginning of the identifier. This is a standard SQL requirement for the embedded form of SQL. In the previous example, :i_count is required in the SQL statement to make the reference to the script variable i_count. Always place the colon immediately before the identifier. Two examples follow:

```
int i_invoice_no
string s_company
int i_company_id
i_invoice_no = 123
SELECT company, id INTO :s_company, :i_company_id
WHERE invno = :i_invoice_no; FROM company
```

```
DoSomething(s_company)
//////////////////////////////////////
string s_image, s_type, s_path
int i_version
string s_image_name = 'pic123'
SELECT image, type, version, path
    INTO :s_image, :s_type, :i_version, :s_path FROM images
    WHERE image = :s_image_name AND version = 1;
```

You can also select values directly into PowerBuilder controls. In the following example. the query places the result in a single-line edit control:

```
SELECT company INTO :sle_1.text FROM company WHERE invno =
:i_invoice_no;
```

The next example selects an integer directly into a single-line edit control. PowerBuilder converts the integer into a string automatically:

```
SELECT Id INTO :sle_1.text FROM company WHERE company = 'Best';
```

Cursor operations are also supported in embedded SQL:

```
DECLARE cursor1 CURSOR FOR
    SELECT company, id FROM company;
OPEN cursor1;
DO
    FETCH cursor1 INTO :s_company, :i_company_id;
LOOP WHILE SQLCA.SQLCode = 0  //rc = 100 at end
CLOSE cursor1;
```

Notice the placement of the semicolons in this example. The loop will continue to execute as long as the Fetch is successful (the SQLCode = 0).

## Embedded SQL Statements

PowerBuilder supports the following SQL statements in embedded SQL.

### Noncursor SQL Operations

CONNECT, SELECT, INSERT, UPDATE, DELETE, COMMIT, ROLLBACK, DISCONNECT

### Cursor Operations

DECLARE, OPEN, FETCH, UPDATE WHERE CURRENT OF, DELETE WHERE CURRENT OF, CLOSE

### Procedure Operations

DECLARE, EXECUTE, FETCH, CLOSE

# CREATING SQL STATEMENTS

PowerBuilder provides utilities to assist in the creation of your SQL statements. These utilities provide a graphical method for selecting the tables and columns in which you are interested. Each utility works interactively with the database and requires that you are connected to the target database. Each utility is available from within the PowerScript painter for inserting code at the current cursor position. For the following discussion, we assume that you are in the PowerScript painter.

## Paste SQL

If you select the **Edit|Paste SQL** menu option or click on the **Paste SQL** icon on the PainterBar, you will open the SQL Statement Type dialog box (Figure 7.1). The SQL Statement Type dialog box displays three types of SQL statements: cursor, noncursor, and procedure.

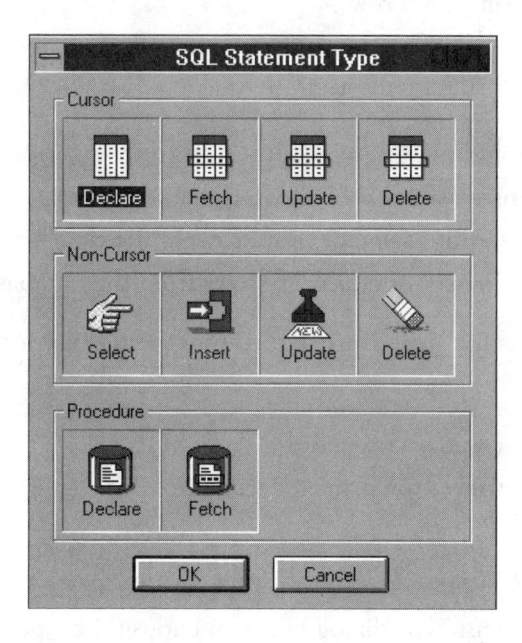

*Figure 7.1  SQL Statement Type dialog box.*

## The SQL Statement Type Dialog Box

This dialog box displays the options for creating SQL statements in three groups. The top row presents the options for creating statements that use a cursor, the second row presents the noncursor version of SQL statements, and the third row lists options that are specific to the DBMS, such as stored procedures.

The cursor statements include:

- **Declare**—creates and names a cursor
- **Fetch**—retrieves one row from the database
- **Update**—modifies a row
- **Delete**—removes a row

The noncursor statements are:

- **Select**—the singleton select, it returns only one row
- **Insert**—inserts a row into the database
- **Update**—modifies one or more rows in the database
- **Delete**—removes one or more rows from the database

The last section is for stored procedure statements (if your DBMS supports procedures).

- **Declare**—creates a procedure
- **Fetch**—retrieves the procedure result

## *SQL Statement Type*

In the SQL Statement Type dialog box, you choose the type of SQL statement that you want to create simply by double-clicking on one of the icons. This opens another tool (which varies according to the statement type) that assists you in creating the statement, and when you have finished, it pastes the SQL statement into your code.

# Cursor SQL Statements

## Declare Cursor

Figure 7.2 shows the Declare Cursor painter that opens after double-clicking on the **Declare Cursor** icon.

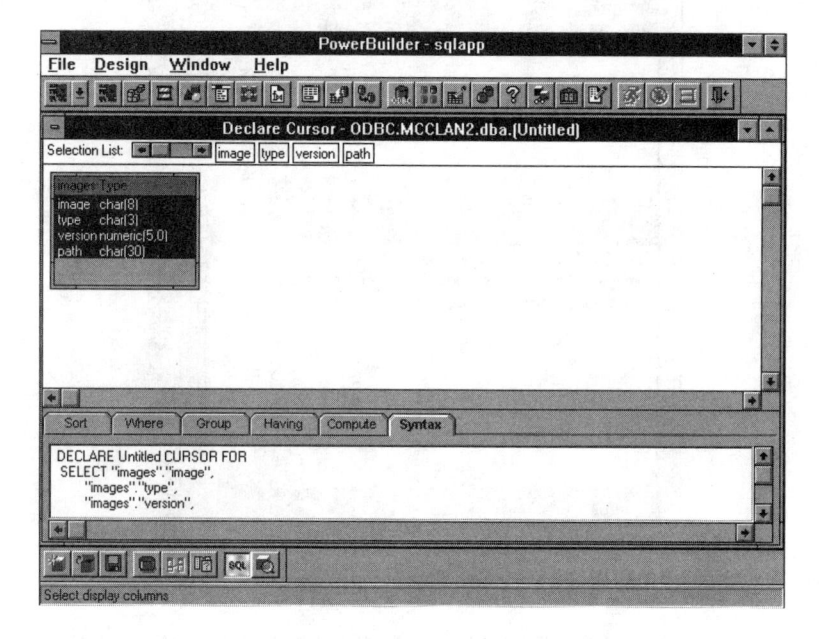

*Figure 7.2  Declaring a cursor.*

This is essentially the same as the Query painter described in the DataWindow chapter. In this painter, you will open one or more tables for the declare cursor statement. Next, you will add columns to the select clause and then specify the join condition (if there are two or more tables): where, group by, having, and order by clauses. These steps are covered in detail in the section on the Query painter.

## Fetch Cursor

Choose the **Fetch cursor** option from the SQL Statement Type dialog box and the Select Declared Cursor dialog box opens as shown in Figure 7.3.

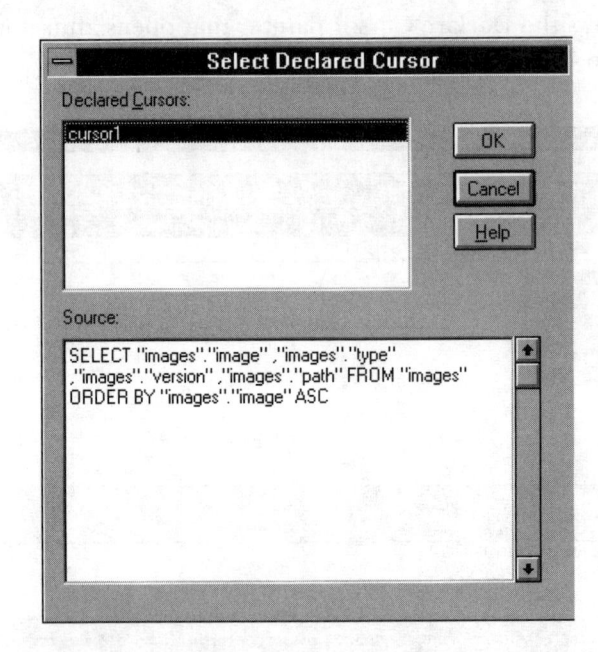

*Figure 7.3  The Select Declared Cursor dialog box.*

In this dialog box you must select a previously declared cursor from the list presented in the listbox. The Source edit box displays the source code for the cursor that is selected in the Declared Cursors listbox. Selecting a cursor opens the Into Variables dialog box shown in Figure 7.4.

The Into Variables dialog box displays the cursor source code at the bottom left of the window. Each item in the select list is presented in the Selected Column list in the same order in which they are referenced in the cursor source statement. You must assign a program variable to hold each select list item. The program variable can be a script variable or an object attribute. The Program Variable listbox assists you in locating the name of a variable (or attribute). You can paste the name of the variable into the Program Variable field by clicking on your selection in the Program Variable listbox. Notice that the listbox has already prepended a colon to the name of each item in the list.

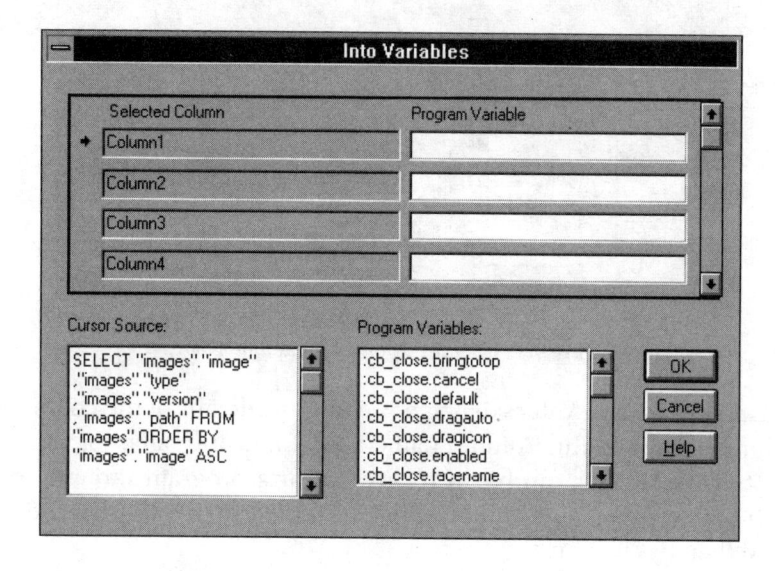

*Figure 7.4  Into Variables dialog box.*

## Update Cursor

Choose the **Update cursor** option from the SQL Statement Type dialog box and the Select Declared Cursor dialog box opens as shown in Figure 7.3. In this dialog box, you must select a previously declared cursor from the list presented in the listbox. The Source edit box displays the source code for the cursor that is selected in the Declared Cursors listbox. Selecting a cursor opens the Update Column Values dialog box shown in Figure 7.5.

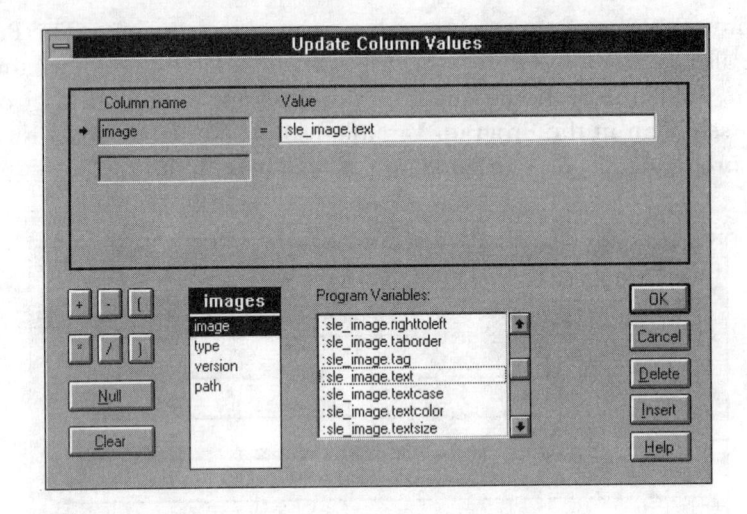

*Figure 7.5 Update Column Values dialog box.*

In the Update Column Values dialog box, you can add any of the columns from the column listbox to the Column name field. Enter the value for the column in the Value field. This can be an expression or a program variable. You can select the value from the Program variables listbox by scrolling to the correct item and then by clicking it.

## Delete Cursor

Choose the **Delete cursor** option from the SQL Statement Type dialog box and the Select Declared Cursor dialog box opens, as shown in Figure 7.3. After you select a previously declared cursor (from the list presented in the listbox), the delete statement is immediately pasted into your code. No other dialog box is associated with this option.

## Noncursor SQL Statements

### Select

Choose the **Noncursor Select** option from the SQL Statement Type dialog box and the Singleton Select dialog box opens, as shown in Figure 7.6. This is essentially the same as the Query painter (covered in detail in the DataWindow chapter). In this painter, you will open one or more tables for the select statement. Next you will specify the join condition (if there are two or more tables), add columns to the select clause, and then define the where, group by, having, and order by clauses.

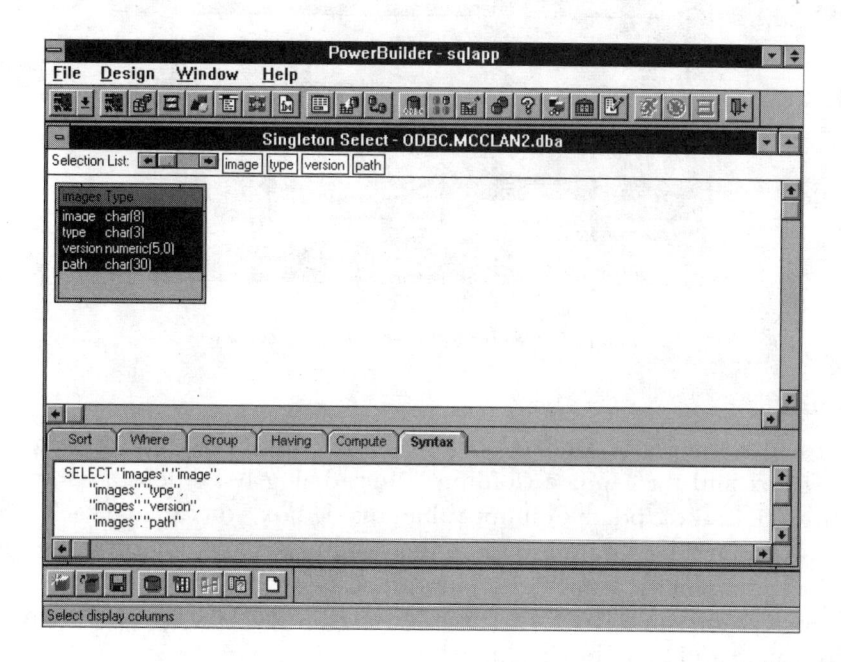

*Figure 7.6 Defining a singleton select statement.*

The result set for this SQL select statement can contain only a single row. This is called a *singleton select statement*, and the system generates an error if the statement execution results in more than a single row.

## Insert

Choose the **Noncursor** Insert option from the SQL Statement Type dialog box and the Insert Column Values dialog box opens, as shown in Figure 7.7. In this dialog box, you must assign a value to each of the columns in the Column Name list. Enter the value for the column in the Value field. This can be an expression or a program variable. Select the value from the Program variables listbox by scrolling to the correct item and clicking on it.

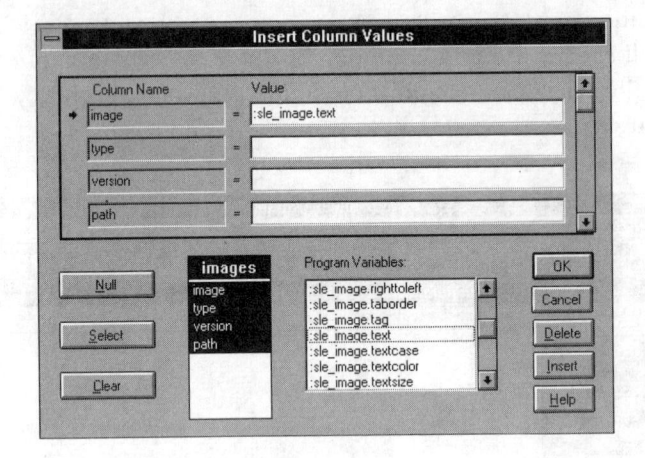

*Figure 7.7 Insert Column Values dialog box.*

## Update

Choose the **Noncursor Update** cursor option from the SQL Statement Type dialog box and the Update Column Values dialog box opens, as shown in Figure 7.8. In the Update Column Values dialog box, you can add each of the columns from the column listbox to the column name field. Enter the value for the column in the Value field. This can be an expression or a program variable. Select the value from the Program variables listbox by scrolling to the correct item and them by clicking on it.

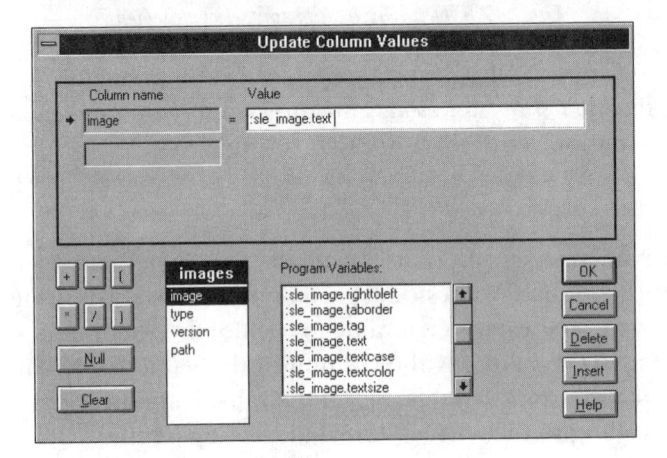

*Figure 7.8 Update Column Values dialog box.*

## Delete

Choose the **Noncursor Delete** option from the SQL Statement Type dialog box and the Where Criteria dialog box opens, as shown in Figure 7.9. In this dialog box, you specify the WHERE clause for the delete statement. This determines which rows are deleted from the selected table.

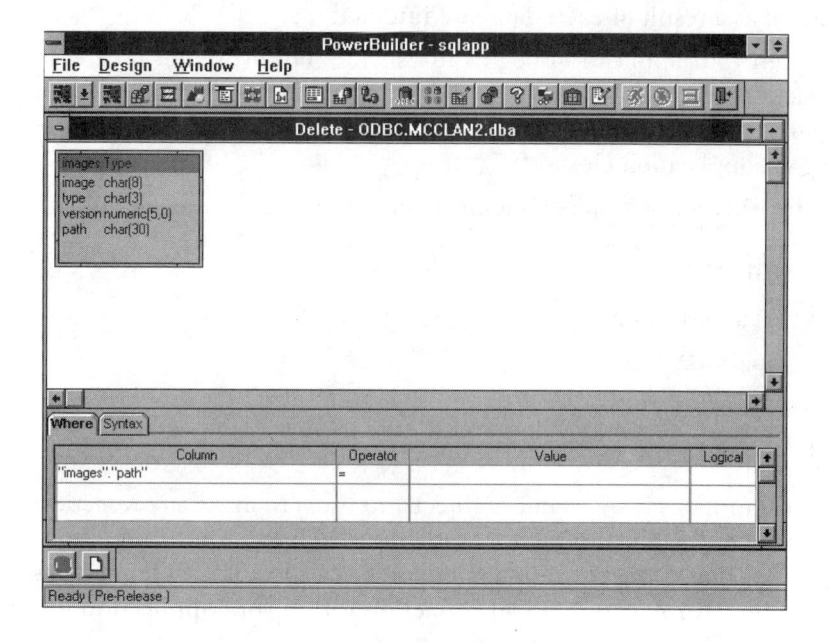

*Figure 7.9 Defining a WHERE clause.*

# QUERY PAINTER

The PowerBuilder Query painter is another tool that you can use to create SQL SELECT statements. This is available on the PowerBar and on the PowerPanel. The Query painter will create SQL SELECT statements that can be saved and used later. You will also use the Query painter when you define DataWindow objects. This will be described in detail in Chapter 11.

## Transaction Objects

A transaction object is required for all database access in PowerBuilder applications. The transaction object is like the SQL communications area in systems such as Oracle. It holds the information that is required to connect to the database, and it holds the return code and other information that is returned as a result of each database interaction.

When your application begins to execute, PowerBuilder creates a global transaction object called SQLCA. This transaction object usually serves as the primary transaction object for your application. It is destroyed automatically when the application closes.

The transaction object contains connection parameters including:

- DBMS
- Database name
- login ID
- Password
- SQLCode

You must initialize a transaction object and use it to make a connection to the database before any interaction with the database. The transaction object represents one connection to a database (to a specific DBMS, database, and user account). You can share a transaction within your application for access to the same DBMS, database, and account.

The attributes of a transaction object are described in Table 7.1.

*Table 7.1* Transaction Object Attributes

| Attribute | Data Type | Description |
| --- | --- | --- |
| DBMS | String | The vendor name (or ODBC); this is a name such as Oracle or Sybase |
| Database | String | Database name—the name of the database to which this transaction object will connect |
| UserId | String | Database login ID |
| DBParm | String | DBMS specific parameters |
| DBPass | String | Database password—the password associated with the User ID |
| Lock | String | Specifies the isolation level |
| LogId | String | The server login ID |
| LogPass | String | The server password—the password associated with the LogId |
| ServerName | String | The server name—the node name for the DBMS |
| AutoCommit | Boolean | Set this flag to **True** to perform automatic commits; if it is False (which is normal) you must explicitly issue commit (or rollback) statement |
| SQLCode | Long | Status code—0 if success, –1 failure; +100 means that there were no more rows available as the result of a SELECT |
| SQLNRows | Long | The number of rows affected by the last operation |
| SQLDBCode | Long | Vendor-specific error code; Oracle (and most systems) return 0 for successful operations |
| SQLErrText | String | Vendor-specific error message; this returns the text associated with SQLDBCode |
| SQLReturn | String | Vendor-specific, but used to return data or data return codes |

You can create other transaction objects in your script code as needed for your application. For example, you may access two different databases from within an application. Doing this requires you to create another transaction object for the second database. The syntax is:

```
transaction sqlca2
sqlca2 = create transaction
CONNECT using sqlca2;
//use sqlca2
COMMIT using sqlca2; // or ROLLBACK
DISCONNECT using sqlca2;
destroy sqlca2
```

## The SQLCode

The transaction object also reports the status after each SQL statement is executed. You must check the status by examining the SQLCode attribute value in the transaction object. The value will be 0 (zero) if the statement was executed successfully. It will be −1 if there was an error, and 100 if a command succeeded but did not alter the database (such as a fetch after the last row has already been retrieved).

If there is an error, you can gather additional information from the transaction object by examining the SQLDBCode and SQLErrText attributes. These attributes contain the DBMS-specific error code and error text. For example, if you executed the following fetch statement without first opening the cursor, an error would occur:

```
FETCH Cursor1 INTO :s_image, :s_type, :i_version, :s_path;
IF SQLCA.SQLCode < 0 THEN
     db_err_handler()
END IF
```

After this statement, the `SQLCA.SQLCode` has a value of –1. (For the Sybase SQL Anywhere database, this would result in a `SQLCA.DBCode` of 0, and the `SQLCA.DBErrText` would be 'Cursor is not open'.)

You must check the `SQLCode` after each embedded statement. You can also use the `SQLNRows` attribute to check the number of rows affected by the operation. For example, consider the following statement:

```
UPDATE images SET version = 1 WHERE version = 0
```

After the update, you can check the `sqlca.SQLNRows` attribute (assuming the `SQLCA.SQLCode` was 0). If the value of `SQLNRows` is 0, you will know that no rows were updated as a result of the `UPDATE` statement.

## THE APPLICATION INITIALIZATION FILE

Each application should have its own initialization file (sometimes called a *profile* file). This file contains application parameters such as database connection information, default value, and other information that is specific to an application but which you do not wish to hard-code into the application. This lets you change parameters at run time without having to recompile the program. In the initialization file, you can also store state information about the application. In this way, your application may "remember" the specific options that the user used in the previous session with the application. This can save time for the user, because they can avoid having to set up preferences every time they use the application.

By convention, the name given to the initialization file is the same as the application and the initialization file is given the extension INI. An initialization file is often called the *ini* file, the *init* file, or sometimes the *dot ini* file (.INI). The init file should be placed in the same directory as the application executable or in the Windows directory. For example, if you create the sample application FirstApp, you create an init file called **FIRSTAPP.INI**. You place this in the same directory as the firstapp library and executable, which is **C:\PB5\MCCLAN2**.

The initialization file is an ASCII text file and is in the same format as other Window's INI files. The file consists of a number of sections and key entries. Each section is labeled with a statement of the form [Section label]; the brackets signify a section label. Each section contains a number of entries that are lines of text with a key label, an equal sign, and a value such as `dbms=ODBC`. Each entry is in the context of a section. Sections can be in any order; the order has no significance. The same is true of key entries in each section. Key names are unique within each section. For example:

```
IMAGEDB.INI
[sqlca]
dbms=ODBC
database=mcclan2
userid=dba
dbpass=sql
logid=
logpass=
servername=
DbParm=ConnectString='DSN=mcclan2;UID=dba;PWD=sql'
;this is a comment
[application]
firsttime=no
dbms=sqlca
```

In this example, there are two sections, `[sqlca]` and `[application]`. The key entries are not ordered in any specific order within the section. The section tile and key names are case insensitive. The values, though, may be case sensitive depending on how the values are used. Comments can be added by beginning the line with a semicolon. This causes all text on that (single) line to be ignored.

You can use the PowerBuilder functions for reading and writing to the initialization file. All access is done by using a section label and a key name. The `ProfileString` function returns a string value (the key value) from a call where you have specified the fully qualified file name, a section label, and the key name within the section. You can also specify an option default value that will be returned if the entry cannot be found.

```
returned_string = &
ProfileString(file_path,section_label,key_name,default_value)
```

The `ProfileInt` call is similar to the `ProfileSting` function, except that it returns the key value as an integer:

```
returned_integer = &
ProfileInt(file_path,section_label,key_name,default_value)
```

You can write to the ini file with the SetProfileString function:

```
returned_code = &
SetProfileString(file_path,section_label,key_name,value)
```

An Application Open event could contain the following code:

```
s_text = ProfileString(s_init_file,"application",&
"firsttime","error")
IF s_text = 'error' THEN
     MessageBox ("error", "init file not found")
     HALT CLOSE
END IF
IF Upper(s_text) = "YES" THEN
     HALT // set up the parameters
ELSE
     sqlca.DBMS        = ProfileString(s_init_file,"sqlca", &
"dbms","")
     sqlca.database    = ProfileString(s_init_file,"sqlca", &
"database","")
     sqlca.userid      = ProfileString(s_init_file,"sqlca", &
"userid","")
     sqlca.dbpass      = ProfileString(s_init_file,"sqlca", &
```

```
"dbpass","")
    sqlca.logid      = ProfileString(s_init_file,"sqlca", &
"logid","")
    sqlca.logpass    = ProfileString(s_init_file,"sqlca", &
"logpass","")
    sqlca.servername = ProfileString(s_init_file,"sqlca", &
"servername","")
    sqlca.dbparm     = ProfileString(s_init_file,"sqlca", &
"dbparm","")
END IF
CONNECT USING SQLCA;
if sqlca.sqlcode <> 0 then
    MessageBox ("Cannot Connect to Database!", &
sqlca.sqlerrtext)
    fw_db_status ( -1,-1, "no database")
    return  // or halt close
end if
fw_db_status ( 0,0, "DB Mcclan2")
```

## EXAMPLE: SQLAPP

SQLApp is an application that demonstrates the basic database functionality provided by embedded SQL. This application will allow you to retrieve, insert, update, and delete rows with the image table.

### Running SQLApp

Before you build your version of this application, run the sample application from the PowerBuilder environment. To do this, launch PowerBuilder (if necessary) and go to the Application painter (click on the **Appl** icon on the PowerBar). Select the **Open** icon from the Application painter PainterBar. In the Select Application Library dialog box select **C:\PB5\MCCLAN2** in the directories listbox. Then select the **SQLAPP.PBL** library in the File Name listbox and click the **OK** button. This opens the Select Application dialog box and should

# Embedded SQL 265

display "SQLAPP" in the Applications field. Select **SQLApp** and click on **OK** to return to the Application painter.

In the Application painter, check that the window caption is "Application-sqlapp." Click on the **Run** icon (on the PowerBar or the PowerPanel) to run the application. When the application runs, you will see the main window displayed on the screen (as shown in Figure 7.10)

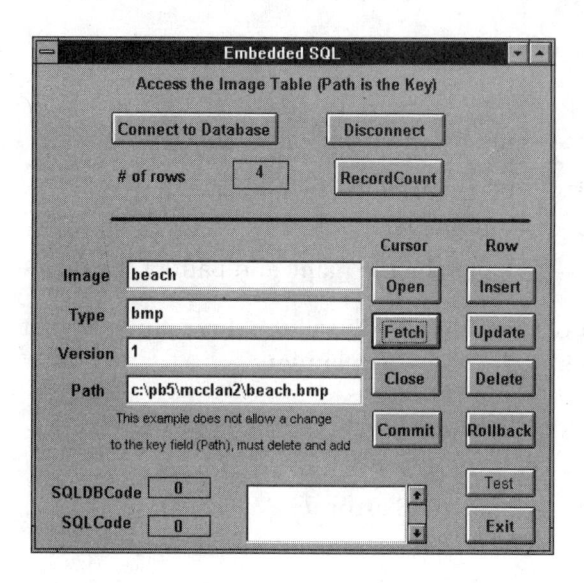

**Figure 7.10** *The SQLApp application.*

On this window, you can click a number of buttons. They are:

cb_connect—establishes a new connection to the database

cb_disconnect—closes the database connection

cb_count—returns the number of rows in the IMAGES table

cb_open—opens the Cursor, executing a SELECT statement that retrieves all rows in the IMAGES table

cb_fetch—steps to the next row in the cursor

cb_close—closes the cursor

cb_insert—inserts a new row into the IMAGES table

cb_update—applies changes to the current row in the IMAGES table `cb_delete`—deletes the current row in the IMAGES table

`cb_commit`—ends the current transaction, lock in all the changes to the database

`cb_rollback`—ends the current transaction, undo the changes that have been made to the `database`.

`cb_exit`—Closes the SQLApp application

Four single-line edit controls are used to input and/or display row data for the IMAGES table:

`sle_image`—contains the name of the image

`sle_type`—stores the type of image

`sle_version`—an integer

`sle_path`—contains the file name and path of the image

At the bottom of the window, you will see three controls that will display the status code after each database operation:

`st_dbcode`—the DBMS code

`st_sqlcode`—the SQL code

`mle_dbtext`—the DBMS error text

## Using SQLApp

Run the application.

> **NOTE** If the application cannot find the **IMAGEDB.INI** file, it is probably because it is not in the current working directory. To set the current directory back to the examples directory (MCCLAN2), just reopen the application in the application painter.

When the window is displayed, click on the **Connect to Database** command button. This should connect the application to the example database. Click the **RecordCount** button to display the number of rows in the IMAGES table.

## Cursor Operations

Click on the **Open** cursor command button. This executes the following query:

```
SELECT image, type, version, path FROM images ORDER BY image;
```

Next, you can click on the **Fetch** button to step through the result set. Notice that the set is ordered by image name. When you reach the end of the set, the SQLCode will return +100. Click the **Close cursor** command button. You can reopen the cursor by clicking the **Open cursor** command button.

## Insert Row

Click on the **Close cursor** command button and then the **Open cursor** command button to clear the single-line edit controls. Path is the primary key for the IMAGES table, so the path that you enter must not be already in the table. Now enter the following:

```
sle_image - asdf
sle_type - bmp
sle_version - 1
sle_path - asdf.bmp
```

Next, click on the **Insert row** button. Check the SQLCode, it should be 0. Click the **RecordCount** button, and the count should be one higher than before. You can click the **Commit** command button to end the transaction and lock in the changes to the database, or you can click the **Rollback** command button to end the transaction and undo any changes (the new record would be removed).

## Update Row

Click on the **Close cursor** command button and then click the **Open cursor** command button to open the cursor. Click the **Fetch** button, and then make some modifications to the **Image**, **Type**, and/or **Version** fields (remember you cannot alter a primary key field, so don't change the Path). Next, click on the **Update row** button. Check the SQLCode; it should be 0.

### Delete Row

Click on the **Close cursor** command button and then click the **Open cursor** command button to open the cursor. Click the **Fetch** button to locate the asdf record that we added previously. Click the **Delete row** button. Close the cursor. Reopen the cursor and step through the rows; the asdf record will be missing. You can now commit or rollback that deletion.

### Disconnect

Click on the **Disconnect** command button to close the connection.

## SQLApp—Step-by-Step

Now you can create your own version of SQLApp. Just follow the next set of instructions.

### Create the Application and Library

1. Start PowerBuilder (if necessary).
2. If you are not in the Application painter, click on the **Appl** icon on the PowerBar.
3. In the Application painter, select the **File|New** menu option.
4. In the Select New Application Library dialog box, set the directory to **C:\PB5\MCCLAN2** and enter the name `ZSQLAPP.PBL` for the library file name. Click on **OK**.
5. In the Save Application dialog box:
   a. In the Applications: field enter SQLApp.
   b. Tab to the comments field and enter `My SQLApp version 1`.
   c. Be sure that the Application Library name is still **zsqlapp.pbl**, if not, select it.
   d. Click on **OK**.
6. PowerBuilder asks if you wish to generate an application template. Click on **No** in this dialog box, as in all the examples for this book (except one in the MDI chapter).

This returns you to the Application painter. You have created the SQLApp application object and the `zsqlapp` library.

## Create the Main Window

Click on the **Window** icon on the PowerBar to open the Window painter. In the Select Window dialog box, click on the **New** button to create a new window. In the Window painter, double-click on the new window to open the Window Style dialog box (or select the **Edit|Properties** menu option).

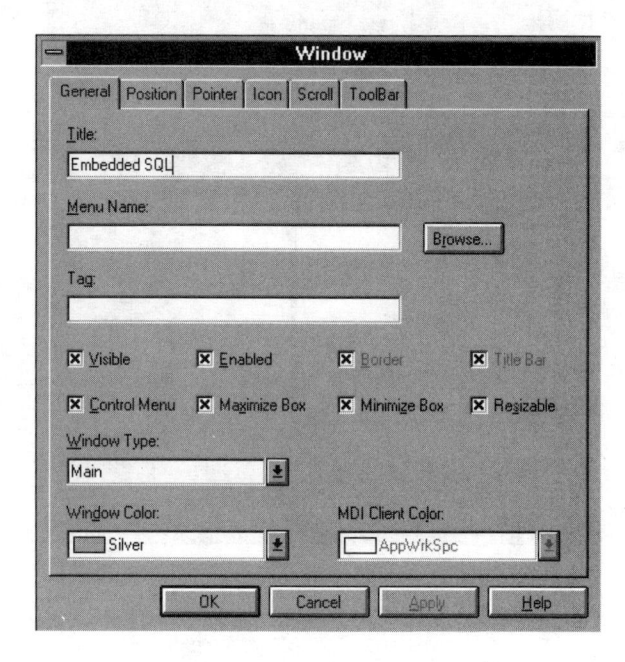

*Figure 7.11 Defining the window style.*

In this dialog box, in the Title editbox enter `Embedded SQL` as the text. Then select **Main** from the Window Type dropdown listbox. This defines the type for the new window. The other options should match those in Figure 7.11. Set these changes by clicking the **Apply** button.

Next, click the **Position** tab (in the Window Properties dialog box) to open the Window Position dialog box.

In this dialog box, set the position (and size) of the window, as shown in Figure 7.12. The position of a Main window is relative to the display area of your monitor's screen. In this example, the position of the main window is set to the upper left of the screen.

Close the dialog box by clicking on **OK**. In the Window painter, select the **File|Save As** menu option. Check to be sure that the library is set to **ZSQLAPP.PBL**, and then enter the name w_embedded_sql and click the **OK** button. Now, close the Window painter.

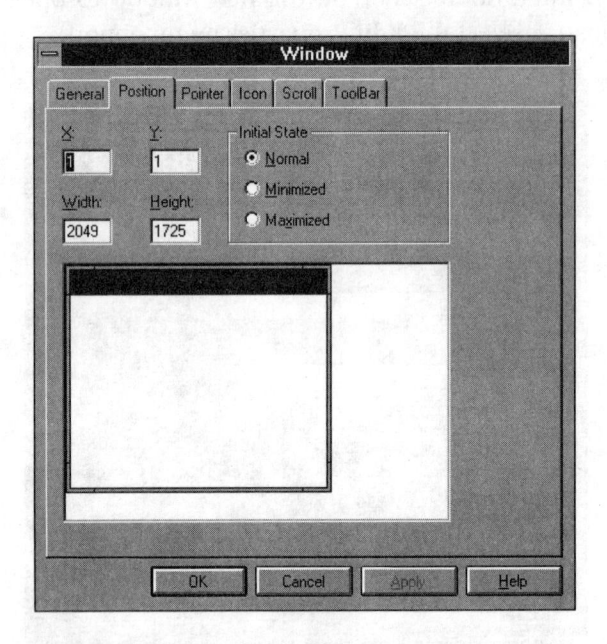

*Figure 7.12  The Window Position dialog box.*

## Add Code to the Application Open Event

Go to the Application painter. To enter the new code, click the **Script** icon on the Application PainterBar. This opens the Script painter. The Script editor should display "Script-open for sqlapp" on the title bar; if not, pull down the SelectEvent dropdown menu and select **Open**. Edit the code until it matches the following exactly:

```
string s_text
string s_init_file
SetPointer (HourGlass!)
s_init_file = "imagedb.ini"
```

```
s_text = ProfileString(s_init_file,"application","firsttime","error")
IF s_text = 'error' THEN
    MessageBox ("error", "init file not found")
    HALT CLOSE
END IF
IF Upper(s_text) = "YES" THEN
    HALT
ELSE
    sqlca.DBMS     = ProfileString(s_init_file,"sqlca","dbms","")
    sqlca.database = ProfileString(s_init_file,"sqlca","database","")
    sqlca.userid   = ProfileString(s_init_file,"sqlca","userid","")
    sqlca.dbpass   = ProfileString(s_init_file,"sqlca","dbpass","")
    sqlca.logid    = ProfileString(s_init_file,"sqlca","logid","")
    sqlca.logpass  = ProfileString(s_init_file,"sqlca","logpass","")
    sqlca.servername = ProfileString(s_init_file,"sqlca","servername","")
    sqlca.dbparm   = ProfileString(s_init_file,"sqlca","dbparm","")
END IF
open(w_embedded_sql)
```

When it is correct, click the **Return** icon.

## *Commentary on the Open Script*

The `SetPointer` function sets the Windows' pointer to the **HourGlass** icon. This lets the user know that the application has started and is doing some initialization before the main window displays. The next lines read the **IMAGEDB.INI** profile file. This file will be used by a number of applications that need to access the example database (**MCCLAN2.DB**). The first `ProfileString` function call is looking for the `firsttime` value in the application section of the profile file. If the call cannot locate the file, the section, or the key, the value of the last function argument, it will return "error." If the key is found, the next section of code reads the SQLCA parameters into the SQLCA transaction object. The application will use the SQLCA to establish the connection to the database. Finally, the last statement opens the main window, `w_embedded_sql`.

Run the application.

**NOTE** In production development, I would not place all this code in the Open event. I would divide this code into functions, and then have only a few function calls in this event. In general, you should place as little code as possible in each event. Partitioning the code into functions makes the application easier to maintain and better structured. For simplicity, this example places most of the application code in the events.

## Add Code to the Window

Click on the **Window** icon on the PowerBar to open the Window painter. In the Select window, select the `w_embedded_sql` window. In the Window painter, add the controls, as shown in Figure 7.13.

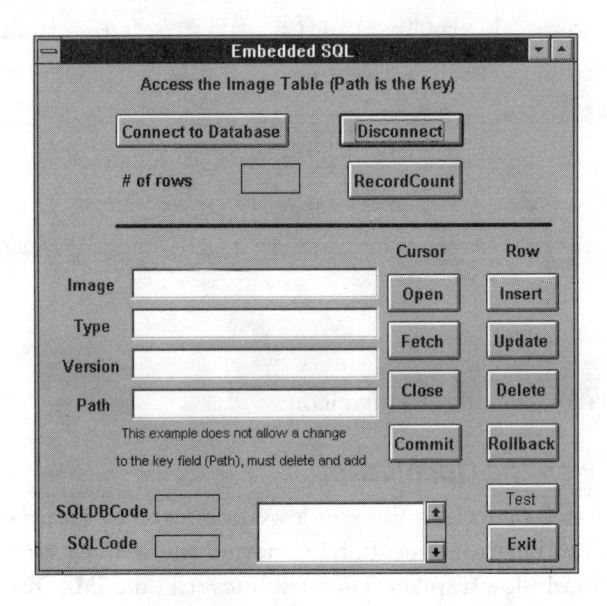

*Figure 7.13  Adding controls to the window.*

## Add Code to the `w_embedded_sql` Window

Next, add code to the `w_embedded_sql` window. You will add code to the `Clicked` event for each of the command buttons. You will also write two window-level functions, `fw_clear`, and `fw_db_status`. You will also define one instance variable, the cursor.

## fw_db_status

You will create a function to update the database status display fields after each database operation. In the Window painter, select the **Declare|Window Function** menu option. Select **New**, and then declare the function as:

```
long fw_db_status ( long al_sqlcode, long al_sqldbcode, string as_sqlerrtext )
```

Your function declaration should look identical to Figure 7.14. Then click on **OK**.

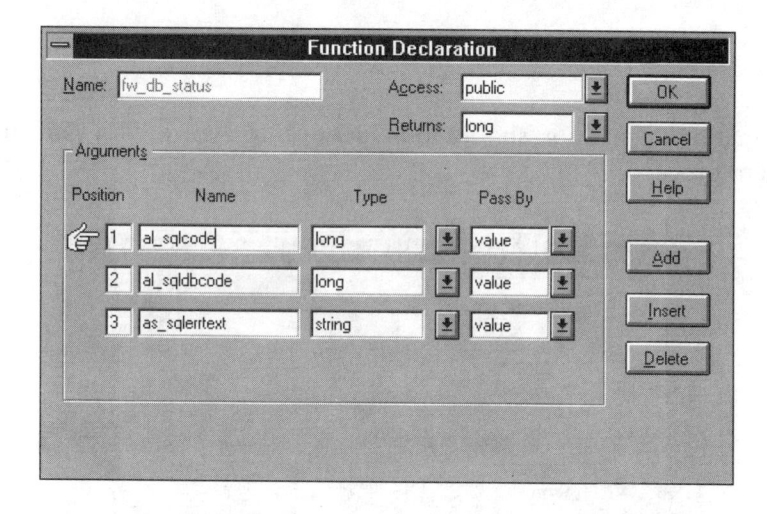

*Figure 7.14* The `fw_db_status` *Function.*

Enter the following code for `fw_db_status`:

```
st_dbcode.text = ''
st_sqlcode.text = ''
mle_dbtext.text = ''
st_dbcode.text = string(al_sqldbcode)
st_sqlcode.text = string(al_sqlcode)
mle_dbtext.text = as_sqlerrtext
return al_sqlcode
```

## Chapter 7

The first three lines of this code just blank out the database return code fields. The next two lines assign the numeric values to the static text fields. The string function is required to convert the long integer variables to a string. The next line assigns the `as_sqlerrtext` string to the multiline edit box. The last line returns a `al_sqlcode` (a long).

### fw_clear

The next function clears the row data fields. In the Window painter, select the **Declare|Window Function** menu option. Select **New**, and then declare the function as:

```
int fw_clear ( )
```

Your function declaration should look identical to Figure 7.15. Click the **OK** button to proceed.

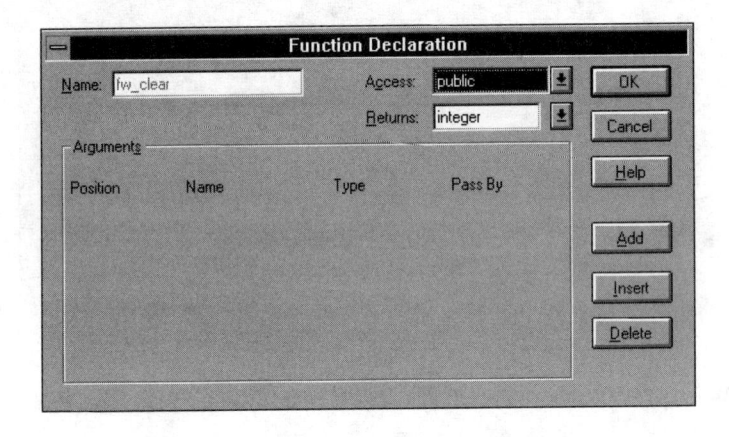

*Figure 7.15* The `fw_CLEAR` *Function.*

Enter the following code for the function:

```
sle_image.text = ''
sle_path.text = ''
```

```
sle_type.text = ''
sle_version.text = ''
return 1
```

### cb_connect

On the Window painter, click the right-mouse button on `cb_connect`, and select the **Script** menu option. For the `Clicked` event of this button (be sure that you are in the correct event), enter the following code:

```
connect;
IF sqlca.sqlcode <> 0 THEN
     fw_db_status ( sqlca.sqlcode, sqlca.sqldbcode, sqlca.sqlerrtext)
ELSE
     fw_db_status ( sqlca.sqlcode, sqlca.sqldbcode, "DB Connected & (Mcclan2)")
END IF
```

This code uses the SQLCA (by default) to connect to the database. The `fw_db_status` function will display the status code. The first line could explicitly specify the transaction object as follows:

```
connect using SQLCA;
```

### cb_disconnect

For the `Clicked` event of this button, enter the following code:

```
disconnect;
fw_db_status ( sqlca.sqlcode, sqlca.sqldbcode, sqlca.sqlerrtext)
```

This will disconnect from the database.

## cb_count

For the `Clicked` event of this button, enter the following code:

```
SELECT count(*)
    INTO :st_count.text
    FROM "images"  ;
fw_db_status ( sqlca.sqlcode, sqlca.sqldbcode, sqlca.sqlerrtext )
```

This will display the number of rows currently in the IMAGES table. You could also use the **Paste SQL** option to create this `SELECT` statement.

## Define the Instance Variable Cursor1

In the Window painter, select the **Declare|Instance Variables** menu option. We must declare the cursor as an instance variable so that various command buttons will have access to the cursor. If the cursor was declared as a local variable inside the Open cursor button, the other buttons (Fetch and Close) would not be able to reference the cursor.

In the Declare Instance Variables dialog box, double-click the **Cursor** icon (under the Declare label). This will open the Declare Cursor dialog box. In the Select Tables dialog box, select the images table and click the **Open** button. Add all of the columns to the Selection list (image, type, version, path). You can do this most easily by clicking the **right-mouse** button at the top of the images table box, and then by selecting **Select All** from the popup menu.

Next, click the **Sort** tab (at the bottom of the window) to define a sort order. Drag the image column from the left side of the Sort dialog box, over to the empty area on the right side (where the Ascending checkbox is located), and drop the icon. This will tell the DBMS to sort the result of this query by the image name.

Close the Declare Cursor dialog box (answer yes to the popup "Return to Script Painter with SQL statement"). When prompted, name this cursor `cursor1`. This should paste the cursor definition into the Declare Instance Variables dialog box. If you have any problems creating the cursor in the Declare Cursor painter, you can type the definition into the Instance Variables dialog box:

```
DECLARE cursor1 CURSOR FOR
    SELECT "images"."image",
```

# Embedded SQL

```
            "images"."type",
            "images"."version",
            "images"."path"
    FROM "images"
ORDER BY "images"."image" ASC  ;
```

While still in the Declare Instance Variables dialog box, add the following lines after the cursor declaration (use the **Ctrl+Enter** key to add a new line without closing the dialog box):

```
string is_path, is_image, is_type
integer ii_version
```

We will use these instance variables to hold the column data from each fetch.

### cb_open

For the `Clicked` event of this button, enter the following code:

```
sle_image.text = ""
sle_type.text      = ""
sle_version.text   = ""
sle_path.text = ""
OPEN Cursor1;
fw_db_status ( sqlca.sqlcode, sqlca.sqldbcode, sqlca.sqlerrtext )
```

This will open the cursor (executing the SELECT statement) and report the status.

### cb_fetch

For the `Clicked` event of this button, enter the following code:

```
//instance vars>> string is_image, is_type, is_path    integer
//ii_version
// you could also fetch directly into the sle.text fields
// use the is_path to hold the key field
```

```
FETCH Cursor1 INTO :is_image, :is_type, :ii_version, :is_path;
fw_db_status (sqlca.sqlcode, sqlca.sqldbcode, sqlca.sqlerrtext )
IF SQLCA.SQLCode = 0 THEN
     sle_image.text = is_image
     sle_type.text      = is_type
     sle_version.text     = string(ii_version)
     sle_path.text = is_path
ELSE
     sle_image.text = ""
     sle_type.text      = ""
     sle_version.text     = ""
     sle_path.text = ""
END IF
```

You could use the **Paste SQL** icon to create the `Fetch` statement or just type it in. This statement fetches a row into the instance variables defined in the previous step. If the fetch is successful, then values are moved into the window controls; otherwise the controls are just blanked out.

### cb_close

For the `Clicked` event of this button, enter the following code:

```
CLOSE Cursor1;
fw_db_status ( sqlca.sqlcode, sqlca.sqldbcode, sqlca.sqlerrtext )
```

This will close the cursor and report the status.

### cb_insert

For the `Clicked` event of this button, enter the following code:

```
int i_version
i_version = integer(sle_version.text)
   INSERT INTO "images"
         ( "image",
```

```
              "type",
              "version",
              "path" )
    VALUES ( :sle_image.text,
             :sle_type.text,
             :i_version,
             :sle_path.text) ;
fw_db_status ( sqlca.sqlcode, sqlca.sqldbcode, sqlca.sqlerrtext)
```

You can use the **Paste SQL** icon to create the INSERT statement or just type it in. This will insert a new row into the IMAGES table (providing that the path is not already in the table). We move the version number into the i_version local variable because a conversion is required (from string to integer).

### cb_update

For the Clicked event of this button, enter the following code:

```
UPDATE "images"
    SET "image" = :sle_image.text,
        "type" = :sle_type.text,
        "version" = :sle_version.text
    WHERE  path = :sle_path.text;
fw_db_status ( sqlca.sqlcode, sqlca.sqldbcode, sqlca.sqlerrtext )
```

You can use the **Paste SQL** icon to create the UPDATE statement or just type it in. It will update a row in the IMAGES table. The value of the Path field will determine which row is updated.

### cb_delete

For the Clicked event of this button, enter the following code:

```
DELETE FROM "images"
   WHERE path = :sle_path.text;
fw_db_status ( sqlca.sqlcode, sqlca.sqldbcode, sqlca.sqlerrtext )
```

You can use the **Paste SQL** icon to create the DELETE statement or just type it in. This will delete the row with the specified path from the IMAGES table.

### cb_commit

For the Clicked event of this button, enter the following code:

```
commit;
fw_db_status ( sqlca.sqlcode, sqlca.sqldbcode, sqlca.sqlerrtext )
```

This will end the current transaction, commit the changes to the database, and begin a new transaction.

### cb_rollback

For the Clicked event of this button, enter the following code:

```
rollback;
fw_db_status ( sqlca.sqlcode, sqlca.sqldbcode, sqlca.sqlerrtext )
```

This will end the current transaction, undo the changes to the database, and begin a new transaction.

## Save the Window and Run the Application

Close the w_embedded_sql window and save the changes to that window. Then run the application from the development environment. If you are prompted to save the changes (to the Application object), answer yes. If everything runs OK, you may wish to create a new executable, as you did in the previous chapter. If you have any problems, compare your code closely to the code in the **SQLApp.pbl**.

Now you have created a complete client-server application in PowerBuilder.

## Selecting and Updating Blobs

In the SqlApp example, the names of the images were stored in the database, but the actual images were DOS files. It is possible to store binary (or text) data in some DBMSs. The Sybase SQL Anywhere engine supports the long binary data type, which can be used to store images such as the BMP files that were used in the SqlApp example. PowerBuilder provides a Blob (Binary Large Object) data type that is used in this manner. In the next example, BMP images are stored in the database as LONG BINARY data. The images are then selected into a Blob variable and displayed in a picture control.

You cannot use the normal SQL SELECT and INSERT statements with blob variables. PowerBuilder provides two additional SQL statements specifically for the use with blob variables. The SELECTBLOB statement allows you to retrieve data into a blob variable and the UPDATEBLOB statement allows you to move the contents of a blob variable to the database (either for an initial insert or a subsequent update).

The format of the SELECTBLOB SQL statement is:

```
SELECTBLOB column_name INTO :blb_variable
     FROM tablename WHERE expression {USING TransactionObject} ;
```

You may also include a host indicator variable (in the INTO list of target parameters) to check for an empty blob.

This statement selects one column with the Blob data type (long binary in Sybase SQL Anywhere) and only one row from the selected table. You must test the SQLCA.SQLCode after this statement to check for successful execution.

```
blob      blb_bmp
SELECTBLOB imagedata INTO :blb_bmp FROM imagebmp
        WHERE filepath = :s_path;
IF sqlca.sqlcode <> 0 THEN
    MessageBox('read blob',"Database SelectBlob failure")
ELSE
    p_1.SetPicture (blb_bmp)
END IF
```

This example selects an image into blb_bmp. If the sqlcode is 0 (successful), the picture control, p_1, is set to display the image.

## UPDATEBLOB SQL Statement

The format of the UPDATEBLOB SQL statement is:

```
UPDATEBLOB table_name SET column_name = :blob_variable
       WHERE expression;
```

This statement updates one column with the Blob data type (long binary in Sybase SQL Anywhere) in the named table. You must test the SQLCA.SQLCode after this statement to check for successful execution.

For example:

```
UPDATEBLOB Imagebmp SET imagedata = :blb_bmp
       WHERE filepath = :s_path;
IF sqlca.sqlcode <> 0 THEN
    messagebox('blob',"database insert failed")
    rollback;
ELSE
    commit;
END IF
```

This example updates (or inserts) the contents of the blb_bmp into the ImageBmp table. If the SQLCode is 0 (successful), the following code applies the update to the database and commits the transaction.

To load an image into the blob from a DOS file, you could use:

```
blob blb_bmp, blb_tmp
string s_path
long l_len, l_pos
int i_file, n_bytes
s_path = uo_1.fu_get_filepath()
IF len(s_path) < 5 THEN
     return
END IF
```

```
l_len = FileLength(s_path)
i_file = FileOpen(s_path,StreamMode!,Read!,LockReadWrite!)
IF i_file > 0 THEN
    n_bytes = FileRead(i_file, blb_tmp)
    DO WHILE n_bytes > 0
        blb_bmp = blb_bmp + blb_tmp
        l_pos = l_pos + n_bytes
        FileSeek(i_file,l_pos, FromBeginning!)
        n_bytes = FileRead(i_file, blb_tmp)
    LOOP
    FileClose(i_file)
ELSE
    return
END IF
```

## CHAPTER 8

# Menus

## INTRODUCTION TO THE MENU PAINTER

Most Windows applications use menus rather than CommandButtons. CommandButtons are okay to use in simple applications and in response windows. However, in most of your applications use menus in the place of CommandButtons and checkboxes.

In this chapter, we will cover the following:

- ✦ How to create menus and menu items
- ✦ Adding script to menu events
- ✦ Cascading menus
- ✦ Dynamic menus
- ✦ Popup menus
- ✦ Menu item properties
- ✦ MDI Microhelp
- ✦ Adding a menu to a window
- ✦ The example MENU application

## Chapter 8

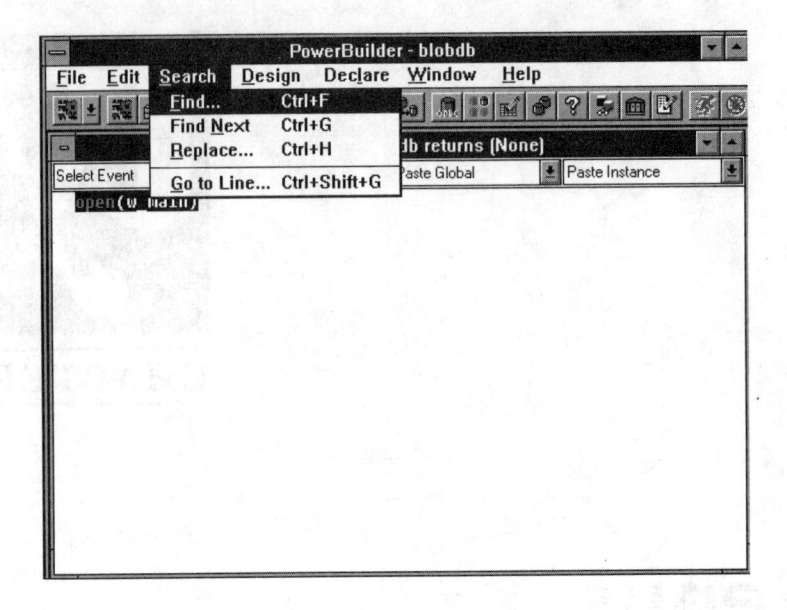

*Figure 8.1  The PowerScript painter search menu.*

Figure 8.1 shows the menu in the PowerScript painter. The menu bar contains one entry (called *menu bar items* or *menu names*) for each dropdown menu. In this example, the menu bar contains the items: File, Edit, Search, Window, and Help (among others). When you select a menu bar item (**Search** in this example), the dropdown menu opens, displaying a set of menu options called the *menu items*. Most of the menu items will perform some immediate action when selected. It is also possible that a menu item will open another window (usually a dialog box) or a cascading menu. The menu items that open other windows are marked with an ellipsis. For example, in Figure 8.1, the item Find Text... opens a dialog box to accept the search criteria.

If the menu item opens another cascading menu, a right triangle symbol is displayed next to the menu item to mark it (Figure 8.11 shows an example). Cascading menus are not often used, but can be useful.

Popup menus are another type of menu that you can create for your applications. These are menus that appear in a window, not related to a menu bar. By now, you are very familiar with the PowerBuilder RMB popup menu which is opened by clicking the right mouse button.

## CREATING MENUS

Building menus in PowerBuilder is a simple process. To create a new menu, click on the **PowerBar** (or **PowerPanel**) menu icon to open the Select Menu dialog box (Figure 8.2).

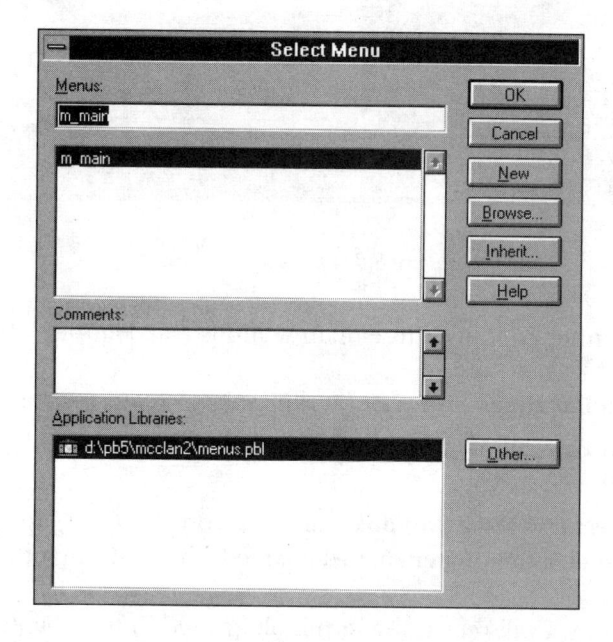

*Figure 8.2* The Select Menu dialog box.

Click on the **New CommandButton** to open the Menu painter (Figure 8.3).

**288** Chapter 8

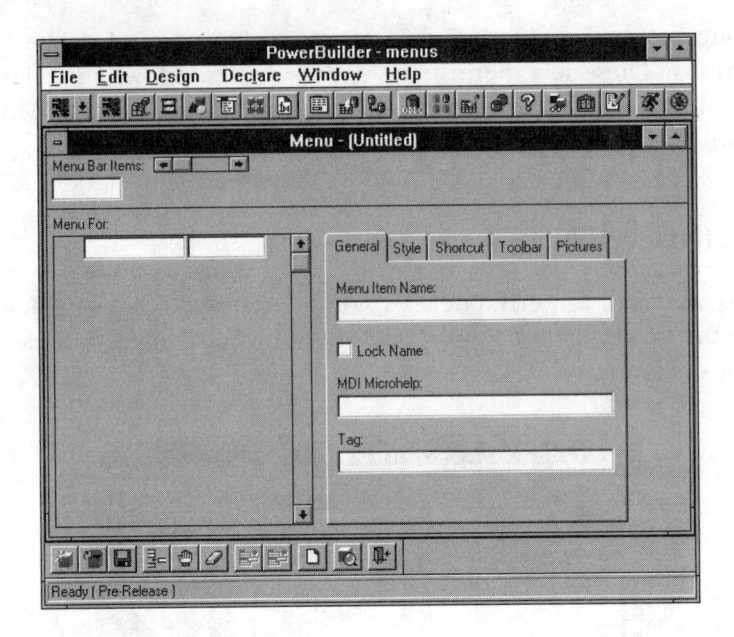

*Figure 8.3* The Menu painter.

The menu painter contains three main sections (see Figure 8.3):

1. **Menu Bar Items**—an area (at the top) to create a menu bar.
2. **Menu For**—an area (on the left) to build the dropdown (or cascading) menu.
3. **Properties Tab dialog box**—an area (on the right) to specify attributes such as menu item name, enabled, checked, and other properties.

To ensure clarity, I will repeat the terminology used in this chapter. The Menu painter calls each component of the menu bar and the dropdown (or cascading) menu calls a menu item. The menu items that are on the menu bar are called menu bar items or menu names.

To create a menu, add an item to the menu bar and then add the items to the dropdown menu. You must then add PowerScript code to implement the commands and menu options. This code will be added to the Clicked event for each menu item. You have a number of other options, such as accelerators, that are also covered in this chapter.

## ADDING MENU BAR ITEMS

When you add a menu to one of your windows, the menu bar items appear in the menu bar across the top of the window (just below the Title bar). The exact design for each menu varies from application to application, but the menu bar for most Windows applications typically includes the entries File, Edit, Window, and Help, as shown in Figure 8.1. Your first task in creating a menu, is to add the first menu bar item. Your menu bar must, of course, contain at least one item. Enter the text for the menu bar item in the first field of the Menu Bar Items area (such as File). The Menu painter will suggest a name for the menu bar item, such as m_file.

Add additional menu bar items by clicking just to the right of the last menu bar entry. This opens the SingleLineEdit box where you can enter the label for the new menu bar item. You can also insert a new menu bar item at any point by clicking on an existing menu bar item, and then by clicking the PainterBar's **insert** icon or by selecting the **Edit|Insert** menu option.

You can also delete or move menu bar items using menu options or by clicking **Menu PainterBar** icons.

## Adding Menu Items

Add items to the menu in the second area of the Menu painter window under the label "Menu For." Test in this example. Use the **Tab** key or click the right-mouse button to jump to the Menu For area. Enter the menu item label and then set the other attributes in the Properties Tab dialog box. More details are provided in the following section on menu item properties.

### Menu PainterBar Icons

The most common menu operations are available on the Menu painter PainterBar. The insert, move, delete, and script icons work for both menu items and menu bar items.

The PainterBar icons include:

- **Insert**—adds a new menu item at the current location. This shifts all entries (if any) from this point down one row (or to the right if you are working with menu bar items).
- **Move**—relocates a menu item.
- **Delete**—removes a menu item.

- **New level**—steps down into the next lower level of a cascading menu.
- **Prev level**—steps up to the next higher level in a cascading menu.
- **New**—creates a new menu.
- **Open**—opens an existing menu.
- **Save**—saves the current menu.
- **Script**—edits the code for a menu item event.
- **Preview**—views the menu.

## Menu Item Events

There are only two events for Menu items.

- **Selected**—triggered when the user highlights the menu item, either with the mouse or with a keyboard combination. You will not usually code for this event. If you do, it will probably be to present some additional information to the user.
- **Clicked**—triggered when the user selects a menu item, either with the keyboard or with the mouse. Every menu item (except those that trigger a cascading menu) will have PowerScript code associated with it. This is where the command is executed or the menu option is set. This is equivalent to the Clicked event in a CommandButton.

For the menu bar items, the Clicked event can be used to set the options (enabled, disabled) for the menu items on the dropdown menu.

## Creating Cascading Menus

The first step to create a cascading menu is to add a menu item which will trigger the cascading menu (**Show Many** in our example Figure 8.4).

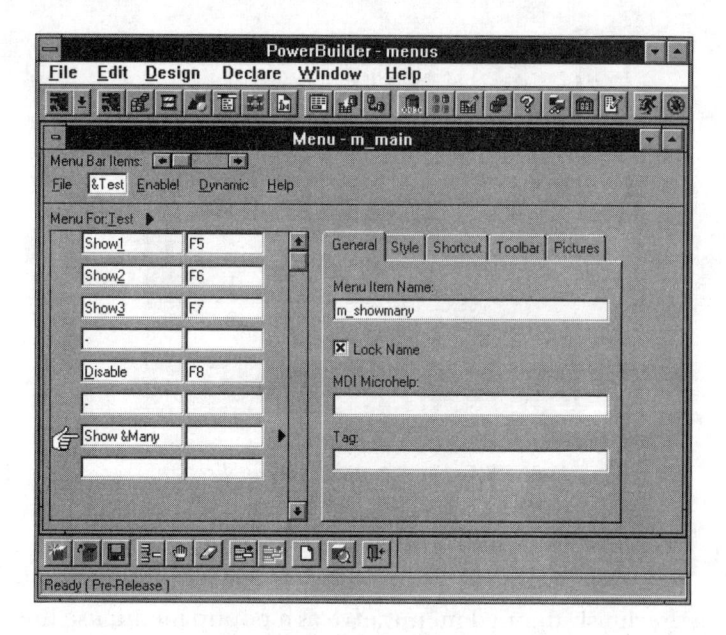

*Figure 8.4  Creating a menu.*

While that menu item is selected, click on the **NextLvl** icon or select the **Edit|Next Level** menu option. The second area (Menu For) of the Menu painter displays the levels that have been created and also changes to display a new dropdown menu. Enter the menu items in this menu, just as you did for the first level. You can add additional levels in the same manner. In general, you should avoid multiple-level cascaded menus, as they can be difficult to navigate. To return to the next higher level in the cascading menu, just click on the **Prior Lvl** icon or selected the **Edit|Prior Level** menu selection. Figure 8.5 shows the final result.

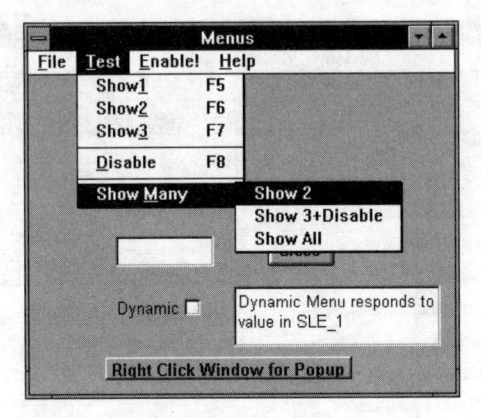

*Figure 8.5  The Menu example application.*

## Creating Popup Menus

To make a previously defined menu serve as a popup menu, use the Popup( ) function. In the example, the following line of code is added to the window's RButtonDown event.

```
m_main.M_test.PopMenu(PointerX( ), PointerY( ))
```

This opens the m_test menu (from the m_main menu) at the current pointer position in the window. Figure 8.6 shows the popup menu.

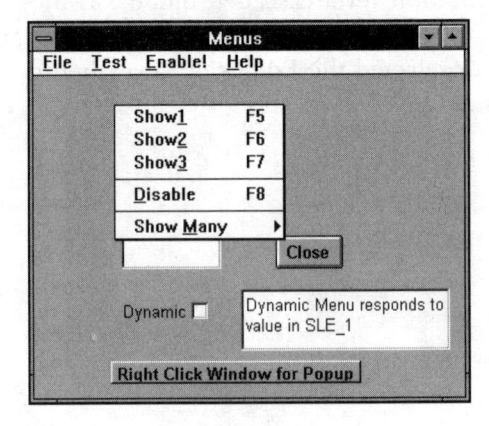

*Figure 8.6  A popup menu.*

# Menu Item Properties

Use the Properties Tab dialog box to set the various attributes for each menu item. You must first select a menu item (using the mouse or the keyboard), and then click the tabs to access various properties for the selected menu item. You can set other characteristics for the style of a menu item on the Style tab of the Properties Tab dialog box.

## General Attributes

Each menu item must be named as you add them to a menu. This name lets you reference the menu item from within your PowerScript code. This is most useful for enabling and disabling menu items as a result of another selection. The Menu painter will create a default name for each menu item. The name for the menu item is a PowerScript identifier and must follow the constraints for identifiers. Look at the General tab on the Properties dialog box for the menu.

The Lock Name option tells the Menu painter to keep the current name of the menu item even if the text associated with that menu item is later changed. When you assign a label to a menu item, the name of the menu item is created. Later you may change the text that is displayed for that menu item, but you may already have coded references to that menu item name in one or more of the events (or in a function). In that case, you would not want to rename the menu item based on the modification that you just made to the label. The Lock Name option prevents any change to the menu item name. If you have not coded any references to the menu item, you can change the name by deselecting the **Lock Name** checkbox and entering the new name. However, I find that the Menu painter often creates problems for the developer when you change the name of a menu item, or even delete an item.

The Tag attribute can be used to associate any text with a menu item. The MDI Microhelp attribute will be discussed in the section on MDI applications later in this chapter.

## Style Attributes

You can set other characteristics for the style of a menu item on the Style tab of the Properties Tab dialog box. In this section, you define the initial state for the menu item and other attributes.

- **Checked**—specifies that the item is checked or unchecked.
- **Enabled**—sets the initial state, to enable or disable the menu item.

- **Visible**—sets the initial state as either visible or invisible.
- **Shift Over\Down**—determines the insertion location for items added in descendant. Set this option to cause this item to shift down (or over) when new items are added (in descendant menus). More details are found in the chapter. on Inheritance.
- **Menu Merge option**—select Exclude, Merge, or other menu options.
- **Type option**—choose from Normal, Exit, or About.

## Shortcut Keys and Accelerators

In the Shortcut section, you can define a shortcut key for the menu item. Pressing this key (or key combination) is the same as selecting this menu option. Select the key from the Key dropdown listbox. You may optionally add the **Alt**, **Ctrl**, or **Shift** key to the shortcut by clicking the corresponding checkbox. The shortcut key works whenever the menu is displayed and no menu items are currently selected, such as when you are working elsewhere in the window. Figure 8.7 shows the common window shortcut keys for the editor's functions. You can copy the selected text by pressing **Ctrl+C**, cut text by pressing **Ctrl+X**, and Paste text by pressing **Ctrl+V**. All these functions are available when the Edit menu is not opened.

*Figure 8.7 The Editor Menu.*

You can also define accelerators for each menu item. You do this by inserting an ampersand (&) into the menu item name, immediately preceding the character that you wish to be the accelerator. This character will display with an underline to mark it as the Accelerator key for that menu item. You can then select that item by pressing the **Accelerator** key while holding down the

**Alt** key. Accelerator keys only work when the menu item is visible. Figure 8.7 shows the Accelerator keys for the common window editor functions. The Accelerator key for Cut is "t" (triggered by **Alt+t**). This accelerator is only available when the Edit menu is open.

> **NOTE** Generally, you use shortcut keys for a few frequent selections, and you define an Accelerator key for every item.

### Separator Lines

You can add a separator line between a menu to partition the menu items into related groups. To add a separator, add a menu item, and use a hyphen (-) for its name. Figure 8.7 shows the Edit menu from the PowerScript editor. Notice the grouping of similar functions, divided by the separator lines.

> **NOTE** The default name for the first separator that you add will be m_-. Additional separators may have names such as m_-1, m_-2, etc.. This is a legal menu item name if you have set the **Allow Dashes in Identifiers** option (in the Properties dialog box for the editor). If you later decide not to allow dashes in identifiers (by unsetting this option), these names become illegal, and then you would encounter an error when you next work with a menu with items containing a dash (hyphen). The error message may not be obvious, so you may receive a message such as "Compiler Errors: Forward Declarations Syntax error." In this case, you will have to rename all the separator menu items.

## Toolbar Tab

The Toolbar tab will only be used with MDI applications. Use the Toolbar tab (with the Pictures tab) to add an entry to the toolbar.

- **Text**—specifies text that will be displayed for the toolbar button.
- **Space Before**—sets the space before the button.
- **Order**—sets the ordering of the buttons on the toolbar.
- **Visible**—makes the button visible.
- **Display Down**—set this to display the button as down (pressed).
- **Object Type**—determines if the button will cascade by selecting Menu or MenuCascade.

## Chapter 8

- **Bar Index**—the number of the toolbar on which this button will be placed.
- **Columns**—sets the number of columns in the dropdown if you selected the MenuCascade object type.
- **Drop Down**—set this to make the button a dropdown toolbar button.

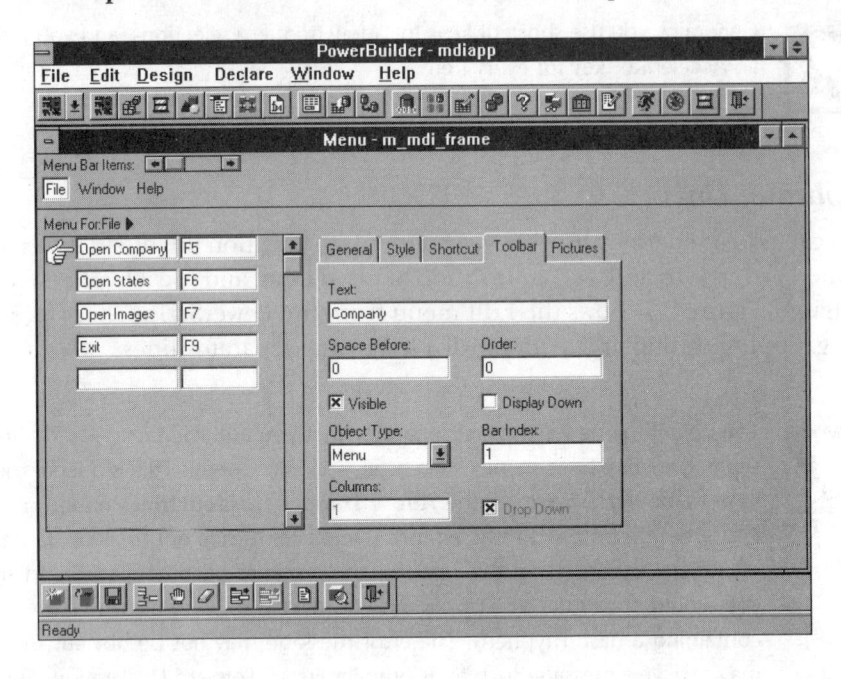

*Figure 8.8  The Toolbar tab.*

## Pictures Tab

The Pictures tab will only be used with MDI applications. Use the Pictures tab to add an entry to the toolbar.

- **Toolbar Item**—this area displays the picture for the toolbar item.
- **Picture Name**—the picture (either a stock picture or a disk file (BMP, RLE, or WMF) image).

- **Browse**—use this to select the disk file for the Picture Name field.
- **Stock Pictures**—use this to assign a stock picture to the Picture Name field.
- **Down Picture Name**—the image to be used for the down (pressed) image.

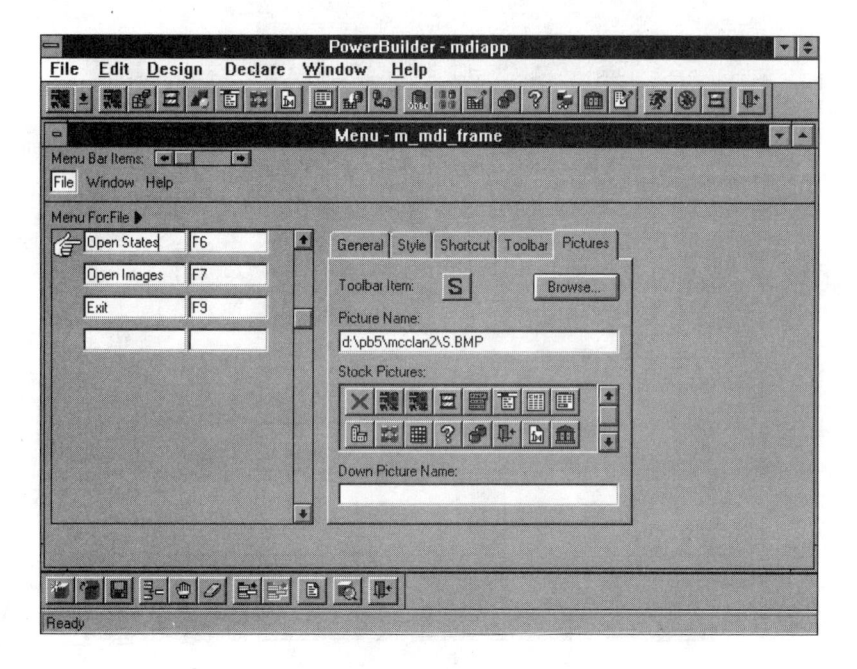

*Figure 8.9* The Pictures tab.

# MDI APPLICATIONS

MDI applications, as a characteristic of their style, use menus and not CommandButtons. MDI application are covered in a later chapter. The next section briefly covers the MDI features.

## Adding MDI Microhelp

When creating a menu for an MDI style application, you can add Microhelp text to be displayed when the menu item is selected. Just add the text to the MDI Microhelp field on the General tab. In the MDIApp example program (from the MDI chapter), text was added for Microhelp (Figure 8.10).

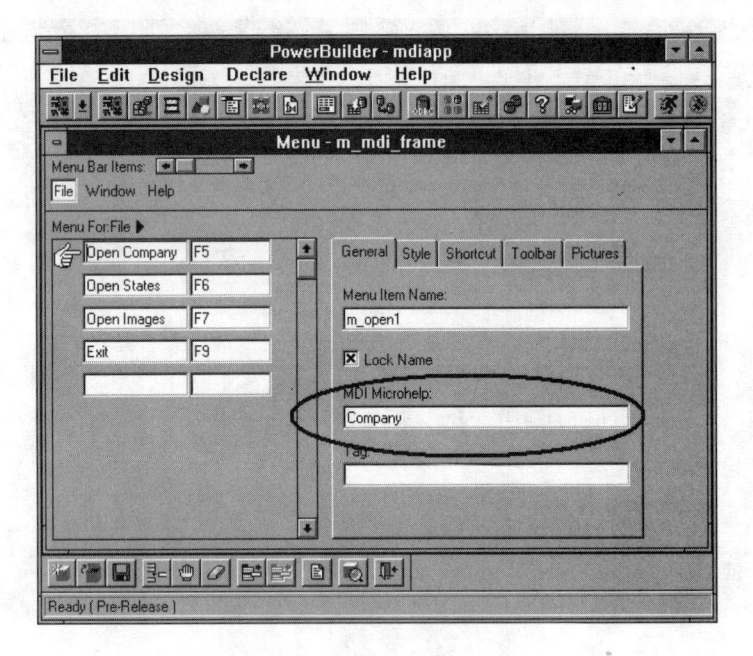

*Figure 8.10  Adding Microhelp text.*

## The MDI Toolbar

MDI applications may have *toolbars*. For example, the PowerBuilder PowerBar is a toolbar. Toolbars contain icons for the most important menu items, and are, in effect, the MDI implementation of CommandButtons. Clicking the **toolbar** icon is the same as clicking the menu item with which it is associated.

You can add an icon for any menu item to your application's toolbar by using the Toolbar tab options to create the toolbar entry and then the Pictures tab to select the picture. First you must define the attributes for the Toolbar item in the Toolbar tab dialog box.

On the Pictures tab, you can select a predefined icon (picture) or a picture file. In Figure 8.11, an icon was added for the Open3 Menu item.

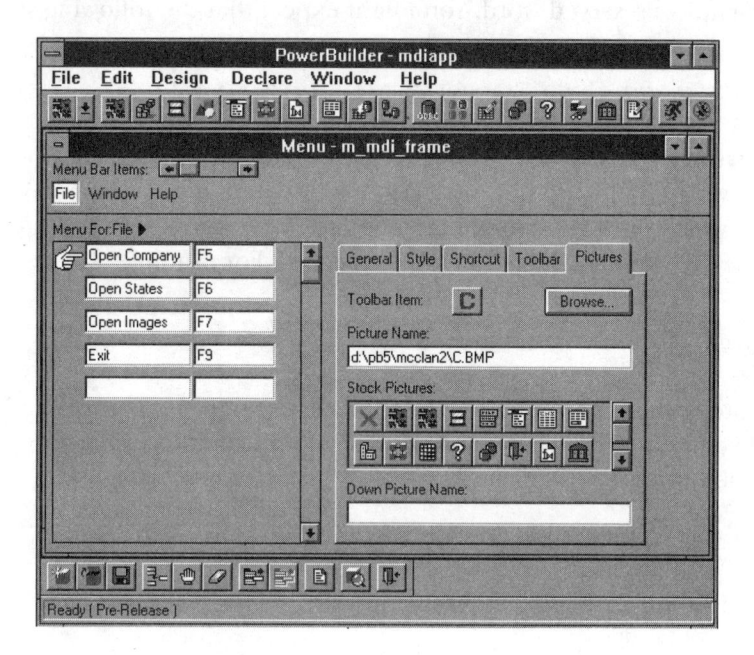

*Figure 8.11  MDI toolbar.*

## ADDING SCRIPTS

The scripts that you write will be similar to the scripts that you have written for the Clicked event of CommandButtons (such as cb_close). The most important difference is that you cannot use the reserved word Parent to refer to the window that contains the menu. To make this type of reference from within a menu requires the ParentWindow reserved word. In the Menu item script, use ParentWindow to refer to the window that the menu is in.

You can refer to the attributes of the parent window using the ParentWindow reserved word as follows:

```
ParentWindow.X = 1
```

The major drawback to menus is that the Menu item event scripts cannot make a reference to the controls on the parent window using the ParentWindow reserved word. You might expect that the following statement

```
ParentWindow.cb_close.TriggerEvent('Clicked')
```

would trigger the Clicked event for the **cb_close** CommandButton on the w_main window. It does not work because the data type of ParentWindow is window, which does not contain any controls. One solution to this is to explicitly name the window which is being referenced. For example:

```
w_main.cb_close.TriggerEvent(Clicked!)
```

Fortunately, there is a better solution. You can assign the ParentWindow to a variable of the required type of window. For our example application, declare a variable w_x of type w_main.

```
w_main w_x
```

```
w_x = ParentWindow
w_x.cb_close.TriggerEvent(Clicked!)
```

This works, and it has the advantage of not requiring the explicit naming of the window. Generally, we do not like to hard-code object names into our scripts, and this technique only requires specifying the **type** of the window (w_main in this example). You could also use the IsValid function after the window assignment to verify that w_x was a valid object.

## PREVIEWING THE MENU

Preview the final presentation form for the menu by selecting the **Design|Preview** menu option or the **Preview** icon on the PainterBar. The preview mode only presents the menu; however, it does not execute any of the script code. You can select menu bar items to: drop down the menu, select menu options, and pull down cascading menus. To actually test the code in the menu, you need to save it, attach it to a window, and then run (or debug) the application.

## SAVING THE MENU

Select the **File|Save** (or **File|Save As**) menu option to save the menu or click the **Save** icon on the PainterBar. Select the **PowerBuilder** library in which you wish to save the menu. Give the menu a name (such as m_main) and click on **OK**.

## ATTACHING THE MENU TO A WINDOW

To add a menu to a window, go to the Window painter where you have the option of adding a menu to the window. Select the **Edit|Properties** menu option or use the RMB popup menu to open the Window Properties dialog box. In this dialog box, on the General tab, use the **Browse** button to select the name of the menu. This will add the menu to the window. Run the application to test the newly created menu.

## MENU ITEM ATTRIBUTES

Menu items have the following attributes:

- **Checked**—this Boolean value specifies whether the menu item has a checkmark displayed next to it.
- **Enabled**—this Boolean value determines whether the menu item is active and can be selected.
- **Item[]**—an array of menu items that appear under the corresponding menu item.
- **MicroHelp**—the text that will be used for the Microhelp line when this item is selected.
- **ShortCut**—a key (or key combination) that will initiate the Clicked! script for the item.
- **ParentWindow**—determines the window that owns the menu item.
- **Tag**—a text field associated with a menu item (but not displayed).
- **Text**—the text that is displayed for the menu item.
- **ToolbarItemDown**—a Boolean value, that determines whether the item will remain in the down position when it is clicked. If so, click it again to raise it.

- **ToolbarItemDownName**—the toolbar icon used when the item is down.
- **ToolbarItemName**—the toolbar picture used for this item on the toolbar.
- **ToolbarItemOrder**—determines the order of the item on the toolbar.
- **ToolbarItemSpace**—sets the spacing between toolbar items.
- **ToolbarItemText**—sets the text for the item on the toolbar.
- **ToolbarItemVisible**—a Boolean that determines whether the toolbar item is visible.
- **Visible**—a Boolean value. Set to **True** to make the menu item visible. Set to **False** to remove the menu item from the menu.

## MENU ITEM FUNCTIONS

The following functions apply to Menu items:

- **Check**—adds a check mark next to the menu item.
- **ClassName**—returns the name of the menu item.
- **Disable**—disables the menu item.
- **Enable**—enables the menu item.
- **Hide**—makes a CommandButton invisible.
- **PopMenu**—opens a menu as a popup window.
- **PostEvent**—places an event on the menu item's event queue and continues (asynchronously).
- **Show**—makes the menu item visible.
- **TriggerEvent**—triggers an event immediately (synchronously).
- **TypeOf**—returns the enumerated type of this control (menu item!).
- **Uncheck**—removes the check mark next to the menu item.

## THE MENUS EXAMPLE

The MENUS example demonstrates most of the functionality for menus. The details that apply to MDI applications will be demonstrated later in the MDI chapter example. Run the MENUS program. When the window opens (Figure 8.12), click the **Dynamic** checkbox and notice that a new menu bar item (Dynamic) appears.

Menus 303

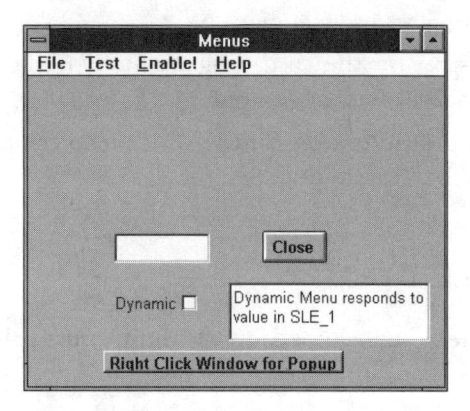

*Figure 8.12* The Menus Example w_main.

Click the **Test** menu (Figure 8.13), and then select **Show1**, **Show2** or **Show3**. This will insert a value in the single-line edit field. This also determines the options that will be visible on the Dynamic dropdown menu. Select the **Test|ShowMany** option to open a cascading menu. You can click the **Show All** option on the cascading menu to display all the Dynamic menu options.

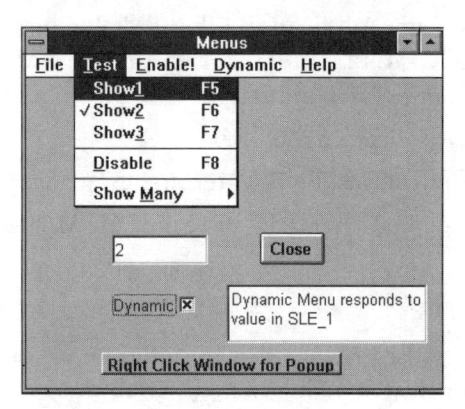

*Figure 8.13* The Test menu.

The Test menu also uses check marks to note the previously selected menu item. You can disable the Test menu by selecting **Test|Disable**. This can then be enabled by selecting the **Enable!** menu bar option. This option immediately executes the Enable command and does not have a dropdown menu. For that reason, the Enable! menu bar option includes the exclamation mark; this is a standard symbol.

You can also disable the Test|Show Many menu option by selecting the **Show3+Disable** option on the cascading menu. To enable the Show Many option, click the **Enable!** menu bar item.

Click the right-mouse button on the window to open the popup menu. This is the same as the Test menu.

# MENUS—STEP-BY-STEP

Now you can create your own version of Menus, just follow the next set of instructions.

## Create the Application and Library

1. Start PowerBuilder (if necessary).
2. If you are not in the Application painter, click on the **Appl** icon on the PowerBar.
3. In the Application painter, select the **File|New** menu option.
4. In the Select New Application Library dialog box, set the directory to (**C:\PB5\MCCLAN2**) and enter the name **ZMENUS.PBL** for the library file name. Click on **OK**.
5. In the Save Application dialog box:
   a. In the Applications: field, enter **menus**.
   b. Tab to the comments field and enter **My Menus version 1**.
   c. Be sure that the Application library name is still zmenus.pbl; if not, select it.
   d. Click on **OK**.
6. PowerBuilder asks if you wish to generate an application template. Click on **No** in this dialog box, as in all the examples for this book (except 1 in the MDI chapter).

This returns you to the Application painter. You have created the menus application object and the zmenus.pbl library.

### Create Menu m_main

Go to the Menu painter (click the **Menu** icon on the PowerBar or PowerPanel). Now create the m_main menu by selecting the **New** button in the Select Menu dialog box. Create the following menu bar items: File, Test, Enable!, Dynamic, Help. To do this, type **File** in the Menu Bar Items area. Then click the mouse on the space just to the right of the File menu bar item. This opens a new item, enter **Test** and then continue the process to create the menu bar. When you are finished, click back on the File menu bar item (Figure 8.14).

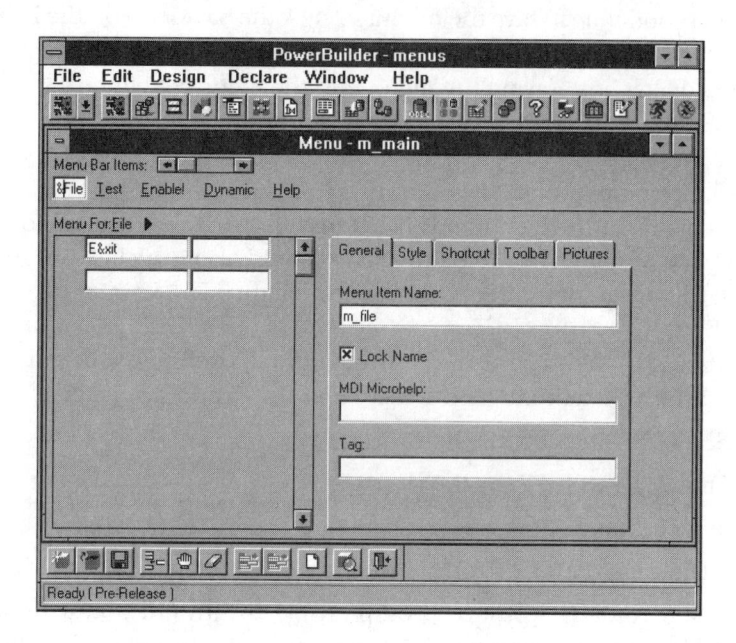

*Figure 8.14* The Menu Bar Items.

## The File Menu

With the cursor on the File menu bar item, hit the **Tab** key once to move to the Menu For File area of the painter (you could also just click on this field). Enter **E&xit** for the menu item name. This creates a label of Exit for this menu item and defines the "x" character as the Accelerator key for this item. The Menu painter will give the menu item the name "m_exit." Open the Script editor for this menu item's Clicked event. To do this, click the **Script** icon (on the PainterBar), or select the **Edit|Script** menu option. Check that you are in the Clicked event (in the editor window's title bar). If not, select **Clicked** from the Select Event dropdown menu. Enter the following line of code:

```
close(ParentWindow)
```

Close the Script editor (click the **Return** icon on the PainterBar). Now add accelerators for each of the menu bar items. Click on each item and add an ampersand (**&**) as the first character of each, so that you have &File, &Test, &Enable!, &Dynamic, &Help. Notice that an underscore is placed under the first character of each menu bar item.

This is a good time to save the menu, so click the **Save** icon on the PainterBar (or select the **File|Save** menu option). Give this menu the name, m_main, in the Save Menu dialog box (saving the menu into the menus.pbl library).

## The Test Menu

With the cursor on the Test menu bar item, hit the **Tab** key once to move to the Menu For Test area of the painter (you could also just click on this field). Enter the following menu items on the Test menu:

1. **Show&1**—with F5 for the shortcut key. (To define a shortcut key, click on the Shortcut tab, and select F5 in the dropdown listbox).
2. **Show&2**—with F6 for the shortcut key.
3. **Show&3**—with F7 for the shortcut key.
4. -a separator.
5. **&Disable**—with F8 for the shortcut key.
6. -a separator (if you are prompted by the Invalid Menu Item Name dialog box, this is to avoid a duplicate name. Just click the **OK** button to accept the suggested name change).
7. **Show&Many**—a cascading menu.

Next, create the cascading menu for the Show Many menu item. To do this, click on the **Show Many** menu item, and then click the **Next Level** icon on the PainterBar (or choose the **Edit|Next Level** menu option). Enter the following menu items on the next level of the cascading menu.

1. **Show2**—this will be named m_show21. (Just click **OK** for the name change when prompted by the Invalid Menu Item Name dialog box).
2. **Show3+Disable**—(this will be named m_show3disable)
3. **Show&All**—(this will be named m_showall)

## The Dynamic Menu

Click on the **Dynamic menu bar** item. With the cursor on the Dynamic menu bar item, hit the **Tab** key once to move to the Menu For Dynamic area of the painter (you could also just click on this field). Enter the following menu items on the Dynamic menu:

1. 1a
2. 1b
3. 2a
4. 2b
5. 2c
6. 3a
7. 3b

Next, create the cascading menu for the 2a menu item. To do this, click on the **2a** menu item, then click the **Next Level** icon on the PainterBar (or choose the **Edit|Next Level** menu option). Enter the following menu items on the next level of the cascading menu.

1. 22a
2. 22b

## The Help Menu

Click on the **Help menu bar** item. With the cursor on the Help menu bar item, hit the **Tab** key once to move to the Menu For Help area of the painter (you could also just click on this field). Enter the following menu items on the Test menu:

1. **&Contents**—with F1 as the shortcut key.
2. -a separator.
3. **&About...**—don't forget the ellipses.

F1 is the standard key used to access the Help system for an application. The About menu option will open the About dialog box, which is signified by the ellipse.

Now save the menu (m_main), and close the Menu painter. You will return to complete the menu (by adding code to a number of the menu items) after you create the main window.

## Create the Main Window

Click the **Window** icon on the PowerBar to open the Window painter. In the Select Window dialog box click on the **New** button to create a new window. In the Window painter double-click on the new window to open the Window Style dialog box (or select the **Edit|Properties** menu option).

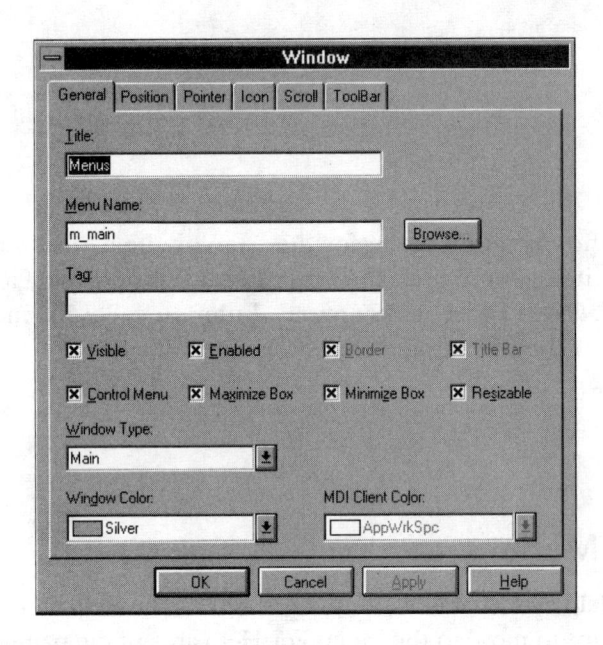

*Figure 8.15* Defining the w_main style.

In this dialog box, in the Title editbox enter **"Menus"** as the text. Then select **Main** from the Window Type dropdown listbox (if it is not already selected). This defines the type for the new window. The other options should match those in Figure 8.15. Set these changes by clicking the **Apply** button.

Next, click the **Position** tab (in the Window Properties dialog box) to open the Window Position dialog box.

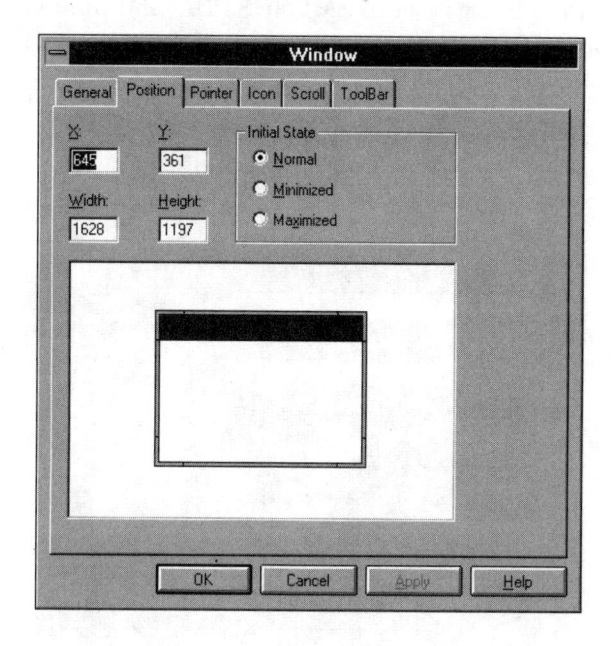

*Figure 8.16 Positioning the w_main style.*

In this dialog box, set the position (and size) of the window, as shown in Figure 8.16. The position of a Main window is relative to the display area of your monitor's screen. In this example, the position of the main window is set near the center of the screen. You can exactly center the screen by clicking the right-mouse button on the window, and then selecting **Center Horizontally** and then **Center Vertically**.

## Attach m_menu to the w_main Window

To add the m_main menu to this window, select the **General** tab and then use the **Browse** button to select the name of the menu. Click **OK**; this will attach the m_main menu to the window.

Close the dialog box by clicking on **OK**. In the Window painter, click the **Save** icon on the PainterBar (or select the **File|Save As** menu option). Check to be sure that the library is set to **ZMENUS.PBL**, and then enter the name **w_main** and click the **OK** button.

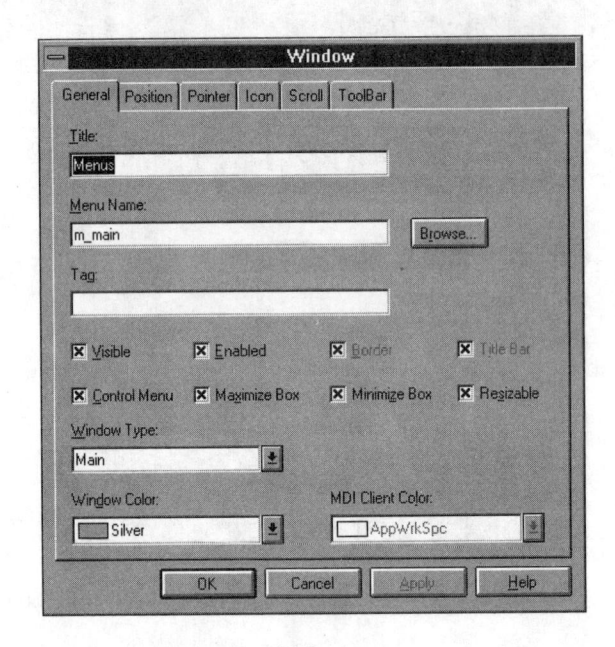

*Figure 8.17  Assigning the menu.*

In the Window painter (for w_main), add the following controls to the window (see Figure 8.18).

> `sle_1`—a single-line edit that will display numeric values assigned from menu items.
>
> `cbx_dynamic`—a checkbox that will activate (make visible) the dynamic menu.
>
> `mle_1`—a multi-line edit, "Dynamic Menu responds to value in SLE_1."
>
> `st_1`—a static text field, "Right Click Window for Popup."
>
> `cb_close`—a button to close the window.

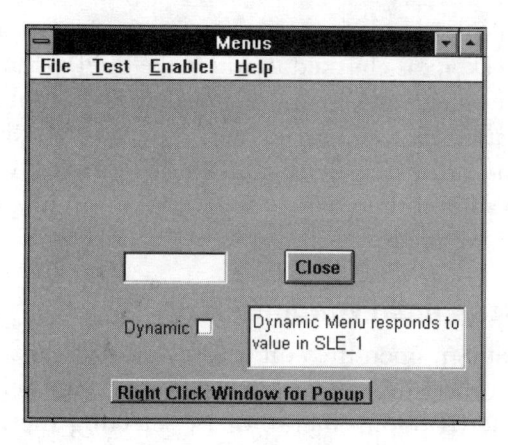

*Figure 8.18  The w_main window.*

To name the controls, `cbx_dynamic` and `cb_close`, just double-click on the control to open the Properties dialog box. Enter the name in the Name field. Also enter the Text field "Dynamic" for `cbx_dynamic`, and enter the Text field "Close" for `cb_close`. Set the text for the **st_1** and **mle_1**, as shown in Figure 8.18.

## Add Code to two w_main Controls

In the Window painter, enter the following code in the specific control events. In the Clicked event for the cb_close button:

```
close(Parent)
```

This will close the w_main window when the cb_close button is clicked.

In the clicked event for the cbx_dynamic checkbox:

```
IF This.Checked THEN
     m_main.m_dynamic.visible = True
ELSE
     m_main.m_dynamic.visible = False
END IF
```

This code will make the Dynamic menu visible (an active) when the `cbx_dynamic` checkbox is checked. It will make the Dynamic menu invisible (and inactive) when the checkbox is unchecked. The Automatic option is set for the `cbx_dynamic` checkbox (on the Properties tab dialog box, on the General tab). This automatically toggles the checkmark on and off in the checkbox. This is a good time to save the `w_main` window again, to save the changes that you have made.

### Add Code to the w_main Window Events

In the Window painter, open the editor for window events. Do this by right-mouse clicking on the surface of the window and then selecting the **Script** option from the RMB popup menu; or by selecting the **Edit|Script** menu option in the Window painter. In the editor, select the `rbuttondown` event from the Select Event dropdown listbox. Enter the following single-line of code for the `w_main rbuttondown` event:

```
m_main.m_test.PopMenu(PointerX( ), PointerY( ))
```

This code will be triggered when the user clicks the right-mouse button on the surface of the `w_main` window. The PopMenu function will open the `m_test` menu (from `m_main`) at the current position of the mouse pointer on the window. The functions PointerX and PointerY return the X and Y positions of the mouse when this event is triggered. Now switch over to the open event for the `w_main` window. You can do this without leaving the editor by selecting the open event from the Select Event dropdown list. This will compile the current script in the `rbuttondown` event before switching to the open event. If you made an error, you will have a chance to fix it.

In the Window painter, enter the following code for the `w_main` open event:

```
integer idx

FOR idx = 1 to UpperBound(m_main.m_dynamic.item[])
    m_main.m_dynamic.item[idx].visible = False
NEXT
```

This code will be triggered when the w_main window opens. The purpose of this code is to hide (initially) all the menu items on the Dynamic menu. We will add code to turn on (activate) each menu item programmatically (determined by the value in the w_main sle_1 (1, 2, 3, or 4)). The m_dynamic.item[] array, is a variable-length array that contains an entry for each menu item on this menu (m_dynamic). The UpperBound function determines the size of the array, and therefore the number of menu items (on the m_dynamic menu). The next line of code makes each menu item invisible. Menu items will be turned on or off (made visible or invisible) in the fm_set_dynamic function in the m_main menu (in a following step). Close the Script editor. Save the window.

## Add Code to the Application Open Event

Go to the Application painter (if you did not close it earlier, you can just select it under the Window menu (Application-menus)). To enter the new code, click the **Script** icon on the Application painter PainterBar; this opens the Script painter. The Script editor should display Script-open for menus, on the title bar. If not, pull down the SelectEvent dropdown menu and select **Open**.

Enter the following single-line of code:

```
open(w_main)
```

You have just coded one of the standard system events for the menus Application object. The Application Open event is triggered as soon as the application is started. When you are finished in the editor, click the **Return** icon.

## Add a Function to m_main

Go to the Menu painter. Now create the following function by selecting the **Declare|Menu Functions** menu option and then by clicking **New** in the Select Function dialog box. The function is named fm_set_dynamic, has no arguments, and returns an integer (1).

```
Function:      fm_set_dynamic
Access:        public
Returns:       Integer
Arguments:     none
```

```
m_main.m_dynamic.m_1a.visible = False
m_main.m_dynamic.m_1b.visible = False
m_main.m_dynamic.m_2a.visible = False
m_main.m_dynamic.m_2b.visible = False
m_main.m_dynamic.m_2c.visible = False
m_main.m_dynamic.m_3a.visible = False
m_main.m_dynamic.m_3b.visible = False

CHOOSE CASE trim(w_main.sle_1.text)
    CASE '1'
        m_main.m_dynamic.m_1a.visible = True
        m_main.m_dynamic.m_1b.visible = True
    CASE '2'
        m_main.m_dynamic.m_2a.visible = True
        m_main.m_dynamic.m_2b.visible = True
        m_main.m_dynamic.m_2c.visible = True
    CASE '3'
        m_main.m_dynamic.m_3a.visible = True
        m_main.m_dynamic.m_3b.visible = True
    CASE ELSE
        m_main.m_dynamic.m_1a.visible = True
        m_main.m_dynamic.m_1b.visible = True
        m_main.m_dynamic.m_2a.visible = True
        m_main.m_dynamic.m_2b.visible = True
        m_main.m_dynamic.m_2c.visible = True
        m_main.m_dynamic.m_3a.visible = True
        m_main.m_dynamic.m_3b.visible = True
END CHOOSE
return 1
```

Close the Menu Function editor. After you have created this function, it is available in the Object Browser for pasting into your code. You could do this in the next menu function, described below. To do so, first position the cursor at the point in your script where you wish to paste the code. Next, open the Object Browser, click on the **menu tab**, and click on **m_main** (in the left listbox). Double-click on **Functions** in the right listbox, click on **fm_set_dynamic**, and then click the **Paste** button. This will paste the function declaration into your code.

## Add Another Function to m_main

Go to the Menu painter (if you're not already there). Now create the following function by selecting the **Declare|Menu Functions** menu option and then by clicking **New** in the Select Function dialog box. The function is named fm_test_action, has one integer argument (ai_number), and returns an integer (1).

```
Function:     fm_test_action
Access:       public
Returns:      Integer
Arguments:    ai_number     integer     by value

w_main.sle_1.text = string(ai_number)

m_main.m_test.m_show1.checked = false
m_main.m_test.m_show2.checked = false
m_main.m_test.m_show3.checked = false
m_main.m_test.m_showmany.checked = false
CHOOSE CASE ai_number
    CASE 1
        m_main.m_test.m_show1.checked = true
    CASE 2
        m_main.m_test.m_show2.checked = true
```

```
      CASE 3
            m_main.m_test.m_show3.checked = true
      CASE 4
            m_main.m_test.m_showmany.checked = true
END CHOOSE
this.fm_set_dynamic ()
return ai_number
```

Close the Menu Function editor. This function unchecks the items on `m_test`, and then checks the one corresponding to the `ai_number` argument. This will display the most recently selected menu option. Then the function calls the `fm_set_dynamic` function to change the `m_dynamic` menu in response to the value chosen.

## Copy Windows to zmenus.pbl

In this step, you will copy several windows from the example library (**MENUS.PBL**) to your **ZMENUS.PBL**. You can also copy a global function, `f_get_env`, rather than code it if you wish. The windows are: `w_about`, `w_environment`, and `w_help` (these windows are all launched from the Help menu).

Go to the Library painter (click the **Library** icon on the PowerBar or the PowerPanel). Locate the example **MENUS.PBL** library. Double-click on the **MENUS.PBL** (if necessary) to expand the display of the objects within the library. You should now see a display, similar to Figure 8.19.

In the Library painter, select the function **f_get_env** and windows `w_about`, `w_environment`, and `w_help`. To do this, you can use the standard Windows' additive selection technique (**Ctrl+click**). While holding the **Ctrl** key, click on each of these objects; all four should then be highlighted. To copy theses objects to your **ZMENUS.PBL**, click the **Copy** icon on the PainterBar (or select the **Entry|Copy** menu option) while these objects are highlighted. This will open the Select Library dialog box where you locate the destination library to which you wish to copy these objects. Locate your **ZMENUS.PBL** library in this dialog box, and then click **OK**. This will copy (duplicate) the function and three windows to your example library.

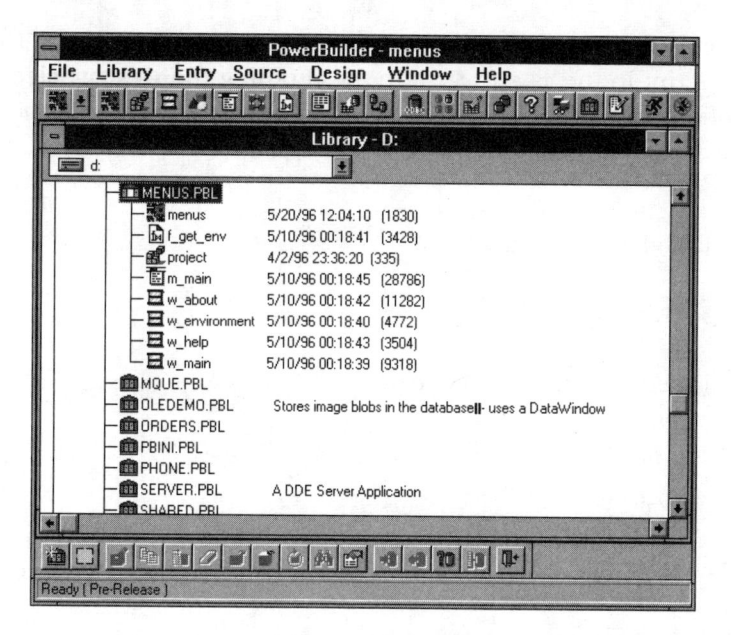

*Figure 8.19 The Library painter.*

To verify the success of the copy, locate the **ZMENUS.PBL** in the Library painter. If the **ZMENUS.PBL** is expanded, double-click it to close it (this will refresh the display). Next, expand the display by double-clicking on the **ZMENUS.PBL** icon. You should see f_get_env, w_about, w_environment, and w_help. If not, go back and copy the missing objects from the **MENUS.PBL**.

After copying these objects, you can proceed to complete the **ZMENUS.PBL**. Be sure to close the Library painter.

### Add Code to m_main Menu Item Events

Go to the Menu painter (click the **Menu** icon on the PowerBar). Now add the following code to the menu items' Clicked event.

### Adding Code to the Test Menu Items

Click on the Test menu bar item to open the Test menu. For the Clicked event for m_show1:

```
fm_test_action(1)
```

For the Clicked event for m_show2 (you can move directly from the m_show1 script to the m_show2 script by choosing the **Design|Select Object** menu option, and then selecting m_show2 in the Select Object listbox):

```
fm_test_action(2)
```

For the Clicked event for m_show3:

```
fm_test_action(3)
```

For the Clicked event for m_disable:

```
fm_test_action(0)
Parent.Disable()
```

For the Clicked event for m_show21 (on the m_showmany cascading menu):

```
fm_test_action(2)
```

For the Clicked event for m_show3disable (on the m_showmany cascading menu):

```
fm_test_action(3)
Parent.Disable()
```

For the Clicked event for m_showall (on the m_showmany cascading menu):

```
fm_test_action(4)
```

Close the script editor.

## *Adding Code to the Help Menu Items*

For the Clicked event for m_contents:

```
open(w_help)
```

For the Clicked event for m_about:

```
open(w_about)
```

## Adding Code to the Enable! Menu Bar Item

For the Clicked event for m_enable:

```
m_main.m_test.enable()
m_main.m_test.m_showmany.enable()
```

Close the Script editor. Close the Menu painter. Now you can run your application.

## The w_environment Window

This section explains the w_environment window and how it works. The open event for the w_environment window contains the following code.

```
string s_text
int i_rc

i_rc = f_get_env(s_text)
IF i_rc <> 1 THEN s_text = 'Error'
mle_1.text = s_text
```

The function f_get_env has the following code:

```
string s_text, s_os, s_cpu, s_pb, s_win16
environment env
integer rc

rc = GetEnvironment(env)
IF rc = 1 THEN

CHOOSE CASE env.OSType
     CASE     AIX!
          s_os = 'AIX'
     CASE     HPUX!
          s_os = 'HPUX'
```

```
        CASE    Macintosh!
            s_os = 'Mac'
        CASE    OSF1!
            s_os = 'OSF1'
        CASE    SOL2!
            s_os = 'SOL2'
        CASE    Windows!
            s_os = 'Windows'
        CASE    WindowsNT!
            s_os = 'Windows NT'
END CHOOSE

CHOOSE CASE env.pbtype
     CASE Desktop!
         s_pb = 'Desktop'
     CASE Enterprise!
         s_pb = 'Enterprise'
END CHOOSE

CHOOSE CASE env.win16
     CASE True
         s_win16 = 'True'
     CASE False
         s_win16 = 'False'
END CHOOSE

CHOOSE CASE env.CPUType
     CASE    Alpha!
         s_cpu = 'Alpha'
     CASE    Hppa!
         s_cpu = 'Hppa'
     CASE    I286!
```

```
            s_cpu = 'I286'
    CASE    I386!
            s_cpu = 'I386'
    CASE    I486!
            s_cpu = 'I486'
    CASE    M68000!
            s_cpu = 'M6800'
    CASE    M68020!
            s_cpu = 'M68020'
    CASE    M68030!
            s_cpu = 'M68030'
    CASE    M68040!
            s_cpu = 'M68040'
    CASE    Mips!
            s_cpu = 'Mips'
    CASE    Pentium!
            s_cpu = 'Pentium'
    CASE    Powerpc!
            s_cpu = 'Powerpc'
    CASE    RS6000!
            s_cpu = 'RS6000'
CASE    Sparc!
            s_cpu = 'Sparc'
END CHOOSE

s_text = 'ScreenWidth =~t' + string(env.screenwidth) + &
    '~r~nScreenHeight =~t' + string(env.screenheight) + &
    '~r~nNumberOfColors =~t' + string(env.NumberOfColors) + &
    '~r~nOSType =~t' + s_os + &
    '~r~nOSFixesRevision =~t' + string(env.OSFixesRevision) + &
    '~r~nOSMajorRevision =~t' + string(env.OSMajorRevision) + &
```

## Chapter 8

```
            '~r~nOSMinorRevision =~t' + string(env.OSMinorRevision) + &
            '~r~nwin16 =~t' + s_win16 + &
            '~r~nPBType =~t' + s_pb + &
            '~r~nPBMajorRevision =~t' + string(env.PBMajorRevision) + &
            '~r~nPBMinorRevision =~t' + string(env.PBMinorRevision) + &
            '~r~nPBFixesRevision =~t' + string(env.PBFixesRevision) + &
            '~r~nCPUType = ' + s_cpu
END IF

as_return_string = s_text
return rc
```

This function calls the PowerBuilder GetEnvironment(), which populates the env environment structure. The following code interprets the values and builds a string describing the results. This will describe the environment where your PowerBuilder application is running.

**CHAPTER 9**

# Introduction to DataWindows

The DataWindow is PowerBuilder's high-level construct that encapsulates data access into a powerful, intelligent, datacentric object. You will use DataWindows for nearly all of your data access. This chapter contains a general introduction to DataWindows. The following two chapters continue this introduction to DataWindows.

## DATAWINDOW CONCEPTS

Basically the DataWindow stands between your application and the database (or other data source) and retrieves, manipulates, and presents the data as required by your application. Figure 9.1 shows the relation between these objects.

**324** Chapter 9

```
    PowerBuilder Application
              ↕
         DataWindow
              ↕
            data
```

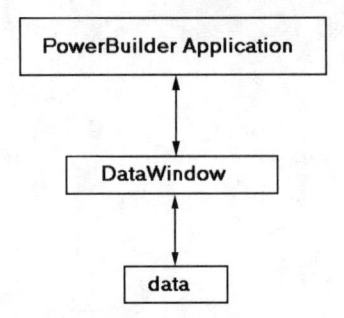

*Figure 9.1  PowerBuilder Applications use DataWindows to access data.*

It is essential that every PowerBuilder programmer become fluent with DataWindows. The DataWindow object is at the center of PowerBuilder's power. Initially you can think of the DataWindow as sort of a multicolumn listbox. The DataWindow is very intelligent, and contains the definitions that it needs to populate itself with data from the database (or another nondatabase data source). Once populated, the DataWindow allows easy manipulation of that data and is great for searching, sorting, filtering, and printing data. PowerBuilder provides functions that let you import and export data between DataWindows and a variety of data sources. These sources include:

- **Clipboard!**—Windows's clipboard
- **CSV!**—comma-separated text
- **Clipboard!**—Windows' clipboard
- **dBASE2!** and **dBASE3!**—dBASE-II && III format
- **DIF!**—Data Interchange Format
- **Excel!**—Microsoft Excel format
- **HTML!**—Text with HTML formatting
- **PSREPORT!**—Powersoft Report format
- **SQLInsert!**—SQL syntax
- **SYLK!**—Microsoft Multiplan format
- **Text!**—tab-separated columns with a return at the end of each row
- **WKS!**—Lotus 1-2-3 format
- **WK1!**—Lotus 1-2-3 format
- **WMF!**—Windows Metafile format

## DataWindow Objects and Controls

Look at the PowerBar and the PainterBar in the Window painter (see Figure 9.2) and notice that both have a DataWindow icon. These two icons actually refer to two different constructs. The first icon (contained in the PowerBar) refers to a **DataWindow object**, and the second icon (contained in the PainterBar) refers to a **DataWindow control**. The PowerBar icon opens the DataWindow object painter, where you define the object. You use the Window painter PainterBar icon to add a DataWindow control to a window, just like adding any other graphical control to a window. The next section clarifies the difference between the DataWindow object and the DataWindow control.

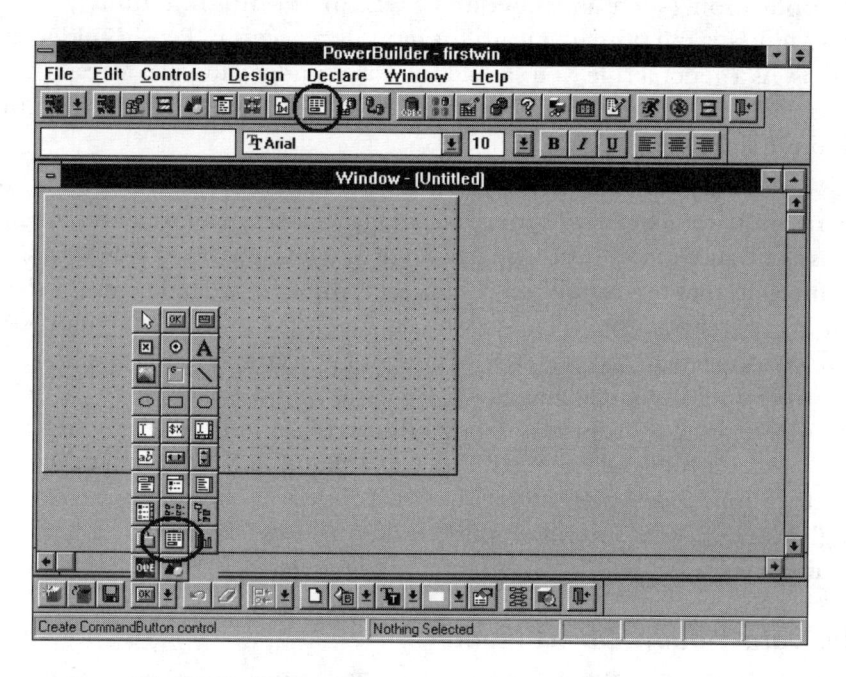

*Figure 9.2 The DataWindow painter icon on the PowerBar, the DataWindow control icon is on the Window painter toolbar.*

Think of the *DataWindow object* as the encapsulation of the data source, and the *DataWindow control* as the connection between a window (and therefore your application) and a DataWindow object. You might think of the DataWindow object as a picture and the DataWindow control as a picture frame. DataWindow objects have attributes. DataWindow controls have attributes, functions, and events. There are functions to read or modify DataWindow object attributes (Describe and Modify); these functions though, are applied to DataWindow controls.

## DataWindow Objects

DataWindow objects represent the data source for your application. The DataWindow encapsulates your database access into a high-level object that handles the retrieval and manipulation of data. The DataWindow also offers a wide range of presentation styles for your data, and the presentation can be customized to a large degree. There are other techniques for accessing data in an application (such as embedded SQL, or the file functions), but the DataWindow is the primary means for most data access in PowerBuilder applications. As a general rule, you should use DataWindows for all your data access. If you choose not to use a DataWindow, you should have good, clearly defined reasons to justify your decision.

You can also use a DataWindow instead of a group of Window controls. There are a number of advantages to defining a set of output and/or input fields as a DataWindow instead of as a set of SingleLineEdits or EditMasks. One advantage is that the DataWindow control is drawn as a single control (by the Windows system), rather than individually for each control. DataWindows also allow you to change the edit style of a field. For example, you can change the style from an Edit (single-line edit style) to an EditMask simply by changing a selection in a fields Properties dialog listbox. To do this same modification to a window control would require that you delete the SingleLineEdit control, create a new EditMask control, and move any event code from the SingleLineEdit to the new EditMask. DataWindows also provide a great deal of functionality for the fields, as mentioned earlier.

### *The DataWindow Object Painter*

Clicking on the **DataWindow** icon on the PowerBar opens the DataWindow painter. You create and modify DataWindow objects in the DataWindow painter. When created, DataWindows are defined as independent objects: They are not necessarily limited to a particular window, or even to a single application. They are much more tightly bound to the database manager and the table(s) to which they refer. DataWindow objects can be, and often are, shared between windows. You will use the same DataWindow objects in different applications that need to access the same tables.

The default prefix for DataWindow object names is d_. The name of the DataWindow object should reflect its purpose, or perhaps the name of the table that it accesses. If a DataWindow accesses the employee table, then you could name it d_employee or d_emp_hr_view.

## DATAWINDOW CONTROLS

The DataWindow icon on the Window painter PainterBar is a reference to a DataWindow control. You add a DataWindow control to a window just like any other control. You drop it on the window, and then position and size it. Then you link (associate) the DataWindow control to a specific DataWindow object. This makes the DataWindow object available to your application. You then code scripts to manipulate the DataWindow control. These scripts control the retrieval, manipulation, and presentation of the data. Often you will add CommandButtons or menu options to the window to trigger the retrieval, updating, and deleting of rows of data from the data source. You could also trigger the initial retrieval in the application or window open events. This is covered in great detail in the chapter "DataWindow Controls."

DataWindow control names have a default prefix of dw_, such as dw_employee. The Window painter assigns a default name, such as dw_1 or dw_2, to the new DataWindow control in the same manner as it names other controls. With most of the other controls, you will probably prefer to give the object a more descriptive name than the one the Window painter assigned. DataWindow controls are a little different in this regard. You may wish to keep the default DataWindow control names that are assigned by the Window painter. An example would be when you are writing scripts and creating windows that you would like to be available for reuse in other applications. If you name the primary DataWindow for each window dw_1, it makes it easier for code references to be generalized. For example, if you write common functions and scripts that refer to dw_1 and dw_2, those references will be general enough to allow you to reuse the same code for different DataWindow controls. Examples of this will be shown along with some alternative methods for obtaining the same generality.

Figure 9.3 shows the relationship between a window, a DataWindow control, a DataWindow object, and the data source.

```
        PB Application Window
                ↕
        DataWindow Control
                ↕
        DataWindow Object
                ↕
            data source
```

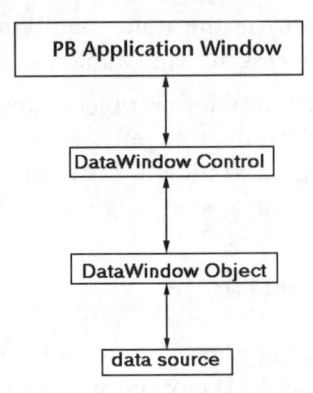

*Figure 9.3* The DataWindow control, DataWindow object, and data source.

The DataWindow control is contained in one of your application windows. The DataWindow control is linked to a particular DataWindow object, which has been defined for a specific data source.

## CREATING A NEW DATAWINDOW OBJECT

To create a DataWindow object for database access, you must be able to successfully connect to the database. You create DataWindows interactively with the database, so you must be connected to the database and be able to access the target table(s) when you are in the design process. This has the advantage of closely coupling the creation of the DataWindow object with the data source, but it also means that you cannot create or update a DataWindow if you cannot access the database. This can be a hindrance, such as when the server is down in a networked development environment.

PowerBuilder also creates its own repository in the database for storing the details about the columns and the tables in the database. This includes information such as data validation rules, presentation formats, edit masks, column labels, and field headings. This repository lets you share these definitions between DataWindows and between other developers to help establish standards across your applications.

When you define the attributes of the DataWindow object, you specify everything that the DataWindow object needs to know about accessing, presenting, formatting, validating, and manipulating the data. You may already have defined some of this information in the Database painter. PowerBuilder stored the definitions that you specified for each column in its repository. Later, when you (or another developer) make another reference to one of these columns, the information about that column will be available, without re-entering it. This helps to build more consistent, easier to maintain applications. For example, you can avoid having one report with a column heading of Employee ID, while another report calls the same column an Employee Number by storing and using the column headings in the repository. More details about the repository are in the chapter on the Database painter. You can override many of the repository defaults in the DataWindow painter.

## DataWindow Creation

Click on the **DataWnd** icon on the PowerBar to begin the process of creating a DataWindow. Watch the status line and you will see that PowerBuilder first connects to the database before opening the DataWindow painter. By default, the connection is to the database to which you last connected in the Database painter. If the connection is to the wrong database, close the painter and go into the Database painter and make the correct connection (see the chapter on the Database painter for more details). Then click again on the **DataWnd** icon on the PowerBar.

The Select DataWindow dialog box opens, as shown in Figure 9.4. To create a new DataWindow, click on the **New** CommandButton.

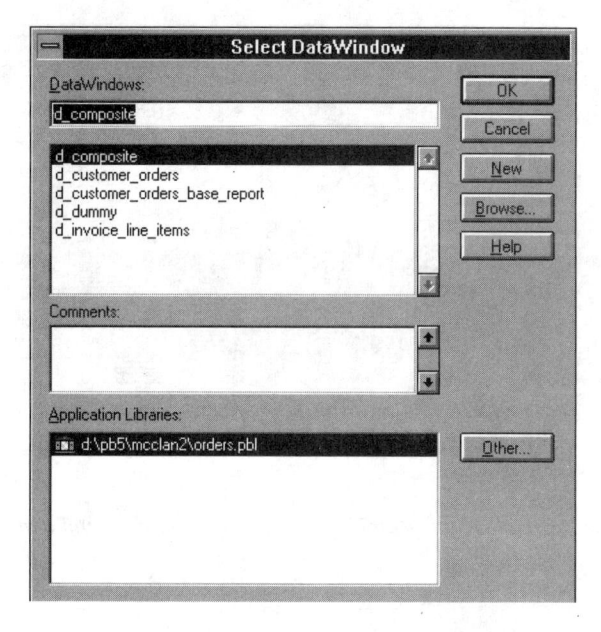

*Figure 9.4* The Select DataWindow dialog box.

The creation of a new DataWindow is divided into two aspects. The first is the definition of the *data source*, and the second is the definition of the *presentation* style. The definition of the data source most often consists of graphically creating a **SQL SELECT** statement, but there are other possibilities (such as file access, hard-coded values, API calls for data access, or programmatic generation).

The definition of the presentation style involves selecting a style and then customizing the appearance of the DataWindow in the DataWindow painter. This painter is somewhat similar to the Window painter; the DataWindow object is presented as a window, to which you add and modify various objects such as columns, computed fields, and labels. The list of available objects is different than the objects that can be added to a window, and the DataWindow object itself is designed to handle data, and is therefore much more complex than a window.

## The Data Source and Presentation Style

After clicking the **New** CommandButton in the Select DataWindow dialog box (Figure 9.4), the next step involves selecting the data source and presentation style. Make these two choices in the New DataWindow dialog box shown in Figure 9.5.

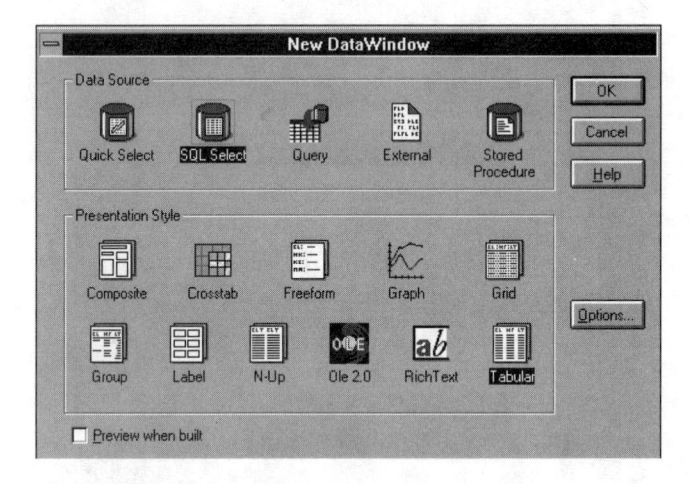

*Figure 9.5 The New DataWindow dialog box; select a data source and a presentation style.*

First you choose a data source. The data source specifies the origin of the data (where PowerBuilder will find the data). In most cases, data comes from a database, but other sources are possible (External data sources are covered later). You will edit (define) the data source in the Quick Select dialog box, the Query painter, or the Result Set dialog box, depending on the choice that you make for the data source.

Next you must specify the presentation style for the new DataWindow object. The presentation style is the format for displaying and accessing the data. You will customize the presentation style details in the DataWindow Presentation painter.

The most common choices in the New DataWindow dialog box are a SQL Select data source and a Tabular presentation style. You must be fluent with these choices as quickly as possible. You can learn more about the other options after you have mastered these two fundamentals.

## Data Sources

The choices for the data source fall into two categories, database sources and external (nondatabase) sources.

The New DataWindow dialog box lists the following data sources:

- Quick Select
- SQL Select
- Query
- External
- Stored Procedure (this is only available with some DBMSs)

All of these are database sources except for the External. The database source can be almost any of the currently available relational DBMSs such as Oracle, Sybase, Informix, SQLBase, or Watcom SQL. Local database managers (such as FoxPro, Paradox, dBase) or other data sources (such as text files) are available through the use of ODBC drivers. The Stored Procedure data source option is only displayed if the DBMS supports stored procedures. If you select a database source, you need only define a SQL SELECT statement. PowerBuilder automatically generates the UPDATE, DELETE, and INSERT statements that are required for the DataWindow.

The External data source includes all nondatabase sources. This includes data sources such as flat files, DDE, PowerScript arrays, API calls, and could even be data built by hard-coding values, programmatic calculations, or user input.

## Presentation Style

The DataWindow object has a wide variety of presentation styles to choose from. The most commonly used presentation style is tabular. The presentation style determines the manner in which data is presented to the user, and it also determines some of the interface options that the user has (such as the ability to resize a column dynamically). Each presentation style has an initial appearance that will be set up by default. The developer can customize the style and can modify many of the presentation details. In PowerBuilder, there is no other report generator separate from the DataWindow painter. DataWindow objects also serve as the source of all the reports that you generate.

The choices for presentation style are:

- Composite
- Crosstab
- Freeform
- Graph
- Grid
- Group
- Label
- N-Up
- Ole 2.0
- RichText
- Tabular

The most important presentation styles are Tabular, Freeform, and Group. You should become familiar with these types first.

## DataWindow Data Sources

This section presents information on all the available choices for data sources.

## Quick Select

The Quick Select data source is used to create simple queries. This is a fast and easy way to create SQL SELECT statements, but it is limited to queries that have no computed columns, and that have no retrieval arguments (but you may specify fixed selection criteria). Quick Select does allow the option of sorting the result set, but does not support the GROUP BY option. You can use multiple tables only if a foreign key has been defined in the Database painter. The join condition is set automatically.

Choose **Quick Select** on the New DataWindow dialog box and click on **OK**. The Quick Select dialog box appears (Figure 9.6).

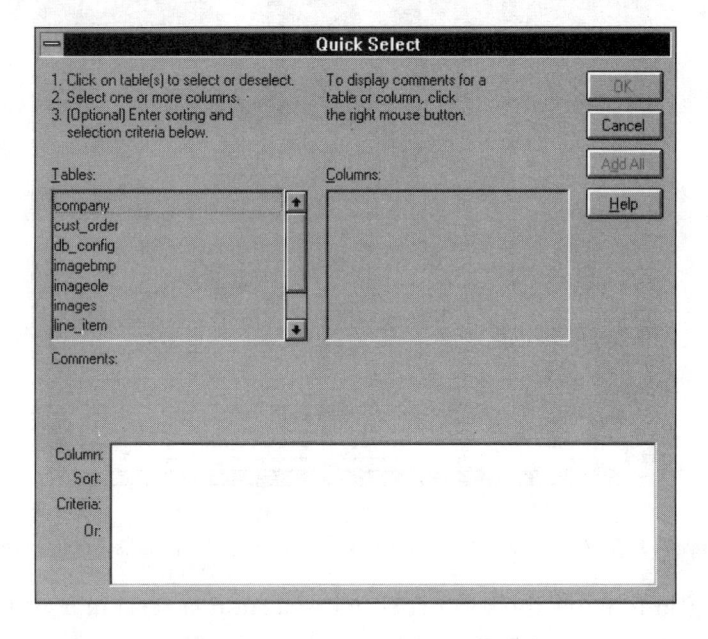

*Figure 9.6 The Quick Select dialog box.*

It takes only a couple of simple steps in this dialog box to define the SQL statement. The grid (at the bottom of the window) is similar to a QBE (Query By Example) matrix. Though this option is limited to rather simple queries, you should take time to explore the Quick Select dialog box because the QBE format is also available to you as a DataWindow mode. You may find the QBE technique to be a useful function to add to your DataWindows.

## The Quick Select Dialog Box

First, you must select a table from the Tables ListBox. PowerBuilder accesses the database to load the list of columns. Next you select the column(s) that you wish to retrieve from the Columns ListBox. Click on each column to select it or you can click on the **Add All** button if you wish to select every column in the table. To remove a column from the list, click on it and it is deselected. The columns that you select are added to the grid at the bottom of the window (see Figure 9.7).

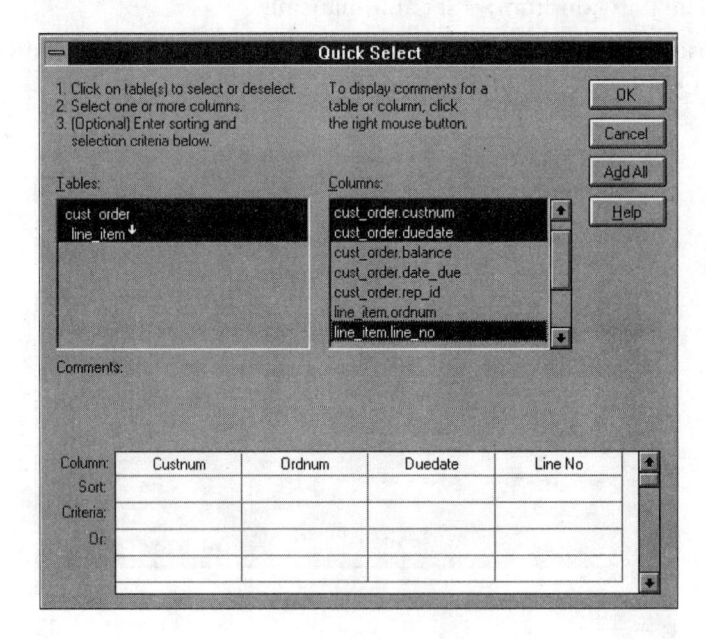

*Figure 9.7  Building a SELECT statement for the line_item and cust_order tables.*

Use this grid to enter the sort order and selection criteria in a QBE fashion. You can reorder the columns in the grid by selecting the column heading (with the mouse) and dragging it to its new position. You may enter selection criteria to restrict the rows that will be selected. It is important to note that any criteria specified on this grid are then hard-coded into the SELECT statement. If you want to define retrieval arguments (variable arguments), then you must use the Query painter to define the SELECT statement.

You can also specify a sort order for the result set. If there are no selection criteria (to be added to the WHERE clause) and no requirement to sort the data (to create an ORDER BY clause), then as soon as you choose the table and the columns, you are finished.

## Joins

You can select more than one table in the Quick Select dialog box only if they share a key relationship. The dialog box will help to find related tables. When you select a table, the Columns box and the Tables box will list all tables that have a foreign key that is related to the selected table. If you select a table from the indented list of related tables, the columns in that table are added to the list in the Columns box. The list in the Tables box will be updated to show only the tables that have a foreign key related to the newly selected table. If you want to return to the original table list, just click the first selected table at the top of the list. The join condition will be defined from the primary/foreign key relationship. You cannot enter the join condition directly.

## Sort Order

Add an ORDER BY clause to the SQL statement by defining a sort order. To do this, click in the grid at the bottom of the Quick Select dialog box. Make entries in the first row of the grid to set the sort order. Click under the column that you wish to use to determine the sort order; this opens a dropdown listbox (Figure 9.8).

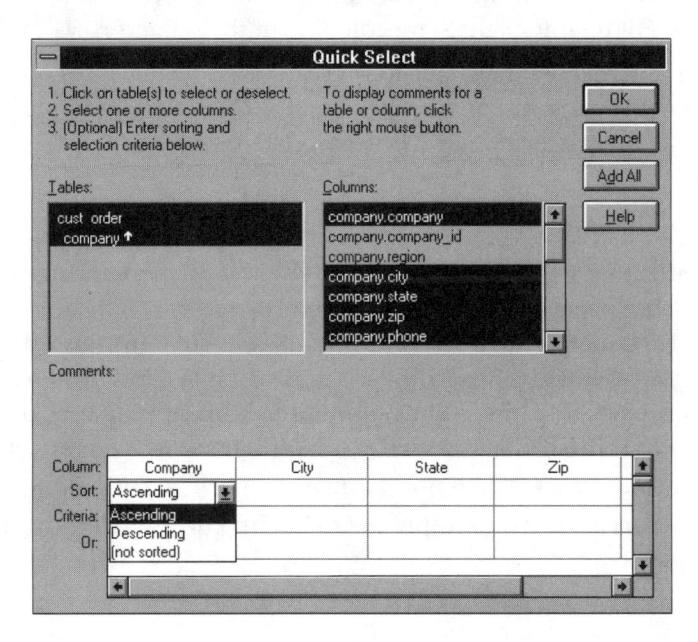

***Figure 9.8*** *Defining a sort order for the Company column.*

You have the option to select the **Ascending** or **Descending** order (or not sorted) from the dropdown listbox. The database sorts the query result rows by any fields that you have specified in this manner. If you use multiple columns in your sort specification, the ORDER BY uses the columns in the order as listed from left to right. You can reorder the columns by clicking on the column heading and dragging it to its new location; this also reorders the columns in the presentation.

## Select Criteria

Add selection criteria in the second and succeeding rows to restrict the rows in the result set. The selection criteria are placed in the WHERE clause of the generated SQL statement. The criteria that you are entering here are fixed criteria, always to be applied to the SELECT statement. If you want to add dynamic values, don't try to enter them here. You can do that later by adding Retrieval Arguments after the statement has been created (in the Query painter). The process is the same as is used for the SQL SELECT option for the data source, covered in the next section.

If the selection criteria is for equality, then just enter the value in the second row of the corresponding column. For example, to select rows from Ohio, enter OHIO under the state column (in the second row of the grid).

For conditions other than equality, you can enter the relational operator to be used for the comparison. For example, enter **< OHIO**, to list all the states that come before Ohio alphabetically. The legal relational operators are

```
=, <>, >, >=, <, <=, LIKE, IN
```

Use wildcards to create a search pattern. Use the % (percent sign) to signify any set of characters, and the _ (underscore) to represent any one, single character. For example, %a% selects any entry that contains the letter a. Th_s, returns any entry that begins with a Th as the first two letters and an s as the fourth letter (such as This or Thus). To find all the cities that begin with a C, you would enter **LIKE C%** in the city column. The search is case sensitive.

The entries in each row (after the first row) are added together to create the criteria. Succeeding rows imply an OR conjunction and let you build more complex queries.

For example, in Figure 9.9 the entry in the second row limits the result to those records with cities that start with the letter C and where the state is equal to OHIO. The third row adds an OR conjunction and adds all records which have a city starting with the word New (from any state) to the result set.

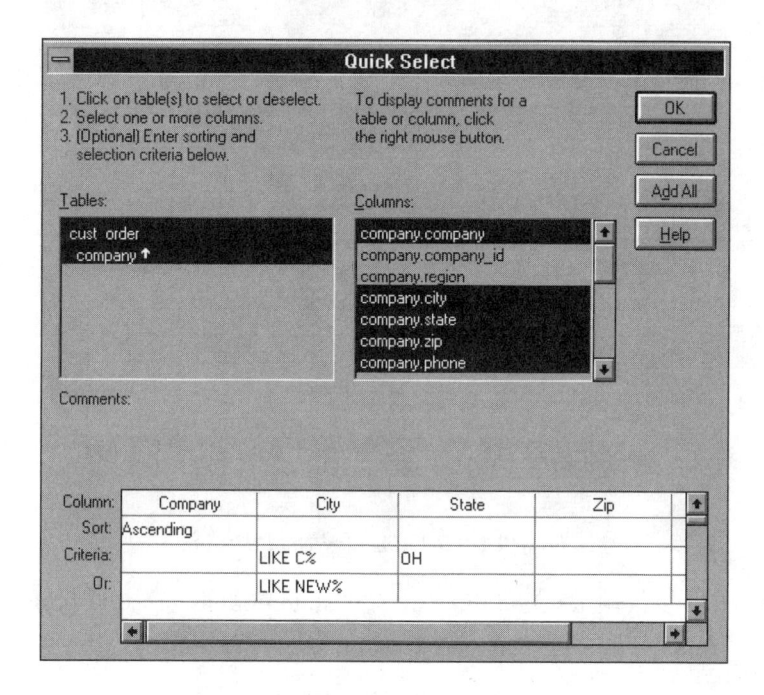

*Figure 9.9  Defining Select criteria.*

As a result of this criteria, the Quick Select creates the following SQL statement:

```
SELECT * FROM company
WHERE (city LIKE 'C%' AND state = 'OH') OR city LIKE 'New%'
SORT BY company;
```

You can also override the OR conjunction that is implicit between rows by inserting an **AND**. Figure 9.10 shows an example where the city must be between Akron and Dayton (alphabetically).

## Chapter 9

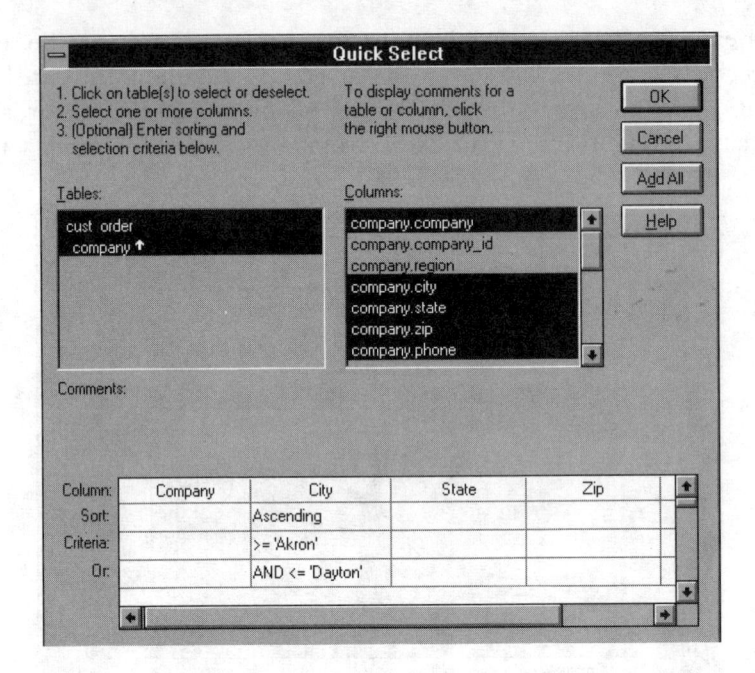

*Figure 9.10 Defining a selection criteria.*

The Quick Select creates the following SQL statement as a result of this criteria:

```
SELECT * FROM company
WHERE (city >= 'Akron' AND city <= 'Dayton')
SORT BY city;
```

In review, the Quick Select can be used to create queries with the follow limitations:

- simple columns only, no computed fields
- not dynamic retrieval arguments
- no subqueries
- no GROUP BY
- ORDER BY is allowed

## The SQL Select Data Source Option

The SQL Select data source option allows the creation of more powerful (and more complex) SELECT statements. Choose the **SQL Select** option if you need to create queries that use multiple tables, computed columns, GROUP BY clauses, or if you need to specify retrieval arguments. Many, if not most, of your DataWindow queries will be too complicated to be created in the Quick Select window.

To use this option, choose **SQL Select** on the New DataWindow dialog box for the data source. PowerBuilder opens the Query painter. The first step is to choose one or more tables from the Select Tables dialog box (Figure 9.11).

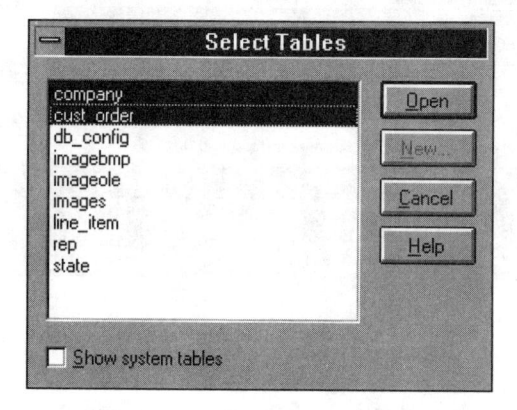

*Figure 9.11 The Select Tables dialog box.*

This dialog box presents a listbox containing all of the tables in the database to which you are connected. Clicking the **Show System Tables** checkbox on that dialog box adds the system tables to the listbox. Normally you don't wish to access the system tables and the default is not to include them in the listbox. This list includes both views and tables.

In this dialog box, you select the table(s) that will be used in the SQL SELECT statement. After selecting the table(s), click on the **Open** CommandButton to open the table(s) and the Query Painter (Figure 9.12).

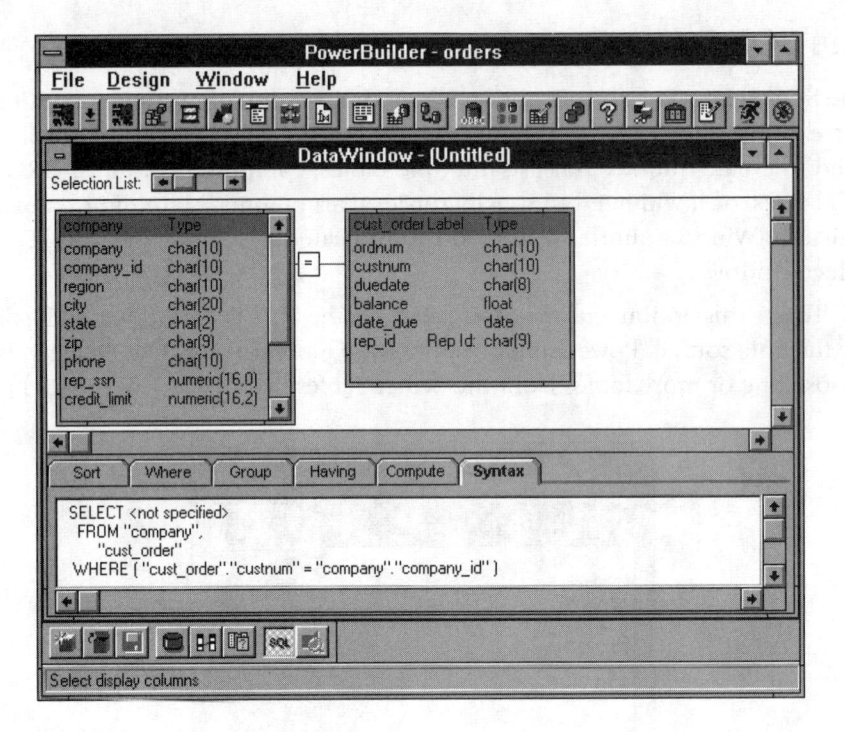

*Figure 9.12  The Query Painter utility.*

Next, continue with the selection of the columns from these tables, and then define any additional requirements for the SELECT statement. You can also use the Query painter to modify SQL statements, including those that you created with the Quick Select dialog box. If you have selected more than one table, you need to specify a join condition for each table.

## The SQL Toolbox

Note the tab dialog box at the bottom of the Query painter; this is the SQL toolbox. You can choose to display or hide the SQL toolbox using the **Design|Show|SQL Toolbar** menu item, or by clicking the **Painter bar Toolbox** icon. The SQL Toolbox gives you access to the following components of the current SQL SELECT statement:

- The syntax of the current SELECT statement
- The SELECT statement's WHERE clause

- The GROUP BY clause
- The HAVING clause (for a GROUP BY)
- The Sort specification (ORDER BY)

Each of these tabs will be covered in the next sections of this chapter.

## Joins

The tables that you have selected are dropped onto the Query painter's work area. If you have selected two or more tables, PowerBuilder will attempt to determine the join conditions to be used between the tables. The join conditions are presented graphically in the work area as a line drawn between the joining columns; the relational operator is contained in a box on that line. You may have to scroll the column list for each table to see which column(s) is being referenced by the line.

Add a join condition by clicking on the **Join** icon on the Painter bar. Click on the column name in the first table and then click on the column name in the second table. This adds the graphical representation of the join to the display, and also adds the join condition to the WHERE clause. The Query painter assumes that the join condition is equality (which is usual). Change the operator by clicking on the join's relational operator square (|=| in Figure 9.12). This opens the Join dialog box shown in Figure 9.13. In this window, you can change the operator or delete the join condition entirely, or specify an outer join (if outer joins are supported by your database).

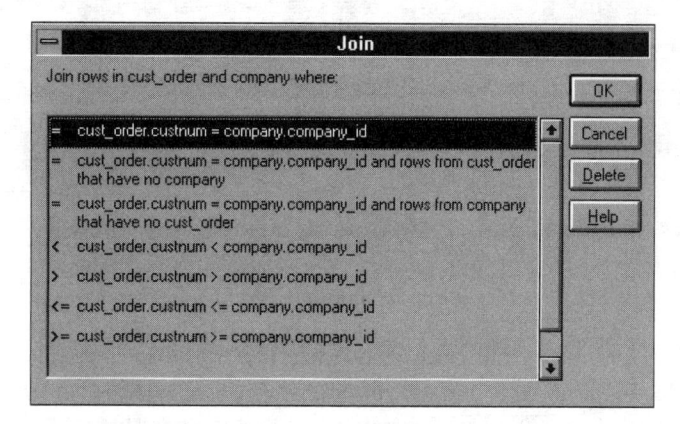

**Figure 9.13** *Selecting the JOIN condition.*

## Selecting Columns

Add columns to the select statement by clicking the column name from the table on the Query painter work area (Figure 9.12). Add all the columns from a table by selecting **Select All** from the control menu (available on each table). The name of each column is highlighted when it is added to the select clause. Remove columns from the list by selecting the column name again. As you add columns, they are added to the selection list area at the top of the Query painter window as labeled rectangles. Reorder columns by clicking and dragging the column's rectangle to its new location. Figure 9.14 shows an example where two columns have been added from the company table; and the next step is to add all the columns in the `cust_order` table using **Select All** on the `cust_order` control menu.

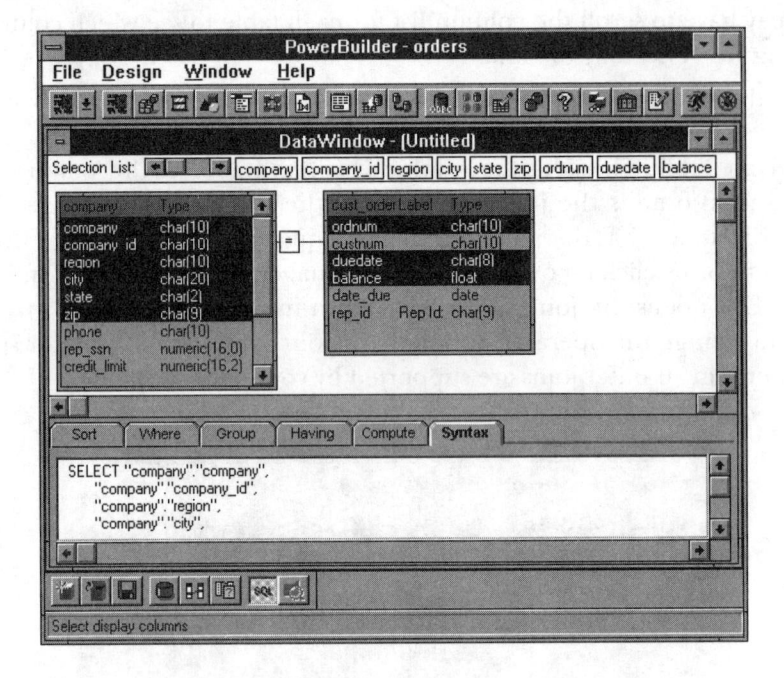

*Figure 9.14 Adding columns to the SELECT statement.*

> **NOTE** You may return to the SQL painter to add more columns at a later time. If you do so, the added columns may not be set to **updatable** by default. You can fix this in the Presentation painter under the Rows|Update Properties menu option covered later in this chapter.

## Computed Columns

To add a computed column to the SELECT clause, click on the **Compute** tab on the SQL Toolbox. Use the right mouse button to open a popup menu with options that help build SQL expressions (Figure 9.15).

To build computed columns, you can paste column names, SQL functions arguments into a Computed Columns edit field to build the expression for the new column.

If you add the DISTINCT option, the result returns only unique values for the column. Click on the **Design|Distinct** to add the DISTINCT option to the computed column.

When you define a computed column in the Query painter, you specify a calculation that is to be performed by the DBMS. Later (on the presentation side) you have the option to create calculations to be computed in the DataWindow. These calculations are computed by PowerBuilder after the data retrieval.

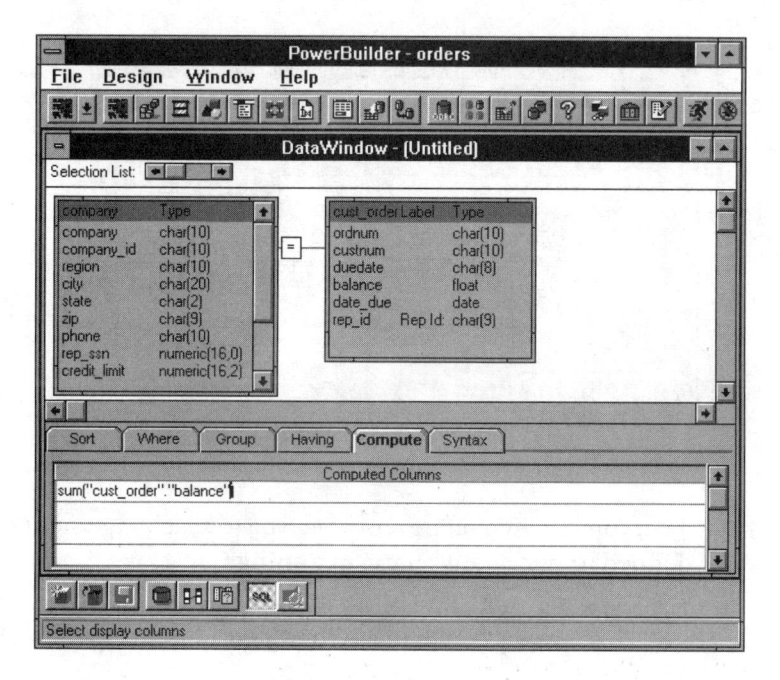

**Figure 9.15** *The Create Computed Column dialog box.*

**NOTE:** If you want to have an additional field on your DataWindow that is accessible in the same way as a table column, create a 'dummy' column in the SQL Select clause. These columns are accessible by any functions that you can use on a regular column (`SetItem()` or `GetItem()`), and have the same set of attributes, such as DisplayAsBitmap. Regular calculated columns in the DataWindow do not have this capability.

## WHERE Clause Criteria

You can specify any selection criteria to be added to the WHERE clause. This restricts the rows that are selected from the database. You can specify conditions with constants or with variables (called *retrieval arguments*) that will be passed into the DataWindow when the query is actually executed. If you are going to use variables in the WHERE clause, then you must declare retrieval arguments before making a reference to them (in the WHERE clause).

To define retrieval arguments, select the **Design|Retrieval Argument** menu option. This opens the Specify Retrieval Arguments dialog box (Figure 9.16).

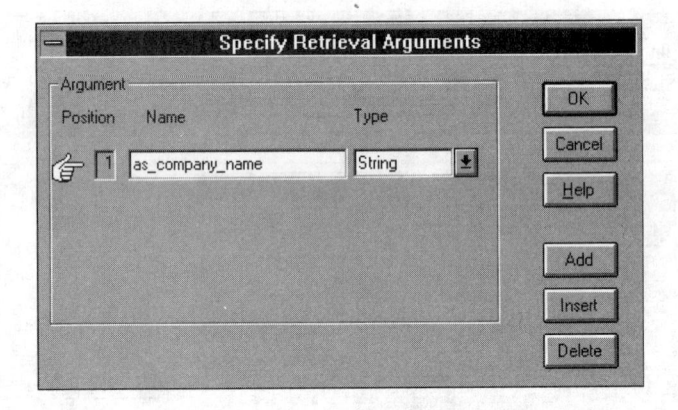

*Figure 9.16 Defining retrieval arguments.*

In this dialog box, you specify a name and data type for each argument. In this example, we defined `as_company_name` as a string.

To add search criteria to the WHERE clause, click on the **Where** tab on the SQL toolbox. This opens the Where tab showing Column, Operator, Value, and Logical.

In this dialog box, you build expressions from column names, SQL Functions, operators, and retrieval arguments. Click the left mouse button on the next row in the Columns column to select the Column name from a listbox. You may use the RMB popup to add Columns, Functions, Arguments, or to clear the entry. You may also type a value directly into the field. Next you will click in the Operator column to display a listbox of possible choices.

Open the RMB popup in the Value field to choose from **Columns**, **Functions**, **Arguments**, or **Select**. Use the **Select** option to create subqueries (nested queries). You may also type values directly into the Value field.

At the end of each line you must choose either the AND or the OR conjunction to link to the next line (if any). You can also add parenthesis in the expression as necessary to specify the evaluation order of the expression.

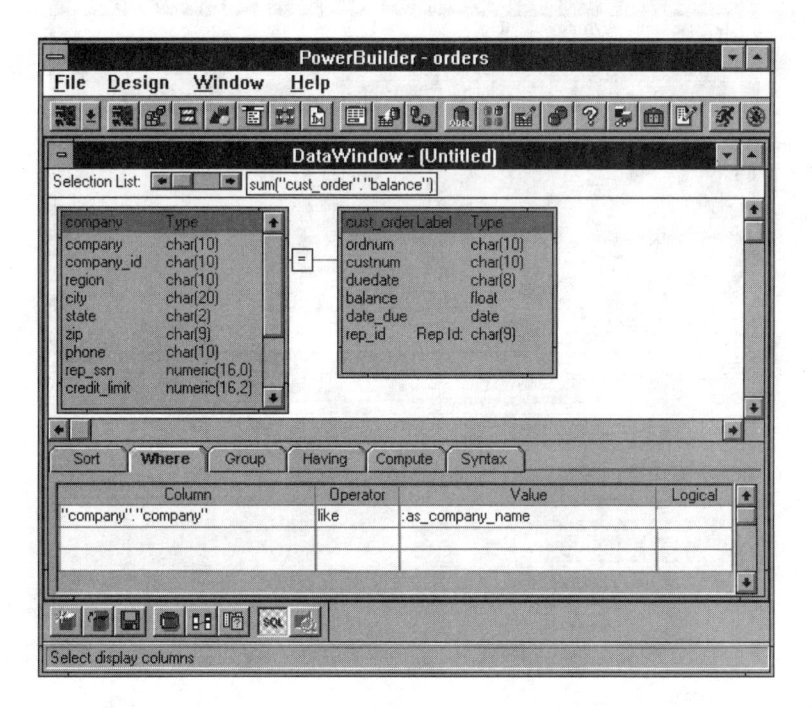

*Figure 9.17 Defining the WHERE criteria.*

## Viewing the SQL Statement

View the SQL statement that the Query painter has created by selecting the **Syntax** tab. This displays the SQL statement that has been generated as a result of the work you have completed so far in this painter, as in the example in Figure 9.18.

If a join is displayed in the work area, the join condition will be added to the WHERE clause. Edit the SQL statement text if necessary (but you can't do that in the Syntax tab). To edit the SQL statement, select the **Design|Convert to Syntax** menu option. This opens the editor where you can make changes in syntax (text) mode.

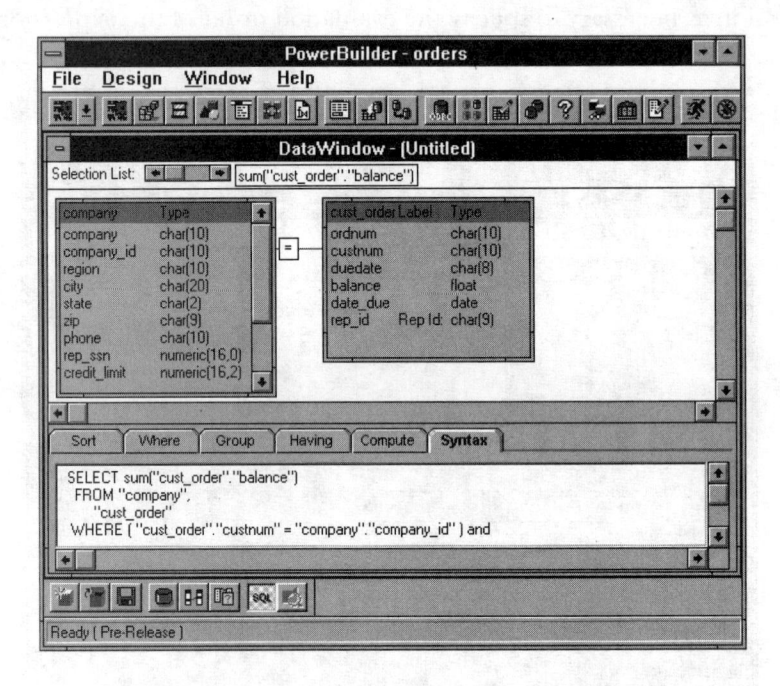

*Figure 9.18 Displaying the SELECT statement.*

When you have finished with the editing, you must select the **Design| Convert to Graphics** menu selection to move the query back to the Query painter. (I have found this to be one of the rougher sections of the PowerBuilder environment. Sometimes PowerBuilder is unable to convert legal SQL statements to graphics.)

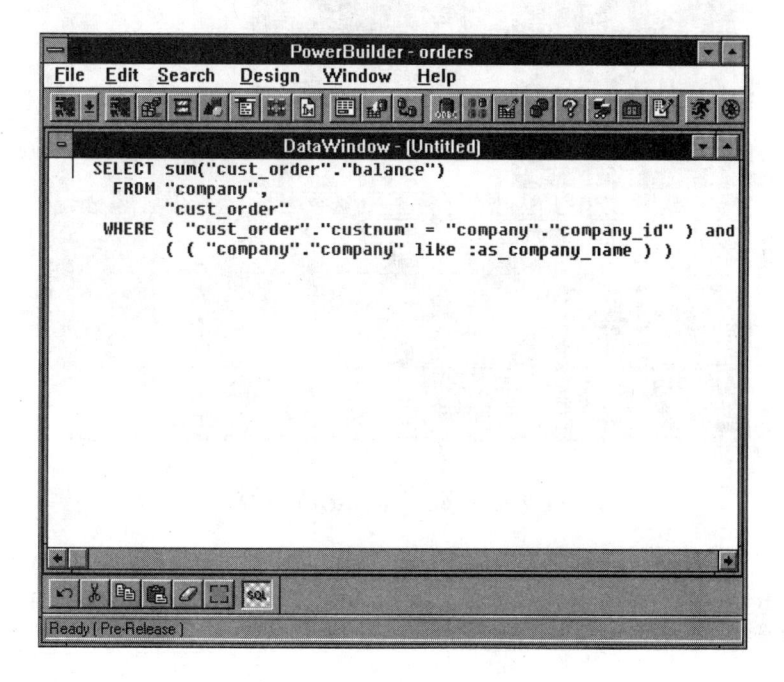

*Figure 9.19  Editing a SQL SELECT statement.*

## Group By

You specify a grouping for the result set by clicking on the **Group** tab on the SQL toolbox. This opens the dialog box shown in Figure 9.20.

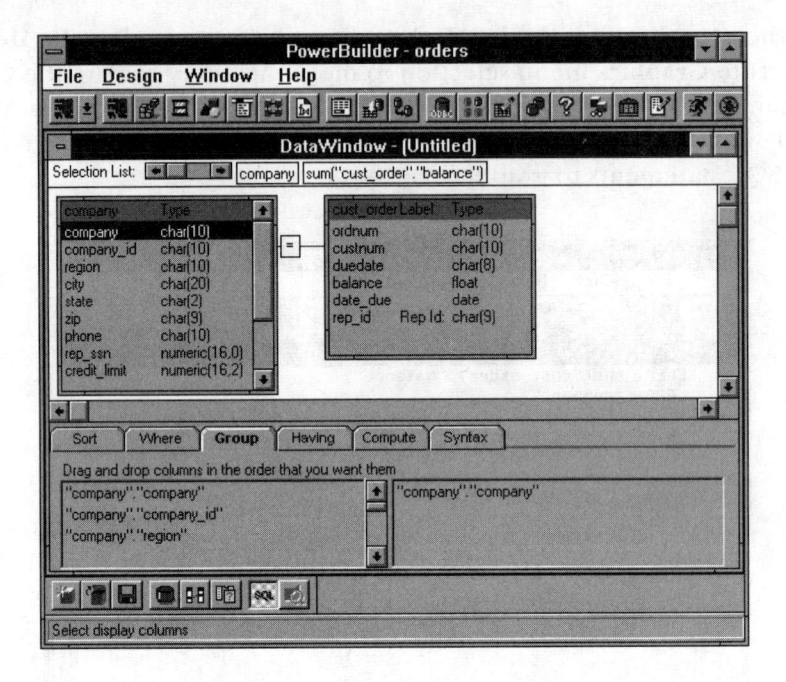

*Figure 9.20  Defining a GROUP BY clause.*

Add the column names in the order that you want for the GROUP BY clause. To insert an item into the list, drag the column(s) to the right-hand listbox. To remove an item, drag it back to the left listbox.

> **NOTE** Note the following limitations for the SELECT clause when you add a GROUP BY clause. In a SQL statement that has a GROUP BY clause, the items in the select list are limited to the items that are also in the GROUP BY clause, and the aggregate column functions such as MIN, MAX, AVG, SUM, etc.

## Having

After you add the GROUP BY condition, you can add a HAVING clause which creates a filter based on the GROUP BY results. Click on the **Having** tab on the SQL toolbox; this opens the Having dialog box shown in Figure 9.21.

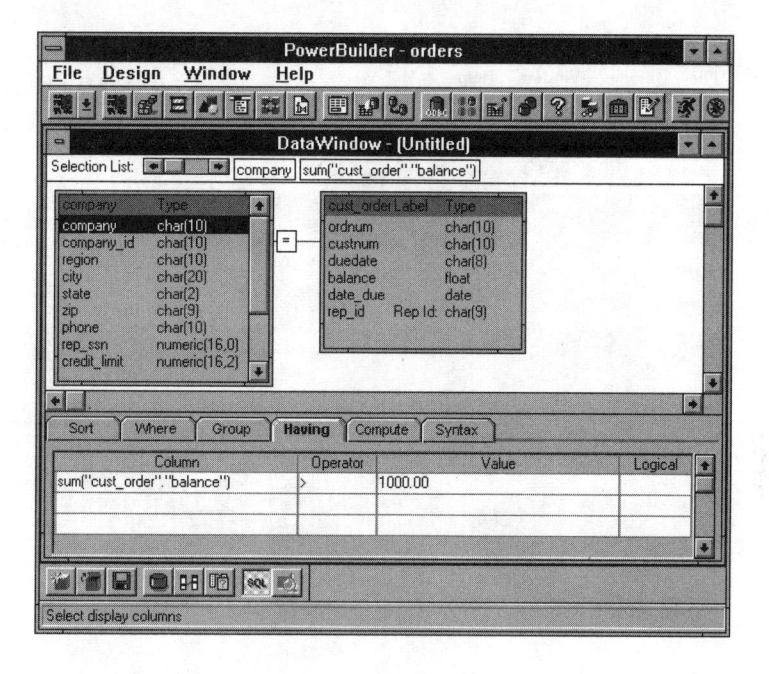

*Figure 9.21 Defining the HAVING clause for a SELECT statement.*

The operation of this dialog box is almost the same as the Where Criteria dialog box, but it is actually a little simpler. In this dialog box, you can restrict the rows that are added to the result set as a result of a criteria placed on the GROUP BY calculation. In the example shown in Figure 9.21, the result set is limited to companies with a balance greater than $100.00.

## Order By

To add an ORDER BY clause to the SQL statement, click on the **Sort** tab on the SQL toolbox. This opens the Sort dialog box (Figure 9.22). A ListBox provides the choices that you have for sorting. Drag a column from the listbox and drop it in the listbox on the right side to add it to the ORDER BY list. In the list, you can select to sort in either ascending or descending order (for each column). To insert an item in the list, just drag to the point in the list where you want insert an item. You can also reorder the columns using drag and drop. To remove an item, just drag it back to the left listbox.

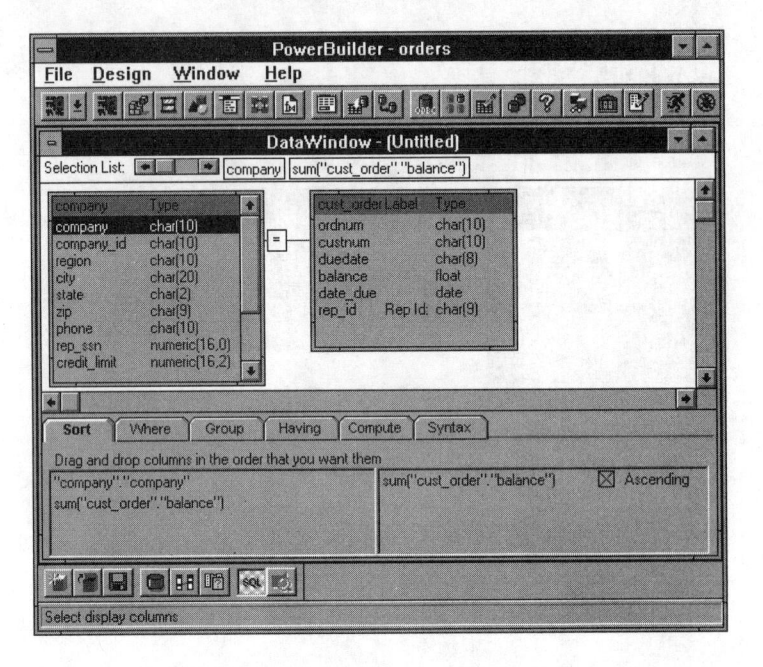

*Figure 9.22* Defining a sort order.

## Unions

You can add UNIONs to your SELECT statements. This option is found on the Design|Unions menu selection. The column count and types must match for each SELECT statement in the UNION.

When you have completed the SQL Statement, click on **Design|Data Source** (or **Painter bar SQL** icon) to go to the design window. But before you do that, you may wish to save the current SELECT statement as a query.

## Saving a Query

If you use the query for other DataWindows, then you can save this query into a PowerBuilder library by selecting the **File|Save Query As** menu option. You will be prompted to set the library and name the query. By convention, query names use the `prefix q_`, such as `q_customer_invoices`.

## The Query Data Source Option

Another Data Source option in the New DataWindow dialog box is Query. The Query data source option lets you use a previously defined SELECT statement as the data source. This could be a query that was created as the result of the SQL SELECT data source option that you saved for later reuse. It could also be a SELECT statement that was created in the Query painter, or one that was originally created in a text editor and converted in the Query painter. The predefined query must reside in a PowerBuilder library. Figure 9.23 shows the Select Query dialog box.

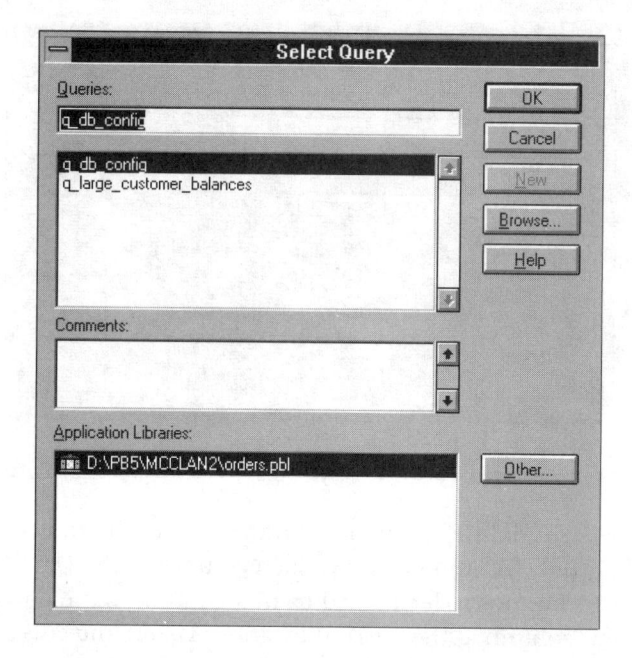

*Figure 9.23* The Select Query dialog box.

Select the library (using the Directories and Libraries listboxes), and then select the query. The DataWindow painter then opens. You can modify the SELECT statement by clicking on the **SQL Select** icon (on the PainterBar) or by selecting the **Design|Edit Data Source** menu option.

## The External Data Source Option

Another Data Source option in the New DataWindow dialog box is External. The External data source option lets you use a nondatabase source for a DataWindow. This can be from a variety of sources including files, the clipboard, DDE, and even hard-coded values. You can also use External DataWindows as an alternative to a group of standard window controls on a window. In this manner, you can package a set of controls into a unit.

When you select the external data source option, PowerBuilder opens the Result Set Description dialog box.

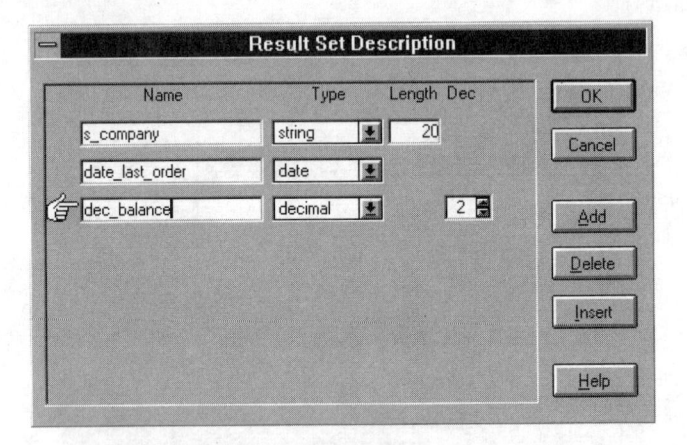

*Figure 9.24 Defining a result set.*

In this window, you define the name, data type, length, and the number of decimal places (only for numerics) for each column of the DataWindow. This window provides buttons to let you Add a new column to the end of the result set, Insert a new column at the current location, Delete the currently selected column, or to receive Help on using this dialog box. When you have defined all of the columns, click on **OK**; this opens the DataWindow painter.

In the case of External DataWindows, you will be responsible for writing the code necessary to populate the DataWindow, or you can use the **Rows|Data** menu option to select data.

## The Stored Procedure Data Source Option

The Stored Procedure data source option is only available if your DBMS supports stored procedures. If so, you can select a stored procedure as a database source for a DataWindow. The DataWindow executes the stored procedure and display: the result set based on that procedure. After you choose the **Stored Procedure** data source option, PowerBuilder opens the Select Stored Procedure dialog box. In this dialog box, pick one procedure from the listbox. You can view the source code for the stored procedure in the Source edit box at the bottom of the dialog box. After you select a stored procedure, define the result set in the Result Set dialog box as described in the previous section on external data sources. If a stored procedure computes more than one result set, you may specify which result set you want to populate the DataWindow. When you finish defining the result set and click on **OK**, the DataWindow painter opens and you can continue with the editing of the presentation style.

## PRESENTATION STYLES

After defining the new DataWindow's data source, your next task is to specify the details of the presentation style. The presentation style determines the layout of the data and specifies the general manner in which the user interacts with that data. You can modify the presentation style to a large, almost unlimited degree. PowerBuilder provides you with ten presentation styles to choose from; each is different in the way that it presents the data.

The choices for presentation style are:

- **Composite**—combines DataWindow reports.
- **Crosstab**—presents the data in a cross tabulation format. This is most useful for calculating totals by groups. Crosstab presents data in a manner similar to spreadsheet programs.
- **Freeform**—this is the "forms"-like presentation. Generally, you use the freeform presentation style to enter, update, delete, and display individual records. The DataWindow presents all of the fields (column values) of a single record with a field label.
- **Graph**—PowerBuilder has an excellent selection of graphs, similar to the graphs available in Microsoft Excel.
- **Grid**—the grid style is similar to the tabular presentation style. The user can reorder and resize the columns in the DataWindow. This provides the advantages of the tabular presentation style, and also allows the user to adjust the display. The disadvantage of the grid style is that while the user can rearrange columns, the developer is not able to modify the layout in the flexible manner available in the tabular style. This style is most often used for display only purposes.

- **Group**—the group presentation style makes it very easy to create reports with group summations. The format is attractive and immediately useful if it matches your requirements. The display is divided into groups with headings and summation rows predefined. The report includes page header, time, and page count.
- **Label**—presents data in a simple mailing label format.
- **N-Up**—presents data in columns across the screen like a newspaper. When a column reaches the bottom of the screen, the data continues in the next column (left to right). The exception to this is that sorted data is presented across the columns in rows.
- **OLE 2.0**—this is a very powerful option which provides support for Microsoft's standard OLE 2.0. This OLE object provides support for Microsoft Word, Graph, and Excel. This version also activates OLE 2.0 containers in place.
- **RichText**—presents data in a Rich Text Format (RTF) editor. You can load and save RTF files, include headers and footers, and provide the multiple fonts and text options in the control. The RTF editor provides enhanced editing functions to the user.
- **Tabular**—the most important, and most often used, presentation style. Data is presented in columns under column headings. Each row is presented in a separate line initially. This presentation allows a great deal of flexibility. You can take a tabular presentation and create a form presentation, or a group presentation very easily. You can create summary bands.

Most commonly used is Select/Tabular, so be sure that you are fluent with this combination before you spend a great deal of time exploring the other options.

The next section presents a sample of the most important presentation styles (you can find an example of the other styles in the DWSTYLES example on the example CD-ROM. The next chapter has details on how to create DataWindows with each of these presentation styles.

## Freeform

This is the "forms"-like presentation. Generally, you use the freeform presentation style to enter, update, delete, and display individual records. The DataWindow presents each of the fields (column values) of a single record with a field label. This format can be customized to a large degree.

Figure 9.25 presents a row from the company table. This form would probably be used to input new records. It could also be used to update, delete, and view records.

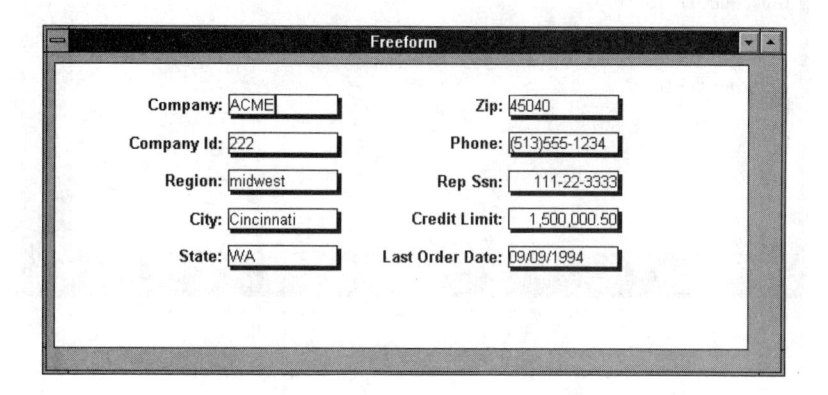

*Figure 9.25  A Freeform report.*

## Tabular

The tabular style is the most important and most often used presentation style. Data is presented in columns under column headings. Each row is presented initially as a separate line. This presentation allows a great deal of flexibility. You can take a tabular presentation and create a form presentation, or a group presentation, very easily.

Figure 9.26 shows an example of a tabular DataWindow. In this example, invoice line items are displayed and grouped together by order number and customer number. The DataWindow also totals the amount of each order.

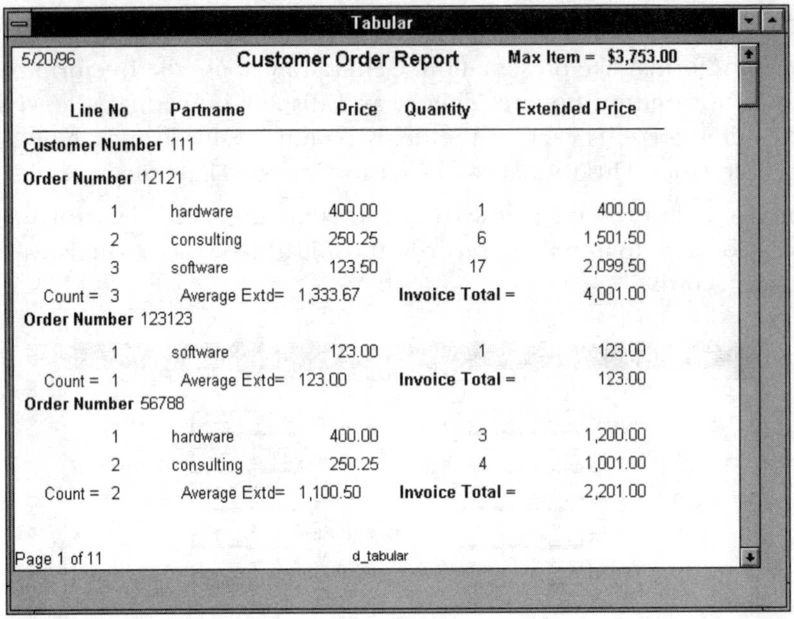

```
                           Tabular
5/20/96               Customer Order Report      Max Item =  $3,753.00

        Line No    Partname       Price    Quantity    Extended Price
Customer Number 111
Order Number 12121
           1       hardware       400.00       1           400.00
           2       consulting     250.25       6         1,501.50
           3       software       123.50      17         2,099.50
     Count = 3     Average Extd= 1,333.67   Invoice Total =  4,001.00
Order Number 123123
           1       software       123.00       1           123.00
     Count = 1     Average Extd=  123.00    Invoice Total =   123.00
Order Number 56788
           1       hardware       400.00       3         1,200.00
           2       consulting     250.25       4         1,001.00
     Count = 2     Average Extd= 1,100.50   Invoice Total =  2,201.00

Page 1 of 11                     d_tabular
```

*Figure 9.26* *The Tabular style.*

# Group

The group presentation style makes it very easy to create reports with group summations. The format is attractive and useful. The display is divided into groups with headings and summation rows predefined. The report includes page header, time, and page count.

It doesn't take very much work to make a great looking presentation with the group presentation style. An example of the group presentation style is shown in Figure 9.27.

This DataWindow groups the line items for each customer (company) and also calculates the total amount for all the invoices for that customer. A final summation has been added to calculate the total of all sales.

|  |  | Group |  |  |  |
| --- | --- | --- | --- | --- | --- |
|  | **Current Customer Orders Report** |  |  |  |  |
| 5/20/96 |  |  |  |  |  |
| Order Number | Line No | Partname | Price | Quantity | Extended Price |
| **Customer Number** 111 |  |  |  |  |  |
| 12121 | 1 | hardware | 400.00 | 1 | 400.00 |
| 12121 | 2 | consulting | 250.25 | 6 | 1,501.50 |
| 12121 | 3 | software | 123.50 | 17 | 2,099.50 |
| 123123 | 1 | software | 123.00 | 1 | 123.00 |
| 56788 | 1 | hardware | 400.00 | 3 | 1,200.00 |
| 56788 | 2 | consulting | 250.25 | 4 | 1,001.00 |
| 6111 | 1 | hardware | 400.00 | 3 | 1,200.00 |
| 9900 | 1 | consulting | 400.00 | 1 | 400.00 |
|  |  |  | Customer Total = |  | 7,925.00 |
| **Customer Number** 222 |  |  |  |  |  |
| 12123 | 1 | hardware | 400.00 | 3 | 800.00 |
| Page 1 of 6 |  |  |  |  |  |

*Figure 9.27* A Group report.

# dwstyles.pbl

You will find an example of all presentation types in the dwstyles application in the **DWSTYLES.PBL**.

**CHAPTER 10**

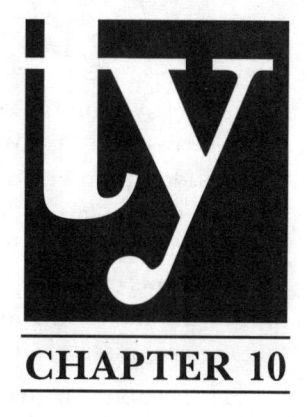

# The DataWindow Painter

The previous chapter presented an overview of the DataWindow object. This chapter focuses on the DataWindow Presentation painter, where you edit the DataWindow object presentation. The DataWindow Presentation painter is similar in complexity to the Window painter. DataWindows serves as the primary interface for data access for the user. DataWindows are also the source for most report generation in PowerBuilder. It is essential to master all the details in order to be able to create the best looking and informative reports. The next chapter covers the programming of DataWindow controls.

# Enhancing DataWindow Objects

After you have completed the definition of the data source, the DataWindow painter creates a DataWindow object. For a tabular presentation style, the DataWindow painter positions the labels, columns, and summation fields (if any) in a default layout. The DataWindow presentation format looks similar to many reports that you have seen before. In the PowerBuilder system, DataWindows can be used to display information on the screen, and to accept input from the user. You can also create Reports in the PowerBuilder system that are essentially read-only (display only) DataWindows.

This chapter discusses the customization of DataWindow objects. Most of this discussion assumes that a DataWindow object was defined with the tabular presentation style, but a great deal of this discussion also applies to the other presentation styles. The tabular presentation is the most often used style, and it has the widest range of customizing abilities. The other presentation styles are covered in the last section of this chapter.

In the tabular presentation style, data is presented in columns under column headings. Each row is presented initially in a separate line; this allows a great deal of flexibility. You can take a tabular presentation and create a form presentation or a group presentation very easily.

## Customizing the DataWindow Presentation

You design and edit the DataWindow object in the DataWindow painter. You can customize the DataWindow presentation by rearranging fields, changing font styles, adding labels, date, time, and page numbers. You can add graphs and other graphical objects (including pictures), and change the font, colors, and the style of presentation for each of the columns. You can also divide the rows into sets of records grouped by the value of one or more columns, and you can add summaries for those groups.

Figure 10.1 shows a DataWindow report.

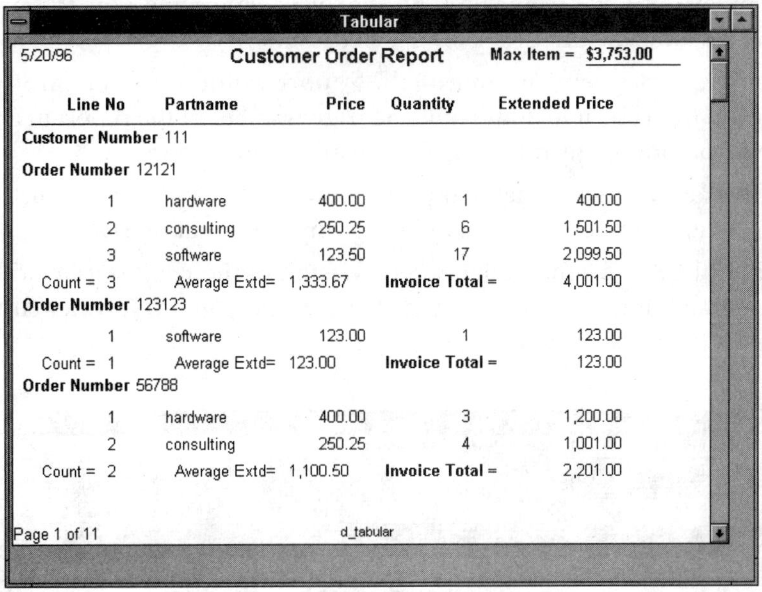

```
┌─────────────────────── Tabular ───────────────────────┐
│ 5/20/96              Customer Order Report    Max Item = $3,753.00 │
│                                                                    │
│        Line No    Partname      Price   Quantity   Extended Price  │
│ Customer Number 111                                                │
│ Order Number 12121                                                 │
│           1       hardware      400.00      1          400.00      │
│           2       consulting    250.25      6        1,501.50      │
│           3       software      123.50     17        2,099.50      │
│     Count = 3     Average Extd= 1,333.67  Invoice Total = 4,001.00 │
│ Order Number 123123                                                │
│           1       software      123.00      1          123.00      │
│     Count = 1     Average Extd= 123.00    Invoice Total = 123.00   │
│ Order Number 56788                                                 │
│           1       hardware      400.00      3        1,200.00      │
│           2       consulting    250.25      4        1,001.00      │
│     Count = 2     Average Extd= 1,100.50  Invoice Total = 2,201.00 │
│                                                                    │
│ Page 1 of 11                     d_tabular                         │
└────────────────────────────────────────────────────────┘
```

*Figure 10.1* *A DataWindow report.*

In the DataWindow in Figure 10.1, notice that the report is divided into sections. At the top of the report (above the horizontal line) there is a heading that contains a label for the report (Customer Order Report) and the date of the report. The heading also contains column headings for the rows of data that appear in the main body (the detail band) of the report. The invoice line items are grouped by customer number and then by order number.

The detail section contains the actual data from the SQL query. This is the main section of the report that presents the details for each line in the invoice.

## Chapter 10

A single line immediately follows each detail section to display the total balance for the invoice. This is a calculated value computed in the DataWindow. A summary line presents the total balance due from the customer and follows after the last order for each customer.

Finally, at the very bottom of the report window, footer information appears. In this case, it includes only the page number of the report in a format that tells you how many total pages there are in this report.

This example uses the tabular presentation style, but has been customized to have an appearance somewhat like a group presentation style.

Figure 10.2 shows the design screen version of the same DataWindow; this is in the DataWindow painter. In the DataWindow painter, you can customize the report to make it exactly what you want.

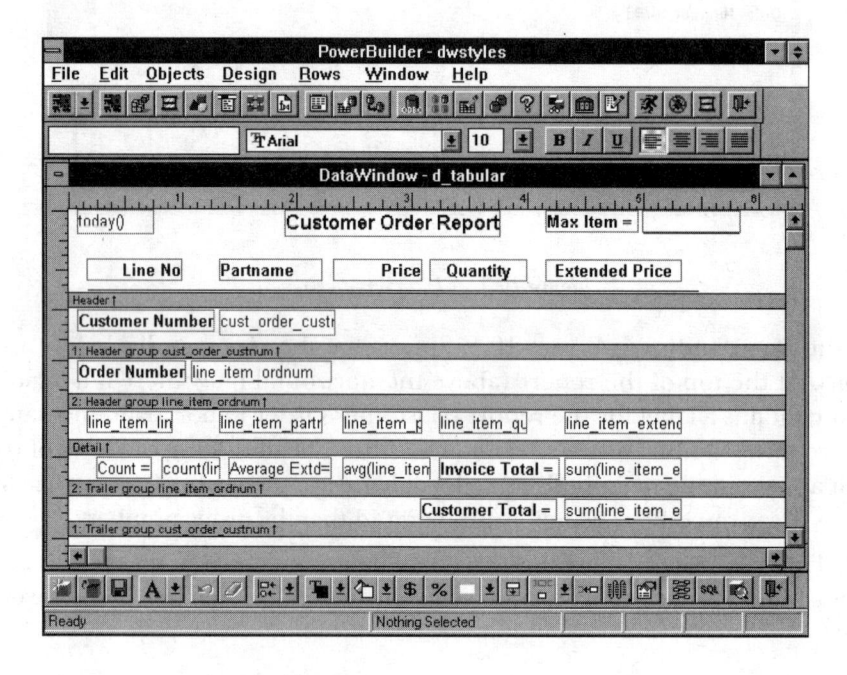

*Figure 10.2* Designing a DataWindow object.

# Bands

The design screen for the DataWindow painter is divided into a number of sections called *bands*. You may recognize the design format; it is presented in a manner similar to that used by a number of database report generators. The tabular display format always has at least four bands: header, detail, summary, and footer bands. Each band represents a section of the final DataWindow report.

Each band has a different function in building the DataWindow presentation. The header band contains column heading, report labels, and other information that is to be displayed at the top of the report. The detail band contains the selection result set (the actual rows from the database), usually presented in rows across the DataWindows. The summary band is used to display summation totals, like the invoice total in Figure 10.1. The footer band is used to present page numbers and other information that is to appear at the bottom of each page. If you create groups in the DataWindow, two additional bands are added for each group. In the example (Figures 12.1 and 12.2), a group for customer number and order numbers were created.

## The Header Band

The header band contains the information that appears at the top the DataWindow and at the top of each page of the report (the printout). This band usually includes a report title, the date, and column headings for the rows of data that appear in the detail band. The header band may also show the report parameters such as the value of the retrieval arguments or the date range for the data. Anything placed in the header band is automatically defined for display only.

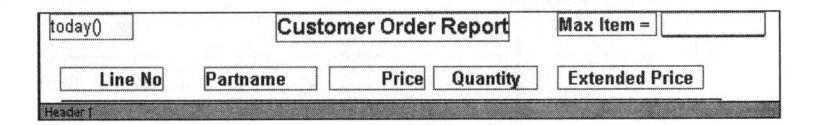

*Figure 10.3* The header band.

In this example, the header contains the report label (Customer Order Report), the date (today()), a label, and static text field for the maximum item in any invoice, and the five column headings for the detail band.

## The Detail Band

The detail band presents the actual data that is the result of the Select statement (or other data source). The detail band displays the result set columns in rows of data across the DataWindow. The DataWindow painter initially adds one SingleLineEdit field for each column in the select list of the Select statement. You can add computed fields to any band, including the detail band. If you add a computed field in the DataWindow painter, the calculation is done by PowerBuilder after the data retrieval has taken place.

*Figure 10.4  The detail band.*

In this example, the detail band contains five columns for the line_item table. These are the line_no, partname, price, quantity, and extended_price columns.

## The Summary Band

The summary band contains information that is presented at the end of the report (or DataWindow), after the display of all the detail records. The summary band is used to present final totals, usually summations, but it could be averages, counts, minimums, or maximums.

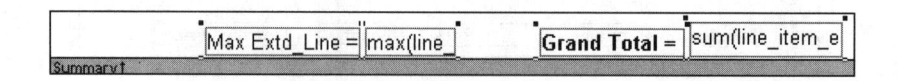

*Figure 10.5  The summary band.*

In this example, the summary band contains the sum of all the extended_price columns, and also the maximum value found in any extended_line field.

## The Footer Band

The footer band holds data that appears at the bottom of each page (on the screen or printout) of the report. The footer usually includes a page number (usually of the form "page 1 of 20"), and sometimes the date of the report. You might also consider adding the name of the DataWindow object to the footer (perhaps using a smaller font size). This label will be useful later when a user shows you a report and asks for some enhancements.

This example footer contains the page number (with the format page 1 of 20), and the name of the DataWindow object.

*Figure 10.6  The footer band.*

## Group Bands

You may choose to subdivide (group) the result set either as part of the presentation or for use in creating aggregate functions such as presenting summations in groups. You define a group by selecting the **Rows|Create Group** menu option and then by defining Group Item Expressions in the Specify Group dialog box (this is covered in the section, The Rows Menu). For each group that you define, the DataWindow painter adds a pair of group bands to your DataWindow.

### Group Header Band

Each grouping that you define adds a corresponding group header band and a group trailer band to the design window. The group header band is where you place the information that you want presented at the start of each new group in the report. Here you usually list the values for the group criteria, and sometimes you may place computed fields for the group in this area.

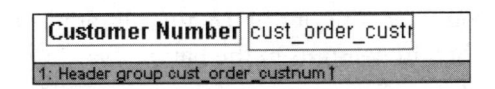

*Figure 10.7  The group header band.*

This example is the group header for group 1 in Figure 10.2 (and Figure 10.1). This header contains the field label and the custnum column. This will appear once for each customer number in the report.

### Group Trailer Band

The group trailer band is where you place information that you want to follow each group in the report. This is most often used to present a calculation, usually a summation based on the subdivision of the detail records. The information in the group trailer immediately follows the set of detail records on which it is based.

There could be multiple pairs of the group bands—remember that there is one pair for each of the groups that you defined for the detail records.

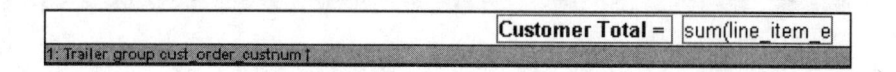

**Figure 10.8** *The group trailer.*

This example is the group trailer for group 1 in Figure 10.2 (and Figure 10.1). This trailer contains a label and the sum of the `extended_line` columns in the detail band for one customer (custnum). This will appear once for each customer number in the report.

## Changing the Design

You can move objects from one band to another simply by dragging the object to its new location. In Figure 10.2, the Customer Number column heading was moved from the Header band to the Group header for `cust_order_custnum`. The custnum column was moved from the detail band to the Group header for `cust_order_custnum`. You can also remove (some) bands or resize any of them. To resize a band, just click on the **band** and drag it. Right click on the band to open the popup menu. The popup menu will let you set the color and the pointer for the band. The detail band popup menu also has a toggle called Autosize height. If you select this, it will dynamically adjust the size of the band to allow for variable height columns in the band.

The design window presents the bands and data in a manner that assists in the customization process. The bands are only used in the design mode and will not be visible in the final object. You can preview the DataWindow, to see what the actual presentation will look like. To do this, select the **Design|Preview** menu option.

## SAVING THE DATAWINDOW OBJECT

Choose the **File|Save** (or **File|Save As**) menu option to save the DataWindow object. The default prefix for DataWindow object names is d_. The name of the DataWindow object should reflect its purpose, or perhaps the name of the table that it accesses. If a DataWindow accesses the employee table, then you could name it d_employee or d_emp_hr_view. Be sure to first select the PowerBuilder library where you want to place the DataWindow object.

## MODIFYING THE DATAWINDOW

You can modify many of the details of the DataWindow presentation including:

- object names
- fonts, field size, field location, field alignment
- set on Autosize Height for a band
- object borders
- color
- background
- add text
- change field edit styles
- format
- pointer
- query criteria
- validation
- bring to front
- send to back
- layer

### Adding DataWindow Objects

Adding objects in the DataWindow painter is similar to how you manipulate objects in the Window painter. To add an object to the DataWindow, select the object type from the Objects menu, and then click at the position in the DataWindow where you wish to drop the new object. There are several exceptions to this process: the Average, Count, and Sum functions. For these objects, you must first select a column to which the function should be applied, the click the menu item. This will drop the object onto the DataWindow.

## Selecting DataWindow Objects

Selecting, moving, and aligning objects in the DataWindow painter is similar to how you manipulate objects in the Window painter.

You select a single control by clicking on it with the mouse. When you select a control, that control is displayed with sizing handles. When you click on another control, the previously selected control(s) is deselected. The **Tab** key can also be used to select a control. Each time that you hit the **Tab** key, the painter selects a different control in the DataWindow. The **Tab** key cycles through all the controls and then starts over again.

## Selecting Multiple Controls

There are several ways to select a set of controls. You can do this by clicking on the first control of the set, and then **Ctrl+click** on each of the additional controls. **Ctrl+click** is a standard way to select multiple objects in Windows applications.

You can also select multiple controls by lassoing the controls with the mouse. To do this, click the mouse on the DataWindow background and then drag the mouse. This creates a "lasso" rectangle that selects all the controls that fall within (even partially) the rectangle's boundaries when you release the button. Beware of using this technique for the functions that depend on the order in which the objects are selected, since it may be difficult to determine which objects were selected first (the first selected is the bottom right object).

## Selecting Objects with the Menu Option

The Edit|Select menu option provides another technique for selecting an object during the design process. Figure 10.9 shows the cascading menu that opens when you select this menu option.

With the following options, you can select all objects, all of the columns, or all of the text:

- **Select All**—selects all objects in the DataWindow.
- **Select Columns**—selects all of the DataWindow columns.
- **Select Text**—selects all of the labels in the DataWindow.

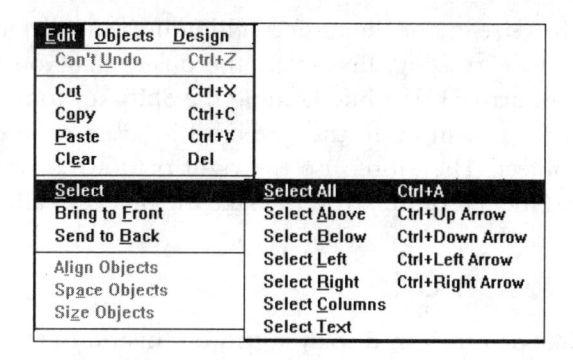

*Figure 10.9  Selecting a set of objects.*

The other options on this menu (Figure 10.9) select a set of objects in relation to the position of the currently selected object(s). To use these options, select an object, and then select the **Edit|Select** menu option. On the cascading menu, you can choose:

- **Select Above**—selects all objects that are located above the selected object.
- **Select Below**—selects all objects that are located below the selected object.
- **Select Left**—selects all objects located to the left of the selected object.
- **Select Right**—selects all objects located to the right of the selected object.

You can also use these functions one after another. For example, you can select all of the objects to the left and below a selected object (or objects).

## Positioning and Sizing Objects

All DataWindow objects are positioned in basically the same manner and can be moved by using either the mouse or the keyboard. To move an object with the mouse, just click within the object and drag it to its new location. To move an object with the keyboard, select the object that you wish to move, and then use the four arrow keys to position it. The keyboard method for moving objects is useful for making small adjustments to the position of an object that might be more difficult with the mouse. (The snap-to-grid option must be off to make the most precise adjustments with the keyboard).

To resize an object with the mouse, click on the object (to select it) and then use the handles that appear around the edges. Drag one of the handles until the object has reached the desired size. The handles on the corners of the object can resize the object simultaneously in two dimensions, while the other handles can only resize in one dimension (either horizontally or vertically). To use the keyboard for resizing, first select the object that you wish to resize. Then use the four arrow keys while holding the **Shift** key to resize the object. The movement for resizing with the keyboard is based on the bottom-right handle of the object. Therefore, use the right or down arrow to make the object larger and the left or up arrow to make the object smaller.

## Using the Design Grid

The DataWindow painter can display a grid of dots on the window that can help with the alignment and relative sizing of objects in the same way that the grid is used in the Window painter. You select this option by choosing the **Design|Options** menu option. This opens the DataWindow Options tab dialog box shown in Figure 10.10.

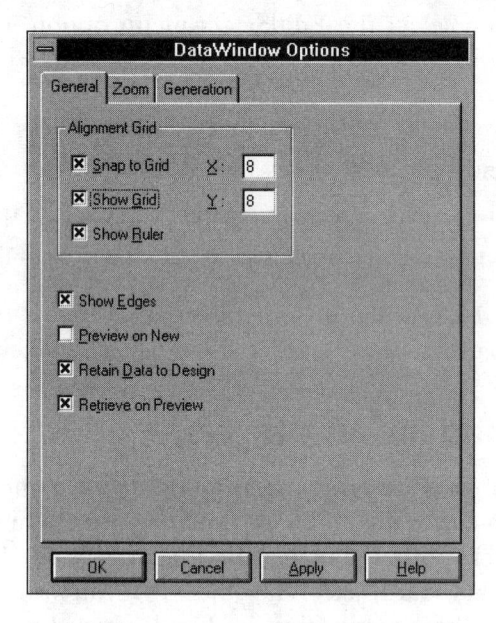

*Figure 10.10  The Options dialog box.*

In the General tab, you can set the display of the grid by checking **Show Grid**. You can also set the distance between the dots (in both the horizontal and vertical planes). The default spacing between dots is eight pixels; a smaller number (like four) will give you finer resolution when placing controls.

## The Snap to Grid Option

Select **Snap to Grid** by checking its checkbox. With Snap to Grid, the DataWindow painter creates a grid for the exact placement of objects. Any objects that you resize or move while this option is active will be placed at the dot which is nearest to the place where you release the object. This makes aligning and relatively sizing objects much easier. If you find that you need to have finer resolution in the placement of the objects, you can decrease the size of the grid cells, just enter smaller values for the X and Y grid options.

*SHORTCUT*

You do not have to make the grid visible to use the snap to grid option. This is something to consider if you want to speed up the display speed, since displaying the grid slows down the environment.

## The Show Ruler Option

Select Show Ruler by checking its checkbox (in the General tab). Show Ruler displays a ruler along the top and left edges of the DataWindow painter. This ruler makes it easier to place objects during the design process, and to predict the final presentation when the report is displayed or printed. This is most useful when designing reports that will be printed on a certain size paper. The unit of measure used on this ruler is set with the DataWindow Object dialog box. Open this dialog box by choosing the **Edit|Properties** menu option (or use the RMB popup on the DataWindow surface, avoiding any objects). In this dialog box, you set the unit of measure to be thousands of an inch or thousands of a centimeter. This dialog box is covered in more detail later in this chapter.

## Using the Zoom Option

You may want to change the viewing size of the DataWindow object which you are creating. PowerBuilder lets you increase or decrease the size of the display of the DataWindow object during the design process. Selecting the **Design|Options** menu option and then selecting the **Zoom** tab opens the Zoom dialog box (Figure 10.11).

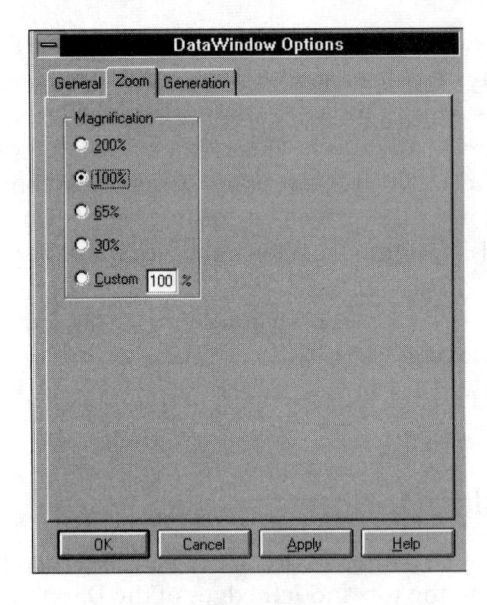

*Figure 10.11  The Zoom dialog box.*

In this dialog box, you can set the Magnification to one of the preset percentages (200%, 100%, 65%, 30%), or you can enter a custom value in the edit field.

## Using the Preview Option

Selecting the **Design|Preview** menu option, or clicking the **Preview** icon on the PainterBar presents a preview of the DataWindow's appearance at run time (Figure 10.12). You may also toggle this option with the **Control+Shift+P** key combination.

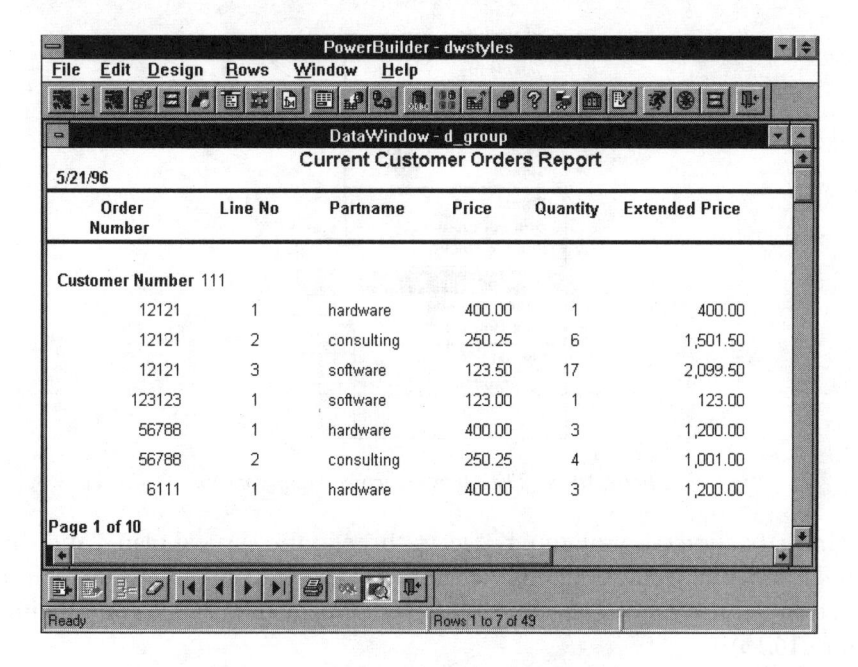

*Figure 10.12 Previewing a DataWindow object.*

If you have defined retrieval criteria in the SELECT statement, you will be prompted for these values when you enter preview mode. When you are in preview mode, the DataWindow painter removes the Preview icon and adds a Design icon to the PainterBar. Clicking on this icon returns you to design mode.

## Aligning Objects with the Alignment Function

The DataWindow painter provides a function to automatically align a set of selected objects. To do this, select a set of objects using one of the methods described above. When you select the objects, you must first select the object that you want to use to govern the alignment of the other objects. After you have selected the objects to be aligned, choose the **Edit|Align Objects** menu option. This displays the align objects cascading menu (Figure 10.13).

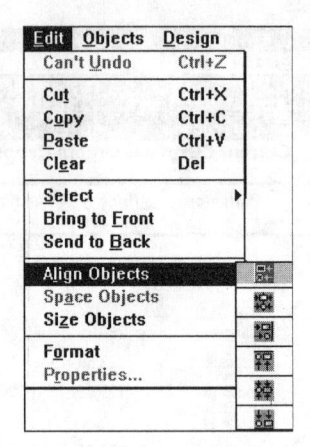

*Figure 10.13 The Align Objects cascading menu.*

You have six choices for aligning objects, three in the vertical plane, and three in the horizontal. You can choose to align the objects in the following manners (listed in the top down order in which they appear in the cascading menu of Figure 10.13):

### Align Vertically

- by the left edge
- centering the objects
- by the right edge

### Align Horizontally

- by the top edge
- centering the objects
- by the bottom edge

Remember that the order in which you select the objects determines the result. Be sure to first select the object that is already in the correct position. After you use this function to align the objects, the objects still remain selected, so that you can reposition the entire group. To do this, just click and drag any one of the selected objects; the entire set will move as you drag that object. To deselect the group, click somewhere else in the DataWindow or just press **Tab**.

## Adjusting the Spacing of Objects

The DataWindow painter can automatically adjust the spacing between a set of selected objects. To do this, first select a set of objects in the same manner as was described earlier in this chapter. In this case, it is also important to select the objects in a specific order because the distance between the first two objects that you select will be the spacing that is applied to the other selected objects. So the procedure is to first set up two adjacent objects with the correct spacing. Then **Ctrl+click** select the objects that are to be spaced similarly.

After you have selected the set of objects, select the **Edit|Space Objects** menu option to display the cascading menu shown in Figure 10.14. You can set the spacing of the selected objects in either the horizontal or vertical dimension.

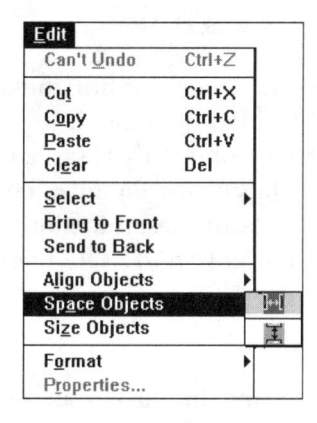

*Figure 10.14  The Space Objects cascading menu.*

The top option in the cascading menu spaces the objects horizontally, based on the distance between the first two objects selected. The second option spaces objects vertically.

## Automatically Sizing of Objects

The DataWindow painter can automatically adjust the size of a set of selected objects to match that of a model object. To do this, first select the object that has the correct size (in either the horizontal or vertical plane) that you wish applied to the other object(s). Then **Ctrl+click** the rest of the objects that you want to size.

After you have selected the set of objects, select the **Edit|Size Objects** menu option. This displays the cascading menu shown in Figure 10.15.

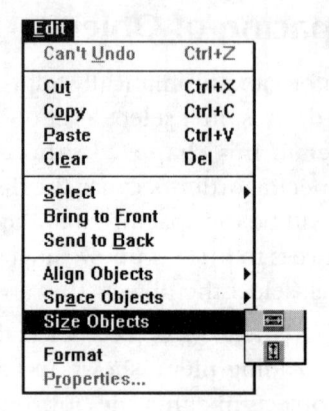

*Figure 10.15 Sizing objects.*

You can size the object(s) in either the horizontal or vertical dimension. Select the first option on the cascading menu to size the selected objects to the horizontal size of the first object that was selected. Select the second option to vertically size the objects. You could, of course, size the object(s) in both dimensions by selecting both these functions, one after the other. You will apply the sizing option most often to a set of fields or labels.

## The Style Toolbar

In the DataWindow painter, you can display an additional toolbar: the *style* toolbar. The style toolbar displays and lets you change the attributes of the text used on the DataWindow. This includes attributes such as the font name, and various options such as underlining, italics, bold, and justification. Figure 10.16 shows the toolbars.

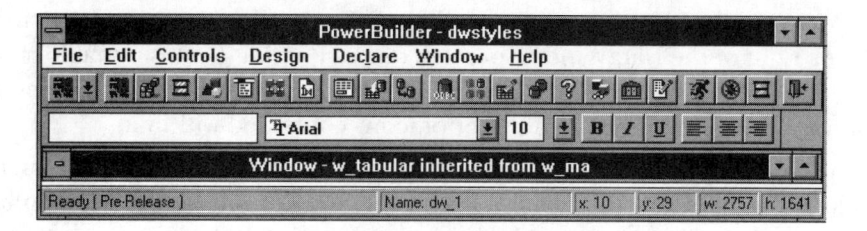

*Figure 10.16  The Style toolbar.*

To show (display) these toolbars, select the **Window|Toolbars** menu option. This opens the Toolbars dialog box (Figure 10.17), where you can choose to show, hide, or relocate any of the toolbars, or customize the contents of the toolbars.

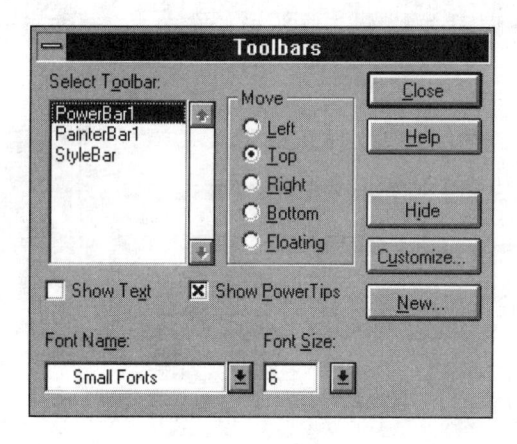

*Figure 10.17  The Toolbars dialog box.*

## Chapter 10

You can display the PowerBar or PainterBar toolbars at the top, bottom, left, or right of the DataWindow painter, or as a floating (repositionable) box. The floating toolbar option is helpful for the PainterBar in the DataWindow painter because of the large number of icons contained within it.

You can reposition the style toolbar or the color bar by selecting a menu option. To reposition the style toolbar, select the **Options|Text Style Toolbar** menu option. You can attach the style toolbar to the frame or to the DataWindow painter, as shown in Figure 10.18.

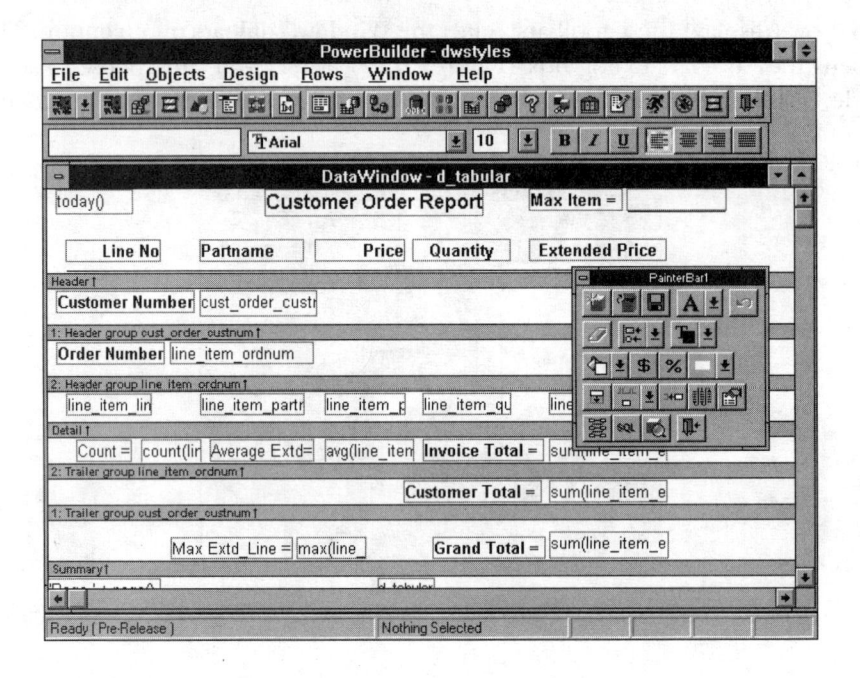

*Figure 10.18* The Text Style Toolbar menu option.

## Colors

A color panel pops up from the PainterBar Foreground Color and Background Color icons. This presents a palette of the color choices for the design process.

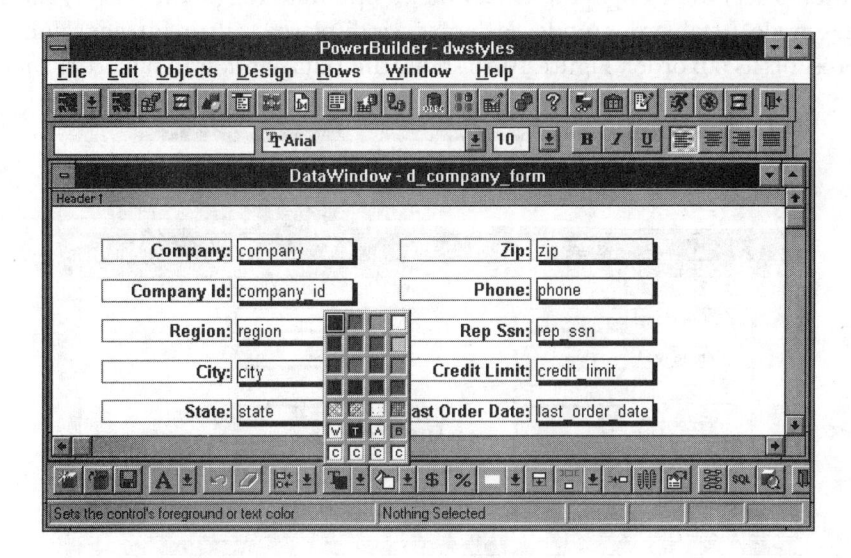

*Figure 10.19  The color panel.*

With the color panel, you can set the color of any selected objects in the DataWindow. First select the object(s) for which you are going to set the color. Then click on the color (on the foreground color panel) that you want to use for the object's text, and then click on a color to set the object's background color (on the background color panel). The icon on the color icons shows the current foreground and background colors.

## Setting the Tab Order

In the DataWindow painter, you can set the tab order for the objects in the same way that you set the tab order for the controls in a window in the Window painter. Select the **Design|Tab Order** menu option to toggle on (or off) the tab order mode. In tab order mode, each object is displayed with an integer value that represents its tab order. Figure 10.20 shows the DataWindow in tab order mode.

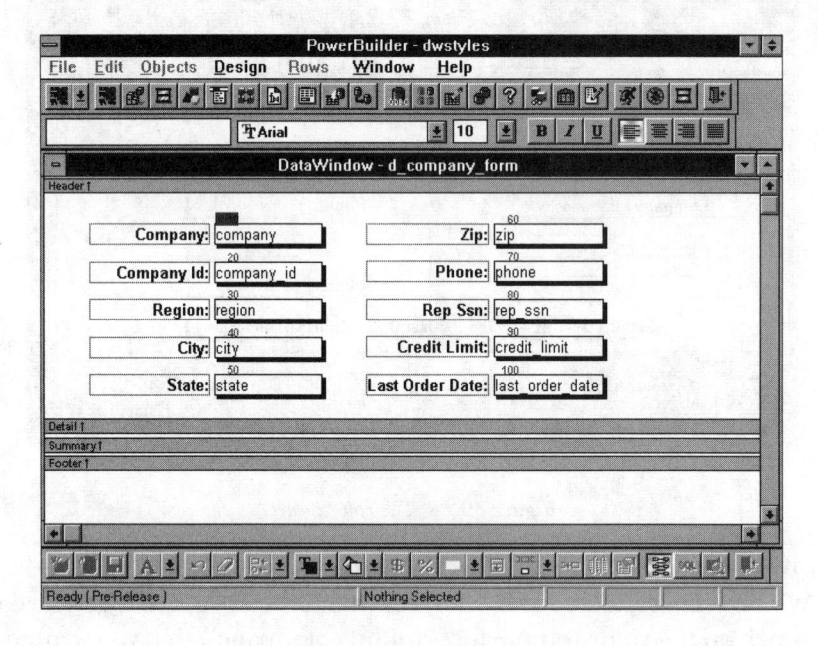

*Figure 10.20  Setting the tab order.*

The tab order determines which object is selected when the user presses the **Tab** key at run time. The object that is selected (receives the focus) is the object with the next highest tab value. After the highest value object has been selected, the selection cycles through the series again. If you don't wish an object to have the focus (such as fields that cannot be edited), set the tab order to **0** for that object. Not all objects in the DataWindow have a tab order; it only applies to objects that the user may need to select.

When you enter tab order mode, the values are initially presented with an increment of 10 between each value. This lets you enter values between existing values to change the tab order. If you exit and then reenter tab order mode, you will notice that the values have been renumbered with a increment of ten. You can set the tab order of objects with the SetTabOrder function (or with the dwModify function for Tabsequence, though this is an advanced technique).

# DataWindow Properties

A DataWindow has a large number of properties that determine its characteristics. These properties define the style of the DataWindow and are controlled in the DataWindow's Object dialog box. To open that dialog box, first click on the surface of the DataWindow, avoiding any objects such as data fields or labels. Next, select the **Design|Properties** menu option from the Window painter menu. This opens the DataWindow Object dialog box, as shown in Figure 10.21.

There is also a shortcut to the DataWindow Style dialog box: just double-click within the DataWindow. You must be sure to actually click on the window area and avoid the objects that have been placed in the DataWindow. If you double-click on an object in the DataWindow, the Properties dialog box will open for that object.

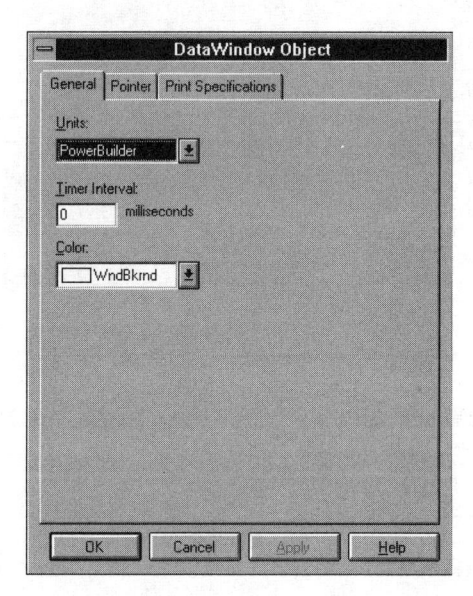

*Figure 10.21  The DataWindow Object dialog box.*

In this dialog box, you can set the unit of measure to PowerBuilder Units (PBUs), pixels, thousandths of an inch, or thousandths of a centimeter. You can also set the timer interval in milliseconds. This attribute controls how often the time is updated in this DataWindow. This applies to objects that use time in a DataWindow. The default (if left at 0) is 1 minute (60,000 milliseconds). You can set the background color of the DataWindow by using the listbox at the bottom of the Style dialog box.

Click on the **Pointer** tab, to open the Pointer dialog box. In this dialog box (Figure 10.22), you can select the icon that will be used when the pointer is over the DataWindow.

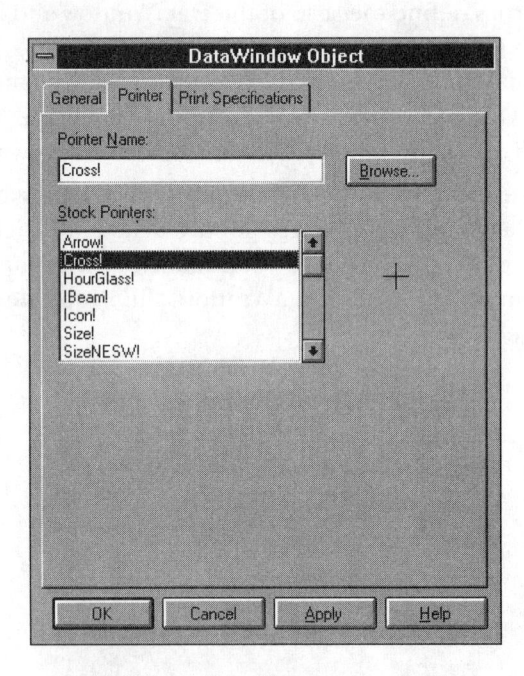

*Figure 10.22  The Select Pointer dialog box.*

In this dialog box, you can choose to use a stock pointer, or you can use a cursor bitmap file (**.CUR** file). The dialog box shows you the currently selected icon in the area just to the right of the listbox.

## Print Specifications

Click on the **Print Specifications** tab to set attributes that are used during the printing of this DataWindow. In this dialog box, you can set Print Queue document name, margins, paper orientation, etc.

## ADDING COMPUTED FIELDS

One of the powerful features of DataWindows is the ability to add computed fields. Computed fields perform a computation within the DataWindow. The calculation is updated as the data in the DataWindow changes. When you add a computed field to your DataWindow, you must define an expression that specifies the computation that is to take place to determine the field's value. In this expression, you can use functions, constants, other columns, and the set of arithmetic operators. The functions that are used here are the PowerScript functions (not SQL functions), since the calculations are done in the DataWindow not on the database server. You can also use user-defined global functions in these computed fields.

Computed fields are useful for calculating values such as the minimum, maximum, average, or a count for a group or the entire result set. They can also be used to concatenate two or more fields into one field.

To add a computed column to a DataWindow, click on the **Compute** icon on the Control Panel or select the **Objects|Computed Field** menu option. Next click on the **DataWindow** at the point where you want to place the computed field. This opens the Computed Object tab dialog box (Figure 10.23).

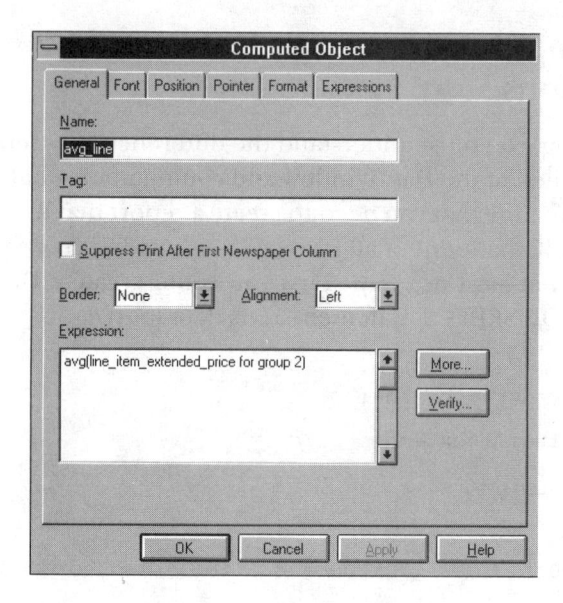

*Figure 10.23  Defining a computed field.*

In this dialog box, you can enter a name for the computed column in this dialog box. If you name the column, you can reference the column in your PowerScript code. There are many examples of where this is useful. See the INVOICE example program for such a reference.

You must also enter the expression for the computed column. Click on the **More** button to open the Modify Expression dialog box. You can paste functions, columns, or operators into the expression using the controls at the bottom of the dialog box. You can refer to a column value in a specific row by using an integer argument with the column name. The integer gives the position of the required row, relative to the current position in the DataWindow. For example, line_item_quantity[-2] is a reference to the value of line_item_quantity in the row which is two rows prior to the current position. line_item_quantity[0] is a reference to the same column in the current row. Line_item_quantity[+3] is a reference to the column in the row which is three rows after the current row.

After you have defined the expression, you can have PowerBuilder validate the expression. Click on **Verify** and you will receive a message that the Expression is OK or that the Expression is not valid. When you are finished, click on **OK**; this closes the dialog box.

## DBMS Computations versus DataWindow Computations

As with grouping, you must understand the difference between computations that are performed in the DataWindow and computations that are performed by the DBMS. Assume that you need to create a report that lists each customer and the total dollar amount of all invoices associated with each customer. You could do this in at least two ways. First you could create a DataWindow with the following SQL SELECT statement as its data source.

```
SELECT "cust_order"."custnum",
       "line_item"."extended_price"
  FROM "cust_order",
       "line_item"
 WHERE ( "cust_order"."ordnum" = "line_item"."ordnum" )
ORDER BY "cust_order"."custnum" ASC;
```

You then create a group in the DataWindow painter on the custnum column. In the group trailer band for custnum, you add a computed field with the expression:

```
sum(line_item_extended_price for group 1)
```

This is similar to a calculation in the DataWindow shown in Figure 10.1. What occurs in this example is that the rows of the invoices are returned sorted by custnum. Each time custnum changes, it creates a new group in the DataWindow. The DataWindow totals the amount off the `extended_price` fields for each group and displays it following the group. Two points are important: First, all of the invoice `line_item` rows are returned in the result set, and second, the actual calculation is done in the DataWindow (on the client machine).

The other alternative would be to create a DataWindow using the following SQL SELECT statement:

```
SELECT "cust_order"."custnum",
       sum("line_item"."extended_price")
   FROM "cust_order",
        "line_item"
  WHERE ( "cust_order"."ordnum" = "line_item"."ordnum" )
GROUP BY "cust_order"."custnum" ASC;
```

In this case, the DBMS returns only one row for each custnum. Each row contains two fields, custnum and the total for the `extended_price` column for all the invoices associated with that custnum. Note the difference in the number of records returned to this DataWindow, and that the computations have taken place on the database server instead of on the client.

Which method you choose depends on several considerations. If the requirement is only to return the customer number and the total invoice sums for each, then you should choose the second method. This reduces the number of records that have to be retrieved and avoids the expense of performing the computations on the client.

If, on the other hand, you have a requirement to display each invoice total in addition to the customer totals, or if you must be able to add or modify rows to the DataWindow and then recalculate the totals, then the first method is required.

## Predefined Calculated Fields

PowerBuilder provides several objects that you can add to your DataWindows that are actually calculated fields of various types. These include the following:

- **Average**—calculates the average value for a given set.
- **Count**—counts the number of items.
- **Page**—displays the current page number.
- **Sum**—calculates the total amount.
- **Today**—displays today's date.

To add an average, count, or sum object, click on one of the columns in the DataWindow, then select the function that you want from the Objects menu. The Sum object is also available as an icon on the PainterBar.

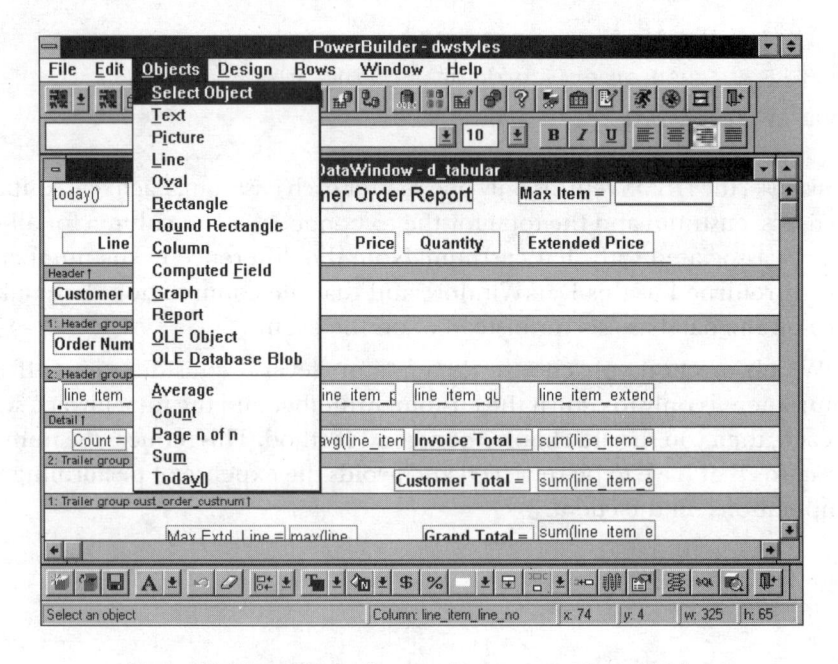

**Figure 10.24** *Adding a Computed column to a DataWindow.*

The Computed Field Definition dialog box opens as shown in Figure 10.24. The expression used to calculate the average of the `extended_price` column in each group is

```
avg(line_item_extended_price for group 1)
// or group 2 if there are 2 groups
```

The Sum Computed field is very handy, and is actually a shortcut for creating a computed column to do the same calculation. If you click on a column in a detail band, and then click on the **Sum** icon, a Sum Computed field is added to the summary band (or the group trailer band if a group has been defined).

The Page and Today objects are easier to use. Just select them from the Objects menu, or click on the **Page** or **Today** icon on the PainterBar, then click at the point in the DataWindow where you want to insert the object. These objects are generally placed in the header or footer bands of a report.

## Adding Database Columns

To add another column to the DataWindow, click on the **Column** icon on the PainterBar or select the **Objects|Column** menu option. Then click in the DataWindow at the position where you want to place the column. This opens the **Select Column** dialog box (Figure 10.25).

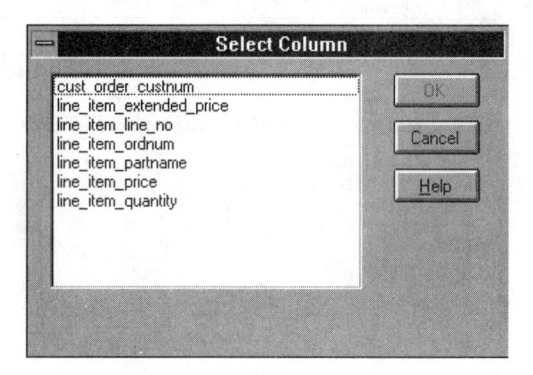

*Figure 10.25* Adding a column to a DataWindow.

Select the column from this dialog box, and then click on **OK** to add the column to the DataWindow.

## The Rows Menu

The DataWindow painter Rows menu is very important to understand. Many powerful features are provided in these menu items.

### Column Specifications

The Rows|Column Specifications menu option opens a dialog box (Figure 10.26), which displays each column and its data type. You can specify an initial value and Validation expression in this dialog box. If an initial value was defined in the Database painter, the dialog box will display that value; you can override that value here. The same is true for the validation rule.

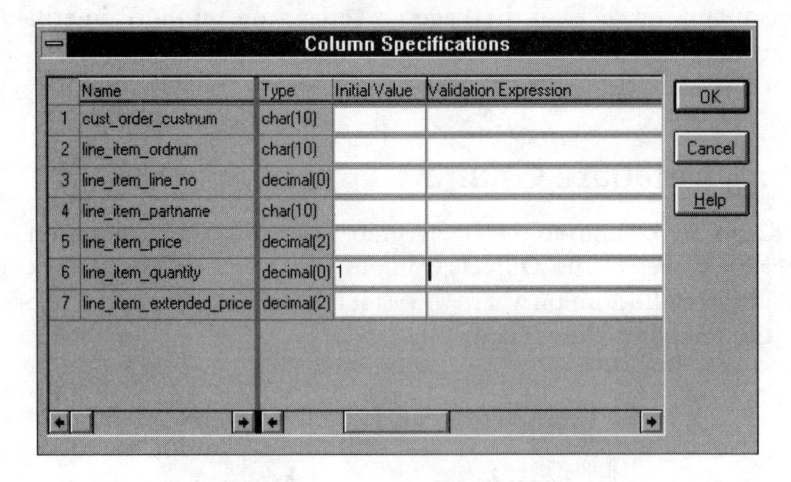

*Figure 10.26* Column Specifications dialog box.

## Data

The Rows|Data menu option opens the Data Retained On Save dialog box (Figure 10.27). In this dialog box, you can define a set of data that is to be retained in the DataWindow object. You have two options for loading this data into this dialog box. You can type the data, row by row; or you can retrieve the data from the database. This is useful for data that doesn't change, or that rarely changes.

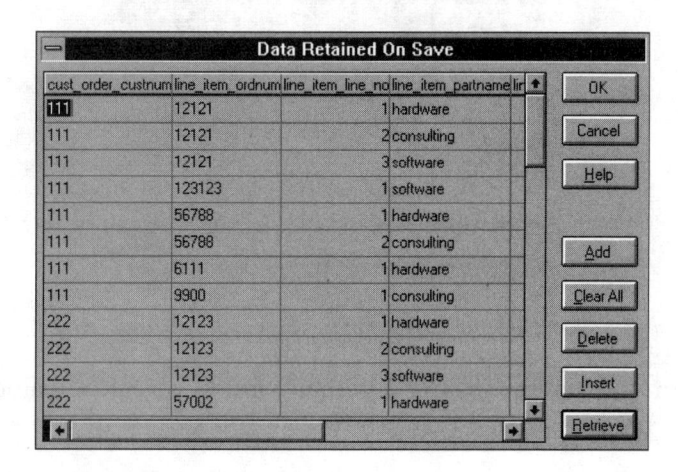

*Figure 10.27 Data Retained On Save dialog box.*

When you close this dialog box, the data is saved in the DataWindow object.

**NOTE** Sometimes it is also used to enter a single, blank row of data into a DataWindow that will be used in a DropDownDataWindow (as a child DataWindow). This single line of text will prevent the automatic retrieval (via the Retrieve DataWindow function) that is triggered by the initial retrieval in the parent DataWindow. This will be discussed in the next chapter.

## Prompt for Criteria

The Rows|Prompt for Criteria menu option opens a dialog box (Figure 10.28) where you can select a set of columns for which you want to specify selection criteria during preview and execution. Click on a column to select it. Click on it again to unselect it.

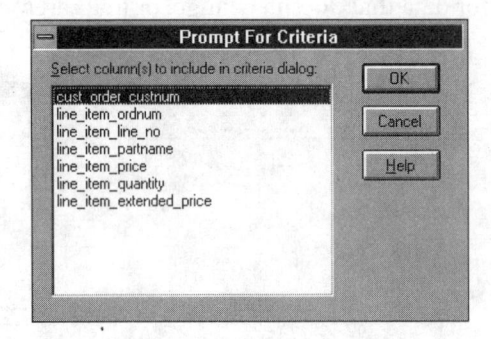

*Figure 10.28  Prompt for Criteria dialog box.*

When the retrieve is issued for this DataWindow object, a dialog box will prompt the user for selection criteria (Figure 10.29).

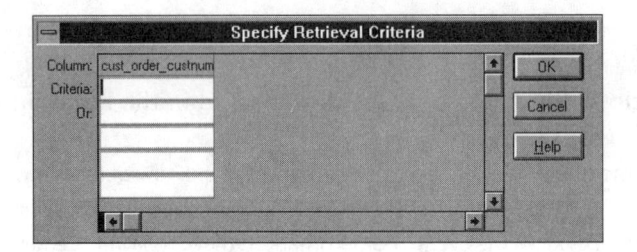

*Figure 10.29  Selection Criteria dialog box.*

## Retrieve

The **Rows|Retrieve** menu option is a cascading menu that opens to display two toggle items (Figure 10.30). The first is **Rows As Needed**. If you set this option, the DataWindow will only retrieve enough rows to fill the DataWindow control. When the user scrolls forward in the DataWindow, more rows will be retrieved as needed. This is most useful in instances where a large number of rows can be expected when the **Retrieve** function is issued.

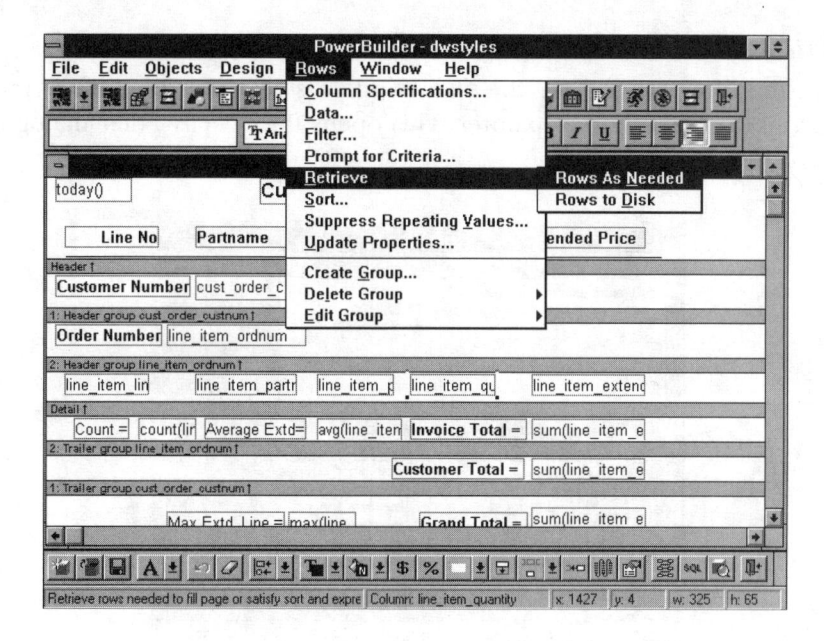

*Figure 10.30* Rows|Retrieve *menu options.*

The second option on the **Rows|Retrieve** cascading menu is **Rows to Disk**. This tells the DataWindow to retrieve the data and store it in a temporary file on the local disk for subsequent access. This option is only available in 32-bit environments.

## Filtering and Sorting

You can filter and sort data in the SQL SELECT statement using the WHERE clause and the ORDER BY clause. However, there may be times when you want to filter and sort data that is already in the DataWindow. As a matter of fact, the filtering and sorting functions in DataWindows are often reason enough to use DataWindows for the presentation of data that doesn't even come from a database. These functions are probably more useful at run time, when you can dynamically restrict the rows displayed in the DataWindow and/or sort the DataWindow in one or more of its columns. The dynamic uses of these functions is covered in the next chapter, on DataWindow controls. The next sections discuss how to use these functions in the DataWindow painter at design time.

### Filtering DataWindow Rows

To set the filter criteria for the DataWindow, select the **Rows|Filter** menu option in the DataWindow painter. This opens the Specify Filter dialog box (Figure 10.31).

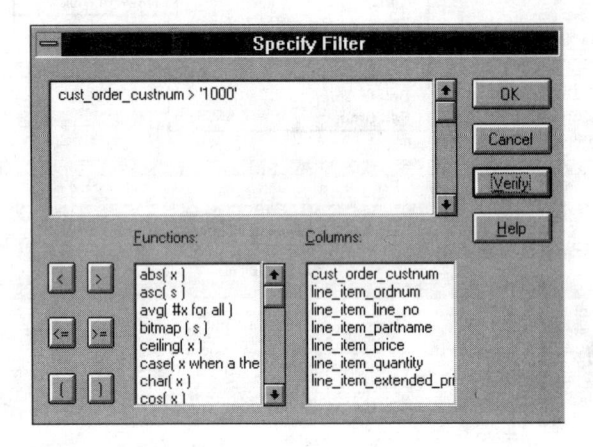

*Figure 10.31 Defining a DataWindow filter.*

In this dialog box, you must enter the expression for the filter condition. You can paste functions, columns, or operators into the expression using the controls at the bottom of the dialog box. When you have completed the expression, click on **Verify** to validate the expression.

### Sorting DataWindow Rows

To set the sort criteria for the DataWindow, select the **Rows|Sort** menu option in the DataWindow painter. This opens the Specify Sort Columns dialog box (Figure 10.32).

In this dialog box, you specify the columns that determine the sort order. You can select the column name from the listbox which contains the names of all the columns in the DataWindow. Add columns to the criteria by dragging a column from the Source Data listbox to the Columns listbox. To insert an item within the current list, just drag to the position. You can delete a Sort column by dragging the column from the Columns listbox back to the Source Data listbox.

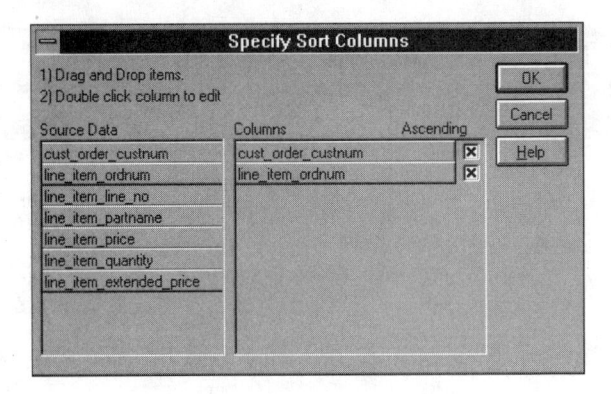

*Figure 10.32  Setting a Sort order.*

You can edit the Sort expression for any column by double-clicking on the column name in the Columns listbox. This will open the Modify Expression dialog box, where you can paste in operators, functions, and column names.

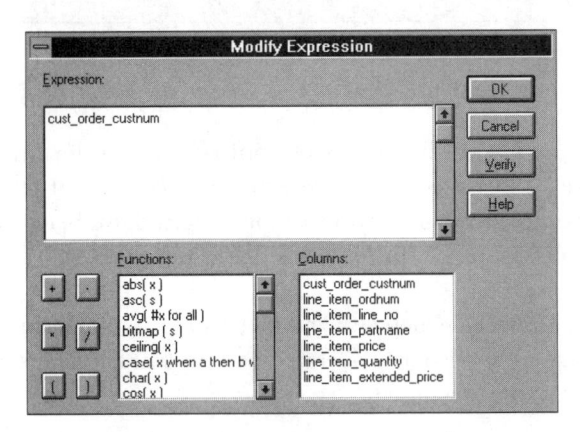

*Figure 10.33  Modifying a Sort expression.*

## Suppressing Repeating Values

You can suppress repeating values in one or more DataWindow columns to improve the appearance and the readability of a report. For example, look at the DataWindow in Figure 10.34.

**394** Chapter 10

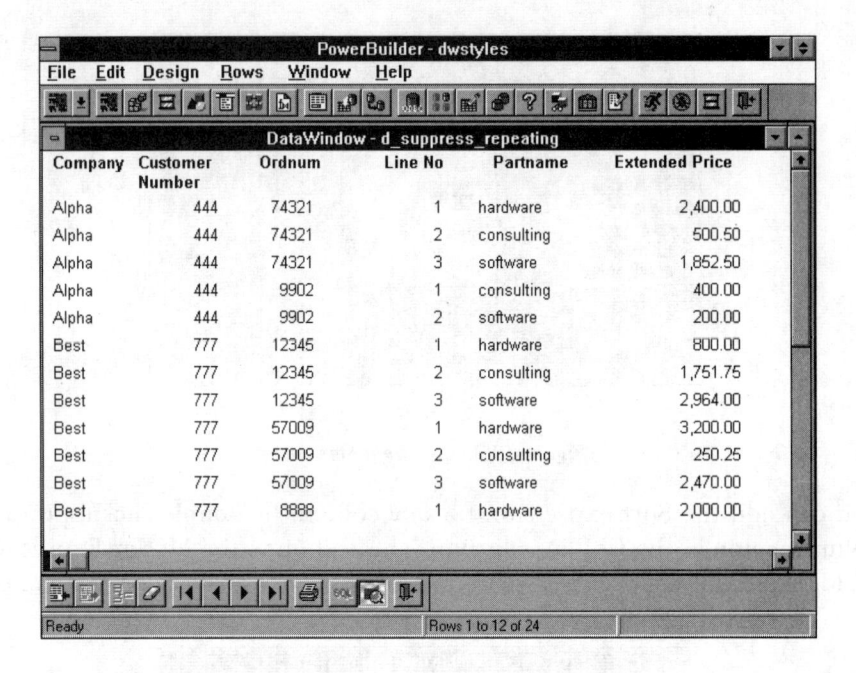

*Figure 10.34  A sample DataWindow.*

This is a list of the invoice line items by company and order number. The next example, Figure 10.35, is exactly the same information, except repeating values in the company, company ID, and order number fields have been suppressed. The improvement in appearance should be obvious, and that result is easily achieved.

NOTE: If the fields that are suppressed have a tab order value greater than zero, the values will be displayed on the screen when the user tabs to the field even though the values are suppressed.

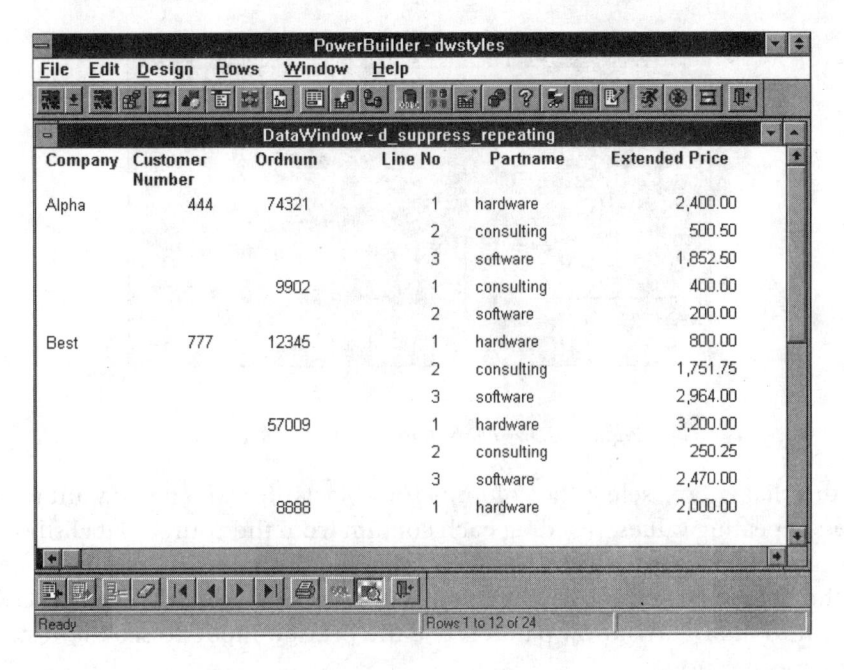

*Figure 10.35 Suppressing repeated values.*

When you choose to suppress a repeating value, the value displays at the start of each new page, and if you are using group levels, each time a value changes in a higher group level.

To suppress repeating values in a DataWindow, select the **Rows|Suppress Repeating Values** menu option. That opens the Specify Repeating Value Suppression List dialog box (Figure 10.36).

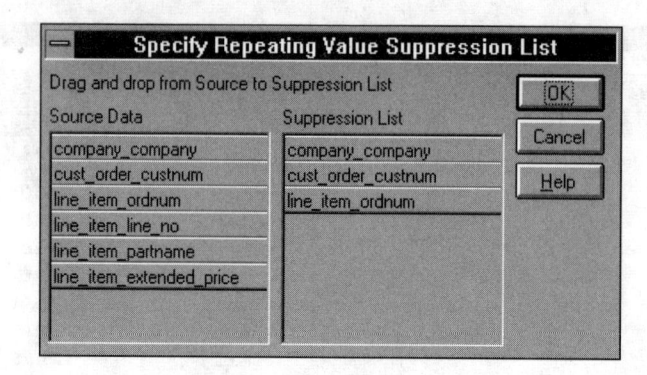

*Figure 10.36  The Suppression List dialog box.*

In this dialog box, select the columns (or objects) for which you want to suppress repeating values. Just drag each column from the Source Data listbox, to the Suppression List listbox. To deselect an item from the list, just drag it back to the Source Data listbox. When you have completed the list, click on **OK** to return to the DataWindow painter. Use the preview mode to see the result of your specification.

## Update Properties

You may have noticed that when you define a DataWindow, you are only required to define a SQL SELECT statement. But as you have seen, besides retrieving rows from the database, a DataWindow can also insert, update, and delete rows against the database. The INSERT, UPDATE, and DELETE statements are generated automatically by the DataWindow Update( ) function that will be covered in detail in the next chapter on DataWindow controls. The details that are necessary for creating these additional SQL statement are called *update properties*. These details are usually handled automatically by PowerBuilder, and often you will not have to deal with these details. There will be times when you will need to change the default behavior that has been defined by the DataWindow. How to specify those update characteristics is the topic of this section.

Select the **Rows|Specify Update Properties** menu option and PowerBuilder opens the Specify Update Properties dialog box (Figure 10.37).

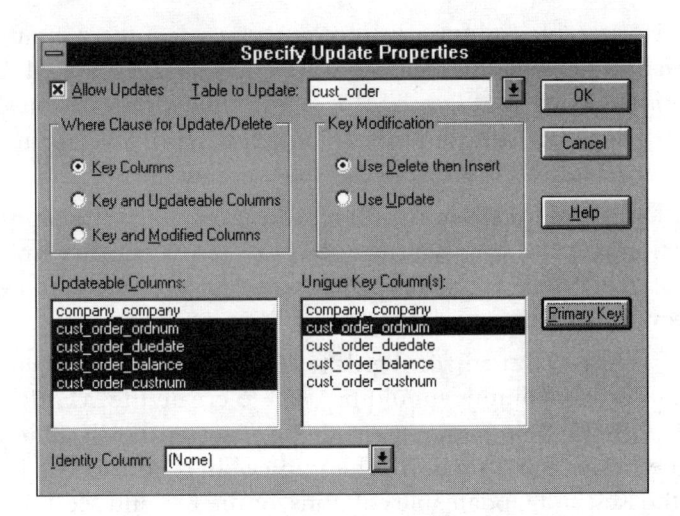

*Figure 10.37 Setting update characteristics.*

This dialog box determines whether or not a table can be updated and if it can, it determines how that update is handled. If you do not want to allow the DataWindow to perform updates to the database, you can uncheck the **Allow Update** option. Normally, for single table queries, the **Allow Update** option is checked by default—if a unique key is chosen or if the table had a primary key and you selected all the columns that make up that key. For multiple table queries, the **Allow Update** option is unchecked, and you must explicitly allow updates by selecting one (and only one) of the tables for update.

The SELECT statement for this example (Figure 10.38) uses a join between two tables (Company and Line_item); Allow Update was initially unchecked when this dialog box was opened. To allow updates, click on the **Allow Update** checkbox. This is required before any of the update characteristics in this dialog box can be changed. The next step is to select the `line_item` table from the Table to Update listbox.

> **NOTE** In this dialog box, only one table can be selected for update; you can programmatically allow the update of multiple tables. Also note that adding columns may require you to update this dialog box.

In the Updateable Columns listbox, you can select the columns that may be updated and deselect the columns which may not be updated. Initially, all the column names are highlighted (for single table queries). You should also change the tab value to **0** for the columns for which you are not allowing updates, or set the Protect attribute for the column.

In the Unique Key Columns listbox, you can change the unique key column selections for the DataWindow object or select another unique key. If you click on the **Primary** key, all changes are canceled and the fields in the Primary key are selected.

In the Where Clause for Update/Delete groupbox, you tell the DataWindow which columns should be used to create the WHERE clause for the SQL Update or Delete statements that are automatically generated when you call the `Update()` function. The choices here are to use just the Key columns, the Key, and Updateable columns, or the Key and Modified columns. Generally Key and Updateable will provide the most stringent data integrity.

In the Key Modification groupbox, you specify the method that is used to update rows when the update involves a change to one (or more) of the columns that make up the primary key. Some DBMSs will not allow you to update a column value that belongs to the Primary key. In that case you should select the **Use Delete then Insert** radiobutton. In this case, PowerBuilder first deletes the original row that you are changing and then inserts the new version of the row. This may not be acceptable in all cases; if you have a DBMS that supports cascading deletes, it is possible to lose records when you delete a row.

## CREATING GROUPS

You can create groups in the DataWindow painter during the design process. This grouping is fundamentally different than GROUP BY (which is available in the SQL statement); and it is important to understand the difference. The grouping created in the DataWindow painter partitions the detail records into groups determined by the group expression that you define in the Specify Group dialog box. This grouping does not reduce the number of rows in the display in any way. It just divides the result set into groups. Each group that you define will have a group header and a group trailer.

If you specified the grouping in the SQL GROUP BY clause, the number of rows returned in the result set will be limited to one row for each group (see the chapter on SQL Basics for a more detailed explanation).

To create a new group, choose the **Rows|Create Group** menu option. This opens the Band Object dialog box shown in Figure 10.38.

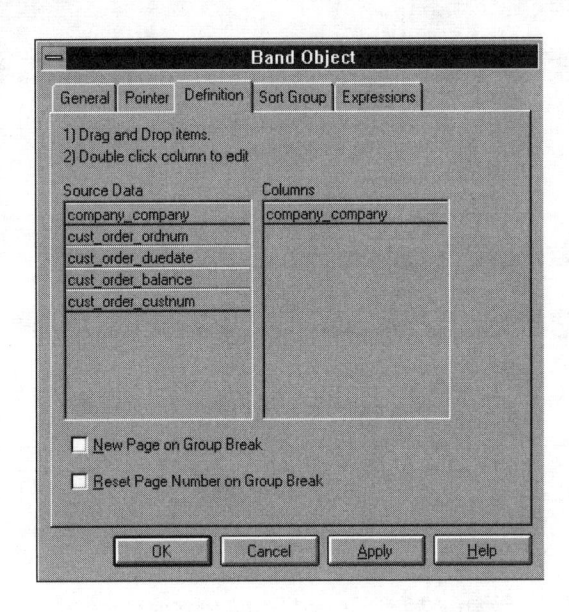

*Figure 10.38 The specify group dialog box.*

Specify the column(s) that create the group in the Columns listbox. To add additional fields, drag a field from the Source Data listbox to the Columns listbox. You may insert a grouping column into the current list by dragging to the desired position. To delete an entry, just drag the column back to the Source Data listbox.

At the bottom of the dialog box, you can select an option to force a new page for each group break. For example, if the grouping is by customer number and you have selected this option, the information for each customer will begin on a new page. You can also select an option to reset the page number for each group. The example in Figure 10.38 shows the criteria that were used for creating the first group for the DataWindow in Figures 12.1 and 12.2. Another group was created for the invoice number column. To create the second group, choose the **Rows|Create Group** menu option again and specify the invoice number grouping as another grouping. If you want to delete or edit a grouping, pick the number of the grouping from a cascading menu, as shown in Figure 10.39.

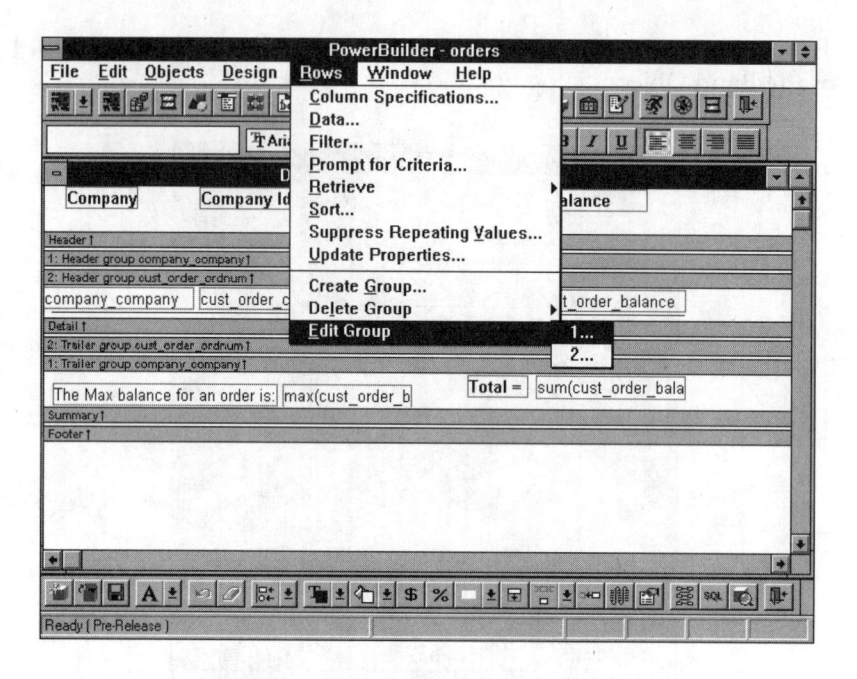

*Figure 10.39* *The Edit Group cascading menu.*

In this case, two groups have been defined for the DataWindow. You can select either 1 or 2 in the cascading menu to edit the group definition. If you delete a group, its group header and group trailer bands will be removed from the DataWindow.

## COLUMN ATTRIBUTES

This section discusses attributes that are common between column styles.

### The Column Popup Menu

If you right click on a column (in the DataWindow painter), the popup menu will display a list of options. Choose **Properties** to open the Column Object dialog box. This has may attributes, some of which will be new to you.

## The DataWindow Painter    401

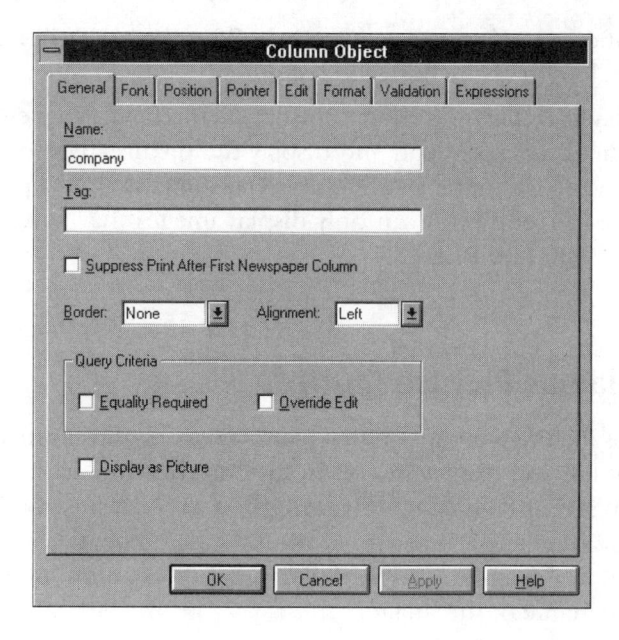

*Figure 10.40  The Column Object dialog box.*

The items in this dialog box are:

- **Name**—you can specify a DataWindow name for the column. All columns should be referenced by name, not by number since the number could change as you modify the DataWindow object. If you later add a column to your SELECT statement, you will need to name using this option.

- **Suppress Print After..**—prevents the object from repeating after the first column in a N-Ups style.

- **Border**—selects the type of border to be used for this column.

- **Alignment**—select from Left, Right, Center, Justify.

- **Query Criteria**—lets you control two details when you are using the DataWindow query mode (described in the next chapter). If you select **Equality Required**, the user can only use equality in the query specification. If you select Override Edit, the user will not be limited to the length of the database column in the QBE cell.

+ **Display as Picture**—interprets the data in this field, as a picture filename. The field will then load and display the picture. This option lets you display images in the DataWindow. It is similar to how a picture control works. Currently you can only display images that have a file type of BMP, WMF, and RLE.

## The Display as Picture Option

The Display as Picture is an option that is applied to an object with a compatible edit style that lets you display images in the DataWindow. The images can be either BMP, WMF, or RLE images that originate as files whose path is stored in the database. When a row is retrieved from the database, the image is loaded and displayed in this column. The data type of this column must be suitable for storing the name of the image.

It is important to understand that in this case the images are stored as files on a disk drive, and it is the name that is stored in the database. You can also store images in the application executable file. This is discussed in the chapter on distributing applications.

### Database Images

You can also store the image itself in the database (if your DBMS provides a binary data type such as blob). You can display it by using a Picture control in the window (outside of the DataWindow). But you cannot display the image directly in the DataWindow. See Chapter 9, "Embedded SQL," for an example which stores images in the database.

That is all there is to the Display as Bitmap option. Just size the object.

> **NOTE** If you update the image through OLE, you cannot use the SetPicture with it.

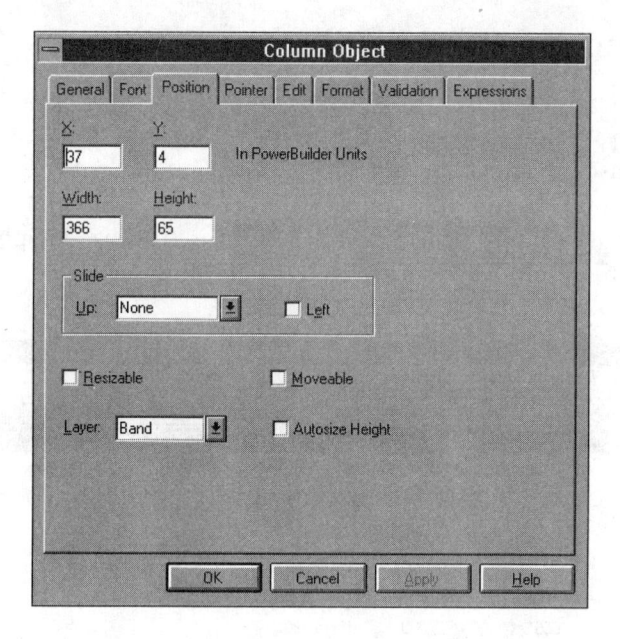

*Figure 10.41  The Column Object Position dialog box.*

The Position tab dialog box controls several important attributes.

- **Slide**—Use this option if you would like to eliminate the unnecessary spaces between two (or more) fields so that they display together. For example, if you have three fields, first_name, middle_initial, last_name, you can use this option to slide the fields together. Select **Slide Up** to adjust vertically positioned fields. Use **Slide Left** to adjust horizontally positioned fields.

- **Autosize Height**—if you have an object that varies in size (such as a variable length string), you can select this option to automatically resize the column's height as necessary. For this to work, you must also check the **Autosize Height** option on the detail band, and turn off the **Auto H Scroll** option and the **AutoVScroll** option in the edit style for the column.

- **Layer**—you can determine the placement of an object as Background, Band, or Foreground.

## Using Autosize Height

If you have a column that varies in size (such as a variable length string), select this option to automatically resize the column's height as necessary. For this to work, you must also check the **Autosize Height** option on the detail band and turn off the **AutoHScroll** option and turn on the **AutoVScroll** option in the edit style for the column. If you do not select the Autosize Height option for detail band the results will be truncated, as shown in Figure 10.42.

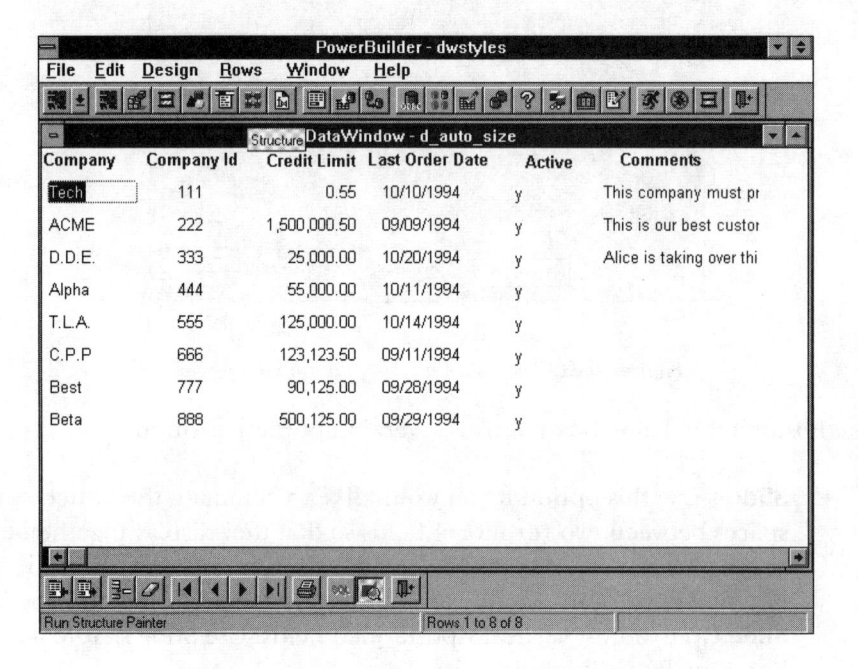

*Figure 10.42* *The comments have been truncated.*

Notice that the comments fields has been sized to be three lines in height. If the text is too large to fit in three lines, it will be truncated, as in this example. If you set the Autosize Height option for the detail band, the size of the band adjusts automatically, as shown in Figure 10.43.

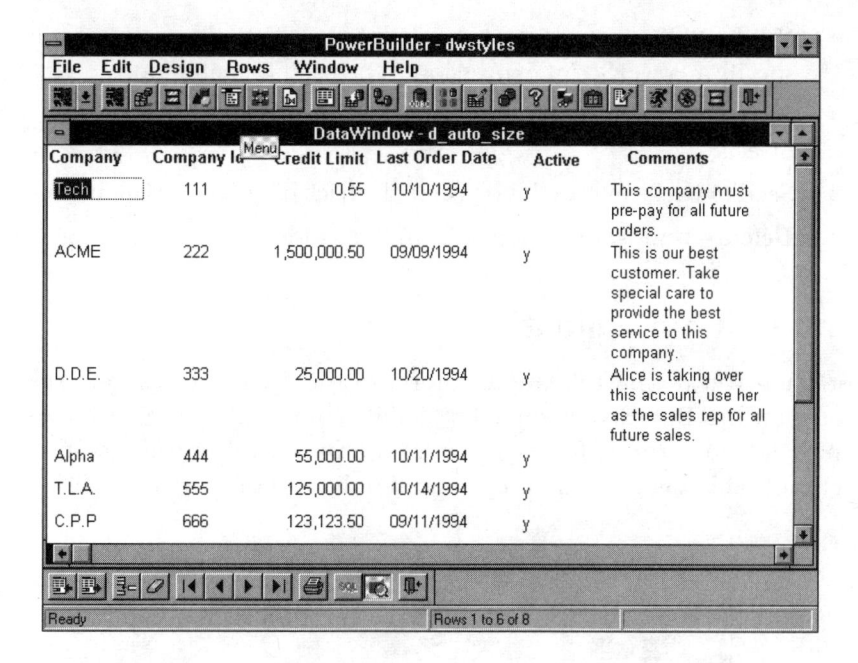

*Figure 10.43  Using a Variable Height field.*

Notice that the complete text for each comment is now visible. The first comment has five lines, the next two have six lines. The band is expanded to allow the correct amount of space for this field.

- **Color**—sets the background and text colors for this column.
- **Edit Styles**—selects a column edit style, as covered below in the section *Column Edit Styles*.
- **Font**—opens the Font dialog box, where you can specify the font characteristics for the text in this column.
- **Pointer**—selects the pointer icon to be used when the pointer is over this column.

- **Validation**—opens the Column Validation dialog box, where you can specify a PowerScript expression to be used for validation.
- **Bring to Front**—moves this object to the front of other overlapping objects.
- **Send to Back**—moves this object to the back of other overlapping objects.
- **Delete**—removes this object from the window.

## Using Column Validation

Most often you define validation criteria in the Database painter (see the chapter on the Database painter for details). You may, however, choose to define validation criteria for a column in the DataWindow painter. To do so, select the **Validation** tab from the Properties dialog box (Figure 10.44).

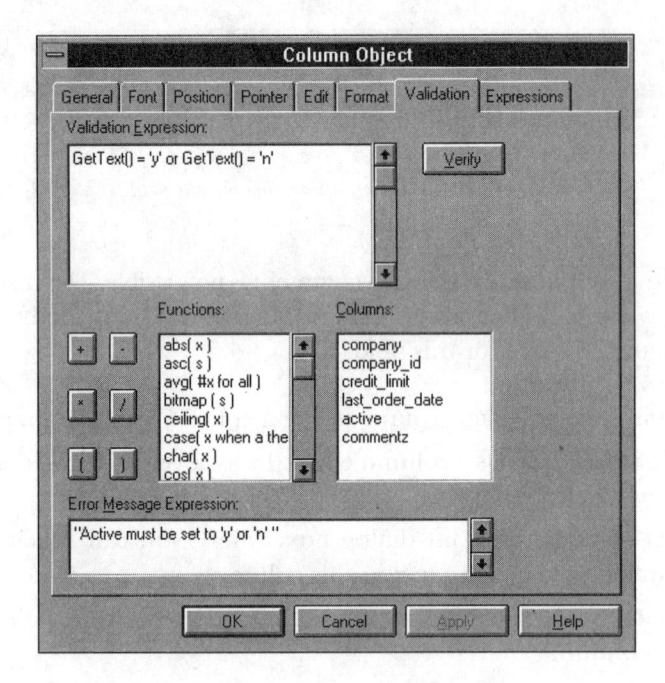

*Figure 10.44 Defining column validation.*

In this dialog box, you enter a Boolean PowerScript expression for the column validation. You can paste functions, columns, or operators into the expression using the controls at the bottom of the dialog box. You can refer to columns outside of the column that is being validated. In this example, the value in the active column must be either y or n.

## COLUMN EDIT STYLES

As a default, each column is given an edit style of Edit when it is added to a DataWindow. This works well for most columns, and is certainly the most common choice, but DataWindows provide a wide range of edit style choices for the columns. The column edit style controls the display of data and the manner in which the user interacts with the data. Select the **Edit** tab from the Properties dialog box to see the choices for column edit styles (Figure 10.45).

The column edit styles are CheckBox, DropDownDataWindow, DropDownListBox, Edit, EditMask, and RadioButton. The first five of these are familiar to you as control types in the Window painter (Edit is essentially a SingleLineEdit). The two others are specific to DataWindows. The DropDownDataWindow is a powerful control that is used to present a list of values for one column of a DataWindow that is derived from the data in another DataWindow.

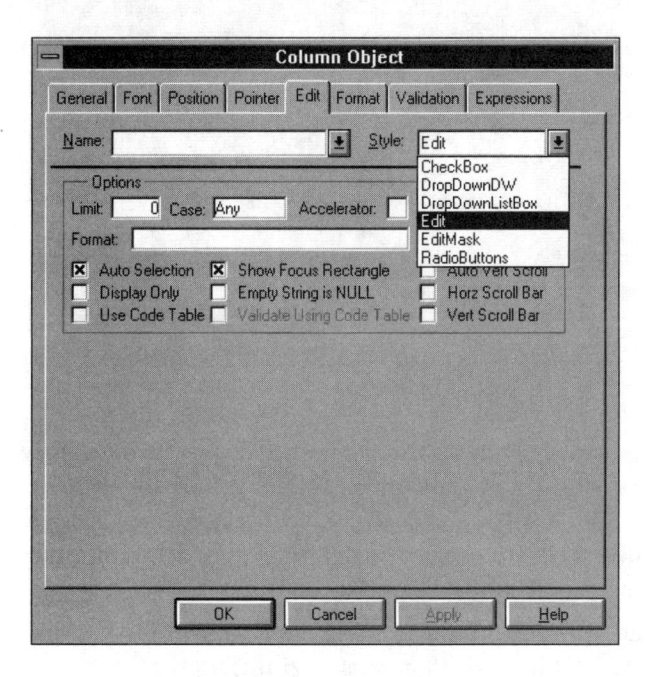

*Figure 10.45 Setting the column edit style.*

You can also define code tables when using DropDownListBox, CheckBoxes, RadioButtons, or Edit. You don't have to define a code table for a DropDownDataWindow; by default it works like one.

## The Default Edit Style

The default edit style (Edit) for a column is basically a SingleLineEdit. If you select the **Edit** option from the cascading menu in Figure 10.45, the Edit Style dialog box will open (Figure 10.46).

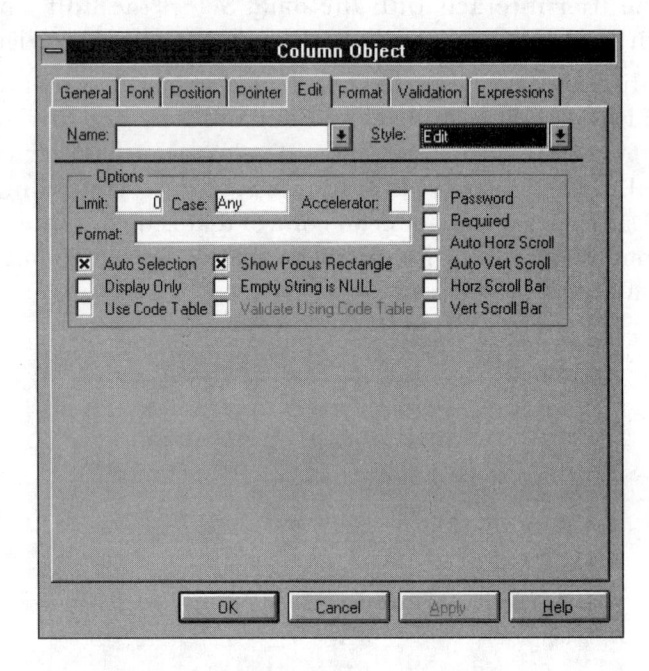

*Figure 10.46 The Edit Style dialog box.*

In the dialog box, you can set the most important attributes for the style. The attributes of the Edit style that you can set in this dialog box are:

✦ **Name**—assigns a previously defined edit style to this object by selecting it from the dropdown listbox.

✦ **Limit**—the maximum number of characters that can be entered in this SingleLineEdit (0 means no limit).

### The DataWindow Painter   409

- **Case**—controls the case of the input text. The choices are Any, lower, and UPPER.
- **Accelerator**—defines a keyboard accelerator for the SingleLineEdit in this field. Enter a character (a, b, etc.) that will be used in conjunction with the Alt key to place the focus in this field.
- **Password**—this option is useful for accepting passwords and other sensitive information in the SingleLineEdit. Checking this box causes the edit field to echo asterisks (*) as text is typed into the field, instead of displaying the actual text.
- **Required Field**—check this if the user must make an entry in this field. If this is checked, the user will not be able to tab away from this field without making an entry.
- **Empty String is NULL**—if this is checked, the DataWindow interprets an empty string in this field to represent a NULL value.
- **AutoHScroll**—if True, this activates automatic scrolling (horizontally) to let the user enter text that is wider than the size of the control.
- **AutoVScroll**—if True, this activates automatic scrolling (vertically) to let the user enter multiple lines of text.
- **H Scroll Bar**—check this option to add a horizontal scroll bar to this object (as needed).
- **V Scroll Bar**—check this option to add a vertical scroll bar to this object (as needed).
- **Display Only**—check this to use the field for display purposes only. This makes the field read-only and does not let the user enter or change the text in the field. But the text can still be selected (highlighted) to cut or copy to the clipboard.
- **Show Focus Rectangle**—check this to display a rectangle around the object when it has the focus.
- **Format**—in this field. you can add a format string to be used with the GetText( ) function. The GetText( ) function is covered in the next chapter.

You could use a code table to map column data values to display values by selecting the **Use Code Table** option. With this option, you enumerate a list of values in a code table. You must specify each possible value in the list. Click **Add** to add a new item at the bottom of the list, **Delete** to remove the current item, and **Insert** to insert an item at the current position in the list. The data value is the value actually read from or written to the database, while the corresponding display values are presented to the user in the object. The data value is optional; if you do not make an entry in that column, the data value will be the same as the display value.

With a code table, you can also use the Validate using Code Table option. With this option selected, the user can only enter values that are in the code table. If the user makes an entry that is not in the table and then tries to tab away from the field, the user receives an error message, and focus returns to the field.

## EditMask Style

The EditMask style is very similar to the SingleLineEdit style, but it has a fixed format built into its definition. Examples of common required formats are phone numbers, social security numbers, or date and time. This control is used like a SingleLineEdit, but to format data that is displayed by, and input into, the field.

The actual edit mask consists of a number of special characters that determine what can be entered in the field. The exact characters that are used vary according to the data type of the data being entered.

### For a number:

#—represents a digit.

0—represents a required digit.

### For a string:

#—represents a digit.

!—represents an uppercase character.

^—represents a lowercase character.

a—represents any alpha-numeric character.

x—allows any character.

Any other characters in the edit mask will be taken literally as punctuation characters used for presentation. For example, the edit mask (###) ###-#### works for phone numbers, and ###-##-#### is a social security number. !!## allows two uppercase characters followed by two digits, and dd/mm/yyyy is a typical date format.

The Edit Mask style dialog box is shown in Figure 10.47. In this case, the predefined EditMask company_phone was selected from the Name listbox. This mask was defined in the Database painter (see the chapter on the Database painter for more details).

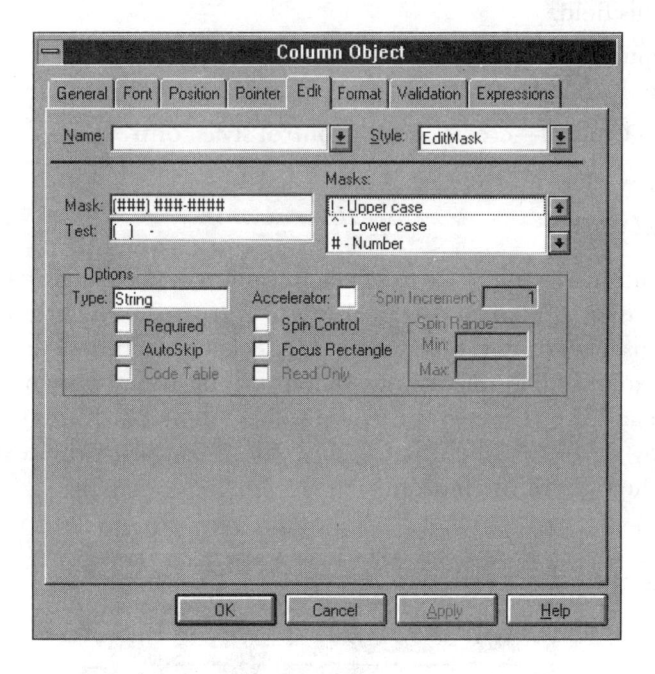

*Figure 10.47 Defining an Edit mask.*

- **Name**—assigns a previously defined edit style to this object by selecting it from the dropdown listbox.
- **Type**—specifies the data type. This can be String, Number, Date, Time, or Datetime; the type is determined by the datatype of the column.
- **Mask**—enters the actual edit mask in this field. Use the values in the Masks listbox (the contents will change according to the data type).

This dialog box also contains a test box where you can enter test values and see the results of the mask that you have specified.

The final options are:

- **Accelerator**—sets the character that is to be used in conjunction with the Alt key as the keyboard accelerator.

- **Focus Rectangle**—click on this to display the focus rectangle on this field when it has the focus.
- **AutoSkip**—causes the focus to jump to the next control in the tab order, when the user has entered the maximum number of characters in this field.
- **Required**—if you check this, it will be a required field. The user will not be able to leave this field (once entered it) without making an entry.
- **Spin Control**—creates a spin control style control.

## RadioButton

Use the RadioButton edit style to select an option from a small set of choices. RadioButtons are grouped together in a groupbox. Only one of the RadioButtons in a group can be selected (checked) at a time. RadioButtons in a group are managed automatically: When you click one of the buttons, it will be checked and the others in the group will be unchecked. You must assign a text (Display Value) to label each RadioButton; you place the text on either the left or the right of the button.

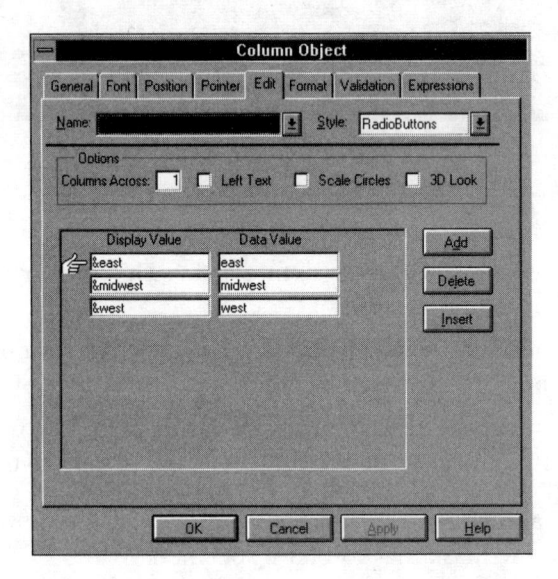

*Figure 10.48* The RadioButton style.

The attributes of the RadioButton style are:

- **Name**—assigns a previously defined edit style to this object by selecting it from the dropdown listbox.
- **Columns Across**—an integer, this is the number of columns used to present the RadioButtons. The default is 1.
- **LeftText**—a Boolean is **True** if the text appears to the left of the button, otherwise the text appears to the right of the button.
- **Scale Circles**—scales the size of the radio buttons to the size of the text.
- **3D**—gives radio buttons a three-dimensional appearance.

The label for each RadioButton is entered in the Display Value column. The actual database value for each RadioButton is entered in the Data Value column.

Click on **OK** and the style is changed to the RadioButton style. You then have to resize the control to display the buttons.

## DropDownListBox Style

A DropDownListBox combines a SingleLineEdit with a listbox. The listbox portion of the control can be dropped down (displayed) or can be closed. The DropDownListBox can be used to display a read-only list for the user to choose from, or it can be setup to allow the input of new values not in the list. To select an item in the list, use the scroll bar to locate and then click on the item. Use the Up and Down arrow keys to scroll through the list; this will select an item as it scrolls.

If the DropDownListBox is set for display-only, a search option is provided for items in the list. The listbox portion displays entries that match the letter that is typed into the SingleLineEdit part of the control. This matches only on the first letter of the items in the list. If there is more than one item beginning with a character, you can cycle through the items that match in the list by repeating the keystroke. You can also use the Up and Down arrow keys to move through the list while in the edit field.

If you select the **DropDownListBox** style the following dialog box opens:

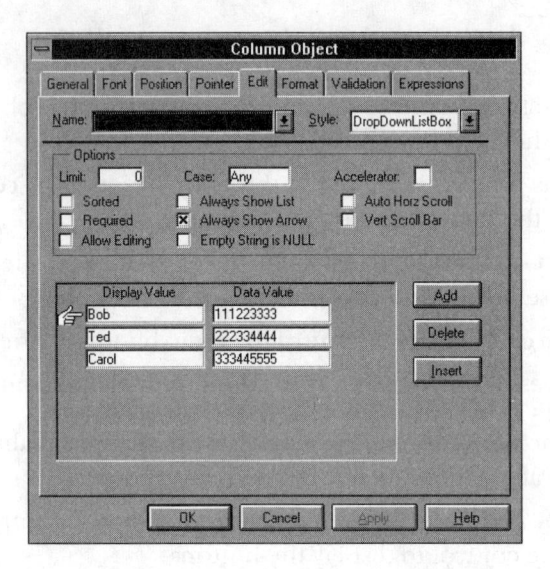

*Figure 10.49  The DropDownListBox style.*

The DropDownListBox Style dialog box is almost the same as the Style dialog box for the listbox. In this dialog box you can change the name of the control. The set of checkboxes is used to set some of the most important attributes.

## DropDownListBox Attributes

The attributes of a DropDownListBox style are:

- **Name**—assigns a previously defined edit style to this object by selecting it from the dropdown listbox. Use an existing edit style as a starting point by selecting its name from this list. After you make a modification to the style, the link to the source style is broken and the Name field is blank.
- **Limit**—specifies the maximum number of characters that can be entered for an new entry (for an editable type control).
- **Accelerator**—to assign an accelerator to this control, enter the character value in this field.
- **Sorted**—checking this attribute alphabetically sorts the list.

- **Allow Editing**—check this to make this an editable dropdown listbox.
- **Required Field**—check this if the user must make an entry in this field. If this is checked, the user will not be able to tab away from this field without making an entry.
- **Empty String is NULL**—if this is checked, the DataWindow will interpret an empty string in this field to represent a NULL value.
- **Always Show List**—causes the listbox portion of the control to always be dropped down and visible when that column has focus. If this is not checked, the user must click the **down arrow** to display the list.
- **Always Show Arrow**—causes the listbox to display the **down arrow** at all times. If this is not checked, the arrow only appears whenever the field has the focus.

You use a code table to map column data values. You enumerate a list of values in a code table and must specify each possible value in the list. Click **Add** to add a new item at the bottom of the list, **Delete** to remove the current item, and **Insert** to insert an item at the current position in the list. The data value is the value actually read from, or written to, the database, while the corresponding display values are presented to the user in the object.

When you click on **OK** the DropDownListBox style is applied to the field. You must size this object (in the DataWindow painter) to represent the size that you want for the ListBox portion of this control when it drops down. If you size this larger than the number of entries in the drop-down portion, it will default to the size needed for the entries.

## DropDownDataWindow Style

The DropDownDataWindow style is very powerful and useful. It connects a column in the DataWindow with a pair of columns in another DataWindow object. The other DataWindow object is called a *DropDownDataWindow* object. Pay careful attention to the terms used here. The DataWindow under construction is referred to as the local DataWindow to clarify this discussion. One of the columns in the local DataWindow has the DropDownDataWindow style and refers to another source DataWindow object called the DropDownDataWindow object.

A column with a DropDownDataWindow style is similar to one with the DropDownListBox style, but the display and data values originate in the database via the DropDownDataWindow object. This is most useful in the case where you want to limit the user's choices for a column's input values, but the list changes from time to time, or is too large to be embedded in a DropDownListBox. For example, the employee table has a column called Department. The list of departments can be stored in another table (the Department table) and the DropDownDataWindow style provides a current list of departments to the user when they need to enter the department for an employee. In an example included with this book, we use a DropDownDataWindow style to provide a list of the states in the Company table. In that case, we also do some filtering based on the region where the company is located, to limit the list of states to those that are in that region.

Previously (prior to PowerBuilder 3.0), this type of relationship had to be implemented through a separate routine and took a great deal of work to create this type of object. Now it is available as a column style and is dramatically easier to implement.

In order to use this style for a column, you must have previously defined the DropDownDataWindow object that will be used as the source for the column. Usually that DataWindow object has to be defined with two columns, the first (left-most) column should be the display values for the column in the local DataWindow. The second column usually serves as the data values for the local DataWindow. The column used for the data value must match the datatype of the local DataWindow object column.

You must create the presentation of the source DataWindow as you want it to be displayed in the dropdown listbox portion of the object. You can control the width of the DropDownDataWindow to control the display of the list. The height is determined automatically. The display column should be the first (left-most) column in the DropDownDataWindow object, because this is what is displayed in the dropdown portion of the column. Regardless of the column that you enter in the Display Column field of the DropDownDataWindow Edit Style dialog box, the first column will be displayed.

To define the attributes of this style, open the DropDownDataWindow Edit Style dialog box (Figure 10.50).

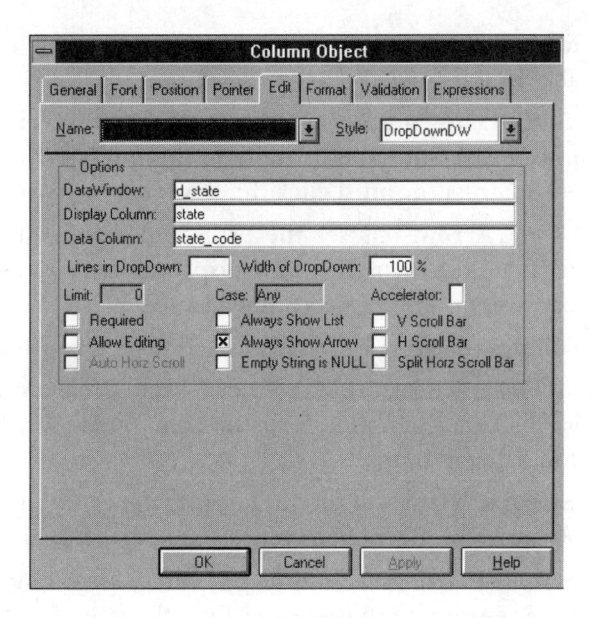

*Figure 10.50  Defining a DropDownDataWindow.*

The attributes of a DropDownDataWindow are:

- **Name**—assigns a previously defined edit style to this object by selecting it from the dropdown listbox. Use an existing edit style as a starting point by selecting its name from this list. After you make a modification to the style, the link to the source style is broken and the Name field will be blank.
- **DataWindow**—this is the name of the source DataWindow object. Select the name from the dropdown listbox.
- **Display Column**—the column in the source DataWindow that is to be used for the display. This column's values are displayed in the line edit portion of the DropDownDataWindow when you select a row in the DropDownDataWindow.
- **Data Column**—the column in the source DataWindow that is to be used for the data values. This column's values will be used as the data value that is actually stored in the database for the column when you update the data source for the local DataWindow.

- **Accelerator**—to assign an accelerator to this control, enter the character value in this field.
- **Always Show List**—causes the listbox portion of the control to always be dropped down and visible when the column has the focus. If this is not checked, the user must click the **down arrow** to display the list.
- **Always Show Arrow**—causes the listbox to display the down arrow whenever it has the focus. This also displays when it doesn't have focus unless you also choose **Always Show List**.
- **Allow Editing**—check this to make an editable DropDownListBox.
- **Required Field**—check this if the user must make an entry in this field. If this is checked, the user will not be able to tab away from this field without making an entry.
- **Empty String is NULL**—if this is checked, the DataWindow interprets an empty string in this field to represent a NULL value.
- **AutoHScroll**—if **True**, this activated automatic scrolling (horizontally) lets the user enter text that is wider than the size of the control.
- **Limit**—the maximum number of characters that can be entered in this SingleLineEdit (0 means no limit).
- **Case**—you can control the case of the input text. The choices are Any, lower, and UPPER.
- **V Scroll Bar**—check this option to add a vertical scroll bar to this object (as needed).
- **H Scroll Bar**—check this option to add a horizontal scroll bar to this object (as needed).
- **Split H Scroll Bar**—check this to display the split bar in the DataWindow object; this lets the user divide the DataWindow into two windows.
- **Width of Drop Down**—specifies the width of the drop-down portion of the DropDownListBox. This is a percent of the width of the column.

# PRESENTATION STYLES

The previous discussion was centered on the Tabular presentation style. While this is the most often used style, there are seven other styles from which to choose. The presentation style determines the layout of the data and specifies the general manner in which the user interacts with that data. This section covers the other presentation styles. PowerBuilder provides you with seven other presentation styles to choose. Each is different in the way that it presents the data.

The other choices for presentation style are:

- **Composite**—combines two or more DataWindow reports.
- **Crosstab**—presents the data in a cross tabulation format. This is most useful for calculating totals by groups. This can present data in a manner similar to spreadsheet programs.
- **Freeform**—this is the "forms"-like presentation. Generally, you use the freeform presentation style to allow individual records to enter, update, delete, and display individual records. The DataWindow presents all of the fields (column values) of a single record with a field label.
- **Graph**—PowerBuilder has an excellent selection of graphs, similar to the graphs available with Microsoft Excel.
- **Grid**—the grid style is similar to the tabular presentation style. The user can reorder and resize the columns in the DataWindow. This has the advantages of the tabular presentation style and also lets the user adjust the display. The disadvantage of the grid style is that while the user can rearrange the columns, the developer is not able to modify the layout in the flexible manner available in the tabular style
- **Group**—the group presentation style makes it very easy to create reports with group summations. The format is attractive and useful. The display is divided into groups with headings and summation rows predefined. The report includes page header, time, and page count.
- **Label**—presents data in a simple mailing label format.
- **N-Up**—presents data in columns across the screen like a newspaper. When a column reaches the bottom of the screen, the data continues in the next column (left to right). The exception to this is that sorted data is presented across the columns in rows.

## Freeform

This is the "forms"-like presentation. Generally, you use the freeform presentation style to enter, update, delete, and display individual records. The DataWindow presents each of the fields (column values) of a single record with a field label. This format can be customized to a large degree.

For this example, a SQL SELECT statement is created in the SQL Painter.

```
SELECT "company"."company",
       "company"."company_id",
       "company"."region",
       "company"."city",
       "company"."state",
       "company"."zip",
       "company"."phone",
       "company"."rep_ssn",
       "company"."credit_limit",
       "company"."last_order_date"
  FROM "company"
ORDER BY "company"."company_id" ASC
```

After defining the SELECT statement, the DataWindow painter opens with the display in Figure 10.51.

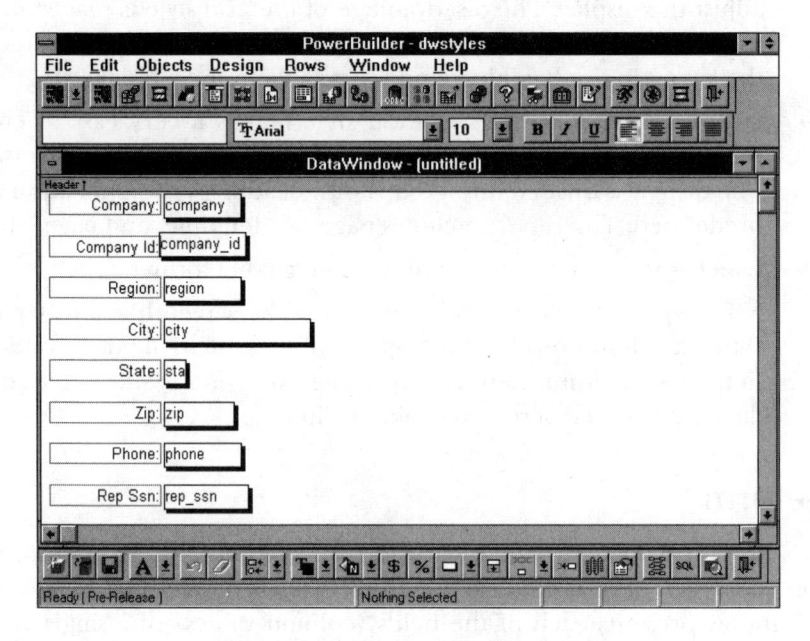

**Figure 10.51** *The DataWindow painter.*

The DataWindow painter initially arranges all the fields in a single column. In this example, there are too many fields to be presented on the screen at one time in this manner. Therefore, we moved five of the fields to the right half of the screen. Figure 10.52 shows the rearranged DataWindow as it will display at run time.

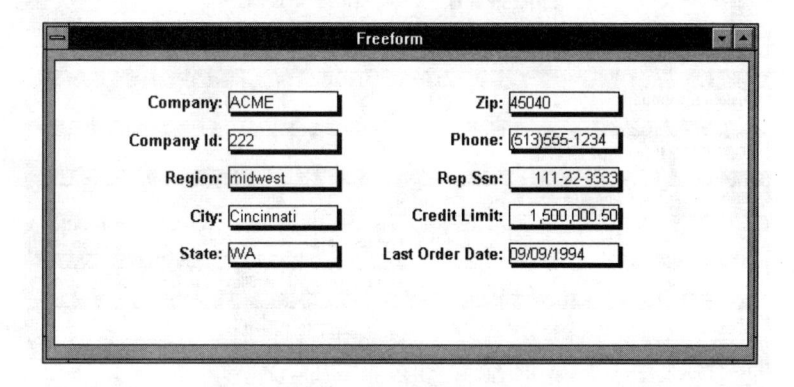

*Figure 10.52* A free-form DataWindow.

## Tabular

Tabular is the most frequently used presentation style. Data is presented in columns under column headings. Each row is initially presented in a separate line. This presentation allows a great deal of flexibility. You can take a tabular presentation and create a form presentation or a group presentation very easily.

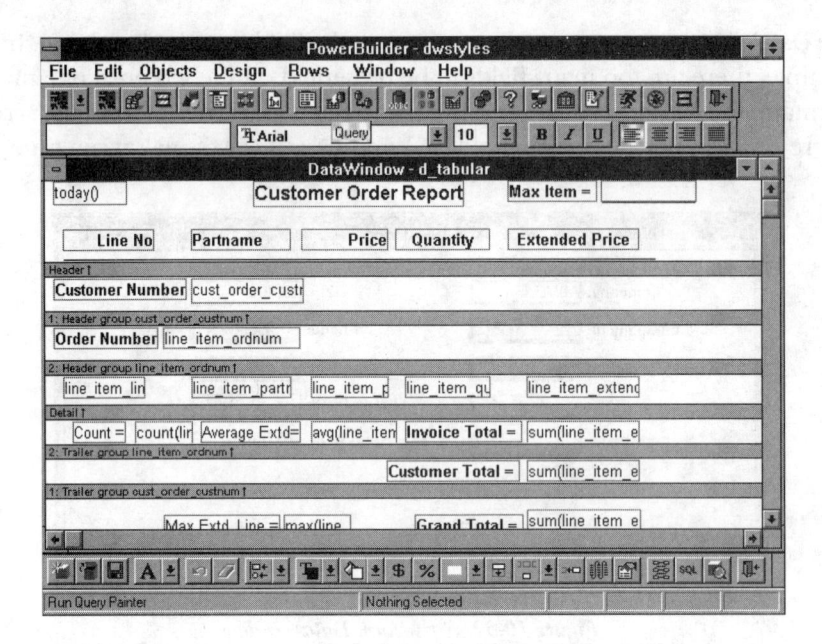

*Figure 10.53* The Tabular Presentation style.

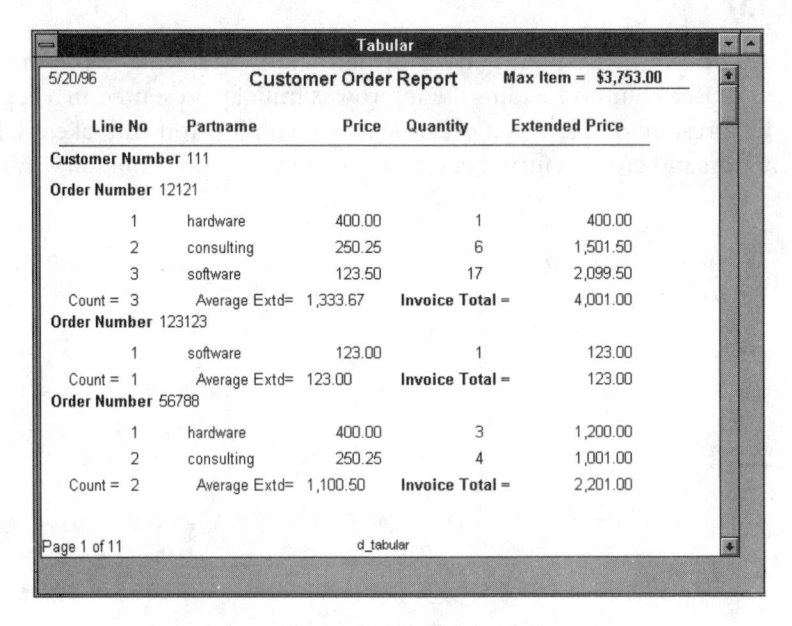

*Figure 10.54* The Final Tabular Report.

## DataWindow Examples

The example applications include a number of PBLs with DataWindow examples. These include **FIRSTDW.PBL**, **CHILDDW.PBL**, **IMAGEDB.PBL**, **BLOBDB.PBL**, and **DWSTYLES.PBL**. Run these applications and try to duplicate each one.

CHAPTER 11

# DataWindow Controls: Adding DataWindows to Your Applications

The previous chapters have covered the creation and customization of DataWindow objects. In order to use a DataWindow *object* in your application, you must add a DataWindow *control* to a window. This chapter covers:

- Overview of DataWindow controls
- Adding DataWindow controls to your windows
- Database Access with DataWindows
- External DataWindows
- Programming DataWindow controls
- DataWindow control properties, events, and functions
- DataStores
- Reports
- DataWindows examples with the most important functions

## Overview: Using DataWindow Controls

You add a DataWindow control to a window and then position and size it like any other control in the Window painter. The next step is unique to DataWindow controls: you must link (associate) the DataWindow control to a specific DataWindow object. Each DataWindow control has a string attribute (DataObject) that specifies the name of the related DataWindow object. This will make the DataWindow object available to your application.

Figure 11.1 shows the relationship between a window, a DataWindow control, a DataWindow object, and the data source.

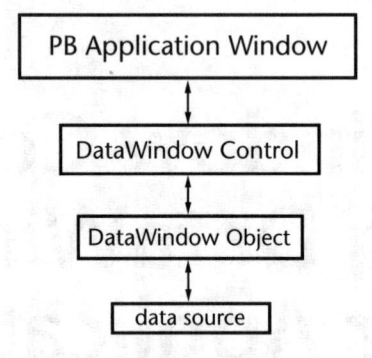

**Figure 11.1** *Relationship between a window, a DataWindow control, a DataWindow object, and the data source.*

The association between a DataWindow control and a DataWindow object is nonexclusive. That is, you can associate more than one control with a particular DataWindow object. You may also change the DataWindow object that is associated with any DataWindow control dynamically at run time.

## DataWindows with a DBMS Source

You will use a set of PowerScript functions with most of the DataWindow controls that you create. When the data source is a DBMS, these functions include:

- **SetTransObject()**—associates a Transaction object with the DataWindow control.

- **Retrieve()**—issues the SQL SELECT statement for the DataWindow object.
- **InsertRow()**—inserts a new row into the DataWindow control.
- **DeleteRow()**—deletes a row from the DataWindow control.
- **Update()**—applies changes made in the DataWindow to the database.

The Retrieve and Update functions automatically generate the necessary SQL statements including:

- SELECT
- UPDATE
- INSERT
- DELETE

You will still use the following embedded SQL Statements in your script code:

- connect;
- commit;
- rollback;
- disconnect;

## DataWindows With an External Source

When the data source is external (not a DBMS), you will not use the SetTransObject or Retrieve functions. You will still use the functions:

- **InsertRow()**—inserts a new row into the DataWindow control.
- **DeleteRow()**—deletes a row from the DataWindow control.

You will write the code to perform the retrieval or generation of the data for external DataWindows. You will also write the code that is required to save the data (if necessary) to a file or other source. External DataWindows may also access databases through an API (such as a HLLAPI). About half the projects on which I have consulted have needed to access legacy data systems on mainframes. In this case, we used external DataWindows to create a PC front-end for existing mainframe applications.

## Adding a DataWindow Control to a Window

In the Window painter, click on the **DataWnd** icon (on the PainterBar's Controls Panel) or select the **Control|DataWindow** menu selection. This tells the Window painter that you are going to add a DataWindow control to the window that you are editing. Then click at the position in the window where you wish to add the DataWindow control. You can then position and size the control as you would any other window control (Figure 11.2).

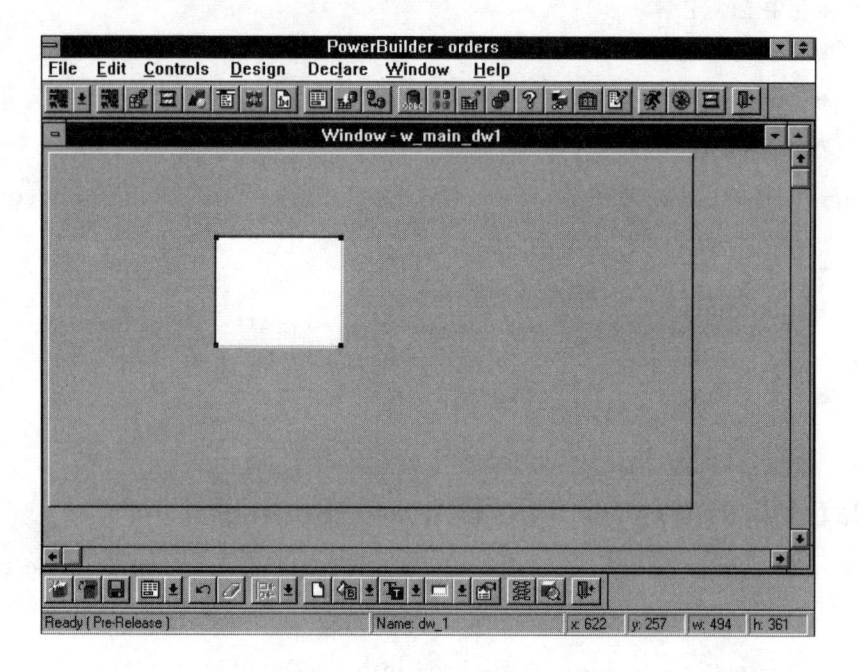

*Figure 11.2 After adding a DataWindow control to a window.*

## DataWindow Control Popup Menu Options

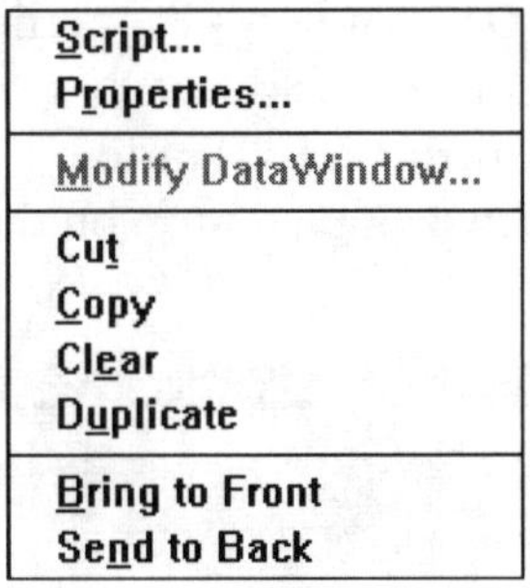

**Figure 11.3** *The DataWindow Popup menu.*

The items in the popup menu (right mouse-click on the control) for a DataWindow control are:

- **Script**—edits a script for a control event.
- **Properties**—opens the Properties Tab dialog box.
- **Modify DataWindow**—opens the DataWindow painter so that you may edit the DataWindow object associated with this control.
- **Cut**—delete the control from the window and move it to the buffer.
- **Copy**—copy this control to the buffer (including scripts).
- **Clear**—removes this control from the window.
- **Duplicate**—makes a copy of this control (including scripts).
- **Bring to Front**—moves this control to the front of other overlapping controls.
- **Send to Back**—moves this control to the back of other overlapping controls.

## Select a DataWindow Object

Each DataWindow control must be associated with a specific DataWindow object. To do this, open the DataWindow's Properties dialog box. Either double-click on the DataWindow control, or select **Properties** from the RMB popup menu (right mouse-click on the DataWindow). To see the list of available DataWindow objects, click the **Browse** button on the General tab (Figure 11.4).

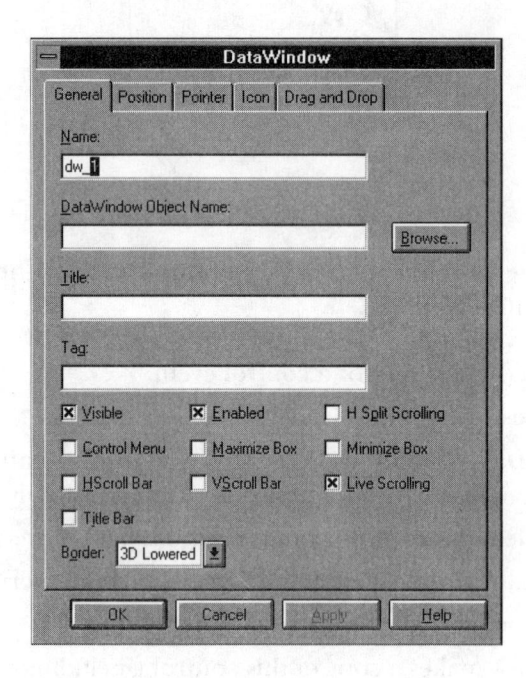

*Figure 11.4* The DataWindow Properties dialog box.

This opens the Select DataWindow dialog box (Figure 11.5).

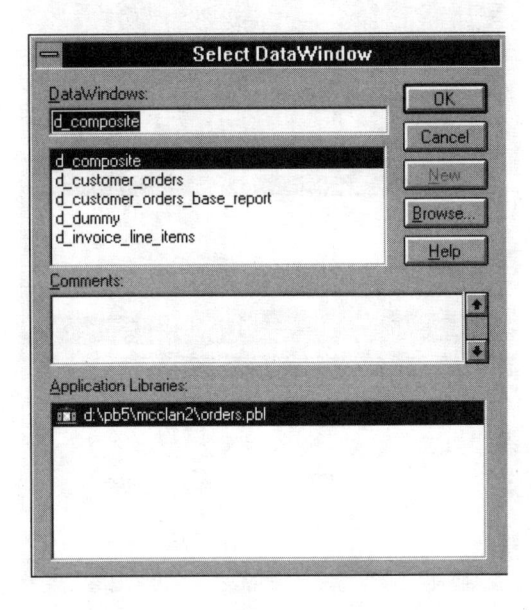

*Figure 11.5  The Select DataWindow dialog box.*

Select the Application library (in the bottom listbox) that holds the DataWindow object. Then select the DataWindow object from the list in the DataWindows listbox (at the top of the dialog box). Click the **OK** button, this links the DataWindow control to the selected DataWindow object. If you need help locating a DataWindow object, you can click on **Browse** (Figure 11.4) to open the Browse DataWindows dialog box (Figure 11.6).

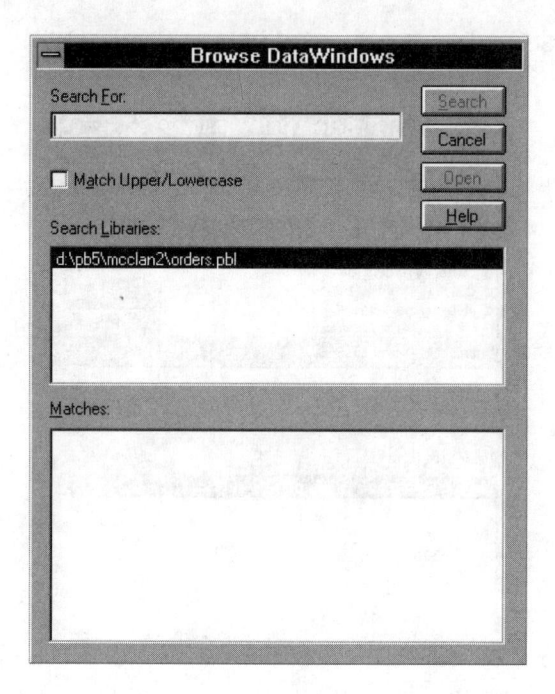

*Figure 11.6  Entering the Browse criteria.*

In this dialog box, first select the libraries (**.PBL** files) that you want to search, then enter the search criteria in the Search For field. Click on **Search** and then the Matches Found ListBox displays all DataWindow objects matching your search criteria. You can make the search case-sensitive by checking the checkbox that is located just below the criteria field. The dialog box will display the matches in the bottom listbox.

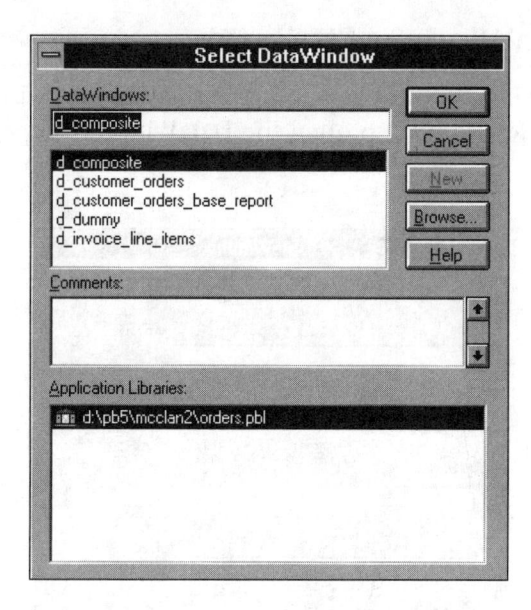

*Figure 11.7  After the search.*

## Modify DataWindow Object

If you wish to edit the DataWindow object (related to a DataWindow control on the current window), note the following shortcut for opening the DataWindow painter. Just select the **Modify DataWindow** option on the RMB popup for the DataWindow control. Right-click the mouse of the DataWindow control (in the Window painter), then select **Modify DataWindow**. This will open the DataWindow painter for the associated DataWindow object.

## Set the DataWindow Attributes

To modify DataWindow control attributes in the Window painter, double-click on the **DataWindow** control to open the DataWindow Properties dialog box (Figure 11.8).

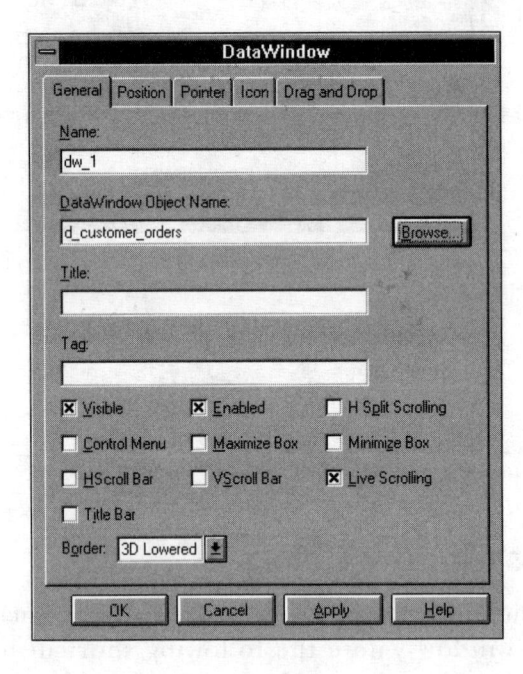

*Figure 11.8 The DataWindow Properties dialog box.*

The attributes of a DataWindow that you can change in this dialog box are:

- **Name**—changes the name of the DataWindow control. PowerBuilder uses the prefix dw_ for DataWindow controls (you should stick with this convention; use the prefix d_ for DataWindow objects).

- **DataWindow Object Name**—contains the name of the DataWindow object that you associated with the control. Click **Browse** to change the associated DataWindow object.

- **Title**—adds a title to the DataWindow. This has the unfortunate side effect of making the DataWindow movable, which is not usually desirable. So, usually you add a static text control to the window instead.

- **Visible**—sets this checkbox to make the control visible.
- **Enabled**—when the control is enabled, it is active and can be selected and receive input. If it is disabled, the control cannot receive input or events and the user cannot tab to the fields within the control.
- **H Split Scrolling**—check this to display the split bar in the DataWindow object; this allows the user to divide the DataWindow into two vertical windows that can be scrolled separately.
- **Control menu**—adds a control menu to the DataWindow. This menu adds functions to let the user move, resize (restore, maximize), minimize, or close the DataWindow. This option is only available if you have added a title bar to the DataWindow.
- **Maximize Box**—adds the Maximize button to the DataWindow. This option is available only if you have added a title bar to the DataWindow.
- **Minimize Box**—adds the Minimize button to the DataWindow. This option is available only if you have added a title bar to the DataWindow.
- **HScroll Bar**—adds a horizontal scroll bar to this control (this appears as needed).
- **VScroll Bar**—check this option to add a vertical scroll bar to this control (this will appear as needed).
- **Live Scrolling**—lets the user move through the rows in the DataWindow using the scroll bar.
- **Title Bar**—adds a title bar to the DataWindow, then add the caption in the Title field.
- **Border**—selects a border for the control (an enumerated value). The choices are 3D Lowered, 3D Raised, Box, None, Resize, and ShadowBox.

If you do not make the DataWindow control resizable, you must size this control (in the Window painter) to be large enough to display what you intended when you created the DataWindow object. You may have to run the application several times to fine-tune the adjustment of the DataWindow size.

The General tab on the DataWindow Properties dialog box contains the most important attributes. The other tabs on this dialog box contain attributes that are essentially the same as for other controls. Use the Position, Pointer, Icon, and Drag and Drop tabs to set these attributes.

# Using DataWindow Controls with a Database

Your application interacts with the DataWindow object through the DataWindow control. To use the DataWindow control with a database (using native DBMS drivers or ODBC), you must initialize a transaction object (such as SQLCA, the global transaction object created by PowerBuilder) and then connect to the database. This part of the process is the same as the process for embedded SQL.

After you make the connection to the database, you must assign the transaction object to a DataWindow control before the DataWindow control can access the database. From this point on, you use DataWindow control functions to retrieve and manipulate the data (instead of using embedded SQL).

For example:

```
i_rc = f_load_sqlca(sqlca) // this initializes the SQLCA &
transation object
IF i_rc = 1 THEN
   CONNECT USING sqlca;
   IF sqlca.sqlcode = 0 THEN
      i_rc = dw_1.SetTransObject(sqlca)
      /// if i_rc = 1 then from this point on, dw_1 has &
access to the tables in the database
```

In this example, we call a global function, `f_load_sqlca`. This function could be written to read the application's profile file (such as **IMAGEDB.INI**), and to assign values found in that file to the SQLCA transaction object. See Chapter 7, "Embedded SQL," for details on using the ProfileString function in this manner, or examine the function `f_load_sqlca` in the DataWindow example applications for this chapter.

## Connecting to the Database

You must have assigned the transaction object parameters that are required to connect to your DBMS before you can use the transaction object to connect to the database. You must also be connected to the database with a transaction object before using that object with the SetTransObject function.

```
CONNECT USING sqlca;
```

## Disconnecting to the Database

You should disconnect from the database before the application terminates.

```
DISCONNECT USING sqlca;
```

# TRANSACTION OBJECTS

A *transaction object* is required for all database access in PowerBuilder applications. The transaction object holds the information that is required to connect to the database, and it holds the return code and other information that is returned as a result of each database interaction.

## SetTransObject

You can set a transaction object for each DataWindow control using the SetTransObject function (do not confuse this with the SetTrans function). The transaction object represents one connection to a database (to a specific DBMS, database, and user account). You can share a transaction object between DataWindows (and embedded SQL) in your application, if they access the same DBMS, database, and account. The syntax for associating the transaction object for a DataWindow control is

```
i_rc = dw_1.SetTransObject ( SQLCA )
```

This statement will assign the SQLCA transaction object to the `dw_1` DataWindow control. This function returns an integer; a value of 1 signals success. When you use SetTransObject, you must take responsibility for managing database transactions. You must issue COMMIT (or ROLLBACK) statements to the database using embedded SQL. You may issue a COMMIT statement immediately after calling the DataWindow Update( ) function (if the Update was successful). You may also keep a transaction open while a particular window is open, and then commit or rollback when the window closes. This makes the changes on the window one logical unit of work. The disadvantage of this technique is that rows may be locked in the database until the transaction ends.

## SetTrans

It is possible to set the transaction object with another (seldom used) function, SetTrans( ). In addition to setting the transaction object, this function takes over the transaction management by issuing COMMIT statements after each database operation. The SetTrans function also connects before each database operation and disconnects after each operation. This also means that each database operation must open a new connection (with SetTrans), and the application will suffer a rather large performance penalty. Usually, this is not desirable, so use the SetTransObject function. The only time to consider using the SetTrans function to specify the transaction object is when you are running short on connections to the database. Since SetTransObject commits and disconnects after each operation, the connects are closed more often.

If you use SetTrans, you do not need to issue the CONNECT, DISCONNECT, COMMIT, or ROLLBACK statements or call the Update function since this is handled internally. We will not use the SetTrans function in our examples, and for the rest of this book you can assume that we are using SetTransObject.

## Data Manipulation

The DataWindow functions that you use for data manipulation (with a DBMS) are:

- **Retrieve**—issues the SQL Select statement for this DataWindow and populates the DataWindow with rows from the database.
- **InsertRow**—adds a new row to the DataWindow at a specified location. This function also initializes any of the columns in the new row with values that you specified as default (initial) values in the Database painter.
- **DeleteRow**—this function removes a specific row from the DataWindow.
- **Update**—applies all the changes (additions, deletions, modifications) made to the rows in the DataWindow back to the database.

> **NOTE:** These are DataWindow PowerScript functions, not embedded SQL statements.

Use the Retrieve function to issue the SELECT statement against the database and populate the DataWindow. For example,

```
l_rows = dw_1.Retrieve()
```

or perhaps

```
l_rows = dw_1.Retrieve('OH', i_account) // with two arguments
```

The second example passes two retrieval arguments to the SQL Select statement. Notice that the functions are applied to the DataWindow control, not to the DataWindow object. The Retrieve function returns a long value, which is the number of rows returned to the DataWindow.

You can insert and delete rows in the DataWindow using the InsertRow and DeleteRow functions.

```
i_rc = dw_1.DeleteRow(14) // delete row 14 from the DataWindow
...
i_rc = dw_1.InsertRow(1) // add a row to the DataWindow,
                         // just before...the current row 1
```

You can also allow the update of fields in the DataWindow.

```
i_rc = dw_1.UpdateRow()   // apply changes to the database
```

Often you will add CommandButtons or menu options to the window to trigger the retrieval, inserting, updating, and deleting of rows of data from the database. You could also trigger the initial retrieval in the application or window open events, but you must populate the DataWindow explicitly (or store data in the DataWindow object with the **Rows|Data** menu option in the DataWindow control painter). During the design process the population of the DataWindow object was automatic when you selected the **Design|Preview** menu option in the DataWindow painter. Remember, that to access the database, each DataWindow needs a transaction object. DataWindows can share transaction objects.

**NOTE:** The changes caused by editing fields in the DataWindow and by issuing the InsertRow and DeleteRow functions are made to rows of data **in the DataWindow**, not to the database.

It is essential that you understand that the InsertRow and DeleteRow functions only directly affect the DataWindow control and not the database. When you want to apply the DataWindow changes to the database, use the Update function. For example:

```
i_rc = dw_1.Update()
IF i_rc = 1 THEN
    commit;
ELSE
    rollback;
END IF
```

The Update function issues the necessary INSERT, UPDATE, and/or DELETE SQL statements to the database (depending on the changes that have been made to the DataWindows). After the Update, you can issue a COMMIT statement to make the changes to the database permanent; otherwise you can issue a ROLLBACK statement to cancel them. You may also delay the COMMIT or ROLLBACK until later, but in general you should make transactions as short as possible.

## DATABASE ERROR HANDLING IN DATAWINDOWS

Chapter 7, "Embedded SQL," covered error handling using the SQLCA.SQLCode attribute. This applies only to embedded SQL and not to the DataWindow database functions. There is a different technique for handling database errors in DataWindows.

When a database error occurs as a result of a DataWindow database function (such as Retrieve or Update), the DBError event will be triggered in the DataWindow control. In that event, you receive several arguments that carry information about the database error.

For example, if you placed the following statement in the Clicked event for a CommandButton (cb_retrieve):

```
l_rows = dw_1.Retrieve(start_date, end_date)
```

and a database error occurred, the DBError event in dw_1 would be triggered. In that event you could place the following code:

```
st_status.text = "DB Error:" + string(sqldbcode) + ' '&
   + sqlerrortext,StopSign!)
return 1 // this will override the default error message
```

The return values for the DBError event are:

0—display an error message. This is the default.
1—do not display an error message.

The arguments for the DBError event are:

**sqldbcode**—a long variable, the number of the database error (from the DBMS).
**sqlerrtext**—a string, the text message associated with the error code.
**sqlsyntax**—a string, the associated SQL statement.
**buffer**—the dwbuffer for the DataWindow.
**row**—a long value. The current row number.

# UPDATING DATA IN A DATAWINDOW

It is important to understand how the DataWindow works to display and update rows in the database. The DataWindow has three buffers:

1. **primary**—the currently available data in the DataWindow
2. **filter**—rows that have been filtered out
3. **delete**—rows that have been deleted

After the initial SELECT (resulting from the Retrieve function call), all data is held in the primary buffer. When you apply a filter condition, some rows may be moved to the filter buffer. When you delete a row, it is moved to the delete buffer.

PowerBuilder also keeps a copy of the original values that were retrieved into the DataWindow. You can access the original retrieval set by asking for the Original value (rather than the current) value of the Primary! buffer. See the section on DataWindow Items for more information.

It is important to note that changing the data in the DataWindow does not change the database! To apply DataWindow changes to the database, you must call the Update function to update the database from the DataWindow and then commit the transaction.

Use the following code to apply changes to the database:

```
rc = dw_1.Update()
```

When you execute the Update function PowerBuilder examines the DataWindow buffers to decide what changes need to be applied to the database. PowerBuilder then generates the necessary SQL statements, including INSERT, DELETE, and UPDATE statements and sends them to the database.

You control the updateability of the data in a DataWindow on a column-by-column basis. To allow the update of a field, set a tab value greater than 0 for that column (in the DataWindow painter) to make it accessible. You can also set the column's Protect attribute to **1** to prevent the editing of a field.

## THE DATAWINDOWS EDIT CONTROL

As the user tabs through the DataWindow fields, an edit control (which is more like a multiline edit control) is placed over the field that has the focus. Only one field may have the focus in a DataWindow at any given moment. The field data is moved into the edit control when the field receives the focus. Then the user can enter or modify data in the selected field. When the user types into the edit control, that text is held in the edit control. The text in the edit control is not in any of the DataWindow buffers (as long as it is being edited).

When the cursor leaves the field (such as when the user presses the **Tab** key), the text in the edit control will either be moved into the primary buffer or rejected, retaining the initial value. The data will be moved into the primary buffer only if the entry is of the correct data type and if it passes the validation rules (if any).

The following functions work with the edit control located at the current row and column in the DataWindow:

| | |
|---|---|
| `dw_1.GetText()` | This returns a string containing the text currently in the edit control. |
| `dw_1.SetText("hello")` | This function assigns a string to the edit control. |
| `dw_1.AcceptText()` | This function moves the text from the edit control into the current buffer cell. |

The data type of the data in the edit control is string, regardless of the column data type. The text will be converted to the appropriate data type when it is moved into the DataWindow buffer. If you are accessing the edit control text, you will have to do the conversion (if required). For example:

```
i_size = Integer(dw_1.GetText())
```

This would convert the edit control text to an integer.

You can also use other MultiLineEdit functions:

- Clear, Copy, Cut, Paste, SelectText, Undo
- CanUndo, LineCount, Position, ReplaceText
- Scroll, Selection
- Undo

# AcceptText

Generally, the AcceptText is performed automatically by the DataWindow, such as when the user tabs to another field, clicks on another field, or hits the **Up** or **Down** arrow keys. The Update function also issues an AcceptText function call for the DataWindow (by default). Sometimes it is necessary to use this function (to lock in the last item that was entered). For example, if you activate another window after modifying a field in a DataWindow, the newly activated window will not see that last modification unless you issue an AcceptText call. See the **IMAGEDB.PBL** for an example.

## Updating a Row in a DataWindow

In this section, we will present the sequence of steps required to update a row in a database using a DataWindow.

At this point, data is displayed in DataWindow. The focus is set to a field on the DataWindow.

## The DataWindow Edit Control

Item data is moved to text in the edit control. The user moves to the field (item) that they wish to edit. The user then updates the edit control text. The events that are typically triggered include:

**RowFocusChanged**—triggered when a new row gets the focus.

**ItemFocusChanged**—triggered when a new item (field) gets the focus.

**EditChanged**—triggered on each keystroke, as the user modifies the edit control text.

Next, the user attempts to move to another field (by tabbing or clicking elsewhere on the screen) or just hits the **Enter** key. This sets a number of actions into motion. These actions and DataWindow events are very important to understand.

PowerBuilder may trigger several DataWindow events during this process. They are:

- **AcceptText**—triggered when the user moves the focus away from the field after making a change.
- **ItemChanged**—triggered when the accept text moves the edit control data into the item value.
- **ItemError**— triggered when the new data fails the validation (or data conversion).
- **ItemFocusChanged**—triggered when the focus changes.

The DataWindow performs an implicit AcceptText (unless you write a ItemChanged event). First, PowerBuilder checks to see if the text in the edit control has been changed (from the original value that was copied from the item). If no change has taken place, the DataWindow allows the ItemFocusChanged event and may also trigger the RowFocusChanged event (assuming the focus remains in the DataWindow).

If a change has taken place, the edit control text is converted to the correct data type and validated. If the data conversion or validation fails, PowerBuilder triggers the DataWindow ItemError event. Otherwise, the buffer item is set to the new value.

PowerBuilder allows the focus to change if everything was successful.

## ItemChanged Event

If the new data fails the validation test or the data conversion failed, PowerBuilder will trigger the DataWindow ItemError event. As discussed, the ItemChanged event occurs when the user changes the text in the edit control and then moves away from the field (or hits **Enter**). You may write your own code to handle this event, or you may use the default processing, which is usual. If you use the default processing (do not write your own script), the ItemChanged event will issue an AcceptText function call.

You may want to write your own script so that you can test the data. If you want to reject the data that has been entered, you return a value of 1 (RETURN 1) to override the default processing, reject the entry, keep the focus on the edit control, and trigger the ItemError event. For example:

```
int     i_invoice

i_invoice = Integer(dw_Invoice.GetText( ))
IF i_invoice < i_last_invoice THEN RETURN 1
```

The return values for this event are:

**0**—accepts the data. This is the default.
**1**—reject the data, do not allow the focus to change.
**2**—reject the data, but allows the focus to change.

## ItemError Event

The ItemError event is triggered when the data conversion fails or if the validation fails. The default behavior is to display a message box with an error message and to hold focus on the same field. You can write a script to this event also. The return values for this event are

**0**—rejects the data and displays the error messagebox. This is the default.
**1**—reject the data, but do not display any message.
**2**—accept the data.
**3**—reject the data, but allows the focus to change.

# DATAWINDOW ITEMS

Each field in a DataWindow buffer is called an *item*. Each item can be referenced by field name, or the relative field number. There are several form of the syntax; each is discussed in the next sections.

## Item Reference by Column Number

The syntax for item references is:

`dw_control.Object.Data.{.buffer}{.datasource} [row_number, column_number]`

The components of this item reference syntax is as follows:

**`dw_control`**—the name of the DataWindow control; such as, `dw_1`.

**`Object.Data`**—this part is a required literal text, meaning make a reference to the data value of an object in the DataWindow.

**`buffer`**—an optional field which specifies the DataWindow to which the reference applies. Choices are Primary, Delete, or Filter. The default is Primary.

**datasource**—an optional field which specifies the source of the DataWindow data. Choices are Current or Original. The default is Current.

**row_number**—a required field. This the row number for a DataWindow.

**column_number**—a required field. This the column number in the DataWindow.

A few examples of item references:

**i_count = dw_1.Object.Data[1,2]**—references the data item at Row 1 Column 2 (Primary buffer, Current data source)

**dw_1.Object.Data[1,2] = 123**—references the data item at Row 1 Column 2

**s_name = dw_1.Object.Data.Delete[1,2]**—references the data item at Row 1 Column 2 in the Delete buffer.

**dw_1.Object.Data.Delete[1,2]**—references the data item at Row 1 Column 2 in the Delete buffer.

**l_emp_no = dw_1.Object.Data.Original[1,2]**—references the data item at Row 1 Column 2 in the Original data source (Primary buffer).

## Accessing All Rows

The syntax for references to item in the selected rows by column name is the same but omits the row_number.

dw_control.Object.Data.{.buffer}{.datasource} [column_number]

By omitting the row_number, the data in all rows will be referenced. For example:

**s_array = dw_1.Object.[2]**—references the field in all row(s) 2nd column.

**dw_1.Object.[2] = s_assignment**—references the field in the selected row(s).

### *Accessing Selected Rows*

The syntax for references to item in the selected rows by column name is the same but includes the Selected keyword:

```
dw_control.Object.Data.{.buffer}{.datasource}
[column_number].Selected
```

For example:

- `s_array = dw_1.Object.Selected[2]`—references the 2nd field in the selected row(s).
- `dw_1.Object.Selected[2] = s_assignment`—references the 2nd field in the selected row(s).

## Item Reference by Column Name

The syntax for item references by column name is

```
dw_control.Object.column_name{.buffer}{.datasource}{[row_number]}
```

The components of this item reference syntax are as follows:

- **dw_control**—the name of the DataWindow control; such as, `dw_1`
- **Object**—this part is a required literal text, meaning make a reference to the data value of an object in the DataWindow
- **column_name**—this part is required, the DataWindow column name.
- **buffer**—an optional field which specifies the DataWindow to which the reference applies. Choices are Primary, Delete, or Filter. The default is Primary.
- **datasource**—an optional field which specifies the source of the DataWindow data. Choices are Current, or Original. The default is Current.
- **row_number**—a required field. This is the row number for a DataWindow
- **column_number**—a required field. This is the column number in the DataWindow

A few examples of item references:

**dw_1.Object.company_name[3]**—references the field in Row 3

**dw_1.Object.version.Delete[2]**—references the version field in Row 2 in the Delete buffer.

**dw_1.Object.version.Original[12]**—references the data item at Row 12 in the Original data source (Primary buffer).

## Accessing All Rows

The syntax for references to item in all rows by column name is the same but omits the row_number.

dw_control.Object.column_name{.buffer}{.datasource}

By omitting the row_number, the data in all rows will be referenced. But you must include one of the other optional parameter for this to work correctly. For example:

**s_array = dw_1.Object.company_name**—this will fail

**s_array = dw_1.Object.company_name.Primary**—references the field in the selected row(s).

**dw_1.Object.sales_rep = s_assignment**—references the field in the selected row(s).

## Accessing Selected Rows

The syntax for references to item in the selected rows by column name is the same but includes the Selected keyword:

dw_control.Object.column_name{.buffer}{.datasource}.Selected

For example,

**s_array = dw_1.Object.company_name.Selected**—references the field in the selected row(s).

**dw_1.Object.sales_rep.Selected = s_assignment**—references the field in the selected row(s).

The **IMAGEDB.PBL** example program shows an example of copying the values in a specific column (all rows) into a string array.

## Ranges of Item References by Column Number

The syntax for referencing a set of items by column number is

```
dw_control.Object.column_name{.buffer}{.datasource}{[starting_row_
number, ending_row_number]}
```

The components of this item reference syntax is as follows:

- **dw_control**—the name of the DataWindow control; such as, `dw_1`.
- **Object.Data**—this part is a required literal text, meaning make a reference to the data value of an object in the DataWindow.
- **buffer**—an optional field which specifies the DataWindow to which the reference applies. Choices are Primary, Delete, or Filter. The default is Primary.
- **datasource**—an optional field which specifies the source of the DataWindow data. Choices are Current, or Original. The default is Current.
- **starting_row_number**—a required field. This the first row number for a DataWindow.
- **ending_row_number**—a required field. This the last row number in the DataWindow.

A few examples of range item references:

**s_arry = dw_1.Object.comany_name[1,22]**—references the data item from Row 1 through Row 22.

**dw_1.Object.sales_rep[1,22] = s_assignment**—assigns the data item from Row 1 through Row 22.

### Item Access Functions

You can also reference items with the GetItem and SetItem functions. For example:

```
dw_1.GetItemDate(row, "start_date");
GetItemDatetime(row, 2);
GetItemDecimal(row, "cost", Delete!, True);
GetItemNumber(row, "age", Filter!, False);
SetItem(row, 2, 'ACME');
GetItemTime(GetRow(), 4);
```

The GetItem functions take the row and column (either as a number or a column name) as required arguments. You may also specify the buffer (Primary is the default), and you may add an argument to obtain the original value that was retrieved from the database. Do not use GetItem or SetItem functions. Use the field addressing techniques described in the previous sections.

## STATUS CODES

As mentioned, each row has a buffer:

- Primary!
- Delete!
- Filter!

Each item (in each buffer) also has a status code. The values are enumerated as:

| Status Code | Value Means |
| --- | --- |
| NotModified! | Unchanged |
| DataModified! | Updated by the user |
| New! | Newly inserted item |
| NewModified! | A new item that has been modified |

Rows also have a status: The enumerated values are:

| Status Code | Value Means |
|---|---|
| New! | Added |
| NewModified! | A newly added row has also been modified |
| DataModified! | Contains a modified field |
| notModified! | Unchanged since retrieval |

You can determine the status of an item using the GetItemStatus (dwGetItemStatus in PowerBuilder 3) function.

When rows are initially retrieved into a DataWindow, all rows and columns are initially marked with a status of NotModified! When you update an item's value, the column and row status will change to DataModified!

When you insert a new row into a DataWindow, the row's status will be initialized to New! Its columns will be initialized to NotModified! if there is no default value or to DataModified! if there is a default value. If a column status is set to DataModified!, then the row's status will follow.

A new row's status will change to NewModified! when you update any item in that row; the column will be DataModified!.

Use the GetItemStatus function to read a column or row status. For example,

```
dwItemStatus    ItemStatus, RowStatus

ItemStatus = dw_1.GetItemStatus(dw_1.GetRow(), "name", PRIMARY!)
RowStatus = dw_1.GetItemStatus(dw_1.GetRow(), 0, PRIMARY!)
```

You can use the SetItemStatus function to change the status for a DataWindow's row or column. If you change a row's status to NotModified! or New!, the status of all the columns will change to NotModified! You can use the SetItemStatus after you copy a row from one DataWindow to another.

# DataWindow Programming

This section covers the major functions and techniques that you use with DataWindow controls. This includes retrieving data, inserting and deleting rows, and applying updates to the database. Additional functions will provide print, query, import, and export functionality. For this discussion, we assume that the code is being placed in a CommandButton, but you can use the code in menu item scripts, object events, or script functions.

## Retrieve()

In the script for the Clicked event for a CommandButton (`cb_retrieve`), you could place the following code to retrieve data into the DataWindow using the SQL SELECT statement that is associated with the DataWindow object. You may also place this code in a window's Open event if you want the DataWindow to be populated as soon as the window opens:

```
long l_rows // rows Retrieved
l_rows = dw_1.Retrieve ( )
// l_rows will be >= 0 if successful
```

In this script, the Retrieve function populates the DataWindow and returns the count (a long value) of rows retrieved if successful or a −1 in the case of an error. The Retrieve function also does a Reset on the DataWindow by default. A reset clears all the rows (if any) from the DataWindow. You can suppress this Reset if you wish, to have the retrieval append the rows to the end of the current set.

If you had declared arguments for the DataWindow's SELECT statement (in the select or SQL painter), then you may include arguments for the Retrieve function:

```
long l_rows
l_rows = dw_1.Retrieve ('OH', 1 )
// l_rows will be >= 0 if successful
```

or

```
long l_rows
string s_state
char c_active_account
```

```
s_state = 'OH'
c_active_account = 'y'

l_rows = dw_1.Retrieve (s_state, c_active_account )
// l_rows will be > 0 if successful
```

If you use a CommandButton to perform the Retrieve, the focus will be set on the button after the retrieval is executed. In that case, you may wish to add the following line of code to set the focus to the DataWindow control:

```
dw_1.SetFocus ( )
```

## InsertRow()

In the script for the Clicked event for a CommandButton (cb_insert), you could place the following code to insert a new row in the DataWindow:

```
long l_row
l_row = dw_1.InsertRow (0)
// insert a new row after the last row
IF l_row > 0 THEN
    dw_1.Object.version[ l_row] = 1// initialization
    dw_1.ScrollToRow ( l_row )
        // also does a dw_1.SetRow ( l_row)
    dw_1.SetColumn ('version') // set focus
END IF
dw_1.SetFocus ( )
```

In this script, the InsertRow function adds a new row to the DataWindow (but not to the database). The argument for the InsertRow function specifies the number of the row where you wish to add the new row. For example, a 5 will insert a row at the fifth position, the row that is currently fifth will become sixth and so on. A 0 (zero) tells the function to add the row at the bottom of the DataWindow. The InsertRow function returns the number of the new row or a −1 if an error occurred. In this code example, if the return value was greater than zero, we initialize the value of the version column to 1 using the dot notation addressing of the data value. This could have been done in the Database painter by setting an initial value for the column.

The next line of code scrolls the window to the new row and does an implicit SetRow. This scrolling is necessary since the row may have been added out of the range of rows currently displayed in the DataWindow. In the next line, we set the current column to be the version column so that the user may edit the assigned value if necessary.

Clicking the `cb_insert` CommandButton sets the focus onto the CommandButton, so the `dw_1.SetFocus()` line sets the focus back on the DataWindow control. This is not necessary for any of this code to work correctly; it is added so the user can begin typing a new entry in the DataWindow without having to tab to (or click on) the DataWindow.

## DeleteRow()

In the script for the Clicked event for a CommandButton (`cb_delete`), you could place the following code to delete the current row from the DataWindow:

```
rc = dw_1.DeleteRow (0 )
```

The argument for DeleteRow is the row number (a long) that you want to delete. The 0 (zero) means that the current row should be deleted. This function returns an integer 1 if it is successful.

## Update()

In the script for the Clicked event for a CommandButton (`cb_update`), you could use the following code to apply the changes against the database:

```
rc = dw_1.Update()
// if rc <> 1 then the DBError event will be triggered
IF rc = 1 THEN
    Commit;
ELSE
    Rollback;
END IF
IF sqlca.sqlcode <> 0 THEN
```

```
    MessageBox ("Transaction Failure", sqlca.sqlerrtext)
    w_main.st_status.text = "Trans Failed"
    return   // or halt close
END IF
```

If the return code is 1 (successful), then we commit the changes to the database, otherwise we cancel the transaction. The COMMIT (or ROLLBACK) is an embedded SQL statement that requires checking the SQLCode value.

## COMMIT

The COMMIT statement is an embedded SQL statement, not a DataWindow function. This means that this statement requires a semicolon, and you check the success of the COMMIT by checking the SQLCode value. The COMMIT statement makes all changes applied to the database by the Update function in the current transaction permanent. It also ends the current transaction and begins a new one.

## ROLLBACK

The ROLLBACK statement is an embedded SQL statement, not a DataWindow function. This statement requires a semicolon, and you check the success of the ROLLBACK by checking the SQLCode value. The ROLLBACK statement cancels all changes applied to the database by the Update function in the current transaction permanent. It also ends the transaction and begins a new one.

### Sharing Data between DataWindows

You can share data between DataWindow (and DataStores covered later) that have the same number and type of columns. The owner (primary) DataWindow calls the function ShareData with the secondary DataWindow as an argument. ShareData returns an integer value of 1 if it is successful.

```
dw_2.DataObject = 'd_company'
i_rc = dw_1.ShareData(dw_2)
```

The first line of this example assigns the d_company DataWindow object to the dw_2 DataWindow control. In the second line, the ShareData function activates the sharing of a DataWindow buffer between two DataWindows. Notice that no SetTransObject was required for the dw_2. In this example, dw_1 is the primary owner of the data. If you make changes to the data in the secondary DataWindow (dw_2), the changes are applied through the primary DataWindow.

To end sharing, call the ShareDataOff function with the secondary DataWindow as an argument. In the next example, dw_2 and dw_3 are sharing data with dw_1. Then after dw_2 has completed its use of the data, the ShareDataOff function terminates the data sharing.

```
i_rc = dw_1.ShareData(dw_2)
i_rc = dw_1.ShareData(dw_3)
f_do_something(dw_2)
i_rc = dw_1.ShareDataOff(dw_2)
```

See the **ORDERS.PBL** example for an example of data sharing between a DataStore and a DataWindow.

## SaveAs

The SaveAs function will allow the user to export the contents of the DataWindow. The user will be presented with a list of export file types:

- **Clipboard!**—Windows' clipboard
- **CSV!**—comma-separated text
- **dBASE2!** and **dBASE3!**—dBASE-II && III format
- **DIF!**—Data Interchange Format
- **Excel!**—Microsoft Excel format
- **HTMLTable!**—Text with HTML formatting
- **PSReport!**—Powersoft Report format
- **SQLInsert!**—SQL syntax
- **SYLK!**—Microsoft Multiplan format
- **Text!**—tab-separated columns with a return at the end of each row

- **WKS!** and **WK1!**—Lotus 1-2-3 formats
- **WMF!**—Windows Metafile format

The code is just a single line of text.

```
dw_1.SaveAs ( )
```

## Print

You can print the contents of the DataWindow in several manners. The simplest solution is to add the single line:

```
dw_1.Print()
```

This will print the entire contents of DataWindow `dw_1`. You can also open a print job. That involves a few more lines of code as follows:

```
int i_job
i_job = PrintOpen("Report")
PrintDataWindow(i_job, dw_1)
PrintClose(i_job)
```

The format of the printout is determined in the DataWindow painter. In the painter you would select the **Design|Print Specifications** menu option. This opens the Print Specifications dialog box, where you can specify margins, paper orientation, and so on. If you click the **Prompt** before printing checkbox, the user will be prompted for this information when the print is triggered.

In the DataWindow painter, you can set the print units of measure to inches or centimeters. Set this parameter under the Design|DataWindow Style menu option.

## Dynamically Assigning DataWindow Objects

You can also change the associated DataWindow object for the DataWindow control at run time. To do this, assign the name of the DataWindow object to the DataWindow control attribute named DataObject:

```
dw_1.DataObject = 'd_company'
i_rc = dw_1.SetTransObject(SQLCA)
```

The first line of this example assigns the d_company DataWindow object to the `dw_1` DataWindow control. The second line reassigns the transaction object for the control as described below (the reassignment of the transaction object must be done after changing the DataWindow object). Using this technique, you could offer the user a selection of reports (DataWindow objects) to choose from in one of your windows. Then you would dynamically assign the DataWindow object to the DataWindow control on that window, instead of creating separate windows for each report. The DataWindow objects must be stored in libraries on the application search path so that PowerBuilder can find them at run time; see the chapter, "Distributing Your Applications," for more details.

## Filter Functions

You can apply filter expressions to the DataWindow control to reduce the number of rows to those that match you filter criteria. This is somewhat similar to a SELECT clause on a SQL SELECT statement with several important differences. First, the filter is applied to the rows in the DataWindow *after* the retrieval has occurred. Second, the filter uses PowerScript DataWindow functions, not SQL. So the syntax is not that of the SQL language, but that of PowerScript code. The filtering process requires two DataWindow functions.

```
i_rc = dw_1.SetFilter(s_expression)
i_rc = dw_1.Filter()
```

The first line of this example sets the filter expression to the string, s_expression. The next line actually applies the filter expression. You can set the filter expression to an empty string (with SetFilter) and then issue the Filter function to remove all filtering.

The filter expression is a string. In our **PHONE.PBL** example, we wish to search four phone number fields in each row for the criteria. The actual expression will be something like this:

```
"left(phone,3) = '398' OR left(carphone,3) = '398' OR left(fax,3) = '398' OR left(pager,3) = '398' "
```

That expression is built as follows (s_number has the partial search number as a string):

```
s_size = string(len(s_number))
s_expression = 'left(phone,' + s_size + ") = '" + s_number + " ' "
s_expression = s_expression + 'OR left(carphone,' + s_size + ") & ='" + s_number + " ' "
s_expression = s_expression + 'OR left(fax,' + s_size + ") & = '" + s_number + " ' "
s_expression = s_expression + 'OR left(pager,' + s_size + ") & = '" + s_number + " ' "
// then the following
i_rc = dw_1.SetFilter(s_expression)
IF i_rc <> 1 THEN
    MessageBox('Filer Error', s_expression)
ELSE
    dw_1.Filter( )
    dw_1.Sort()
    dw_1.SetFocus()
END IF
```

See the **PHONE.PBL** application for examples.

## Sort Functions

You can apply sort expressions to the DataWindow control to the rows by the values in one or more rows. This is somewhat similar to a ORDER BY clause on a SQL SELECT statement with several important differences. First, the sort is applied to the rows in the DataWindow *after* the retrieval has occurred. Second, the sort uses PowerScript DataWindow functions, not SQL. So the syntax is not that of the SQL language, but that of PowerScript code. The sorting process requires the use of two DataWindow functions.

```
i_rc = dw_1.SetSort(s_expression)
i_rc = dw_1.Sort()
```

The first line of this example sets the sort expression to the string, s_expression. The next line actually applies the sort expression. The sort expression is fairly simple, just the column name and a letter to set "A"scending or "D"escending ordering.

The sort expression is a string, such as

```
"company A, phone D"
```

In our **PHONE.PBL** example, we wish to sort on any single field. In that example, we just sort on the current column in the DataWindow. That expression is built as follows (s_number has the partial search number as a string):

```
string s_column
int i_rc

s_column = dw_1.GetColumnName()
IF IsNull(s_column) THEN
     s_column = 'phone'
END IF
i_rc = dw_1.SetSort(s_column)
IF i_rc <> 1 THEN
```

```
        MessageBox('Error', 'SetSort Error')
ELSE
        dw_1.Sort( )
        dw_1.SetColumn(s_column)
        dw_1.ScrollToRow(1)
        dw_1.SetFocus()
END IF
```

In the `rbuttondown` event, I used the same code, but changed one line to sort in "D"escending order.

```
i_rc = dw_1.SetSort(s_column + ' D')
```

See the **PHONE.PBL** application for examples.

## The Find Function

You can apply search expressions to the DataWindow control to locate the first row that matches your find criteria. Then you can continue the search, or in the case of a sorted column, you may just scroll to that position in the DataWindow. The filtering process requires the use of the Find DataWindow function.

```
i_rc = dw_1.Find(s_expression)
```

Just call the Find function with the search expression (the string, s_expression). In our **PHONE.PBL** example, we allow a search on any field, and then scroll to the first matching row (after sorting on the same column). The actual expression for the Find will be something like this:

```
"Left(Company,1) >= 'M' "
```

That expression is built as follows (s_value has the search string):

```
long l_row

s_column = dw_1.GetColumnName()
IF NOT IsNull(s_column) THEN
    SetPointer(HourGlass!)
    Parent.SetRedraw(False)
    cb_sort.TriggerEvent(Clicked!)
    OpenWithParm(w_search, "Enter Search Criteria and hit [Enter]")
    s_value = message.stringparm
    IF s_value = 'cancel' THEN return
    s_len = string(len(s_value))
    s_expression = ' "' + s_column + ' like ' + s_value + ' " '
    l_row = dw_1.Find( "left("+s_column+"," +s_len +") &
>='"+s_value+"'", 1, dw_1.RowCount())

    IF l_row <= 0 THEN
        beep(1)
    ELSE
        dw_1.setfocus ( )
        dw_1.scrolltorow ( l_row )
    END IF
    Parent.SetRedraw(True)
END IF
```

See the **PHONE.PBL** application for examples.

# DataWindow Events

In this section, we will discuss the events that are important for DataWindows.

## Retrieving Data into a DataWindow

First you must populate a transaction object (SQLCA in this example) and connect to the database. Then assign the transaction object to the DataWindow and retrieve rows into the DataWindow (this example leaves out the error checking):

```
connect using SQLCA;
dw_1.SetTransObject(SQLCA)
dw_1.Retrieve()
```

The events that are triggered thus far would be as follows:

- **Constructor**—before the window open event, all window object constructor are triggered.
- **GetFocus**—only triggered if the DataWindow has the lowest tab order value.
- **RetrieveStart**—the SQL SELECT statement is about to be executed as a result of `dw_1.Retrieve()`.
- **SQLPreview**—this event makes the SQL statement(s) that are about to be issued to the DBMS available. You can examine these, or modify them programmatically if you wish.
- **RetrieveRow**—this event fires once for each row that is retrieved
- **RowFocusChanged**—triggered when a new row gets the focus
- **ItemFocusChanged**—triggered when a new item (field) gets the focus
- **RetrieveEnd**—signals the completion of the SELECT statement

The return values for the RetrieveStart event are as follows:

0—continue. This is the default.

1—cancel the retrieval.

2—do not perform the Reset before the retrieval. Appends the rows to the end of the current set.

The return values for the SQLPreview event are as follows:

0—continue. This is the default.

1—cancel the operation.

2—skip this operation, but continue on to the next one.

The return values for the RetrieveRow event are:

0—continue. This is the default

1—cancel the retrieval.

## Updating the Database

For this discussion, assume that a number of rows have been inserted, modified, and deleted. At some point, the user finally clicks your **Apply Update CommandButton** (for example). In response to this, you issue the following statements:

```
i_rc = dw_1.Update()
IF i_rc = 1 THEN
   commit;
ELSE
   rollback;
END IF
```

The Update applies the changes to the database, and the COMMIT makes the changes permanent.

**NOTE** The Update function performs an AcceptText by default.

The events that are triggered typically as a result of the Update could be:

- **ItemChanged**—may be triggered as a result of the implicit AcceptText.

- **UpdateStart**—triggered when after the Update function call, but before the update actually begins.
- **SQLPreview**—triggered for each SQL statement that is generate to complete the Update. This could contain statements DELETE, INSERT, and UPDATE.
- **UpdateEnd**—triggered on completion of the update.

The return values for the UpdateStart event are as follows:

0—continue. This is the default.

1—cancel the update.

## Printing a DataWindow

In this section, we will present the events that occur when printing a DataWindow. The events that are typically triggered could be the following:

**PrintStart**—triggered after the Print function was issued.

**PrintPage**—triggered just before each page is printed. The event has an argument, pagenumber, that contains the number of the page about to be printed. You can skip printing of a page by returning 1.

**PrintEnd**—triggered when the print has finished.

The return values for this event are as follows:

0—continue, print this page.

1—skip this page.

## THE OBJECT BROWSER

You can use the Object Browser to display DataWindow controls and DataWindow objects. For a DataWindow control, click the **Window** tab and double-click on the window name that contains the DataWindow control. This will list all the objects in the window. Click the DataWindow control (such as `dw_1`), and then select the DataWindow elements in the right listbox. This includes Properties, Events, Functions, External Functions, Instance Variables, Shared Variables, and Structures.

Click on the DataWindow tab to access the DataWindow object. You can list the properties and functions in the right listbox. Another option is to double-click on the DataWindow object in the left listbox. This expands the DataWindow, listing the components in that DataWindow object. This is very useful for looking up DataWindow object column names. You can also then click on the component (in the left listbox) and list the element attributes in the lower window (Properties and Functions).

## DataWindow Control Attributes

Some of the more important DataWindow control attributes are:

- **DataObject**—changes the DataWindow object that is associated with this control.
- **Enabled**—a Boolean value, set to **True** to enable the control, making it active and able to be selected or clicked and to receive events.
- **HScrollBar**—a Boolean value, **True** if a horizontal scroll bar will be added to this control as needed.
- **LiveScroll**—set this to **True** to allow the user to move through the rows in the DataWindow using the scroll bar.
- **Object**—the DataWindow's object. This allows access to the object attributes.
- **VScrollBar**—a Boolean value; if True, a vertical scroll bar will be added to this control as needed.

## DataWindow Control Events

Some of the more important DataWindow control events are:

- **Clicked**—occurs when the user clicks within the DataWindow.
- **DBError**—triggered when a database error occurs as a result of a DataWindow operation.
- **EditChanged**—occurs when the entry in the DataWindow edit control is changed.
- **ItemChanged**—occurs when the text in the edit control has been changed and the user presses the **Enter**, **Tab**, or **Down Arrow** key or clicks elsewhere on the window.

- **ItemError**—triggered after an ItemChanged event if the validation fails for that field.
- **ItemFocusChanged**—triggered when the user changes the focus to another item in the DataWindow.
- **PrintEnd**—triggered when a DataWindow print ends.
- **PrintPage**—triggered just before each page (of a DataWindow) is printed. You can use this event to skip the printing of each page.
- **PrintStart**—triggered when a DataWindow print begins.
- **RetrieveEnd**—triggered when a DataWindow completes a retrieve operation.
- **RetrieveStart**—triggered when a DataWindow begins a retrieve operation.
- **RowFocusChanged**—triggered each time a different row is selected in the DataWindow.
- **UpdateEnd**—triggered after the updates have been completed against the database.
- **UpdateStart**—triggered when an update is about to be issued against the database.

# DataWindow Control Functions

Some of the more important DataWindow control functions are:

- **AcceptText**—moves the edit control text into the current item buffer cell.
- **DBCancel**—cancels the current database retrieval.
- **DBErrorCode**—returns the DBMS specific error code for the last database operation.
- **DBErrorMessage**—returns the DBMS specific error text for the last database operation.
- **DBHandle**—returns the database connection handle.
- **DeletedCount**—returns the number (count) of rows that have been deleted from the primary DataWindow buffer (that have not yet been deleted from the database).
- **DeleteRow**—removes a row from the DataWindow.
- **Filter**—applies the current filter to the DataWindow.

- **FilteredCount**—returns the number (count) of rows that are in the filtered DataWindow buffer (that have been removed from the primary buffer as a result of the current filter).
- **GetClickedColumn**—returns an integer, the number of the column that was clicked.
- **GetClickedRow**—returns a long, the number of the row that was clicked.
- **GetColumn**—returns the number of the current column.
- **GetColumnName**—returns the name (a string) of the current column.
- **GetRow**—returns the number (a long) of the current row in the DataWindow.
- **GetSelectedRow**—returns the number (a long) of the first selected row in the DataWindow.
- **GetText**—returns a string, the text in the edit control.
- **ImportString**—copies data (in a string) into a DataWindow.
- **InsertRow**—adds a new row to the DataWindow at a specified location, may initialize some of the column values.
- **LineCount**—returns the number (the count) of lines that are in the current field.
- **ModifiedCount**—returns the number (count) of rows that have been changed in the primary DataWindow buffer (that have not yet been updated in the database).
- **Print**—prints a copy of the DataWindow.
- **Reset**—clears the DataWindow.
- **Retrieve**—issues the SQL SELECT statement for this DataWindow.
- **RowCount**—returns the current number of rows in this DataWindow's primary buffer.
- **SaveAs**—writes the rows in this DataWindow out to another format, such as dBASE or Lotus.
- **ScrollToRow**—scrolls (moves) to a specific row number in the DataWindow.
- **SetColumn**—sets the current column.
- **SetFilter**—defines the PowerScript expression used for the Filter function associated with this DataWindow.
- **SetRow**—sets the current row to be the specified row.

- **SetSort**—specifies the criteria to be used for the Sort() function to order the rows in this DataWindow.
- **SetText**—assigns a string to the edit control.
- **SetTransObject**—assigns a transaction object to the DataWindow; you must control the transactions. Use this instead of SetTrans.
- **Sort**—orders the rows in the DataWindow according to the sort criteria defined for the DataWindow (may be set by SetSort).
- **Update**—applies all the changes made to the DataWindow to the database.

# DATASTORES

DataWindows are very powerful objects, as you have seen. There are, however, times that you would like to have the functionality of a DataWindow, but do not need or want the DataWindow control to display the DataWindow object. PowerBuilder has an nonvisual version of the DataWindow, which is called a DataStore, for this purpose. The DataStore is a nonvisual version of a DataWindow control. It has essentially the same attributes, events, and functions as a DataWindow.

# REPORTS

In the preceding discussion, we have used DataWindows as an interactive object. DataWindows are able to display data to, as well as accept data from, the user. DataWindows also serve as the source for reports in PowerBuilder. The only difference is that reports are read-only. The columns in a report all have a tab order of 0 (zero). There are two report icons on the PowerPanel.

- **Report**—launches the Report painter; use this to create and edit reports.
- **RunReport**—use this view to export and print reports.

In the Report painter, you work in essentially the same manner as when you created DataWindows. You can Preview the report the verify it before printing.

The RunReport option presents the report as it will be printed. You cannot edit the report in this mode. You can print the report, adjust print parameters, zoom the display, and apply sorting or filtering. You can also export the report (use the **File|Save Rows As** menu option) to a number of formats including the following:

- **CSV!**—comma-separated text, with or without headers.
- **dBASE2!** and **dBASE3!**—dBASE-II && III format.
- **DIF!**—Data Interchange Format.
- **Excel!**—Microsoft Excel format, with or without headers.
- **HTMLTable!**—Text with HTML formatting.
- **PSReport!**—Powersoft Report format.
- **SQLInsert!**—SQL syntax.
- **SYLK!**—Microsoft Multiplan format, with or without headers.
- **Text!**—tab-separated columns with a return at the end of each row, with or without headers.
- **WKS!** and **WK1!**—Lotus 1-2-3 formats, with or without headers.
- **WMF!**—Windows Metafile format.

## THE DATAWINDOW EXAMPLE PROGRAMS

The example programs include several applications for this chapter:

- **ImageDb**—creates a version of SQLApp (the embedded SQL example from Chapter 7) using a DataWindow. This application demonstrates the basic database functionality of INSERT, UPDATE and DELETE. Image information is stored in the IMAGES table. We also add a window to display the images.
- **Orders**—creates a DataWindow with a two-table join between COMPANY and CUST_ORDER tables. The second version of this application will add a second DataWindow (using the LINE_ITEM table) and create a master-detail relationship with the first. The third version of this example adds another window to demonstrate DataStores and data sharing (between a DataWindow and a DataStore).

- **ChildDw**—creates a DataWindow that demonstrates all the possible edit styles for DataWindow columns. This includes Check Box, DropDownDataWindow (Child DataWindow), DropDownListBox, EditMask, and Radio Button styles.
- **Phone**—an example of a DataWindow that stores data internally (select the **Rows|Data** menu option in the DataWindow painter). This window can be used to locate the source of an incoming phone call (if you have Caller Id). Hit [**Enter**] or click on the **Filter** button. Then simply enter the first few digits of the phone number and the DataWindow will search across all phone number fields. You can also sort, search (scroll), and change the Current Row indicator in this example.
- **BlobDb**—an embedded SQL example that stores blobs (images in this case) in the database.
- **DwStyles**—demonstrates each of the DataWindow presentation styles. This is for display only; you do not build a copy of this example.

Mastering DataWindows is half the process of obtaining PowerBuilder expertise. You should take as much time as possible to study DataWindows. Build the example programs, ImageDb, Orders, ChildDw, and BlobDb. These examples cover all the essentials of DataWindows.

## Example Requirements

All of these examples require several variables and objects. You must create the following global variables:

```
Boolean gb_db_connected = False
string gs_init_file = 'imagedb.ini'
```

The first variable will be True when the application connects successfully to the database. This will let you know when you need to issue a DISCONNECT when closing the application. The gs_init_file is a string that contains the name (and optionally the full path) of the profile file to be used with each of the examples. The **IMAGEDB.INI** file contains information that is needed to establish the connection with the MCCLAN2.DB database. This is the Sybase SQL Anywhere database required by these examples.

The application open event will always contain a single line of text:

```
open(w_main)
```

You should always include the `db_init.pbl` in Libraries Search Path for your version of the examples. To do this, open the Application painter (all other painters must be closed) and open the Properties Tab dialog box. Do this by clicking the **Properties** icon on the PainterBar or select the **Entry|Properties** menu option. In the Properties dialog box, select the **Libraries** tab (Figure 11.9).

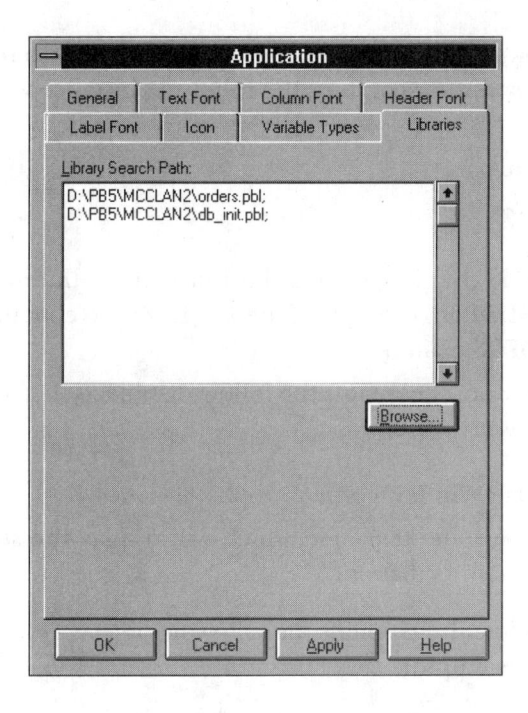

*Figure 11.9 Properties dialog box.*

In the Library Search Path listbox, add the **DB_INIT.PBL** library (last in the list). You can do this by typing the entry, or by clicking the **Browse** button and selecting the **DB_INIT.PBL** from the Select Library dialog box. This will give you access to the functions that read the initialization file and setup the database connection. In this way, you do not have to create the functions, nor do you need to copy them into your application's PBL. This is also instructive, concerning the use of shared PowerBuilder libraries.

## DB_INIT.PBL

The **DB_INIT.PBL** has objects and functions that will help to build these applications. This section will cover the objects in this **DB_INIT.PBL**.

### w_main

This Main window can be copied to a new PBL when you re-create the example applications. This window contains the following instance variables:

```
string is_filepath
string is_invoice
```

The `is_filepath` variable contains the full path to the image used in the IMAGEDB and BLOBDB examples. The `is_invoice` contains a string that is used in the ORDERS example.

The `w_main` window contains the following objects that are used in all the example applications:

**dw_1**—the DataWindow control.

**st_status**—a static text field which will display the status, such as db connection information.

The `w_main` window also contains the following objects (you may delete these for the ORDERS example):

**p_1**—a picture control. Contains the code necessary to open the FileOpen dialog box, and store the results in the set of static text controls.

**st_current_dir**—a static text control that stores the directory from the FileOpen dialog box.

**st_imagename**—a static text control that stores only the filename selected from the FileOpen dialog box.

**st_ext**—a static text control that stores only the file extension from the selection in the FileOpen dialog box.

## wf_db_init

The w_main window contains a window level function, wf_db_init. This function reads the initialization (profile) file, loads the SQLCA object, connects to the database, and then populates the dw_1 DataWindow control. The code for that function is as follows:

```
//fw_db_init (); returns <NONE>
int i_rc
long l_rows
string s_db_section

SetPointer (HourGlass!)

i_rc = f_get_db_section(s_db_section)
IF i_rc <> 1 THEN
    fw_status_message("No dbms specified in Profile [application]")
ELSE
    i_rc = f_load_sqlca ( gs_init_file, s_db_section, sqlca )
    IF i_rc = 1 THEN
        connect;
    ELSE
        sqlca.sqlcode = 1 //connect failed
    END IF

    IF sqlca.sqlcode = 0 THEN
        gb_db_connected = True
        fw_status_message("connected")
        i_rc = This.dw_1.SetTransObject ( sqlca )
        IF i_rc = 1 THEN
            l_rows = This.dw_1.Retrieve ( )
            IF l_rows < 0 THEN fw_status_message("retrieve failed")
        ELSE
```

```
                fw_status_message("SetTransObject failed")
            END IF
        ELSE
            fw_status_message("db connection failed")
        END IF
    END IF
RETURN
```

This function reads the application initialization file (**IMAGEDB.INI**) and locates the KEY for the database information in the profile. It finds this value in the [application] section under the key dbms (this is SQLCA in the IMAGEDB.INI file). It then looks for the transaction object values in that section (SQLCA). It populates a transaction object with these values and then attempts to connect to the database. This function calls wf_status_message to display the result message. If successful, the function continues to populate the dw_1 DataWindow (using the Retrieve function).

## *wf_status_message*

The w_main window contains another window level function, wf_status_message. This function knows how to call SetMicrohelp for MDI windows, and how to use st_status for the w_main main window. All calls to display status text are made to this function. All that you need to place in this function is code to display a status message. The simplest solution would be to use the following in the examples in this chapter:

```
//int wf_status_message(string as_text)
w_main.st_status.text = as_text
return 1
```

For the MDI applications, you would need to change this to:

```
//int wf_status_message(string as_text)
SetMicroHelp(as_text)
return 1
```

The code that I used is a bit more complex and is designed to work for both types of windows (main with a static text field st_status, or MDI with MicroHelp). The code is as follows:

```
//int wf_status_message(string as_text)
integer idx, i_max
string s_name
statictext st_x

IF this.windowtype = mdihelp! THEN
    setmicrohelp (as_text)
ELSE
    i_max = UpperBound(this.control[])
    FOR idx = 1 to i_max
        s_name = ClassName(This.control[idx])
        IF s_name = 'st_status' THEN
            st_x = This.control[idx]
            st_x.text = as_text
            EXIT
          END IF
    NEXT
    IF idx > i_max THEN MessageBox('status', as_text)
END IF
RETURN 1
```

This code first checks to see if the window is a MDI with Microhelp type window. If so, it calls SetMicroHelp to display the as_text string (the only argument to the function). Otherwise, the function searches the window's control array to locate the st_status field. If found, it displays the text in that statictext field and exists. If not found, it uses a messagebox.

## Global Functions

You will find several global functions in the **DB_INIT.PBL** for use in the database examples.

### f_get_db_section

This function reads the application initialization file (**IMAGEDB.INI** in our examples), and locates the KEY for the database information in the profile. It finds this value in the [application] section under the key dbms (this is SQLCA in the **IMAGEDB.INI** file). It returns an integer value 1, if successful.

```
int i_rc
string s_db_section

s_db_section =
ProfileString(gs_init_file,"application","dbms","none")
IF s_db_section = 'none' THEN
    i_rc = f_locate_profile ( gs_init_file, gs_init_file)
    IF i_rc = 1 THEN
        s_db_section =
ProfileString(gs_init_file,"application","dbms","none")
    END IF
END IF

IF s_db_section = 'none' THEN
    MessageBox("Error", "Could not find init file " + gs_init_file)
ELSE
    as_db_section = s_db_section
    i_rc = 1
END IF

RETURN i_rc
```

## f_load_sqlca

It then looks for the transaction object values in that section (SQLCA). This function populates a transaction object (passed as an argument) with the values found in the `as_db_section` of the `as_init_file`. If successful, it returns an integer value 1.

```
//int f_load_sqlca ( string as_init_file, string as_db_section, &
ref transaction atran_object )
int i_rc

IF IsValid(atran_object) THEN
    atran_object.DBMS = ProfileString(as_init_file,as_db_section,"dbms","err")
    IF atran_object.DBMS <> 'err' THEN
        atran_object.database = ProfileString(as_init_file,as_db_section,"database","")
        atran_object.userid = ProfileString(as_init_file,as_db_section,"userid","")
        atran_object.dbpass = ProfileString(as_init_file,as_db_section,"dbpass","")
        atran_object.logid = ProfileString(as_init_file, &
as_db_section,"logid","")
        atran_object.logpass = ProfileString(as_init_file,as_db_section,"logpass","")
        atran_object.servername = ProfileString(as_init_file,as_db_section,"servername","")
        atran_object.dbparm = ProfileString(as_init_file,as_db_section,"dbparm","")
        i_rc = 1
    END IF
END IF
RETURN i_rc
```

## f_locate_profile

This function prompts the user with a standard dialog box in order to locate the application initialization (profile) file (given as argument as_filename). It returns the filepath in as_filepath.

```
//int f_locate_profile ( string as_filename, ref string as_filepath )

integer i_rc
string s_filename, s_filepath

i_rc = GetFileOpenName("Please locate INIT file:" + as_filename, &
            s_filepath, s_filename, "INI", "INI (*.INI), *.INI")
IF i_rc = 1 THEN
    as_filepath = s_filepath
END IF
RETURN i_rc
```

## f_extract_directory

```
//int f_extract_directory ( string as_filepath, ref string &
as_directory )
int i_tmp, i_pos, i_rc

i_tmp = Pos(as_filepath, '\', 1)
DO WHILE i_tmp > 0
    i_pos = i_tmp
    i_tmp = Pos(as_filepath, '\', i_pos + 1)
LOOP
IF i_pos > 0 THEN
    as_directory = Left(as_directory, i_pos - 1)
    i_rc = 1
END IF
RETURN i_rc
```

## f_main_init

This function is not used in the examples. It is just a copy of the `fw_db_init` function for reference.

**CHAPTER 12**

# Multiple Document Interface

This chapter presents an introduction to Multiple Document Interface (MDI) applications. By now you should be familiar with at least one MDI application, PowerBuilder. MDI is a style of application that has become the standard for most larger Windows applications. Microsoft Word and Excel are other familiar examples. The main feature of the MDI style is the use of multiple child windows (called *sheets*) within a parent window (called the *frame*). The components of an MDI application always include a frame window, two or more sheet windows, and one or more menus. MDI applications use menus rather than command buttons. This is a style that you should follow.

## THE MDIAPP EXAMPLE

Run the sample MDI application found in example programs. To do this, run the MDIAPP application in the **MDIAPP.PBL**. Figure 12.1 shows the MDIAPP application's MDI frame window. The status line displays `Connecting to DB...` and then `db connected` if the connection was made successfully. (This application uses the same database functions as the earlier applications. It also uses the **IMAGEDB.INI** profile file and the **MCCLAN2.DB** database).

> **NOTE** If your toolbar icons do not match those in Figure 12.1, then do the following: open the `m_mdi_frame` menu and select each open menu item (on the File menu, click the **Pictures** tab, and enter the correct path to each BMP (see Figure 12.10).

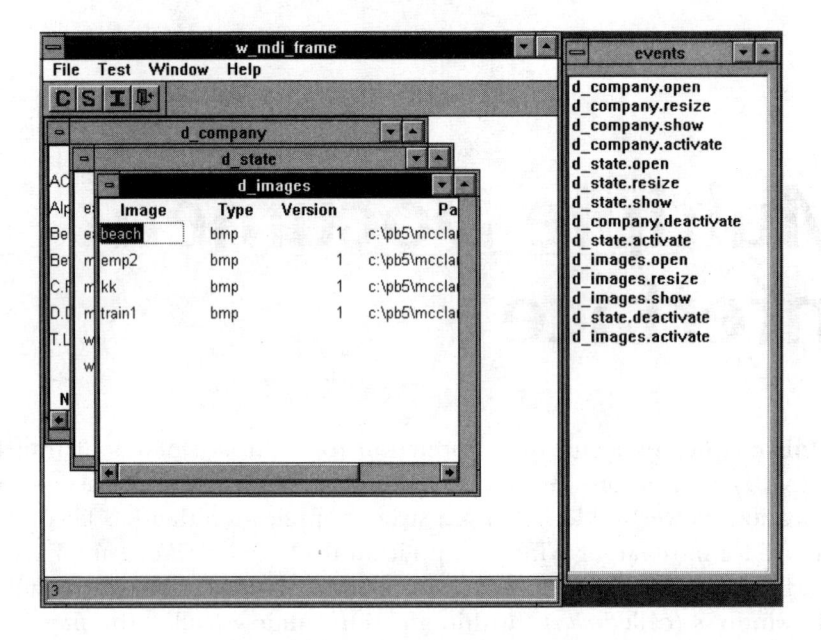

*Figure 12.1  The MDIApp application.*

In this example, the frame window, the menu bar, the toolbar, the client area where the sheets will be opened, and the MicroHelp status line are shown. The example program included on the CD-ROM also opens a second window, Events, which displays the various MDI events that occur. Most of the events that will display are related to the MDI sheets.

Look first at the menu options. Under the File menu, there are options to open three different types of sheets: one for the COMPANY table, one for the STATES table, and one for the IMAGES table. Each option also has an icon on the toolbar. Selecting any one of these will open a sheet and add the name of the sheet to the Window menu. You can also open multiple instances of each type of sheet. Figure 12.2 shows an example where the user has opened two instances of the `d_images` sheet. Notice that the second instance is labeled "[read only]."

After you have opened the first sheet, look at the File menu. Options have been added to insert, delete, or update rows in the table (in the active sheet) to close the *current* sheet or to close all sheets (see Figure 12.3). There is also a Refresh option that will reissue the `Retrieve` statement. Some of these options will be disabled (grayed out) for the read-only sheets.

Pull down the Window menu to find a set of options to arrange the sheets. You will also see a list of the currently open sheets at the bottom (Figure 12.4). If you choose the name of one of the open sheets, it raises the sheet to the top of the stack and makes it the active sheet.

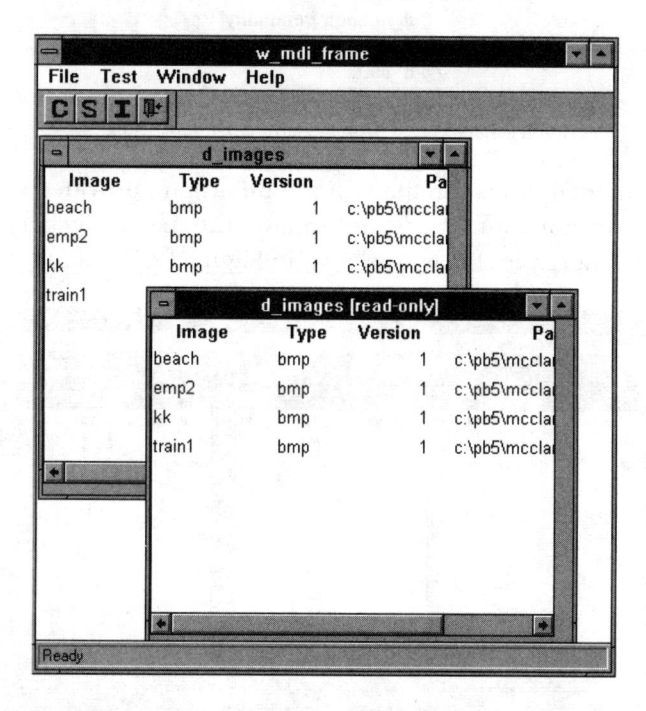

*Figure 12.2 After opening sheets in the MDI application.*

**486** Chapter 12

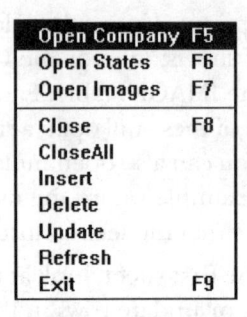

*Figure 12.3  The File menu.*

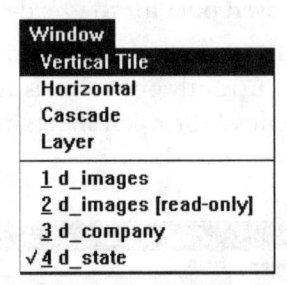

*Figure 12.4  The Window menu listing open sheets.*

The arrangement options (on the Window menu) are provided to let the user tile vertically, tile horizontally, cascade, or layer the sheets. Clicking the **Vertical** tile option arranges the sheets, as shown in Figure 12.5.

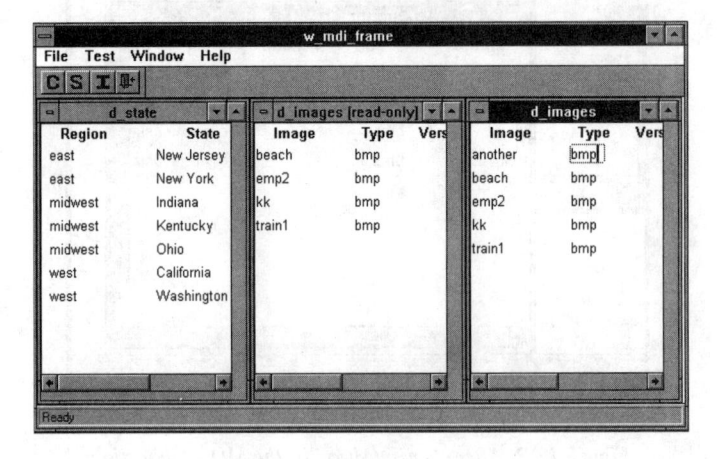

*Figure 12.5  Tiled windows.*

In this example, there are three open sheets. Two are opened for the Images table. Notice that in the d_images, an additional row has been added. This added row does not show up in the other d_images [read-only] sheet. Changes that you make in a DataWindow are not actually applied to the database until you select the **File|Update** menu option. You can then use **File|Refresh** to refresh the data in the read-only sheets if you wish. (You must activate the window before making the menu selection).

Notice the Microhelp text that displays in the frame's status line (at the bottom left of the window) when you select any menu option. Move the pointer over one of the icons on the toolbar. After a second or so, the toolbar item's text will display in a popup.

## The OpenSheet Function

Use the PowerScript function OpenSheet for MDI sheets rather than the Open function that you have used to open non-MDI windows. The advantage of using OpenSheet is that PowerBuilder will then provide the opened sheet with more automatic window management, such as adjustment of size. Otherwise, you would have to handle these details programmatically.

An example of the OpenSheet function is:

```
OpenSheet(w_inv, "Invoice", "w_main", i_list_position, Cascade!)
```

The OpenSheet function has the following arguments:

- Type of window
- Name of the sheet (optional)
- Name of the frame window
- Menu pad number (for listing open windows) default is next-to-last (if you enter 0)
- Opening arrangement (Cascade!, Layered!, Original!)

Sometimes sheets do not have their own menus. Menus (and/or toolbars) are inherited from the previous sheet if a menu is not provided for a newly opened sheet. Therefore, to avoid confusing the user, if any sheet has a menu, all the sheets should have menus. Set the toolbar **Alignment**, **Height**, **Visible**, **Width**, **X**, **Y** in the Window painter.

Another version of this function allows the passing of a parameter to the sheet when it is opened. That function is:

`OpenSheetWithParm(w_sheet[1], open parameter, window type, frame, position, opening arrangement)`

The `OpenSheetWithParm` function has the following arguments:

- The window reference is a window variable that will receive the reference to the open window.
- The parameter is a string, numeric, or powerobject parameter. The opened sheet will receive this parameter in the window open event, as an element of the message object.
- The type of the window is optional.
- Name of the frame window.
- The menu pad number (for listing open windows) is optional. The default is next-to-last (if you enter 0).
- Opening arrangement (`Cascade!`, `Layered!`, `Original!`) is optional. The default is `Cascade!`.

## MDI Events

When you run the MDIAPP, you will have a chance to see the events that occur for the MDI application. When you open a new sheet (the second in this example), the events are:

sheet2.Open

sheet2.Resize

sheet2.Show

sheet2.Activate

When you make another sheet the activate sheet, you will see the following events:

sheet2.Deactivate

sheet1.Activate

If you close sheet1 in this example, you will see the following events:

```
sheet1.CloseQuery
sheet1.Close
sheet1.Deactivate
sheet2.Activate
sheet1.Hide
```

Run the example application (MDIAPP) and observe the events. Minimize the sheets, click on the events window, and try other actions to see the resulting events.

# CREATING AN MDI APPLICATION

Now that you have seen the example, you can create you own MDI application. This section steps you through the construction of the MDIAPP example. Create a new application, MDIAPP, and name the library **ZMDIAPP.BPL**. Immediately add the **DB_INIT.PBL** to the Library list for the application. Do this in the Application painter, open the Properties dialog box, and select the **Libraries** tab.

## Creating the MDI Frame

To create the frame window for this example, create a new window in the Window painter. Open the Window Properties dialog box and select the **MDI Frame with Microhelp** item in the Window Type dropdown listbox. You can create MDI frames with or without MicroHelp. For this example, we will use the option for MicroHelp. Give the window a title, such as MDI Application. Save the window with the name `w_mdi_frame`.

The MDI frame must have a menu. Menus are part of the MDI style. In general, you do not use buttons in MDI applications. There are exceptions of course, but to follow the recommended style, always attempt to place the actions in menu options if possible. Menus will be created in a later step in this chapter. After you create the `m_mdi_frame` menu, add it to the window by again opening the Window Properties dialog box. Click the **Browse** button to open the Select Menu dialog box. Select the menu from the listbox, as shown in Figure 12.6.

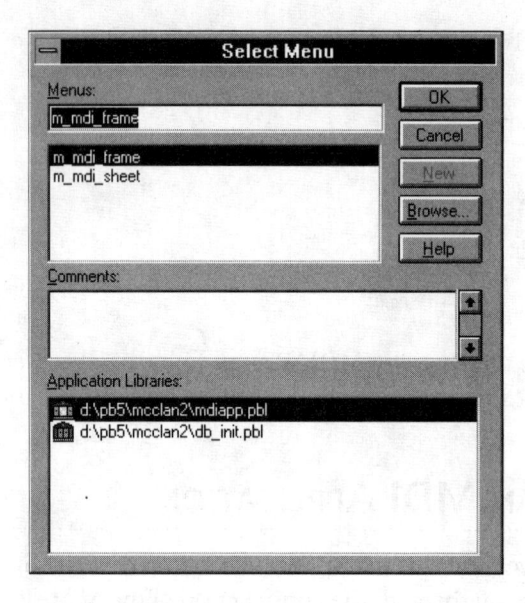

**Figure 12.6** *Adding a menu to a window.*

## Creating the Window Parms Structure

Next, create a structure called `str_win_open_parms`. This structure will carry a set of parameters to each sheet when the frame initially opens the sheet. The scope of this structure definition is global. Open the Structure painter (click the **Structure** icon on the PowerBar or PowerPanel). Define two elements for this structure as:

```
s_window_type  string
b_read_only    boolean
```

Save this structure as `str_win_open_parms`. The advantage of passing a structure to the sheets in the Open event, is that you can later add new elements to this structure.

# Creating the Sheet Window (w_mdi_sheet)

Next, create another new window to serve as the MDI sheet. In the Window Properties dialog box, select the Main option in the WindowType listbox (this is the default). The type of the sheet window can actually be any type other than a MDI frame, but the convention is to select **Main** as the type. All of the sheets in this application will be instances of this window. The use will open the sheets by using the File menu options (or the toolbar icons). Close the Properties dialog box.

Next, add a DataWindow control to the window. The DataWindow object will be assigned dynamically, so do not assign the object at this time. Position the DataWindow in the top-left corner of the window and adjust the size to fill the current window. The DataWindow control will be resized dynamically at run time, so the size is not too important at this time.

## Instance Variable

Next, add an instance variable to the `w_mdi_sheet` window. The instance variable will hold the window-open parameters that are passed to each sheet in its Open event. Define the instance variable as

```
str_win_open_parms istr_win_parms
```

## Window OPEN Event

Add the following script to the `w_mdi_sheet` Open event (also check that you are in the window's events, not the DataWindow control's events):

```
//w_mdi_sheet   Open script
int idx, i_count
istr_win_parms = message.powerobjectparm
IF IsValid(istr_win_parms) THEN
     dw_1.dataobject = istr_win_parms.s_window_type
     this.title = istr_win_parms.s_window_type
```

```
    dw_1.SetTransObject(sqlca)
    dw_1.Retrieve()
    IF istr_win_parms.b_read_only THEN
        This.title = This.title + ' [read-only]'
        i_count = integer(dw_1.Describe("datawindow.column.count"))
        FOR idx = 1 to i_count
            dw_1.Modify("#"+string(idx)+'.protect = 1')
        NEXT
    END IF
END IF
```

This code is triggered when the sheet first opens. The MDI frame window contains a function, `fw_open_sheet`, that will pass the `str_win_open_parms` structure as the `message.powerobjectparm`. The first line of this event assigns that parameter to the instance variable `istr_win_parms`. The next line verifies the structure using the `IsValid` function. From this structure, the sheet gets the name of the DataWindow object, and the title of the sheet. The next lines set up the DataWindow control, `dw_1`.

The `IF` statement checks to see if this is a read-only window. If so, the text *[read-only]* is added to the titlebar. The next statements set the protect attribute for each column to prevent changes. We do this in an instructive manner using the DataWindow `Describe` function. First, we set the integer `i_count` to the number of columns in the DataWindow. We determine this dynamically by querying the DataWindow object with the `Describe` function with the argument `"datawindow.column.count"`. This function always returns a string, so it must be converted to an integer before we can use it. Next, the `FOR` loop steps through each column, assigning the `protect` attribute using the DataWindow `Modify` function. The argument for the `Modify` for the first column would be `"#1.protect = 1"`. Using the `FOR` loop index and the string function creates a general solution to setting the attribute for all the columns.

## Resize Event

Add the following statement to the `w_mdi_sheet` window's `Resize` event:

```
dw_1.Resize(this.WorkSpaceWidth( ) - 64, this.WorkSpaceHeight( ) - 32)
```

This will resize the DataWindow control, `dw_1`, to fill the sheet each time the sheet is resized.

## w_mdi_sheet User Events

We need to be able to issue `Insert`, `Delete`, and `Update` statements for each sheet's DataWindow. We could do this in several ways, but we will use events in this example. Declare three user events for the window, as shown in Figure 12.7.

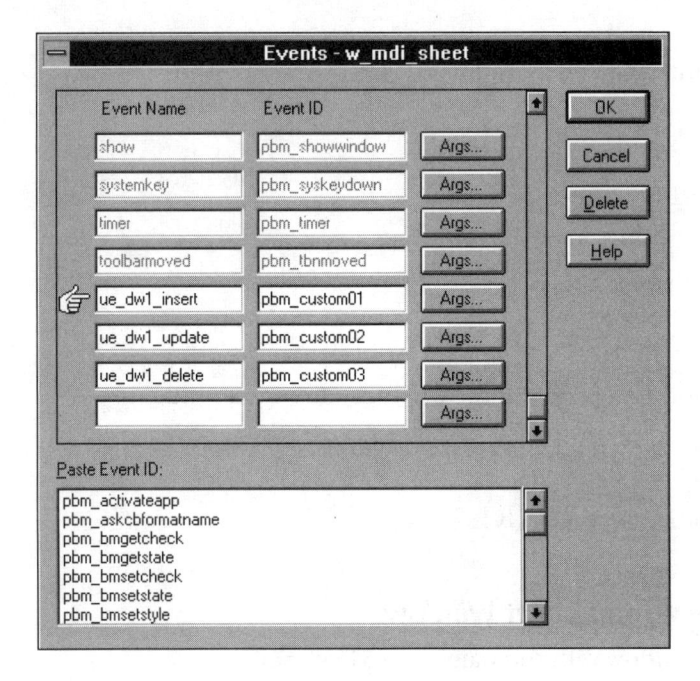

*Figure 12.7  Declaring user events.*

Add the following code to the ue_dw1_insert event:

```
long l_row
int i_rc
SetPointer(HourGlass!)
l_row = dw_1.insertrow (1)
IF l_row > 0 THEN
    i_rc = dw_1.scrolltorow ( l_row )
    // also does a dw_1.setrow
    i_rc = dw_1.setcolumn(1)
    i_rc = dw_1.setfocus ( )
END IF
```

Add the following code to the ue_dw1_update event:

```
IF dw_1.update ( ) = 1 THEN
    commit;
ELSE
    rollback;
END IF
```

Add the following code to the ue_dw1_delete event:

```
int i_rc
i_rc = dw_1.DeleteRow(0)
```

### Save the w_mdi_sheet Window

Save this window with the name w_mdi_sheet.

## w_mdi_frame Instance Variable

Now that you have created the w_mdi_sheet window, you must return to the Window painter to add an instance variable array of this type to the w_mdi_frame window. This array will hold the references to the sheets that are opened. To do this, open the Window painter, select the **w_mdi_frame** window, and then select the **Declare|Instance Variables** menu option. Declare an instance variable array, i_wsheet, of type w_mdi_sheet () as shown:

```
w_mdi_sheet i_wsheet[ ]
```

This is an unbounded, variable-length array of w_mdi_sheet windows. The w_mdi_frame will use this array in its wf_open_sheet function in response to a user request to open a new sheet.

## w_mdi_frame Window-Level Functions

Go back to the Window painter and add a number of functions to the w_mdi_frame. To do this, open the Window painter, if necessary.

### fw_open_sheet

In the painter for the m_mdi_frame window, select the **Declare|Window Functions** menu option. Add a function named fw_open_sheet. Figure 12.8 shows the declaration for that function.

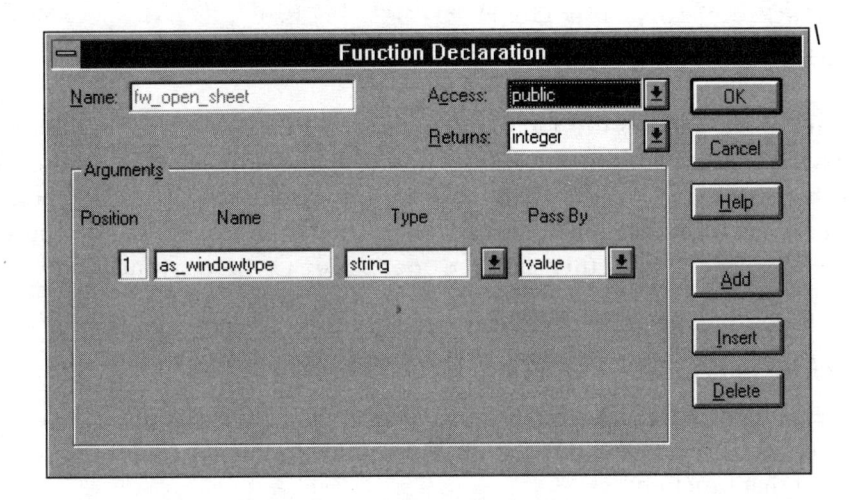

*Figure 12.8* Declaring the fw_open_sheet function.

## Chapter 12

Add the following code to the `fw_open_sheet` function:

```
//integer fw_open_sheet(string as_windowtype)
int idx, i_count, i_max
str_win_open_parms str_parms
i_max = UpperBound(iwin_sheet)
FOR i_count = 1 to i_max
    IF NOT IsValid(iwin_sheet[i_count]) THEN
        idx = i_count
    ELSE
        IF iwin_sheet[i_count].title = as_windowtype THEN
            str_parms.b_read_only = True
        END IF
NEXT
IF i_count > i_max THEN idx = i_count
str_parms.s_window_type = as_windowtype
OpenSheetWithParm(iwin_sheet[idx], str_parms, This)
this.SetMicrohelp(string(idx))
return 1
```

This function searches the `iwin_sheet` array for an empty slot (as the result of having closed a window). If it does not find an empty slot, then it uses the next higher position in the array for the window reference. It then checks to see if a sheet with this name is already opened; if so, it marks the new window as a read-only window. It then calls the `OpenSheetWithParm` function to open the sheet and pass it the `str_win_open_parms` structure.

### fw_close_all_sheets

In the painter for the `m_mdi_frame` window, define another window function, `fw_close_all_sheets`. This function takes no arguments. Add the following code to that function:

```
//fw_close_all_sheets
int idx, jdx, i_max
i_max = UpperBound(iwin_sheet)
```

```
FOR idx = 1 to i_max
   IF IsValid(iwin_sheet[idx]) THEN
      Close(iwin_sheet[idx])
   END IF
NEXT
return 1
```

This code searches the `iwin_sheet` array for open windows using the `IsValid` function. It closes each open window.

### fw_status_message

In the painter for the `m_mdi_frame` window, define another window function, `fw_status_message`. This function takes one argument, the text that you want to display. Add the following code to that function:

```
//integer fw_status_message(string as_text)
This.SetMicroHelp(as_text)
return 1
```

This code sends the text on to the SetMicroHelp function.

### fw_db_init

In the painter for the `m_mdi_frame` window, define another window function, `fw_db_int`. This function takes no arguments, and it is the same function that we have used in previous examples. Declare the function `fw_db_init` with no arguments and returns `[None]` (this is the last option at the bottom of the Returns dropdown listbox). If you wish, you can copy in the code from a file that is included in the example directory. The file is named **dbint2.fun**. To do this (from within the `fw_db_init` function painter, select the **File|Import** menu option and locate the file. The function code is:

```
//fw_db_init
int i_rc
long l_rows
string s_db_section
SetPointer (HourGlass!)
```

```
    i_rc = f_get_db_section(s_db_section)
IF i_rc <> 1 THEN
     fw_status_message("No dbms specified in Profile [application]")
ELSE
     i_rc = f_load_sqlca ( gs_init_file, s_db_section, sqlca )
     IF i_rc = 1 THEN
          connect;
     ELSE
          sqlca.sqlcode = 1 //connect failed
     END IF
     IF sqlca.sqlcode = 0 THEN
          gb_db_connected = True
          fw_status_message("connected")
     ELSE
          fw_status_message("db connection failed")
     END IF
END IF
return
```

This code reads the **IMAGEDB.INI** profile, initializes the SQLCA, and then connects to the database.

### *w_mdi_frame Open Event*

In the painter for the `m_mdi_frame` window, add the following code to the window's Open event:

```
//open event
This.SetMicroHelp('Connecting to DB...')
Post fw_db_init()
```

This code sets the initial Microhelp message and then posts a function call to `fw_db_init` to initialize the database. We post the function call so that the `w_mdi_frame` window will be visible as soon as possible.

## Add Code to the Application Open Event

Add the following code to the application Open event. This code will open the main window, make the connection to the database, and dynamically update the MicroHelp status line:

```
// application open event script
Open (w_mdi_frame)
// end of application open event script
```

## Creating the Menus

Next, create two menus for the MDI application. The first menu, m_mdi_frame, is used when the application opens. It provides the options to open a sheet or the exit the application. The first window is attached to the w_mdi_frame in the Window Style dialog box as shown earlier in Figure 12.6.

The second menu, m_mdi_sheet, is an extension of the first menu. It will be displayed when one or more of the sheets are open. This menu adds options to insert or delete rows in the DataWindow, update changes to the database, and close the current or all sheets. This menu belongs to the w_mdi_sheet window and is placed on the frame whenever a sheet window is open.

Figure 12.9 shows the m_mdi_frame menu. In the MDI MicroHelp field, add the line of text to be displayed in the MicroHelp status area for each menu option.

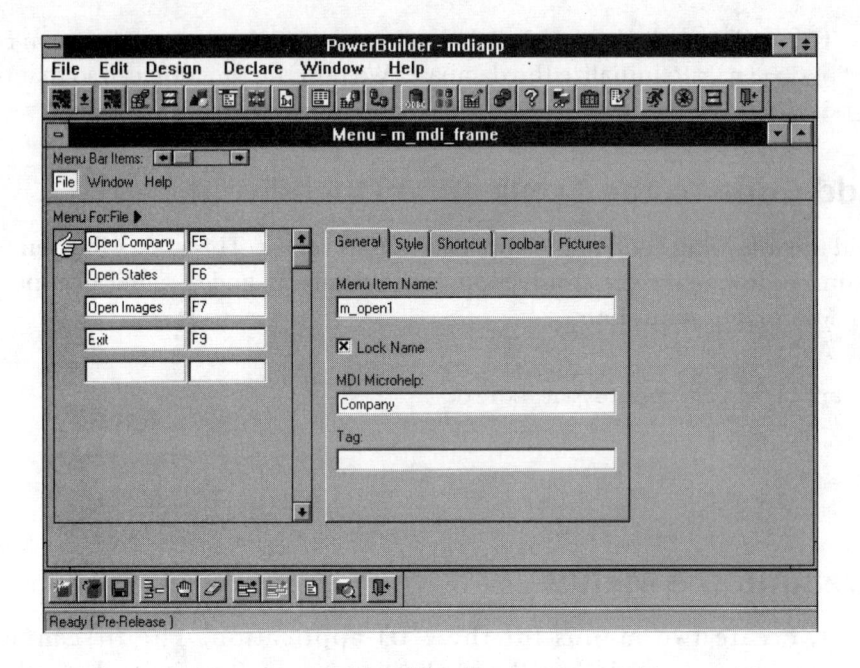

*Figure 12.9* Creating the `m_mdi_frame` menu.

In this example, a menu item is provided to open each window. A Window toolbar item is also provided to open each window, and to exit the application. To add an icon to the MDI frame's toolbar, click on the **Toolbar** tab and enter a word or two for the Text field. Then click the **Pictures** tab to open the dialog box shown in Figure 12.10.

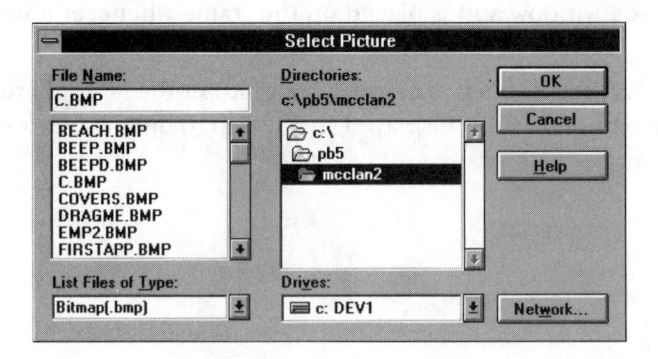

*Figure 12.10* Selecting an icon.

## Multiple Document Interface 501

For this example, you will find three BMP files in our examples directory. Use the `Stock Picture Exit!` for the last toolbar item. The toolbar icons should be:

- **Open Company**—Use the BMP file **C.BMP**. Toolbar text is `Company`.
- **Open States**—Use the BMP file **S.BMP**. Toolbar text is `States`.
- **Open Images**—Use the BMP file **I.BMP**. Toolbar text is `Images`.
- **Exit**—Use the stock picture, Exit! Toolbar text is `Exit`.

Insert MicroHelp text for each menu item (on the General tab, MDI Microhelp field). You can also dynamically set the MicroHelp text using the `SetMicroHelp()` function. Often, the application or window `Open` event uses this technique. You could also have various controls on a window set the MicroHelp using the `SetMicroHelp()` function. This is usually done in the `GetFocus` event for the control. If you do this, you can store the text in the tag attribute for the control. If you set Microhelp text for a control in this event, you should also clear the Microhelp text in the `LoseFocus` event.

For each toolbar item, the most important attributes that you can set are the following:

- Up and down icons (16 x 15 pixels)
- Text (display controlled in app)
- Spacing (if no text)
- Order on bar
- Visible
- Display down (stick, until you set `MenuItem.ToolbarItemDown = FALSE`)

In the script for the `Clicked` event for the Open Company menu option, add the following line of code:

```
w_mdi_frame.fw_open_sheet("d_company")
```

In the script for the `Clicked` event for the Open States menu option, add the following line of code:

```
w_mdi_frame.fw_open_sheet("d_state")
```

In the script for the `Clicked` event for the Open Images menu option, add the following line of code:

```
w_mdi_frame.fw_open_sheet("d_images")
```

In the script for the `Clicked` event for the Exit menu option, add the following line of code:

```
Close(w_mdi_frame)
```

Under the Windows menu, add the options, as shown in Figure 12.11.

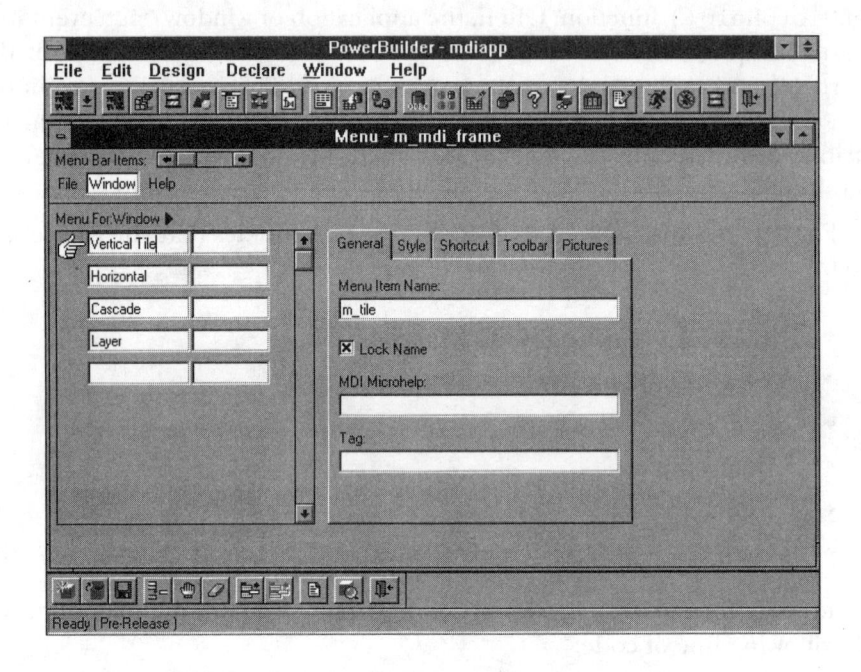

*Figure 12.11  Adding options to the Window menu.*

In the script for the `Clicked` event for the Vertical Tile menu option, add the following line of code:

```
ParentWindow.ArrangeSheets (tile!)
```

In the script for the `Clicked` event for the Tile menu option, add the following line of code:

```
ParentWindow.ArrangeSheets (tilehorizontal!)
```

In the script for the `Clicked` event for the Cascade menu option, add the following line of code:

```
ParentWindow.ArrangeSheets (cascade!)
```

In the script for the `Clicked` event for the Layer menu option, add the following line of code:

```
ParentWindow.ArrangeSheets (layer!)
```

## Creating the m_mdi_sheet Menu

Open the Menu painter and select the **m_mdi_frame** menu. Immediately save the menu as m_mdi_sheet. After saving the menu, any changes that you make will now be to the m_mdi_sheet menu.

> **NOTE** The best solution for creating a menu that extends an existing one would be to inherit the new menu from the previous one. This requires the use of inheritance, a basic object-oriented technique that will be covered in Chapter 14. In this example, we will just duplicate the m_mdi_frame menu to create the m_mdi_sheet menu. If you already know how to inherit a menu, then use the inheritance technique for the following example.

Insert the new options in the File menu, as shown in Figure 12.12. (Notice that the top menu item has been scrolled off the display to show the items that are to be added.)

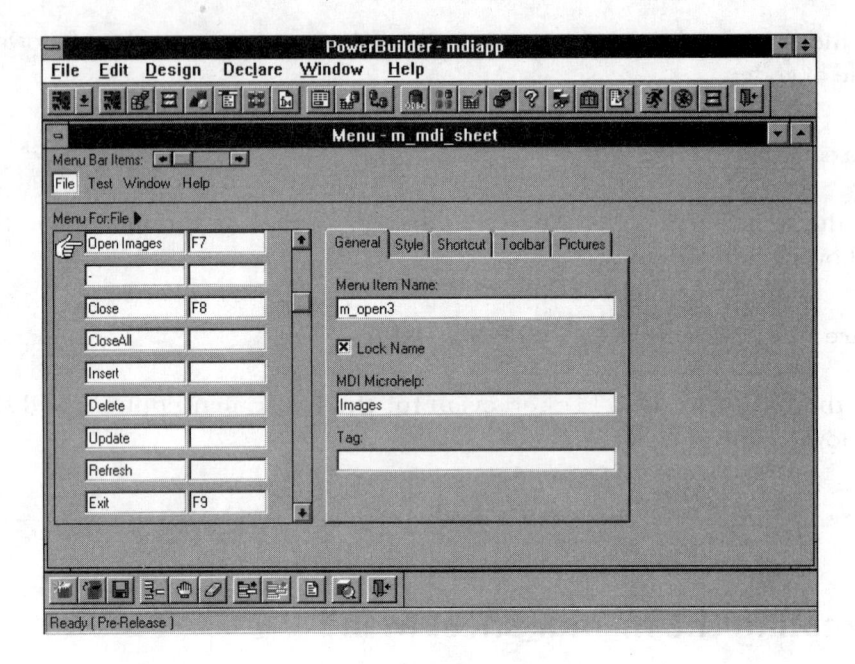

*Figure 12.12 The* `m_mdi_sheet` *menu.*

The separator is created by adding only a single dash as the menu item. It is a good idea to change the name of that menu item, say, to m_1. This is recommended because if you set the `DashesInIdentifier` option to 0, m_- will not be a legal name. Even if that option is currently set to 1, you may find that you want to disallow dashes in identifiers later, and this would cause a problem when you regenerate a menu with menu item names that contain dashes.

In the script for the Clicked event for the Close menu option, add the following line of code:

```
Close(ParentWindow) // this will close the active sheet
```

In the script for the `Clicked` event for the CloseAll menu option, add the following line of code:

```
w_mdi_frame.fw_close_all_sheets()
```

In the script for the `Clicked` event for the Insert menu option, add the following line of code:

```
ParentWindow.TriggerEvent ( "dw1_insert" )
```

In the script for the `Clicked` event for the Update menu option, add the following line of code:

```
ParentWindow.TriggerEvent ( "dw1_update" )
```

In the script for the `Clicked` event for the Refresh menu option, add the following lines of code:

```
w_mdi_sheet w_x
w_x = ParentWindow
IF IsValid(w_x) THEn w_x.dw_1.Retrieve()
```

This code shows another technique for accessing objects in a ParentWindow from a menu item. ParentWindow returns the data type, window. The PowerBuilder window class does not contain a DataWindow control (`dw_1`), so we must assign the ParentWindow to a variable of type `w_mdi_sheet` in order to be able to address the DataWindow control on that type of window.

In the script for the `Clicked` event for the Exit menu option, add the following line of code:

```
close(w_mdi_frame) // exit the application
```

Save this menu (m_mdi_sheet), and then add it to the w_mdi_sheet window (Figure 12.13).

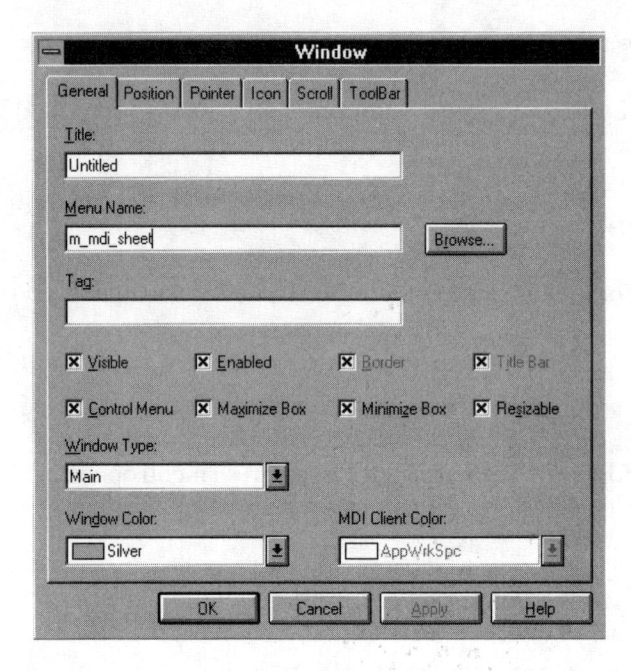

*Figure 12.13* w_mdi_sheet *Properties dialog box.*

## CREATING AN MDI TEMPLATE

When you create a new application, PowerBuilder 5 can create an MDI application template. This creates an application with frame and sheet windows, a menu for the frame, and an About box. To use this option, open the Application painter and select the **File|New** menu option. This opens the Select New Application Library dialog box (Figure 12.14).

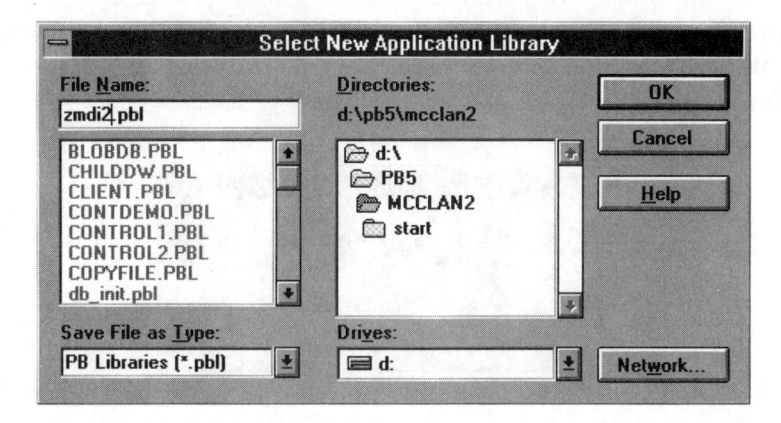

*Figure 12.14 Select the new Application library.*

For this example, enter the name **zmdi2.pbl** for the library and choose **C:\PB5\MCCLAN2** as the directory. Click **OK** to create the **ZMDI2.PBL** and continue on to create the application object. This will open the Save Application dialog box.

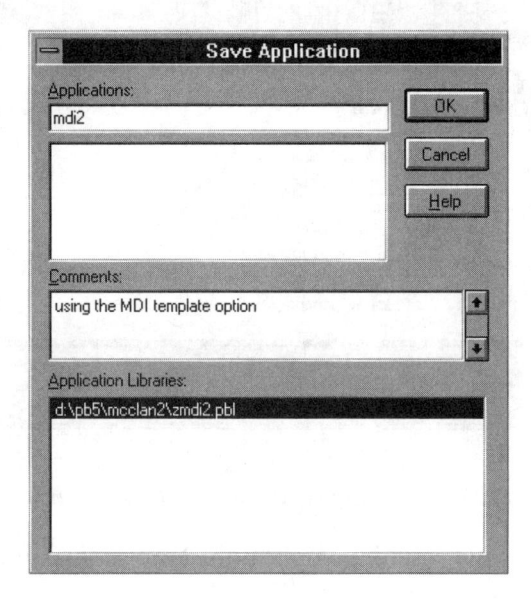

*Figure 12.15 The Save Application dialog box.*

Enter the name of the application, **mdi2**, and a comment in this dialog box. Click **OK**, and PowerBuilder gives you the option of creating an MDI application template (Figure 12.16).

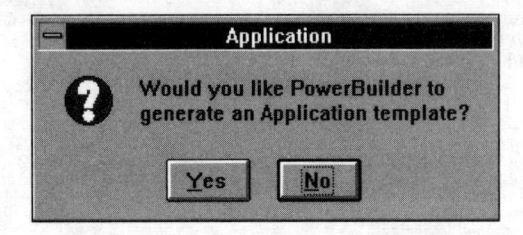

*Figure 12.16  Creating an MDI application.*

Click **Yes** to create an MDI application template. The Application painter shows the components that were added to your application (see Figure 12.17).

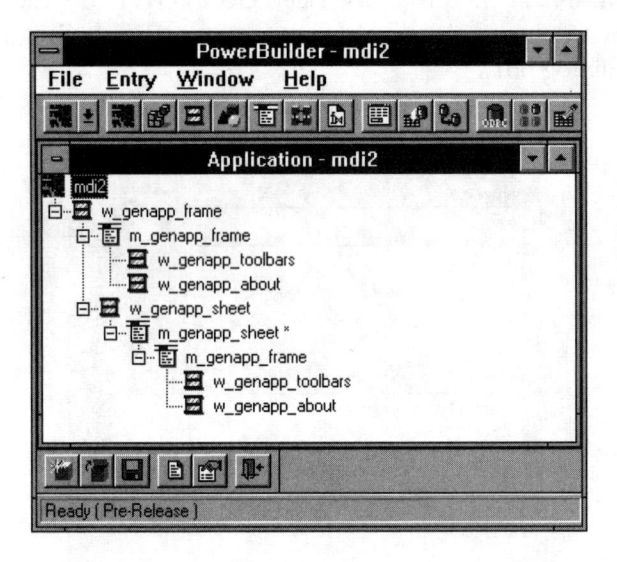

*Figure 12.17  The MDI template objects in the Application painter.*

Figure 12.18 shows the resulting application. You can expand this application as required.

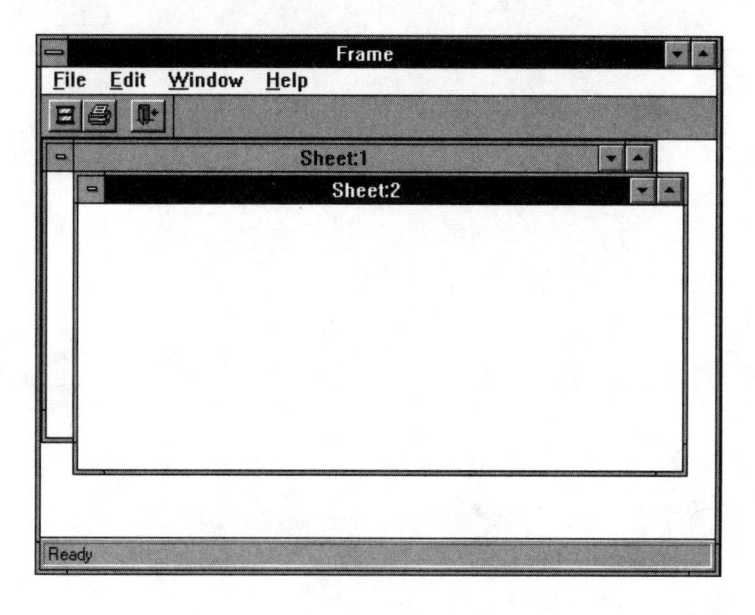

*Figure 12.18* The MDI template application.

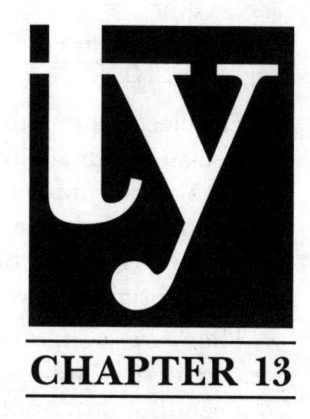

# User Objects

PowerBuilder gives you the ability to create a special type of control called a *user object*, one of the most powerful resources in PowerBuilder. You will find these most useful when you identify a functionality or object that has a usefulness that you would like to share between applications or that you would like to standardize. This chapter includes the following topics:

- User object overview
- Standard visual user objects
- Custom visual user objects
- External visual user objects
- Custom class user objects
- Standard class user objects

# User Objects

A user object is a reusable construct (a class or a control) that you create to encapsulate functionality you would like to use in various places in your applications. You can employ a user object to input or display information to users, respond to mouse or keyboard actions, to encapsulate data processing, and much more. After you build a user object, you can use it almost as if it were one of the original PowerBuilder controls.

There are several types of user objects in PowerBuilder. The most basic ones are derived from one of the standard PowerBuilder objects (such as a CommandButton). Another type of user object is more complex and usually includes multiple objects (SingleLineEdits, CommandButtons, DropDownListBoxes, etc.) within a user object, building a more complex functionality. User objects take full advantage of the object-oriented features of PowerBuilder. You will design the user object to be reusable by generalizing its behavior when you write the script code for its events and internal functions.

User objects have characteristics that are similar to the standard PowerBuilder objects and controls. User objects have the following:

- **Properties**—Attributes or variables, the values of which determine the characteristic of the user object.
- **Events**—Which may contain script code.
- **Functions**—Procedures that serve many purposes such as accessor functions, computations, and data processing.

Events will trigger the execution of your scripts just as in the standard controls. Functions implement the behavior of the user object or provide an interface to the user object (often used to set or obtain the values of user object variables). Functions are part of the definition of the user object. User objects may also contain variables and structures.

## Types of User Objects

There are six types of user objects divided into two general categories. Each type has a different manner of construction and use. The two categories are:

- **Class**—A nonvisual object, created without any PowerBuilder controls. The class user objects are implemented entirely by using user object variables and functions (PowerScript code).
- **Visual**—An object based on PowerBuilder controls, including other user objects. PowerScript code will work with these controls in the same manner as in PowerBuilder windows.

The types of user objects are described in the following sections.

## Class Category

- **Custom**—A nonvisual user object that is not based on any of the built-in PowerBuilder objects but may be inherited from another custom class user object.
- **Standard**—A nonvisual user object that is based on one of the built-in nonvisual PowerBuilder classes such as the Message or Error object.

## Visual Category

- **Standard**—Based on a single standard PowerBuilder control, such as a CommandButton.
- **Custom**—An object (like a window) that can contain multiple standard PowerBuilder controls.
- **External**—Used to access externally defined controls (i.e., external to PowerBuilder).

We often refer to the types of user objects in the following manner: standard class user object, standard visual user object, custom class user object, or custom visual user object. The external type does not really need any further qualification.

You will use the User Object painter to create these types of objects. You can use inheritance to derive a new user object from an existing one. Since one of the main advantages of user objects is reusability, you will most often place user objects in a shared library on the network, where they can be accessed for multiple applications. Sometimes you create application-specific user objects; these are better placed in one of that application's libraries.

## Using Visual User Objects

After you create a visual user object, you can add it to any of your windows in the Window painter. User Object is an option on the Controls menu, and there is a User Object icon on the Window painter controls. When you select one of these, a dialog box presents a list of user objects in the application's libraries. You select a type of user object and place it in a window like any other control. You can then position or size it on the window. You can perform other developmental activities, such as adding script code to its events and communicating between the user object and other PowerBuilder objects.

### Using Class (Nonvisual) User Objects

After you create a class user object, you implement an instance of it by declaring a variable of that type and using the CREATE statement to instantiate the object. This object will be scoped as any other variable. When you are finished with the instance, deallocate the object using the DESTROY statement.

## The Standard User Object

The first and simplest type of user object is the visual standard user object. The standard user object is based on and limited to a single standard PowerBuilder control as its source. It simply packages a standard PowerBuilder control as a reusable control and extends the control's normal behavior.

If you find that you frequently define similar PowerBuilder controls in different windows (or across different applications) for a certain type of use, you should create a standard visual user object to avoid redefining that control and recoding the script(s). Using a user object will also ensure that this type of control will always have the same appearance and behavior. The user object will also make it easier to maintain code and make global changes.

A simple example is the cb_close command button that we have used in many of the windows in our example applications. Each time that we needed to use a button to close a window, we had to define it, set the label, and add the code to the Clicked event to close the parent window. If this button had been defined as a standard user object, we could just drop the button (user object) onto any window and have that functionality.

The steps necessary to build a standard user object are:

- Open the User Object painter (click on the **User Object** icon on the PowerBar). In the Select User Object dialog box, click on the **New** button.

- In the New User Object dialog box, select the Standard Visual user object type (click on **Standard** under the Visual category), then click **OK**.

- The Select Standard Visual Type dialog box lists the standard controls that can be used as the basis for the new object. Select the standard PowerBuilder control on which you wish to build your standard user object. Click on the **OK** button; this opens the User Object painter with the object displayed in a manner similar to the Window painter. Your new user object inherits the attributes and events associated with that control.

- The User Object painter displays the new object in the painter's workspace. In this painter, you can modify the control just as you worked with controls in the Window painter. Size and shape the user object using the sizing handles. In this painter, you can add functions, user events, structures, or variables for the user object. This is the main value of a standard visual user object over a PowerBuilder control. You cannot attach functions, structures, or variables to a standard PowerBuilder control, but you can define any of these for user objects. Double-click on the object to open the Properties dialog box in which there are tabs labeled General, Font, Position, Pointer, and Drag and Drop. All of these attributes are the same as in the Window painter.

- Save the user object to a library. Select **Save** (or **Save As**) from the File menu. Use the prefix **u_** for user objects.

- Add the user object to one of your windows. In the Window painter, select the **Controls|User Object** menu selection (or click the **User Obj** icon on the painter bar). This opens the Select User Object dialog box. Select the user object in this dialog box, and then click in the window to add the object to that window.

A standard user object has the same events as the PowerBuilder control on which it is based. The events inherited from each standard PowerBuilder control will vary but may include events such as:

- Clicked
- Constructor
- Destructor
- DragDrop
- DragEnter
- DragLeave
- DragWithin
- GetFocus
- LoseFocus
- Other
- RButtonDown

## The Example uodemo Program

Run the example program, **uodemo**. This will demonstrate a number of user objects of several different types. The window includes the following visual user objects:

- `u_dw_nav`—Controls the `dw_1` DataWindow
- `u_dw_nav_with_close`—Adds a button (to `u_dw_nav`) to close the application
- `u_lb_with_isearch`—A listbox with incremental search
- `u_cb_close`—Closes the parent window and all related windows

It also includes a nonvisual user object that calculates sales tax.

This chapter presents the steps necessary to re-create this example. So create a new application uo_demo and name the library **zuodemo.pbl**. Create a main window, `w_main_with_uos`. Add the following code to the Application open event:

```
Open(w_main_with_uos)
```

Finally, copy the DataWindow, dw_1, from the **UODEMO.PBL** to your **ZUODEMO.PBL** (do this in the Library painter). This DataWindow has data stored internally, so it will not need to connect to the database or initialize a transaction object to work for this example.

## An Example Standard Visual User Object

For the first example, create a user object (based on a command button) that closes the parent window. A couple of other features will be added to the u_cb_close user object. We will add functions to enable or disable the button (u_cb_close). The button will be disabled when other windows are opened so that the main window can only close if all other windows have closed.

To create the u_cb_close user object, start by clicking on the **User Object** icon on the PowerBar. This displays the Select User Object dialog box shown in Figure 13.1.

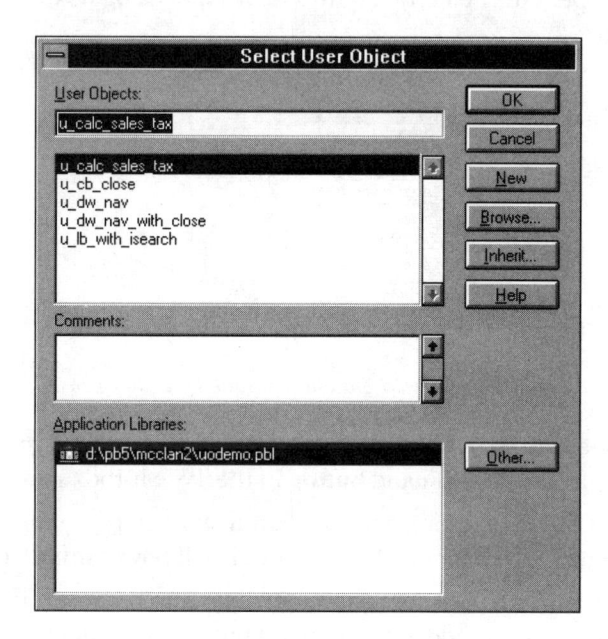

*Figure 13.1* *The Select User Object dialog box.*

Click on the **New** button, which opens the New User Object dialog box (Figure 13.2).

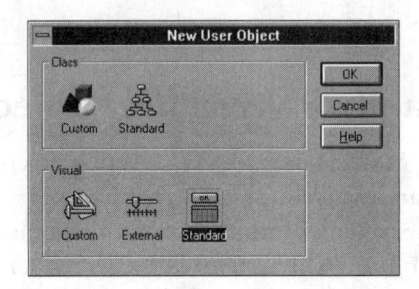

*Figure 13.2  New User Object dialog box.*

When this dialog box opens, select the **Standard user object type** icon in the Visual category. This opens the Select Standard Visual Type dialog box (see Figure 13.3).

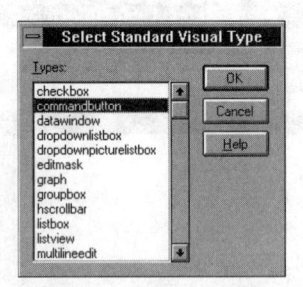

*Figure 13.3  Select Standard Visual Type dialog box.*

This determines the type of control that will be the basis for your new object. For this example, select **command button** in the Type listbox and then click **OK**.

The User Object painter opens with an instance of a command button in the work area (similar to Figure 13.4, except it will have "none" for the label).

Now build your user object in a manner similar to the way you worked in the Window painter after you added a command button to a window. However, in the case of standard user objects, you are limited to working with a single control. You can now modify the command button, add variables, events, object-level functions, and so forth.

# User Objects 519

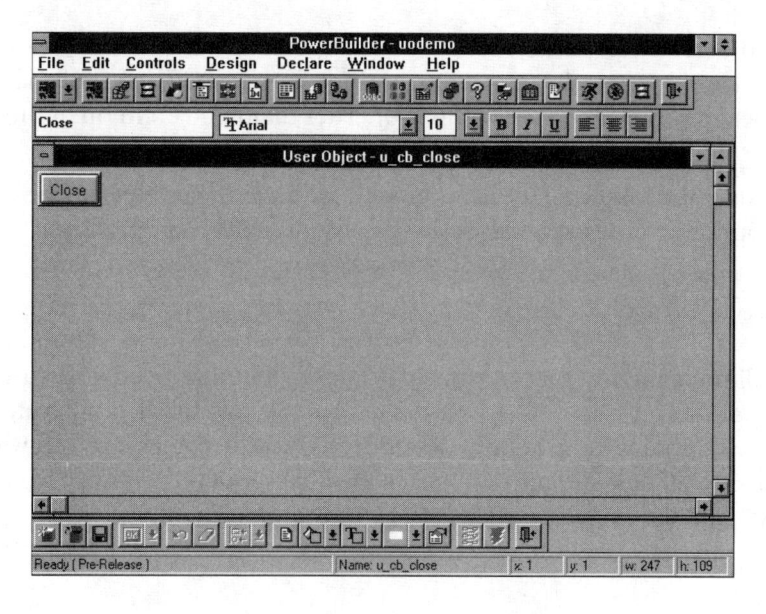

*Figure 13.4* The User Object painter.

Double-click on the user object (the command button) to open the Properties dialog box (Figure 13.5).

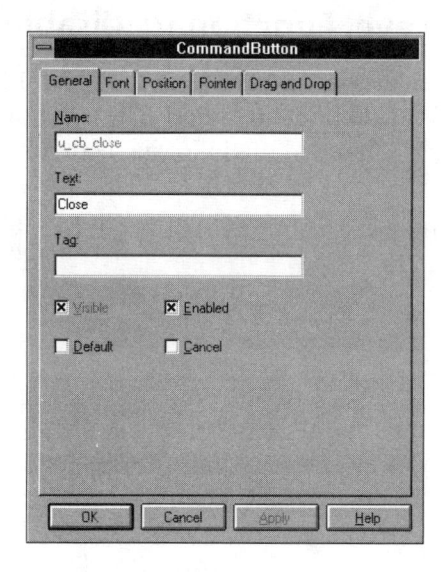

*Figure 13.5* The Style dialog box.

In the Text field, enter **Close**. The name of the object is `u_cb_close`. Notice that the name is grayed and cannot be changed (you will name the object when you save it). Close the Properties dialog box and open the Script editor for the `Clicked` event.

Declare the following instance variable (use the **Declare|Instance Variables** menu option) to the user object:

```
protected integer   ii_count
```

This will track the number of disable requests that have been sent (using the `fu_disable` function). The protected keyword sets the access level, so the `ii_count` variable cannot be accessed from outside the object, but will it be inherited by all descendant classes (see the chapter on inheritance from more details). Add the following code to the `Clicked` event:

```
close(Parent)
```

This code will close the parent window. Now go and create the object-level functions, described in the following sections.

## Create Object-Level Function fu_disable

Next, create an object-level public function (`fu_disable`) by selecting the **Declare|User Object Functions** menu option. The function takes no arguments and returns an integer. Then add the following code to the function:

```
//integer fu_disable
ii_count++
This.enabled = False
return ii_count
```

This function will disable the u_cb_close object. It will also track how many windows are currently open and have made this function call.

## Create Object-Level Function fu_enable

Next, create an object-level public function (`fu_enable`) by selecting the **Declare|User Object Functions** menu selection. The function takes no argument and returns an integer. Then add the following code to the function:

```
//integer fu_enable
IF ii_count > 0 THEN ii_count = ii_count - 1
IF ii_count  = 0 THEN This.enabled = True
return ii_count
```

It will decrement the count of how many windows are currently open. This function will enable the `u_cb_close` object if the count is equal to 0 (zero).

## Create Object-Level Function fu_get_state

Next, create an object-level public function (`fu_get_state`) by selecting the **Declare|User Object Functions** menu selection. The function takes no argument and returns a Boolean that is equal to the enabled state. Then add the following code to the function:

```
//boolean fu_get_state
return This.enabled
```

Close the Script editor. Use the **File|Save** menu option to save and name the object (`u_cb_close`), then close the User Object painter and go back to the Window painter.

Let's review what we have just created. These public functions form the interface for our `u_cb_close` object:

```
integer fu_enable()
integer fu_disable()
boolean fu_get_state()
```

In more complex user objects, you would usually also have a number of internal functions declared with an access level of private (or protected). These internal functions will do internal processing and can be called only from within the object. They will not be visible outside the user object.

## Adding a User Object to a Window

Now you can add an instance of your new user object to the window. To do this, select the **Controls|User Objects** menu option (or click the **User Obj** icon on the PainterBar controls popup menu). This displays the Select User Object dialog box (see Figure 13.6).

In this dialog box select the name of the library where you saved the object (in the Application Libraries listbox), and then select **u_cb_close** in the User Objects listbox.

Next you will click in the window to drop the control, as you have done for the standard PowerBuilder controls. PowerBuilder will name the user object `cb_1` by default. Rename the control to `cb_close` (Figure 13.7). Notice that even though it is a user object, it is named after the type of control on which it was built (this is only the case with Standard Visual user objects).

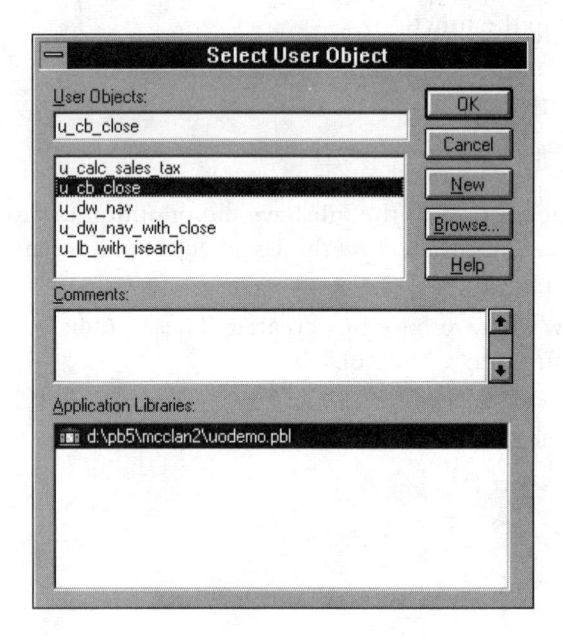

*Figure 13.6* The Select User Object dialog box.

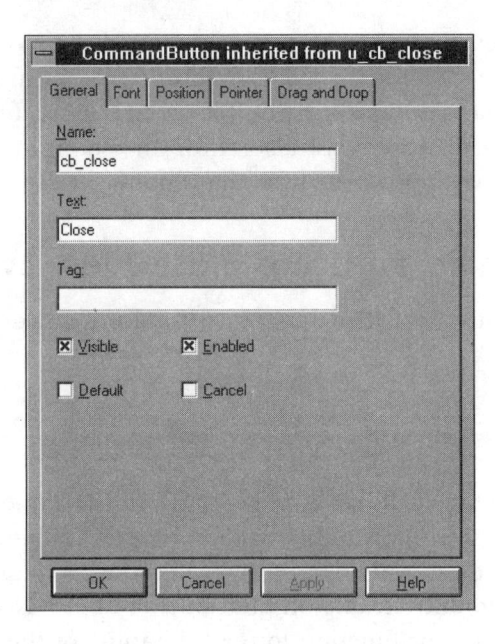

*Figure 13.7  The user object's Properties dialog box.*

Now run the application. When you click on the user object, the window will close.

This example will also show how to use a user-object-level function to communicate from code in the application to the user object. We added several object-level functions to the user object. You can call those functions from within the `w_main_with_uos` window as follows:

```
i_rc = cb_close.fu_disable()
```

In this example, we are calling the `fu_disable` from with the same window. We can call this function from outside the window with the following code:

```
i_rc = w_main_with_uos.cb_close.fu_disable()
```

You could use this example code in a window that was opened by the `w_main_with_uos` window. In that manner, the `cb_close` object would know about the other opened window(s) and would be disabled until those windows have closed. The example program will do this in a later step.

So, with this example, you should understand that communicating with the new user object is fairly simple. Communicating from the user object to other controls in the window is also possible, but it is more difficult. The custom visual user object example will also show an example of an object that manipulates a DataWindow control in the window.

## Edit the w_main_with_uos CloseQuery Event

Now you can add the following code to the `CloseQuery` event (in w_main_with_uos).

```
IF cb_close.fu_get_state() = False THEN return 1
```

This statement will cancel the close for the main window if the `cb_close` button is disabled (this means that another window is open and must be closed first). The `CloseQuery` event will be triggered when the user attempts to close the main window by double-clicking on the Controls Menu. Note that we use the `fu_get_state` accessor function to read the value of the enabled attribute rather than using the following:

```
IF cb_close.enabled = False THEN return 1
```

In general, you will not access attributes (variables) inside user objects in this manner. You should use accessor functions to read and set these variables. This concept is called *data hiding*, and it occurs when details are encapsulated inside the object as much as possible. This is a preferred object-oriented programming practice.

# CUSTOM VISUAL USER OBJECTS

The second type of user object is called a *custom visual user object*. It lets you package two or more standard PowerBuilder controls together as a new reusable control. Creating a custom control is almost an identical process to creating a new window with multiple controls. The User Object painter represents the custom visual control with a window to show its form. After creating this window, the new object combines multiple controls and code into a unit, a new type of control.

The following steps necessary to build a custom user object are:

- Click on the **User Obj** icon on the PowerBar to open the User Object painter. In the Select User Object dialog box, click on the **New** button.
- In the New User Object dialog box, select the **Custom** user object type in the Visual category, and then click **OK**.
- The User Object painter opens in the workspace, and the user object is displayed as a window. In this painter, you can add and modify controls just as you did in the Window painter. You can add functions, events, structures, or variables for the user object.
- Save the user object to a library. Select **Save** (or **Save As**) from the File menu.

Custom user objects have a fixed number of events. The events include:

- `Constructor`
- `Destructor`
- `DragDrop`
- `DragEnter`
- `DragLeave`
- `DragWithin`
- `Other`
- `RButtonDown`

The controls within the user object are not individually addressable from outside the user object, but you can trigger the user object events (including user-defined events), and you can call object-level functions. Examples are user object events and functions.

For the custom visual type of user object, we have included several examples that you may find useful. The first example is named `U_DW_NAV`. We will create a control that can navigate through the rows in a DataWindow. This user object will take the form of a button bar (see Figure 13.8), with buttons for FIRST, PRIOR, NEXT, and LAST record access. The purpose of creating this as a user object is to create a generalized control for reuse. The goal is to allow you to place this custom user object into any window that has a DataWindow and to gain navigation functionality without any additional effort (you will need one line of code to tie the user object control to the DataWindow). In many cases, this control will provide all that is necessary, and you won't need any other controls for navigation. You can easily expand this user object. For example, you could easily add buttons for QBE functionality.

## The U_DW_NAV User Object

Now, create the U_DW_NAV object, start by clicking the **User Object** icon on the PowerBar. This displays the Select User Object dialog box shown in Figure 13.1. Click on the **New** command button to open the New User Object dialog box (Figure 13.2). There, click on the **Custom** icon in the Visual category and then click **OK**. This opens the Custom User Object painter.

In this painter, you will build the user object in a manner similar to the way you add controls to a window in the Window painter. The window in this painter represents the custom user object. Click on the **PainterBar** to select the type of control that you want to add to the user object, drop the control on the window, and then proceed as you would expect. The size of the window in this painter determines the size of the custom object.

For this example, add four command buttons to the window. Arrange and label the buttons as shown in Figure 13.8.

The first problem is that we need to write code for these buttons to manipulate a DataWindow control of which we do not know the name. It could be named dw_1, dw_2, or dw_customer in the window where we want to use the U_DW_NAV control, so we will declare an instance variable of type DataWindow from our code references. Declare an instance variable (using the **Declare|Instance Variables...** menu selection) as:

```
datawindow idw_x
```

The code in the user object will refer to the idw_x instance variable. This idw_x does not currently relate to any specific DataWindow control on any window. We will "hook up" this instance variable when we add the U_DW_NAV control to a window. This is covered later. Add the following lines of code to the First command button's Clicked script:

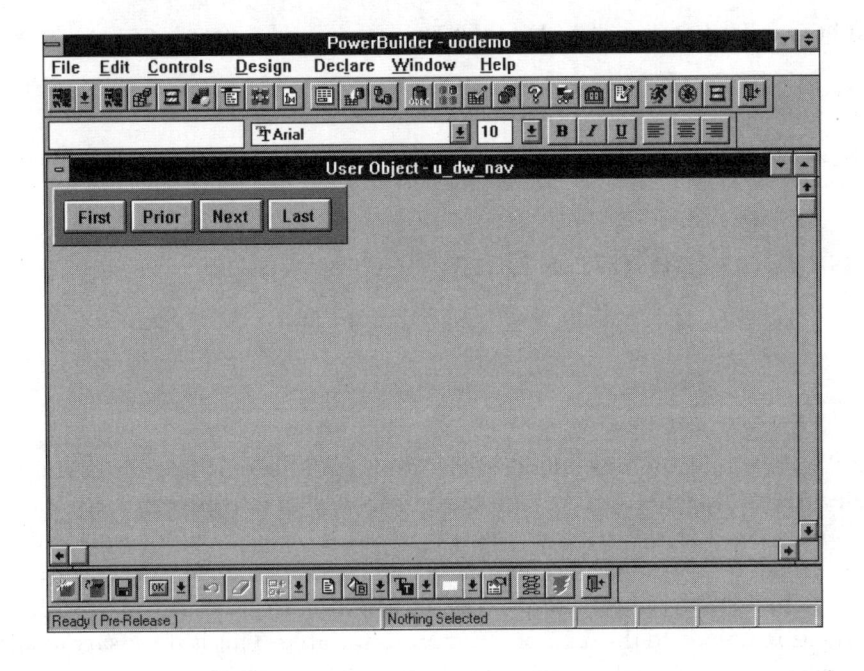

*Figure 13.8 Arranging the command buttons.*

```
idw_x.ScrollToRow(1)
idw_x.SetFocus () // do you see why this line is required
```

Add the following line of code to the Prior command button's `Clicked` script:

```
idw_x.ScrollPriorRow()
idw_x.SetFocus ()
```

Add the following line of code to the Next command button's `Clicked` script:

```
idw_x.ScrollNextRow()
idw_x.SetFocus ()
```

Add the following line of code to the Last command button's `Clicked` script:

```
idw_x.ScrollToRow(idw_x.RowCount())
idw_x.SetFocus ()
```

## Assigning the idw_x DataWindow Value

Let's review this user object. We declared an instance variable as:

```
datawindow idw_x
```

All the code that you just added to the command buttons references this variable. At the moment, `idw_x` is acting as a place-holder for the actual DataWindow that will be controlled by this user object. When you add this user object to a window (containing a DataWindow), it will be necessary to assign the actual DataWindow control, which is to be controlled with this navigation object, to the `idw_x instance` variable. This is necessary to allow the user object to make references to the DataWindow control. When you define the user object, the name of the DataWindow control is not known, and we wish to allow the use of this user object with a DataWindow of any name, so it must be assigned at run time.

There are several ways to accomplish this assignment. I recommend using a Registration function.

## Using a Registration Function (or Event)

The technique we recommend is to add a registration function to the user object. This registration function can be called in the window's open event to initialize the DataWindow control reference variable. The window's `Open` event is triggered only after all the control constructors have been executed, so the reference (to `DataWindow, dw_1`, or whatever it is named) will be valid. You could also use a user-defined event added to this user object to achieve the same result.

To use the object-level registration function, choose the **Declare|User Object Functions** menu selection. Declare the function as shown in Figure 13.9. Be sure to add the function argument `dw_control`, and indicate that its data type is DataWindow.

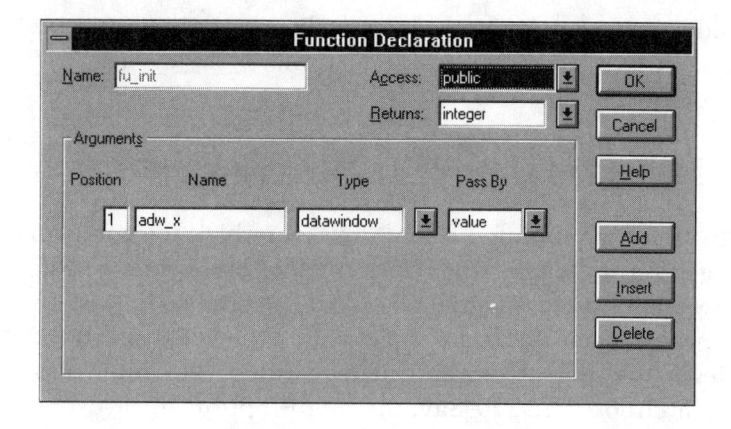

*Figure 13.9  The registration function declaration.*

After creating the `fu_init` user object function, add the following lines of code.

```
IF IsValid(adw_x) THEN
   This.idw_x =adw_x
   return 1
ELSE
   return 0
END IF
```

Save the object as `U_DW_NAV` by selecting the **File|SaveAs** menu option. Now you can close the function and the User Object painter.

To use this registration function, you must add a line of code to your window's open event. For example,

```
uo_1.fu_init(dw_1)
```

Substitute the name of the DataWindow control (if it is not `dw_1`) for the `dw_1` argument (and the name of the user object control if it is not `uo_1`).

Use this technique. Be sure to remove the code provided in the previous example from the constructor event for the user object (if you uncommented the third line).

Consider how you would implement this registration as a user-defined event (in the user object). You can look at the U_DW_NAV user object for an example solution.

## The U_DW_NAV_VERTICAL User Object

Figure 13.10 shows a variation of U_DW_NAV in which the command buttons are arranged vertically instead of horizontally. Create this user object if you may have windows where this design would be preferable. An easy way to create this version is to open the User Object painter and select **U_DW_NAV** as the object. Resize the user object, and then rearrange the buttons in a vertical stack. Then choose the **File|Save As** menu option to save the object as U_DW_NAV_VERTICAL. A better technique for doing this is to use inheritance, which will be discussed in the next chapter.

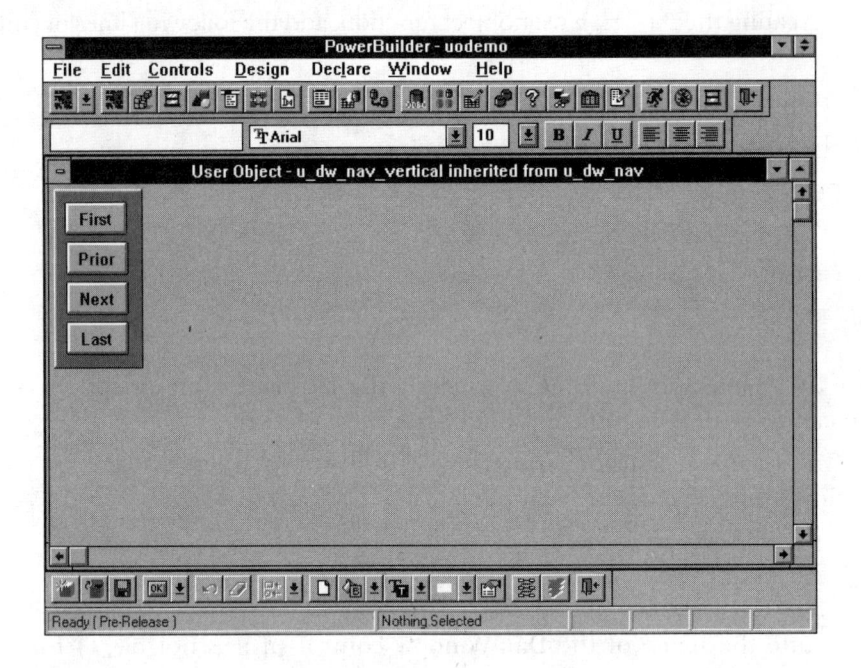

*Figure 13.10* U_DW_NAV_VERTICAL.

# The U_DW_NAV_WITH_CLOSE User Object

This is a version of `U_DW_NAV` that adds a Close command button that closes the parent window. Again, the simplest technique would be to open the `U_DW_NAV` object, make the changes, and then save the user object with the new name. But inheritance is the better solution.

Consider for a moment, how you would implement the Close button on this user object. The point is to realize that the `cb_close` button on the `U_DW_NAV_WITH_CLOSE` must make a reference to the window or a close command button on the window that is unknown at the time this control is created.

## Referencing the User Object's Parent Window

Here is the first technique for closing the parent window from a command button in the user object. Add a user-object-level function to `U_DW_NAV_WITH_CLOSE` by selecting the **Declare|User Object Functions** menu selection. Declare the function as `fu_close_parent_window` without any arguments. Add the following code to the function:

```
//integer fu_close_parent_window
return Close(Parent)
```

To the `Clicked` event for the Close button, add the following line of code:

```
fu_close_parent_window()
```

Your first thought on how to close the window might have been to simply add the following line of code to your Close command button's `Clicked` event:

```
Close(Parent) // this will not work
```

This will not work, and it is very important to understand why. The parent of the Close button is actually the `U_DW_NAV_WITH_CLOSE` user object. If this is confusing, consider that the user object itself is a window (of sorts), much like any other window with controls added to it. If you added a command button to a normal window, that button's parent would be the window. In the same way, the parent of the Close button is the user object.

However, the parent of the user object itself (represented by the window in the User Object painter) is the window to which you add an instance of the user object. The function implemented was declared at the user-object level, so the parent reference in that code is containing window. It is essential that you understand this and the previous paragraphs.

## *Referencing a Window's Controls*

The purpose of the next example is to demonstrate communication between a button on the user object and an object on the window (the window's `cb_close` button). We will place this code in the `U_DW_WITH_CLOSE` user object `CB_CLOSE` button's `rbuttondown` event. We will add a `TriggerEvent(Clicked!)` command to trigger the `Clicked` event for the window's Close button (this version requires that you have a Close button on the parent window in the example).

The first problem we encounter when we are designing the user object is that we don't know the name of the Close button on the window (or the window name). How can we address the trigger from within the user object? The answer is to use an object-level instance variable to hold a reference to the window's Close button. This variable will be assigned the value of the window's command button at run time using a registration function as we did for the reference to the DataWindow control. Create the instance variable by selecting the **Declare|Instance Variable** menu option (in the User Object painter). Add the second line to the instance declarations:

```
datawindow idw_x
command button icb_x
```

The user object must assign these values in a registration function. Continue working in the User Object painter. Add the following code to the user object's Close command button `Clicked` event:

```
IF IsValid(icb_x) THEN icb_x.TriggerEvent(Clicked!)
```

This code first checks to see that the `icb_x` instance variable has been assigned (use the `IsValid` function to check to see if objects have valid values). If the reference is valid, the `TriggerEvent` function is used to trigger the `Clicked` event for the window's command button.

### fu_init

To add an object-level function to register the controls (the window's Close command button and a DataWindow) with the user object, do the following. Choose the **Declare|User Object Functions** menu selection. Declare `fu_init` and add the following code:

```
//int fu_init(DataWindow adw_x, CommandButton acb_x)
int i_rc
IF IsValid(adw_x) THEN
   This.idw_x = adw_x
   IF IsValid(acb_x) THEN
      This.icb_x = acb_x
        i_rc = 1
   END IF
END IF
return i_rc
```

Close the User Object painter. Add the U_DW_NAV_WITH_CLOSE control to the window (name it `uo_dw_nav2`). Then add the following code to the `w_main_with_uos` Open event:

```
uo_dw_nav2.fu_init(dw_1, cb_close)
```

## The U_LB_WITH_SEARCH User Object

The next example of a custom visual user object combines a SingleLineEdit control with a listbox to perform the incremental type of search in the listbox that was implemented in the second window of the CONTROL1 application. In that window, a single-line edit was paired with a listbox to provide an incremental search in the listbox for the first item that began with the letters entered in the edit box. As you enter text in the SingleLineEdit field, the listbox selects the first entry that best matches the entire text (in the edit field). This is useful enough to be packaged together as a user object.

## Chapter 13

To create the U_LB_WITH_ISEARCH object, start by clicking on the **User Object** icon on the PowerBar. This will display the Select User Object dialog box shown in Figure 13.1. Click on the **New** button to open the New User Object dialog box. There, click on the **Custom** icon in the Visual category and click **OK**. This opens the Custom User Object painter.

For this example, add a SingleLineEdit control to the window and then a listbox control. Arrange the controls, as shown in Figure 13.11.

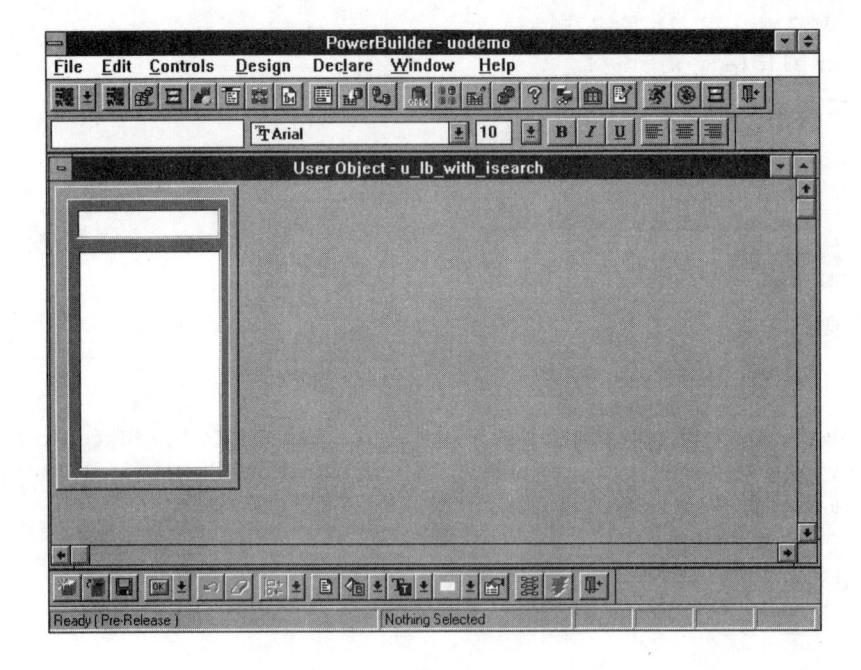

*Figure 13.11* U_LB_WITH_SEARCH.

### sle_1 we_keyup User Event

Add a user event, we_keyup, to the SingleLineEdit box. Do this by opening the Script editor using the popup menu (over the sle). Select the **Declare|User Events** menu option. Name the event we_keyup, and assign it the pbm_keyup Event ID.

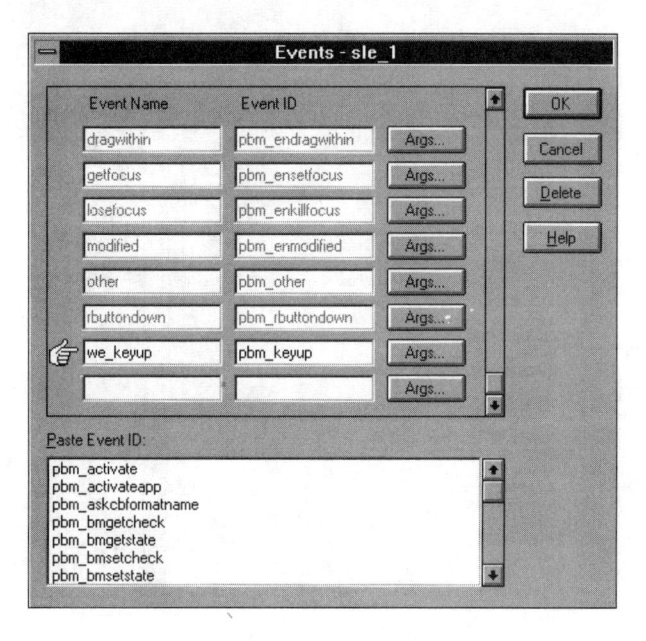

*Figure 13.12* we_keyup.

This adds a new event to the SingleLineEdit control, which maps one of the Window events to it. In the PowerScript editor, select that event (at the bottom of the list), and add the following text to that script:

```
int idx
idx = lb_1.SelectItem(this.text, 0)
```

This event is triggered as each keystroke ends (when the focus is in the SingleLineEdit). The script code searches the items in the list box (lb_1) for a match to the sle_1.text value.

## ue_add_item User Event

Next, add a user event at the user object level (the window in the User Object painter). To do this, select the **Declare|User Events** menu option.

**536** Chapter 13

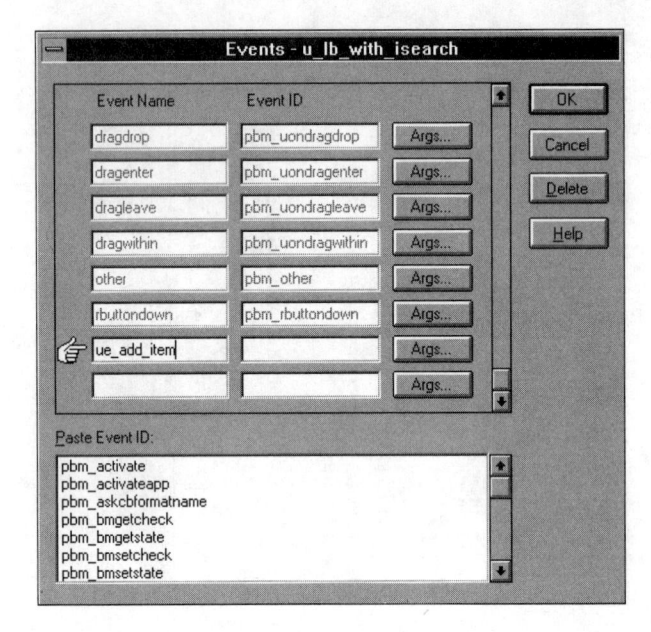

*Figure 13.13* `ue_add_item`.

Add a user event `ue_add_item` and give it no event ID. Click the **Args** button to add the only argument:

```
as_item string value
```

Also set the return value to a long. Now, close the Event Declaration dialog box and the Events dialog box. In the User Object painter, open the Script editor for an event in the user object. Select the new event, **ue_add_item**, from the Select Event drop-down listbox and add the following code:

```
long l_rc
l_rc  = lb_1.AddItem ( as_item )
return l_rc
```

This provides a user-object-level event that can be used to add items to the listbox. Another way to do this would be with a user-object-level function; we will also implement that method for this example.

## fu_add_item

To add that, declare a function at the user object level (use the **Declare|User Object Functions** menu selection). Declare a function, as shown:

The function name is fu_add_item, with a single string argument, as_item. Add the following code for that function:

```
//long fu_add_item(string as_item)
long l_rc
l_rc  = lb_1.AddItem ( as_item )
return l_rc
```

This works the same as the ue_add_item event. Save the object as U_LB_WITH_ISEARCH by selecting the **File|SaveAs** menu option.

## fu_get_selected

Declare another function at the user object level (use the **Declare|User Object Functions** menu selection). Declare a function, as shown:

The function name is fu_get_selected, and it has no arguments. Add the following code for that function:

```
//string fu_get_selected()
return lb_1.selecteditem()
```

This works the same as the ue_add_item event. Save the object as U_LB_WITH_ISEARCH by selecting the **File|SaveAs** menu option.

## Add U_LB_WITH_ISEARCH to the Window

Add one of these new user objects to a window. Name it uo_isearch. To demonstrate both methods of adding items to the listbox, you will also need to add two SingleLineEdit controls to the window.

For the first of the SingleLineEdits, add the following code to the modified event:

```
uo_isearch.fu_add_item(This.text)
This.text = ''
```

For the second of the SingleLineEdits, add the following code to the modified event:

```
uo_isearch.Event ue_add_item(This.text)
This.text = ''
```

Create a window with all these objects, as shown in Figure 13.14. This example also includes a few controls yet to be added.

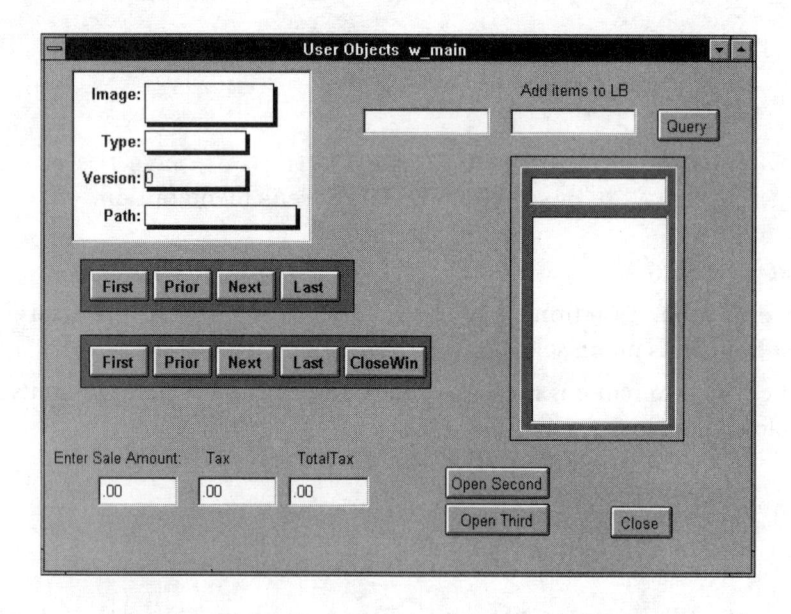

*Figure 13.14* *The example window in the* uo *application.*

## CUSTOM CLASS USER OBJECTS

The next type of user object is a nonvisual user object. It lets you encapsulate a behavior (or functionality) very much like creating a class in the C++ language. You cannot use any of the standard PowerBuilder controls in this type of user object. Instead the user object is composed of PowerScript code, variables, functions, structures, and events. This type of control is used mostly for data processing functions. For example, you might have a customer object that contains functions to handle customer transactions.

The class user object is not added to one of your applications in the Window painter, as were the other types of user objects that we have seen. Instead, you must instantiate an instance of the class type by using the CREATE command.

For example, in a script you would declare a variable of the type u_calc_sales_tax. Then use the CREATE statement to instantiate the uo_tax object:

```
u_calc_sales_tax  uo_tax
uo_tax = CREATE u_calc_sales_tax
// use the object
// for a while
DESTROY uo_tax
```

For the example, we create a custom class user object that calculates the sales tax for a given purchase amount. This object is used in the lower-left section of Figure 13.14. In the section, you enter a sales amount in the field labeled Enter Sales Amount. The sales tax will be calculated by a user object and displayed in the Tax field. The total of all previously calculated tax is displayed in the Prior field.

To create the U_CALC_SALES_TAX user object, start by clicking on the **User Object** icon on the PowerBar. This displays the Select User Object dialog box, shown in Figure 13.1. Click on the **New** button. This opens the New User Object dialog box (Figure 13.2). Click the **Custom** icon in the Class category and click **OK**. This choice specifies that you are creating a nonvisual user object.

The Custom Class object only has only two events:

- constructor
- destructor

The User Object painter opens with a window that represents the user object. You will not be able to add any controls to the window. For this example, declare a shared variable by selecting the **Declare|Shared Variables** menu option. Add the following declaration to the dialog box:

```
decimal {2} sdec_total
```

This will track the total tax calculated so far. It is a shared variable, so that it will retain the current total across instances of `u_calc_sales_tax`.

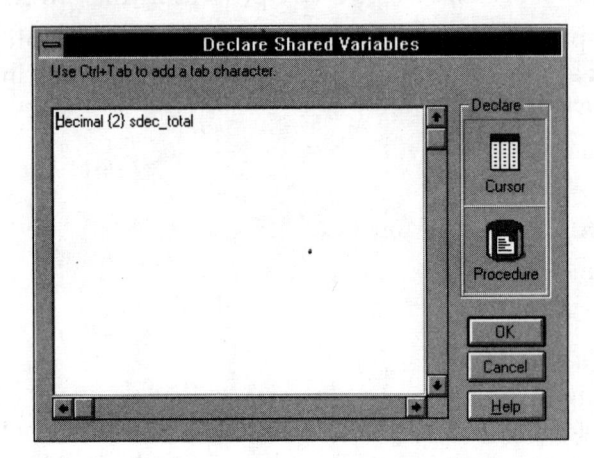

*Figure 13.15 The shared variable.*

Add an instance variable of the decimal type (choose the **Declare|Instance Variables** menu option):

```
decimal{2} idec_rate = 0.055
```

This will store the tax rate.

## *u_calc_sales_tax.fu_amount*

Create an object-level function by selecting the **Declare|User Object Function** menu option. Name the function `fu_amount` and add the decimal argument `adec_sale`. Add the following code to the function:

```
//decimal fu_amount(decimal adec_sale)
decimal{2} dec_out
IF adec_sale = 0 THEN
    sdec_total = 0
ELSE
    dec_out = adec_sale * idec_rate
    sdec_total += dec_out
```

```
END IF
return dec_out
```

This function calculates and returns the sales tax. It also stores the total taxes in `sdec_total`.

### u_calc_sales_tax.fu_get_total

Add another object-level function. Name the function `fu_get_total`. It has no arguments, but it does return a decimal value. Add the following line of code to the function:

```
return (sdec_total)
```

### u_calc_sales_tax.fu_set_rate

Add another object-level function. Name the function `fu_set_rate`. It has one decimal argument, and it does not return a value. Add the following lines of code to the function:

```
//fu_set_rate(decimal adec_rate)
```

### idec_rate = adec_rate

This allows you to change the sales tax rate. Now, save the object as U_CALC_SALES_TAX by selecting the **File|SaveAs** menu option.

### Add to the Window

Add the following instance variable to the `w_main_with_uos` window:

```
u_calc_sales_tax iuo_tax
```

Add the following code to the window's open event:

```
int i_rc
i_rc = uo_dw_nav.fu_init(dw_1)
i_rc = uo_dw_nav2.fu_init(dw_1, cb_close)
iuo_tax = CREATE u_calc_sales_tax
```

Also, before you can use the new user object in the application, you will need to add three edit mask controls to the window. Name the EditMask controls, em_sale, em_tax, and sem_total.

Define the edit mask (for all three) with the data type number and use the following mask:

```
"###,###.00"
```

Add the following script to the Modified event for the EditMask:

```
decimal {2} dec_tax
dec_tax = iuo_tax.fu_amount(dec(This.text))
em_tax.text = String(round(dec_tax, 2))
em_total.text = String(iuo_tax.fu_get_total())
```

Now you can run the application.

## STANDARD CLASS-USER OBJECTS

The next type of user object is also nonvisual. It lets you base the class on one of the PowerBuilder objects such as Message, Error, or Transaction. This user object is built from PowerScript code, variables, functions, structures, and events.

The Standard class object is not added to one of your applications in the Window painter as the visual types of user objects were. You must instantiate an instance of the class type by using the CREATE command as you did for the Custom class user object.

For example, in a script you would declare a variable of the type u_my_message:

```
u_my_message   uo_message
uo_message = CREATE u_my_message
// use the object
// for a while
DESTROY uo_message
```

For our example, we will create a Standard class user object based on the message object. We will add two functions to the user object and an instance variable.

To create the `U_MY_MESSAGE` user object, start by clicking on the **User Object** icon on the PowerBar. This displays the Select User Object dialog box shown in Figure 13.1. Click on the **New** button. This opens the New User Object dialog box (Figure 13.2). Click the **Standard** icon in the Class category and click **OK**. This choice specifies that you are creating a class (nonvisual) user object based on one of the PowerBuilder objects.

The Standard class object has only two events:

- constructor
- destructor

The User Object painter opens with a window that represents the user object. You will not be able to add any controls to the window. For this example, declare an instance variable by selecting the **Declare|Instance Variables...** menu option. Add the following declaration to the dialog box:

```
int ii_Len
```

Create an object-level function by picking the **Declare|User Object Function** menu option. Name the function `fu_set_stringparm` and add a string argument `s_text` passed by value. Add the following code to the function:

```
This.StringParm = s_text
This.ii_Len = len(s_text)
return 0
```

This function stores the `s_text` and the length of the text in the user object.

Add another object-level function and name it `fu_get_stringparm`. It has one string argument, `s_text`, which is passed by reference. This function should return a decimal value. Add the following lines of code to the function:

```
s_text = This.StringParm
return (This.ii_Len)
```

Save the object as U_MY_MESSAGE by selecting the **File|SaveAs** menu option.

Next, we will use the new standard class user object in an application. Open a window and add a command button and a SingleLineEdit control (`sle_1`) to the window.

Add the following code to the button's `Clicked` event:

```
u_my_message uo_message
int i_rc
string s_text, s_text2
s_text = 'Testing'
uo_message = create u_my_message
i_rc = uo_message.fu_set_stringparm('test')
i_rc = uo_message.fu_get_stringparm(s_text2)
sle_1.text = s_text2
destroy uo_message
```

Run the application. When you click the **command** button, the `sle_1` displays the Testing message.

**CHAPTER 14**

# Inheritance

PowerBuilder provides support for the major tenets of object-oriented programming: data abstraction, inheritance, and polymorphism. This chapter provides an introduction to these concepts followed by a detailed explanation of the use of inheritance in PowerBuilder. The object-oriented features in PowerBuilder are very useful and worth investigating. The reusability gained from these features is one of the main advantages of PowerBuilder over competing products (e.g., Visual Basic). This chapter covers:

- Object-oriented concepts
- Window inheritance
- Menu inheritance
- User object inheritance
- MDI inheritance

Inheritance is one of the most powerful features in PowerBuilder, and it will pay to invest the time necessary to implement it in your development process.

## Object-Oriented Concepts

Object-oriented programming encompasses the creation and use of objects as a fundamental part of the development process. What is an object? That will become clearer in the next sections, but essentially an object is a bundle of variables and functions that act as a unit. Objects are embedded with a number of operations that can be used to access and manipulate these variables and to perform other processing. The object is the basic element used to build the application in an object-oriented system. Object types (classes) are identified and documented during the analysis and design phases; therefore successful object-oriented development does require a greater design effort.

It is essential to understand the more important aspects of object orientation before proceeding with the PowerBuilder examples.

## Data Abstraction and Encapsulation

Data abstraction is the definition of a construct, consisting of attributes and functionality (like the object we just described). Once these properties are defined, we have created an abstract data type. In many ways, this is really just a logical extension of structured programming techniques. For example, most languages let the programmer define structures. A structure is a set of variables that are treated as a unit (the beginnings of our object). Data abstraction takes this a step further by adding functions and scoping (of functions and variables) to the structure. These functions perform operations on the structure elements. The data elements and behavior are internal to the object and therefore encapsulated in the object. The internal details are hidden to a large degree, and interaction with the object is through a set of well-defined operations.

In the chapter on user objects, you learned how to package a set of controls into an object and how to add functions to user objects. Each user object that you define is then a new data type that is available for use in your programs.

## Classes

The definition of a type of object is called a *class*. A class creates an object definition (including variables and functions) and defines the interface that is used to access that class of object. Each object handles the manipulation of its own attributes. If another object (external to it) wishes to modify it, that external object would make a request (via a function call or triggered event) to the object to handle it. The code (or external object) that uses this interface becomes the client of the object. It makes requests for retrieving and for setting values to the interface, not by directly manipulating the object's attributes. The object also provides other functionality via the function calls or events.

> **NOTE** Think of a class as a data structure with a set of functions written as an API to access and manipulate the elements of that data structure. All access to the structure is through the API. This API also provides other functionality related to the type (meaning) of the class.

A class is similar to a data type in that it allows the creation of variables of its type, and it provides a number of operations and/or operators to manipulate the objects. Encapsulation makes the object largely independent of things that may affect it, which makes the system more maintainable.

Data abstraction helps you build cleaner, easier-to-extend application, and simplifies their maintenance. But nothing comes for free, and object-oriented programming requires additional design to properly recognize and document the object classes.

## Objects

As we have seen, a class is a type or category of object. An object is an *instantiation* (instance) of a class. In PowerBuilder development, you define both classes and objects. In the early stages, this process is somewhat hidden from the developer (this was mentioned in Chapter 2, "The PowerScript Language," and is covered again in this chapter).

The relationship between a class and an object is similar to the relationship between a data type and a variable of that data type. An even better analogy is the relationship between a structure definition (or a typedef in the C language) and the declaration of a variable of that type of structure. Classes have elements (member variables) that are very much like structures, but classes also contain functions (called *methods* in object-oriented terms) that manipulate the member variables and perform other processing tasks.

For example, consider the following declaration (this example is similar to C++ and is used as a general example):

```
class Person
{
    char first_name[12];
    char last_name[20];
    char phone[20];
    public:
        Person (); // a constructor function with the same
                   // name as the class
        GetFirstName();
        SetFirstName();
        GetLastName();
        SetLastName();
};
Person employee1;
```

In this example, a class has been defined with three data elements (`first_name`, `last_name`, `phone`). The class also contains a number of functions. The first is the constructor that will create an instance of this class (an object). The next two functions provide access to the `first_name` element (the code for these methods would be defined somewhere else). The final line declares an object, `employee1`, of this type.

You could implement this class in PowerBuilder as a user object (either a nonvisual Custom Class or a Visual Custom user object). In this case, we'll consider it to be a nonvisual Custom Class object.

## u_person

Assume that we built a new Custom Class user object. In the u_person user object, the variables are instance variables and the methods are object-level functions:

```
//u_person instance variables
protected string is_last_name
protected string is_first_name
protected string is_phone
```

The set of object-level functions are declared as:

```
public function string fu_get_fname ()
public function string fu_get_lname ()
public function string fu_get_phone ()
public function string fu_get_description ()
public function integer fu_set_fname (string as_lname)
public function integer fu_set_lname (string as_fname)
public function integer fu_set_phone (string as_phone)
protected function string fu_build_full_name ()
```

The public functions form the API for using instances of u_person. In our user object, we have added a new function, fu_get_description. This function returns a string describing the object, which is the concatenation of the last and first name. fu_get_description calls another function, fu_build_full_name, which is not to be visible outside the user object, so it has an access level of protected (private would also work for this example at this point).

Continuing with the Person example, consider the following code in a PowerBuilder application. This could be in a window or a function, but it is outside the u_person user object itself:

```
u_person uo_contact
uo_contact = CREATE u_person
```

```
IF NOT IsValid(uo_contact) THEN return 0
uo_contact.fu_set_lname("Wallace")
uo_contact.fu_set_fname("William")
s_text = uo_contact.fu_get_description()
```

In the first lines of this code, an instance of this class was created (`uo_contact`), and the `is_last_name` and `is_first_name` are assigned values. The class (`u_person`) is used just like a data type in the declaration. The dot notation is used to specify that the `fu_set_lname()` function (a method in the `Person` class) is to be called with the argument `Wallace` and applied to the variable in the `uo_contact` object. The last line calls the `fu_get_description` function to return the last name plus first name string.

The `uo_contact` object encapsulates variables and functions to capture the meaning (behavior) of a `Person`. Each object that is instantiated for this class represents an individual, one unique person (in this case, perhaps the contact person at a company). Notice that instead of directly manipulating the values of the object's data members, the object's `fu_set_lname` + `fu_set_fname` functions were used to update the value. This is an essential part of object-oriented programming. You must (in most cases) access the member variables only through the defined interface (the methods). That encapsulation is essential for partitioning the application.

Another point to remember is to always limit scope and apply restrictive access levels as much as possible. In this example, `fu_build_full_name` is an internal function, which is not to be visible from outside the user object. So it is declared with an access level that would make the following code fail (from outside the user object):

```
uo_contact.fu_build_full_name()
```

The attempt to access the instance variables directly would also fail:

```
uo_contact.is_last_name = 'Smith'
```

The principle of *encapsulation* is perhaps the easiest object-oriented concept to put into practice. Classes partition the application system into logical and functional units with well-defined interfaces. This alone can contribute to better-designed and more manageable applications.

## INHERITANCE

*Inheritance* lets the developer derive a new class (object type) from an existing base class. The descendant class inherits all the attributes (variables) and functions of the ancestor class. The new class will specialize the more general base class in some way, perhaps by adding attributes, or by restricting the ancestor's behavior in some manner. The payoff is that you gain the reusability of existing objects that already have some of the features that you need for the new objects, and you gain the reuse of well-tested code, shortening the development process.

For example, an `Employee` class based on the previously discussed `Person` class can be created. Clearly `Employee` has all the attributes of `Person`, but an employee is a person who has a special kind of relationship with our company. To capture that relationship, an `Employee ID` (`emp_id`) is added with one or more methods to handle `Employee` processing. The next example defines the `Employee` class and creates an instance of that class.

## u_employee

We create a new nonvisual `Custom Class` user object, but this time instead of selecting **New** in the Select User Object dialog box, we selected **Inherit** and then the user object (class) **u_person** as the Inherit From user object. That means that a new descendant user object has been created (`u_employee`) that has all the attributes and functions of ancestor user object `u_person`.

Now we add to the descent class. In the `u_employee` class (user object), we add one instance variable and two object-level functions:

```
//u_employee instance variables
protected string is_emp_id
```

The object-level functions are defined as:

```
public function integer fu_set_id (string as_id)
public function string fu_get_description ()
```

The `fu_set_id` public function provides access to the new `is_emp_id`. We have also added a new version of the function, `fu_get_description`, that returns the concatenation of the last name, first name and the employee ID. In this example, we have overridden a function in the ancestor `u_person` class.

Continuing with the employee example, consider the following code in a PowerBuilder application. This could be in a window or a function, but it is outside the `u_person` user object itself:

```
u_employee uo_emp
uo_emp = CREATE u_employee
IF NOT IsValid(uo_emp) THEN return 0
uo_emp.fu_set_lname("McClanahan")
uo_emp.fu_set_fname("David")
uo_emp.fu_set_emp_id("123456789")
s_text = uo_emp.fu_get_description()
```

In the first lines of this code, an instance of this class was created (`uo_emp`), and the `IsValid` function verifies that the `CREATE` was successful. We then assign values to the `uo_emp`, and then call the `fu_get_description` function to return a string with the information. The `uo_emp` object encapsulates variables and functions to capture the meaning (behavior) of an `Employee`.

The new `Employee` class inherits all the member data elements (public or protected instance or shared variables) and all public and protected member functions from the `Person` class. The `Employee` class is a descendant of the `Person` class, and `Person` is an ancestor of the `Employee` class. An `Employee` is also considered to be a `Person`, as it has all the attributes (and functionality) of the `Person` class. The `Employee` has an employee ID (`is_emp_id`) and a couple of new functions.

> **NOTE** Private variables and functions are not inherited to descendant classes.

## Why Inherit?

The `Employee` class could have been created without using inheritance by defining the entire set of attributes and functions:

```
//u_not_inherited  instance variables
private string is_last_name
private string is_first_name
private string is_phone
private string is_emp_id
```

The set of object-level functions would be

```
public function string fu_get_fname ()
public function string fu_get_lname ()
public function string fu_get_phone ()
public function string fu_get_full_name ()
public function integer fu_set_fname (string as_lname)
public function integer fu_set_lname (string as_fname)
public function integer fu_set_phone (string as_phone)
private function string fu_build_full_name ()
public function integer fu_set_id (string as_id)
public function string fu_get_description ()
```

This would create the same functionality as the `u_employee` class. The advantage of using inheritance is the reusability of the parts that are in common with `Person` and `Employee`. We would not have to redefine the 90% that had already been defined in the `u_person` class. Another benefit is, that if other fields are added to the `Person` class later, such as address, city, state, and zip, the `Employee` class would then automatically gain these attributes. Note that changes would also be inherited. If the length of the `first_name` attribute in the `Person` class is changed, it will also change in the `Employee` class. If new functions are added to the `Person` class, the `Employee` class also gains these functions. If corrections or extensions are made to the `Person` functions, these changes are also inherited in the `Employee` class. Also note that the `Employee` class gains from all the testing that has already been done with the `Person` class, and will therefore be more robust.

You can add elements to the descendant class, and you can override behavior (as demonstrated), but you cannot delete members (variables or functions) from the ancestor when you define a descendant class. This is a fundamental concept of inheritance. It is important to design the classes so that only the elements that are truly in common with all the descendants are placed in the base class.

It would also be possible to create new classes that are inherited from `Employee` and from `Person`, creating an inheritance hierarchy for the classes:

```
Person
     — Employee
          — SalesRep
     — Friends
          — Relatives
```

A class may serve as the source for multiple descendants. In some object-oriented languages, it is possible to create a descendant class that is derived from more than one base (ancestor) class. This is called *multiple inheritance*, but it is not supported in PowerBuilder. You may derive a class only from one ancestor class. This avoids the complexity that is introduced by multiple inheritance. Single inheritance is suitable for most cases.

Sharing a base set of objects can save a great deal of time and effort for a development team and can provide a boost to new PowerBuilder developers.

## POLYMORPHISM

*Polymorphism* is another characteristic of object-oriented programming. This features allows a function's behavior to vary with the type of the object to which it is applied. For example, three different classes (`file`, `directory`, and `fileset`) may all have a method named `Delete`. The behavior of that method varies for each of these object types because the rules (the definition) for the delete will need to vary for each.

An example of polymorphism in PowerBuilder is the `fu_get_description` function in the `u_employee` class. Other examples are provided later in this chapter.

## OBJECT-ORIENTED POWERBUILDER

To become a proficient PowerBuilder developer, you must spend some time learning about and using its object-oriented features. These features provide you with reusable objects and better design modularity, while helping to clarify the function and to ease the maintenance of the systems you develop.

PowerBuilder provides support for each of the major tenets of object-oriented programming. PowerBuilder provides classes (and objects), inheritance, and polymorphism.

### PowerBuilder Classes

When you create a new window (e.g., `w_main`), you are actually creating a class (an object type, a new data type). It is very important to understand this point.

When you open the window,

```
open (w_main)
```

you are actually opening an instance (object) of that window. PowerBuilder has created an instance of the object type `w_main` and given it the same name (`w_main`) as the class. Internally, PowerBuilder has generated the following global statement:

```
w_main w_main
```

The first reference in this statement is to the `w_main` class, the window that you defined. The second `w_main` reference declares a window object of type `w_main`. Now, reconsider the `open(w_main)` statement in the following context:

```
w_main w_main
open(w_main)
```

Here, the `w_main` reference in your open function is a reference to the object (variable), not to the class (data type). PowerBuilder hides this declaration to allow beginning PowerBuilder developers to use the system without having to understand object-oriented details., but it does confuse the terminology (specifically the use of the word *object*), in the PowerBuilder system.

Now that you understand that `w_main` is a class, you could declare your own instances of it as follows:

```
w_main w_main1, w_main2
open(w_main1)
open(w_main2)
```

Notice that `w_main` is used as the data type for the `w_main1` and `w_main2` variables. You could also create instances of a window by creating an array as follows:

```
w_child w_children[10]
int idx
FOR idx = 1 to 10
    open(w_children[idx])
    w_children[idx].x = idx * 100
    w_children[idx].y = idx * 100
NEXT
```

This example creates ten instances of a `w_child` window, cascading the child windows across the parent window. Your sole reference to each window is the `w_children` array. For example,

```
w_children[5].Title = "I'm the 5th w_child window"
```

You can tell if a window is open using the `IsValid` function:

```
IF IsValid(w_children[5]) THEN Close(w_children[5])
```

In the same manner, you can also create instances of any of the predefined object types. These types include:

CheckBox, CommandButton, DataWindow, DropDownListBox, EditMask, Graph, ListBox, MenuItem, MultiLineEdit, Oval, Picture, PictureButton, RadioButton, SingleLineEdit, UserObject, and Window.

All of these object types are part of the system object hierarchy defined by PowerBuilder. You can view the object hierarchy in the browser, as shown in Figure 14.1. Open the browser and select the **System** tab. Then right-mouse click on an object in the left listbox and set the **Show Hierarchy** option in the popup menu to view the PowerBuilder hierarchy.

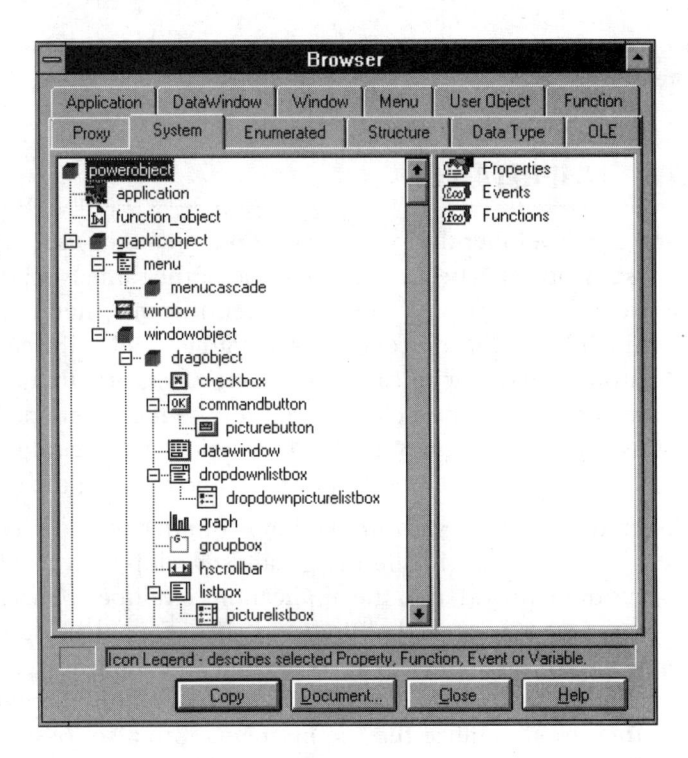

*Figure 14.1 The class browser.*

Use any of these classes as a data type. For example, create a `CommandButton` variable that is assigned the value of an existing command button (`cb_close` in this example). The variable can then be treated as an alias for `cb_close`. This is a fundamental technique. You will use this often, such as when you make references from user objects to other controls in the window (outside the user object):

```
commandbutton cb1
cb1 = cb_close
cb1.text = 'Exit'    // cb_close.text
cb1.enabled = true // cb_close.enabled
```

All of this becomes more important when using the object-oriented features in PowerBuilder.

## WINDOW INHERITANCE

*Inheritance* lets the developer derive a new window, menu, or user object from an already existing object. The ancestor must be of the same type; that is, you can only derive a window from a window, a menu from a menu, and a user object from a user object. The descendant object inherits all of the components of the ancestor object. This includes attributes, variables, structures, functions, events, and script code. The new class specializes the more general base class in some way, usually by adding new items to the object, but it could be limited to modifying the ancestor in some way (such as repositioning the controls).

Most companies involved with sizable PowerBuilder projects have a team of developers who specialize in the design and development of libraries of reusable objects to be provided to the application developers. Sharing a base set of objects can save a great deal of time and effort for a development team and can help to implement standards for PowerBuilder coding and presentation of information. It is usually better to review the current requirements of various projects and then to generalize the requirements into a set of base objects. Sometimes it is possible to create a set of base objects for the most obvious requirements, but it is usually better to create these objects as a direct result of a requirement. Otherwise, you may spend time developing a set of objects that never get used.

Inheritance is one of the features that makes PowerBuilder the leading front-end development tool for developing client/server applications for Windows. You can only use inheritance with windows, menus, and user objects. Any time you create one of these objects, you have the option of using inheritance to derive the object from an existing object rather than starting a new one with the creation of the new object. This gives you a jump-start, since the base (ancestor) object provides a starting point for your new object. Another benefit of inheritance is that it lets you create and promote standards for labels and the presentation of data.

Window inheritance is very useful in this regard. For example, you may create a main window for every application that has the same size and contains some basic controls, such as a command button to close the application. Instead of re-creating this each time, you can create a base window to serve as the ancestor for the descendant windows derived from it. The advantages of this is that you get a window with the attributes, controls, and script code already implemented. To create a new window using inheritance, open the window painter, and select the **Inherit CommandButton** option when you create a new window. When you derive a new window (which I'll call the *descendant* window) from a base window (the parent or ancestor), your new window inherits the attributes, controls, events, and scripts of the base window. Detailed examples are provided throughout this chapter.

## The Snap-to-Grid Option and Inheritance

Be sure to turn on the **Snap to Grid** option. This is essential for inheriting from any visual objects (windows, visual user objects) and is recommended for the following reason: if you move any of the controls on a descendant window, the link between the control in the ancestor and in the descendant will be lost for the position attributes. This means that if the control is moved in the ancestor, its new location will not be passed on to the descendant window. Other attributes of that control, such as the label text or size, will be intact. The connection is lost only for the attributes that you change in the descendent. If you have turned off **Snap to Grid**, it is very easy to accidentally move a control in the descendant window.

You can reestablish the inheritance connection with the original object by selecting the object(s) and selecting the **Edit|Reset Attributes** menu option. To reset the attributes for a descendant window, click on the window and then select the **Edit|Reset Attributes** menu option.

## Updating the Ancestor

In the Window painter, you can only update one level of the hierarchy (one window) at a time. You cannot open an object in a painter if you are editing one of its ancestors (or descendants) in another window. To demonstrate the effect of updating the `w_ancestor` window, do the following exercise. In the `w_main2` window, move the **Close** command button down and to the side. Save the window. Next, open the Window painter for the `w_ancestor` window and move both buttons up an inch or so. Change the label for `cb_close` to **CloseIt**.

Close the window and run the application. You will see the new label, and the `cb_beep` button will be positioned higher in the window. Clearly these changes to the ancestor `w_ancestor` have been applied to the descendants, but notice that the position of `cb_close` is determined by the change you made in `w_main2`. That is because the repositioning in `w_main2` severed the link for the X and Y position of `cb_close`.

### Restoring the Inheritance Link

You can restore the link for the `cb_close` button by resetting its attributes. Do this in the Window painter (for `w_main2`). Click on the **cb_close** button to select it. Then select **Edit|Reset Attributes**. This will place the `cb_close` button back at its original location.

> **NOTE**
> You may wonder when the changes that you make to the ancestor(s) are applied to its descendant(s). The descendant window (`w_main2` in this example) will be updated with any changes that you make to the `w_ancestor` or `w_main` windows. This update occurs when you run the application, edit the `w_main2` window, or build the next application executable. You can explicitly regenerate an object in the Library painter to be sure it is up-to-date.

## Menu Inheritance

You can use inheritance with menus, but this feature is rather limited in PowerBuilder. You can only make additions to the end of the menu bar, add new menu items at the end of each dropdown menu, or insert items at one position in an existing menu. You can override items on a menu, but in general, inheritance is more limited for menus than windows.

For this example, a simple menu is created. The items for the menu bar are: File, Test, and Help. For the Test dropdown menu, add the menu items shown in Figure 14.2.

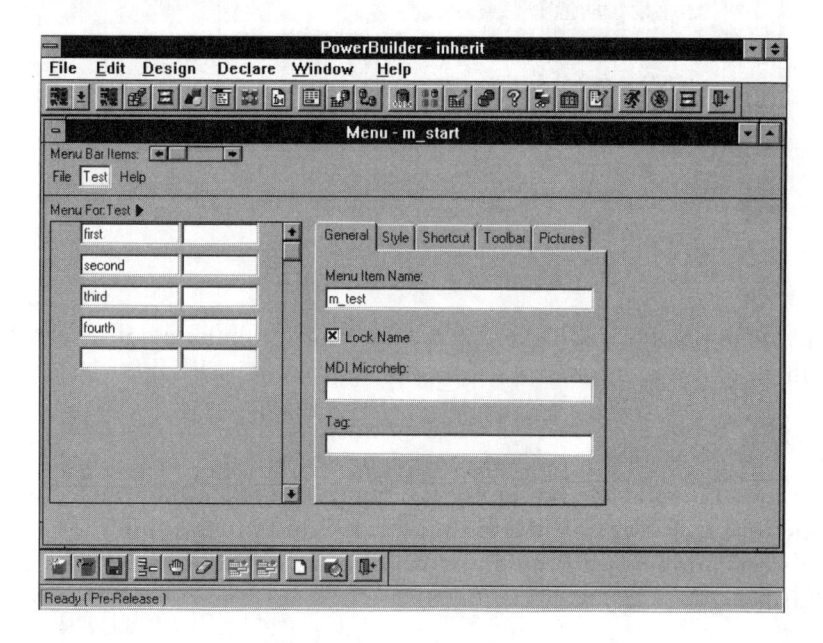

*Figure 14.2  Menu* m_start.

Save the menu as m_start and close the Menu painter. Next, create a new menu, m_start2, as a descendant of the m_start menu. Click on the **Inherit** command button shown in Figure 14.3. Select the m_start menu in the dropdown listbox.

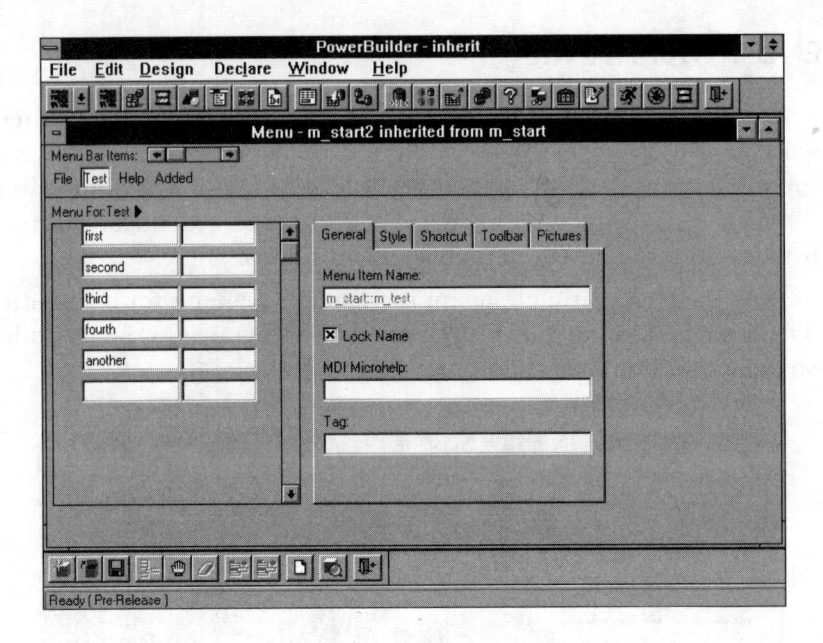

*Figure 14.3 Menu* m_start2.

In the Menu painter, disable and make the "third" menu item invisible. Add a statement to this menu item's script to beep when it is clicked:

```
beep(1)
```

Add a menu item at the bottom of the menu and label it another. Now save the menu as m_start2. Add it to your window and run the application. Select the **Test** menu bar option to pull down the menu. Notice the missing third item (see Figure 14.4).

# Inheritance 563

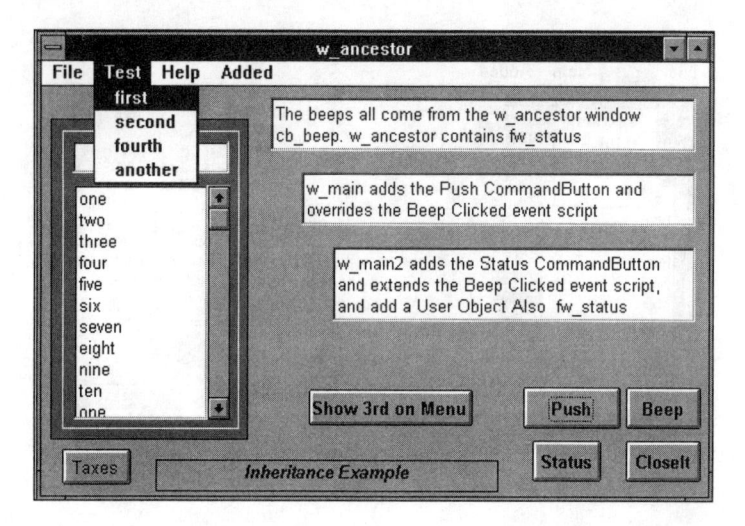

*Figure 14.4  Our example menu.*

Close the application and add a command button to the `w_main2` window. Label the button **Show Third** and add the following code to the `Clicked` event for the button:

```
m_start2.m_test.m_third.show ( )
m_start2.m_test.m_third.enable ( )
```

These lines of code will make the third item visible and then enable it. Run the application again. Check the Test menu as you did before. Now click on **Show Third** and check the menu again. The third menu item appears. Using this technique, you can control the menu dynamically at run time (Figure 14.5).

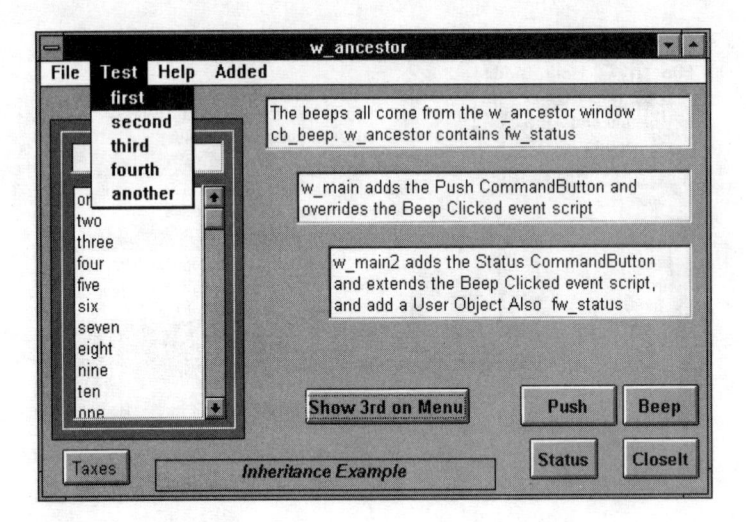

*Figure 14.5  Dynamically changing the Test menu.*

## USER OBJECT INHERITANCE

Inheritance is very useful with user objects. In the chapter on user objects, several versions of the U_DW_NAV user object were created. It would have been better to have used inheritance to create the successive versions, since the variations used most of the components of U_DW_NAV.

For the first example of user object inheritance, the user object that appears in Figure 14.6 will be added. For this example, use the U_LB_WITH_SEARCH user object that was developed in the previous chapter as the ancestor. (This user object can also be found in the **SHARED.PBL** library). The only changes made to the descendant user object are the addition of ten items to the listbox. To create the new user object, click on the **User Obj** icon on the PowerBar. This opens the Select User Object dialog box (Figure 14.18). In this dialog box, click on the **Inherit** command button.

In the Inherit From User Object dialog box, select the library and the U_LB_WITH_SEARCH user object as the ancestor (Figure 14.7).

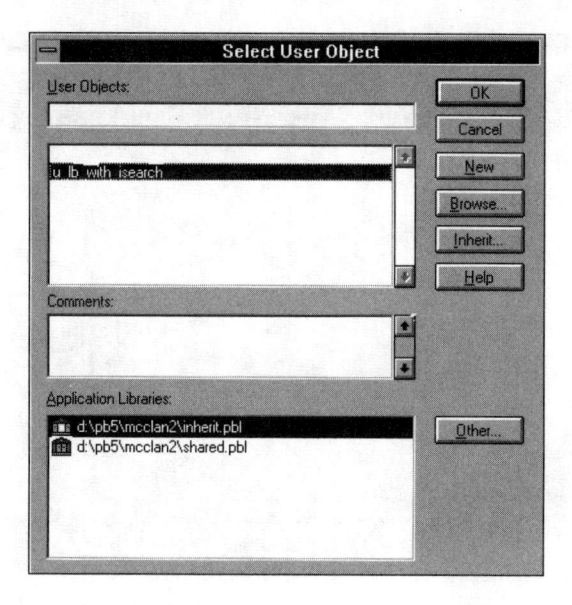

*Figure 14.6* Create a new user object with inheritance.

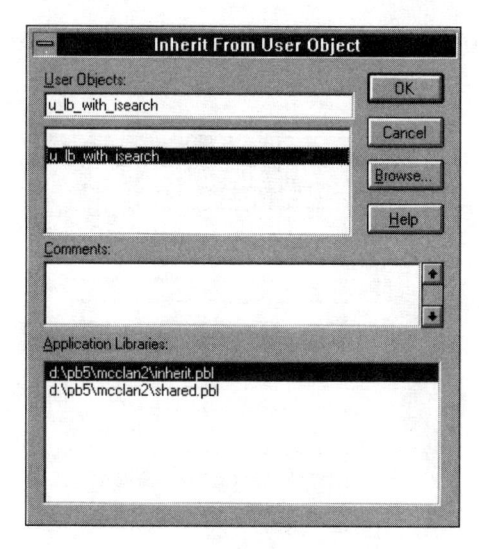

*Figure 14.7* The Inherit From User Object dialog box.

This opens the User Object painter (Figure 14.8).

**566** Chapter 14

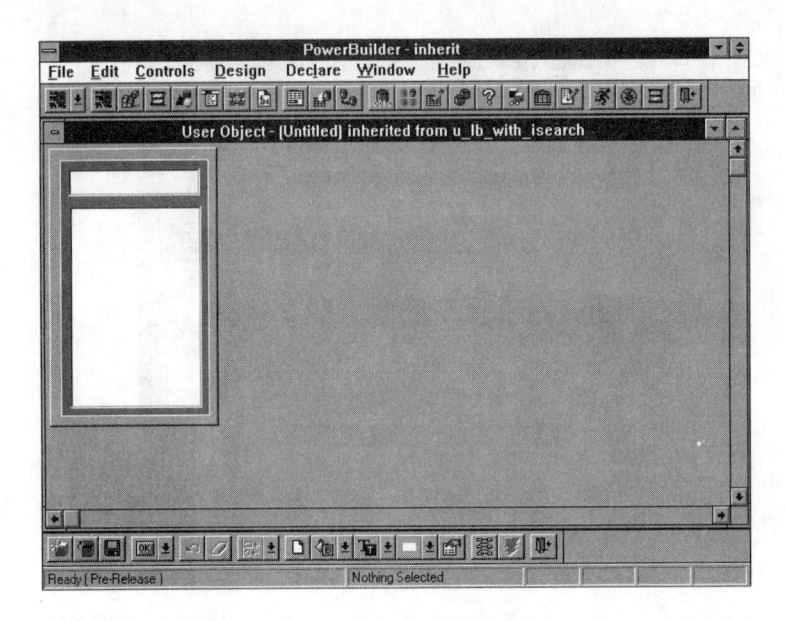

*Figure 14.8  The new user object.*

In this painter, double-click on the **ListBox** control to open the Style dialog box (Figure 14.9).

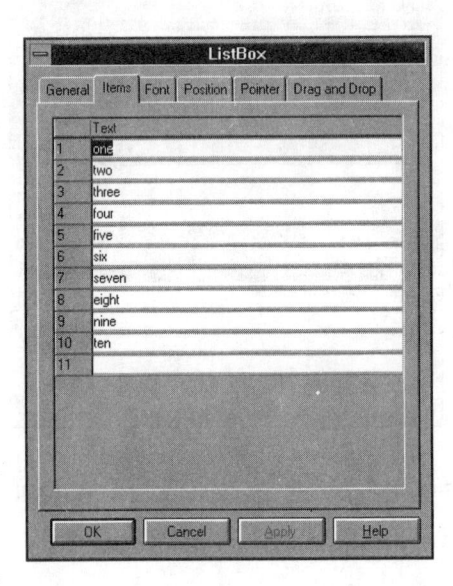

*Figure 14.9  The ListBox style dialog box.*

In the items listbox, add the numbers one through ten, as shown in Figure 14.21. Use the **Ctrl+Enter** key combination between each item or the **OK** command button will be clicked by default. Be sure that the **Sorted** checkbox is marked. Save this user object as U_LB_WITH_SEARCH_INITIALIZED, and then add it to your main Application window.

If you would like to work further with user object inheritance, go back to the U_DW_NAV user object and build user objects U_DW_NAV_VERTICAL and U_DW_NAV_WITH_CLOSE user objects based on inheritance.

## MDI INHERITANCE

MDI applications are often more complex, requiring more design and forethought, and often employ inheritance throughout its core objects, windows, and menus. MDI menus are usually inherited from an ancestor, such as m_mdi_ancestor, to give a base set of menu items to all descendant menus. From this m_mdi_ancestor, I often create two immediate descendants: The first is m_frame, and it serves as the menu for the frame. The second is m_sheet_ancestor, which adds a toolbar and serves as the ancestor for the menus created for the MDI sheets.

The MDI application usually has an ancestor sheet that contains the processing that is in common with all sheets. This usually involves code in the Open event to accept the window open parameters that are passed in from the frame window using the OpenSheetWithParm function. Other events that coded in the ancestor sheet include the activate, close query, and perhaps resize. Often there are instance variables to track the current state, or user-defined events to trigger certain common functions (DataWindow retrieval, etc.).

For example, let's consider the MDIAPP application. In that example, we actually created two menus m_mdi_frame and m_mdi_sheet. m_mdi_sheet was based on a copy of m_mdi_frame, and then we added menu items for the sheets. Obviously, you now know that inheritance would be a better method, since any changes made to the m_mdi_frame menu would also apply (automatically) to m_mdi_sheet.

In the **SHARED.PBL**, you will find the m_mdi_ancestor menu. Create a new menu and inherit it from m_mdi_ancestor. Save it as m_frame. Create another menu and inherit it from m_mdi_ancestor. Save this one as m_sheet_ancestor.

In the **SHARED.PBL**, you will find a window, w_ma_sheet. This is an ancestor for all the sheets in the MDI application.

The example library **MDIAPP2.PBL** has an application based on these objects. Look at this for a model of how to use inheritance in MDI applications.

# APPENDIX A

# The PowerScript Language

This Appendix contains more details on the PowerScript language.

## Data Types

### Boolean

The Boolean data type represents a logical condition. A variable of the Boolean data type can only have one of two values: TRUE or FALSE. Since PowerScript is case-insensitive, you could enter the value as true, false, True, False, etc. Boolean identifiers should begin with the letter b, such as b_first_time or bFirstTime.

## Integer (or Int)

Integers are 16 bit signed whole number values in PowerScript. This means that an integer can hold a value from −32768 to +32767. Integer identifiers should begin with the letter i. For example, i_value or i_count.

## UnsignedInteger (or UInt)

The unsigned integer is a 16 bit unsigned whole number value. It can range in value from 0 to 65535. Unsigned integer identifiers should begin with the letters ui, such as ui_size or ui_size.

## Long

A long integer is a signed 32 bit whole number value. It can hold values from −2,147,483,648 to +2,147,483,647. Long identifiers should begin with the letter l, such as l_size or lSize.

## Unsigned Long (or ULong)

An unsigned long is a 32 bit unsigned whole number. It can hold values from 0 to 4,294,967,295. Unsigned long identifiers should begin with the letters ul, such as ul_size.

## Decimal (or Dec)

The decimal type is a signed number with a decimal point such as _12.123. It has a maximum of 18 digits. To declare a decimal variable, include the number of post-decimal digits in the declaration. For example, to declare an array of five decimal variables that have 2 post-decimal digits, use the following declaration:

```
dec{2} money[5]
```

Decimal identifiers should begin with the letters dec, such as dec_cost.

## Real

The real data type is a signed floating point number, such as 2.2E4. A real has a precision of 6 digits and a range of 1.17E-38 to 3.4E38. Rounding error will effect this type. Real identifiers should begin with the letter r, such as r_total.

## Double

The double is a signed floating point number with 15 digits of precision. It has a range of 2.2E-308 to 1.7E308. Double identifiers should begin with the letter d, such as dValue or d_value.

## Date

The date data type takes the format YYYY-MM-DD, such as 1994-12-31. Date identifiers should begin with the letters date, such as date_start.

## Time

Time is formatted as HH:MM:SS:mmmmmm, such as 14:30:01:123456. Time identifiers should begin with the letter t, such as t_start.

## DateTime

The DateTime data type has a format that combines the date and time into one value. It is most often used to read or write to the database. Use the function DateTime(date, time) to combine a date and time into a DateTime variable. Use Time(datetime), and Date(datetime) to convert a DateTime variable to a time or date data type respectively. DateTime identifiers should begin with the letters dt, such as dt_timestamp.

## Blob

The blob is a binary large object of up to 4,294,967,295 bytes in size. Blobs can contain any binary data, such as images, program files, or text. Blob identifiers should begin with the letters blb, such as blb_image or blb_image.

You can specify a size for a blob variable when you declare it. If you do not specify a size, then PowerBuilder will decide its size when you assign a value to it.

```
Blob{32000} blb_document1
Blob blb_image1
```

The first example declares a blob with a length of 32,000 bytes. If you assign longer text to that blob, it will be truncated. The second declaration causes PowerBuilder to define the size when you assign a value to blb_image1. There are functions to manipulate the contents of a blob, which are covered later in this chapter.

## Char

The char data type is a single ASCII character. You can have an array of type char, but in general you will use the string data type instead. Use the char array when you need to parse the array. Char identifiers should begin with the letter c, such as c_char1 or c_char1.

## String

The string data type is an array of ASCII characters (60,000 maximum). String identifiers should begin with the letter s, such as s_name or s_name.

String literals can use either single or double quote marks for delimiters. This is useful for including quote marks within the string, i.e. 'She said "Yes," before I asked'. String literals have a limit of 1024 characters. You can assign a string literal to a string variable.

PowerBuilder provides a number of functions for string manipulation. If you assign a string to a char variable, only the first character of the source is assigned to the target. You can assign a string to a char array, and you can assign a char array to a string. If the char array is bounded with a size smaller than the length of the string, the text will be truncated.

Strings can be concatenated using the plus sign:

```
string s_full_name  = s_first + ', ' + s_last
```

String comparisons are done directly by using the relational operators:

| | |
|---|---|
| = | equality |
| <> | not equal |
| > | greater than |
| >= | greater than or equal |
| < | less than |
| <= | less than or equal |

```
IF s_text = 'abc' THEN ...
IF s_last_name > 'M' THEN ....
```

You can use a character or character array in any function instead of a string. PowerBuilder will promote the char (or char array) to a string in the process.

## Using Special ASCII Characters

You can assign special characters, such as the backspace, to a char variable by using the following set of codes (the tilde [~] is used as a marker).

| | |
|---|---|
| ~n | newline |
| ~t | tab |
| ~v | vtab |
| ~r | return |
| ~f | formfeed |
| ~b | backspace |
| ~" | quote |
| ~' | tick |
| ~~ | tilde |

You can also assign a value by entering the numeric value for any character by using the tilde.

| | |
|---|---|
| ~256 | decimal |
| ~hFF | hex |
| ~o377 | octal |

## The NULL Value

Since PowerBuilder is primarily for creating database applications, it is necessary for PowerScript to support the NULL value that is used in all relational database systems. A NULL value is not the same as a zero (for integers), and is not the same as a zero length string (for strings). It is a special marker that signifies an UNKNOWN value for a variable. You assign a NULL value to a variable by using the function SetNull(). You test for a NULL value by using the IsNull() function.

```
SetNull(s_company)
b_test = IsNull(s_company)
```

When you read data in from a database it is possible to read in NULL values, you must use the IsNull function to test for that value.

## The Any Data Type

PowerBuilder has added the Any data type which is a flexible type that will take on the data type of the value that is assigned to it. Any type variables can also hold structures., objects, and arrays.

```
any a_value, a_value2, a_value3
string s_text, s_type

a_value = 123.4
a_value2 = 44.3
a_value3 = a_value + a_value2
s_type = ClassName(a_value) //'decimal'
a_value = 'hello'
a_value2 = ' there'
a_value3 = a_value + a_value2
s_type = ClassName(a_value) //'string'
s_text = a_value
```

This examples shows the a_value variable with the any data type. After the first assignment, the data type (shown in s_type) would be decimal, later it is string. Use the ClassName function to determine the data type.

When you use PowerScript operators with Any type variables, the data types much match. In the previous example, you could not add a decimal to a string.

The Any data type is useful, but because of the extra overhead involved in processing and error checking, you should avoid the unnecessary use of this data type.

## DECLARING CONSTANTS

You can add the keyword CONSTANT to any variable declaration to define a constant value. This value is evaluated at compile time, rather than at run-time. The value is fixed for the entire application. You can not reassign the value of a constant in your program code. The standard convention is to use uppercase names for constant variables. Constant variables also have scope (global, shared, instance, or local). Use constants to see limits and parameters, for example:

```
CONSTANT integer MAX_WINDOWS 15
```

This example declares MAX_WINDOWS to be a constant integer with a value of 15. You can place other declarations in your code such as:

```
Window win_array[MAX_WINDOWS]
```

This is the way to define arrays sizes and other limits that you may wish to change in the future. In this way, you can simply change the value assigned in the declaration.

## THE PRONOUN RESERVED WORDS

PowerBuilder has 4 special keywords that are used to make a reference to an object without having to specifies its name. This will allow you to build more robust code with greater reusability.

- This—used for a reflexive reference to the object itself (window, control, or user object).
- Parent—refers to the window that owns or contains the object making the reference.
- ParentWindow—this is a reference from a MenuItem referring to the window to which it is attached.
- Super—refers to the ancestor script.

## This

Use the reserved word This to make a reflexive reference. It is a reference to the object itself (such as a window, control, MenuItem, or user object).

For example, assume that you have a CommandButton labeled "Close Cursor." The purpose of the CommandButton is to close a database cursor after performing a number of fetches against it. In the script for the Clicked event for this CommandButton, you would close the cursor. You could also disable the Close Cursor CommandButton in this script since the cursor could not be closed again (until it was reopened). This is done in the next example; the Open Cursor CommandButton is also enabled. The Close Cursor CommandButton Clicked event would contain the following lines:

```
//in cb_close_cursor clicked event
Close Cursor1;
This.enabled = False        // cursor is closed so
// disable this button
cb_open_cursor.enabled = True // enable that button
```

The second line (This.enabled = False) is equal to:

```
cb_close_cursor.enabled = False
```

## Parent

The reserved word Parent is used most often in the script for an object that is contained in a window. In this case, Parent is a reference to the containing window and is the same as using the name of the window. The object could be a control, such as a CommandButton, a ListBox, or a RadioButton. One of the most common uses is in a CommandButton labeled "Close" placed on a window to close the window. For example:

```
//cb_close Clicked event
Parent.title = "Good-bye"
Close(Parent)
```

The first statement changes the title of the window to "Good-bye" (if only briefly). The second statement closes the window that contains the Close CommandButton. If the window's name was w_main, the statement is the same as the following:

```
w_main.title = 'Good-bye'
Close(w_main)
```

The advantage of using the Parent reserved word is that the same button and code could be used for windows with different names. Another advantage is that it clearly expresses the relationship between the Close button and the unnamed window that it closes.

## Using Parent in a MenuItem

If you use the Parent reserved word in a MenuItem script, it has a different meaning. In this case, the word Parent refers to the menu (the next higher MenuItem) that contains the MenuItem. You can use this to enable or disable a menu. The reserved word This can be used to check or uncheck the MenuItem.

```
This.Checked = True
Parent.Disable( )
```

This example checks the current MenuItem and disables the next higher MenuItem.

For a cascading menu, the following disables the next higher MenuItem and also unchecks it:

```
Parent.Checked = False
Parent.Disable()
```

## Using Parent in a User Object

In a custom user object, the reference Parent (in one of the controls added to the user object) refers to the user object control. This is not really so surprising, the user object control is really a window on which the custom control is built. In a custom user object, you could use the following statements:

```
Parent.enabled = false
Parent.visible = false
```

The first statement disables the entire custom user object, so that none of the controls that it contains can be used.

The second statement hides the user object. If you include the second statement in a normal CommandButton in a window, it makes the window invisible.

If you experiment, you may find that you can use the reserved word Parent with standard user objects, to some degree. In a standard user object (uo_cb) that is based on a CommandButton, the code:

```
this.text = Parent.Class_name()
close(Parent)
```

changes the CommandButton text to the name of the window and then closes the window. This has limited usefulness. The standard user object is actually parented by a "graphicobject" type, which only has two attributes visible and a tag. So these are the only attributes that you can refer to in the scripts for a standard user object (the standard user object's Parent picks up the attributes of a window at run-time).

## ParentWindow

Use the reserved word ParentWindow only in a MenuItem script. In a MenuItem script, ParentWindow is a reference to the window that contains the menu. If window w_main contains menu m_app1, a reference in m_app1 to ParentWindow is like using the name w_main (but with the limitation mentioned in the next paragraph).

In the discussion about the reserved word Parent, an example was given that closed a window with a CommandButton, using the statement Close(Parent). If you want to close a window with a menu option, use the statement:

```
Close(ParentWindow)
```

The ParentWindow reserved word has a limitation. You can not combine it with a control name to access a control's attribute. So the following reference to a CommandButton's enabled attribute is illegal:

```
ParentWindow.cb_test.enabled = False
```

Remember that a MenuItem script is the only place where you can use the ParentWindow reserved word. It is preferred over hard-coding the window name. So instead of the following:

```
w_main_mdi.ArrangeSheets (Cascade!)
```

use:

```
ParentWindow.ArrangeSheets (Cascade!)
```

## Super

Super is a reference used in the script of an inherited object to refer to the script in its immediate ancestor. Super will be discussed in more detail in the chapter on inheritance. Use the keyword as in the following:

```
Call Super::Clicked
```

This example calls the clicked event script in the immediate ancestor of the cb_calculate CommandButton. This is equivalent to the following, more verbose call that does the same thing (assuming the name of the ancestor window is w_ancestor):

```
Call w_ancestor`cb_calculate::Clicked
```

**APPENDIX B**

# Using the Example Applications

This appendix describes the setup process for installing the example files. There is also a discussion about setting up and connecting to the example database (**MCCLAN2.DB**).

## Appendix B

> **NOTE:** You must have already installed Sybase SQL Anywhere with your PowerBuilder installation program before you can use these examples. Most of them use the **MCCLAN2.DB** database.

## THE EXAMPLE APPLICATIONS

The disk that came with this book contains dozens of libraries and other files for the example applications. The example files include a Sybase SQL Anywhere database, **MCCLAN2.DB**, there may also be a **MCCLAN2.LOG** log file. Many of the examples use this database and require that you have installed the Sybase SQL Anywhere database engine and the Sybase SQL Anywhere ODBC driver on your system. If you did not install the Sybase SQL Anywhere database engine, do so before proceeding with the setup of the example applications.

### Run the SETUP Program

Use the **SETUP.EXE** program to copy the files to your local drive and configure ODBC for the example database (**MCCLAN2.DB**). The **SETUP** program must be run from Windows. Start Windows and insert the disk in the disk drive (assumed to be **A:** for this example).

From the Windows File Manager, set the current directory to the disk. Double-click on the **SETUP.EXE** program to begin the installation program. This will install the examples to the directory that you choose. **SETUP.EXE** uses the compressed files in the same directory as **SETUP.EXE**.

The **SETUP** program will present an opening dialog box, as shown in Figure B.1 (Step through the introductry screens).

The setup program will create a directory for the examples, such as **C:\PB5\MCCLAN2**. You may change the destination path for the example files, but it is highly recommended that you use the default. All further references assume **C:\PB5\MCCLAN2** is the installation directory, so adjust these statements according to the actual location you have chosen.

# Using the Example Applications 583

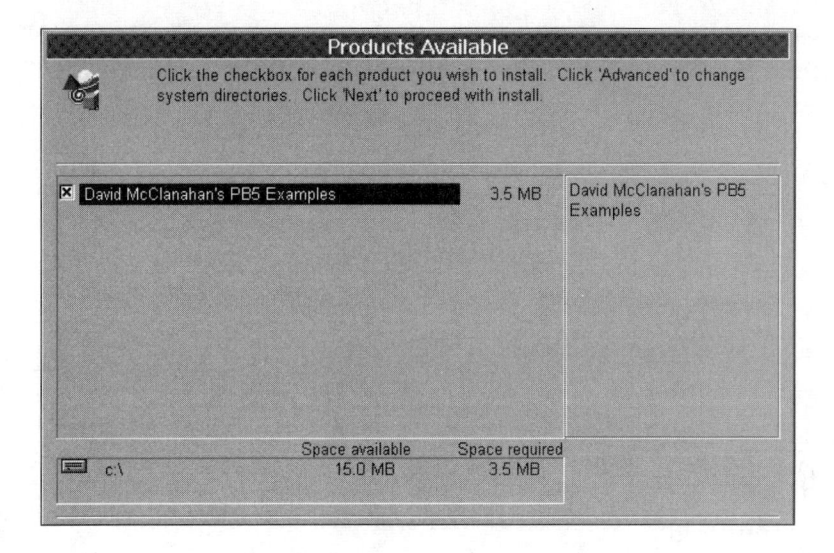

*Figure B.1  The initial SETUP screen.*

**NOTE**  If you are prompted for a disk (with the message "or type the new path"), just enter the drive letter of your floppy drive, such as A: (Figure B.2).

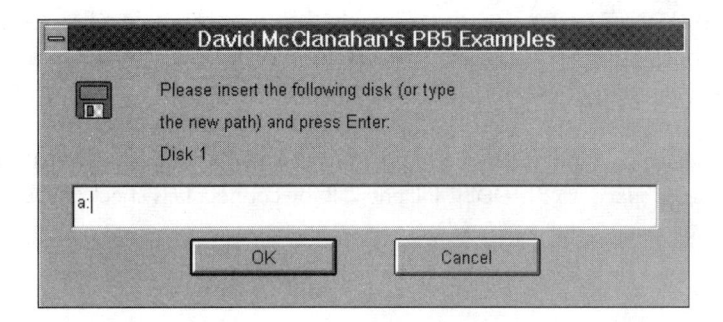

*Figure B.2  A SETUP dialog box.*

Setup will update the **ODBC.INI** file for the example database, **MCCLAN2.DB**. The following lines will be added to the **ODBC.INI** file (but may vary slightly on your system):

```
[ODBC Data Sources]
Mcclan2=Sybase SQL Anywhere 5.0
[MCCLAN2]
Start=dbeng50w
Driver=c:\SQLANY50\WIN\WOD50W.DLL
pwd=sql
uid=dba
databasename=mcclan2
databasefile=C:\PB5\MCCLAN2\mcclan2.db
autostop=yes
```

You may fully qualify the start path as:

```
Start=c:\SQLANY50\WIN\dbeng50w.exe -d -c512
```

The **WOD50W.DLL** will have a different name and path on each platform (such as **WOD50T.DLL**). If you have installed the example file to a directory other than **C:\PB5\MCCLAN2**, the ODBC configuration must match that directory. (You can also edit **ODBC.INI** in a text editor.)

> **NOTE** I have encountered a bug in the PowerBuilder install program that incorrectly adds spaces to the ODBC.INI entry. If the connect fails check ODBC.INI for the following line

```
[ODBC Data Sources]
   Mcclan2=Sybase SQL Anywhere 5.0
```

and change it to the following (just deleted the leading blanks)

```
[ODBC Data Sources]
Mcclan2=Sybase SQL Anywhere 5.0
```

## The PBINI Application

After you have completed the setup for the example files, you should run one of the example programs to complete the process. This application is in the **PBINI.PBL** library, which is in the **C:\PB5\MCCLAN2** directory (or the directory where you installed the example files). If you installed the examples to the default directory (**C:\PB5\MCCLAN2**), you can proceed with this program. Otherwise you may have to adjust the directory entries in the **PBINI.INI** file before running the **PBINI** program. The **PBINI.INI** file is the initialization file that tells **PBINI** where to locate the files it needs during its execution.

### Before Running PBINI

You must verify that the values in the profile file for this application match the directories on your system (only in the `[Dirs]` section). The file is named **PBINI.INI** and will be found in the same directory as the **PBINI.PBL**. (If you installed to the default directory, this file may not any require any changes.)

In **PBINI.INI**, set the `DIRS` values as follows:

+ Set the `PB5` value to point to the directory containing the PowerBuilder initialization file, **PB.INI**.
+ Set both `LOCAL` and `BASE` to point to the directory where you installed the examples.

For Windows 3.1, the default values are:

```
[DIRS]
PB5=C:\PWRS\PB5
LOCAL=C:\PB5\MCCLAN2
BASE=C:\PB5\MCCLAN2
[DBMS]
dbms=Sybase SQL Anywhere 5.0
```

For Windows NT, the default values are:

```
[DIRS]
PB5=C:\PWRS\PB5i32
LOCAL=C:\PB5\MCCLAN2
BASE=C:\PB5\MCCLAN2
[DBMS]
dbms=Sybase SQL Anywhere 5.0
```

The DBMS section contains a value that specifies the DBMS. This will be Sybase SQL Anywhere 5.0 for these examples and will only require a change for a later release of the DBMS.

Once you have reviewed and/or edited the **PBINI.INI** settings, you can run the PBINI program.

### Run the PBINI Program

Start up PowerBuilder and run the **PBINI** application. To run this application, click on the **Application** icon on the PowerBuilder toolbar (shown circled on the PowerBar in Figure B.3).

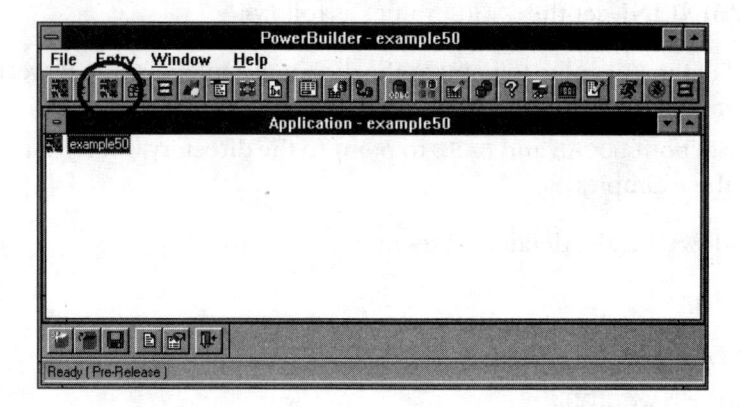

*Figure B.3* Click the **Application** icon on the PowerBar.

This will open the Application painter. Select **File|Open**, then select the **PBINI.PBL** file in the Select Application Library dialog box (Figure A.4) and click **OK**.

## Using the Example Applications 587

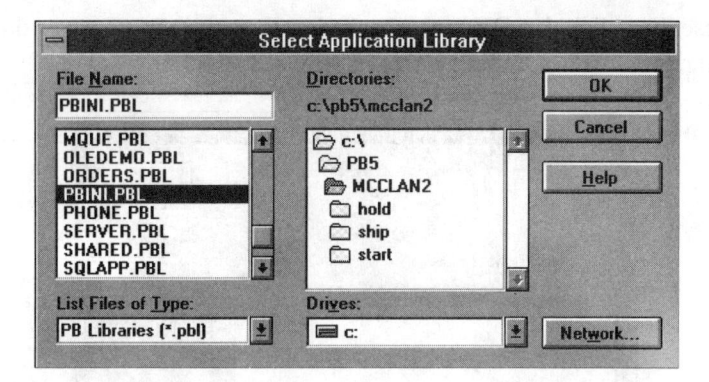

*Figure B.4  Select the **PBINI** application.*

In the Select Application dialog box, select **pbini** (Figure B.5) and click **OK** (this will open the application).

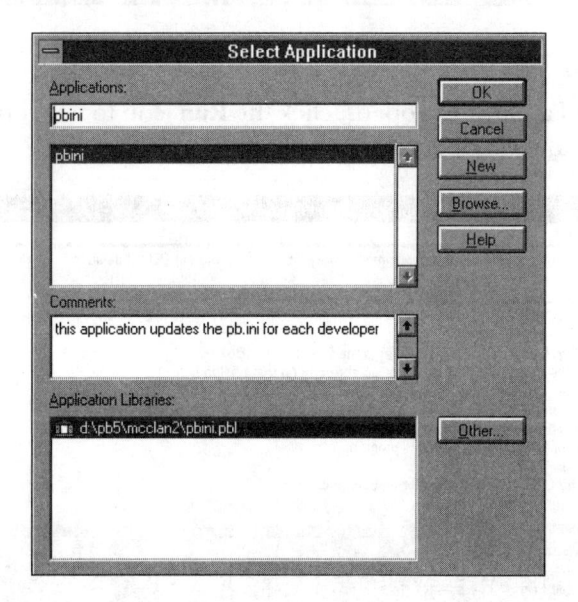

*Figure B.5  To open the **PBINI** application.*

It is possible that the Migrate Application dialog window may open, as shown in Figure A.6. If so, this means that you are working with a version of PowerBuilder 5 that was released later than the version that created the example applications.

## Appendix B

In this case, just click the **OK** button to bring the application up to date. If this dialog window does not appear skip this step.

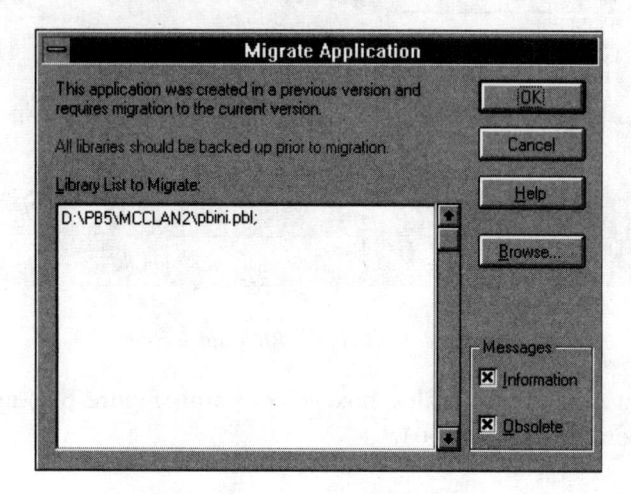

*Figure B.6* To migrate the application.

After the PBINI application opens, click the **Run** icon to begin the application. The main window will open, as shown in Figure B.7.

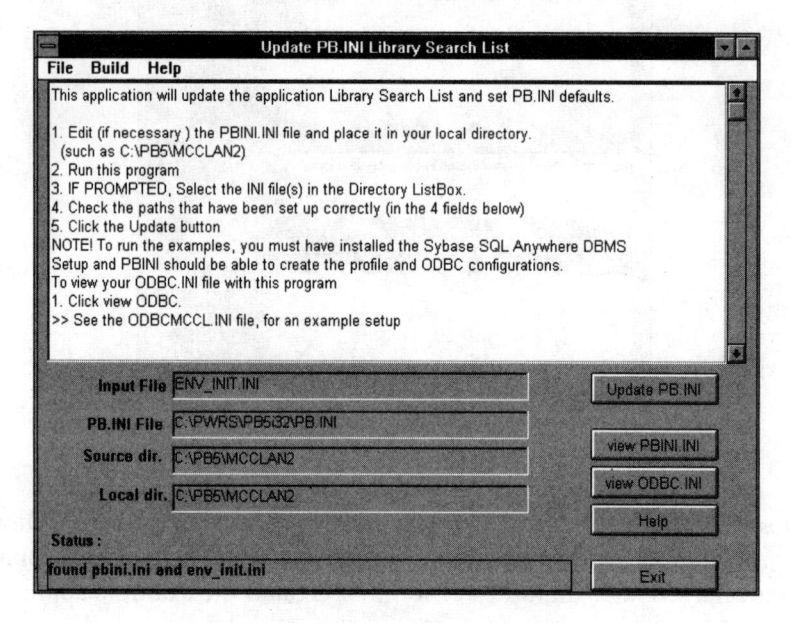

*Figure B.7* The PBINI application.

## Using the Example Applications 589

In the window, you will see the following:

- A `MultiLineEdit`—this displays Help information and INI file entries.
- Four parameter fields—these fields display the input file that will be used to update the **PB.INI**, and the directory locations for **PB.INI** and the **Source** and **Local** directories.
- Status—a `SingleLineEdit` field at the bottom displays status information.
- `CommandButtons`—these buttons are described in the next list.

In the window, you will see the following buttons:

- **Update PB.INI**—click this to update the **PB.INI** file for the example applications.
- **view PBINI.INI**—click this to display the **PBINI.INI** profile settings. These values determine the values of the directory fields on this winow.
- **view ODBC.INI**—click this to see the **ODBC.INI** settings that apply to the example database (**MCCLAN2.DB**).
- **Help**—this redisplays the original text in the multiline edit.
- **Exit**—closes the application.

Check the four parameter fields at the bottom of the window. The *input file* is a file that contains information that will be inserted into your **PB.INI** file. The **PB.INI** file will be in the same directory as the PowerBuilder 5 executable. The **Source** and **Local** directories should be set to the target directory that you selected during the install process (**SETUP.EXE**). When you are sure that the references are correct, click the **Update PB.INI** button.

The PBINI application will back up the **PB.INI** file (to **PB.WAS**), so you may restore the **PB.INI** file if an error should occur. After the backup file is created, the application will update the **PB.INI** file [Application] section for the examples. This application will also add the **MCCLAN2** database profile to your **PB.INI** file. The following is the **MCCLAN2** profile:

```
[PROFILE MCCLAN2]
DBMS=ODBC
Database=
```

```
UserId=
DatabasePassword=
LogPassword=
ServerName=
LogId=
Lock=
DbParm=Connectstring='DSN=MCCLAN2'
Prompt=0
```

This just says that the **Mcclan2** profile uses ODBC and should use the ODBC DSN (data source name) **MCCLAN2** (found in the **ODBC.INI** file). At this point, the installation is complete. For these changes to take effect you must exit and restart PowerBuilder.

To test the installation, run the **IMAGEDB** application in the **IMAGEDB.PBL** library. You will see the status field text change from `Connecting to database ...` to `Connected` if everything is working. If you receive an error message, the connection was not successful. In that case, go through the next sections to correct the problem, or use PowerBuilder to setup the ODBC configuration and the PowerBuilder database profile.

## Viewing the ODBC Configuration

You may also use the **PBINI** application to display the **ODBC.INI** references to the **MCCLAN2.DB** database. To do this, click on the **view ODBC.INI** button.

> **NOTE** If the program cannot find the **ODBC.INI**, it will prompt you to select the **ODBC.INI** file in the Open File dialog box. You will find this file in your main **WINDOWS** directory, such as **C:\WINDOWS** or **C:\WINNT35**.

You should see a display similar to the one in Figure B.8 (for Windows 3.1) or B.9 (for Windows NT).

```
----ODBCINST.INI-----
[Sybase SQL Anywhere 5.0]
Driver=C:\SQLANY50\WIN\WOD50W.DLL
-----ODBC.INI-----
[ODBC Data Sources]
Mcclan2=sybase sql anywhere 5.0
[MCCLAN2]
autostop=yes
databasefile=c:\pb5\mcclan2\mcclan2.db
databasename=mcclan2
driver=c:\sqlany50\win\wod50w.dll
pwd=sql
start= dbeng50w
uid=dba
```

*Figure B.8* Viewing the ODBC configuration in Windows 3.1.

```
----ODBCINST.INI------
[Sybase SQL Anywhere 5.0]
Driver=C:\SQLANY50\win32\WOD50T.DLL
-----ODBC.INI-----
[ODBC 32 bit Data Sources]
Mcclan2=Sybase SQL Anywhere 5.0 (32 bit)
[MCCLAN2]
UID=dba
Start=dbeng50
PWD=sql
Driver32=C:\SQLANY50\win32\WOD50T.DLL
DatabaseName=MCCLAN2
DatabaseFile=c:\PB5\MCCLAN2\MCCLAN2.DB
AutoStop=yes
```

*Figure B.9* Viewing the ODBC configuration in Windows NT.

## Using PBINI to Configure the ODBC

You may also use the PBINI application to configure the **ODBC.INI** file for the **MCCLAN2.DB** database. To do this, be sure that the **PBINI.INI** file is set up properly (as described earlier). You must also check that the **ODBCM-CCL.INI** file is properly set up (found in the **examples** directory).

## Appendix B

**PBINI** uses the **ODBCMCCL.INI** file to initialize the **ODBC.INI** file. Review the **ODBCMCCL.INI** entries before you configure ODBC with the **PBINI** program.

The **ODBCMCCL.INI** file contains the following for Windows 3.1:

```
[mcclan2]
Start=dbeng50w
Driver=c:\SQLANY50\Win\WOD50W.DLL
pwd=sql
uid=dba
databasename=mcclan2
databasefile=LOCAL\mcclan2.db
autostop=yes
[ODBC Data Sources]
Mcclan2=Sybase SQL Anywhere 5.0
```

The **ODBCMCCL.INI** file contains the following for Windows NT:

```
[mcclan2]
start=dbeng50
driver32=c:\SQLANY50\win32\wod50t.dll
pwd=sql
uid=dba
databasename=mcclan2
databasefile=LOCAL\mcclan2.db
autostop=yes
[ODBC 32 bit Data Sources]
Mcclan2=Sybase SQL Anywhere 5.0 (32 bit)
```

Adjust the paths for the Start and Driver entry if necessary before updating the ODBC.INI file with this application. When everything is correct, right-mouse click on the view ODBC.INI button to perform the update.

## AN ALTERNATE INSTALLATION TECHNIQUE

If you have followed the instructions and you still cannot connect to the **MCCLAN2** database, you can use the following technique to install the examples.

If you are able to connect to the **MCCLAN2** database successfully, skip this section.

### Overview

You must have installed the Sybase SQL Anywhere database engine with the PowerBuilder installation program for this technique to work. The directions in the following section will tell you how to temporarily delete the example database files and create a new **MCCLAN2** database in the **Examples** directory using PowerBuilder's Database painter. Creating a new **MCCLAN2** database in the Database painter will automatically set up the ODBC configuration and the database profile. Once the creation of the new **MCCLAN2** database is completed, you will delete the newly created **MCCLAN2** database files and copy the real database files to your example library. The copy process will place the actual **MCCLAN2** database where you created the temporary database and will use the ODBC settings and PowerBuilder database profile you created in the Database painter.

### Temporarily Delete the Example Database Files

Delete the database files, **MCCLAN2.DB** and **MCCLAN2.LOG** log file (if there is one) from the **Examples** directory (such as **C:\PB5\MCCLAN2**). Check to be sure that you have actually removed the database files (**MCCLAN2.DB** and **MCCLAN2**) from the directory. The file attributes for both files are set to mark these as system files, and Windows will prompt you to be sure that you want to delete them. The directory itself must remain on the drive, so if you deleted the directory in the process, re-create it before proceeding.

## Delete the Old ODBC Data Source

Run PowerBuilder. Go to the Configure ODBC dialog box (via the PowerBar icon). In this dialog box, you must select the appropriate driver for the database (Figure B.10). Our sample database uses the **SYBASE SQL ANYWHERE 5.0** driver, so select that entry in the Installed Drivers list box. If **SYBASE SQL ANYWHERE 5.0** does not appear in the Installed Drivers list box, that is the problem, and you must install the Sybase SQL Anywhere engine using the PowerBuilder installation program.

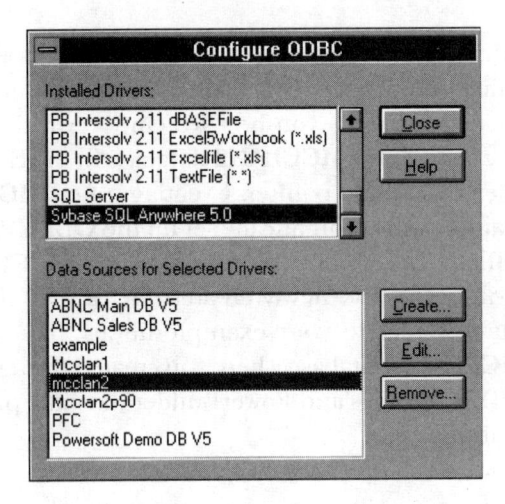

*Figure B.10  The Configure ODBC dialog box.*

After selecting **SYBASE SQL ANYWHERE 5.0**, select **MCCLAN2** in the Data Sources list box. Then click on the **Remove** button. This will delete the old nonfunctional ODBC data source. If **MCCLAN2** does not appear in this list, skip this step and continue with the next. In any case, click on **Close** to exit the dialog box.

## Delete the Old Database Profile

In PowerBuilder, go to the Database Profiles dialog box (via the PowerBar icon) and delete the **MCCLAN2** profile.

In this dialog box (Figure B.11), select the **MCCLAN2** profile and click on **Delete**. This will remove the PowerBuilder **MCCLAN2** database profile from the **PB.INI** file. If **MCCLAN2** is not listed (it may have been deleted by the previous step) in the Profiles list box, skip this step.

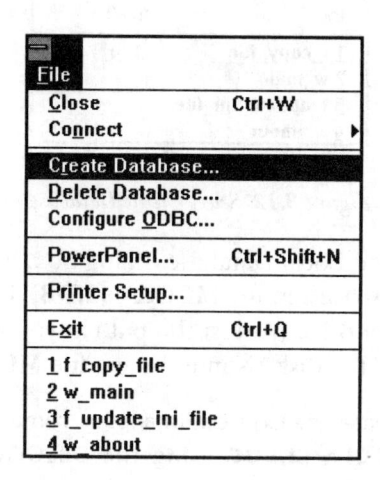

*Figure B.11* The Database Profiles dialog box.

## Create the MCCLAN2 Database

Now you will create a new **Sybase SQL Anywhere** database in the Database painter. This will also create the ODBC data source (**ODBC.INI** configuration) and the PowerBuilder database profile automatically. You are creating an empty database that will be replaced with the example database in the final step of this procedure.

In the Database painter, connect to any database (such as the PowerSoft Demo DB V5 example database), then select **File|Create Database** (Figure B.12).

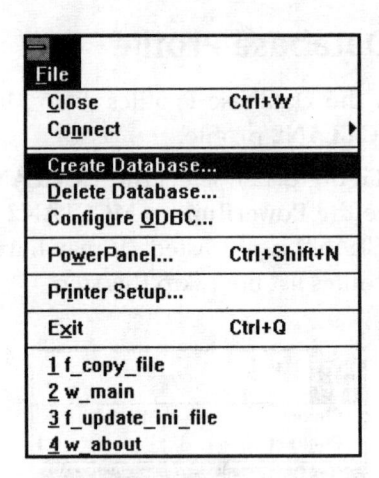

**Figure B.12** *Select Create Database.*

This will open the Create Local Database dialog box. Enter the disk drive letter, full path, and database name (**MCCLAN2.DB**) in the Database Name field, as shown in Figure B.13. (Adjust the path as you wish, but the directory you enter must exist on the disk.) Name the log file **MCCLAN2.LOG**

> **NOTE** If the DBMS creates the log file with another name, such as **MCCLAN2**, then rename it **MCCLAN2.LOG** using the DBLOGW.EXE program in the SQLANY50\WIN directory. For example, use
>
> ```
> DBLOGW.EXE -t MCCLAN.LOG C:\PB5\MCCLAN2\MCCLAN2.DB
> ```
>
> for the command line. Then rename the file in the File Manager.

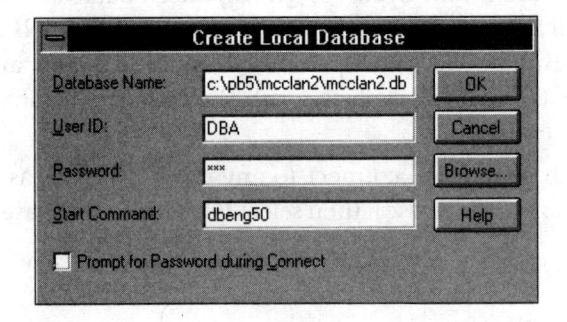

**Figure B.13** *Create the MCCLAN2 database.*

The password for the Sybase SQL Anywhere database is **SQL**. Click **OK** to create the database. If this operation completes successfully, the Database painter will connect to the new **MCCLAN2** database (watch the Database painter status line for this information). When this step is complete, close the Database painter and exit PowerBuilder.

This step will have created the **MCCLAN2** database (for our temporary use), the ODBC data source definition, and the PowerBuilder database profile. All you need to do now is install the example database (only) from the DISKETTE that came with this book.

## Exit PowerBuilder

Now you must exit PowerBuilder and be sure that the Sybase SQL Anywhere database is also closed. If you see the minimized **Sybase SQL Anywhere** icon on the Windows desktop, click on it and select **Close** from the popup menu.

## Delete the Newly Created MCCLAN2 Database Files

Now go to the Windows File Manager and delete the newly created files **MCCLAN2.DB** and **MCCLAN2.LOG** (the log file may have another name such as **MCCLAN2**). Again, check to be sure that they have actually been removed from the **Examples** directory. At this stage, the ODBC configuration and the database profile have been correctly created. Now just copy the example database files (**MCCLAN2.DB** and **MCCLAN2.LOG**) to the **examples** directory from uncompressed sources on the DISKETTE: **\WIN16\FILES** (for Windows 3.1) or **\WIN32\FILES** (for Windows NT and Windows 95).

## Run PowerBuilder

The next time you run PowerBuilder, you will be able to successfully connect to the example database (**MCCLAN2.DB**). This technique will work if you have correctly installed the Sybase SQL Anywhere database engine.

## Run the PBINI Application

Now run the **PBINI** application as described earlier in this appendix.

## AutoStop

You can set an option in the ODBC configuration that will tell the Sybase SQL Anywhere engine to close the database when you exit PowerBuilder. Otherwise, the database remains open (you will see the minimized icon on the desktop after you close PowerBuilder). To set this option, select the **Configure ODBC** icon from the PowerBar. Select **SYBASE SQL ANYWHERE 5.0** for the driver and **MCCLAN2** as the data source. Select the **Edit** option to open the ODBC Configuration dialog box (Figure B.14).

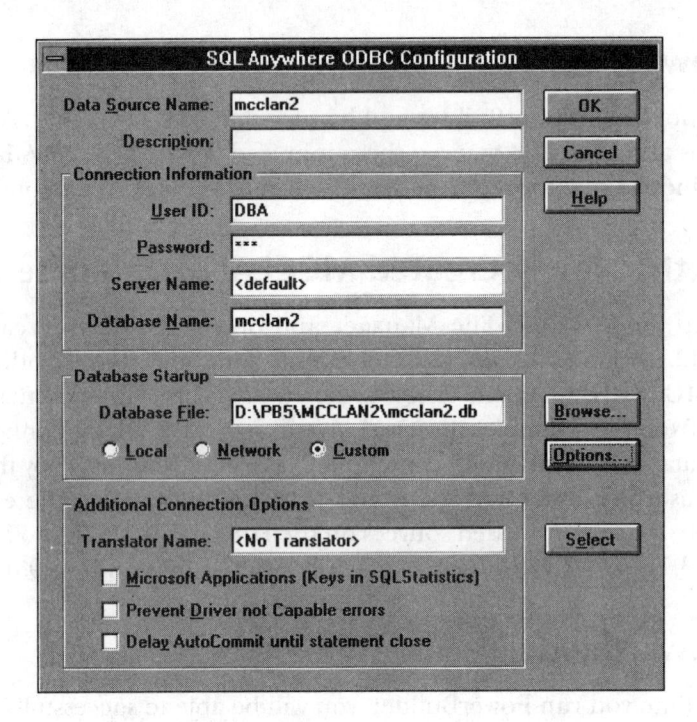

*Figure B.14  The ODBC configuration for the MCCLAN2 database.*

Click on the **Custom** radio button. Then click on the **Options** command button to open the Startup Options dialog box (Figure B.15).

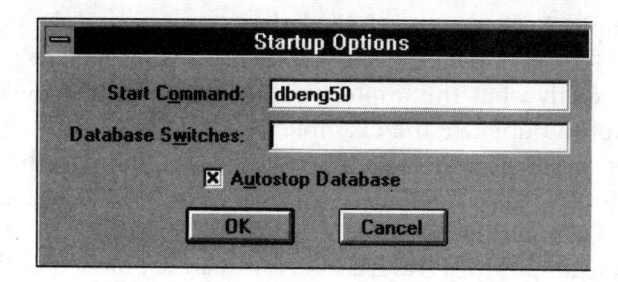

*Figure B.15 The options.*

In this dialog box, click the **AutoStop Database** check box.

## Installing to a Nondefault Directory

If you install the example files to a directory other than **C:\PB5\MCCLAN2**, you will have to make a number of changes to the applications. For example, in the Application Open event for many of the example applications, you may find a reference to an initialization (**INI**) file for the application. Usually, there will be a statement that defines the path and file name, such as:

```
gs_init_file = "C:\PB5\MCCLAN2\IMAGEDB.INI"
```

You will need to modify the path to match the directory where you installed the example files. Some PowerBuilder objects, such as PictureButtons or Picture controls, may also contain the path for the associated **MCCLAN2**. You will need to open the Style dialog box for those objects and modify the path. The setup for the example database may also need to be changed.

The best solution is to accept the default directory for the installation. If you install to a different directory and cannot connect to the database, you can use the alternate installation technique presented in this appendix.

## The Example Applications

All the database examples use a Sybase SQL Anywhere database **C:\PB5\MCCLAN2\MCCLAN2.DB** (and the **MCCLANL.LOG** log file). The **SETUP.EXE** program can set up the ODBC configuration properly in most cases.

The examples have been carefully designed to cover all the essential areas of PowerBuilder development. You should run each example so that you understand exactly what the application does and how it looks. Next you should attempt to duplicate the example application as precisely as possible. Name your versions of each application library the same as the sample, but prefix each library name with the letter z. You are limited to eight-character names in the DOS file system, so you may have to truncate the name by one character. For example, for **FIRSTAPP**, create a library named **ZFIRSTAP.PBL**. Later, if you want to create other versions, you can create a library named **ZFIRSTA2.PBL** and so on. You can name all the objects (including windows and application objects) exactly the same as in the exercise text.

You should be able to create each application from the knowledge you have gained by reading the text and using the PowerBuilder Help system. If you cannot complete the exercise in that manner, open the example application and examine the source code. It would be helpful to print out a listing of each application. You can do this in the Library painter.

Throughout this text, we assume that the path to the sample application is **C:\PB5\MCCLAN2**. If that is not the case (perhaps you placed them in directory **D:\pbsample**), you will have to adjust all references to **C:\PB5\MCCLAN2** accordingly. The **PBINI** application program will allow you to place the example files in any directory.

## A Word about Programming Style

These examples have been coded to demonstrate the important topics as clearly as possible. Occasionally you may notice sections of code that could be optimized, such as:

```
s_text = ProfileString(s_init_file, s_section, s_key, 'notfound')
st_display.text = s_text
```

which could be coded in a single statement as:

```
st_display.text = ProfileString(s_init_file, s_section, s_key, 'not-found')
```

The reason for coding this in two statements is so that you (or students in my classes) can more easily observe the workings of the code in the debugger. The first example allows easy viewing of the result of the ProfileString function.

I generally only allow several lines of code to be placed into a control event (such as a command button's `Clicked!` event). I tend to organize most code into functions and subroutines that are called from the few lines of code that exist in the controls. The code in the controls is limited to manipulating that control and to calling functions. These examples often have all the code in the button that performs a certain action, so you can see the entire section as one function. In practice, it can be difficult to track down code when you have to look through many events in many objects, and structuring the code into functions is necessary. The next step is to extend the use of object-oriented programming and encapsulate the code into classes.

Also note that there is much more code in the example programs that will provide valuable instruction if you look closely at the examples.

# INDEX

## A

abstraction, inheritance, 546
Accelerators
  for window controls
    defining command button accelerator, 153, 154
    SingleLineEdit properties dialog box, 155
  menu item properties, 294, 295
    separator lines, 295
AcceptText, DataWindow controls, 443
adding window controls, 141, 142. *See also* controls, windows
  adding a control to a window, 142, 143
    control button, positioning and sizing, 145
    control status, 145
    Controls List dialog box, 144
    Controls Menu, 142
    design grid, using, 145
    multiple controls, selecting, 144, 145
    selecting controls, 143, 144
    unselecting controls, 144
  aligning controls with alignment function, 146, 147
    Align Controls menu, 147
  automatically sizing controls, 149
    Size Controls cascading menu, 149
    undoing control movement or sizing, 150
  Control Palette, 141
  spacing of controls, adjusting, 148
    Space Controls cascading menu, 148
  working with controls, 142
Align Controls menu, 147
alignment function
  aligning objects, DataWindow, 373
    horizontal alignment, 374
    vertical alignment, 374
  using to align controls, 146, 147
ampersand (&), line continuation, 23
ancestor (inheritance), updating, 560

inheritance link, restoring, 560
Any data type, 574
API, data structure access, 547
application and library, creating
  CONTROL1, 191
  Events2, 232
  FirstWin, 127
  MENUS, 304-306
  SQLApp, 268
Application Error Object, 81, 82
application initialization file, 83, 84
  embedded SQL, 261-264
application-level events, 80-82
application object events, 79
application object properties, 79
application open event, adding code to
  CONTROL1, 193, 194
  Events2, 235
  MENUS, 313
  SQLApp, 270-272
Application painter, 76-78
Application SystemError event, 81
applications, creating PowerBuilder
  Application Error Object, 81, 82
    PowerBuilder Error Codes, 82
  application initialization file
    format, 83
    naming of, 83
    ProfileInt() function, 84
    ProfileString() function, 84
    purpose of, 83
    SetProfileString() function, 84, 85
  application-level events, 80-82
    Application Close event, 80
    Application Idle event, 80, 81
    application object events, 79
    application object functions, 81
    Application Open event, 80
  application object events, 79

603

## Index

application object properties, 79
  dot notation properties, 79
Application painter, 76-78
  application executable, 78
  application objects, 77
  application programs, 77
  described, 76, 77
  PowerBuilder application libraries, 77
Application SystemError event, 81
building applications, 85
  creating new application, 85, 86
  developing the exercise applications, 86
  colors in PowerBuilder applications, 158
    basic color set, 159
    color values, 158, 159
    show invisible, 160
    3D look, 160
  components of, 76
  described, 76
  FirstApp example, 86-98
  Library painter, 99, 100
  properties, events, and functions, 78, 79
arrays, PowerScript language, 28
ASCII character, using special, 573
autoresize height, 404-406

### B

bands, DataWindow painter, 363-366
blob
  data types, 571, 572
  selecting and updating, 280, 281
block comments, nesting, 24
bookmarks, online help, 14
Boolean, data types, 569
breakpoints, adding, 70
  breakpoint status, 71, 72
  Select Script dialog box, 71
Browse Object dialog box, 65
Browse OLE Classes dialog box, 67
Browser dialog box, 63
buttons, 165. *See also* CommandButtons

### C

cascading menus, creating, 290-292
cb_changes clicked field, adding code to, 203
cb_close, 200, 278
cb_commit, 280
cb_connect, 275
cb_count, 276
cb_delete, 279, 280
cb_disconnect, 275
cb_fetch, 277, 278
cb_file_list, 198
cb_insert, 278, 279
cb_load_file, 198
cb_open, 200, 277
cb_rollback, 280
cb_update, 279
cbx_enalbe, 197
changing attributes, window controls, 155, 156
char, data types, 572

CheckBox controls, 180
child window, 483
  creating Windows, 109, 111
  creating in FirstWIn example, 129-131
CHOOSE CASE statement, 36, 37
class, 547
  browser, 557
clear, text editing, 55
color
  colors in PowerBuilder applications, 158
    basic color set, 159
    color values, 158, 159
    show invisible, 160
    3D look, 160
  modifying DataWindow, 379
column attributes, DataWindow painter, 400-418
Column Object Dialog Box, 401
Column Object Position dialog box, 403
column popup menu, 400-402
Column Specification dialog box, 388
column specifications, rows menu, 388
column validation, using, 406, 407
columns, data sources, 342
  computed, 343, 344
Command Button Style dialog box, 151
CommandButtons. *See also* controls, window
  adding to a window, 165, 166
  CommandButton dialog box, 166-168
    opening, 166
  defined, 165
  events, 169, 170
  functions, 170, 171
  properties, listed, 168, 169
comments, PowerScript language
  block, nesting, 24
  multiline, 23, 24
  single-line, 23, 24
COMMIT statement, DataWindow
  controls, 456
complex objects, 217
computed
  columns, data sources, 343, 344
  fields, DataWindow painter, 382-387
constants, declaring, 574, 575
context sensitive
  help, 62, 63
  online, 14
  popup menu
    activating, 15
    availability of, 16
  using, 7
control. *See also* controls, windows
  Accelerators for, 153-155
  attributes, setting, 153
  automatic sizing of, 149
    Size Controls cascading menu, 149
    undoing control movement or sizing, 150
  button, positioning and sizing, 145
  copying to another window, 164
  duplicating, 156, 157

# Index

naming, 151, 152
popup menu options, 163, 164
status, 145
text, setting in a window control, 152
   setting style, 153
working with, 142
Control Properties dialog box, 150
   Command Button Style dialog box, 151
   control attributes, setting, 153
   naming a control, 151, 152
   text, setting in a control, 152
      setting style, 153
CONTROL1, example program, 188-190
CONTROL1, step-by-step, 191.
*See also* window controls
   application and library, creating, 191
   application open event, adding code to, 193, 194
   main window, creating, 191, 192
   running the application, 206
   w_first window, returning to, 195, 196
      cb_close, adding code to, 200
      cb_file_list, adding code to, 198
      cb_load_file, adding code to, 198
      cb_open, adding code to, 200
      cbx_enalbe, adding code to, 197
      ddlb_1, adding code to, 199
      declare str_win_open_parms, 199
      instance variable, adding code to, 196
      pb_beep, adding code to, 197
      RadioButton, adding code to, 199
      window timer event, adding code to, 196, 197
   w_second window, creating, 194, 195
   w_second window, returning to, 200
      cb_changes clicked field, adding code to, 203
      function, adding a, 201, 202
      lb_list other event, adding code to, 204
      open event, adding code to, 201
      p_1 constructor event, adding code to, 203
      sle_insert modified event, adding code to, 202, 203
      sle_isearch other event, adding code, 202
      st_target dragdrop event, adding code to, 204, 205
   window, defining, 192
controls, window, 137-206. *See also* user objects
   Accelerators for, 153-155
   adding controls to a window, 140-150
   changing attributes, 155, 156
   CheckBox controls, 180
   colors in PowerBuilder applications, 158-160
   CommandButtons, 164-171
   Control Properties dialog box, 150-153
   description, properties, events, and functions, 160, 161
   drag and drop, 184-188
   DropDownListBox controls, 175, 176
   DropDownPictureListBox controls, 176
   duplicating controls, 156, 157
   EditMask control, 172, 173
   GroupBox controls, 179
   HScrollBar control, 180
   Line controls, 181
   ListBox controls, 174, 175
   ListView controls, 177, 178
   MultiLineEdit control, 173
   Oval controls, 181, 182
   overview, 137-140
   Picture Controls, 176, 177
   PictureButtons, 171
   PowerBuilder controls and objects, 139, 140
   PowerBuilder units (PBUs), 157
   RadioButton controls, 179
   Rectangle controls, 182
   RichTextEdit control, 174
   RoundRectangle controls, 182
   SingleLineEdit controls, 172
   StaticText controls, 177
   Tab controls, 183
   TreeView controls, 178
   VScrollBar control, 181
   window controls, 161-164
Controls List dialog box, 144
Controls Menu, 142
copy, text editing, 55
criteria prompt, rows menu, 390
cursor operations, SQL statements, 247, 248
cursor SQL statements
   Declare cursor, 251
   Delete cursor, 254
   Fetch cursor, 252, 253
   Noncursor SQL statements
      Delete, 257
      Insert, 255, 256
      Select, 254, 255
      Update, 256
   Update cursor, 253, 254
custom
   class user objects, 538-541
   event, creating, 221-223
   visual user object, 525-538
Customize dialog box, 11
customizing
   toolbars, 8, 11
cut, text editing, 55

## D

data
   abstraction, inheritance, 546
   encapsulation, inheritance, 546
   retrieving, DataWindow controls, 464, 465
   rows menu, 389
   sharing between DataWindows, 156, 457
   source, DataWindows, 330, 331, 332
   types, 27, 569-576
   updating, DataWindow controls, 441, 442
database, using DataWindow controls, 436
database error handling, DataWindow controls, 440, 441
DataStores, DataWindow controls, 470

# 606 Index

datatypes, PowerScript language, 27
DataWindow, introduction, 323-357. *See also*
DataWindow controls; DataWindow painter
  concepts, 323
    DataWindows, importance of, 324
    importing and exporting data, 324
  controls
    described, 325
    differences vs. objects, 327
    relationship within DataWindow, 328
  data sources, 332
    columns, selecting, 342
    computed columns, 343, 344
    External Data Source option, 352
    GROUP BY condition, 347, 348
    HAVING clause, 349
    joins, 335, 341
    ORDER BY clause, 349
    Query Data Source Option, 351
    Quick Select, 333
    Quick Select dialog box, 333, 334
    saving query, 350
    select criteria, 336-338
    sort order, 335, 336
    SQL Select data source option, 339, 340
    SQL Toolbox, 340, 341
    Stored Procedure data source option, 352, 353
    UNIONs, 350
    viewing SQL statement, 346, 347
    WHERE clause criteria, 344, 245
  described, 323
  object
    described, 325
    differences vs. controls, 326, 327
    relationship within DataWindow, 328
  object, creating, 328, 329
    data source, 330-332
    DataWindow creation, 329, 330
    presentation style, 330-332
  presentation styles, 353
    choices for, 353, 354
    dwstyles.pbl, 357
    freeform, 355
    group, 356, 357
    tabular, 355, 356
DataWindow computations vs. DBMS computations, 384-386
DataWindow controls, adding to applications, 425-481. *See also* DataWindow; DataWindow edit control; DataWindow painter adding to a window, 428
    DataWindow control popup menu options, 429
    selecting DataWindow object, 430-433
  COMMIT statement, 456
  database error handling, 440, 441
  DataStores, 470
  DataWindow events, 464
    printing a DataWindow, 466
    retrieving data into, 464, 465
  updating the database, 465, 466
  DataWindow example programs, 471, 472
    DB_INIT.PBL, 474-478
    global functions, 478-481
    requirements, 472-474
  DataWindow Items, 446
    item reference by column name, 448-450
    item reference by column number, 446-448
  DataWindow objects, dynamically assigning, 459
  DataWindow programming, 452, 453
    DeleteRow(), 455
    InsertRow(), 454, 455
    Retrieve(), 453, 454
    Update(), 455, 456
  DataWindows edit control, 442-445
    AcceptText, 443
    ItemChanged event, 445
    ItemError event, 446
    updating rows, 444
  events, 467, 468
  functions, 468-470
  modifying DataWindow object, 433
  Object Browser, 466, 467
  overview, using datawindow controls, 426
    DataWindows with a DBMS source, 426, 427
    DataWindows with an external source, 427
  Reports, 470, 471
  ROLLBACK statement, 456
    filter functions, 459, 460
    find function, 462, 463
    print, 458
    SaveAs function, 457, 458
    sharing data between DataWindows, 156, 457
    sort functions, 461, 462
  setting DataWindow attributes, 434, 435
  Status codes, 451, 452
  transaction object
    data manipulation, 438-440
    defined, 437
    SetTrans, 438
    SetTransObject, 437, 438
  updating data, 441, 442
  using with a database, 436
    connecting to a database, 436, 437
    disconnecting from the database, 437
DataWindow events, 464
DataWindow Items, 446-450
DataWindow Object dialog box, 381
DataWindow objects
  dynamically assigning, 459
  enhancing, 360
DataWindow painter, 359-423. *See also*
DataWindow; DataWindow controls
  bands
    changing design, 366
    described, 363
    detail band, 364
    footer band, 365

## Index  607

group bands, 365, 366
header band, 363, 364
summary band, 364
column attributes, 400
  autoresize height, using, 404-406
  column popup menu, 400-402
  column validation, using, 406, 407
  Display as Picture option, 402, 403
  DropDownDataWindow style, 415-418
  DropDownListBox attributes, 414, 415
  DropDownListBox style, 413, 414
  EditMask style, 410-412
column edit styles, 407, 408
  default edit style, 408-410
computed fields
  adding, 382, 383
  database columns, adding, 387
  DBMS computations vs. DataWindow computations, 384-386
  defining, 383
  predefined calculated fields, 386, 387
enhancing DataWindow objects, 360
  customizing DataWindow presentation, 360-362
  DataWindow report, 361
  designing DataWindow object, 362
groups, creating, 398-400
modifying DataWindow, 367
  adding DataWindow objects, 367
  alignment function, 373, 374
  colors, 379
  objects, selecting with menu option, 368, 369
  positioning objects, 369, 370
  review option, 372, 373
  selecting DataWindow objects, 368
  show ruler option, 371
  sizing objects, 369, 370, 375, 376
  snap to grid option, 371
  spacing of objects, adjusting, 375
  style toolbar, 376-378
  tab order, 380
  using design grid, 370, 371
  zoom option, 272
overview, 360
presentation styles, 418, 419
  freeform, 419-421
  RadioButton style, 412, 413
  tabular, 421, 422
properties, 381, 382
  print specifications, 382
rows menu, 388
  column specifications, 388
  criteria prompt, 390
  data, 389
  filtering and sorting, 391-393
  retrieve, 390, 391
  suppressing repeat values, 393-396
  update properties, 396-398
saving DataWindow object, 367
DataWindow presentation, customizing, 360-362

DataWindow programming, 452, 453
DataWindow Properties dialog box, 430, 434
DataWindow report, 361
date, data types, 571
DateTime, data types, 571
DB_INIT.PBL, DataWindow example programs, 474
  w_main, 474
  wf_db_init, 475, 476
  wf_status_message, 476, 477
DBMS computations vs. DataWindow computations, 384-386
ddlb_1, adding code to, 199
decimal, data types, 570
Declare cursor, 251
Declare menu, PowerScript painter, 58
declare str_win_open_parms, 199
Delete cursor, 254
DeleteRow(),DataWindow controls, 455
descendant classes, 552
description, window controls, 160
design grid
  modifying DataWindow, 370, 371
  using in window controls, 145
Design menu, PowerScript painter, 58
detail band, DataWindow painter, 364
development environment
  displaying text labels in toolbar, 7, 8
  overview, 6
  MicroHelp, displaying, 9
  PowerBuilder Painters, 6, 7
  PowerTips, displaying, 9
Display as Picture option, column attributes, 402, 403
.DLL file extension, 78
DO...LOOP, 37
  forms, 38
dot ini (.INI) file extension, 83
dot notation
  addressing, applications object properties, 79
  syntax, PowerScript language, 24-26
  with instance variables, using
    accessing instance variable externally, 31, 32
    labeling scope in identifiers, 32
    passing variables in function cells, 33, 34
    shared scope, 32
    variable access levels, 32
double, data types, 571
drag and drop
  CONTROL1, step-by-step, 191. *See also* window controls
  application and library, creating, 191
  application open event, adding code to, 193, 194
  main window, creating, 191, 192
  running the application, 206
  w_first window, returning to, 195-200
  w_second window, creating, 194, 195
  w_second window, returning to, 200-206
  window, defining, 192

## Index

described, 184
draggable object attributes, 184
dragged object, 184
functions
　drag, 187
　dragged object, 187, 188
　target object, 184
draggable object attributes, window controls, 184
drop down listboxes, 48, 49. *See also* programming
edit menu, 50
　Paste Function dialog box, 51
Paste Argument, 50
Paste Global, 49
Paste Instance, 49
Paste Object/Window, 50
Paste Shared, 49
Paste SQL, 51
　SQL Statement dialog box, 60
Paste Statement, 52, 53
　Paste Statement dialog box, 52
Select Event, 49
DropDownDataWindow style, column attributes, 415-418
DropDownListBox attributes, column attributes, 414, 415
DropDownListBox controls, 175, 176
DropDownListBox style, column attributes, 413, 414
DropDownPictureListBox controls, 176
duplicating controls, 156, 157
dwstyles.pbl, 357
dynamic menu, 307

### E

edit field control, 172
Edit Group cascading menu, 400
Edit menu, PowerScript painter, 57, 58
Edit Style dialog box, 408
EditMask control, 172, 173
　spin controls, defining, 173
EditMask style
　column attributes, 410-412
　DataWindow painter, 410
　　for a number, 410
　　for a string, 410
Editor Properties dialog box, 61
embedded SQL. See SQL, embedded
embedded SQL statements, 248
entering and editing text. *See also* programming
　cut, copy, clear, or replace, 55
　keyboard shortcuts, 55, 56
　pasting text, 55
　selecting text, 54
enumerated datatypes, PowerScript language, 27, 28
Events1, PowerBuilder application, 208-211
　experiments with, 211, 212
Events2 example program, 231
Events2, step-by-step, 231-243

application and library creating, 232
application open event, adding code to, 235
lb_1, adding another user event, 241
lb_1, adding user event to, 239
lb_1 we_mousemove event, adding code to, 241
main window, creating, 232-234
sle_1 dragdrop event, adding code to, 242
sle_1 modified event, adding code to, 240, 241
ue_add_item event, adding code, 240
ue_init event, adding code to, 237, 238
w_main, adding a function to, 234
w_main open event, 236, 237
w_main window, assign user event, 235, 236
window, adding controls to, 238, 238
events
　creating PowerBuilder applications, 78
　DataWindow controls, 467, 468
　initiating, 229-231
　window controls, 160
events, functions, and user events, 207-243
　Events1, PowerBuilder application, 208-211
　　experiments with, 211, 212
　Events2, step-by-step, 231-243
　Events2 example program, 231
　events-driven programming, 208
　functions and events, initiating, 229-231
　overview, 207
　PowerBuilder events, 212-219
　user events, defining, 219-229
events-driven programming, 208. *See also* events, functions, and user events
　messages, 208
executable, creating, 96, 97
　running from Windows, 98
Exit Script dialog box, 60
exporting text from scripts to DOS, 58, 59. *See also* programming
External Data Source option, data sources, 352

### F

f_extract_directory, global function, 480, 481
f_get_db_section, global function, 478
f_load_sqlca, global function, 479
f_locate_profile, global function, 480
Fetch cursor, 252, 253
File menu, PowerScript painter, 57
File/Toolbars menu option, 8
filter functions, DataWindow controls, 459, 460
filtering and sorting
　DataWindow painter, 391
　　filtering DataWindow rows, 392
　　sorting DataWindow rows, 392, 393
　rows menu, 391-393
find function, DataWindow controls, 462, 463
Find option, online help, 12, 13
FirstApp example, 86, 87
　executable, creating
　　defining executable, 97

Project painter, 97
Select Project dialog box, 96
opening the application, 87, 88
Select Application dialog box, 88
Select Application Library dialog box, 87
run executable from Windows, 98
run the application, 95
running FirstApp, 88-91
code for, 90, 91
step-by-step, 91-95
adding code to close event, 93, 94
adding code to open event, 92, 93, 94, 95
creating application and library, 91, 92
FirstWin example
FirstWin application, 125
running FirstWin, 126
step-by-step
application and library creation, 127
child window, creating, 129-131
code, adding to application open event, 134
code, adding to w_main window, 135
main window, creating, 127, 128
popup window, creating, 131, 132
response window, crating 132-134
running the application, 135
Window Position dialog box, 129
FOR...NEXT loop, 398
footer band, DataWindow painter, 365
frame, MDI, 483
freeform, presentation styles, 355, 419-421
fu_disable (object-level) function, creating, 520
fu_enable (object-level) function, creating, 521, 522
fu_get_state (object-level) function, creating, 522, 523
function
access level, 45
argument list, 44
PowerBuilder events, 217
declarations, 68, 69
return value type, 41
PowerBuilder events, 216, 217
functions. *See also* events, functions, and user events
creating PowerBuilder applications, 78, 79
DataWindow controls, 468-470
initiating, 229-231
window controls, 161
Functions Declaration dialog box, 68
fw_clear, 274, 275
fw_db_status, 273, 274

## G
General Tab dialog box, 104
General (Window Style) dialog box, 108
global functions, DataWindow example programs, 478-481
f_extract_directory, 480, 481
f_get_db_section, 478

f_load_sqlca, 479
f_locate_profile, 480
global scope, 29
group, presentation styles, 356, 357
group bands, DataWindow painter, 365
group header band, 365, 366
group trailer band, 366
GROUP BY condition, data sources, 347, 348
GroupBox controls, 179
groups, DataWindow painter, 398-400

## H
HALT statement, 40
HAVING clause, data sources, 349
header band, DataWindow painter, 363, 364
Help
context sensitive, 62, 63
MicroHelp, displaying, 9
online help, 11-15
accessing, 11
bookmarks, using, 14
context sensitive help, 14
Find option, 12, 13
Help button, using, 14, 15
Help Contents dialog box, 12
Help Option, 15
overview, 11, 12
HScrollBar control, 180

## I
idec_rate = adec_rate, 541
identifiers, PowerScript language, 26, 27
idw_x DataWindow value, assigning, 528
IF statements, 34, 35
importing text to scripts, 58, 59. *See also* programming
File Import dialog box, 59
inheritance, 545-567
data abstraction and encapsulation, 546
classes, 547
object, 547-550
descendant classes and, 552
described, 551
MDI inheritance, 567
importance in PowerBuilder, 546
menu inheritance, 561-564
object oriented builder, 555
PowerBuilder classes, 555-558
object-oriented concepts, 546
polymorphism, described, 554, 555
u_employee, 551, 552
user object inheritance, 564-567
using, 553, 554
window inheritance, 558, 559
ancestor, updating. 560
snap-to-grid option, 559, 560
Inheritance From User Object dialog box, 565
.INI file extension, 83
initialization file, 83
Insert Column Values dialog box, 256
InsertRow(),DataWindow controls, 454, 455

## Index

instance variables, 30, 31
   adding code to, 196
   instance variable, MDI, 491
   using dot notation with, 31-34
Int, data types, 570
Integer, data types, 44, 570
ItemChanged event, DataWindow controls, 445
ItemError event, DataWindow controls, 446
Into Variables dialog box, 253

### J
joins, data sources, 335, 341

### K
keyboard shortcuts, text editing, 55, 56

### L
lb_1, adding another user event, 241
lb_1, adding user event to, 239
lb_1 we_mousemove event. adding code to, 241
lb_list other event, adding code to, 204
Library painter, 99, 100
line continuation, PowerScript language, 23
Line controls, 181
ListBox controls, 174, 175
ListBox style dialog box, 566
ListView controls, 177, 178
local scope, 30
long, data types, 570
looping, implementing, 37
LOOPING constructs. *See also* programming
   DO...LOOP, 37
      forms, 38
   FOR...NEXT loop, 398
   HALT statement, 40
   implementing looping, 37
   RETURN statement, 40

### M
main window, creating
   CONTROL1, 191, 192
   Events2, 232-234
   FirstWin, 127, 128
   MENUS, 308-313
   SQLApp, 269, 270
mathematical operators, precedence of, 35
MDI (Multiple Document Interface), 483-509
   creating MDI application, 489
      creating menus, 499-503
      m_mdi_sheet menu, creating, 503-506
      MDI frame creation, 489, 490
      sheet window, creating, 491-494
      w_mdi_frame instance variable, 494, 495
      w_mdi_frame window-level functions, 495-499
      window parms structure, creating, 490
   inheritance, 567
   MDI style, main features, 483
   MDIAPP example, 484-487
      MDI events, 488, 489
      OpenSheet function, 487, 488

template, creating, 506-509
MDI applications, menus, 297
MDI frame window, creating Windows, 109, 110, 112, 113
   general attributes, 293
   Pictures tab, 296, 297
   shortcut keys, 294
   Toolbar tab, 295, 296
menu
   creating menus, 287, 288
   MDI applications, 297
   MDI MicroHelp, adding, 298, 299
   menu bar items, adding, 289-292
   menu item attributes, 301, 302
   menu item functions, 302
   menu item properties, 293-297
   menu painter, introduction to, 285-287
   MENUS, step-by-step, 304-322
   MENUS example, 302-304
   Pictures tab, 296, 297
   shortcut keys, 294
   style attributes, 293, 294
   Toolbar tab, 295, 296
menu inheritance, 561-564
menus, 285-322
   adding scripts, 299, 300
   attaching menu to a window, 301, 302
   creating menus, 287, 288
   MDI applications, 297
   MDI MicroHelp, adding, 298, 299
   menu bar items, adding, 289-292
   menu item attributes, 301, 302
   menu item functions, 302
   menu item properties, 293-297
   menu painter, introduction to, 285-287
   MENUS
      example, 302-304
      step-by-step, 304-322
   previewing, 301
   saving, 301
MENUS, example, 302-304
MENUS, step-by-step
   application and library, creating, 304
   file menu, 305, 306
   m_main menu, creating, 304, 305
   application open event, adding code to, 313
   copy windows to zmenus.pbl, 316, 317
   enable menu bar item, adding code to, 319
   help menu items, adding code to, 318
   m_main menu item events, adding code to, 317
   test menu items, adding code to, 317, 318
dynamic menu, 307
help menu, 307, 308
m_main
   adding a function to, 313-315
   adding another function to, 315, 316
main window, creating, 308, 309
   m_menu, attaching to w_main window, 309-311
   w_main controls, adding code to, 311, 312
   w_main window events, adding code to, 312, 313

# Index 611

test menu, 306
w_environment window, 319-322
messages, events-driven programming, 208
message object, 228, 229
MicroHelp, displaying, 9
multiline comments, 23, 24
MultiLineEdit control, 173

## N

naming a control, window controls, 151, 152
New User Object dialog box, 518
noncursor SQL operations, SQL statements, 248
Noncursor SQL statements
  Delete, 257
  Insert, 255, 256
  Select, 254, 255
  Update, 256
NULL value, 573, 574

## O

object, 547-550
  described, 547, 548
  u_person, 549, 550
Object Browser, 46. *See also* programming
  as a search tool, 65
  Browse Object dialog box, 65
  Browse OLE Classes dialog box, 67
  Browser dialog box, 63
  DataWindow controls, 466, 467
  described, 63
  function declarations, 68, 69
    Functions Declaration dialog box, 68
    Object Browser dialog box for Functions, 66
  object types, 64
  selecting other objects, 67, 68
    Select Object dialog box, 68
  uses for, 65, 66
Object Browser dialog box for Functions, 66
object-function access level,
  PowerBuilder events, 218
object-level functions, 43, 44
  PowerBuilder events, creating, 216
object oriented builder, inheritance, 555
object-oriented concepts, inheritance, 546
online help, 11-15
  accessing, 11
  bookmarks, using, 14
  context sensitive help, 14
  Find option, 12
    entering search criteria, 12, 13
    matching words, selecting, 13
    Search dialog box, 13
    topic, selecting, 13, 14
  Help button, using, 14, 15
  Help Contents dialog box, 12
  Help Option, 15
    Find Dialog Box, 15
  overview, 11, 12
open event, adding code to, 201
operator precedence, 35, 36
Options dialog box, DataWindow painter, 370
ORDER BY clause, data sources, 349

other event, 227, 228
Oval controls, 181, 182

## P

p_1 constructor event, adding code to, 203
parametized custom event, creating
  new name, specifying, 224
  parameters, defining, 224
  steps in creating, 223
parent
  pronoun reserved word, 576, 577
    using in MenuItem, 577
    using in user object, 577, 578
  window, MDI, 483
ParentWindow, pronoun reserved words, 578, 579
Paste Argument, drop down listboxes, 50
Paste Function dialog box, 51
Paste Global, drop down listboxes, 49
Paste Instance, drop down listboxes, 49
Paste Object/Window, 50
Paste Shared, drop down listboxes, 49
Paste SQL, 51, 249
  SQL Statement Type, 250
  SQL Statement Type dialog box, 249, 250
paste Statement, 52, 53
Paste Statement dialog box, 52
pasting text, 55
pb_beep, adding code to, 197
.PBL extension, 76
PBUs (PowerBuilder Units), 157
pibbles, (.PBL file extension), 76
Picture controls, 176, 177
PictureButtons, window controls, 71
Pictures tab, menu item properties, 296, 297
polymorphism, inheritance, 554, 555
popup menu
  activating, 15
  creating, 292
  customizing toolbars, 8
  options, 429
  options in, 8
  window painter, 120
  using, 7
popup window, creating Windows, 109, 111
  creating in FirstWin example, 131, 132
positioning objects, DataWindow, 369, 370
PowerBar toolbar, 6
  display text option, 8
  icons on, 7
  launching icons, 10
  making visible, 10
PowerBuilder. *See also* programming
  initial window, 6
  launching application, 6
PowerBuilder application libraries, 77
PowerBuilder applications, creating. *See also*
  applications, creating PowerBuilder
PowerBuilder classes, inheritance, 555-558
PowerBuilder controls and objects, 139, 140
PowerBuilder Error Codes, 82
PowerBuilder events. *See also* events,
  functions, and user events

# Index

function argument list, 217
function return value type, 216, 217
object-function access level, 218
object-level functions
  creating, 216
overview, 212, 213
sample function, 218, 219
standard user objects, 217, 218
user-defined functions, 213, 217, 218
  creating global function, 214
  editing global function, 214
  function declarations, editing, 215
  function name prefixes, recommended, 215
  Select Function dialog box window, 214
PowerBuilder functions. *See also* programming
  Object Browser, 46
  overview, 40
  user-defined functions
    creating, 40-42
    editing, 41
    function access level, 45
    function argument list, 44
    function return value type, 41
    object-level functions, 43, 44
    sample function, 45, 46
    Select Function dialog box, 41
    standard user-objects, 44, 45
PowerBuilder inheritance, 546
PowerBuilder painters, 6, 7, 16-19
  described, 17
  painter descriptions, 18, 19
  painter utilities, 17
PowerBuilder Units (PBUs), 157
PowerPanel
  dialog box, 10
  drop down list, opening, 10
PowerScript code, compiling, 59-62. *See also* programming
  customizing the editor, 61, 62
    Editor Properties dialog box, 61
  Exit Script dialog box, 60
PowerScript debugger. *See also* programming
  activating, 69, 70
  breakpoints, adding, 70
    breakpoint status, 71, 72
    Select Script dialog box, 71
  features, 69
  limitations of, 69
  running the debugger, 72
  uses of, 69
  variables, displaying and modifying, 73
    adding variables to watch window, 73
    locating window instance variables, 73
PowerScript language. *See also* programming
  Any data type, 574
  arrays
    creating, 28
    unbounded, 28
  ASCII character, using special, 573
  data types, 27, 569-576
    blob, 571, 572
    Boolean, 569

    char, 572
    date, 571
    DateTime, 571
    decimal, 570
    double, 571
    enumerated, 27, 28
    Int, 570
    Integer, 570
    long, 570
    real, 570
    string, 572, 573
    time, 571
    unsigned long, 570
    ULong, 570
  comments
    block, nesting, 24
    multiline, 23, 24
    single-line, 23, 24
  constants, declaring. 574, 575
  dot notation syntax
    control name, 26
    general form, 24
    using for other function, 25, 26
  embedded SQL and, 245
  identifiers
    defined, 26
    minus sign, use in, 26, 27
    uses of, 26
  line continuation, 23
  NULL value, 573, 574
  pronoun reserved words, 575
    Parent, 576-578
    ParentWindow, 578, 579
    Super, 579
    This, 575, 576
  text
    entering, 22
    spacing and, 22
    underscore character, 23
  similarities with other languages, 22
  triggering code execution, 22
PowerScript language statements. *See also* programming
  CHOOSE CASE statement, 36, 37
  IF statements, 34, 35
  operator precedence, 35, 36
PowerScript painter. *See also* programming
  described, 47
  menu options, 56
    Declare menu, 58
    Design menu, 58
    Edit menu, 57, 58
    File menu, 57
    Search menu, 58
  opening, 47
  title bar, 48
Powersoft program group, 6
PowerTips, displaying, 9
presentation style
  data sources, 353-357
  DataWindows, 330-332, 418-422
previewing menus, 301
print, DataWindow controls, 458

# Index 613

printing a DataWindow, 466
private access, object-function access level, 218
procedure operations, SQL statements, 248
profile file, 83, 261
ProfileInt() function, 84
ProfileString() function, 84
programming, PowerBuilder 5
　context sensitive help, 62, 63
　dot notation with instance variables, using, 31-34
　drop down listboxes, 48-53
　import and export, 58, 59
　LOOPING constructs, 37-40
　Object Browser, 63-69
　PowerBuilder functions, 40-46
　PowerScript
　　code, compiling, 59-62
　　debugger, 69-73
　　language, 22-28
　　language statements, 34-37
　　painter, 47, 48, 56-58
　　text, entering and editing, 53-56
　　variable scope options, 29-31
Project painter, 97
Prompt for Criteria dialog box, 390
pronoun reserved words, 575
　Parent, 576-578
　ParentWindow, 578, 579
　Super, 579
　This, 575, 576
properties
　creating PowerBuilder applications, 78
　window controls, 160
properties, DataWindow, 381, 382
protected access, object-function access level, 218
public access, object-function access level, 218

## Q

Query Data Source Option, data sources, 351
Query painter. *See also* SQL, embedded
　creating SELECT statements, 257
　SQL code, 260, 261
　transaction objects, 258
　　attributes of, 259
　　creating other transaction objects, 260
　utility, DataWindows, 340
Quick Select, data sources, 333
Quick Select dialog box, data sources, 333, 334

## R

RadioButton
　adding code to, 199
　controls, 179
real, data types, 570
Rectangle controls, 182
reference variable, declaring, 34
registration function, using, 528-530
relational operators, 35
　precedence of, 35
replace, text editing, 55

Reports, DataWindow controls, 470, 471
resize events, MDI, 493
resizing new window, creating windows, 116
　automatic centering, 118
　initial state, 118
　scroll bars, 119
　sizing for different resolution monitors, 118, 119
　Window Position dialog box, 117
response window, creating Windows, 109, 111, 112
　creating in FirstWIn example, 132-134
retrieval arguments, defining, 344
retrieve, rows menu, 390, 391
Retrieve(), DataWindow controls, 453, 454
RETURN statement, 40
review option, modifying DataWindow, 372, 373
RichTextEdit control, 174
right mouse button (RMB), 7
RMB (right mouse button), 7
　popup, window controls, 163
ROLLBACK statement, DataWindow controls, 456-462
RoundRectangle controls, 182
rows menu, DataWindow, 388-398

## S

Save Application dialog box, 507
SaveAs function, DataWindow controls, 457, 458
saving
　DataWindow object, 367
　menus, 301
　query, data sources, 350
　windows, 119, 120
scope
　labeling in identifiers, 32
　shared, 32
script. *See* PowerScript
scripts, adding to menus, 299, 300
Search menu, PowerScript painter, 58
Select Application dialog box, 88
Select Application Library dialog box, 87
select criteria, data sources, 336-338
　defining Select criteria, 337
Select Data Window dialog box, 329, 431
Select Declared Cursor dialog box, 252
Select Event, drop down listboxes, 49
Select Function dialog box, 41
Select Object dialog box, 68
Select Painter dialog box, 282
Select Project dialog box, 96
Select Query dialog box, 351
Select Standard Visual Type dialog box, 518
SELECT statement
　displaying, 346
　editing, 347
　Query painter, 257
Select Tables dialog box, 339
Select User Object dialog box, 517
Select Window dialog box, 102

## 614  Index

selecting
  DataWindow objects, modifying
    DataWindow, 368
  text, 54
Selection Criteria dialog box, 390
SetProfileString() function, 84, 85
SetTrans, DataWindow controls, 438
SetTransObject, DataWindow controls,
  437, 438
sheet, MDI, 483
sheets and menus, creating Windows, 113
  recommendations for, 113
sheet window, creating MDI, 491-494
  instance variable, 491
  resize events, 493
  w_mdi_sheet user events, 493, 464
  w_mdi_sheet window, saving, 494
  window open event, 491, 492
shortcut keys, menu item properties, 294
show ruler option, modifying DataWindow, 371
single-line comments, 23
SingleLineEdit
  controls, 172
  properties dialog box, 155
sizing objects, modifying DataWindow,
  369, 370, 375, 376
sle_1 dragdrop event, adding code to, 242
sle_1 modified event, adding code to, 240, 241
sle_insert modified event, adding code to,
  202, 203
sle_isearch other event, adding code, 202
snap to grid option
  inheritance, 559, 560
  modifying DataWindow, 371
sort functions, DataWindow controls, 461, 462
sort order, data sources, 335, 336
spacing of objects, modifying DataWindow, 375
Specify Group dialog box, 399
spin controls, 173
SQL, embedded, 245-283
  application initialization file, 261-264
  cursor SQL statements, 251-257
  PowerScript and, 245
  Query painter, 257-261
  SQL statements, 246-248
    creating, 248-250
  SQLApp example, 264-268
    step-by-step, 268-283
SQL code, Query painter, 260, 261
SQL Select data source option, data sources,
  339, 340
SQL Statement dialog box, 50
SQL Statement Type dialog box, 249, 250
SQL statements. *See also* SQL embedded
  cursor operations, 247
  embedded SQL statements, 248
    cursor operations, 248
    noncursor SQL operations, 248
    procedure operations, 248
  embedding in PowerScript code, 246
  statement requirements, 246

SQL statements, creating, 248. *See also*
  SQL, embedded
  Paste SQL, 249
    SQL Statement Type, 250
    SQL Statement Type dialog box, 249, 250
SQL Toolbox, data sources, 340, 341
SQLApp example, 264. *See also* SQL, embedded
  buttons, 265, 264
  running SQLApp, 264, 265
  using SQLApp, 266
    cursor operations, 267
    delete row, 268
    disconnect, 2268
    insert row, 267
    update row, 267
SQLApp step-by-step, 268.
  *See also* SQL, embedded
  application and library, creating, 268
  application open event, adding code to,
    270, 271
    open script commentary, 271, 272
  blobs, selecting and updating, 280, 281
  code, adding to window, 272
  main window, creating, 269, 270
  running application, 280
  saving window, 280
  UPDATEBLOB SQL statement, 282, 283
  w_embedded_sql window, adding code to,
    272
    cb_close, 278
    cb_commit, 280
    cb_connect, 275
    cb_count, 276
    cb_delete, 279, 280
    cb_disconnect, 275
    cb_fetch, 277, 278
    cb_insert, 278, 279
    cb_open, 277
    cb_rollback, 280
    cb_update, 279
    fw_clear, 274, 275
    fw_db_status. 273, 274
    instance variable cursor1, defining, 276, 277
st_target dragdrop event, adding code to,
  204, 205
standard class objects, 542-544
standard user-objects, 44, 45, 514-516
  PowerBuilder events, 217, 218
StaticText controls, 177
Status codes, DataWindow controls, 451, 452
Stored Procedure data source option,
  data sources, 352, 353
string, data types, 572, 573
style, defining Windows, 107. *See also*
  Windows, creating
  child, 109, 111
  General (Window Style) dialog box, 108
  main, 108, 109, 110
  MDI, 109, 110, 112, 113
    Frame with MicroHelp, 115
    sheet window types, 114

# Index

popup, 109, 111
response, 109, 111, 112
sheets and menus, 113
  recommendations for, 113
Window Type, 108
style attributes, menu item properties, 293, 294
Style dialog box, 519
style toolbar
  DataWindow painter, 377
  Window painter, 105
summary band, DataWindow painter, 364
Super, pronoun reserved words, 579
suppressing repeat values, rows menu, 393-396
Suppression List dialog box, 396

## T

Tab controls, 183
tab order, modifying DataWindow, 380
tabular, presentation styles, 355, 356, 421, 422
tag attribute, window controls, 164
target object, window controls, 184
text
  entering and editing. *See also* programming
    cut, copy, clear, or replace, 55
    keyboard shortcuts, 55, 56
    pasting text, 55
    selecting text, 54
  PowerScript language, 22, 23
  setting in a window controls, 152
    setting style, 153
This, pronoun reserved words, 575, 576
3D look, Window painter, 104
time, data types, 571
toolbar
  closing display, 10
  customizing, 8, 11
  displaying, 10
  displaying text labels in, 7, 8
Toolbar
  MDI, 298, 299
  tab, menu item properties, 295, 296
toolbars, Window painter, 104, 105
Toolbars dialog box, 8, 9, 11
  DataWindow painter, 377
  Window painter, 107
transaction objects
  DataWindow controls, 437-440
  Query painter, 258
    attributes of, 259
    creating other transaction objects, 260
TreeView controls, 178

## U

ucalc_sales_tax.fu_amount, 540, 541
ucalc_sales_tax.fu_get_total, 541
ucalc_sales_tax.fu_set_rate, 541
U_DW_NAV user object, 526-528
U_DW_NAV VERTICAL user object, 530
U_DW_NAV_WITH_CLOSE user object, 531-533
  fu_init, 533

parent window, referencing user object's, 531, 532
windows controls, referencing, 532
u_employee, inheritance, 551, 552
U_LB_WITH_SEARCH user object, 533, 534
  adding U_LB_WITH_ISEARCH to the window, 437, 538
  fu_add_item, 537
  fu_get_selected, 537
  sle_1 we keyup user event, 534, 535
  ue_add_item user event, 535, 536
ue_add_item event, adding code, 240
ue_init event, adding code to, 237, 238
ULong, data types, 570
UNIONs, data sources, 350
unsigned long, data types, 570
uodemo program, 516, 517
update characteristics, setting, 397
Update Column Values dialog box, 254
Update cursor, 253, 254
update properties, rows menu, 396-398
Update(), DataWindow controls, 455, 456
UPDATEBLOB SQL statement, 282, 283
updating rows, DataWindow controls, 444
user-defined functions, PowerBuilder events, 213, 217, 218
  creating global function, 214
  editing global function, 214
  function declarations, editing, 215
  function name prefixes, recommended, 215
  Select Function dialog box window, 214
user events, creating, 219, 220
  custom events, user-defined, 221
  parametized events, user-defined, 221
  predefined system events, 220, 221
  system events, user-defined, 221
user events, defining 219.
  *See also* events, functions, and user events
  custom event, creating, 221-223
  message object, 228, 229
  other event, 227, 228
  parametized custom event, creating
    new name, specifying, 224
    parameters, defining, 224
    steps in creating, 223
  user events, creating, 219, 220
    custom events, user-defined, 221
    parametized events, user-defined, 221
    predefined system events, 220, 221
    system events, user-defined, 221
  windows event, mapping, 226, 227
user object inheritance, inheritance, 564-567
User Object Painter, 519
user objects
  described, 512
  categories, 512, 513
    adding user object to a window, 522-524
    characteristics, 512
    class, 513
    fu_disable (object-level) function, creating, 520

fu_enable (object-level) function, creating, 521, 522
fu_get_state (object-level) function, creating, 522, 523
visual, 513
standard user object, 514-516
using, 514
uodemo program, 516, 517
visual user objects, using, 514
w_main__with_uos CloseQuery event, editing, 524
custom class user objects
  described, 538-540
  idec_rate = adec_rate, 541
  ucalc_sales_tax.fu_amount, 540, 541
  ucalc_sales_tax.fu_get_total, 541
  ucalc_sales_tax.fu_set_rate, 541
custom visual user object
  assigning idw_x DataWindow value, 528
  building, 525
  described, 524
  event, using, 528-530
  registration function, using, 528-530
  U_DW_NAV user object, 526-528
  U_DW_NAV VERTICAL user object, 530
  U_DW_NAV_WITH_CLOSE user object, 531-533
  U_LB_WITH_SEARCH user object, 533-538
standard class objects, 542-544

## V
variable
  access levels, 32
  scope options, declaring
    global scope, 29
    instance variables, 30
    local scope, 30, 31
variables, displaying and modifying, 73
  adding variables to watch window, 73
  locating window instance variables, 73
visual user objects, using, 514
VScrollBar control, 181

## W
w_main
  adding a function to, 234
  DB_INIT.PBL, 474
  open event, 236, 237
  window, assign user event, 235, 236
w_main__with_uos CloseQuery event, editing, 524
w_mdi_frame window-level functions, 495-499
  fw_close_all_sheets, 496, 497
  fw_db_init, 497
  fw_open_sheet, 495, 496
  fw_status_message, 497
  w_mdi_frame open event, 498, 499
w_mdi_sheet user events, MDI, 493, 464
w_mdi_sheet window, saving MDI, 494
wf_db_init, DB_INIT.PBL, 475, 476
wf_status_message, DB_INIT.PBL, 476, 477

WHERE
  clause, defining, 257
  criteria, defining, 345
window attributes, 122
window attributes, other, 115-119. *See also* Windows creating
  options in defining window style, 115, 116
  resizing new window, 116
    automatic centering, 118
    initial state, 118
    scroll bars, 119
    sizing for different resolution monitors, 118, 119
    Window Position dialog box, 117
  Window Style dialog box, 115
window controls. *See also* controls, windows
  control popup menu options, 163, 164
    copying control to another window, 164
    RMB popup, 163
    tag attribute, 164
  controls by category, 162, 163
  example, 161
window events, 120, 121
window functions, 121
window inheritance, inheritance, 558, 559
window open event, MDI, 491, 492
window options, other, 119
Window painter, 102, 103. *See also* Windows, creating 3D look, 104
  color options, setting, 105, 106
    Toolbars dialog box, 107
  General Tab dialog box, 104
  popup menu, 120
    window scripts, 120
  Select Window dialog box, 102
  style toolbar, 105
  toolbars, 104, 105
  Window painter dialog box, 103
Window painter dialog box, 103
Window Position dialog box, 117, 129, 193
Window Style dialog box, 115
window type, creating Windows, 108
Window variables, 122-124
  creating instances of windows, 123
  object scope assignments, 122
Windows, creating, 101-136
  attributes, other window, 115-119
  FirstWin example, 125-135
  saving the window, 119, 120
  window attributes, 122
  window events, 120, 121
  window functions, 121
  window options, other, 119
  Window painter, 102-107
  Window painter popup menu, 120
  Window variables, 122-123
  Windows, style, defining, 107-114
windows event, mapping, 226, 227

## Z
Zoom dialog box, 372
zoom option, modifying DataWindow, 272